Handbook of Big Data

Chapman & Hall/CRC
Handbooks of Modern Statistical Methods

Series Editor

Garrett Fitzmaurice

Department of Biostatistics

Harvard School of Public Health

Boston, MA, U.S.A.

Aims and Scope

The objective of the series is to provide high-quality volumes covering the state-of-the-art in the theor and applications of statistical methodology. The books in the series are thoroughly edited and preser comprehensive, coherent, and unified summaries of specific methodological topics from statistics. Th chapters are written by the leading researchers in the field, and present a good balance of theory an application through a synthesis of the key methodological developments and examples and case studie using real data.

The scope of the series is wide, covering topics of statistical methodology that are well developed an find application in a range of scientific disciplines. The volumes are primarily of interest to researcher and graduate students from statistics and biostatistics, but also appeal to scientists from fields where th methodology is applied to real problems, including medical research, epidemiology and public healt engineering, biological science, environmental science, and the social sciences.

Published Titles

Handbook of Mixed Membership Models and Their Applications
Edited by Edoardo M. Airoldi, David M. Blei, Elena A. Erosheva, and Stephen E. Fienberg

Handbook of Markov Chain Monte Carlo
Edited by Steve Brooks, Andrew Gelman, Galin L. Jones, and Xiao-Li Meng

Handbook of Big Data
Edited by Peter Bühlmann, Petros Drineas, Michael Kane, and Mark van der Laan

Handbook of Discrete-Valued Time Series
Edited by Richard A. Davis, Scott H. Holan, Robert Lund, and Nalini Ravishanker

Handbook of Design and Analysis of Experiments
Edited by Angela Dean, Max Morris, John Stufken, and Derek Bingham

Longitudinal Data Analysis
Edited by Garrett Fitzmaurice, Marie Davidian, Geert Verbeke, and Geert Molenberghs

Handbook of Spatial Statistics
Edited by Alan E. Gelfand, Peter J. Diggle, Montserrat Fuentes, and Peter Guttorp

Handbook of Cluster Analysis
Edited by Christian Hennig, Marina Meila, Fionn Murtagh, and Roberto Rocci

Handbook of Survival Analysis
Edited by John P. Klein, Hans C. van Houwelingen, Joseph G. Ibrahim, and Thomas H. Scheike

Handbook of Missing Data Methodology
Edited by Geert Molenberghs, Garrett Fitzmaurice, Michael G. Kenward, Anastasios Tsiatis, and Geert Verbeke

Chapman & Hall/CRC
Handbooks of Modern
Statistical Methods

Handbook of Big Data

Edited by

Peter Bühlmann
Petros Drineas
Michael Kane
Mark van der Laan

CRC Press
Taylor & Francis Group
Boca Raton London New York

CRC Press is an imprint of the
Taylor & Francis Group, an **informa** business
A CHAPMAN & HALL BOOK

Reprint, 2019

CRC Press
Taylor & Francis Group
6000 Broken Sound Parkway NW, Suite 300
Boca Raton, FL 33487-2742

ISBN 978-0-367-24070-7 (hbk)

Digitally Printed at Replika Press Pvt. Ltd

Visit the Taylor & Francis Web site at
http://www.taylorandfrancis.com

and the CRC Press Web site at
http://www.crcpress.com

For sale in India, Pakistan, Nepal, Bhutan, Bangladesh and Sri Lanka only.

Contents

Preface xi

Editors xiii

Contributors xv

I General Perspectives on Big Data 1

1 The Advent of Data Science: Some Considerations on the Unreasonable Effectiveness of Data 3
Richard J.C.M. Starmans

2 Big-*n* versus Big-*p* in Big Data 21
Norman Matloff

II Data-Centric, Exploratory Methods 33

3 Divide and Recombine: Approach for Detailed Analysis and Visualization of Large Complex Data 35
Ryan Hafen

4 Integrate Big Data for Better Operation, Control, and Protection of Power Systems 47
Guang Lin

5 Interactive Visual Analysis of Big Data 61
Carlos Scheidegger

6 A Visualization Tool for Mining Large Correlation Tables: The Association Navigator 73
Andreas Buja, Abba M. Krieger, and Edward I. George

III Efficient Algorithms 103

7 High-Dimensional Computational Geometry 105
Alexandr Andoni

8 IRLBA: Fast Partial Singular Value Decomposition Method 125
James Baglama

9 Structural Properties Underlying High-Quality Randomized Numerical Linear Algebra Algorithms 137
Michael W. Mahoney and Petros Drineas

10 Something for (Almost) Nothing: New Advances in Sublinear-Time Algorithms 155
Ronitt Rubinfeld and Eric Blais

IV Graph Approaches 169

11 Networks 171
Elizabeth L. Ogburn and Alexander Volfovsky

12 Mining Large Graphs 191
David F. Gleich and Michael W. Mahoney

V Model Fitting and Regularization 221

13 Estimator and Model Selection Using Cross-Validation 223
Iván Díaz

14 Stochastic Gradient Methods for Principled Estimation with Large Datasets 241
Panos Toulis and Edoardo M. Airoldi

15 Learning Structured Distributions 267
Ilias Diakonikolas

16 Penalized Estimation in Complex Models 285
Jacob Bien and Daniela Witten

17 High-Dimensional Regression and Inference 305
Lukas Meier

VI Ensemble Methods 321

18 Divide and Recombine: Subsemble, Exploiting the Power of Cross-Validation 323
Stephanie Sapp and Erin LeDell

19 Scalable Super Learning 339
Erin LeDell

VII Causal Inference 359

20 Tutorial for Causal Inference 361
Laura Balzer, Maya Petersen, and Mark van der Laan

21 A Review of Some Recent Advances in Causal Inference 387
Marloes H. Maathuis and Preetam Nandy

VIII Targeted Learning 409

22 Targeted Learning for Variable Importance 411
Sherri Rose

23 Online Estimation of the Average Treatment Effect **429**
Sam Lendle

24 Mining with Inference: Data-Adaptive Target Parameters **439**
Alan Hubbard and Mark van der Laan

Index **453**

Preface

The purpose of this book is to describe some modern approaches to analyzing and understanding the structure of datasets where their size outpaces the computing resources needed to analyze them using traditional approaches. This problem domain has become increasingly common with the proliferation of electronic devices that collect increasing amounts of data along with inexpensive means to store information. As a result, researchers have had to reimagine how we make sense of data; to identify fundamental concepts in statistics and machine learning and translate them to the new problem domain; and, in some cases, to come up with entirely new approaches. The result has been an explosion in new methodological and technological tools for what is colloquially known as *Big Data*. We have carefully selected representative methods and techniques to provide the reader not only with a wide-ranging view of this landscape but also the fundamental concepts needed to tackle new challenges. Our intent is that this book will serve to quickly orient the reader and provide a working understanding of key statistical and computing ideas that can be readily applied for applications and research.

A tremendous amount of research and progress in the broadly understood area of *Big Data* has been made over the past few decades. The data management community in particular has made important contributions to the issue of how to effectively store and access data. This book acknowledges these new computational capabilities and attempts to address the question, "given that we can access and store a vast, potentially complex dataset, how can we understand the statistical relationships within it?"

With this in mind, we have set out to accomplish three distinct tasks. First, to identify modern, scalable approaches to analyzing increasingly large datasets. By representing the state of the art in this centralized resource, we hope to help researchers understand the landscape of available tools and techniques as well as providing the fundamental concepts that make them work. The second task is to help identify areas of research that need further development. The practice is still evolving, and rigorous approaches to understanding the statistics of very large datasets while integrating computational, methodological, and theoretical developments are still being formalized. This book helps to identify gaps and explore new avenues of research. The third goal is to integrate current techniques across disciplines. We have already begun to see *Big Data* sub-specialties such as genomics, computational biology, search, and even finance, ignoring inter-community advances, both in computational statistics and machine learning. We hope that this book will encourage greater communication and collaboration between these sub-specialties and will result in a more integrated community.

In designing this book, we have tried to strike the right balance not only between statistical methodology, theory, and applications in computer science but also between the breadth of topics and the depth to which each topic is explored. Each chapter is designed to be self-contained and easily digestible. We hope it serves as a useful resource for seasoned practitioners and enthusiastic neophytes alike.

This project could not have been completed without the encouragement, guidance, and patience of John Kimmel of Chapman & Hall/CRC Press. We express here our gratitude and thanks.

Peter Bühlmann
ETH Zürich
Petros Drineas
Rensselaer Polytechnic Institute
Michael Kane
Yale University
Mark van der Laan
University of California, Berkeley

Editors

Peter Bühlmann is a professor of statistics at ETH Zürich, Switzerland. His research interests are in causal and high-dimensional statistical inference, machine learning, and applications in the life sciences. Together with Sara van de Geer, he has written the book *Statistics for High-Dimensional Data: Methods, Theory and Applications.* He is a fellow of the Institute of Mathematical Statistics and an elected member of the International Statistical Institute. His presentations include a Medallion Lecture at the Joint Statistical Meetings 2009, a read paper to the Royal Statistical Society in 2010, the 14th Bahadur Memorial Lectures at the University of Chicago, and some other named lectures. He is a 2014 "Highly Cited Researcher in Mathematics" by Thomson Reuters. Besides having served on various editorial boards, he was the editor of the *Annals of Statistics* from 2010 to 2012.

Petros Drineas is an associate professor in the Computer Science Department of Rensselaer Polytechnic Institute. He earned a PhD in computer science from Yale University, New Haven, Connecticut, in 2003 and a BS in computer engineering and informatics from the University of Patras, Greece, in 1997. His research interests lie in the design and analysis of randomized algorithms for linear algebraic problems, as well as their applications to the analysis of modern, massive datasets. Professor Drineas is the recipient of an Outstanding Early Research Award from Rensselaer Polytechnic Institute, Troy, New York, as well as an NSF CAREER award. He was a visiting professor at the U.S. Sandia National Laboratories during the fall of 2005; a visiting fellow at the Institute for Pure and Applied Mathematics at the University of California, Los Angeles, in the fall of 2007; a long-term visitor at the Simons Institute for the Theory of Computing at the University of California, Berkeley, in the fall of 2013; and has also worked for industrial labs (e.g., Yahoo Labs and Microsoft Research). From October 2010 to December 2011, he served the U.S. National Science Foundation as the program director in the Information and Intelligent Systems Division and the Computing and Communication Foundations Division. He has presented keynote talks and tutorials in major conferences (e.g., SIAM Applied Linear Algebra conference, ACM Knowledge Discovery and Data Mining conference, International Conference on Very Large Databases, and SIAM Data Mining conference) and has made over 60 invited colloquium and seminar presentations in the United States and Europe. He received two fellowships from the European Molecular Biology Organization for his work in population genetics, and his research has been featured in various popular press articles, including *SIAM News*, *LiveScience*, *ScienceDaily*, *Scitizen*, and *Yahoo! News*. Professor Drineas has co-organized the widely attended workshops on Algorithms for Modern Massive Datasets in 2006, 2008, 2010, 2012, and 2014.

Michael Kane is a member of the research faculty at Yale University. He earned PhD and MA degrees in statistics from Yale University, New Haven, Connecticut, along with an MS degree in electrical engineering and a BS degree in computer engineering from Rochester Institute of Technology, Rochester, New York. His research interests are in the areas of scalable statistical/machine learning and applied probability. He is a winner of the American

Statistical Association's Chambers Statistical Software Award for The Bigmemory Project, a set of software libraries that allow the R programming environment to accommodate large datasets for statistical analysis. He is a grantee on the Defense Advanced Research Projects Agency's XDATA project, part of the White House's Big Data Initiative, and on the Gates Foundation's Round 11 Grand Challenges Exploration. Dr. Kane has collaborated with companies including AT&T Labs Research, Paradigm4, Sybase (a SAP company), and Oracle.

Mark van der Laan is the Jiann-Ping Hsu/Karl E. Peace professor of biostatistics and statistics at the University of California, Berkeley. He is the inventor of targeted maximum likelihood estimation, a general semiparametric efficient estimation method that incorporates the state of the art in machine learning through ensemble method super learning. He is the recipient of the 2005 COPPS Presidents' and Snedecor Awards, the 2005 van Dantzig Award, as well as the 2004 Spiegelman Award. His research covers a wide range of areas, including causal inference, censored data, computational biology, multiple testing, machine learning, and semiparametric efficient methods and theory. He is the founding editor of the *International Journal of Biostatistics* and the *Journal of Causal Inference*, and has co-authored a variety of books and more than 250 publications.

Contributors

Edoardo M. Airoldi
Department of Statistics
Harvard University
Cambridge, Massachusetts

Alexandr Andoni
Department of Computer Science
Columbia University
New York City, New York

James Baglama
Department of Mathematics
University of Rhode Island
Kingston, Rhode Island

Laura Balzer
Division of Biostatistics
University of California, Berkeley
Berkeley, California

Jacob Bien
Department of Biological Statistics and Computational Biology
and
Department of Statistical Science
Cornell University
Ithaca, New York

Eric Blais
David R. Cheriton School of Computer Science
University of Waterloo
Waterloo, Ontario, Canada

Andreas Buja
Department of Statistics
The Wharton School
University of Pennsylvania
Philadelphia, Pennsylvania

Ilias Diakonikolas
School of Informatics
University of Edinburgh
Edinburgh, Scotland

Iván Díaz
Department of Biostatistics
Johns Hopkins University
Baltimore, Maryland

Petros Drineas
Computer Science Department
Rensselaer Polytechnic Institute
Troy, New York

Edward I. George
Department of Statistics
The Wharton School
University of Pennsylvania
Philadelphia, Pennsylvania

David F. Gleich
Department of Computer Science
Purdue University
West Lafayette, Indiana

Ryan Hafen
Department of Statistics
Purdue University
West Lafayette, Indiana

Alan Hubbard
Division of Biostatistics
University of California, Berkeley
Berkeley, California

Abba M. Krieger
Department of Statistics
The Wharton School
University of Pennsylvania
Philadelphia, Pennsylvania

Erin LeDell
University of California, Berkeley
Berkeley, California

Sam Lendle
Division of Biostatistics
University of California, Berkeley
Berkeley, California

Guang Lin
Department of Mathematics
School of Mechanical Engineering
Purdue University
West Lafayette, Indiana

Marloes H. Maathuis
Seminar for Statistics
ETH Zürich
Zürich, Switzerland

Michael W. Mahoney
Department of Statistics
University of California, Berkeley
Berkeley, California

Norman Matloff
Department of Computer Science
The University of California, Davis
Davis, California

Lukas Meier
Seminar for Statistics
ETH Zürich
Zürich, Switzerland

Preetam Nandy
Seminar for Statistics
ETH Zürich
Zürich, Switzerland

Elizabeth L. Ogburn
Department of Biostatistics
Johns Hopkins University
Baltimore, Maryland

Maya Petersen
Divisions of Biostatistics and Epidemiology
University of California, Berkeley
Berkeley, California

Sherri Rose
Department of Health Care Policy
Harvard Medical School
Boston, Massachusetts

Ronitt Rubinfeld
Department of Electrical Engineering and Computer Science
Massachusetts Institute of Technology
Cambridge, Massachusetts

Stephanie Sapp
Google Inc.
Boulder, Colorado

Carlos Scheidegger
Department of Computer Science
University of Arizona
Tucson, Arizona

Richard J.C.M. Starmans
Department of Information and Computing Sciences
Utrecht University
Utrecht, the Netherlands

Panos Toulis
Department of Statistics
Harvard University
Cambridge, Massachusetts

Mark van der Laan
Division of Biostatistics
University of California, Berkeley
Berkeley, California

Alexander Volfovsky
Department of Statistics
Harvard University
Cambridge, Massachusetts

Daniela Witten
Departments of Statistics and Biostatistics
University of Washington
Seattle, Washington

Part I

General Perspectives on Big Data

1

The Advent of Data Science: Some Considerations on the Unreasonable Effectiveness of Data

Richard J.C.M. Starmans

CONTENTS

1.1 Preamble: Wigner versus Google 3
1.2 Big Data and Data Science 5
1.3 Project of Computer Science 7
1.4 The Apory of Complete Knowledge 9
1.5 Bacon and the Emergence of Data Science 11
1.6 Herald of the Controversy 13
1.6.1 Exploratory Data Analysis 13
1.6.2 Thesis 14
1.6.3 Antithesis 14
1.6.4 Synthesis 15
1.7 Plea for Reconciliation 16
References 18

1.1 Preamble: Wigner versus Google

In 1960, the Hungarian-American physicist and later Nobel laureate Eugene Paul Wigner (1902–1995) published his by now celebrated essay "The Unreasonable Effectiveness of Mathematics in the Natural Sciences," which appeared in *The Communications of Pure and Applied Mathematics* (Wigner, 1960). In this article, the author discusses the universal scope of mathematics, a discipline that was coined and famously proclaimed *Queen and Servant of Science* by E.T. White in 1938 (White, 1938). In particular, Wigner expresses his astonishment that almost all physical notions, as well as highly complex, nearly incomprehensible physical phenomena or processes can be described, understood, explained, or predicted with relatively simple, elegant mathematical concepts, techniques, and models. The predicate *unreasonable* is used to express the author's conviction that this situation is no less than a marvel, inconceivable, and so far unexplained, despite the fact that for more than 2000 years philosophers, mathematicians, and physicists have been discussing and pondering the Pythagorean universe we live in, including Pythagoras, Plato, Archimedes, Descartes, Galilei, Kant, Pearson, Einstein, and Heisenberg. Be that as it may, the article became a touchstone (or at the least a milestone) in reflections and debates on the mathematization of the world picture and mathematical-reductionist or physicalist approaches in epistemology. It goes without saying that Wigner's work was a prelude to zealous arguments put forward by those advocating this type of unification in science, but it also has put into motion the pens of those who felt themselves bent under the yoke of a physicalist or otherwise founded reductionism. Resistance within the natural sciences manifested itself primarily in the life sciences, because the complexity, variety, and variability in living nature complicate and set hurdles to such a straightforward reduction, at least according to the antagonists. For example, the mathematical biologist Israel Gelfand is frequently cited as well, for openly alluding to Wigner's catch phrase: "There is only one thing which is more unreasonable than the unreasonable effectiveness of mathematics in physics, and this is the unreasonable ineffectiveness of mathematics in biology" (Lesk, 2000). However, most opponents can unsurprisingly be found in the social sciences and humanities, claiming a much more multifaceted, rich, and diverse field of activity, which demands other methodological standards and rules. For example, Vela Velupillai in his turn scorned the *unreasonable ineffectiveness of mathematics in economics*, among other things, by emphasizing that mathematical assumptions are usually invalid from an economic point of view, and proposed more realistic models habitually intractable (Velupillai, 2005).

On somewhat different grounds, the Google researchers Alon Halevy, Peter Norvig, and Fernando Pereira appear among the opponents of the Wigner thesis. With a quip to Wigner's essay, the three authors wrote an equally lucid, but due to simplifications also controversial, paper titled "The Unreasonable Effectiveness of Data" published in 2009 in the journal *IEEE Intelligent Systems* (Halevy, 2009). When it comes to sciences concerned with people rather than with elementary particles, the authors contend, simple formulas and elegant mathematical physical theories are usually of limited use. According to Halevy cum suis (2009), the same applies to parametric statistical models. To understand complex human behavior and predict it, it is better to rely on many petabytes of often crude, unannotated, unstructured, or even distorted data, which are forged into knowledge through smart algorithms. In fact, "we should stop acting as if our goal is to author extremely elegant theories and instead embrace complexity and make use of the best ally we have, the unreasonable effectiveness of data." The authors fulfill their apologetic task with plenty of verve, and their plea shows more and more the character of an *oratio pro domo*. In doing so, they conveniently ignore important developments in both the philosophy of science and the history of statistic of the past 100 years, and they hardly seem worried in committing the fallacy of *false dilemma* or the fallacy of the *straw man*. Rather than supplying arguments, they basically proclaim the dichotomy. Be that as it may, *The unreasonable effectiveness of data* is so frequently and persistently quoted that it almost seems to be one of the *Federalist Papers* of the current data era, at least for those afflicted with any sense of history and not reluctant to a light pathos. In addition, admittedly, there are several reasons why it may serve as a preamble to the underlying essay on data science and big data. First, it cogently illustrates that we are currently witnessing a genuine rehabilitation of the concept of data, with respect to the classical triptych *Data–Information–Knowledge*, three concepts that co-occur with an increasing order of complexity and importance since the evolution of computer science in general and of artificial intelligence (AI) in particular. Data are raw, unsophisticated, and are related to the physical, acoustic, or orthographic level. They primarily serve as a basis for information, which is the second and at a far more interesting level of the triptych, dealing with semantics, interpretation, and human understanding. Information is generally considered a key concept in foundational research of virtually all sciences. The third and highest level deals with knowledge, the eminent field of justified true belief, which warranted convictions, reliability, and validity. We are entering the elevated realms of epistemology associated with the pursuit of truth, the ultimate goal of science to formulate unified *Grand Theories*. Even more than information, knowledge presumes the *homo mensura* principle. Nature is intelligible, accessible by human perception, cognition and consciousness, and language. Apart from epistemology, this idea has been utilized in computer science as well as in distinguished fields such as knowledge representation and reasoning, strong AI, and multiagent systems, the latter based on the metaphor of computers as autonomous subjects, equipped with high-level cognitive functions, including language, perception, consciousness, intelligence, and morality, and interacting with their environment. Be that as it may, the current focus on big data and data science may suggest that this development from *data oriented* toward *knowledge oriented* has stopped or has even been reversed. Second, it is remarkable that neither the concept of big data nor that of data science is actually used by Halevy cum suis, although both concepts had already been coined many years before and were used at a modest scale. It suggests that only recently the idea of a revolution, a newly established paradigm or scientific discipline, has got shape. Third, and most importantly, it must be emphasized that despite its rough simplifications, the *Wigner versus Google* dichotomy put forward by Halevy seems recognizable in everyday practice of data analysis and scientific research, which is regrettable and avoidable, but appears to be an excellent starting point for this chapter, which will put the advent of data science and big data in a historical–philosophical perspective.

1.2 Big Data and Data Science

Due to their frequent and often simultaneous appearance in the media, the concepts of big data and data science seem closely related, if not inseparable. They equally adorn national and international research agendas, strategic plans of governments, and they control economics and business, both in industry and in service sectors. Academic data science centers spring up like mushrooms after rain. New courses on big data, both academic and commercial, are developed and are offered at a rapid pace; many set themselves up as self-proclaimed experts, consultants, or apologists of the big data era. Many commercial products and services are developed, accompanied and supported by conferences, numerous books, and other publications. Whether it comes to science, economy and prosperity, public health, environmental and climate issues, justice, or national security, the vital importance of big data and data science for the current time is most vigorously stressed, and sometimes it is even proclaimed a panacea for problems of various kinds. For example, in their recent book *Big Data: A Revolution That Will Transform How We Live, Work and Think* (2013), Viktor Mayer-Schönberger and Kenneth Cukier appear to be strongly committed to this tradition. In a compelling and catchy way, they sketch the outlines of a dataficated world, in which reality in its full size will gradually be encoded into data, making it accessible and knowable, resulting in better predictions and true knowledge. Unquestionably, they commit themselves to Hastely's postulated and cherished contrast between traditional mathematics and statistics on the one hand and data science on the other. But, they surpass the pretensions of Halevy tremendously, because they suggest that *la condion humaine* is to alter, due to the new revolution. According to a recent article written by Thomas Davenport and D.J. Patil, which was published in the *Harvard Business Review*, data scientists will appear to be the sexiest profession in the twenty-first century (Davenport and Patil, 2012), and the opportunities of the new profession are nearly daily hailed in numerous publications in the popular media. Of course, according to these protagonists, the human quest for self-realization, progress, and prosperity can only find its eudaimonic completion due to the labors and the supervision of the data scientist.

Be that as it may, the interplay between the concepts of big data and data science can be studied from various perspectives, especially since both are under development and are claimed or even annexed by many. Conceptual confusion seems inevitable. For example, the concept of big data appears to be a notoriously unruly concept with several dimensions and connotations; it is therefore *functionally vague*. It seems to be neither well defined nor very new. Roughly spoken, it typically refers to *more* or *too much* data than what we are used to, or which can be managed, accessed, analyzed, interpreted, and validated by conventional means, as a basis for useful information or reliable knowledge. Even the deliberate choice for the wooly adjective big in *big data* implies a dynamic and shifting meaning, depending on possibly highly individual circumstances, advancing technology, available storage capacity, processing power, and other cultural or historical contingencies. This connotation of a *moving target*, however, concerns not only the *volume* of data but also the other dimensions that lie hidden in the concept of big data: the *variety* of data (various formats, types, and sources), the *variation in quality and status*, the *continuous generation* and production of data, which are seemingly *unsolicited* and sometimes unintentionally available, and the *velocity* with which data are produced and analyzed, and may or must be used, and not the least their often *distributed* nature, that is, data can be produced and stored nearly everywhere and sources need to be found and integrated. All of these factors suggest a kind of ubiquity of data, but also contain a *functionally vague* understanding, which is situationally determined, and because of that it can be deployed in many contexts, has many advocates, and can be claimed by many as well. Partly because of this context-sensitive definition of the concept of big data, it is by no means a time phenomenon or novelty, but has a long genealogy that goes back to the earliest civilizations. Some aspects of this phenomenon will be discussed in the following sections.

In addition, we will show in this chapter how big data embody a conception of data science at least at two levels. First of all, data science is the technical-scientific discipline, specialized in managing the multitude of data: collect, store, access, analyze, visualize, interpret, and protect. It is rooted in computer science and statistics; computer science is traditionally oriented toward data structures, algorithms, and scalability, and statistics is focused on analyzing and interpreting the data. In particular, we may identify here the triptych database technology/information retrieval, computational intelligence/machine learning, and finally inferential statistics. The first pillar concerns database/information retrieval technology. Both are core disciplines of computer science since many decades. Emerging from this tradition in recent years, notably researchers of Google and Yahoo have been working on techniques to cluster many computers in a data center, making data accessible and allowing for data-intensive calculations: think, for example, of BigTable, Google File Systems, a programming paradigm as Map Reduce, and the open source variant Hadoop. The paper of Halevy precedes this development as well. The second pillar relates to intelligent algorithms from the field of computational intelligence (machine learning and data mining). It comprises a variety of techniques such as neural networks, genetic algorithms, decision trees, association rules, support vector machines, random forest, all kinds of ensemble techniques, and Bayesian learning. Put roughly, this pillar fits the tradition of subsymbolic AI. The third pillar is the field of mathematical inferential statistics, based on estimation theory, the dualism of sample and population (the reality *behind* the data), thus allowing to reason with uncertain and incomplete information: parameter estimation, hypothesis testing, confidence intervals p values, and so on.

But data science has a more far-reaching interpretation than just a new discipline; it proclaims a new conception of science, in which the essence of knowledge is at stake and the classic questions in epistemology are reconsidered or reformulated. What is knowledge, how do you acquire this, how do you justify it, which has methodological consequences? What is the status of scientific theories? How do they relate to reality? Do they exist independently of the human mind? Data science has an impact on many classical themes in epistemology: the structure of theories, causality, laws and explanations, completeness and uncertainty of knowledge, the scientific realism debate, the limits of confirmation theory, rationality and progress in science, unification of science, and so on. We will argue that in view of both the meanings of data science, the regrettable distinction between statistics and computational data analysis appears as a major bottleneck not only in data science but also in research methodology and epistemology. Moreover, this problem is historically inspired. Some aspects of the genealogy of data science, including the current debate, will be shown by subsequently considering the project of computer science, the apory of complete knowledge, Francis Bacon's preoccupation with the bounds of knowledge, and John Tukey's ideas on exploratory data analysis (EDA). To conclude, we discuss the possible resolution of the Wigner–Google controversy and some prerequisites for a reconciliation.

1.3 Project of Computer Science

Partly because of the vague and context-sensitive definition of the concept of big data, it is not a time phenomenon, but has a long genealogy, which dates back to the earliest civilizations and started with the invention of scripture and a numeric system. At that particular moment, history began and simultaneously the project of computer science started when the need to manage data emerged. For practical and scientific reasons, man has always sought to collect, count, measure, weigh, store, and analyze data in the struggle for life, for warfare, to build up societies that are more complex, and to gain or retain power. Due to some evolutionary determined cognitive limitations, *Homo faber* has always looked for tools to support the management of large amounts of data, and therefore computer project was heralded long before microelectronics, the concept of the Turing machine or the digital computer, had been introduced. Those who were involved were confronted with the two faces of big data problems: either you do need data, but do not know how to obtain them, or you do have the data, intended or unintended, but you do not know how to manage them. In the former case, data are not available because they do not exist, or they are lost, hidden, or forbidden for religious or ethical reasons (too dangerous), for economic reasons (too expensive), or for technical reasons (lack of proper measurement equipment or other tools to search for, to produce, or to obtain them). In the latter case, data are abundantly available, unasked; however, we have no means to access, analyze, interpret, and employ them. The aspect of scalability immediately arises at both sides; we need a certain magnitude, but once this has been obtained, one must find ways to deal with it. This was as much a problem in antiquity concerning the storage or calculations with an abacus, as it is the issue nowadays in complexity theory or in data management, storage, and retrieval at data centers. Accordingly, many *ancient* professions and organizations had to deal with big data: astronomers and astrologists, kings and generals, merchants and sea captains, tax surveyors and alchemists, accountants and legal administrators, archivists and librarians, officials occupied with censuses, the creation of baptismal registries and mortality statistics, or the introduction of civil registrations. Many breakthroughs and discoveries in the history of computer science, mathematics, and statistics were the result of or at least related to big data problems, or could be interpreted as such. They are well documented in the history of science, namely, the Arab–Indian number system, the introduction of zero, the invention of the printing press, the system of double bookkeeping, and so on. In the seventeenth century, Johannes Kepler had to deal with a big data problem in his astronomical calculations on data supplied by Tycho Brahe; the logarithms of John Napier offered the solution. The many hitherto hardly used data from the baptismal registers and other demographic data inspired John Graunt, William Petty, and others in the seventeenth century to develop their statistics. Johan de Witt and Johannes Hudde required big data to construct their life insurance policy and to lay the foundations for actuarial science. The father of Blaise Pascal was a tax collector and benefited from the mechanical calculator that his son had developed. Bernoulli laid one of the mathematical foundations behind the *more is better* philosophy of the current big data era with his empirical law of large numbers, bridging the gap between the observable and the underlying real world, thus paving the way for inferential statistics. His contemporaries, John Arbuthnot, Bernard Nieuwentijt, and Patrick Sussmilch among others, in the eighteenth century concluded after a big data analysis, combining many distributed sources, that due to divine intervention the proportions of newly born boys and girls seemed to be fixed. At the end of the nineteenth century, the famous American census caused a serious big data problem for the government; Herman Hollerith developed his famous mechanical tabulating machine based on punch cards to tackle it. In about the same period, it was the British statistician Karl Pearson who got at his disposal large amounts of complex and very diverse biometrical data, systematically collected by his friend and maecenas Francis Galton. Being one of the founding fathers of nineteenth-century statistics himself, Galton convinced Pearson that the intrinsic variability in living nature did allow a mathematical treatment without deprecatory interpretations of deviations and error functions (Starmans, 2011). Pearson understood that in order to do justice to the variability and complexity of nature, variation should be identified not just in the errors of measurement, but in the phenomena themselves, encoded in data, unlike his predecessors Pierre-Simon Laplace and Adolphe Quetelet, who tried to correct or repair the phenomena to make them fit the normal distribution. Studying the large collections for data supplied by Galton, Pearson found that phenomena were not normally distributed, but were intrinsically skewed. He showed that they could well be described by using his by now famous four parameters (mean, standard deviation, skewness, and kurtosis) and in fact could be classified by families of skewed distributions. The *animated* power to deal with these big data was supplied by the so-called compilatores, a group of women employed by Pearson, who had to calculate the four parameters in a kind of atelier. Indeed, Pearson gave the probability distribution a fundamental place in science, as the mechanism that generated the data, but for Pearson, it was in fact a substitute for reality due to his extreme empiricism and idealism. He contemplated the world at a different level of abstraction, where data, variation in data, data-generating mechanisms, and more specifically the four parameters encode or build up a reality. Rather than representing or describing the alleged material reality, they replaced it. The clouds of measurements became the objects of science, and material reality was replaced by the concept of a probability distribution. It was an abstract world, identified with data and thus, accessible, intelligible, and knowledgeable through the observation of big data. The distribution was essentially a summary of the data. In this monist position, the whole idea of statistical inference was basically a form of goodness-of-fit testing (Starmans, 2011, 2013). In addition, Ronald Fisher, Pearson's enemy and in some ways his successor, famously arrived in 1919 at the Rothemstad Experimental Station in Hertfordshire, England, and found many data systematically collected and archived, but they were left untouched because no one was able to analyze them properly. They enabled Fisher to develop his ideas on the design of experiments and to write his studies on crop variation. The *avalanche of numbers*, eloquently proclaimed by the philosopher Ian Hacking, shows many instances of the nineteenth century. This very short, unavoidably unbalanced, and far from representative anthology can easily be expanded, but it illustrates the many dimensions of scalability, including reciprocal relations and mutual dependencies, both in practical and scientific matters. Sometimes, big data caused the problem, and sometimes they led the way to the solution, exhibiting an alternating technology push and pull. We need data to gain insight and knowledge, we need tools to manage the data, but if more data become available, sometimes unintended, new tools and techniques are required, thus encouraging the application of computer science and the emergence of statistics.

1.4 The Apory of Complete Knowledge

From a philosophical perspective, the genealogy of big data has another important aspect: the underlying knowledge ideal based on the ancient quest for complete and certain knowledge. This knowledge ideal carries a dual apory, because knowledge is usually inherently uncertain and inherently incomplete. The question is of course whether the idea of complete knowledge is still incoherent in modern times in an almost dataficated world. The ubiquity of data got stature and was prepared by developments in computer science over the past 20 years, ranging from embedded systems and distributed computing to ambient intelligence ubiquitous computing and smart environments and as a next step the Internet of Things. But big data not only exist by the grace of practical and scientific issues but also express a human preoccupation. It is nothing but a manifestation of the age-old human aspiration to capture everything: collect, store, analyze, interpret, and prevent it from oblivion in order to acquire knowledge and to control nature, thereby challenging the Creator's crown, a typical case of *vana curiositas*, or even *hubris*. The underlying ideal of knowledge involves a quest for certain and complete knowledge, which man from that day would take with great perseverance, but which has a dual apory. Knowledge is usually inherently uncertain and incomplete. It is uncertain because it often involves probability statements, which mostly are approximately true; testimony can be unreliable, canonical sources turn out to be false, experts are unmasked, so sometimes the truth seems just contingent, time- and culture-bound and the validity of knowledge is limited. Simultaneously, knowledge is incomplete in the sense that we do not know most of what is the case or which is true, and despite intensive efforts, it is also hardly obtainable and may not even be knowable. We cannot see, perceive, understand, remember, deduce, detect, avoid oblivion, collect, store, make available, and integrate everything. In a way, uncertainty primarily concerns the nature and quality of knowledge, whereas incompleteness refers to the acquisition, or rather, the availability and the quantity of the knowledge. The notion of full knowledge is notoriously problematic in many respects. She alludes to the omniscience of the Creator and can thus be regarded as an expression of hubris, she ignores finiteness and temporality, but also the limits of human cognition and condition. It also raises political and social questions (publicity, privacy, and equality) is computationally *intractable* and therefore from epistemological standpoint elusive, if not utopian, incoherent, or illusory. It therefore comes as no surprise that epistemology since ancient times has focused almost exclusively on the more manageable problem of secure, valid, and reliable knowledge.

The alleged apory of complete knowledge finds its antithesis along two roads. First, it can be argued that in specific, precisely defined contexts, it has indeed a meaningful interpretation. For example, in formal logic, a system is said to be complete if each proposition that is true in a particular class of models is also derivable, that is to say, it can be found with the aid of a system of derivation rules. Complementary to this system is called a *sound* if each proposition that is derivable is also true. In computer science, researchers in the field of information retrieval use related criteria for the evaluation of search results. Using the concepts of recall and precision, two core questions can be answered. If a document is relevant (*true*), what is the probability that it will be found/retrieved (*derived*)? Conversely, if the term is found, what is the probability that it is relevant? The notion of completeness is strictly defined and conditional: if something is true, it can be found. This is obviously only a prelude to a full quantitative approach to information such as the Shannon information theory-based entropy, which is considered by many as the universal notion of information, and the theory of Kolmogorov complexity, which measures the amount of information by the ease with which a compression of a string of *characters* can be implemented and that complexity is identified with *minimal description length*.

All this will not convince the critics. A second way to challenge the apory takes many forms and manifestations of the pursuit of full knowledge, both in the narrative tradition and in the history of science. Often, this is done under the influence of new technologies: writing, printing, photography, film, computer, and the Internet. We can touch upon only a few *issues* here. First, the *Atlantis motif*, ranging from the rediscovery of the old *perfect* knowledge that had been lost (the Renaissance) to the anamnesis of Plato, and prevention of that knowledge from falling prey to oblivion. In addition, the *Borges motif*, namely the abundance of knowledge, is embodied in the notion of *information overload* and is themed and depicted in Borges's Library of Babel Labyrinth. Next, we may identify the *Eco-motif*, which concerns hidden, secret, or forbidden knowledge, reserved only for initiates (the Pythagoreans, the Rosicrucian order, etc.), aptly described by Umberto Eco in his best-selling novel *The Name of the Rose* published in 1980. These and other *aspects* are manifest from early antiquity to the present: the textbooks of Varro (agriculture) and Vitruvius (engineering), *compilatores* as Pliny the Elder, even Euclid and Ptolemy, which in geometry or astronomy actually realized synthesis. The development formed the famous Library of Alexandria through the 18th emancipator project of *Diderot's Encyclopedia* toward the twentieth-century Gutenberg project and the ideal of *liberalized* knowledge, underlying the principle of *collaborative writing and editing* of Wikipedia. Moreover, in this respect, the quest for complete knowledge seems an indispensable aspect of the *homo mensura* principle, and it cannot be omitted in a reflection on the genealogy and philosophy of big data, although we can only touch upon it in this chapter. The latter specifically applies to one particular feature of the idea of complete knowledge: its pejorative reading in the narrative tradition, not unlike other technical innovations, as we already mentioned. Through the ages, often the dark side of it is emphasized: *vana curiositas* hubris or arrogance and faustian preoccupations. In many myths, religious texts, legends, literary, and other cultural expressions, the disobedience to the gods or to nature has been formulated and depicted as a preventive warning, and is dominantly reflected in the design or use of technical artifacts. The myth of Prometheus, the Fall of Icarus, the solar car of Phaeton, and the biblical story of the Tower of Babel have almost become archetype in this regard. That applies equally to the ultimate goal of human beings to create artificial life or *to own image* to build new people. In Ovid's *Pygmalion* and Carlo Collodi's *Pinocchio*, all seemed to be rather innocent, as established by divine or supernatural intervention. In contrast, *Mary Shelley's Frankenstein* knew no *deus ex machina*; here it was the science itself that brought about the transformation, and the consequences were significantly more terrifying. The horror and science fiction literature for a substantial part exists by virtue of these human preoccupations, and it exploits the fears for uncontrollable robots or computers that take over the human mind completely. In the footsteps of Jules Verne and H. G. Wells, a genre has been created, whose best manifestations and appearances are so often as elaborate as real futurological studies. Profound scientific and technological knowledge is linked to an unbridled imagination, which often even in old philosophical problems is thematic and deep. The actual dystopia usually will consider only when the threat concerns the social and political order, but it also touches the human condition. The genre now has many modern classics, some of which have become rather iconic, including *2001: A Space Odyssey* (1968) or more recently *The Matrix*, a film that appeared in 1999 (Starmans, 2015a). It is remarkable that many dystopias in the narrative tradition since ancient times show a strong big data component. It paradoxically started already with Plato. Noteworthy is a passage in his dialog the *Phaedrus*, in which King Thamos is deeply worried about the invention of writing, because he fears that it allows man to rely less on his memory and that is precisely an essential part of the essence of man, according to Plato. Undoubtedly, the fundamental importance that Plato ascribes to the memory (anamnesis) in the process of knowledge acquisition can account for this. Given the extensive work that he has written himself, his lament is probably intended as a prophylactic warning for bold authors. Later manifestations of the big data dystopia include George Orwell's classical novel *1984*, the film *Minority Report* (2002), or perhaps even *Moneyball* (2011), although the latter could also be interpreted as a sign of progress.

Be that as it may, from a philosophical point of view, one may debate whether the supposed incoherence of complete knowledge is still defendable due to improved storage, retrieval, processing power, intelligent algorithms, and statistical techniques. Large amounts of very heterogeneous data come available continuously and at high speed. Operational systems monitor millions of online transactions, sensors perform many millions of times per second, and search engines compare billions of searches. This constantly puts new demands on storage, retrieval, and analysis, but the reciprocal relationship between software and hardware constantly shifts the limits of feasibility. The ubiquity of the data, wherein the reality is dataficated, means that everything that exists, or at least is of interest, is encoded in data. In the philosophical sense, this implies the old idea that reality is not described or represented so much in data, but it could be identified and constructed from data. As stated previously, it has already been anticipated in computer science for a long time: building on embedded systems and distributed computing via ambient intelligence, ubiquitous computing, and smart environments to the Internet of Things.

1.5 Bacon and the Emergence of Data Science

In addition to the genealogy of big data in general, the Wigner versus Google dichotomy can also be traced back to sources that are more ancient. Summarizing the debate, on the one hand, there is computational data analysis, dominated by computer science and AI, and on the other hand, classical mathematical statistics, based on hypothesis testing, parameter estimation, confidence intervals, p values, and so on. Many data and algorithms versus statistical mathematical models, computation versus estimation. Opposite to the *monism* of the data analysis with an observable reality, encoded and in a way replaceable or maybe even existent in data, there is the *dualism* of inferential statistics with a perceptible sample and the underlying *theoretical* population. Put differently, *the data speak for themselves* versus the statistical theory, including all kinds of assumptions and ceteris paribus clauses. A reality accessible through data or maybe even identical with data, versus a reality accessible through (mathematical) theory. In a nutshell, this fits the classical distinction between empiricism versus rationalism, but also—regarding the truth pretense that often occurs—the opposition empiricism versus (scientific) realism. After all, classical statistics, other than Bayesianism, considers the parameter as a fixed and unknown quantity to be estimated, and the model should contain (approximation of) the true data generating probability distribution. In the Pythagorean universe in which we (allegedly) live, this division is real. Clearly, epistemology for the most part exists because of the postulated or experienced tension between empiricism and theory, the observations, the data, the *special*, and the concrete on the one hand versus the law-like statements, the theories, and the abstract on the other hand. As such, it also takes little effort to identify classical issues from the philosophy of science, such as Hume's notorious problem of induction, the issue of underdetermination, the Quine–Duhem thesis, the theory-ladenness of perception, and the scientific realism debate as fundamentals in the data science debate. More importantly, however, there are many attempts made to eliminate this kind of contradictions, arguing that it indeed is a false dilemma, which can only exist by sketching a caricature of the opponent's vision. Formulated more benevolently: efforts to reach a synthesis. The contours of empiricism and rationalism as a method for learning were already apparent in antiquity itself and the tension would be discussed throughout the history of ideas by many thinkers, including Plato, Aristotle, Thomas Aquinos, Descartes, Hume, Kant, Mach, and Stuart Mill; the logical positivists and pragmatists such as Peirce; and naturalists such as Quine. Here we have to restrict ourselves to one shining example, and precisely because of the methodological implications of the debate, we seek the help of the seventeenth-century philosopher Francis Bacon (1561–1626), who struggled with similar problems. In his *New Organon* (1620), we find the following oft-quoted passage:

> Those who have handled sciences have been either men of experiment or men of dogmas. The men of experiment are like the ant, they only collect and use; the reasoners resemble spiders, who make cobwebs out of their own substance. But the bee takes a middle course: it gathers its material from the flowers of the garden and of the field, but transforms and digests it by a power of its own. Not unlike this is the true business of philosophy; for it neither relies solely or chiefly on the powers of the mind, nor does it take the matter which it gathers from natural history and mechanical experiments and lay it up in the memory whole, as it finds it, but lays it up in the understanding altered and digested. Therefore from a closer and purer league between these two faculties, the experimental and the rational (such as has never yet been made), much may be hoped.

Here too we observe a flawed opposition, if not a false dilemma. The spider and the ant are opposites, but obviously caricatures and no serious options; the bee is the only reasonable alternative. First, Bacon denounces *idols* that afflict humans and impede the progress of knowledge: cognitive limitations, prejudices, errors, unclear language, and misplaced trust in authority. He distinguishes the idols of the tribe, the grotto, the marketplace, and the theater. The latter links to the belief in authority and canonical texts of antiquity, especially those of Aristotle. As an antidote, Bacon advocates a natural history, which deals with systematic and unbiased collection of data, from which knowledge can be distilled. Bacon believes that induction is a process of generalization, but in a dialogic or maybe even in a dialectical way with a systematic search for counterexamples, a process that is embodied in his famous tables of affirmation, denial, and comparison. He believes that in this way the *form*, the real causes of the phenomena, automatically becomes visible. Bacon objects to both metaphysics and mathematics, which he associates with the spider, but also makes efforts to act not as a naive empiricist in the footsteps of the ant either. He works out his method in such a fashion that it preludes what is now known is the hypothetico-deductive model. With his tables, he uses a kind of dialog logic, with the systematic search for counterexamples (pejorative entities) being central. If the tables would yield contradictory causes or explanations, Bacon states, a critical test should provide definitive, thereby anticipating the *crucial experiments*, which the famous experimenter Robert Hooke would propagate a few decades later. Because of his dialectical and testing-oriented approach, Bacon was as much a hypothetico-deductivist *avant la lettre* as an exponent of a naive inductivist, the latter partly because of his infamous disinterest of mathematics in research methodology. He connects observation and theory and empiricism and rationalism; he tries to reconcile with each other, albeit in a completely different way than Immanuel Kant 150 years later. It could be argued that Bacon on the eve of the scientific revolution was fairly successful. Moreover, because of the direct methodological importance, he inadvertently gave a preamble to the contemporary data science debate, which takes place on the eve of a new revolution, proclaimed in science (Starmans, 2015b). In the next sections, it will be argued that the debate requires after the thesis of classical statistics and antithesis of the computational data analysis a synthesis in a kind of Hegelian triad, anticipated by Bacon.

1.6 Herald of the Controversy

Although Bacon could clearly be considered an ancestor of the debate, we will now confine ourselves to a specific and contemporary statistical understanding and elucidation of the issue, and the key figure is undoubtedly the American mathematician John W. Tukey (1915–2000). In the annals of the history of science, he is primarily chronicled for his contributions in the field of statistics and data analysis. In 1977, his now classic monograph *Exploratory Data Analysis* (*EDA*) saw the light (Tukey, 1977), however, he was already successful in many areas inside and outside of statistics. Originally a chemist, he shifted his attention to mathematics and earned his PhD at Princeton on a topological subject. His interest in metamathematics led to contributions to logic and model theory (Tukey's lemma), his investigations in spectral analysis of time series resulted among others in the famous algorithm for the fast Fourier transform. In statistics, his name has been associated with the post hoc test of the variance analysis (e.g., the Tukey range test), a resampling method as the jackknife and of course to many descriptive, often-graphic techniques, ranging from box plots and stem-and-leaf plots to smoothing techniques and all kinds of new descriptive metrics. Tukey worked with various renowned scientists such as the physicist Richard Feynman, the computing pioneer John von Neumann and Claude Shannon, Turing Award laureate Richard Hamming, and statistician Samuel Wilks. Among the many concepts and notions introduced by Tukey, *bits* and *software* are undoubtedly the most famous ones. Of the many other neologisms attributed to him, some will probably be apocryphal, but they indisputably illustrate Tukey's influence on the times in which he lived. With respect to the themes addressed in this chapter, an essential aspect of his legacy concerns the fact that he appears the herald of the current controversy. In fact, he ushered in a new phase in the development of statistics and data analysis, which as a Hegelian process is taking place now and has to be completed in the era of big data (Starmans, 2013). This triptych of thesis–antithesis–synthesis will be briefly discussed in the next sections.

1.6.1 Exploratory Data Analysis

We start with the publication of *EDA*, a remarkable and in many ways unorthodox book, which is very illustrative for the underlying debate. First, it contains no axioms, theorems, lemmas, or evidence, and even barely formulas. Given Tukey's previous theoretical mathematical contributions, this is striking, though he certainly was not the first. Ronald Fisher, who wrote *Statistical Methods for Research Workers* (1925), which went through many reprints and in fact can be considered as the first methodological and statistical manual, was his predecessor. This book provided many practical tips for conducting research, required only a slight mathematical knowledge, and contained relatively few formulas. Partly as a result, Fisher's methods in biology, agronomy, and psychology were quickly known and canonized, well before the mathematical statistics had codified these insights. However, Tukey was in many ways different from Fisher, who of course was a theoretical statistician at heart. *EDA* hardly seems comparable to traditional statistical handbooks. It contains no theoretical distributions, significance tests, p values, hypotheses, parameter estimates, and confidence intervals. There were no signs of confirmatory or inferential statistics, but purely the understanding of data, looking for patterns, relationships, and structures in data, and visualizing the results. According to Tukey, a detective has to go to work like a contemporary Sherlock Holmes, looking for clues, signs, or hints. Tukey maintains this metaphor consistently throughout the book and provides the data analyst with a toolbox full of methods for the understanding of frequency distributions, smoothing techniques, scale transformations, and, above all, many graphic techniques, for exploration, storage, abstraction, and illustration of data. Strikingly, *EDA* contains a large number of neologisms, which Tukey sometimes tactically or polemically uses, but which may have an alienating effect on the uninitiated reader. He chooses the words because of his dissatisfaction with conventional techniques and nomenclature, which according to him are habitually presented as unshakable and sacred by his statistical colleagues to the researcher. Finally, the bibliography of *EDA* has remarkably few references for a voluminous study of nearly 700 pages. There are only two of these: a joint article by Mosteller and Tukey and the Bible.

1.6.2 Thesis

The unorthodox approach of Tukey in *EDA* shows a rather fundamental dissatisfaction with the prevailing statistical practice and the underlying paradigm of inferential/confirmatory statistics. The contours of this tradition began to take shape when the probabilistic revolution during the early twentieth century was well under way: first, with the probability distributions and goodness-of-fit procedures developed by Karl Pearson, then the significance tests and maximum likelihood estimation (MLE) developed by Ronald Fisher, the paradigm of hypothesis testing by Jerzy Neyman and Egon Pearson, and the confidence intervals of Neyman. These techniques combined with variance and regression analysis showed a veritable triumphal procession through the empirical sciences, and often not just methodologically. Biology and psychology sometimes seemed to be transformed or reduced to applied statistics. According to some researchers, inferential/testing statistics became virtually synonymous with the *scientific method* and appeared *philosophically justified* since the 1930s, especially with the advancement of the hypothetical-deductive method and Popper's concept of falsifiability. The success inevitably caused a backlash. This is not only because many psychologist and biologists rejected the annexation of their field by the statisticians without a fight but also because of intrinsic reasons. The embrace of the heritage of Pearson, Fisher, and Neyman did not cover up the fact that various techniques were contradictory, but were presented and used as a seemingly coherent whole at the same time. In spite of the universal application, there were many theoretical and conceptual problems regarding the interpretation and use of concepts such as probability, confidence intervals, and other (alleged) *counterintuitive* concepts, causing unease and backlash that continue even to this day. The emergence of nonparametric and robust statistics formed a prelude to a countermovement, propagated by Tukey since the 1960s.

1.6.3 Antithesis

Although Tukey in *EDA* does his best to emphasize the importance of confirmatory tradition, the antagonism becomes manifest to the reader in the beginning of the book. Moreover, he had already put his cards on the table in 1962 in the famous opening passage from *The Future of Data Analysis.*

> For a long time I have thought that I was a statistician, interested in inferences from the particular to the general. But as I have watched mathematical statistics evolve, I have had cause to wonder and to doubt. And when I have pondered about why such techniques as the spectrum analysis of time series have proved so useful, it has become clear that their 'dealing with fluctuations' aspects are, in many circumstances, of lesser importance than the aspects that would already have been required to deal effectively with the simpler case of very extensive data where fluctuations would no longer be a problem. All in all, I have come to feel

> that my central interest is in data analysis, which I take to include, among other things: procedures for analyzing data, techniques for interpreting the results of such procedures, ways of planning the gathering of data to make its analysis easier, more precise or more accurate, and all the machinery and results of mathematical statistics which apply to analyzing data. (...) Data analysis is a larger and more varied field than inference, or allocation.

Also in other writings, Tukey makes a sharp distinction between statistics and data analysis, and this approach largely determines the status quo. First, Tukey unmistakably contributed to the emancipation of the descriptive/visual approach, after a pioneering work of William Playfair (eighteenth century) and Florence Nightingale (nineteenth century) after the rise of *inferential power* in the previous period. In addition, it can hardly be surprising that many see in Tukey a pioneer of computational disciplines such as data mining and machine learning, although he himself assigned a modest place to the computer in his analyses. More importantly, however, Tukey, because of his alleged antitheoretical stance, is often regarded as the person who tried to undo the Fisherian revolution. He could thus be regarded as an exponent or precursor of today's erosion of the concept model, with the view that all models are wrong, that the classical concept of truth is obsolete, and pragmatic criteria as predictive success should come first in data analysis.

1.6.4 Synthesis

This one very succinct opposition has many aspects that cannot be discussed in this chapter. We focus on three considerations. Although it almost sounds like a platitude, it must first be noted that *EDA* techniques nowadays are implemented in all statistical packages either alone or sometimes by using hybrid inferential methods. In current empirical research methodology, *EDA* has been integrated in different phases of the research process. In the second place, it could be argued that Tukey did not undermine the revolution initiated and set forward by Galton and Pearson, but on the contrary he grasped the ultimate consequences to this position. Indeed, it was Galton who had shown 100 years before that variation and change are intrinsic in nature, urging to search for the deviant, the special or idiosyncratic, and indeed it was Pearson who realized that the straitjacket of the normal distribution (Laplace and Quetelet) had to be abandoned and replaced by many (classes of) skewed distributions. Galton's heritage suffered a little by the successes of the parametric, strong model assumptions-based Fisherian statistics and was partly restored by Tukey. Finally, the contours of a Hegelian triad became visible. The nineteenth-century German philosopher G.F.W. Hegel postulated that history goes through a process of formation or development, which evokes a thesis and an antithesis, both of which are then to be brought to a higher level to be *completed*, thereby leading to a synthesis. Applied to the less metaphysically oriented present issue, this dialectical principle seems very apparent in the era of big data, which evokes a convergence between data analysis and statistics, creating similar problems for both. It sets high demands for data management, storage, and retrieval; has a great influence on the research of efficiency of machine learning algorithms; and also involves new challenges for statistical inference and the underlying mathematical theory. These include the consequences of misspecified models, the problem of small, high-dimensional datasets (microarray data), the search for causal relationships in nonexperimental data, quantifying uncertainty, efficiency theory, and so on. The fact that many data-intensive empirical sciences depend heavily on machine learning algorithms and statistics makes the need for bridging the gap compelling for practical reasons. It appears so in a long-standing philosophical opposition, which manifests the scientific realism debate. Roughly put, the scientific realist believes in a *mind-independent* objective reality that can be known and from which true statements can be made. This applies equally to postulated theoretical entities. In contrast, the empiricist/instrumentalist, who accepts no reality behind the phenomena, doubts causality and has a more pragmatic vision of truth. Thus considered, Fisher belonged to the first tradition. He shows himself as a dualist in the explicit distinction between sample and population; the statistic is calculated in the sample. It has a distribution of its own based on the parameter, a fixed but unknown quantity that can be estimated. It focuses on the classic problems of *specification*, *estimation*, and *distribution*. From this point of view, the empiricist and anticausalistic Karl Pearson belonged to the second tradition. He also replaced the material reality by the probability distribution, but according to him, this distribution was observable in the data, not as an expression or other narrative for an underlying *real* world. Although Pearson was far from antitheoretical, Tukey and his conception of data analysis resemble more as the anticausalistic, goodness-of-fit-oriented, monist Pearsonian tradition than as the causalistic, estimation-oriented, dualist Fisherean approach.

1.7 Plea for Reconciliation

In the previous sections, we showed how the issue of current practice of data analysis has certain aspects that can be traced back to classical epistemic positions. They have traditionally played a role in the quest for knowledge, the philosophy of science, and in the rise of statistics: the ancient dichotomy between empirism and rationalism, the Baconian stanza, the Pearson–Fisher controversy, Tukey's sharpening of the debate, and most recently the Wigner–Google controversy. It also appeared that not all controversies are based on the same dimension, there is no one-to-one correspondence, and many seem to suffer from the fallacy of the false dilemma, as may be concluded from the many attempts to rephrase the dilemma. Perhaps the coexistence of positions is a precondition (in the Hegelian sense) for progress/synthesis, but the latter is not always manifest in practice. Due to the growing dependency on data and the fact that all sciences, including epistemology, have experienced a probabilistic revolution, a reconciliation is imperative. We have shown that the debate has many aspects, including, among other things, the erosion of models and the predicament of truth, the obscure role of the dualist concept of estimation in current data analysis, the disputed need for a notion of causality, the problem of a warranted choice for an appropriate machine learning algorithm, and the methodology required to obtain data. Here, we will discuss such an attempt for reconciliation, restricting ourselves to a few aspects, which are typical for current practice of data analysis and are also rooted in the tradition we have sketched. We then outlined briefly how to ensure such a step toward reconciliation from the proposed methodology such as targeted maximum likelihood estimation (TMLE), combined with super learning (SL) algorithms (Van der Laan and Rose, 2011; Starmans and van der Laan, 2013; Van der Laan, 2013).

Typically, the current practice of statistical data analysis relies heavily on parametric models and MLE as an estimation method. The unbiasedness of MLE is of course determined by the correct specification of the model. An important assumption is that the probability distribution that generated the data is known up to a finite number of parameters. Violation of this assumption and misspecification of the model may lead to unbiased and extremely difficult interpretation of estimators, often identified with coefficients in a (logistic) regression model. This cannot be repaired by a larger sample size or big data.

In this respect, George Box's famous dictum that "Essentially, all models are wrong, but some are useful" is often quoted, but there really is a clear erosion of the model concept in statistics, sometimes making the classic concept of truth obsolete. Models often demonstrably do not obtain the (approximation of the) true data generating distribution and ignore the available realistic background knowledge. The models must therefore be *bigger*, which makes the MLE problematic. Essential here is the fact that the maximum likelihood estimators are typically nontargeted, but do not have to be estimated to answer almost any conceivable research question, requiring only a low-dimensional target parameter of the distribution. Because of a nontargeted approach, an evaluation criterion is used, which is focused on the fit of the entire distribution, and the error is spread over the entire distribution. The MLE of the target parameter is then not necessarily unbiased, especially in high-dimensional datasets (e.g., microarray data) and/or data with thousands of potential covariates or interaction terms. The larger the statistical model, the more problematic the nontargeted approach.

Targeted learning starts with the specification of a nonparametric or semiparametric model that contains only the realistic background knowledge and focuses on the parameter of interest, which is considered as a property of the as yet unknown, true data generating distribution. This methodology has a clear imperative: model and parameter of interest must be specified in advance. The (empirical) research question needs to be translated in terms of the parameter of interest. Additionally, a rehabilitation of the model concept is realized. Subsequently, targeted learning involves an estimation procedure that takes place in a data-adaptive, flexible way in two steps. First, an initial estimate is searched on the basis of the relevant part of the true distribution, which is needed to evaluate the target parameter. This initial estimator is found using the SL algorithm. In short, this is based on a library of many diverse analytical techniques, ranging from logistic regression to ensemble techniques, random forest, and support vector machines. Because the choice of one of these techniques is generally subjective and the variation in the results of the different techniques is usually considerable, a kind of weighted sum of the values is calculated by means of cross-validation. On the basis of this initial estimator, the second stage of the estimation procedure can then be started, wherein the initial fit is updated with the objective of an optimum bias-variance trade-off for the parameter of interest. This is accomplished with a targeted maximum likelihood estimator of the fluctuation parameter of a selected submodel parameter by the initial estimator. The statistical inference is then completed by calculating standard errors on the basis of the *influence-curve theory* or resampling techniques. Thus, parameter estimation keeps, or rather regains, a crucial place in the data analysis. If one wants to do justice to variation and change in the symptoms, one cannot deny Fisher's unshakable insight that randomness is intrinsic and implies that the estimator of the parameter of interest itself has a distribution. Big data, and even census survey or other attempts to discount or encrypt the whole of reality in the dataset, cannot replace it. After doing justice to the notion of a model, and the restoration of the dualist concept of estimation in the practice of data analysis, two methodological criteria are at stake: a specifically formulated research question and the choice of the algorithm, which is less dependent on personal preferences. Finally, some attention has to be paid to the notion of causality, which is always a difficult area in statistics, but is now associated with this discipline and, of course, in the presence of big data is considered to be unnecessary and outdated. (Correlations are sufficient!) It cannot be overemphasized that the experience of cause–effect relationships in reality is inherent to the human condition, and many attempts to exclude it, including those of Bertrand Russell and Karl Pearson, have dramatically failed. Most of the data analyses include impact studies or have other causal connotations. The TMLE parameter can be interpreted statistically in the statistical model. By the addition of nontestable assumptions, the parameter can, however, also be causally interpreted and be connected to the estimation theory.

Of course, in this brief exposé, only some aspects of the issue could be addressed, including a few historical–philosophical considerations on the genealogy of big data, and some methodological problems related to statistical/data analytic practice, arguing that statistics and computational data analysis in a dataficated world are two sides of the same coin, rather than contradicting each other.

References

Bacon, F. 1620. *Novum Organon*. Edition: The New Organon. Cambridge University Text, 2000, p. 79.

Davenport, T.H., D.J. Patil. 2012. Data scientist: The sexiest job of the 21st century. *Harvard Business Review*, 90(10): 70–76.

Fisher, R. 1925. *Statistical Methods for Research Workers*. Edinburgh, Scotland: Oliver and Boyd.

Halevy, A., P. Norvig, F. Pereira. 2009 March/April. The unreasonable effectiveness of data. *IEEE Intelligent Systems*, 24(2): 8–12.

Lesk, A.M. 2000. The unreasonable effectiveness of mathematics in molecular biology. In *The Mathematical Intelligencer*, Volume 22, pp. 28–37.

Mayer-Schönberger, V., K. Cukier. 2013. *Big Data: A Revolution that Will Transform How We Live, Work and Think*. Boston, MA: Houghton Mifflin Harcourt.

Starmans, R.J.C.M. 2011. Models, inference and truth: Probabilistic reasoning in the information era. In M.J. Van der Laan, S. Rose (Eds.), *Targeted Learning: Causal Inference for Observational and Experimental Data*, pp. 1–20, 648p. New York: Springer.

Starmans, R.J.C.M. 2013. Picasso, Hegel and the era of big data (in Dutch). *STAtOR*, 24(2).

Starmans, R.J.C.M. 2015a. Contemporary dystopias: The fall of icarus and the wrath of the machines. *Filosofie*, 25(1).

Starmans, R.J.C.M. 2015b. The ant, the spider and the bee; Bacons unintended preamble to the data science debate (in Dutch). *Filosofie*, 25(3).

Starmans, R.J.C.M., M.J. van der Laan. 2013. Inferential statistics versus machine learning: A prelude to reconciliation (in Dutch). *STAtOR*, 24(2).

Tukey, J.W. 1962. The future of data analysis. *The Annals of Mathematical Statistics*, 33: 1–67.

Tukey, J.W. 1977. *Exploratory Data Analysis*. Pearson.

van der Laan, M.J., S. Rose. 2011. *Targeted Learning: Causal Inference for Observational and Experimental Data*. Springer Series in Statistics. New York: Springer.

van der Laan, M.J., R.J.C.M. Starmans. 2014. *Entering the Era of Data Science: Targeted Learning and the Integration of Statistics and Computational Data Analysis*. Advances in Statistics, 20p. New York: Hindawi Publishing Corporation.

Velupillai, V. 2005. The unreasonable ineffectiveness of mathematics in economics. *Cambridge Journal of Economics*, 29(6): 849–872.

White, E.T. 1938. *Mathematics: Queen and Servant of Science* (ed. 1951). New York: McGraw-Hill.

Wigner, E. 1960 February. The unreasonable effectiveness of mathematics in the natural sciences. *Communications in Pure and Applied Mathematics*, 13(1): 1–14. New York: John Wiley & Sons.

2

Big-n *versus Big*-p *in Big Data*

Norman Matloff

CONTENTS

2.1 No Need for Statistics with Big Data? 21
2.2 Notation and Notions of Dimensionality 22
2.3 Toward a Rough Taxonomy of Big Data 22
2.4 Case of Big-n 23
2.4.1 Basic Method 23
2.4.2 Validity of the SA Method 24
2.4.3 Complexity Analysis 24
2.4.4 Examples 25
2.5 Case of Big-p 26
2.5.1 Running Examples: Linear Regression and PCA 26
2.5.2 Curse of Dimensionality 26
2.5.2.1 Data Sparsity 26
2.5.2.2 Variable Sparsity May Ameliorate the COD 27
2.5.3 Principle of Extreme Values 28
2.5.4 What Theoretical Literature Tells Us 29
2.5.5 Example 30
2.6 Conclusion 30
References 31

What do we—or should we—mean by the word *big* in the phrase *Big Data*? And to what degree are the problems of Big Data solved, being solved, or have a poor outlook for solution? These questions will be discussed in this chapter, examining some analyses in the research literature along with some simple models, with the goal of clarifying some issues for practical but careful data scientists.

Consider the classical setting of n observations in p variables, stored in an $n \times p$ matrix A. Though the popular image of Big Data involves Big-n settings, typical Big Data applications also involve Big-p. Both Big-n and Big-p will be treated here, in different senses, the former from a computational point of view and the latter in a statistical context.

2.1 No Need for Statistics with Big Data?

A commonly held myth is that statistical inference is not an issue with Big Data. It is believed that the sample size n is so large that standard errors of estimates are essentially 0, and thus the problems of Big Data are only computational in nature, not statistical. But this view is inaccurate. Standard errors, especially relative to effect size, can indeed be large even with Big Data.

For a quick, simple example, consider Figure 1.D in [17]. It shows very wide error bars for some types of graph configurations, in spite of n having a value of over 54 million. One would find large standard errors in other kinds of analyses on this data, say for coefficients of dummy variables in a linear regression model.

Similarly, the standard errors of coefficients in linear regression tend to grow as p increases, so for very large p, standard errors do become an issue. Indeed, the familiar problems of *multiple comparisons* or *simultaneous inference* worsen as p grows, for large but fixed n.

Thus, the Big-p problem is just as important as Big-n. Indeed, a central issue will be the size of p relative to n. Though a plethora of procedures have been developed in recent years for Big-p settings, we will view these methods from a safe distance, in order to understand their goals and possible pitfalls.

2.2 Notation and Notions of Dimensionality

Many authors, such as [3,10], like to use the term *high-dimensional data* rather than *Big Data*. This is an allusion to the importance of the Big-p problem. In this section, we develop our first notions along such lines, to be elaborated upon as the chapter progresses.

The usual setting will be assumed: We have n observations in p variables, stored in an $n \times p$ matrix A. The dimensionality of the problem is then taken to be p.

This formulation is somewhat narrow, in at least two senses, which can be described as follows:

- Many of today's applications have less regularity than this. For instance, there may be a varying number of quantities per observation.
- The statistical dimensionality of the problem may be different from, often greater than, the number of variables.

The second item above is especially important. In modeling, a distribution is a mixture of k Gaussians; for example, we could easily have $k > p$. Even more to the point, in nonparametric modeling for regression or classification, the effective dimensionality is infinite.

Nevertheless, the $n \times p$ setting will suffice for the discussion here. In some cases, though, p will denote the dimensionality of a parameter space.

2.3 Toward a Rough Taxonomy of Big Data

It would be useful to establish a working definition of Big Data, in terms of the relation between n and p. Let us focus on parametric models here, with $\theta \in R^p$ denoting the parameter vector to be estimated. For instance, θ could be the vector of coefficients in a linear model.

The results of [14] are very relevant here. For p-dimensional parametric exponential families, Portnoy showed that maximum likelihood estimators will be asymptotically normal in the usual sense if $p^2/n \to 0$ as $p, n \to \infty$. Since, as noted above, there are still reasons to be concerned about standard errors in Big Data, this criterion is appealing, and we might define Big-p as $p > \sqrt{n}$.

On the other hand, if one is willing to assume *variable sparsity*, meaning that most components of θ are zero or small, one can at least obtain consistency results even if $p \gg n$ [3]. (It will be explained below why we call this concept *variable* sparsity, i.e., sparsity in the variables.)

But what about nonparametric approaches? Indications here are dismal, as will be discussed in Section 2.5.2, though a possible remedy is proposed there.

In other words, there is no hard-and-fast definition of Big-p. One's definition depends on one's goals and assumptions. There will be an elaboration on this point in the following sections.

2.4 Case of Big-n

One of the first aspects of Big-n that comes to mind is computation time. Here, we discuss the elements of a simple yet very powerful method to reduce that computation, which will be referred to as *software alchemy* (SA). For further details, including software for the method and references to work by various authors related to SA, see [13].

2.4.1 Basic Method

Suppose one has a certain estimator one wishes to apply to one's data. For concreteness; say, for example, we are finding an estimated coefficient vector in logistic regression using the R **glm()** function. Instead of applying **glm()** to all n observations, we break the data into r groups of size k, apply **glm()** to each group, then average the resulting r estimated coefficient vectors.

If we have a multicore machine or other parallel system that allows parallel computation of degree r, then the computation done in this manner can be much faster than if we were to simply apply **glm()** to the full dataset.

More formally defined, the method is as follows. Let $X_1, X_2, ..., X_n$ be i.i.d., with common distribution F_X, and let θ be some function of F_X. Both X and θ could be vector-valued.

Let $\widehat{\theta}$ be an estimator of θ based on n observations, and divide the data into r groups, and let $k = \lfloor n/r \rfloor$. Specifically, the first group consists of $X_1, ..., X_k$, the second comprises $X_{k+1}, ..., X_{2k}$, and so on. (If r does not evenly divide n, the last group will of size larger than k.) Now compute the analogs of $\widehat{\theta}$ on each group, yielding $\tilde{\theta}_1, \tilde{\theta}_2, ..., \tilde{\theta}_r$. Finally, take the average of these values:

$$\overline{\theta} = \frac{1}{r}\sum_{i=1}^{r} \tilde{\theta}_i \tag{2.1}$$

This becomes our estimator.

The utility of this method also extends to distributed databases, such as the Hadoop Distributed File System. There our data are already stored in chunks, and thus ready for using the above method.

Note carefully the i.i.d. assumption. In some datasets, there has been some preprocessing performed that invalidates this assumption. For instance, the data may be stored in an order determined by the sorted values of one of the variables. This is the case, for example, with the flight delay data used later in this chapter, which is stored in date order. In such a setting, the data must be randomized before applying the method.

In the parallel processing literature, the term *embarrassingly parallel* (EP) refers to applications in which computation may be split into chunks whose computation can be done independently of each other. For instance, finding the sum of elements of a vector has the EP property, whereas complex sorting algorithms do not. The above-described method has a big advantage in that it in essence can convert a non-EP statistical problem into an EP one, as the computation of the $\tilde{\theta}_i$ above can be done independently of each other, hence the term SA—converting non-EP problems to (statistically equivalent) EP ones.

R code implementing SA is available in [13].

2.4.2 Validity of the SA Method

The speedup in computation would of course be useless if $\overline{\theta}$ were less statistically accurate than $\widehat{\theta}$. Fortunately, that is not the case. In [13], it was shown that the SA method works well for any asymptotically normal estimator, in the sense that SA achieves the same statistical accuracy as that estimator:

> Fix r while letting n and k go to ∞. If $\widehat{\theta}$ is asymptotically multivariate normally distributed with asymptotic covariance matrix Σ, then the same holds for $\overline{\theta}$.

In other words, $\overline{\theta}$ has the same statistical accuracy as that of $\widehat{\theta}$, and thus our speedup in computation does not come at the expense of statistical accuracy. This result is intuitively clear, and is proven using characteristic functions in [13].

It is clear that the SA method also works if p is growing, as long as one has asymptotically normal estimators. For this reason, a rough criterion for usability of the method might be taken to be $p < \sqrt{n}$, the Portnoy criterion discussed above; a more conservative criterion would be to apply the above to the groups, that is, require $p < \sqrt{n/r}$.*

Concerning the asymptotic nature of the SA method, note that it is used only in situations in which n is large enough for SA to bring a computational speedup, settings in which n should be large enough for the asymptotics to have taken hold. SA was applied to a variety of estimators in [13], and excellent agreement between $\overline{\theta}$ and $\widehat{\theta}$ was found, with proportional difference always being under 0.001 and in most cases much smaller.

Note that another reason for restricting use of the method to Big-n is bias, which may be more prominent in smaller samples. See Section 2.5.3 for a discussion of this in the principal components analysis (PCA) setting.

Since the data groups are independent, it is straightforward to calculate an estimated covariance matrix for $\overline{\theta}$; we simply take the sample covariance of the r quantities $\tilde{\theta}$, divided by r. The R code available in [13] does this.

2.4.3 Complexity Analysis

Suppose the work associated with computing $\widehat{\theta}$ is $O(n^c)$. This would be the case, for instance, in computation of any *U-statistic*, in which one must apply some function to all possible (X_i, X_j) pairs of observations in our data, so that we must do $O(n^2)$ amount of computation. If the r chunks are handled simultaneously on a parallel machine, say multicore, SA reduces the time complexity of an $O(n^c)$ problem to roughly $O(n^c/r^c)$.

Thus, statistical applications with computational time complexity greater than or equal to $O(n)$ will be major beneficiaries of SA. Examples of such applications investigated in [13] include quantile regression, estimation of hazard functions with censored data, and so on.

For $c > 1$ SA brings a *superlinear* speedup, meaning a speedup that is faster than linear in r; the latter would only reduce the time to $O(n^c/r)$. Another noteworthy point is that

*One sometimes hears that Tukey recommended that one use not more than $\sqrt{n}$ predictor variables in regression analyses, but the author has not found a reference for this.

a similar analysis shows that we attain a speedup for $c > 1$ even if the groups are handled serially on a uniprocessor machine, with time $r\ O(n^c/r^c) = O(n^c/r^{c-1})$.

However, in some applications, the run-time complexity depends substantially on p, not just r. In the linear regression case, for example, the run time is first $O(np^2)$ to form sums of squares and cross products, and then $O(p^3)$ time to perform matrix inversion. Using QR factorization instead of matrix inversion, the latter time may be $O(p^2)$, depending on which quantities are computed, but the point is that the situation is not so simple as considering the time effects of n. The case of PCA is similar.

One of the investigations performed in [13], for instance, simulated linear regression computation with $n = 200{,}000$ and $p = 125$. SA yielded a speedups of 1.70 and 2.49 with 4 and 16 cores, respectively.* By contrast, the simulations done for quantile regression exhibited superlinear behavior: For a problem size of $n = 50{,}000$ and $p = 75$, speedups of 8.06 and 25.55 were obtained with 4 and 16 cores.

2.4.4 Examples

In [13], the SA method was investigated via simulation. Here, let us look at some real data, specifically the airline flight delay data (http://stat-computing.org/dataexpo/2009).

The approximately 500,000 records of the 2008 dataset were used in this example. The R **glm.fit()** function was used to predict whether a flight will be more than 10 minute late, using the variables ActualElapsedTime, DepDelay, DepTime, Distance, Month, TaxiIn, and TaxiOut as predictors. A much more sophisticated prediction model could be developed, say by converting Month to seasonal dummy variables, but here the goal was to illustrate the SA method.

The run times in seconds, and values of the estimated coefficient for the DepDelay variables were as follows:

Cores	**Time**	**DepDelay coef.**
1	195.593	0.203022181
4	123.331	0.203025159
8	82.160	0.203027800
16	85.454	0.203032682

Substantial speedups were obtained up through 8 cores, though using 16 cores did not help further. The latter behavior is typical in the parallel processing world; after a certain point, additional parallelization does not bring benefit, and may actually reduce speedup. In addition, the estimated DepDelay coefficients obtained using SA were in very close agreement with that of applying **glm.fit()** to the full data. The same is held for the estimated coefficients of the other predictor variables, which are not shown here.

Next, consider ridge regression, using the implementation of the CRAN package *ridge*. Here, the ridge parameter λ is set via an algorithm, so computation can be lengthy. The results have been tabulated as follows:

Cores	**Time**	**ActualElapsedTime coef.**
1	90.173	0.3643521
4	53.336	0.3643433
8	39.584	0.3643375
16	47.696	0.3643163

Again, substantial speedups are obtained, and the SA estimator is virtually indistinguishable from the non-chunked one.

*Here and in Section 2.4.4, the machine used was a 16-core system with a hyperthreading degree of 2, thus with parallel computation capability approaching 32. The machine was running OpenBLAS for matrix operations.

2.5 Case of Big-p

Our focus now shifts to statistical consideration, in Big-p settings. The Big-p case has become commonplace, even central, to the Big Data field. Yet the problems with this situation are not always clearly identified and discussed. We will explore such points in the following sections.

2.5.1 Running Examples: Linear Regression and PCA

As running examples to cite for concreteness, let us take linear regression models and PCA. Linear models are important due to their ubiquity, and due to the fact, noted in Section 2.5.2, that nonparametric regression methodology may be problematic in Big-p settings. PCA plays a major role in many analyses of Big Data, ironically because it is often used for *dimensionality reduction*—turning Big-p into Small-p.

We will assume the standard notation for the regression case: We have a matrix X of predictor variable data and vector Y of response variable data, and the usual formula

$$\widehat{\beta} = (X'X)^{-1}X'Y \tag{2.2}$$

gives us the vector of estimated coefficients.

2.5.2 Curse of Dimensionality

The curse of dimensionality (COD), an old notion due to Bellman, is often mentioned in Big Data contexts. Indeed, Bellman's concept may be viewed as the forerunner of Big-p research.

2.5.2.1 Data Sparsity

A major aspect of the COD is the idea that most points in a bounded region of high-dimensional space are distant from each other. For instance, consider nearest-neighbor regression, in which we predict the response variable—the *Y value*—of a new observation to be the average of the responses of the k observations in our training set whose predictor variables are closest to the new one. With high values of p, one can show that those neighboring observations tend to be far from the new one [2]. They thus tend to be *unrepresentative*. especially at the edges of the data space.

These considerations are described dramatically in [18, p. 101]: "To maintain a given degree of accuracy of [a nonparametric regression] estimator, the sample size must increase exponentially with [p]." This is quite an irony. Early researchers in nonparametric regression methods would have envied analysts who enjoy today's Big-n datasets, as the nonparametric methods need large n to be effective, for fixed p. But the COD implies that all this can be lost if we are also in a Big-p setting. Thus, parametric models turn out to be useful even with Big Data.

However, arguably the impact of the COD is not yet fully clear. For example, a common explanation for the COD is that as $p \to \infty$, the volume of the unit hypersphere relative to that of the unit hypercube goes to zero [4]. Therefore, if the variables have, say, a uniform distribution on the hypercube, the probability that a point is within 0.5 unit of the center goes to 0. This supports the notion that data for large p are *sparse*, a condition we will refer to here as *data sparsity*, to distinguish it from the notion of variable sparsity introduced earlier.

Yet as pointed out in [12], this data sparsity argument depends crucially on choosing the l_2 (Euclidean) metric

$$d[(x_1, ..., x_p), (y_1, ..., y_p)] = \sqrt{(x_1 - y_1)^2 + ... + (x_p - y_p)^2} \tag{2.3}$$

If one instead uses the l_∞ metric

$$d[(x_1, ..., x_p), (y_1, ..., y_p)] = \max(|x_1 - y_1|, ..., |x_p - y_p|) \tag{2.4}$$

then *all* points are within 0.5 of the center, so that the volume argument no longer implies sparsity.

However, there are other arguments for sparsity that do not involve a specific metric. In [7], for instance, it is shown, again with the unit hypercube as our data space, that the size of a subcube needed to contain a certain fraction of our data grows with p. The results in [2] apply to general metrics.

2.5.2.2 Variable Sparsity May Ameliorate the COD

The work showing data sparsity in Section 2.5.2.1 has one common assumption: all variables/dimensions should be treated identically. Revisiting this assumption may be the key to dealing with the COD.

In nonparametric prediction applications, for instance, it may be that the unweighted sums in Equations 2.3 and 2.4 should be replaced by weighted ones, with the more important predictor variables carrying larger weights, say

$$d[(x_1, ..., x_p), (y_1, ..., y_p)] = \sqrt{w_1(x_1 - y_1)^2 + ... + w_p(x_p - y_p)^2} \tag{2.5}$$

Then as p grows, neighbors of a given point are mainly those points that are close for the important predictor variables. Sparsity is then not an issue, and the COD becomes less relevant [12]. In essence, the effective value of p remains bounded as the actual value increases.

Of course, finding the proper set of weights would be a challenge. If one knows the rough order of importance of the predictors in a regression setting, one might try, say, $w_i = i^\gamma$, and choose γ by cross-validation, for instance. But in any case, the above argument at least shows that, in principle, the COD may not be as large an obstacle as presently thought.

Another approach to the COD has been assumptions of variable sparsity. In regression, this may be a reasonable assumption, motivated as follows. Suppose

$$E(Y|X_1, X_2, ...) = \sum_{i=1}^{\infty} \beta_i X_i \tag{2.6}$$

say with the X_i i.i.d. $N(0,1)$. Then, the simple existence of the right-hand side implies that $\beta_i \to 0$ as $i \to \infty$. In other words, only a finite number of the β_i are *large*, fitting our definition of variable sparsity. And typically our predictors are correlated, with this again reducing the effective value of p.

This is part of the motivation of LASSO regression [16]. Here, we choose $\widehat{\beta}$ to minimize

$$||Y - X\widehat{\beta}||^2 \tag{2.7}$$

as usual, except now with the constraint

$$\sum_i |\widehat{\beta}_i| \leq \lambda \tag{2.8}$$

This typically yields an estimator with many 0s, that is, a sparse solution.

The situation is not so clearcut in the case of PCA. To see why, first recall that the eigenvalues in PCA represent an apportionment of the total variance of our p variables. Many analysts create a *scree plot*, displaying the eigenvalues in decreasing order, with the goal of determining an effective value of p. This produces good results in many cases, especially if the data have been collected with regression of a specific variable as one's goal. The above discussion involving Equation 2.6 suggests that a scree plot will begin to flatten after a few eigenvalues.

By contrast, consider a dataset of people, for instance. Potentially there are a virtually limitless number of variables that *could* be recorded for each person, say: height, weight, age, gender, hair color (multivariate, several frequencies), years of education, highest degree attained, field of degree, age of first trip more than 100 miles from home, number of surgeries, type of work, length of work experience, number of coworkers, number of times filing for political office, latitude/longitude/altitude of home, marital status, number of marriages, hours of sleep per night and many, many more. While there are some correlations between these variables, it is clear that the effective value of p can be extremely large.

In this kind of situation, the total variance can increase without bound as p grows, and there will be many strong principal components. In such settings, PCA will likely not work well for dimensional reduction. Sparse PCA methods, for example, [19], would not work either, since the situation is not sparse.

Another approach to dealing with the COD that may be viewed as a form of variable sparsity is to make very strong assumptions about the distributions of our data in application-specific contexts. A notable example is [5] for genomics data. Here, each gene is assumed to have either zero or nonzero effect, the latter with probability ϕ, which is to be estimated from the data. Based on these very strong assumptions, the problem becomes in some sense finite-dimensional, and significance tests are then performed, while controlling for false discovery rates.

2.5.3 Principle of Extreme Values

In addition to sparsity, the COD may be viewed as a reflection of a familiar phenomenon that will be convenient to call the principle of extreme values (PEV):

> PEVs: Say $U_1, ..., U_p$ are events of low probability. As p increases, the probability that at least one of them will occur goes to 1.

This is very imprecisely stated, but all readers will immediately recognize it, as it describes, for example, the problem of multiple comparisons mentioned earlier. It is thus not a new concept, but since it will arise often here, we give it a name.

The PEV can be viewed as more general than the COD. Consider, for instance, linear regression models and the famous formula for the covariance matrix of the estimated coefficient vector,

$$\text{Cov}(\widehat{\beta}) = \sigma^2(X'X)^{-1} \tag{2.9}$$

Suppose all elements of the predictor variables were doubled. Then, the standard errors of the estimated coefficients would be halved. In other words, the more disperse our predictor variables are, the better. Thus, data sparsity is actually helpful, rather than problematic as in the nonparametric regression case.

Thus, the COD may not be an issue with parametric models, but the PEV always comes into play, even in the parametric setting. Consider selection of predictor variables for a linear regression model, for example. The likelihood of spurious results, that is, of some predictors appearing to be important even though they are not, grows with p, again by the PEV.

There is potential trouble in this regard for PCA as well. Say we are working with variables $W_1, ..., W_p$, and write $W = (W_1, ..., W_p)'$. The largest eigenvalue is

$$\lambda_1 = \arg\max_u \mathrm{Var}(u'\mathrm{W}) = \arg\max_u u'\mathrm{Cov}(\mathrm{W})u, \quad ||u]] = 1 \tag{2.10}$$

Our estimate of λ_1 will be calculated using the sample covariance matrix $\widehat{\mathrm{Cov}(\mathrm{W})}$ of W in Equation 2.10, that is,

$$\widehat{\lambda_1} = \arg\max_u u'\widehat{\mathrm{Cov}(\mathrm{W})}u, \quad ||u]] = 1 \tag{2.11}$$

The PEVs then come into play for large p relative to n. Since we are maximizing, the estimate of λ_1 will be greatly biased upward. For example, suppose $X_1, X_2, ...$ are i.i.d. $N(0,1)$. Let $W_1 = X_1 + X_2$, with $W_i = X_i$ for $i > 1$. In this case, the true population value of λ_1 is 2.62 (independent of p), while in simulated samples for various p, the following values of $\widehat{\lambda_1}$ were obtained:

p	$\widehat{\lambda_1}$
50	2.62
500	4.34
5000	17.17

In other words, the PEV will likely result in severe distortions in PCA.

2.5.4 What Theoretical Literature Tells Us

There is a vast theoretical literature on the Big-p case. No attempt is made here to summarize it, but again as a guide to our thoughts, here are just a few citations (somewhat arbitrarily chosen):

- The 1988 paper by Portnoy [14] has already been mentioned. It roughly finds that we are *safe* if p is $o(\sqrt{n})$. But it does not exclude the possibility that methods might be found that allow much larger values of p than this.

- One common way to deal with Big-p settings in regression modeling is to do variable selection, thus reducing p. A component in many variable selection techniques is *cross-validation.* To assess a model, we repeatedly fit the model to one part of the data and use the result to predict the remaining, *left out,* portion. To the surprise of many, if not all, researchers in this field, work in 1993 by Shao [15] showed that cross-validation does not work unless the size k of the *left out* portion, relative to n, goes to 0 as n goes to infinity. While this is not a major impediment in practice, the surprising nature of Shao's result suggests that our intuition may be weak in finding good methods for the Big-p case, many of which are based on choosing a tuning parameter by cross-validation.

  Arguably, Shao's result is yet another consequence of the PEVs: Unless k becomes small, there will be so many of subsamples in our cross-validation process that enough of them will contain extreme values to distort the final extimator.

- Work such as [8] in 2009 has investigated conditions under which PCA estimates are consistent for fixed n and $p \to \infty$. They consider *spiked* patterns of eigenvalues, as proposed by Johnstone. Their results are positive but the technical conditions would likely be quite difficult (or impossible) to verify in practice.

- Indeed, difficult-to-verify technical conditions plague the entire theoretical literature in Big-p topics. Moreover, some of the results are negative, that is, showing potential lack of consistency of the LASSO, as in [9].

This issue of verifying technical assumptions is key. For example, consider [8], the PCA analysis cited above. First, they assume a ρ-mixing condition. Roughly speaking, this says that there is some permutation of our variables such that any pair of the (newly indexed) variables are less correlated if their indices are distant from each other, with the correlation going to zero as the distance goes to infinity. This may be a natural assumption in a time series context, but questionable in many others. Moreover, the assumption would be difficult to verify empirically, since the PEVs implies there will be a lot of spurious correlations.

Another assumption made in that paper is that

$$\frac{\sum_{i=1}^{p} \lambda_{ip}^2}{(\sum_{i=1}^{p} \lambda_{ip})^2} \to 0 \quad \text{as } p \to \infty \tag{2.12}$$

where λ_{ip} is the ith-largest eigenvalue for the first p variables. Again, the PEV is a problem here, as it causes, as noted earlier, large biases in the estimated eigenvalues, a big obstacle to verifying the assumption.

The list of assumptions of course does not stop there. One result, for instance, makes an assumption of *uniformly bounded eighth moments* on components of a certain complicated matrix expression.

To be sure, in a mathematical sense work such as this has been deep and very highly impressive. However, its connection to practical data analysis is unclear.

2.5.5 Example

An approach this author has found useful in explaining Big-p issues to data analysts has been that of Foster and Stine at Wharton [6]. Interested in the effects of overfitting, they added noise variables to the data, completely unrelated to the data. After performing a linear regression analysis, every one of the fake predictor variables was found to be *significant.* This is an excellent illustration of the PEVs, and of the use of significance testing for variable selection.

This author ran a similar analysis using LASSO, specifically the R **lars** package. The dataset is from Census 2000, for those working as programmers or engineers in Silicon Valley counties. There were 20,009 observations, and 10 variables, such as age and education, with wage income taken as the response variable. In the spirit of the Wharton study, 50 noise variables were added, i.i.d. $N(0,1)$. The original data were centered and scaled.

After running LASSO on the augmented dataset, the value of λ in Equation 2.8 that minimized the Mallows Cp value occurred at Step 20. The latter corresponded to inclusion of variables 6, 1, 8, 3, 5, 9, 2, 48, 26, 45, 27, 33, 14, 21, 58, 55, 49, 38, and 42 (in that order). In other words, LASSO identified 12 of the fake variables as important predictors. It also failed to pick up two of the real variables: 7 and 10.

The invention of the LASSO spawned many refinements, such as elastic net, SCAD, and so on. But it is clear that the PEV is problematic for any such procedure in practice.

2.6 Conclusion

This chapter had the goal of clarifying the problems of Big-n and Big-p in Big Data. Though there is an effective method for dealing with the computational issues in Big-n, it is argued that the statistical issues with Big-p continue to loom large. The data analyst should not conclude from the large number of methods developed in recent years that the problems have been solved.

Though profoundly impressive theoretical research has been done, the assumptions tend to be difficult, or arguably impossible, to verify in real applications. This, along with lack with the capability to perform statistical inference and other concerns, led Berk to write in 2008 [1] that shrinkage estimators such as the LASSO seem to primarily be *niche players.**

In addition, efforts to circumvent the Big-p problem via methods for dimension reduction, notably PCA, may produce substantial distortions, giving the data analyst a false sense of security. These methods tend to have the same problems as with other Big-p methodology.

Yet the problem of Big-p is here to stay, of course. In the end, the data analyst must do *something.* He/she may try various methods, but must keep in mind that we are still very much in uncharted territory here.

References

1. Richard A. Berk. *Statistical Learning from a Regression Perspective.* Springer, New York, 2008.
2. Kevin S. Beyer, Jonathan Goldstein, Raghu Ramakrishnan, and Uri Shaft. When is "nearest neighbor" meaningful? In *Proceedings of the 7th International Conference on Database Theory, ICDT '99*, pp. 217–235, London. Springer-Verlag, Berlin, Gernamy, 1999.
3. Peter Bühlmann and Sara van de Geer. *Statistics for High-Dimensional Data: Methods, Theory and Applications.* Springer Series in Statistics. Springer, New York, 2011.
4. Bertrand S. Clarke, Ernest Fokoué, and Hao H. Zhang. *Principles and Theory for Data Mining and Machine Learning.* Springer, New York, 2009.
5. Bradley Efron. *Large-Scale Inferencef: Empirical Bayes Methods for Estimation, Testing, and Prediction.* Institute of Mathematical Statistics Monographs. Cambridge University Press, Cambridge, 2010.
6. Dean P. Foster and Robert A. Stine. Honest confidence intervals for the error variance in stepwise regression. *Journal of Economic and Social Measurement*, 31:89–102, 2006.
7. Trevor Hastie, Robert Tibshirani, and Jerome Friedman. *The Elements of Statistical Learning: Data Mining, Inference, and Prediction.* Springer, New York, 2003.
8. Sungkyu Jung and J. Stephen Marron. PCA consistency in high dimension, low sample size context. *The Annals of Statistics*, 37(6B):4104–4130, 2009.
9. Keith Knight and Wenjiang Fu. Asymptotics for lasso-type estimators. *The Annals of Statistics*, 28(5):1356–1378, 2000.
10. Inge Koch. *Analysis of Multivariate and High-Dimensional Data.* Cambridge University Press, New York, 2013.

*A 2014 paper [11] provides a procedure for significance testing with the LASSO, but again with restrictive, hard-to-verify assumptions.

11. Richard Lockhart, Jonathan Taylor, Ryan J. Tibshirani, and Robert Tibshirani. A significance test for the lasso. *The Annals of Statistics*, 42(2):413–468, 2014.

12. Norman Matloff. Long live (big data-fied) statistics! In *Proceedings of JSM 2013*, pp. 98–108, The American Statistical Association, 2013.

13. Norman Matloff. Software alchemy: Turning complex statistical computations into embarrassingly-parallel ones. arXiv:1409.5827, 2014.

14. Stephen Portnoy. Asymptotic behavior of likelihood methods for exponential families when the number of parameters tends to infinity. *The Annals of Statistics*, 16:356–366, 1988.

15. Jun Shao. Linear model selection by cross-validation. *Journal of the American Statistical Association*, 88(422):486–494, 1993.

16. Robert Tibshirani. Regression shrinkage and selection via the lasso. *Journal of the Royal Statistical Society, Series B*, 58:267–288, 1994.

17. Johan Ugander, Lars Backstrom, Cameron Marlow, and Jon Kleinberg. Structural diversity in social contagion. *Proceedings of the National Academy of Sciences of the United States of America*, 109(16):5962–5966, 2012.

18. Larry Wasserman. *All of Statistics: A Concise Course in Statistical Inference*. Springer, New York, 2010.

19. Hui Zou, Trevor Hastie, and Robert Tibshirani. Sparse principal component analysis. *Journal of Computational and Graphical Statistics*, 15(2):265–286, 2006.

Part II

Data-Centric, Exploratory Methods

3

Divide and Recombine: Approach for Detailed Analysis and Visualization of Large Complex Data

Ryan Hafen

CONTENTS

3.1 Introduction 35
3.2 Context: Deep Analysis of Large Complex Data 36
3.2.1 Deep Analysis 36
3.2.2 Large Complex Data 37
3.2.3 What is Needed for Analysis of Large Complex Data? 37
3.3 Divide and Recombine 38
3.3.1 Division Approaches 39
3.3.2 Recombination Approaches 39
3.3.3 Data Structures and Computation 40
3.3.4 Research in D&R 41
3.4 Trelliscope 41
3.4.1 Trellis Display/Small Multiples 41
3.4.2 Scaling Trellis Display 41
3.4.3 Trelliscope 42
3.5 Tessera: Computational Environment for D&R 43
3.5.1 Front End 43
3.5.2 Back Ends 43
3.5.2.1 Small Scale: In-Memory Storage with R MapReduce 44
3.5.2.2 Medium Scale: Local Disk Storage with Multicore R MapReduce 44
3.5.2.3 Large Scale: HDFS and Hadoop MapReduce via RHIPE . 44
3.5.2.4 Large Scale in Memory: Spark 44
3.6 Discussion 45
References 45

3.1 Introduction

The amount of data being captured and stored is ever increasing, and the need to make sense of it poses great statistical challenges in methodology, theory, and computation. In this chapter, we present a framework for statistical analysis and visualization of large complex data: divide and recombine (D&R).

In D&R, a large dataset is broken into pieces in a meaningful way, statistical or visual methods are applied to each subset in an embarrassingly parallel fashion, and the results of these computations are recombined in a manner that yields a statistically valid result. We introduce D&R in Section 3.3 and discuss various division and recombination schemes.

D&R provides the foundation for Trelliscope, an approach to detailed visualization of large complex data. Trelliscope is a multipanel display system based on the concepts of Trellis display. In Trellis display, data are broken into subsets, a visualization method is applied to each subset, and the resulting panels are arranged in a grid, facilitating meaningful visual comparison between panels. Trelliscope extends Trellis by providing a multipanel display system that can handle a very large number of panels and provides a paradigm for effectively viewing the panels. Trelliscope is introduced in Section 3.4.

In Section 3.5, we present an ongoing open source project working toward the goal of providing a computational framework for D&R and Trelliscope, called *Tessera*. Tessera provides an R interface that flexibly ties to scalable back ends such as Hadoop or Spark. The analyst programs entirely in R, large distributed data objects (DDOs) are represented as native R objects, and D&R and Trelliscope operations are made available through simple R commands.

3.2 Context: Deep Analysis of Large Complex Data

There are many domains that touch data, and hence several definitions of the terms *data analysis*, *visualization*, and *big data*. It is useful therefore to first set the proper context for the approaches we present in this chapter. Doing so will identify the attributes necessary for an appropriate methodology and computational environment.

3.2.1 Deep Analysis

The term *analysis* can mean many things. Often, the term is used for tasks such as computing summaries and presenting them in a report, running a database query, processing data through a set of predetermined analytical or machine learning routines. While these are useful, there is in them an inherent notion of knowing *a priori* what is the right thing to be done to the data. However, data most often do not come with a model. The type of analysis we strive to address is that which we have most often encountered when faced with large complex datasets—analysis where we do not know what to do with the data and we need to find the most appropriate mathematical way to represent the phenomena generating the data. This type of analysis is very exploratory in nature. There is a lot of trial and error involved. We iterate between hypothesizing, fitting, and validating models. In this context, it is natural that analysis involves great deal of visualization, which is one of the best ways to drive this iterative process, from generating new ideas to assessing the validity of hypothesized models, to presenting results. We call this type of analysis *deep analysis*.

While almost always useful in scientific disciplines, deep exploratory analysis and model building is not always the right approach. When the goal is pure classification or prediction accuracy, we may not care as much about understanding the data as we do about simply choosing the algorithm with the best performance. But even in these cases, a more open-ended approach that includes exploration and visualization can yield vast improvements. For instance, consider the case where one might choose the best performer from a collection of algorithms, which are all poor performers due to their lack of suitability to the data, and this lack of suitability might be best determined through exploration. Or consider an analyst with domain expertise who might be able to provide insights based on explorations that vastly improve the quality of the data or help the analyst look at the data from a new perspective. In the words of the *father of exploratory data analysis*, John Tukey:

> Restricting one's self to planned analysis – failing to accompany it with exploration – loses sight of the most interesting results too frequently to be comfortable. [17]

This discussion of deep analysis is nothing new to the statistical practitioner, and to such our discussion may feel a bit belabored. But in the domain of *big data*, its practice severely lags behind the other analytical approaches and is often ignored, and hence deserves attention.

3.2.2 Large Complex Data

Another term that pervades the industry is *big data*. As with the term *analysis*, this also can mean a lot of things. We tend to use the term *large complex data* to describe data that poses the most pressing problems for deep analysis. Large complex data can have any or all of the following attributes: a large number of records, many variables, complex data structures that are not readily put into a tabular form, or intricate patterns and dependencies that require complex models and methods of analysis.

Size alone may not be an issue if the data are not complex. For example, in the case of tabular i.i.d data with a very large number of rows and a small number of variables, analyzing a small sample of the data will probably suffice. It is the complexity that poses more of a problem, regardless of size.

When data are complex in either structure or phenomena generating the data, we need to analyze the data in detail. Summaries or samples will generally not suffice. For instance, take the case of analyzing computer network traffic for thousands of computers in a large enterprise. Because of the large number of actors in a computer network, many of which are influenced by human behavior, there are so many different kinds of activity that can be observed and modeled such that downsampling or trying to summarize will surely result in lost information. We must address the fact that we need statistical approaches to deep analysis that can handle large volumes complex data.

3.2.3 What is Needed for Analysis of Large Complex Data?

Now that we have provided some context, it is useful to discuss what is required to effectively analyze large complex data in practice. These requirements provide the basis for the approaches proposed in the remainder of the chapter.

By our definition of deep analysis, many requirements are readily apparent. First, due to the possibility of having several candidate models or hypotheses, we must have at our fingertips a library of the thousands of statistical, machine learning, and visualization methods. Second, due to the need for efficient iteration through the specification of different models or visualizations, we must also have access to a high-level interactive statistical computing software environment in which simple commands can execute complex algorithms or data operations and in which we can flexibly handle data of different structures.

There are many environments that accommodate these requirements for small datasets, one of the most prominent being R, which is the language of choice for our implementation and discussions in this chapter. We cannot afford to lose the expressiveness of the high-level computing environment when dealing with large data. We would like to be able to handle data and drive the analysis from a high-level environment while transparently harnessing distributed storage and computing frameworks. With big data, we need a statistical methodology that will provide access to the thousands of methods available in a language such as R without the need to reimplement them. Our proposed approach is D&R, described in Section 3.3.

3.3 Divide and Recombine

D&R is a statistical framework for data analysis based on the popular split-apply-combine paradigm [20]. It is suited for situations where the number of cases outnumbers the number of variables. In D&R, cases are partitioned into manageable subsets in a meaningful way for the analysis task at hand, analytic methods (e.g., fitting a model) are applied to each subset independently, and the results are recombined (e.g., averaging the model coefficients from each subset) to yield a statistically valid—although not always exact—result. The key to D&R is that by computing independently on small subsets, we can scalably leverage all of the statistical methods already available in an environment like R.

Figure 3.1 shows a visual illustration of D&R. A large dataset is partitioned into subsets where each subset is small enough to be manageable when loaded into memory in a single process in an environment such as R. Subsets are persistent, and can be stored across multiple disks and nodes in a cluster. After partitioning the data, we apply an analytic method in parallel to each individual subset and merge the results of these computations in the recombination step. A recombination can be an aggregation of analytic outputs to provide a statistical model result. It can yield a new (perhaps smaller) dataset to be used for further analysis, or it can even be a visual display, which we will discuss in Section 3.4.

In the remainder of this section, we provide the necessary background for D&R, but we point readers to [3,6] for more details.

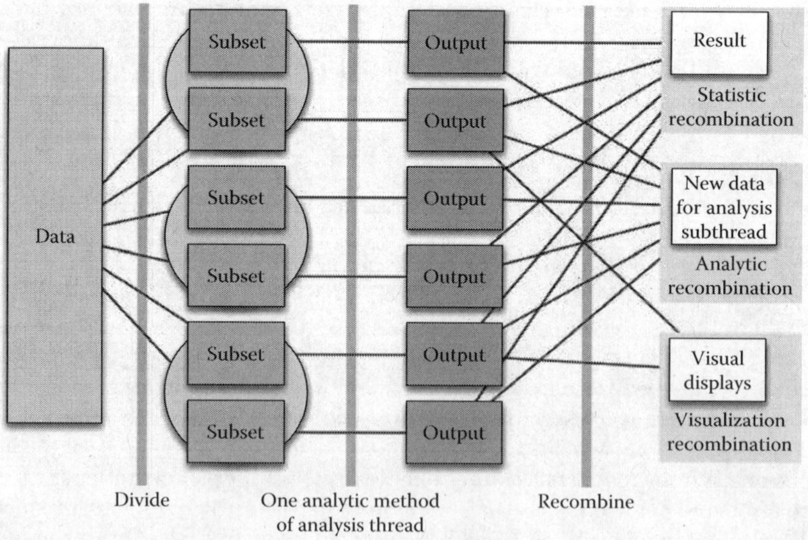

FIGURE 3.1
Diagram of the D&R statistical and computational framework.

3.3.1 Division Approaches

Divisions are constructed by either *conditioning-variable* division or *replicate* division.

Replicate division creates partitions using random sampling of cases without replacement, and is useful for many analytic recombination methods that will be touched upon in Section 3.3.2.

Very often the data are *embarrassingly divisible*, meaning that there are natural ways to break the data up based on the subject matter, leading to a partitioning based on one or more of the variables in the data. This constitutes a conditioning-variable division. As an example, suppose we have 25 years of 90 daily financial variables for 100 banks in the United States. If we wish to study the behavior of individual banks and then make comparisons across banks, we would partition the data by bank. If we are interested in how all banks behave together over the course of each year, we could partition by year. Other aspects such as geography and type or size of bank might also be valid candidates for a division specification.

A critical consideration when specifying a division is to obtain subsets that are small enough to be manageable when loaded into memory, so that they can be processed in a single process in an environment like R. Sometimes, a division driven by subject matter can lead to subsets that are too large. In this case, some creativity on the part of the analyst must be applied to further break down the subsets.

The persistence of a division is important. Division is an expensive operation, as it can require shuffling a large amount data around on a cluster. A given partitioning of the data is typically reused many times while we are iterating over different analytical methods. For example, after partitioning financial data by bank, we will probably apply many different analytical and visual methods to that partitioning scheme until we have a model we are happy with. We do not want to incur the cost of division each time we want to try a new method.

Keeping multiple persistent copies of data formatted in different ways for different analysis purposes is a common practice with small data, and for a good reason. Having the appropriate data structure for a given analysis task is critical, and the complexity of the data often means that these structures will be very different depending on the task (e.g., not always tabular). Thus, it is not generally sufficient to simply have a single table that is indexed in different ways for different analysis tasks. The notion of possibly creating multiple copies of a large dataset may be alarming to a database engineer, but should not be surprising to a statistical practitioner, as it is a standard practice with small datasets to have different copies of the data for different purposes.

3.3.2 Recombination Approaches

Just as there are different ways to divide the data, there are also different ways to recombine them, as outlined in Figure 3.1. Typically for conditioning-variable division, a recombination is a collation or aggregation of an analytic method applied to each subset. The results often are small enough to investigate on a single workstation or may serve as the input for further D&R operations.

With replicate division, the goal is usually to approximate an overall model fit to the entire dataset. For example, consider a D&R logistic regression where the data are randomly partitioned, we apply R's `glm()` method to each subset independently, and then we average the model coefficients. The result of a recombination may be an approximation of the exact result had we been able to process the data as a whole, as in this example, but a potentially small loss in accuracy is often a small price to pay for the simple, fast computation. A more lengthy discussion of this can be found in [6], and some interesting research is discussed in Section 3.3.4.

Another crucial recombination approach is visual recombination, which we discuss in Section 3.4.

3.3.3 Data Structures and Computation

In addition to the methodological concerns of D&R, there are also computational concerns. Here, we define the minimal conditions required for a D&R computational environment.

Data structures are the first important consideration. Division methods can result in partitions where subsets can have nontabular data structures. A generic storage mechanism for data with potentially arbitrary structure is a *key-value store*. In a key-value store, each key-value pair constitutes a subset of the data, and typically the key is a unique identifier or object that describes the subset, and the value contains the data for the subset. When the data are large, there are many distributed key-value store technologies that might be utilized such as the Hadoop Distributed File System (HDFS) [14]. It is important to have the ability to store data in a persistent state on these systems, and useful to have fast random lookup of any subset by key.

A data set that has been partitioned into a collection of subsets stored as key-value pairs, potentially distributed across machines or disks of a cluster, is called a *distributed data object* (DDO). When the data for each subset of a DDO is a slice of a data frame, we can more specifically call such an object a *distributed data frame*.

For D&R computation, we need to compute on a distributed key-value store in parallel and in a way that allows us to shuffle data around in a division step, apply analytic methods to the subsets, and combine results in a recombination step. Environments that implement MapReduce [4] are sufficient for this. In MapReduce, a *map* operation is applied to a collection of input key-value pairs in parallel. The map step outputs a transformed set of key-value pairs, and these results are *shuffled*, with the results being grouped by the map output keys. Each collection of data for a unique map output key is then sent to a *reduce* operation, again executed in parallel. All D&R operations can be carried out through this approach. Systems such as Hadoop [8] that run MapReduce on HDFS are a natural fit for D&R computation.

D&R is sometimes confused as being equivalent to MapReduce. This is not the case, but D&R operations are *carried out* by MapReduce. For example, a division is typically achieved by a single MapReduce operation—the map step reassigns records to new partitions, the shuffle groups the map output by partition assignment, and the reduce collates each partition. The application of an analytic method followed by recombination is a separate MapReduce operation, where the analytic method is applied in the map and the recombination is done in the shuffle and reduce. Recall that division is independent of recombination and typically a division persists and is used for many different recombinations.

A common question that arises when discussing the use of systems such as Hadoop for D&R computation is that of Hadoop being a *batch* processing system. As we discussed in Section 3.2, this fits the purpose of the type of deep analysis we are doing, which is typically *offline* analysis of historical data. Of course, the models and algorithms that result from a deep analysis be adapted and integrated into a real-time processing environment, but that is not the use case for D&R, where we are doing the actual discovery and validation of the algorithms. But speed is still important, and much work is being done to improve the speed of these type of systems, such as Spark [23], which can keep the data in memory distributed across machines, avoiding the most expensive time cost present in Hadoop; reading and writing data to disk multiple times throughout a MapReduce operation.

3.3.4 Research in D&R

The D&R paradigm provides fertile ground for new research in statistical analysis of big data. Many ideas in D&R are certainly not new, and there is a lot of research independent of ours that fits in the D&R paradigm that should be leveraged in a D&R computational environment.

The key for D&R research is to find pairs of division/recombination procedures that provide good results. Existing independent research that relates to D&R that can serve as a platform for new research includes Bayesian consensus Monte Carlo [13], bag of little bootstraps [11], alternating direction method of multipliers [2], and scatter matrix stability weighting [10]. It is important to note that we seek methods that require a very minimal amount of iteration, preferably none, as every MapReduce step can be very costly. There are also many domains of statistics that remain to be studied, including spatial, time series, and nonparametric statistics. There is a great opportunity for interesting research in this area.

3.4 Trelliscope

Visualization is crucial throughout the analysis process. This could not be more true than in the case of large complex data. Typical approaches to visualizing large data are either very specialized tools for data from a specific domain, or schemes that aggregate various aspects of the data into a single plot. Specialized tools generally do not work for deep analysis because of the flexibility required to make any imaginable plot we might deem useful. Visualizations of summaries are indispensable, but alone are not enough. Summaries can hide important information, particularly when the data are complex. We need flexible, detailed visualization that scales. Trelliscope is an approach that addresses these needs.

3.4.1 Trellis Display/Small Multiples

Trelliscope is based on the idea of Trellis display [1]. In Trellis display, the data are split into meaningful subsets, usually *conditioning* on variables of the dataset, and a visualization method is applied to each subset. The image for each subset is called a *panel.* Panels are arranged in an array of rows, columns, and pages, resembling a garden trellis.

The notion of conditioning in Trellis display manifests itself in several other plotting systems, under names such as *faceted* or *small multiple* plots. Trellis display for small data has proven to be very useful for uncovering the structure of data even when the structure is complicated and in making important discoveries in data not appreciated in the original analyses [1]. There are several reasons for its success. One is that it allows the analyst to break a larger or higher dimensional dataset into a series of two-dimensional plots, providing more visual detail. Second is the ability to make comparisons across different subsets. Edward Tufte, in discussing multipanel displays as *small multiples*, supports this benefit, stating that once a viewer understands one panel, they immediately understand all the panels, and that when arranged adjacently, panels *directly depict comparisons* to *reveal repetition and change, pattern and surprise* [16].

3.4.2 Scaling Trellis Display

The notion of conditioning to obtain a multipanel display maps naturally to D&R. We can divide the data in any manner and specify a panel plotting function to be applied to each subset with the recombination being a collation of the panels presented to view. But there is a problem here. Typically in D&R, we are dealing with very large datasets, and typically divisions can result in thousands to hundreds of thousands of subsets. A multipanel display would have as many panels. This can happen even with data of small to moderate size. It is easy to generate thousands of plots, but it is not feasible to look at all of them.

The problem of having more visualizations than humanly possible to cognitively consume is a problem that pioneering statistician John Tukey realized decades ago. Since it is impossible to view every display in a large collection, he put forth the idea of asking the computer to sort out which ones to present by judging the relative interest of showing each of them [18]. He proposed computing diagnostic quantities with the help of a computer to determine which plots to show. In his words, "it seems natural to call such computer guiding diagnostics *cognostics*. We must learn to choose them, calculate them, and use them. Else we drown in a sea of many displays" [18]. Hence, we use the term *cognostic* to mean a single metric computed about a single plot that captures a behavior of interest that can be used by the computer to bring interesting plots to our attention. For any collection of plots, we may be interested in several behaviors, and will therefore compute several cognostics.

There has been interesting research on cognostics for scatterplots, called *scagnostics*, that has yielded metrics that quantify different shapes or behaviors that might present themselves in a scatterplot [21,22]. Beyond scatterplots, there are many useful metrics that might be computed to guide the selection of plots. Many such cognostics may be context-dependent. For example, when dealing with displays of quantile plots, metrics such as the median, first and third quartile, and range might be good cognostics. Or when dealing with time series plots, calculations of slope, autocorrelation coefficient, variance of first-order differences, and so on might be good cognostics. Often, choosing a useful cognostic is heavily based on the subject matter of the data and the particular plot being made. For example, consider a collection quantile plots, one for each county in the United States, showing the age distribution for male and female. For each quantile plot, a useful cognostic might be the difference in median age between genders.

How does the computer use cognostics to determine which plots we should view? There are many possibilities. One is *ranking* or *sorting* the plots based on the cognostics. For example, we can effectively understand the data at extremes of the median age difference by gender by calling up panels with the largest or smallest absolute age difference cognostic. Another possibility is *sampling* plots across the distribution of a set of cognostics, for example, looking at a representative set of panels that spans the age difference distribution. Another action is to *filter* panels of a display to only panels that have cognostics in a range of interest. There are many possible effective ways to get a good representation of *interesting* panels in a large display, particularly when combining cognostics. For example, if we want to find interesting panels with respect to a collection of cognostics, we can, for example, compute projections of the set of cognostics into two dimensions, plot the projection as a scatterplot, and select panels based on interesting regions of the projection. Another possibility is to apply a clustering algorithm to a set of cognostics to view panels representative of each of the clusters.

3.4.3 Trelliscope

Trelliscope is a computational system that implements the ideas of large-scale multipanel display with cognostics for effective detailed display of large complex data [9]. In Trelliscope, the analyst creates a division of the data, specifies a plotting function to be applied to each subset, and also specifies a cognostics function that for each subset will compute a set of metrics. The cognostics are collected from every subset and are used in an interactive viewer allowing the user to specify different actions with the cognostics (sort, filter, and sample) in different dimensions, thereby arranging panels in a desired way.

Trelliscope's multipanel visual recombination system has been influenced by work in *visualization databases* [7]. A visualization database can be thought of as a large collection of many different displays that are created throughout the course of a data analysis, many of which might be multipanel displays. In addition to needing a way to effectively view panels within a single display, we also need ways to store and organize all of the *visual artifacts* that are created during an analysis. Trelliscope provides a system for storing and tagging displays in a visualization database, so that they can easily be sorted through and retrieved for viewing or sharing with others.

3.5 Tessera: Computational Environment for D&R

Tessera is an open source project that implements D&R in a familiar high-level language at the front end and ties to various distributed storage and computing at back ends. Development of Tessera began out of necessity when tackling applied statistical problems involving big data by researchers at Purdue University and has expanded to include statisticians and computer scientists at Pacific Northwest National Laboratory. Development of Tessera has been part of the US government *big data* initiatives including funding from Defense Advanced Research Projects Agency and Department of Homeland Security. In this chapter, we introduce and discuss the components of Tessera. For several examples of how to use Tessera, the reader is encouraged to visit the Tessera website: http://tessera.io/. The website is a more suitable medium than this chapter for providing interactive reproducible tutorials and up-to-date examples.

3.5.1 Front End

The front end of Tessera is the R statistical programming environment [12]. R's elegant design makes programming with data very efficient, and R has a massive collection of statistics, machine learning, and visualization methods. Further supporting this choice is the large R user community and its popularity for statistical analysis of small data. We note, however, that the D&R approach could easily be implemented in other languages as well.

Tessera has two front-end R packages. The first is `datadr`, which is a domain-specific language for D&R operations. This package provides commands that make the specification of divisions, analytic methods, and recombinations easy. Its interface is abstracted from different back-end choices, so that commands are the same whether running on Hadoop or on a single workstation. In `datadr`, large DDOs behave like native R objects. In addition to division and recombination methods, `datadr` also provides several indispensable tools for reading and manipulating data, as well as a collection of division-independent methods that can compute things such as aggregations, quantiles, or summaries across the entire dataset, regardless of how the data are partitioned.

The second front-end package is `trelliscope`. This package provides a visualization database system for storing and managing visual artifacts of an analysis, as well as a visual recombination system for creating and viewing very large multipanel displays. Trelliscope displays can be viewed in an interactive viewer that provides several modes for sorting, filtering, and sampling panels of a display.

3.5.2 Back Ends

The `datadr` and `trelliscope` packages are interfaces to distributed computing back ends. They were designed to be extensible to be able to harness new technology as it comes along.

As discussed in Section 3.3.3, a back end for D&R needs to be able to do MapReduce over a distributed key-value store. Additionally, there needs to be a mechanism that *connects* R to these back ends, as we need to be able to run R code inside of the map and reduce steps. Tessera currently has implemented support for four different back ends which we will discuss in the following sections: in-memory storage with R MapReduce (small), local disk storage with multicore R MapReduce (medium), HDFS storage with Hadoop MapReduce via RHIPE (large), and HDFS storage with Spark MapReduce via SparkR (large).

3.5.2.1 Small Scale: In-Memory Storage with R MapReduce

D&R is not just useful for large data. When dealing with small datasets that fit within R's memory comfortably, the in-memory Tessera back end can be used to store and analyze DDOs (although in this case, the term *distributed* does not really apply). A nonparallel version of MapReduce has been implemented in R to handle all D&R operations for this back end. A nice feature of the in-memory back end is that the only requirements are the `datadr` and `trelliscope` packages, making it an easy way to start getting familiar with Tessera without the need for a cluster of machines or to install other back end components such as Hadoop, which can be a difficult task.

This back end is useful for very small datasets, which in our current experience has typically meant tens or hundreds of megabytes or less. As data gets larger than this, even though it may still be much smaller than the available memory on the machine, the lack of parallel computation and the growing size of objects in memory from making copies of subsets for each thread becomes a problem. Even with parallel in-memory computing in R, we have found the strategy of *throwing more memory at the problem* to not scale.

3.5.2.2 Medium Scale: Local Disk Storage with Multicore R MapReduce

When the data are large enough that they are difficult to handle in memory, another option is to use the local disk back end. The key-value store in this case is simply a collection of files stored in a directory on a hard drive, one file per subset. Computation is achieved with a parallel version of MapReduce implemented in R, making use of R's `parallel` package [12]. As with the in-memory back end, this back end is also useful for a single-workstation setup, although it could conceptually be used in a single network of workstations [15] setting where every workstation has access to the disk.

We have found this back end to be useful for data that is in the range of a few gigabytes.

3.5.2.3 Large Scale: HDFS and Hadoop MapReduce via RHIPE

RHIPE is the R and Hadoop Integrated Programming Environment [5]. RHIPE is an R interface to Hadoop, providing everything from reading, writing, and manipulating data on HDFS, to running Hadoop MapReduce jobs completely from within the R console. Tessera uses RHIPE to access the Hadoop back end for scaling to very large datasets.

Hadoop has been known to scale to data in the range of petabytes. Leveraging RHIPE, Tessera should be able to scale similarly, although the largest amount of data we have routinely used for it is in the multi-terabyte range.

3.5.2.4 Large Scale in Memory: Spark

Another large-scale back-end option that is becoming very popular is Spark. Spark is a general distributed execution engine that allows for keeping data in memory, greatly improving performance. Spark can use HDFS as a distributed storage mechanism. It provides many more data operations than MapReduce, but these operations are a strict superset of MapReduce, and therefore Spark is a suitable back end for Tessera. The additional data operations are a bonus in that the same data being used for D&R can be used for other parallel computing purposes. Tessera connects to Spark using the SparkR package [19], which exposes the Spark API in the R console.

Support in Tessera for Spark at the time of this writing is very experimental—it has been implemented and works, and adding it to Tessera is a testament of Tessera's flexibility in being back end agnostic, but it has only been tested with rather small datasets.

3.6 Discussion

In this chapter, we have presented one point of view regarding methodology and computational tools for deep statistical analysis and visualization of large complex data. D&R is attractive because of its simplicity and its ability to make a wide array of methods available without needing to implement scalable versions of them. D&R also builds on approaches that are already very popular with small data, particularly implementations of the split-apply-combine paradigm such as the `plyr` and `dplyr` R packages. D&R as implemented in `datadr` is future proof because of its design, enabling adoption of improved back-end technology as it comes along. All of these factors give D&R a high chance of success. However, there is a great need for more research and software development to extend D&R to more statistical domains and make it easier to program.

References

1. Richard A. Becker, William S. Cleveland, and Ming-Jen Shyu. The visual design and control of trellis display. *Journal of Computational and Graphical Statistics*, 5(2):123–155, 1996.

2. Stephen Boyd, Neal Parikh, Eric Chu, Borja Peleato, and Jonathan Eck-stein. Distributed optimization and statistical learning via the alternating direction method of multipliers. *Foundations and Trends® in Machine Learning*, 3(1):1–122, 2011.

3. William S. Cleveland and Ryan Hafen. Divide and recombine (D&R): Data science for large complex data. *Statistical Analysis and Data Mining: The ASA Data Science Journal*, 7(6):425–433, 2014.

4. Jeffrey Dean and Sanjay Ghemawat. Mapreduce: Simplified data processing on large clusters. *Communications of the ACM*, 51(1):107–113, 2008.

5. Saptarshi Guha and William S. Adviser-Cleveland. Computing environment for the statistical analysis of large and complex data. PhD thesis, Department of Statistics, Purdue University, West Lafayette, IN, 2010.

6. Saptarshi Guha, Ryan Hafen, Jeremiah Rounds, Jin Xia, Jianfu Li, Bowei Xi, and William S. Cleveland. Large complex data: Divide and recombine (D&R) with rhipe. *Stat*, 1(1):53–67, 2012.

7. Saptarshi Guha, Paul Kidwell, Ryan Hafen, and William S. Cleveland. Visualization databases for the analysis of large complex datasets. In *International Conference on Artificial Intelligence and Statistics*, pp. 193–200, 2009.

8. Apache Hadoop. Hadoop, 2009.

9. Ryan Hafen, Luke Gosink, Jason McDermott, Karin Rodland, Kerstin Kleese-Van Dam, and William S. Cleveland. Trelliscope: A system for detailed visualization in the deep analysis of large complex data. In *IEEE Symposium on Large-Scale Data Analysis and Visualization (LDAV)*, pp. 105–112. IEEE, Atlanta, GA, 2013.

10. Michael J. Kane. Scatter matrix concordance: A diagnostic for regressions on subsets of data. *Statistical Analysis and Data Mining: The ASA Data Science Journal*, 2015.

11. Ariel Kleiner, Ameet Talwalkar, Purnamrita Sarkar, and Michael I. Jordan. A scalable bootstrap for massive data. *Journal of the Royal Statistical Society: Series B (Statistical Methodology)*, 2014.

12. R Core Team. *R: A Language and Environment for Statistical Computing.* R Foundation for Statistical Computing, Vienna, Austria, 2012.

13. Steven L. Scott, Alexander W. Blocker, Fernando V. Bonassi, Hugh A. Chipman, Edward I. George, and Robert E. McCulloch. Bayes and big data: The consensus Monte Carlo algorithm. In *EFaB@Bayes 250 Conference*, volume 16, 2013.

14. Konstantin Shvachko, Hairong Kuang, Sanjay Radia, and Robert Chansler. The Hadoop distributed file system. In *IEEE 26th Symposium on Mass Storage Systems and Technologies*, pp. 1–10. IEEE, Incline Village, NV, 2010.

15. Luke Tierney, Anthony Rossini, Na Li, and Han Sevcikova. *SNOW: Simple Network of Workstations.* R package version 0.3-13, 2013.

16. Edward R. Tufte. *Visual Explanations: Images and Quantities, Evidence and Narrative*, volume 36. Graphics Press, Cheshire, CT, 1997.

17. John W. Tukey. *Exploratory Data Analysis.* 1977.

18. John W. Tukey and Paul A. Tukey. Computer graphics and exploratory data analysis: An introduction. *The Collected Works of John W. Tukey: Graphics: 1965–1985*, 5:419, 1988.

19. Shivaram Venkataraman. *SparkR: R frontend for Spark.* R package version 0.1, 2013.

20. Hadley Wickham. The split-apply-combine strategy for data analysis. *Journal of Statistical Software*, 40(1):1–29, 2011.

21. Leland Wilkinson, Anushka Anand, and Robert L. Grossman. Graph-theoretic scagnostics. In *INFOVIS*, volume 5, p. 21, 2005.

22. Leland Wilkinson and Graham Wills. Scagnostics distributions. *Journal of Computational and Graphical Statistics*, 17(2):473–491, 2008.

23. Matei Zaharia, Mosharaf Chowdhury, Michael J. Franklin, Scott Shenker, and Ion Stoica. Spark: Cluster computing with working sets. In *Proceedings of the 2nd USENIX Conference on Hot Topics in Cloud Computing*, pp. 10–10, 2010.

4

Integrate Big Data for Better Operation, Control, and Protection of Power Systems

Guang Lin

CONTENTS

4.1 Introduction 47
4.1.1 Types of Big Data in Power Systems and Acquisition 48
4.1.2 Big Data Integration Quality Challenges in Power Systems 48
4.2 Integrating Big Data for Model Reduction and Real-Time Decision Making 48
4.2.1 Data Analysis Algorithms for Model Reduction 49
4.2.1.1 *k*-Means Clustering-Based Model Reduction 49
4.2.1.2 Dynamic-Feature Extraction, Attribution, and Reconstruction Algorithm for Model Reduction 49
4.2.1.3 Case Study 52
4.3 Summary 59
4.4 Glossary 59
References 60

As deploying the smart grid infrastructure to power systems, new challenges rise in handling extremely large datasets for better decision making. It is critical to utilize such large datasets in a power system for better operation, control, and protection. In particular, we will focus on discussing data types and acquisition, data management and how to integrate big data for feature extraction, systematic integration, and contingency analysis of power systems.

4.1 Introduction

The term *big data* usually refers to large datasets that are difficult to store, process, and analyze with traditional database and analysis tools. As we are building the smart grid infrastructure, we are facing new challenges in analyzing *big data* for more accurate and robust operation, control, and protection. There are three characteristics of big data in power systems as indicated in [9]: large volume, high velocity, and increasing variety. While building smart grid infrastructure, many metering devices have been introduced to the power systems, which dramatically increase the data volume. In addition, many phasor measurement units (PMU) or synchrophasors have been employed into power systems, which significantly increase the data velocity. The PMU device measures the electrical waves on an electricity grid, using a common time source for synchronization. Time synchronization allows synchronized real-time measurements of multiple remote measurement points on the grid. The PMU device can measure 50/60 Hz AC waveforms (voltages and currents) typically at a rate of 48 samples per cycle (2880 samples per second). The collection of many different types of meter data dramatically increases the variety of big data and places additional difficulty on analyzing such big datasets.

4.1.1 Types of Big Data in Power Systems and Acquisition

Various types of data are tagged with metadata and annotations. Metadata consist of additional information that would help data use, security, and validation. For example, the interpretation, the ownership, the meter device, and the collection location and the date are part of the metadata. Annotations to data can greatly enhance the data search capability and enable better collaboration and workflow development.

The types of acquired data in power systems are equipment parameters, network topology, and connectivity information among different power system components, and anomalous network conditions.

The data in power systems could be either static or real time. Static information is often used for planning for which steady-state data are sufficient. On the other hand, real-time data contain the information that is operational such as current, voltage, and power flow. Such real-time data are often used for real-time operation and control, and in close collaboration with independent system operators and regional transmission organizations, and so on. If big datasets are employed for improving reliability and emergency response, real-time data are required. In contrast, data that require minimal updating can be used for research and planning efforts.

4.1.2 Big Data Integration Quality Challenges in Power Systems

Anomalies in grid data and inconsistencies among data sources must be resolved before applying the data. Inconsistencies may exist in data from different sources. The dataset must pass through rigorous data validity and quality assurance procedures. The structure and requirements of this process affect model acceptance, validity, and credibility.

4.2 Integrating Big Data for Model Reduction and Real-Time Decision Making

Past lessons learned from large blackouts that affect the grid in recent years have shown the critical need for better situation awareness about network disturbances such as faults, sudden changes from renewable generation, and dynamic events. Hence, integrating big data for real-time decision making will greatly enhance the efficiency and security of grid operation. However, the dynamic state estimation model for a large power network is computational expensive, which cannot meet the need for real-time decision making. To achieve this objective, in interconnected power systems, dynamic model reduction can be applied to generators outside the area of interest (i.e., study area) to reduce the computational cost associated with transient stability studies using the real-time big data. Our approach is to utilize real-time big data to reduce a large system of power grid governing equations to a smaller systems for which the solution is an approximate solution to the original system. Our goal is to employ big data that show how generators are behaving to (1) cluster the generators based on similar behavior, and then (2) choose a representative element from each cluster. In doing this we have reduced the system model from the full number of generators to a smaller set of generators. When the full system is too computationally intensive to simulate for forecasting, islanding, contingency analysis, or other simulation activities to support real-time decision making, we can use the reduced system that contains all of the same fundamental behaviors as the full grid. Using this reduced system allows us to save computational time, which is a necessary reduction for real-time decision making.

One of the big data in interconnected power systems is PMU datasets, which collect data synchronously across the power grid. These units are deployed to many systems throughout the grid and are time synchronized so that measurements taken at different locations can be correlated together. The data that we care about, collected from the PMUs, are rotor angle data. These data are collected at the millisecond resolution and give a picture of the oscillation of the rotor angle at each generator. For each generator a time series of rotor angles is collected, $\vec{\delta_i} = \langle \delta_i^{(1)}, \delta_i^{(2)}, \ldots, \delta_i^{(m)} \rangle$, where $\delta_i^{(j)}$ is the rotor angle of generator i at the jth time.

4.2.1 Data Analysis Algorithms for Model Reduction

In this section, we describe several algorithms we use for model reduction of power systems and characteristic generator identification using real-time big data, PMU data.

4.2.1.1 *k*-Means Clustering-Based Model Reduction

k-means clustering is a standard clustering technique [14] and is widely used in many applications [8,10]. The general idea is a recursive algorithm that, in each step, computes centroids of each of the clusters and then reassigns points to the cluster whose centroid it is closest to. This needs an initialization of cluster centroids, which is often done randomly. The algorithm then runs as follows: assign each point to the cluster whose randomly chosen centroid is closest, recompute centroids, reassign points to clusters, recompute centroids, and so on. This is repeated for some predetermined number of steps, or until clusters do not change and the algorithm has converged. One problem with *k*-means clustering is that there is no guarantee that it will terminate in a globally optimal clustering; it is possible to get stuck in a local minimum. Because the initialization is done randomly, there can be multiple clusterings from the same input data.

4.2.1.2 Dynamic-Feature Extraction, Attribution, and Reconstruction Algorithm for Model Reduction

The dynamic-feature extraction, attribution, and reconstruction (DEAR) algorithm [15] is based on the singular value decomposition (SVD) or randomized algorithm [13] to extract the first few principal components for model reduction. The DEAR model reduction method can be summarized as follows:

- *Step 1*: Dynamic-feature extraction—analyze the dynamic response vectors of the original system for a disturbance, and use the SVD or randomized algorithm to extract the first few principal components as the optimal orthogonal bases of these responses.

- *Step 2*: Feature attribution—determine characteristic generators by identifying generators with responses that are highly similar to the optimal orthogonal bases.

  Analyze the similarity between δ_i and x_i; those δ_i with the highest similarity to x are selected to form a subset of δ, which is called a set of characteristic generators.

- *Step 3*: Feature reconstruction—use characteristic generators to describe the full model. Responses of the noncharacteristic generator are approximated by linear combinations of characteristic generators so that only dynamic equations of characteristic generators are kept and a reduced model is obtained.

4.2.1.2.1 Dynamic-Feature Extraction: Finding the Optimal Orthogonal Bases

Here, we discuss the concept of optimal orthogonal bases of a system's dynamic responses and how to identify them using dynamic PMU big dataset.

For convenience, the classical generator model is assumed, and rotor angles, δ, are the state variables. The magnitude of the generator internal voltage, E', is assumed to be constant. Suppose $\delta_1, \delta_2, \ldots, \delta_i, \ldots, \delta_m$ are the m rotor angles of the system to be reduced. The term δ_i is a normalized n-dimensional row vector representing the dynamic of rotor angle δ_i following a disturbance. Its elements are time series: $\delta_i(t_1), \delta_i(t_2), \ldots, \delta_i(t_n)$. Define

$$\delta = [\delta_1; \delta_2; \ldots; \delta_m] \tag{4.1}$$

Here, δ is an $m \times n$ matrix. Suppose $x = [x_1; x_2; \ldots; x_i; \ldots; x_r]$ is the first r principal components from SVD. Here x_i is an n-dimensional row vector, and $r < m$. *Optimal* means that for any $r < m$, δ_i can be approximated by a linear combination of x, and the errors between the approximation, $\hat{s}$, and the actual responses are minimized. In other words, given any $r < m$, we need to find an optimal x, such that $\hat{s} = \kappa x$, where κ is an $m \times r$ matrix, and

$$||\delta - \hat{s}||_2 = \sum_{i=1}^{m} (\delta_i - \hat{s}_i)^T (\delta_i - \hat{s}_i) \tag{4.2}$$

is minimized. We adopt the SVD algorithm for a moderate size of dataset or employ a randomized algorithm [13] for big data to solve the above problem. In particular, through SVD we get

$$\delta = UDW^T \tag{4.3}$$

where U is an $m \times m$ unitary matrix, D is an $m \times n$ rectangular diagonal matrix with nonnegative real numbers on the diagonal, and W^T is an $n \times n$ unitary matrix. The first r^2 rows of W^T constitute the optimal orthogonal bases, which can be used to approximate δ. The diagonal elements of D (i.e., singular values of δ) in descending order are scaling factors indicating the strength or energy of the corresponding row vectors of W^T. Define

$$\begin{aligned} x &= W^T(1:r,:) \\ \kappa &= T(:,1:r) \end{aligned} \tag{4.4}$$

where $T = UD$; κ is the first r columns of T. As a result, δ can be approximated by $\hat{s} = \kappa x$. For any $r < m$, the SVD algorithm can guarantee that Equation 4.2 is minimized.

Remark 4.1 *Although there may exist thousands of modes in the mathematic model of a large-scale power system, usually only a small fraction of them are noticeably excited by a disturbance. We refer to these modes as* dominant modes, *and the rest as* dormant modes. *Usually,* dominant modes *have strong oscillation energy (shown as the* features *in system dynamics), while* dormant modes *have weak energy and are hard to observe. Here, SVD is used to extract the features composed of those* dominant modes, *which correspond to the first r diagonal elements of matrix D in Equation 4.3, unlike how it is used in traditional linear system model reduction methods (e.g., balanced truncation [11] or Hankel norm reduction [7]). More details about the SVD algorithm can be found in [4] and [2].*

4.2.1.2.2 Feature Attribution: Determine Characteristic Generators

The r optimal orthogonal basis vectors found in the feature extraction step will result in minimal errors when used to approximate δ. If each of these basis vectors exactly matches the dynamic angle response of one of the generators, then the angle dynamics of the other generators must have very minimal energy impact (because their corresponding singular values are smaller). This means that we can just keep these r generators in the model and ignore the other generators. Although this will not happen in a real system because generators usually participate in multiple oscillation modes, we still will try to match an optimal basis with the generator whose dynamic response has the highest similarity to this *oscillation pattern*, and will call the generator a characteristic generator. We will then use the set of characteristic generators as suboptimal bases to represent the entire system. To determine the characteristic generators, we need to find a subset of $\delta = [\delta_1; \delta_2; \ldots; \delta_m]$ such that this subset has the highest similarity to x, the optimal orthogonal set. In other words, we need to find

$$\xi = [\delta_p; \delta_q; \ldots; \delta_z] \quad (r = z - p + 1) \tag{4.5}$$

such that ξ is highly similar to x. According to the last subsection, any δ_q can be approximated by a linear combination of the optimal orthogonal bases:

$$\begin{aligned} \delta_p &\approx \kappa_{p1}x_1 + \kappa_{p2}x_2 + \cdots + \kappa_{pi}x_i + \cdots + \kappa_{pr}x_r \\ &\vdots \\ \delta_q &\approx \kappa_{q1}x_1 + \kappa_{q2}x_2 + \cdots + \kappa_{qi}x_i + \cdots + \kappa_{qr}x_r \end{aligned} \tag{4.6}$$

Here, x is the optimal orthogonal basis and δ is normalized [1]. A larger $|\kappa_{qi}|$ indicates a higher degree of collinearity between the two vectors (δ_q and x_i). For example, if $|\kappa_{qi}| > |\kappa_{pi}|$, it indicates that the similarity between x_i and δ_q is higher than that between x_i and δ_p. δ_q will have the highest similarity to x_i, if the inequality in Equation 4.7 holds.

$$|\kappa_{qi}| > |\kappa_{pi}| \quad for \ \forall p \in \{1, 2, \ldots, m\} \quad p \neq q \tag{4.7}$$

By doing so, a rotor angle response of the highest similarity can be identified for each optimal orthogonal basis. As a result, ξ in Equation 4.5 is determined.

Remark 4.2 *The same characteristic generator can appear two or more times in Equation 4.5 when using the criteria in Equation 4.7. For example, if δ_q has the highest similarity to both x_i and x_j, then we will have two δ_q entries in Equation 4.5. In that case, delete one of the entries, and thus, $r = r - 1$.*

Remark 4.3 *From an engineering perspective, some generators may be of particular interest, and detailed information about them is preferred. Dynamic equations for these generators can be kept in the reduced model without being approximated if they are not identified as characteristic generators.*

4.2.1.2.3 Feature Reconstruction: Model Reduction Using the Linear Combination of Characteristic Generators

According to Equations 4.3–4.7, δ can now be arranged as Equation 4.8:

$$\delta = \begin{bmatrix} \xi \\ \bar{\xi} \end{bmatrix} \approx \begin{bmatrix} \kappa_{\xi} \\ \kappa_{\bar{\xi}} \end{bmatrix} x$$

where δ is an $m \times n$ matrix defined in Equation 4.1, ξ is an $r \times n$ matrix defined in Equation 4.5, representing rotor angle dynamics of characteristic generators, and $\bar{\xi}$ is an

$(m-r) \times n$ matrix representing the dynamics of noncharacteristic generators; x is an $r \times n$ matrix and can be calculated from Equation 4.5; and κ_{ξ} is an $r \times r$ square matrix; $\kappa_{\bar{\xi}}$ is an $(m-r) \times r$ matrix. Normally, κ_{ξ} is invertible. We have two different approaches to finding the approximate linear relations between $\bar{\xi}$ and ξ. The first approach is to solve the following overdetermined equation:

$$\bar{\xi} = C\xi \tag{4.8}$$

where C is an $(m-r) \times r$ matrix and can be determined by the least-squares method, namely, $C = \bar{\xi}[(\xi\xi^T)^{-1}\xi]^T$. Another approach is to use the approximate linear relations in Equation 4.8. According to Equation 4.8, we have

$$\xi \approx \kappa_{\xi} x \tag{4.9}$$

and

$$\bar{\xi} \approx \kappa_{\bar{\xi}} x \tag{4.10}$$

Premultiplying κ_{ξ}^{-1} on both sides of Equation 4.9 yields

$$x \approx \kappa_{\xi}^{-1} \xi \tag{4.11}$$

Substituting Equation 4.11 into 4.10 yields

$$\bar{\xi} \approx \kappa_{\bar{\xi}} \kappa_{\bar{\xi}}^{-1} \xi \tag{4.12}$$

Equation 4.8 or 4.12 establishes the approximate linear relations between the rotor angle dynamics of characteristic generators and that of noncharacteristic generators. The dynamics of all generators in the original system then can be reconstructed by using only the dynamic responses from characteristic generators.

4.2.1.2.4 Generalization to High-Order Models

In classical models, it is assumed that the magnitude of the generator internal voltage E' is constant, and only its rotor angle δ changes after a disturbance. In reality, with the generator excitation system, E' will also respond dynamically to the disturbance. The dynamics of E' can be treated in the same way as the rotor angle δ in the above-mentioned model reduction method to improve the reduced model, except that the set of characteristic generators needs to be determined from δ. This way, both δ and E' of noncharacteristic generators will be represented in the reduced model using those of the characteristic generators.

4.2.1.2.5 Online Application of the DEAR Method

For offline studies, the DEAR process can be performed at different conditions and operating points of the target system (external area) to obtain the corresponding reduced models. For online applications, however, computational cost may be very high if SVD has to be calculated every time the system configuration changes. A compromise can be made by maintaining a fixed set of characteristic generators, which is determined by doing SVDs for multiple scenarios offline and taking the super set of the characteristic generators from each scenario. During real-time operation of the system, the approximation matrix C from Equation 4.8 used for feature reconstruction, is updated (e.g., using the recursive least-squares method) based on a few seconds data right after a disturbance. This way, SVD is not needed every time after a different disturbance occurs.

4.2.1.3 Case Study

In this section, the IEEE 145-bus, 50-machine system [5] in Figure 4.1 is investigated. There are 16 and 34 machines in the internal and external areas, respectively. Generator 37 at

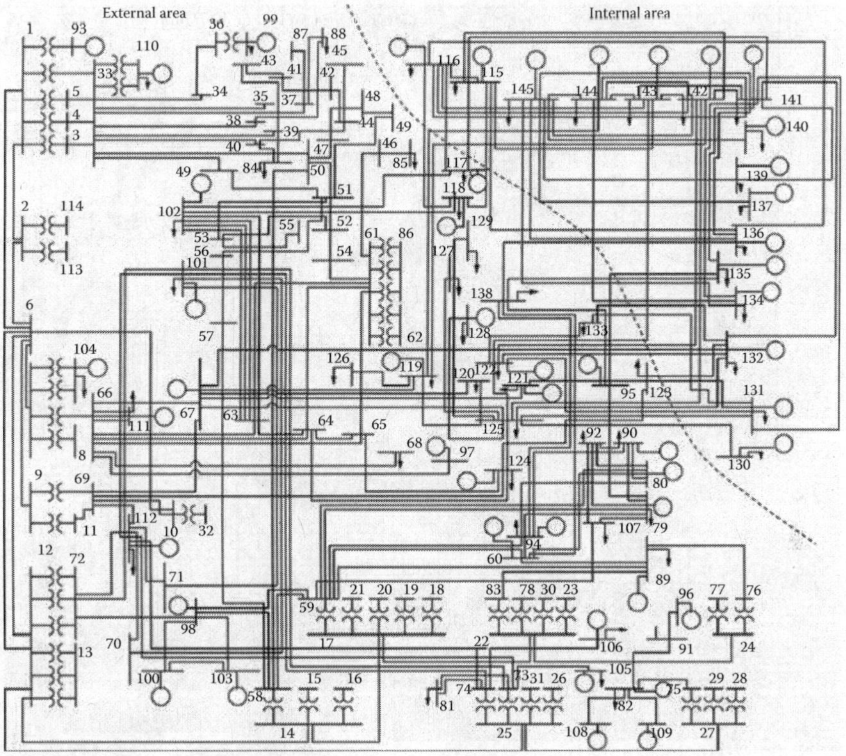

FIGURE 4.1
IEEE 50 machine system. (From S. Wang et al., *IEEE Trans. Pattern Anal. Mach. Intell.*, 29, 2049–2059, 2014.)

Bus 130 in the internal area is chosen as the reference machine. All generators are modeled using classical models. A three-phase, short-circuit fault (F1) is configured on Lines 116–136 at Bus no. 116 at $t = 1$ s. The fault lasts for 60 ms, and then the line is tripped to clear the fault. Postfault rotor angle dynamics in the time interval of $1.2 \leq t \leq 5$ s are analyzed to perform model reduction, using inertial aggregation [6] (one of the coherency-based reduction methods) and the DEAR method, so that their performance can be compared. Many methods are available for coherency identification. In this case study, the principal component analysis method presented by Anaparthi et al. [1] and Moore [12] is chosen to identify coherency groups, and the MATLAB® clustering toolbox is used to aid the analysis. Clustering results according to the rotor angle dynamics in the external area are shown in Figure 4.2. In Figure 4.2, the horizontal axis represents generator numbers, and the vertical axis scales distances between generator groups. Here the distance is defined in the three-dimensional Euclidean space expanded by the first three columns of the matrix T in Equation 4.5. Depending on the distance selected between clusters, different number of coherency groups can be obtained. For example, at a distance larger than 9, two groups are formed (level-2 clustering). Generators 23, 30, and 31 comprise one group, and the other generators comprise another group. Similarly, there are 10 generator groups at level 10, which are shown in the following: Group 1 (generators 30, 31); Group 2 (generator 23); Group 3 (generators 9 and 10); Group 4 (generator 16); Groups 5 (generators 7, 13, and 15); Group 6 (generator 3); Group 7 (generators 32 and 36); Group 8 (generators 8, 18, 25, 33, 34, and 35); Group 9 (generators 2 and 6); Group 10 (generators 1, 4, 5, 11, 12, 14, 17, 19–22, 24, 26,

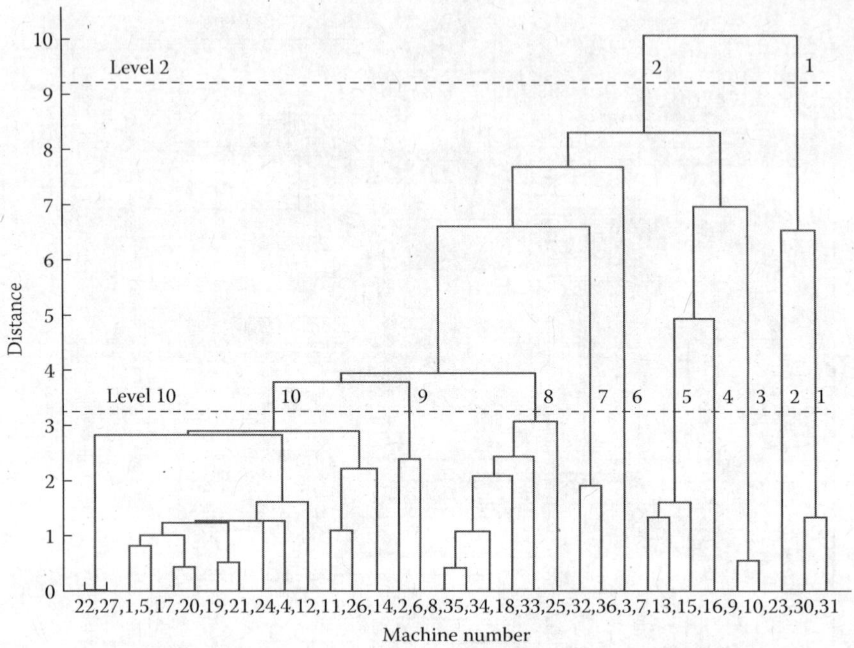

FIGURE 4.2
Coherent groups clustering. (From S. Wang et al., *IEEE Trans. Pattern Anal. Mach. Intell.*, 29, 2049–2059, 2014.)

and 27). Fewer groups result in a simpler system. The normalized (i.e., subtracted by the mean value of the data and divided by its standard deviation) angle dynamics of the 10 groups at level 10 are shown in Figure 4.3, where coherency can be observed between generators in the same group. These coherent machines are then aggregated using the inertial aggregation method reported by Chow et al. [6]. Finally, we obtain a reduced system with 10 aggregated generators for the external system. Following the procedure described above, the optimal orthogonal bases are first obtained by Equations 4.3 and 4.5 and by setting $r = 10$. These 10 basis vectors are shown as the blue solid lines in Figure 4.4. Then, the corresponding 10 characteristic generators are identified using Equation 4.7. The rotor angle dynamics of these characteristic generators are shown as dashed red lines in Figure 4.4. An approximate linear relation between the characteristic generators and the noncharacteristic generators is then established to get the reduced model. Notice that, in this case, δ_2 has the highest similarity to orthogonal bases x_7 and x_8. Therefore, the set of characteristic generators contains only nine elements, which is $\xi = [\delta_{27}\ \delta_3\ \delta_{15}\ \delta_{30}\ \delta_{36}\ \delta_{23}\ \delta_2\ \delta_{18}\ \delta_4]^T$. With the reduced models developed using both coherency aggregation and the DEAR method, the performance of these two methods can be compared. Under the forgoing disturbance, the dynamic responses of generator G42 (connected to the faulted line) from these two reduced models and from the original model are shown in Figure 4.5. The blue solid line represent the original model. The red dashed-dotted line represents the reduced model by coherency aggregation, and the black dotted line by the DEAR method. The reduced model by the DEAR method appears to have smaller differences from the original model, and outperforms the coherency aggregation method. Another important metric for evaluating the performance of model reduction is the reduction ratio, which is defined as

$$R = \frac{(N_F - N_R)}{N_F} \tag{4.13}$$

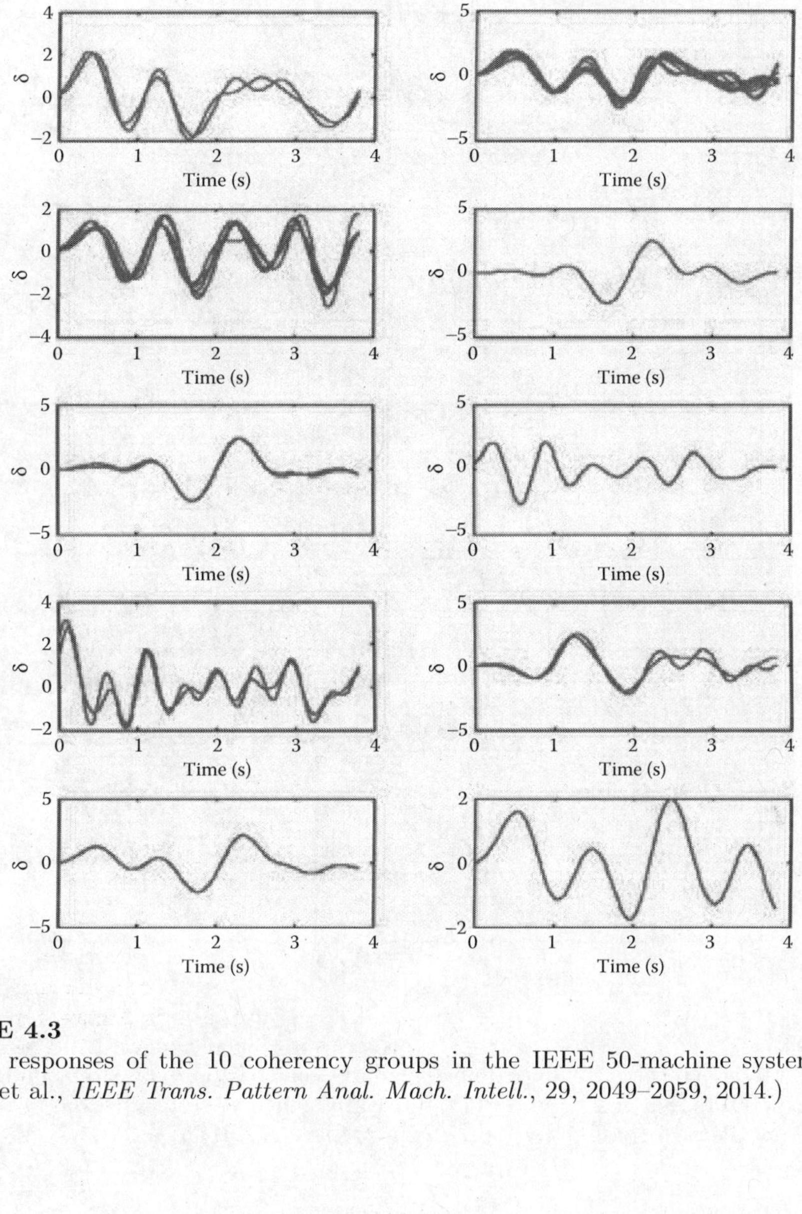

FIGURE 4.3
Dynamic responses of the 10 coherency groups in the IEEE 50-machine system. (From S. Wang et al., *IEEE Trans. Pattern Anal. Mach. Intell.*, 29, 2049–2059, 2014.)

where:

- N_R is the total number of state variables of the reduced model of the external system
- N_F is that of the original model

The mismatch between the black dotted line and the blue solid line in Figure 4.5 is 0.1630, and the reduction ratio defined by Equation 4.13 is $R = (34-9)/34 = 0.7353$, both of which represent the performance of the DEAR method. The mismatch between the red dashed-dotted line and the blue solid line in Figure 4.5 is 0.4476 and $R = (34-10)/34 = 0.7059$, both representing the performance of the coherency aggregation method. Therefore, it can be concluded that the DEAR method performs better, even under a slightly higher reduction ratio. We now investigate if the same conclusion can be drawn under different reduction ratios and for generators other than G42 shown in Figure 4.5. Define a comprehensive metric shown in Equation 4.14 for all the internal generators.

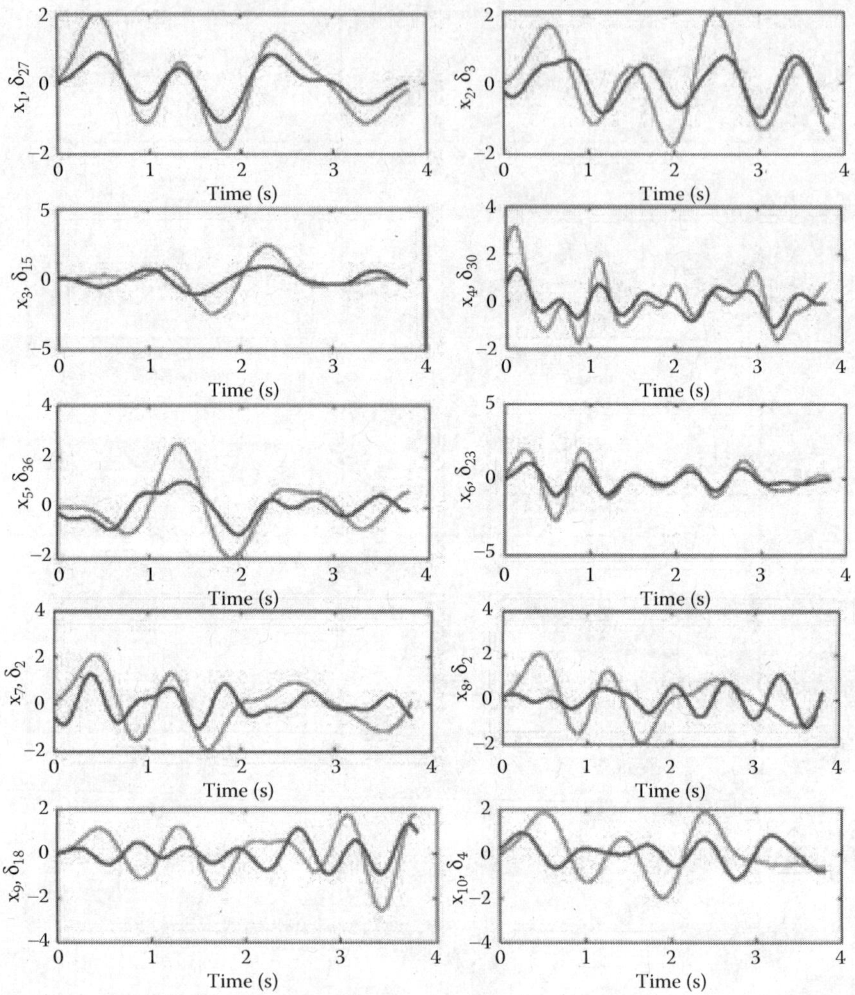

FIGURE 4.4
Optimal orthogonal bases (blue solid lines) and dynamic responses of corresponding characteristic generators (red dashed lines) in the IEEE 50-machine system. (From S. Wang et al., *IEEE Trans. Pattern Anal. Mach. Intell.*, 29, 2049–2059, 2014.)

$$J(i) = \frac{1}{N}\sum_{i\in\varphi} J_s(i) \tag{4.14}$$

where φ is the set of all the generators in the internal system, N is the total number of these generators, and $J_s(i) = \sqrt{\frac{1}{(t_2-t_1)}\int_{t_1}^{t_2}[\delta_i^a(t) - \delta_i^f(t)]^2 dt}$. A performance comparison of the DEAR method and the traditional coherency aggregation is shown in Figure 4.6, in which the horizontal axis represents the reduction ratio defined in Equation 4.13, and the vertical coordinates represent the error defined in Equation 4.14. It is apparent that the DEAR method consistently performs better than the coherency method. To demonstrate the basic idea of a super set of characteristic generators in Section III.F, three faults (three-phase fault lasting for 60 ms) are configured on Lines 116–136, Lines 116–143, and Lines 115–143,

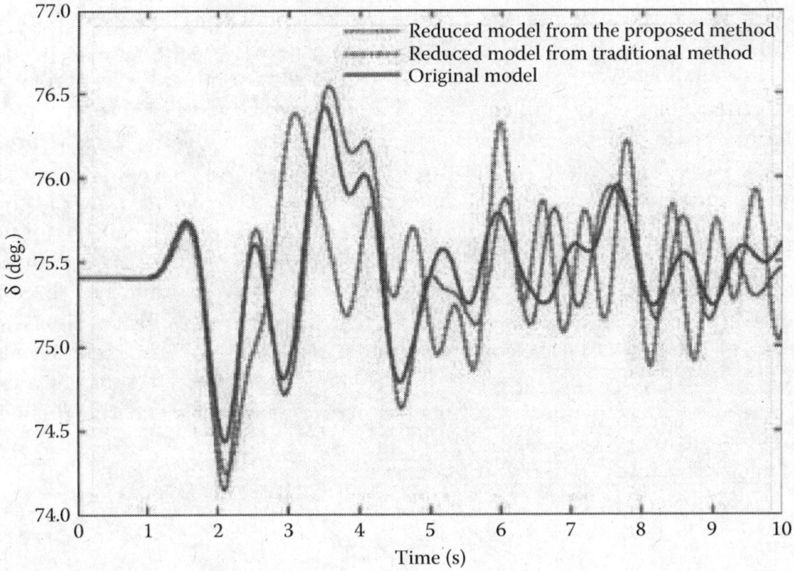

FIGURE 4.5
Rotor angle dynamics of generator 42 (on Bus 136) following fault F1. (From S. Wang et al., *IEEE Trans. Pattern Anal. Mach. Intell.*, 29, 2049–2059, 2014.)

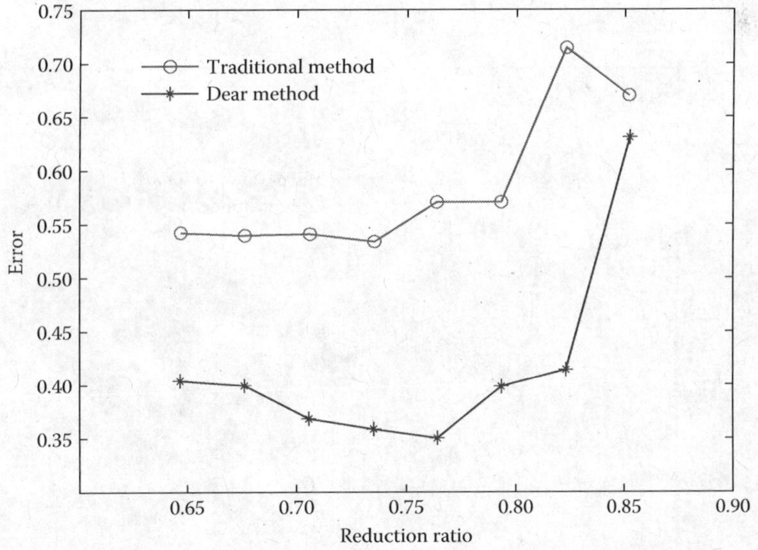

FIGURE 4.6
Performance comparison between the coherency aggregation method and the DEAR method. (From S. Wang et al., *IEEE Trans. Pattern Anal. Mach. Intell.*, 29, 2049–2059, 2014.)

respectively. Choose the size r of the characteristic generator set for each fault scenario to be 9 here. Define D_g as the number of times each generator appears as a characteristic generator after analyzing the system dynamic response to a fault. For example, generator 2 is a characteristic generator in all the three fault scenarios; it, therefore, has a D_g of 3. D_g of each characteristic generator is shown in Table 4.1. Select $D_g = 2$ as a threshold, that is, generators with $D_g \geq 2$ are chosen to form the super set of characteristic generators. The following generators are selected: generators 2, 15, 18, 23, 30, 3, 4, 22, and 36. With the super set, three different coefficient matrices C in Equation 4.8 can be obtained for the three faults, denoted by C_1, C_2, and C_3. Then a rough estimation of a generalized C can be obtained by, for example, letting $C_g = (C_1 + C_2 + C_3)/3$. When another three-phase fault takes place, for example, F4 on Lines 141–143, measurement data for the first 3 s after fault clearance can be used to refine the coefficient matrix C_g. Applying the recursive least-squares method, C_g is replaced by the more accurate coefficients in C_4. We thus get a new reduced model, represented by the super set of characteristic generators and the coefficient matrix C_4, without performing SVD. The performance of the new reduced model is illustrated in Figure 4.7 using the rotor dynamics of generator 42.

TABLE 4.1
D_g of characteristic generators.

D_g	3	3	3	3	3	2	2	2	2	1	1	1	1
Gen. no.	2	15	18	23	30	3	4	22	36	11	27	31	32

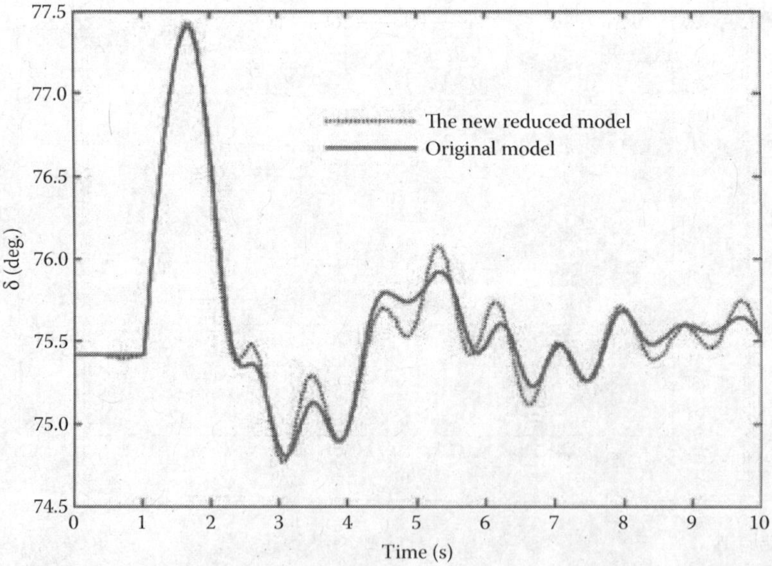

FIGURE 4.7
Rotor angle dynamics of generator 42 (on Bus 136) following fault F4. (From S. Wang et al., *IEEE Trans. Pattern Anal. Mach. Intell.*, 29, 2049–2059, 2014.)

4.3 Summary

In this chapter, types of big data in power systems and acquisition are introduced. Several big data analysis algorithms to integrate real-time big dataset for model reduction and real-time decision making are illustrated. Both k-means clustering and DEAR methods are presented. The network model is unchanged in the DEAR method, which makes online applications relatively easier and more flexible (e.g., generators of interest can be retained in the reduced model). Tests on the IEEE standard system shows that the DEAR method yields better reduction ratios and smaller response errors under both stable and unstable conditions than the traditional coherency-based aggregation methods. The introduced data analysis tools can effectively integrate real-time big data for better operation, and control and protection of power systems.

4.4 Glossary

Phasor measurement unit: A phasor measurement unit (PMU) or synchrophasor is a device that measures the electrical waves on an electricity grid, using a common time source for synchronization. Time synchronization allows synchronized real-time measurements of multiple remote measurement points on the grid. In power engineering, these are also commonly referred to as synchrophasors and are considered one of the most important measuring devices in the future of power systems.

k-Means clustering: k-means clustering is a method of vector quantization, originally from signal processing, that is popular for cluster analysis in data mining. k-means clustering aims to partition n observations into k clusters in which each observation belongs to the cluster with the nearest mean, serving as a prototype of the cluster.

Singular value decomposition: In linear algebra, the singular value decomposition (SVD) is a factorization of a real or complex matrix, with many useful applications in signal processing and statistics. Formally, the SVD of an $m \times n$ real or complex matrix M is a factorization of the form $M = U\Sigma V*$, where U is an $m \times m$ real or complex unitary matrix, Σ is an $m \times n$ rectangular diagonal matrix with nonnegative real numbers on the diagonal, and $V*$ (the conjugate transpose of V, or simply the transpose of V if V is real) is an $n \times n$ real or complex unitary matrix. The diagonal entries $\Sigma_{i,i}$ of Σ are known as the singular values of M. The m columns of U and the n columns of V are called the left-singular vectors and right-singular vectors of M, respectively.

Randomized algorithm: A randomized algorithm [13] is an algorithm that employs a degree of randomness as part of its logic. The algorithm typically uses uniformly random bits as an auxiliary input to guide its behavior, in the hope of achieving good performance in the average case over all possible choices of random bits.

Model reduction: Model reduction [3] is used to produce a low-dimensional system that has the same response characteristics as the original system with far less storage requirements and much lower evaluation time. The resulting reduced model might be used to replace the original system as a component in a larger simulation or it might be used to develop a low-dimensional controller suitable for real-time applications.

References

1. K. K. Anaparthi, B. Chaudhuri, N. F. Thornhill, and B. Pal. Coherency identification in power systems through principal component analysis. *IEEE Trans. Power Syst.*, 20(3):1658–1660, 2005.

2. A. C. Antoulas. *Approximation of Large-Scale Dynamical Systems.* SIAM Press, Philadelphia, PA, 2005.

3. A. C. Antoulas, D. C. Sorensen, and S. Gugercin. A survey of model reduction methods for large-scale systems. *Contemp. Math.*, 280:193–219, 2001.

4. D. P. Berrar, W. Dubitzky, and M. Granzow. *A Practical Approach to Microarray Data Analysis.* Springer, New York, 2002.

5. C. A. Canizares, N. Mithulananthan, F. Milano, and J. Reeve. Linear performance indices to predict oscillatory stability problems in power systems. *IEEE Trans. Power Syst.*, 19(2):1104–1114, 2004.

6. J. Chow, P. Accari, and W. Price. Inertial and slow coherency aggregation algorithms for power system dynamic model reduction. *IEEE Trans. Power Syst.*, 10(2):680–685, 1995.

7. K. Glover. All optimal Hankel norm approximation of linear multivariable systems, and their L^{∞}-error bounds. *Int. J. Control*, 39(6):1145–1193, 1984.

8. M. Honarkhah and J. Caers. Stochastic simulation of patterns using distance-based pattern modeling. *IEEE Trans. Pattern Anal. Mach. Intell.*, 42(5):487–517, 2010.

9. M. Kezunovic, L. Xie, and S. Grijalva. The role of big data in improving power system operation and protection. In *2013 IREP Symposium*, pp. 1–9. IEEE, Rethymno, Greece, 2013.

10. D. Lin and X. Wu. Phrase clustering for discriminative learning. *Annual Meeting of the ACL and IJCNLP*, pp. 1030–1038, Suntec, Singapore, 2009.

11. S. Liu. *Dynamic-Data Driven Real-Time Identification for Electric Power Systems.* University of Illinois, Urbana, IL, 2009.

12. B. Moore. Principal component analysis in linear systems: Controllability, observability, and model reduction. *IEEE Trans. Autom. Control*, AC-26(1):17–32, 1981.

13. A. Nazin and B. Polyak. A randomized algorithm for finding eigenvector of stochastic matrix with application to PageRank problem. In *Control Applications, (CCA) & Intelligent Control*, pp. 412–416. IEEE, Saint Petersburg, Russia, 2009.

14. S. Z. Selim and M. A. Ismail. K-means-type algorithms: A generalized convergence theorem and characterization of local optimality. *IEEE Trans. Pattern Anal. Mach. Intell.*, PAMI-6(1):81–87, 1984.

15. S. Wang, S. Lu, N. Zhou, G. Lin, M. Elizondo, and M. A. Pai. Dynamic-feature extraction, attribution and reconstruction (DEAR) method for power system model reduction. *IEEE Trans. Pattern Anal. Mach. Intell.*, 29(5):2049–2059, 2014.

5

Interactive Visual Analysis of Big Data

Carlos Scheidegger

CONTENTS

5.1 Introduction 61
5.2 Binning 64
5.3 Sampling 67
5.4 Graphical Considerations 68
5.5 Outlook and Open Issues 68
References 69

5.1 Introduction

In this chapter, we discuss *interactive visualization* of big data. We will talk about why this has recently become an active area of research and present some of the most promising recent work. We will discuss a broad range of ideas but will make no attempt at comprehensiveness; for that, we point readers to Wu et al.'s vision paper [25] and Godfrey et al.'s survey [9]. But before we get there, let us start with the basics: why should we care about visualization, and why should it be interactive?

The setting we are considering is that of *data analysis*, where the *data analyst* hopes to understand and learn from some real-world phenomenon by collecting data and working with a variety of different techniques, statistical and otherwise. As the analyst creates different hypothesis in his or her head to try and understand the data, he or she will generate possibly many different visualizations from the dataset. We also restrict ourselves here to *big data*, and we use the term somewhat loosely to mean "big enough that repeated full scanning through the dataset is painful." As a consequence (and this is a good thing), whether or not you have big data depends on the computer that will be generating the visualizations. It is also why only recently have we truly had to care about big data visualization as a research problem: for the past 40 years or so, computer technology has outpaced our ability to gather data for analysis. But this has now changed. The main constraint in interactive analysis is one of *latency*: if it takes significantly longer to wait for a command than it does to express this command to the computer, the analyst risks missing important information about the dataset [16].

Even in the smallest of cases, *visual* presentation is a powerful means to understanding. We follow Tukey's philosophy here that data graphics force us to ask questions we did not even know we wanted to ask [23]. Consider the venerable example of Anscombe's quartet [3]. Anscombe famously observed that numeric summaries of a dataset can be highly misleading: with as few as 11 observations, it is possible to create different datasets with exactly the same means, medians, linear fits, and covariances (see Figure 5.1). Looking at the plots

x1		y1		x2		y2	
Min.	: 4.0	Min.	: 4.260	Min.	: 4.0	Min.	:3.100
1st Qu.	: 6.5	1st Qu.	: 6.315	1st Qu.	: 6.5	1st Qu.	:6.695
Median	: 9.0	Median	: 7.580	Median	: 9.0	Median	:8.140
Mean	: 9.0	Mean	: 7.501	Mean	: 9.0	Mean	:7.501
3rd Qu.	:11.5	3rd Qu.	: 8.570	3rd Qu.	:11.5	3rd Qu.	:8.950
Max.	:14.0	Max.	:10.840	Max.	:14.0	Max.	:9.260

Coefficients:		Coefficients:	
(Intercept)	x1	(Intercept)	x2
3.0001	0.5001	3.001	0.500

x3		y3		x4		y4	
Min.	: 4.0	Min.	: 5.39	Min.	: 8	Min.	: 5.250
1st Qu.	: 6.5	1st Qu.	: 6.25	1st Qu.	: 8	1st Qu.	: 6.170
Median	: 9.0	Median	: 7.11	Median	: 8	Median	: 7.040
Mean	: 9.0	Mean	: 7.50	Mean	: 9	Mean	: 7.501
3rd Qu.	:11.5	3rd Qu.	: 7.98	3rd Qu.	: 8	3rd Qu.	: 8.190
Max.	:14.0	Max.	:12.74	Max.	:19	Max.	:12.500

Coefficients:		Coefficients:	
(Intercept)	x3	(Intercept)	x4
3.0025	0.4997	3.0017	0.4999

Summaries

	x1	y1	x2	y2
1	10	8.04	10	9.14
2	8	6.95	8	8.14
3	13	7.58	13	8.74
4	9	8.81	9	8.77
5	11	8.33	11	9.26
6	14	9.96	14	8.10
7	6	7.24	6	6.13
8	4	4.26	4	3.10
9	12	10.84	12	9.13
10	7	4.82	7	7.26
11	5	5.68	5	4.74

	x3	y3	x4	y4
1	10	7.46	8	6.58
2	8	6.77	8	5.76
3	13	12.74	8	7.71
4	9	7.11	8	8.84
5	11	7.81	8	8.47
6	14	8.84	8	7.04
7	6	6.08	8	5.25
8	4	5.39	19	12.50
9	12	8.15	8	5.56
10	7	6.42	8	7.91
11	5	5.73	8	6.89

Tabular views

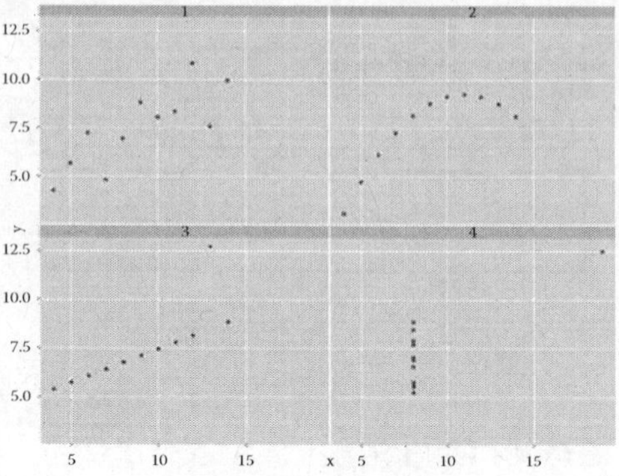

Graphical displays

FIGURE 5.1
Anscombe's quartet [3] shows a fundamental shortcoming of simple summaries and numeric tables. Summaries can be exactly the same, and numeric tables all *look* similar, but the data they hold can be substantially different. This problem is sharply accentuated in big data visualization, where the number of data points easily exceeds the number of pixels in a computer screen.

makes it clear that the different datasets are generated by fundamentally different processes. Even though tables of the raw numeric values area in this case are small, they do not convey for human consumers, in any effective way, the structure present in the data. As we here are going to talk about datasets with arbitrarily large numbers of observations (and, in current practice, easily in the range of billions), the numeric tables are more obviously a bad idea.

Still, can we not just draw a scatterplot? No, unfortunately we cannot: the first problem naive scatterplots create is that the straightforward implementation requires at least one entire pass over the dataset every time the visualization is updated (and, at the very least, one pass over the set of points to be plotted). In an exploratory setting, we are likely to try different filters, projections, and transformations. We know from perceptual experiments that latencies of even a half-second can cause users to explore a dataset less thoroughly [16]. Big data visualization systems need to be *scalable*: aside from some preprocessing time, *systems should run in time sublinear on the number of observations.*

Suppose even that scanning were fast enough; in that case, *overplotting* becomes a crippling problem, even if we had infinite pixels on our screens: there are just too many observations in our datasets and too few photoreceptors in the human eye. Using semi-transparent elements, typically via alpha blending [19], is only a solution when the amount of overplotting is small (see Figure 5.2). A better solution is to use *spatial binning* and visual encodings based on per-bin statistics. Binning has two desirable characteristics. First, if the binning scheme is sensible, it will naturally pool together similar observations from a dataset into a single bin, providing a natural *level-of-detail* representation of a dataset. In addition, binning fits the pixel-level limitations of the screen well: if we map a specific bin to one single pixel in our scheme, then there is no need to *drill down* into the bin any further, because all the information will end up having to be combined into a single pixel value anyway. As we will see, one broad class of solutions for big data visualization relies on binning schemes of varying sophistication. More generally, we can think of binning as a general scheme to apply computational effort in a way more aligned to human perceptual principles: if we are unable to perceive minute differences between dataset values in a zoomed-out scatterplot, it is wasteful to write algorithms that treat these minute differences as if they were as big as large-scale ones.

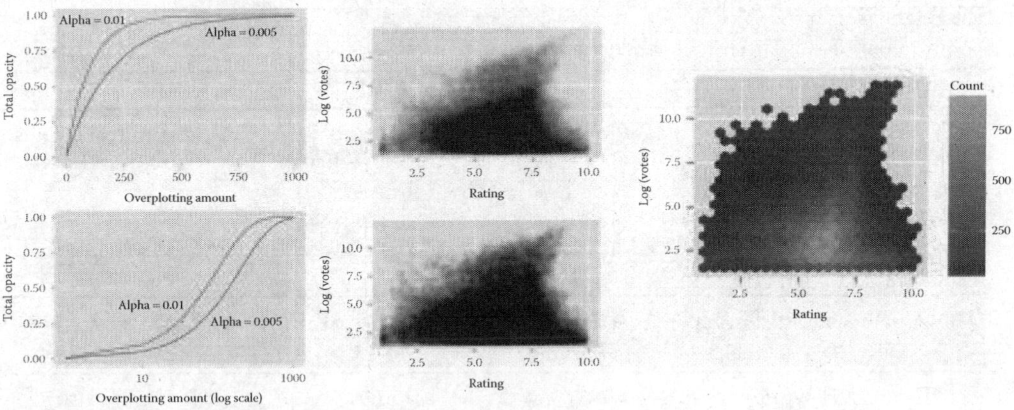

FIGURE 5.2
Overplotting becomes a problem in the visualization of large datasets, and using semitransparent shapes is not an effective solution. The mathematics of transparency and its perception work against us. Most of the perceptual range (the set of different possible total opacities) is squeezed into a small range of the overplotting amount, and this range depends on the specific per-point opacity that is chosen (*left column*). As a result, different opacities *highlight* different parts of the data, but no single opacity is appropriate (*middle column*). Color mapping via bin counts, however, is likely to work better (*right column*).

Finally, any one single visualization will very likely not be enough, again because there are simply too many observations. Here, *interactive* visualization is our current best bet. As Shneiderman puts it, overview first, zoom, and filter the details on demand [20]. For big data visualizations, *fast interaction, filtering, and querying of the data are highly recommended*, under the same latency constraints for visualization updates.

Besides binning, the other basic strategy for big data visualization is *sampling*. Here, the insight is similar to that of resampling techniques such as jackknifing and bootstrapping [7]: it is possible to take samples from a dataset of observations as if the dataset were an actual exhaustive census of the population, and still obtain meaningful results. Sampling-based strategies for visualization have the advantage of providing a natural *progressive* representation: as new samples are added to the visualization, it becomes closer to that of the population.

This is roughly our roadmap for this chapter, then. First, we will see how to *bin* datasets appropriately for exploratory analysis and how to turn those bins into visual primitives that are pleasing and informative. Then we will briefly discuss techniques based on sampling, and finally we will discuss how exploratory modeling fits into this picture. Table 5.1 provides a summary of the techniques we will cover in this chapter.

With the material presented here, you should be able to apply the current state-of-the-art techniques and visualize large-scale datasets, and also understand in what contexts the available technology falls short. The good news is that for one specific type of approach, many open-source techniques are available. The techniques we present in this chapter have one main idea in common: if repeated full scans of the dataset are too slow to be practical, then we need to examine the particulars of our setting and extract additional structure. Specifically, we now have to bring the visualization requirements *into* our computation and analysis infrastructure, instead of making visualization a separate concern, handled via regular SQL queries or CSV flat files. One crucial bit of additional structure is that of the *visualization technique* itself. Although not explored to its generality in any of the techniques presented

TABLE 5.1
A summary of the three techniques discussed in the chapter.

Technique	Software Type	Speed	Interaction	Binning Scheme
Bigvis	R package	Good	No	Per-analysis, dense
imMens	HTML + WebGL	Best	Active brush limited to two attributes	Fixed, dense
Nanocubes	HTTP server	Better	Yes	Hierarchical, sparse

Technique	Table Scan	Memory Usage	Modeling	Number of Data Dimensions
Bigvis	Per-analysis	Good	Some	Does not care
imMens	Once	Best	None	Does not care
Nanocubes	Once	Worst (for server)	None	Uses progressively more memory

Technique	Data Insertion	Data Deletion	Scan Speed
Bigvis	Yes, rescan	Yes, rescan	1–3MB rows/s
imMens	No	No	Unreported
Nanocubes	Yes	No	10–100KB rows/s

Note: See text for a more thorough discussion. Categories are meant to be neither objective nor exhaustive.

here, a large opportunity for future research is to encode human perceptual limitations computationally, and design algorithms that quickly return *perception approximate* results (an example of this technique is the sampling strategy used by Bleis et al., to be further discussed in Section 5.3 [14]. Combined with our (limited, but growing) knowledge of the visual system, this would enable end-to-end systems that quickly return approximate results indistinguishable from the exact ones.

Because of space limitations, this chapter will not touch every aspect of large-scale data visualization. Specifically, there is one large class of data visualization techniques that is not going to be covered here, namely visualization of data acquired from imaging sensors and numerical simulations of physical phenomena. These include, for example, 3D tomography datasets, simulations of the Earth's atmospheric behavior, or magnetic fields in a hypothetical nuclear reactor. Researchers in *scientific visualization* have for a long time developed techniques to produce beautiful images of these very large simulations running on supercomputers; see, for example, the recent work of Ahrens et al. [2]. By contrast, we will here worry about large-scale *statistical* datasets, which we are going to assume are either *independent samples* from a population, or in fact the entire population itself, where each observation is some tuple of observations.

5.2 Binning

Histograms have been used as a modeling and visualization tool in statistics since the field began; it is not too surprising, then, that binning will play a central role in the visualization of big data. All techniques in this section produce histograms of the datasets. The main innovation in these techniques, however, is that they all preprocess the dataset so that histograms themselves can be computed more efficiently than a linear scan over the entire dataset.

All techniques in this section exploit one basic insight: at the end of the day, when a visualization is built, *there are only a finite number of pixels in the screen.* If any two samples were to be mapped to the same pixel, then we will somehow have to combine these samples in the visualization. If we design a preprocessing scheme that does some amount of combination ahead of time, then we will need to scan the samples individually every time they need to be plotted. This observation is simple, but is fruitful enough that all techniques in this section exploit it *differently.* As a result, no one technique dominates the other, and choosing which one to use will necessarily depend on other considerations.

We will go over three techniques. Bigvis is an R package developed by Hadley Wickham that, in addition to visualization of large datasets, allows for a limited amount of efficient *statistical modeling* [24]. Liu et al. have created imMens, a JavaScript-based library that leverages the parallel processing of graphics processing units (GPUs) to very quickly compute aggregate sums over partial data cubes [17]. Finally, Lins et al. have developed nanocubes, a data structure to represent multiscale, sparse data cubes [15]. Both imMens and nanocubes are built on *data cubes* [10]. In a relational database, a data cube is a materialization of every possible column summarization of a table (Microsoft Excel's pivot tables are a simple form of data cubes) (see Figure 5.3 for an example).

The biggest disadvantage of general data cubes is their resource requirements. Just in terms of space usage, an unrestricted data cube will take space exponential in the number of dimensions. This is easy to see simply because for each of n columns, an entry in a column of a datacube table can be either *All* or one of the entries in the original table, giving a potential blowup of 2^n. There have been many papers that try to improve on this worst-case behavior [21], and the biggest difference between imMens and nanocubes lies on the trade-offs they choose to take in order to curb the resource usage.

We start our discussion with imMens. The basic representation of imMens is that of a dense, *partial* data cube: out of all possible aggregations in n dimensions, the preprocessing

Relation (A)

Country	Device	Language
The United States	Android	en
The United States	iPhone	ru
South Africa	iPhone	en
India	Android	en
Australia	iPhone	en

Aggregation (B)

Country	Device	Language	Count
All	All	All	5

Group by on Device, Language (C)

Country	Device	Language	Count
All	Android	en	2
All	iPhone	en	2
All	iPhone	ru	1

Cube on Device, Language (D)

Country	Device	Language	Count
All	All	All	5
All	Android	All	2
All	iPhone	All	3
All	All	en	4
All	All	ru	1
All	iPhone	ru	1
All	Android	en	2
All	iPhone	en	2

Equivalent to group by on all possible subsets of {Device, Language}

FIGURE 5.3
A simple relation from a database and some of its possible associated aggregations and data cubes. (Data from Lins, L. et al., *IEEE Trans. Vis. Comput. Graphics*, 19, 2456–2465, 2013.)

step for imMens computes all possible sums where the *All* placeholder appears in at least $n-4$ of the columns. In other words, imMens's partial data cubes are at most four dimensional. There is a very good reason for this particular choice: imMens was built to enable extremely fast *brushing* as a form of interactive exploration [4]. In this mode, a user moves his or her mouse over one particular two-dimensional projection of a dataset, and the position of the mouse implies a *restriction* on the values they are interested in.

So that is one restricted dimension for the X position and another dimension for the Y position. Now, for every *other* plot in a brushed multidimensional histogram, we want to compute the sum of events in any particular bin. Those are, potentially, two extra dimensions for a total of four. Because most of the interactive exploration in scatterplots happens with one active brush, the representation in imMens works precisely in the right way. When higher levels of aggregation are necessary (for storage reasons, sometimes imMens only computes *three*-dimensional tables), imMens uses the GPU parallel power to perform this aggregation quickly. As a result, after the data tiles are loaded on the client, imMens can sustain interaction rates of 50 frames per second for datasets with hundreds of millions to billions of events.

Another defining characteristic of imMens's storage is that its binning scheme is dense: bins in which no events are stored take as much space as bins in which many events are stored. This limits the *effective resolution* of imMens's binning scheme and is a significant limitation. Many datasets of interest have features at *multiple scales*: in time series analysis, for example, features can happen at week-long scales or at hour-long scales.

Nanocubes, by contrast, uses a *sparse, multilevel* scheme for its address space, essentially computing a nested sequence of 2^d-ary trees (binary trees for single-dimensional values, quad-trees for spatial values, etc.) [15]. In order to avoid the obvious exponential blowup, nanocubes *reuse* large portions of the allocated data structures: the algorithm detects that further refinements of a query do not change the output sets and share those portions across the data structure. As a simplified example, consider that every query for "rich men in Seattle" will include "former CEOs of Microsoft" Bill Gates. It makes no sense, then, to store separate results for "rich men in Seattle AND former CEOs of Microsoft" and "rich men in Seattle": the two result sets are identical. The construction algorithm for nanocubes is essentially a vast generalization of this kind of rule and results in large storage gains. Specifically, datasets that would take petabytes of storage to precompute in dense schemes can be stored in a nanocube in a few tens of gigabytes.

Both nanocubes and imMens expose their application program interface (API) via web-based visualization. Compared to imMens, the main disadvantage of nanocubes is that it requires a special server process to answer its queries. imMens, however, preprocesses the dataset into data tile files, which are served via a regular web server; all of the subsequent computation happens on the client side. For deployment purposes, this is a very favorable setup.

In addition, both nanocubes and imMens (in their currently available implementations) share a limitation in the format of the data stored *in* their multivariate bins: these techniques only store event counts. Wickham's bigvis, by contrast, can store (slightly) more sophisticated event statistics of events in its bins [24]. As a result, bigvis allows users to easily create multivariate histogram plots where each bin stores a sample mean (or sample variance, or other such simple statistics). This is a significant improvement in flexibility, particularly during exploratory analysis, where better statistics might help us find important patterns in the data.

At the same time, bigvis does not employ any precomputation strategy. It relies on the speed of current multicore processors in desktops and workstations, and every time the user changes the *axes* used for plotting, bigvis recreates the addressing scheme and rescans the data. Unlike the one for imMens and nanocubes, the addressing scheme in bigvis is exceedingly simple, and thus scanning through the dataset is relatively fast. In addition, the richer statistics stored in bigvis's bins enable it to provide *statistical modeling* features completely absent in nanocubes and imMens. It is possible, for example, to do linear regressions and LOESS curve fits over bigvis's data structures.

It should be noted that data cubes *do* allow for these more general statistics. Specifically, their data can live in any commutative monoid, and there has been some recent work exploring connections between algebraic structures and allowable statistical and machine learning algorithms [13]. Besides enabling nanocubes and imMens to perform more sophisticated analyses, these connections provide an exciting avenue for future work. We envision a world where exploratory statistics, in general, are assumed to have access to a data cube like imMens's or nanocubes. It is plausible that techniques that require repeated scanning through the dataset (EM, clustering, stochastic gradient descent) can benefit from judicious preaggregation.

5.3 Sampling

Instead of preaggregation, the other general class of strategy for low-latency visualization is that of *sampling*. The idea again is simple: if we are interested in understanding the behavior of a large *population* (in this case, our dataset), then it should be enough for us to study a small subset of this population, intuitively for the same reason that it is enough, in many statistical analyses, to study a sample instead of the entire population.

In the context of general interactive query engines, BlinkDB is the best known and current state of the art [1]. BlinkDB provides a typical SQL querying interface enriched by *time bound* or *error bound* clauses. Its engine then builds a multidimensional stratified sample that is updated in a streaming fashion until either of the bounds are satisfied. The main complication lies in building indices capable of efficiently updating pieces of the stratified sample, using a generalization of Hellerstein et al.'s online aggregation algorithms [12] that take into account the additional knowledge available from the requested bounds. Fisher et al.'s experiment with analysts in sampleAction [8] suggests that incremental results and confidence bounds are typically interpreted correctly. This provides evidence that the faster cycle "query, examine results, think something new, repeat" is not happening at the expense of a significantly worse data analysis capacity.

Another significant advantage of sampling engines, as opposed to aggregation engines, is that it is much simpler to design a sampling engine that (at some level) has full row-level access to the database. This usually means that the *type* of query returned by sampling engines can be richer than that of aggregation engines. This retained flexibility means potentially richer visualizations, but also simpler integration with existing visualization systems. If your application requirements include having (eventual, when the sampling engine *converges*) access to full-resolution elements of a dataset, then a sampling engine is probably a safer choice.

Nevertheless, sampling engines present one serious shortcoming for interactive visualization purposes that must be kept in mind. Simply put, in the current state of the art, it is not straightforward to generate high-confidence, low-error samples for many visualizations of interest. For example, in a two-dimensional heatmap to be presented on a typical laptop screen, the database engine would have to run about one million independent stratified sampling runs (one for each pixel). It is not clear that the approaches in the literature scale well to a large query set of this kind. If the system simply chooses to provide a simple incremental sampling without replacement (such as sampleAction [8]), then the risk is that this sampling will never actually produce acceptable error rates. This happens because the heatmap being presented might have a colormap that portrays a wide dynamic range of possible values. Consider, for example, a logarithmically increasing density plot: the range of cardinalities in each pixel can easily go from tens to hundreds of thousands. The first example from Liu et al.'s paper showcases this problem very elegantly: a naive sample from a geographical dataset destroys much of the high-resolution structure that makes a visualization valuable in the first place.

5.4 Graphical Considerations

The final class of techniques we will discuss exploits the peculiarities of the human visual system to produce faster results. In other words, these techniques settle for approximate results, but approximate in a *perceptual* sense. This is done in an attempt to save work that would not have produced any perceptible change in the final image. This is an attractive proposition in principle, but in practice it requires tight integration between the visualization and the querying system, because even a change in the visualization that is typically considered innocuous, such as a change in the color scale or the transformation of one of the axes of the plot (from linear to logarithmic, for example), can cause the computational trade-offs behind the perceptibility approximations to change wildly.

The techniques discussed in this (admittedly shorter) section are the closest to current research and, as such, do not appear to be readily available in any open-source software package. Nevertheless, they point to important problems in current systems and in the direction of where we can expect future advances to happen.

The first system we highlight is Battle et al.'s *Scalr*, which introduces knowledge about the perceptually relevant variables directly into the *query optimizer* of a database engine [25]. This allows scalr to transform an exact query into an approximate one by a variety of different means, including both aggregation and sampling as discussed above. scalr is implemented on top of SciDB [22], whose focus on array data provides attractive operators for the manipulation of multiresolution constructs that tend to be relevant in visualization settings such as images and heatmaps.

The second technique we highlight is Kim et al.'s sampling with ordering guarantees [14]. This is an application of the general strategy of sampling, but done under a specific perceptual constraint. The authors assume that a visualization will be consumed mostly for the *ordering* relationships it depicts. In other words, they assume that the bulk of the visual information to be processed in a bar chart is the relative ordering of the bar heights. With that assumption in mind, they design an online streaming update algorithm that very quickly converges (about 25× faster than other sampling strategies, for a total time of below 1 s and 10^{10} entries in the dataset) to the *perceptually correct* result. Whether or not ordering is a realistic perceptual component to be preserved can be set aside for now: the fundamental innovation here is that knowledge about perceptual properties is driving the algorithm. In principle, this technique should be generalizable to other settings, and it shows significant promise for the future of big data visualization.

5.5 Outlook and Open Issues

Let us take a step back and look at the area more broadly, now that we know what are the main techniques at our disposal. Binning strategies attack the problem by observing that screen resolution is finite, and that careful precomputation can be sufficiently efficient and *rich.* Sampling strategies, by contrast, try to spend data-accessing effort only where the *result uncertainty* is largest, quickly converging to an approximation of the result in a statistical sense. Notice, then, that both classes of techniques are actually trying to build effective *approximations* of the exact result without requiring a full scan of the data.

We believe that the overall strategy of approximate query processing is the best hope for interactive data analysis. Specifically, we believe that *perceptual approximations* are going to become a central part of the design of algorithms for interactive visualization. We seek an infrastructure where richer mathematical descriptions of perceptual characteristics—take, for example, Harrison et al.'s recent generalization of Weber's law for perception of correlation [11] or Demiralp et al.'s crowdsourcing of perceptual kernels [6]—can be translated into potential efficiency gains by *expressing the perceptual landscape of the visualizations in the computing language itself.*

In essence, we are advocating here for a concerted effort at pushing the visualization concerns into the back end (be it an analysis back end or a database back end), rather than being relegated to front ends. This will certainly bring its own set of problems, not the least of which being that separating the back end from the front end is currently done for very good engineering reasons: modularity, separation of concerns, etc. Still, the current situation of state-of-the-art visualization APIs provides a good illustration of the problems we face. We enjoy a large degree of modularity and independence: the *de facto* front end for visualizations has become the web browser, by means of modern APIs such as d3 [5] and HTML5 features such as scalable vector graphics [18]. Web browsers, by design, provide automatic distributed operation, and data back ends vary widely in sophistication. At the same same, these libraries fail to scale properly when datasets grow, eventually requiring the very solutions we discussed earlier in this chapter, special purpose as they are. So although we look forward to one day having general, modular, *and* scalable visualization back ends, our best bet for the near-term future seems to be on a tightly integrated front-end–back-end design based on perceptual considerations of the final visual artifact being displayed.

We also look forward to a deeper consideration of perceptual limitations of the outputs of data analysis algorithms themselves. As a naive example, if the output of a clustering algorithm will be displayed on a screen, then we do not need to know the values of cluster centers to a resolution finer than that of the screen. The same argument holds for many other potentially costly operations such as model fitting and supervised learning algorithms.

References

1. Sameer Agarwal, Barzan Mozafari, Aurojit Panda, Henry Milner, Samuel Madden, and Ion Stoica. BlinkDB: Queries with bounded errors and bounded response times on very large data. In *Proceedings of the 8th ACM European Conference on Computer Systems*, pp. 29–42, Prague, Czech Republic, 2013.

2. James Ahrens, Sébastien Jourdain, Patrick O'Leary, John Patchett, David H. Rogers, and Mark Petersen. An image-based approach to extreme scale in situ visualization and analysis. In *Proceedings of the International Conference for High Performance Computing, Networking, Storage and Analysis*, pp. 424–434, Piscataway, NJ, 2014.

3. Francis J. Anscombe. Graphs in statistical analysis. *The American Statistician*, 27(1):17–21, 1973.

4. Richard A. Becker and William S. Cleveland. Brushing scatterplots. *Technometrics*, 29(2):127–142, 1987.

5. Michael Bostock, Vadim Ogievetsky, and Jeffrey Heer. D^3: Data-driven documents. *IEEE Transactions on Visualization and Computer Graphics*, 17(12):2301–2309, 2011.

6. Cagatay Demiralp, Michael Bernstein, and Jeffrey Heer. Learning perceptual kernels for visualization design. *IEEE Transactions on Visualization and Computer Graphics*, 20(12):1933–1942, 2014.

7. Bradley Efron and Robert J. Tibshirani. An Introduction to the Bootstrap. Chapman & Hall/CRC Press, Boca Raton, FL, 1994.

8. Danyel Fisher, Igor Popov, Steven Drucker, and M.C. Schraefel. Trust me, I'm partially right: Incremental visualization lets analysts explore large datasets faster. In *Proceedings of the SIGCHI Conference on Human Factors in Computing Systems*, pp. 1673–1682, ACM, New York, 2012.

9. Parke Godfrey, Jarek Gryz, and Piotr Lasek. Interactive visualization of large data sets. Technical Report EECS-2015-03, York University, Toronto, Canada, 2015.

10. Jim Gray, Surajit Chaudhuri, Adam Bosworth, Andrew Layman, Don Reichart, Murali Venkatrao, Frank Pellow, and Hamid Pirahesh. Data cube: A relational aggregation operator generalizing group-by, cross-tab, and sub-totals. *Data Mining and Knowledge Discovery*, 1(1):29–53, 1997.

11. Lane Harrison, Fumeng Yang, Steven Franconeri, and Remco Chang. Ranking visualizations of correlation using Weber's law. *IEEE Transactions on Visualization and Computer Graphics*, 20(12):1943–1952, 2014.

12. Joseph M. Hellerstein, Peter J. Haas, and Helen J. Wang. Online aggregation. *ACM SIGMOD Record*, 26(2):171–182, 1997.

13. Michael Izbicki. Algebraic classifiers: A generic approach to fast cross-validation, online training, and parallel training. In *Proceedings of the 30th International Conference on Machine Learning*, pp. 648–656, Atlanta, GA, 2013.

14. Albert Kim, Eric Blais, Aditya Parameswaran, Piotr Indyk, Samuel Madden, and Ronitt Rubinfeld. Rapid sampling for visualizations with ordering guarantees. *ArXiv e-prints*, December 2014.

15. Lauro Lins, James T Klosowski, and Carlos Scheidegger. Nanocubes for real-time exploration of spatiotemporal datasets. *IEEE Transactions on Visualization and Computer Graphics*, 19(12):2456–2465, 2013.

16. Zhicheng Liu and Jeffrey Heer. The effects of interactive latency on exploratory visual analysis. *IEEE Transactions on Visualization and Computer Graphics*, 20(12): 2122–2131, December 2014.

17. Zhicheng Liu, Biye Jiang, and Jeffrey Heer. imMens: Real-time visual querying of big data. In *Proceedings of the 15th Eurographics Conference on Visualization, Computer Graphics Forum*, vol. 32, pp. 421–430, John Wiley & Sons, Chichester, 2013.

18. Mozilla Developer Network. SVG: Scalable Vector Graphics. https://developer.mozilla.org/en-US/docs/Web/SVG.

19. Thomas Porter and Tom Duff. Compositing digital images. *SIGGRAPH Computer Graphics*, 18(3):253–259, January 1984.

20. Ben Shneiderman. The eyes have it: A task by data type taxonomy for information visualizations. In *IEEE Symposium on Visual Languages, 1996 Proceedings*, pp. 336–343, Boulder, CO, September 1996.

21. Yannis Sismanis, Antonios Deligiannakis, Nick Roussopoulos, and Yannis Kotidis. Dwarf: Shrinking the petacube. In *Proceedings of the ACM SIGMOD International Conference on Management of Data*, pp. 464–475. ACM, New York, 2002.

22. Michael Stonebraker, Paul Brown, Alex Poliakov, and Suchi Raman. The architecture of scidb. In *Scientific and Statistical Database Management*, pp. 1–16. Springer, Berlin, Germany, 2011.

23. John W. Tukey. *Exploratory Data Analysis*. Addison-Wesley, Reading, MA, 1977.

24. Hadley Wickham. Bin-summarise-smooth: A framework for visualising large data.

25. Eugene Wu, Leilani Battle, and Samuel R. Madden. The case for data visualization management systems: Vision paper. *Proceedings of the VLDB Endowment*, 7(10):903–906, June 2014.

6

A Visualization Tool for Mining Large Correlation Tables: The Association Navigator

Andreas Buja, Abba M. Krieger, and Edward I. George

CONTENTS

6.1 Overview 73
6.2 Introduction 74
6.3 Graphical Displays 75
6.3.1 Graphical Display of Correlation Tables: Blockplots 75
6.3.2 Graphical Overview of Large Correlation Tables 78
6.3.3 Other Uses of Blockplots: p-Values 80
6.3.4 Other Uses of Blockplots: Fraction of Missing and Complete Pairs of Values 81
6.3.5 Marginal and Bivariate Plots: Histograms/Barcharts, Scatterplots, and Scatterplot Matrices 82
6.3.6 Variations on Blockplots 85
6.4 Operation of the AN 86
6.4.1 Starting Up the AN 87
6.4.2 Moving Around: Crosshair Placement, Panning, and Zooming 87
6.4.3 Graphical Parameters 88
6.4.4 Correlations, p-Values, and Missing and Complete Pairs 89
6.4.5 Highlighting: Strips 90
6.4.6 Highlighting: Rectangles 90
6.4.7 Reference Variables 91
6.4.8 Searching Variables 91
6.4.9 Lenses: Scatterplots and Barplots/Histograms 92
6.4.10 Color Brushing in Scatterplots 94
6.4.11 Linear Adjustment 94
6.4.12 Future of AN 98
Appendix A: Versatility of Correlation Analysis 98
Appendix B: Creating and Programming AN Instances 100
Acknowledgments 102
References 102

6.1 Overview

The *Association Navigator* (AN for short) is an interactive visualization tool for viewing large tables of correlations. The basic operation is zooming and panning of a table that is presented in a graphical form, here called a *blockplot*.

The tool is really a toolbox that includes, among other things, the following: (1) display of p-values and missing value patterns in addition to correlations, (2) markup facilities to highlight variables and sub-tables as landmarks when navigating the larger table, (3) histograms/barcharts, scatterplots, and scatterplot matrices as *lenses* into the distributions of variables and variable pairs, (4) thresholding of correlations and p-values to show only strong and highly significant p-values, (5) trimming of extreme values of the variables for robustness, (6) *reference variables* that stay in sight at all times, and (7) wholesale adjustment of groups of variables for other variables.

The tool has been applied to data with nearly 2000 variables and associated tables approaching a size of 2000×2000. The usefulness of the tool is less in beholding gigantic tables in their entirety and more in searching for interesting association patterns by navigating manageable but numerous and interconnected sub-tables.

6.2 Introduction

This chapter describes the AN in three sections: (1) In this introductory section, we give some background about the data analytic and statistical problem addressed by this tool; (2) in Section 6.3, we describe the graphical displays used by the tool; and (3) in Section 6.4, we describe the actual operation of the tool. We start with some background:

An important focus of contemporary statistical research is on methods for large multivariate data. The term *large* can have two meanings, not mutually exclusive: (1) a large number of cases (records, rows), also called the *large*-n *problem*, or (2) a large number of variables (attributes, columns), also called the *large*-p *problem*. The two types of largeness call for different data analytic approaches and determine the kinds of questions that can be answered by the data. Most fundamentally, it should be observed that increasing n, the number of cases, and increasing p, the number of variables, each has very different and in some ways opposite effects on statistical analysis. Because the general multivariate analysis problem is to make statistical inference about the association among variables, increasing n has the effect of improving the certainty of inference due to improved precision of estimates, whereas increasing p has the contrary effect of reducing the certainty of inference due to the multiplicity problem or, more colorfully, the *data dredging fallacy*. Therefore, the level of detail that can be inferred about association among variables improves with increasing n, but it plummets with increasing p.

The problem we address here is primarily the large-p problem. From the above discussion, it follows that, for large p, associations among variables can generally be inferred only to a low level of detail and certainty. Hence, it is sufficient to measure association by simple means such as plain correlations. Correlations indicate the basic directionality in pairwise association, and as such they answer the simplest but also the most fundamental question: are higher values in X associated with higher or lower values in Y, at least in tendency?

Reliance on correlations may be subject to objections because they seem limited in their range of applicability for several reasons: (1) they are considered to be measures of linear association only; (2) they describe bivariate association only; and (3) they apply to quantitative variables only. In Appendix A, we refute or temper each of these objections by showing that (1) correlations are usually useful measures of directionality even when the associations are nonlinear; (2) higher-order associations play a reduced role especially in large-p problems; and (3) with the help of a few tricks of the trade (*scoring* and *dummy coding*), correlations are useful even for categorical variables, both ordinal and nominal. In view of these arguments, we proceed from the assumption that correlation tables, when used creatively, form quite general and powerful summaries of association among many variables.

In the following sections, we describe first how we graphically present large correlation tables, and then how we navigate and search them interactively. The software written to this end, the AN, implements the essential displays and interactive functionality to support the *mining* of large correlation tables. The AN software is written entirely in the R language.*

All data examples in this chapter are drawn from the phenotypic data in the *Simons Simplex Collection* (SSC) created by the Simons Foundation Autism Research Initiative (SFARI). Approved researchers can obtain the SSC dataset used in this chapter by applying at https://base.sfari.org.

6.3 Graphical Displays

6.3.1 Graphical Display of Correlation Tables: Blockplots

Figure 6.1 shows a first example of what we call a *blockplot*† of a dataset with $p = 38$ variables. This plot is intended as a direct and fairly obvious translation of a numeric correlation table into a visual form. The elements of the plot are as follows:

- The *labels* in the bottom and left margins show lineups of the same 38 variables: `age_at_ados_p1.CDV`, `family_type_p1.CDV`, `sex_p1.CDV`,.... In contrast to tables, where the vertical axis lists variables top down, we follow the convention of scatterplots where the vertical axis is ascending, and hence the variables are listed bottom up.

- The blue and red squares or blocks represent the pairwise correlations between variables at the intersections of the (imagined) horizontal and vertical lines drawn from the respective margin labels. The magnitude of a correlation is reflected in the *size* of the block and its sign in the *color*; positive correlations are shown in blue and negative correlations in red.‡ Along the ascending 45° *diagonal* are the correlations +1 of the variables with themselves; hence, these blocks are of maximal size. The closeness of other correlations to +1 or −1 can be gauged by a size comparison with the diagonal blocks.

- Finally, the plot shows a small comment in the bottom left, *Correlations (Compl. Pairs)*, indicating that what is represented by the blocks is correlation of complete—that is, non-missing—pairs of values of the two variables in question. This comment refers to the missing values problem and to the fact that correlation can only be calculated from the cases where the values of both variables are non-missing. The comment also alludes to the possibility that very different types of information could be represented by the blocks, and this is indeed made use of by the AN software (see Sections 6.3.3 and 6.3.4).

---

*http://www.cran.r-project.org.

† This type of plot is also called *fluctuation diagram* (Hofmann 2000). The term *blockplot* is ours, and we introduce it because it is more descriptive of the plot's visual appearance. We may even dare propose that blockplot be contracted to *blot*, which would be in the tradition of contracting *scatterplot matrix* to *splom* and *graphics object* to *grob*.

‡ We follow the convention from finance where *being in the red* implies negative numbers; the opposite convention is from physics where red symbolizes higher temperatures. Users can easily change the defaults for blockplots; see the programming hints in Appendix B.

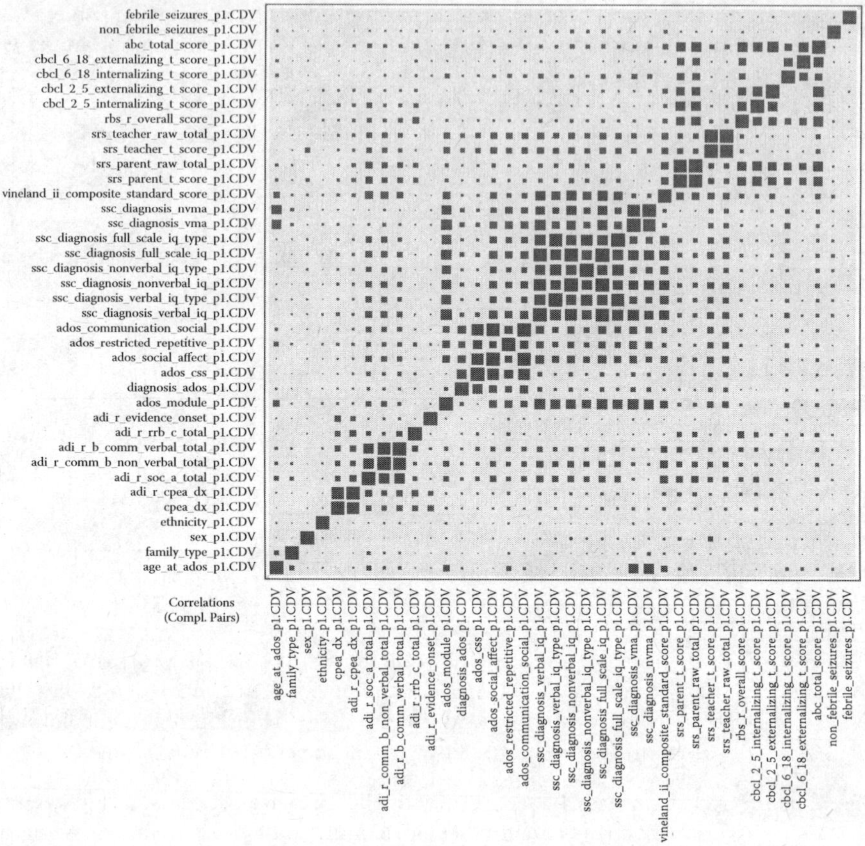

FIGURE 6.1
A first example of a *blockplot*: labels in the bottom and left margins show variable names, and blue and red blocks in the plotting area show positive and negative correlations.

As a *reading exercise*, consider Figure 6.2: this is the same blockplot as in Figure 6.1, but for ease of pointing, we marked up two variables on the horizontal axis*:

`age_at_ados_p1.CDV`, `ados_restricted_repetitive_p1.CDV`

which means "age at the time of the administration of the Autism Diagnostic Observation Schedule," and "problems due to restricted and repetitive behaviors," respectively. Two other variables are marked up on the vertical axis:

`ssc_diagnosis_vma_p1.DCV`, `ssc_diagnosis_nvma_p1.DCV`.

which means *verbal mental age*, and *nonverbal mental age*, respectively, which are related to notions of intelligence quotient (IQ). For readability, we will shorten the labels in what follows.

As for the actual reading exercise, in the intersection of the left vertical strip with the horizontal strip, we find two blue blocks, of which the lower is recognizably larger than the upper (the reader may have to zoom in while viewing the figure in a PDF reader), implying that the correlation of `age_at_ados..` with both `..vma..` and `..nvma..` is positive, but more strongly with the former than the latter, which may be news to the nonspecialist: verbal

* This dataset represents a version of the table `proband_cdv.csv` in version 9 of the phenotypic SSC. The acronym `cdv` means *core descriptive variables*.

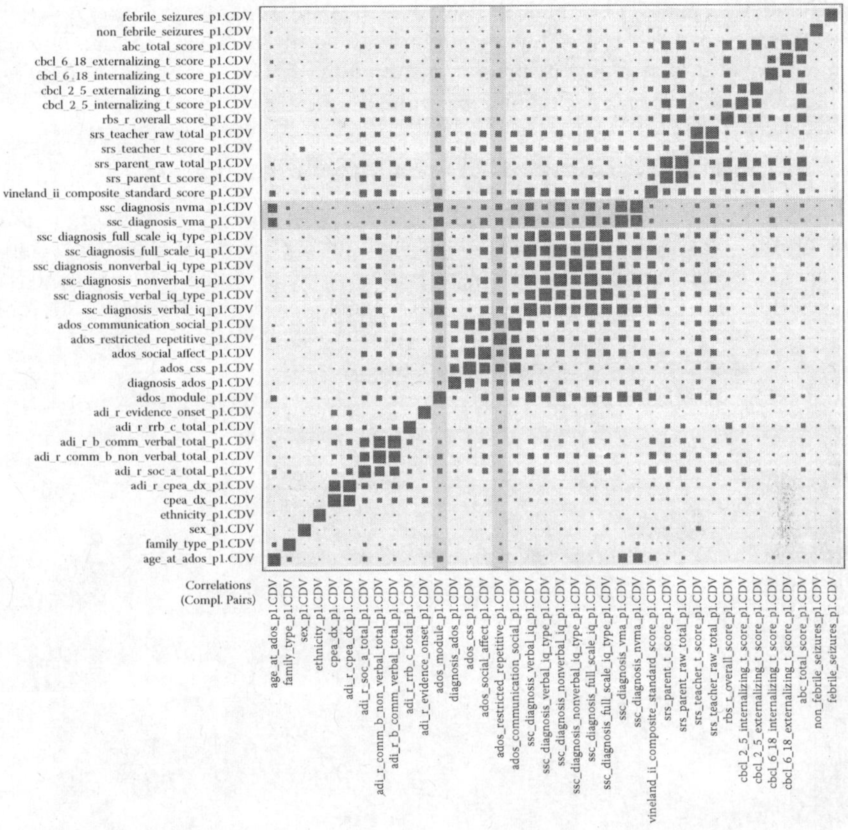

FIGURE 6.2
A reading exercise illustrated with the same example as in Figure 6.1. The salmon-colored strips highlight the variables `age_at_ados_p1.CDV` and `ados_restricted_repetitive_p1.CDV` on the horizontal axis, and the variables `ssc_diagnosis_vma_p1.DCV` and `ssc_diagnosis_nvma_p1.DCV` on the vertical axis. At the intersections of the strips are the blocks that reflect the respective correlations.

skills are more strongly age related than nonverbal skills. (Strictly speaking, we can claim this only for the present sample of autistic probands.) Similarly, following the right vertical strip to the intersection with the horizontal strip, we find two red blocks, of which again the lower block is slightly larger than the upper, but both are smaller than the blue blocks in the left strip. This implies that `..restricted_repetitive..` is negatively correlated with both `..vma..` and `..nvma..` but more strongly with the former, and both are more weakly correlated with `..restricted_repetitive..` than with `age_at_ados..`. All of this makes sense in light of the apparent meanings of the variables: Any notion of *mental age* is probably quite strongly and positively associated with chronological age; with hindsight we may also accept that problems with specific behaviors tend to diminish with age, but the association is probably less strong than that between different notions of age.

Some other patterns are quickly parsed and understood: the two 2×2 blocks on the upper-right diagonal stem from two versions of the same underlying measurements, *raw_total* and *t_score*. Next, the alternating patterns of red and blue in the center indicate that the three IQ measures (*verbal*, *nonverbal*, *full_scale*) are in an inverse association with the corresponding IQ types. This makes sense because IQ types are dummy variables that indicate whether an IQ test suitable for cognitively highly impaired probands was applied. It becomes apparent that one can spend a fair amount of time wrapping one's mind around the visible blockplot patterns and their meanings.

6.3.2 Graphical Overview of Large Correlation Tables

Figure 6.1 shows a manageably small set of 38 variables, which is yet large enough that the presentation of a numeric table would be painful for anybody. This table, however, is a small subset of a larger dataset of 757 variables, which is shown in Figure 6.3. In spite of the very different appearance, this, too, is a blockplot drawn by the same tool and by

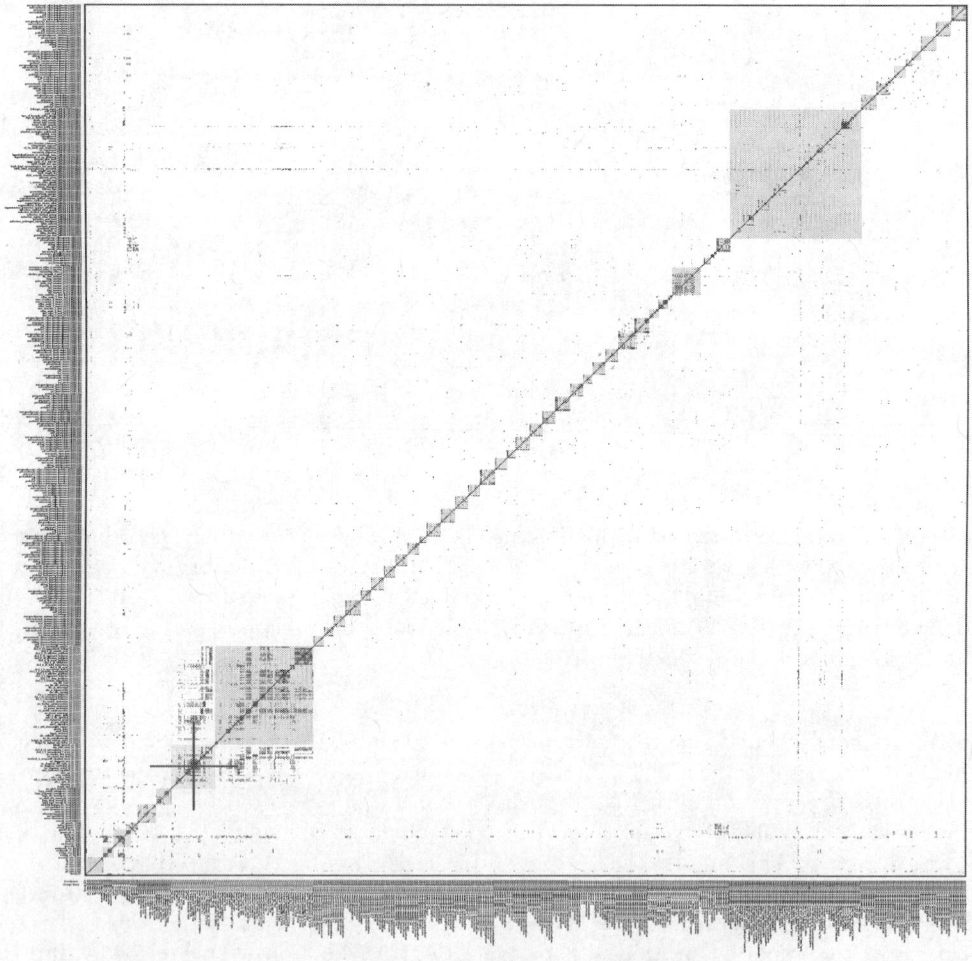

FIGURE 6.3
An overview blockplot of 757 variables. Groups of variables are marked by background highlight squares along the ascending diagonal. The blockplot of Figure 6.1 is contained in this larger plot and can be found in the small highlight square in the lower left marked by a faint crosshair. Readers who are viewing this chapter in a PDF reader may zoom in to verify that this highlight square contains an approximation to Figure 6.1.

the same principles, with some allowance for the fact that $757^2 = 573,049$ blocks cannot be sensibly displayed on screens with an image resolution comparable to 757^2. When blocks are represented by single pixels, blocksize variation is no longer possible. In this case, the tool displays only a selection of correlations that are largest in magnitude. The default (which can be changed) is to show 10,000 of the most extreme correlations, and it is these that give the blockplot in Figure 6.3 the characteristic pattern of streaks and rectangular concentrations.

The function of this blockplot is not so much to facilitate discovery as to provide an overview organized in such a way that meaningful subsets are recognizable to the expert who is knowledgeable about the dataset. The tool helps in this regard by providing a way to group the variables and showing the variable groups as diagonal highlight squares. In Figure 6.3, two large highlight squares are recognizable near the lower left and the upper right. Closer scrutiny should allow the reader to recognize many more much smaller highlight squares up and down the diagonal, each marking a small variable group. In particular, the reader should be able to locate the third largest highlight square in the lower left, shown

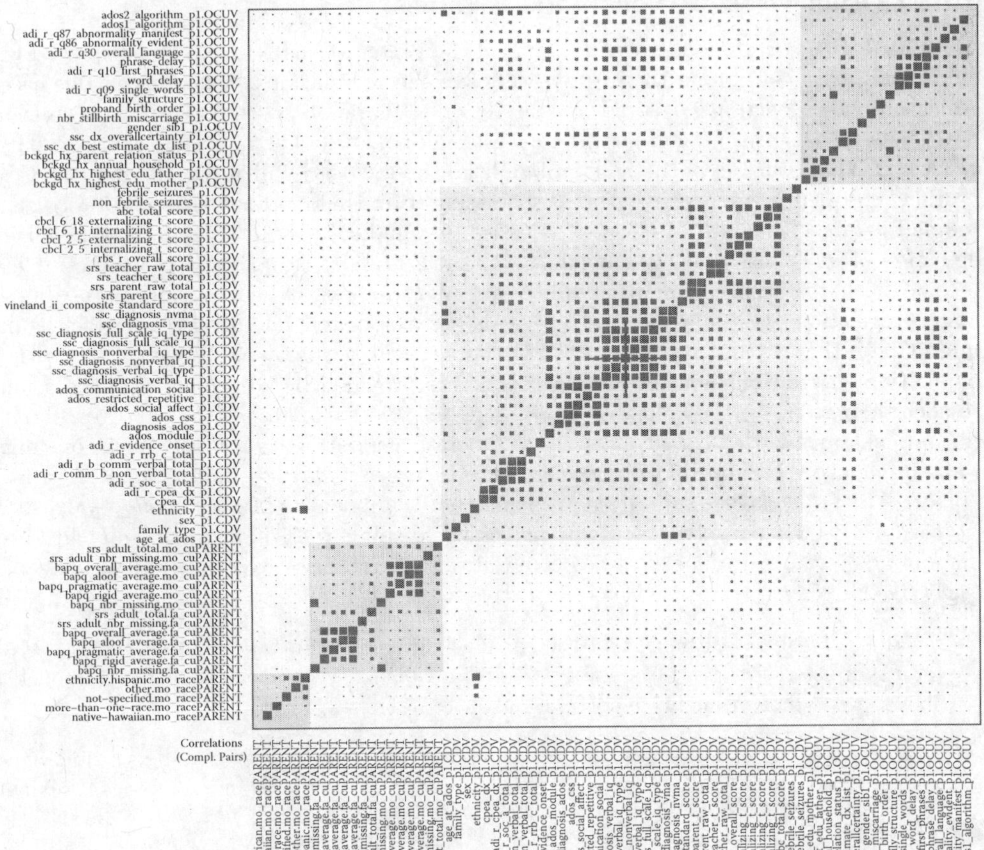

FIGURE 6.4

The 38-variable group of Figure 6.1 in the context of the neigboring variable groups.

in turquoise as opposed to gray and pointed at by a faint crosshair: this square marks the group of 38 variables shown in Figures 6.1 and 6.2.

The mechanism by which variable grouping is conveyed to the AN is a naming convention for variable names: to define a variable group, the variables to be included must be given names that end in the same suffix separated by an underscore "_" (default, can be changed), and the variables must be contiguous in the order of the dataset. As an example, Figure 6.4 shows the 38-variable group of Figure 6.1 in the context of its neighbor groups: This group is characterized by the suffix `p1.CDV`, whereas the neighbor group on the upper right (only a small part is visible) has the suffix `p1.OCUV`, and the two groups on the lower left have suffices `cuPARENT` and `racePARENT`.* The background highlight squares cover the intra-group correlations for the respective variable groups. As in Figure 6.3, the highlight square for the 38-variable group is shown in turquoise, whereas the neighboring highlight squares are in gray.

Figures 6.1 through 6.4 are a prelude for the zooming and panning functionality to be described in Section 6.4.

6.3.3 Other Uses of Blockplots: *p*-Values

Associated with correlations are other quantities of interest that can also be displayed with blockplots, foremost among them the *p*-values of the correlations. A *p*-value in this case is a measure of evidence *in favor of* the assumption that the observed correlation is spurious, that is, its deviation from zero is due to chance alone, although the population correlation is zero.† *p*-Values are hypothetical probabilities; hence, they fall in the interval $[0, 1]$. As *p*-values represent evidence *in favor of* the assumption that *no* linear association exists, it is small *p*-values that are of interest, because they indicate that the chance of a spurious detection of linear association is small. By convention, one is looking for *p*-values at least below 0.05, for a *type I error* probability of 1 in 20 or less. When considering *p*-values of many correlations on the same dataset—as is the case here—one needs to protect against *multiplicity*, that is, the fact that 5% of *p*-values will be below 0.05 even if in truth all population correlations vanish. Such protection is provided by choosing a threshold much smaller than 0.05, by the conservative Bonferroni rule as small as 0.05/#correlations. In the data example with 757 variables, the number of correlations is 286,146; hence one might want to choose the threshold on the *p*-values as low as 0.05/286,146 or about 1.75 in 10 million. The point is that in large-*p* problems, one is interested in *very small* *p*-values.‡

p-Values lend themselves easily to graphical display with blockplots, but the direct mapping of *p*-values to blocksize has some drawbacks. These drawbacks, however, can be easily fixed:

- *p*-Values are blind to the sign of the correlation: correlation values of $+0.95$ and -0.95, for example, result in the same two-sided *p*-values. We correct for this drawback by showing *p*-values of negative correlations in red color.

- Of interest are small *p*-values that correspond to correlations of large magnitude; hence, a direct mapping would represent the interesting *p*-values by small blocks, which is

* These suffices abbreviate the following full-length meanings: "proband 1, core descriptive variables"; "proband 1, other commonly used variables"; "commonly used for parents"; and "race of parents". These variable groups are from the following SSC tables: `proband_cdv.csv`, `proband_ocuv.csv`, and `parent.csv`.

† Technically, the (two-sided) *p*-value of a correlation is the hypothetical probability of observing a future sample correlation greater in magnitude than the sample correlation observed in the actual data—assuming that in truth the population correlation is zero.

‡ The letters 'p' in *large*-p and *p*-value bear no relation. In the former, *p* is derived from *parameter*, but in the latter from *probability*.

visually incorrect because the eye is drawn to large objects, not to large holes. We therefore invert the mapping and associate blocksize with the complement $1-(p\text{-value})$.

- Drawing on the preceding discussion, our interest is really in very small p-values, and one may hence want to ignore p-values greater than .05 altogether in the display. We therefore map the interval [0, .05] inversely to blocksize, meaning that p-values below but near .05 are shown as small blocks and p-values very near .00 as large blocks.

The resulting p-value blockplots are illustrated in Figure 6.5. The two plots show the same 38-variable group as in Figure 6.1 with p-values truncated at .05 and .000,000,1, respectively, as shown near the bottom-left corners of the plots. The p-values are calculated using the usual normal approximation to the null distribution of the correlations. In view of the large sample size, $n \geq 1800$, the normal approximation can be assumed to be quite good, even though one is going out on a limb when relying on normal tail probabilities as small as 10^{-7}. Then again, p-values as small as this are strong evidence against the assumption that the correlations are spurious.

6.3.4 Other Uses of Blockplots: Fraction of Missing and Complete Pairs of Values

Missing values are so common that they require special attention and special tools for understanding their patterns. They are sometimes approached with imputation methods, but in view of the large number of variables we wish to explore, we use simple deletion methods that rely on the largest number of available values. For correlations, this means that we use for a given pair of variables the full set of complete pairs of values. Another common and more stringent deletion method is to use only cases that are complete on all variables, but in the large-p problem, this is not a viable approach because complete cases may well not exist when the number of variables reaches into the hundreds or thousands.

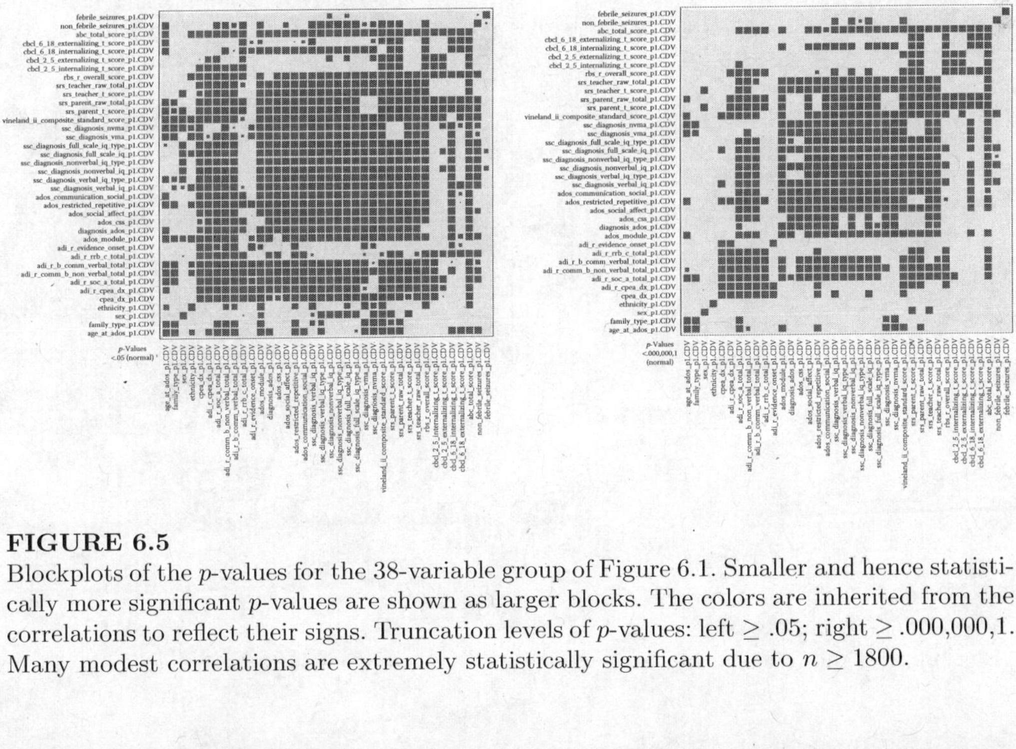

FIGURE 6.5
Blockplots of the p-values for the 38-variable group of Figure 6.1. Smaller and hence statistically more significant p-values are shown as larger blocks. The colors are inherited from the correlations to reflect their signs. Truncation levels of p-values: left $\geq .05$; right $\geq .000,000,1$. Many modest correlations are extremely statistically significant due to $n \geq 1800$.

An issue with calculating correlations from maximal sets of complete pairs of values is that this set may vary from correlation to correlation because it is formed from the overlap of non-missing values in both variables. Thus, associated with each correlation $r(x, y)$ are the following:

- The number $n(x, y)$ $(\leq n)$ of complete pairs from which $r(x, y)$ is calculated.
- The number $m(x, y) = n - n(x, y)$ of incomplete pairs where at least one of the two, x or y, is missing.

Just like the correlations $r(x, y)$, the values $n(x, y)$ and $m(x, y)$ form $n \times n$ tables; hence, they can be easily visualized with blockplots in their fractional forms $n(x, y)/n$ and $m(x, y)/n$. An example of each is shown in Figure 6.6, again for the same 38-variable group of Figure 6.1. Apparently four variables have a major missing value problem.

Depending on whether the number of complete or incomplete pairs dominates, one or the other plot is more sensible in that it uses less ink. Finally, we note that in this case of a blockplot, the diagonal is not occupied by a constant but contains instead the fraction of non-missing $(n(x, x)/n)$ and missing $(m(x, x)/n)$ values, respectively, for each individual variable X. The two tables have inverse relationships between the diagonal and off-diagonal elements: $n(x, x) \geq n(x, y)$ and $m(x, x) \leq m(x, y)$. That is, in the $n(x, y)$ table, the diagonal dominates its row and column, whereas in the $m(x, y)$ table, the diagonal is dominated by its row and column.

6.3.5 Marginal and Bivariate Plots: Histograms/Barcharts, Scatterplots, and Scatterplot Matrices

The correlation of a pair of variables is a simple summary measure of association between two variables; hence, one often wonders about the detailed nature of the association. The full details can be learned from a scatterplot of the two variables. Often the association is constrained by the marginal distribution; hence, we also show histograms and barcharts. Figure 6.7 shows three examples of triples consisting of a pairwise scatterplot and two

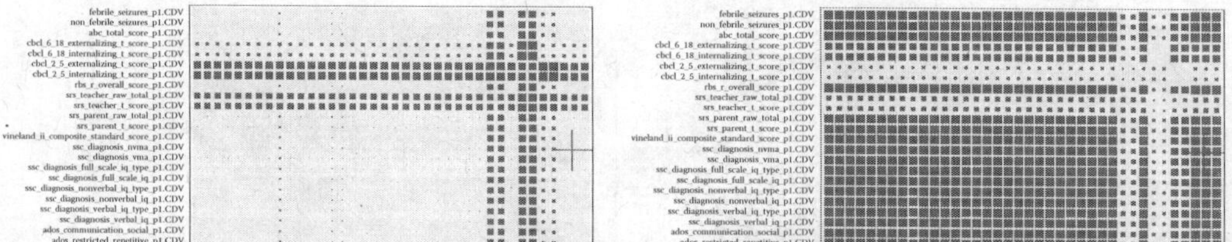

FIGURE 6.6
Blockplots of the fractions of missing (*left*) and complete (*right*) pairs of values.

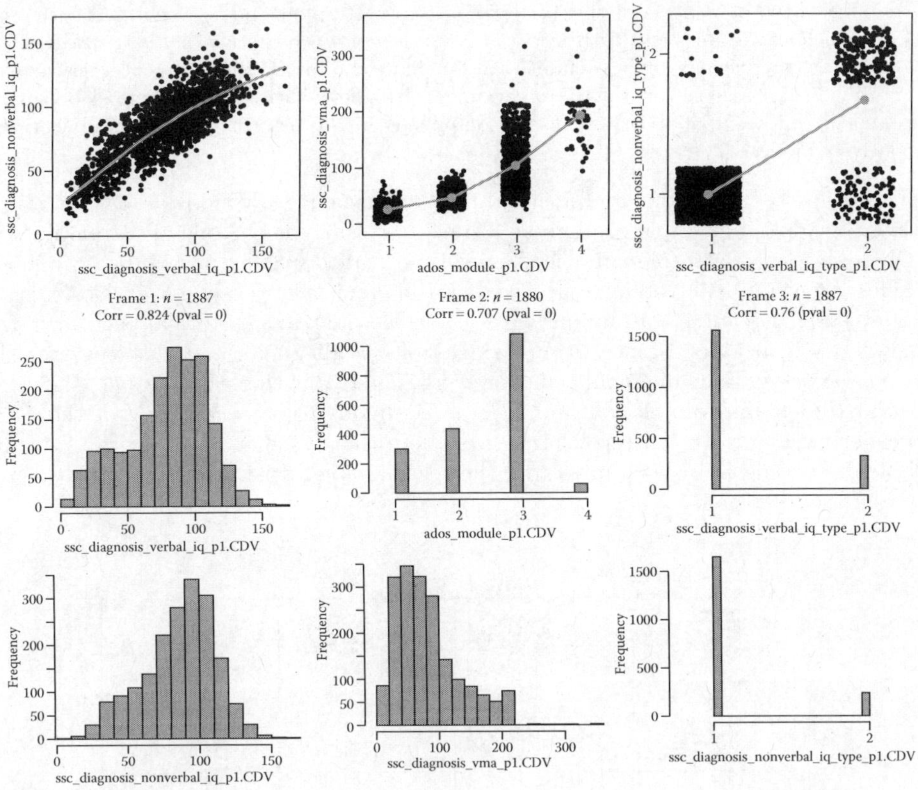

FIGURE 6.7
Scatterplots and histograms/barplots for three variable pairs. Corr, correlation; pval, p-value.

marginal histograms (for quantitative variables) and barcharts (for categorical variables). From Figure 6.7, we can draw a few conclusions and recommendations:

- A most basic use of the plots is to note the *type* of the variables: In Figure 6.7, both variables on the left (`..nonverbal_iq..` and `..verbal_iq..`) and the y-variable in the center (`..vma..`) are *quantitative*; the x-variable in the center (`ados_module..`) is apparently *ordinal* with four levels, and both variables on the right (`nonverbal_iq_type` and `verbal_iq_type`) are *binary*. Quantitative variables can have strong marginal features: it might be of interest to observe that the x-variable on the left is slightly bimodal, with a major mode around $x = 90$ and a minor mode around $x = 30$.* The y-variable in the center scatterplot is partially censored on the upper side at about $y = 210$, as can be seen both in the scatterplot and in the (lower) histogram.
- *Categorical variables*, when scored numerically, can be gainfully displayed in scatterplots. It is useful to *jitter* them to avoid being misled by overplotting. In Figure 6.7, jittering is applied to the x-variable in the center scatterplot and to both binary variables in the right-hand scatterplot.

* The bimodality of the IQ distribution is a measurement artifact: for cognitively highly impaired probands, a different and more appropriate IQ test is administered. In theory, this alternative test should be scaled to cohere with the test administered to the majority, but in practice it creates a minor mode in the low end of the IQ distribution, more so for verbal IQ than for nonverbal IQ.

- To enhance the perception of the *association*, the scatterplots can be decorated with *smooths* for continuous variables and with *traces of group means* when the x-variable is categorical with fewer than, say, eight groups (default, can be changed). In the left and center scatterplots of Figure 6.7, the associations of the y-variables with the x-variables are seen to be somewhat nonlinear, but compared to the linear component of the association, the nonlinearities are relatively modest.*

The AN shows scatterplots and histograms/barcharts in a window separate from the blockplot window, one triple of plots at a time. To overcome the one-at-a time limitation, the AN also offers scatterplot matrices (sometimes called *sploms*) of arbitrary numbers of variables. An example, involving four variables (different from those in Figure 6.7), is shown in Figure 6.8. For readers not familiar with scatterplot matrices, note that each variable pair is shown twice, in plots located symmetrically off the diagonal, and with reverse roles as x- and y-variables. Each diagonal cell shows a variable label that indicates (1) the common x-axis in the column of the cell and (2) the common y-axis in the row of the cell. For the reader familier with scatterplot matrices, note that we show the vertical order of the variables ascending from bottom to top, the reason being consistency with the convention we use in the blockplots.

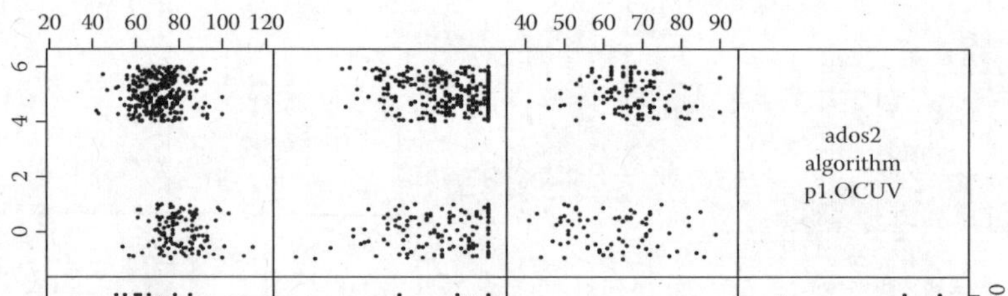

FIGURE 6.8
Scatterplot matrix of four variables. (Note the convention for the vertical order of the variables: bottom to top, for consistency with the blockplots.)

* The nonlinearity on the left could be due to the marginal distributions. The nonlinearity in the center is expected by the expert: verbal mental age (`vma`) on the y-axis should be considerably higher on average in ADOS modules 3 and especially 4 because these modules or levels are formed from a simple test of language competence.

As for particulars of the scatterplot matrix shown in Figure 6.8, the visually most striking features concern marginal distributions, not associations: The first variable is capped at the maximal value +90, and the fourth variable is binary. Otherwise the associations look simply monotone and seem well summarized by correlations.

6.3.6 Variations on Blockplots

Blockplots are not the most common visualizations of correlation tables. As a Google search of *correlation plot* reveals, the most frequent visual rendering of correlation tables is in terms of *heatmaps* where square cells are always filled and numeric values are coded on a gray or color scale. An example is shown in the left frame of Figure 6.9; for comparison, the right frame shows the corresponding blockplot. Here are a few observations about the two types of plots:

- Color or gray scale is generally a weaker visual cue than size. This argument favors blockplots as long as the blocks are not too small, that is, as long as the view is not zoomed out too much. The superiority of blockplots over heatmaps is also noted by Wickham et al. (2006, Figure 2).
- In heatmaps, color fuses adjacent cells when they are close in value. This may or may not be a problem for the trained eye, but there is a loss of identity of the rows and columns in heatmaps.
- Heatmaps do not permit markup with background color because they fill the square or rectangular cells completely. This problem can be overcome by shrinking the heatmap cells somewhat to allow some surrounding space to be freed up that can be filled with background color for markup, as shown in the center frame of Figure 6.9. This method of rendering, however, seems to further decrease the crispness of heatmaps.
- Heatmaps perform nicely when the view is heavily zoomed out, in which case the individual blocks are so small that size is no longer visually functional as a cue. In this case, color coding works well and gives an accurate impression of global structure. We solve this problem for blockplots by showing only 10,000 or so of the largest correlations when heavily zoomed out. Thinning the table in this manner works well even when the visible table is so large that each cell is strictly speaking below the pixel resolution of a raster screen.

Because none of the two types of plots—blockplots or heatmaps—may be uniformly superior at all scales, the AN provides both, and with one keystroke, one can toggle between the two rendering methods. Varying block size allows for the mixed variant shown in the center of Figure 6.9.

Visualization of correlation tables has a small literature in statistics. An early reference that addresses large correlation tables is Hills (1969), who applies half-normal plots to tell statistically significant from insignificant correlations and clusters variables visually in two-dimensional projections. Closer to the present work are articles by Murdoch and Chow (1996) and Friendly (2002). Both propose relatively complex renderings of correlations with ellipses or augmented circles that may not scale up to the sizes of tables we have in mind but may be useful for conveying richer information for tables that are smaller, yet too large for numeric table display. Blockplot coding, which uses squares, has the advantage that these shapes can completely fill their cells to represent extremal correlations as these are geometrically similar to the shapes of the containing cells (at least if the the default aspect ratio of the blockplot is maintained), whereas all other shapes leave residual space even when maximally expanded.

What we prefer to call descriptively *blockplots*, possibly contracted to *blots*, has previously been named *fluctuation diagrams* (Hofmann 2000). Under this term, one can find a static implementation in the R-package `extracat` on the `CRAN` site authored by Pilhoefer

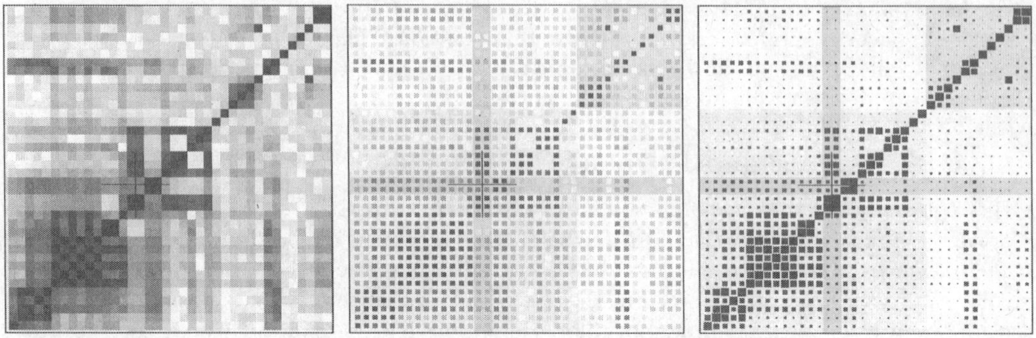

FIGURE 6.9
A heatmap (*left*) compared with a corresponding blockplot (*right*), as well as a *shrunk heatmap* (*center*).

and Unwin (2013). Static software for heatmaps is readily available, for example, in the R-function `heatmap()`. Heatmaps are often applied to raw data tables, but they can be equally applied to correlation tables. Many variations of glyph coding can be found in the classic book by Bertin (1983).

An interesting aspect of blockplots is that there exists science regarding the perception of area size. A general theory holds that most continuous stimuli (*continua* such as length, area, volume, weight, brightness, and loudness) result in perceptions according to *Stevens' power law* (Stevens 1957; Stevens and Galanter 1957; Stevens 1975). That is, a quantitative stimulus x translates to a quantitative perception $p(x)$ through a law of the form $p(x) = c\,x^{\beta}$. As discussed by Cleveland (1985, p. 243) with reference to Stevens (1975), for area perception the power is about $\beta = 0.7$, meaning that an actual area ratio of 2:1 is on average perceived as a ratio of $(2{:}1)^{0.7} \approx 1.62$. This law can be leveraged to determine the transformation that should be used to map correlations to squares in a blockplot. In R the symbol size is parametrized in terms of a linear expansion factor called `cex` (*character expansion*). Our goal is to use block sizes such that their perceived ratios faithfully reflect the ratios of respective correlations. This results in the condition $\text{cor} \sim p(\texttt{cex}^2) = (\texttt{cex}^2)^{0.7} = \texttt{cex}^{1.4}$; hence, $\texttt{cex} \sim \text{cor}^{1/1.4} \approx \text{cor}^{0.7}$. This is indeed the default power transformation in the AN, although users can change it (see Appendix B). If most correlations are very small, a power closer to zero will expand the range of small values, resulting in enhanced discrimination at the low end at the cost of attenuated discrimination at the high end.

6.4 Operation of the AN

The purpose of the AN is to generate the displays described above in rapid order and even with real-time motion. Numerous real-time operations are under mouse and keyboard control, while a few text-based operations are under dialog and menu control. Further parameters can be controlled from the R language (see Appendix B), but this will not be necessary for most users. This section describes the operations of the AN, the purposes they serve, as well as a minimal set of R-related instructions that concern one-time setup, regular starting up, and saving of state. The software will be available as an R-package, but the instructions below do not reflect this and get the reader going by sourcing the software from the first author's site.

6.4.1 Starting Up the AN

In order to simply see some AN running, the reader may paste the following code into an R interpreter:

```
source("http://stat.wharton.upenn.edu/~buja/association-navigator.R")
p <- 200
mymatrix <- matrix(rnorm(20000),ncol=p)
colnames(mymatrix) <- paste("V", 1:p, "_", c(rep("A",p/2),rep("B",p/2)), sep="")
a.n <- a.nav.create(mymatrix)
a.nav.run(a.n)
```

This code will download and source the software, generate an artificial data matrix of normal random numbers, generate an instance of an AN from it, and start up by creating a window showing a blockplot of correlations as they arise from pure random association among 100 variables given a sample size of 200, divided into two blocks of 100 variables each, suffixed A and B, respectively. The reader may left-drag the mouse in the plot to see a first real-time response.

To prevent confusion in the operation of an AN, users should note the following fundamental points:

- *Important*: While the AN is running, the R interpreter (R Gui) is blocked by the execution of the AN's event loop! All interactions must be directed at the master window of the AN, which usually shows a blockplot.
- *Quitting the AN* and returning to the R interpreter is done by typing the capital letter `Q` into the AN master window. The master window will remain as a passive R plot window. It will no longer respond to user input, but the R interpreter (R Gui) will be responsive again. (A live AN can also be stopped violently by typing interrupt characters `ctrl-C` into the R interpreter or by killing the AN master window, but an educated R user wouldn't be this crude.)
- *Help*: On typing the letter `h` into a live AN, a help window will appear with terse documentation of all AN interactions. The window is meant to give reminders to previously initiated AN users, not introductions to beginners. The help window is actually a menu such that selecting a line documenting a keystroke will emulate the effects of the keystroke. Because the help window is a menu, it must be closed in order to regain the AN's attention. (This behavior will be changed in a future version.)
- *Notion of* state: An AN instance has an internal state. As a consequence, whenever a user stops a live AN and restarts it, it will resume in the exact state in which it was stopped.
- *Saving* state: From the previous point follows that state of an AN is saved across R sessions if the core image has been saved (`save.image()`) before quitting the R sessions.

6.4.2 Moving Around: Crosshair Placement, Panning, and Zooming

When an AN is run for the first time, it shows an overview of the complete correlation table, which may comprise hundreds of variables. Most likely the variables will be organized in variable groups that are characterized by shared suffixes of variable names and visually form a series of highlight squares along the ascending diagonal. The first order of business is to zoom in and pan up and down the ascending diagonal to gain an overview of these sub-tables. Here are the steps:

- *Crosshair*: Place it by left-clicking anywhere in the plotting area. All subsequent zooming is done with regard to the location of the crosshair; it is also the reference point for some panning operations. Repeat left-clicking a few times for practice. The last location of the crosshair will be the target for zooming, described next.
- *Zooming*: Hit the following for a single step of zooming, or keep depressed for *continuous* zooming.
  - `i` for zooming in (alternate: `=`).
  - `I` for accelerated zooming in (alternate: `+`).
  - `o` for zooming out (alternate: `-`).
  - `O` for accelerated zooming out (alternate: `_`).

  Accelerated zooming changes the visible range by a factor of 2, whereas regular zooming is adjusted such that 12 steps change the visible range by a factor of 2. Thus, the accelerated zooms are usually done discretely with single keystrokes, and the regular zooms in *continuous* mode with depressed keys. For practice, zoom in and out a few times with your choice of key alternates.
- *Panning* (shifting, translating) is most frequently done by dragging the mouse, but keystrokes are sometimes useful for vertical, horizontal, and diagonal searching.
  - Left-depress the mouse and drag; the plot will follow. When heavily zoomed out from a large table, the response may be slow. The response to mouse dragging will be swifter the more zoomed in the view is.
  - ←, →, ↑, ↓ for translation in the obvious directions by one block/variable per keystroke
  - `d`/`D` for diagonal moves down/up the ascending 45° diagonal
  - " ", the space bar for accelerated panning by doing the last single-step keyboard move in jumps of five blocks/variables instead of one
  - "`.`" to pan so the crosshair location becomes the center of the view
  - `[`", "`]`, `{`", "`}` to pan so the crosshair location becomes, respectively, the bottom left, the bottom right, the top left, or the top right of the view.

  Yet another method of panning will be described below under *Searching Variables*. Combined pan/zoom based on focus rectangles is described in Section 6.4.3.

6.4.3 Graphical Parameters

Graphical parameters that determine the aesthetics of a plot are rarely gotten right by automatic algorithms. The problem of aesthetics is particularly difficult when zooming in and out over several orders of magnitude. The AN, therefore, makes no attempt to guess at pleasing and much less optimal values for such graphical parameters as font size of variable labels and margin size in blockplots. Instead, the user gets to choose them by trial and error as follows:

- *Block size in the blockplot*: hit or depress
  - `b` to decrease
  - `B` to increase

  After starting up a new AN, adjusting the block size is usually the second operation after zooming in.

- *Crosshair size*: hit or depress
  - `c` to decrease
  - `C` to increase

  Exploding the crosshair by depressing `C` is an effective method for reading the variable names of a given block in the margins.

- *Font size of the variable labels*: hit or depress
  - `f` to decrease
  - `F` to increase

  Important: When the font size is large in relation to the zoom, the variable labels get *thinned out* to avoid gross overplotting (only every second, third, etc. label might be shown). This allows viewers to at least identify the variable group from the suffix.

- *Margin size for the variable labels*: hit or depress
  - `m` to decrease
  - `M` to increase

  Margin size needs adjusting according to the prevalent label length and font size. A dilemma occurs when, for example, the x-variable labels are much shorter than the y-variable labels. For this situation, we want the following:

- *Differential margin size for the variable labels*: hit or depress
  - `n` to decrease the left/y margin and increase the bottom/x margin
  - `N` to increase the left/y margin and decrease the bottom/x margin

6.4.4 Correlations, p-Values, and Missing and Complete Pairs

By default, the blockplot of an AN represents correlations, but the user can choose them to represent p-values or fraction of missing (incomplete) pairs or fraction of complete pairs as follows: Hit

- `ctrl-O` for observed correlations
- `ctrl-P` for p-values of the correlations (Section 6.3.3)
- `ctrl-M` for fraction of missing/incomplete pairs (Section 6.3.4)
- `ctrl-N` for fraction of complete pairs (Section 6.3.4)

As discussed in Section 6.3.3, p-values can be thresholded to obtain Bonferroni-style protection against multiplicity. The thresholds are confined to a ladder of *round* values. Stepping up and down the ladder is achieved by repeatedly hitting

- `>` to lower the threshold and obtain greater protection
- `<` to raise the threshold and lose protection.

Recall Figure 6.5 for two examples of p-value blockplots that differ in the threshold only. Thresholding also applies to correlation blockplots, in which case `>` raises the threshold on the magnitude of the correlations that are shown and `<` lowers it.

Sometimes, it is useful to compare magnitudes of the blocks without the distraction of color; hence, it may be convenient to hit

- `ctrl-A` to toggle between showing all blocks in blue (ignoring signs) and showing the negative correlations (and their p-values) in red.

6.4.5 Highlighting: Strips

Highlight strips are horizontal or vertical bands that run across the whole width or height of the blockplot. They help users search the associations of a given variable with all other variables. Cross-wise highlight strips are also often placed to maintain the connection between a given block and the labels of the associated variable pair. By default, the color of highlight strips is *lightgoldenrod1* in **R**. Their appearance is shown in Figure 6.2. Highlight strips can coexist in any number and combination, horizontally and vertically. The mechanisms for creating and removing them are as follows:

- Right-click the mouse on
  - A block in the blockplot to place *a horizontal and a vertical* highlight strip through the block.
  - An x-variable label on the horizontal axis to place a *vertical* highlight strip through this variable.
  - A y-variable label on the vertical axis to place a *horizontal* highlight strip through this variable.
- Hit `ctrl-C` to clear the strips and start from scratch.

Instead of clicking, one can right-depress and drag the mouse across the blockplot with the effect that horizontal and vertical strips are placed across all blocks touched by the drag motion.

Vertical highlight strips lend themselves to convenient searching of associations between a fixed variable on the horizontal axis and all variables on the vertical axis. To this end, it is useful to pan vertically with ↑, ↓, and the space bar as accelerator (Section 6.4.2).

6.4.6 Highlighting: Rectangles

A highlight rectangle is a rectangular area in the blockplot selected by the user for highlighting. Highlight rectangles are meant to help the user focus on the associations between contiguous groups of variables on the horizontal and the vertical axis. By default, the color of highlight rectangles is *lightcyan1* in R. Their appearance is that of the center square in Figure 6.4. In the case of this figure, the highlight rectangle coincides with the highlight square for the variable group defined by the suffix `p1.CDV`. Unlike highlight squares, which mark predefined variable groups, highlight rectangles can be placed (and removed from) anywhere by the user. The mechanisms to this end are as follows:

- Define a highlight rectangle in arbitrary position by placing two opposite corners:
  - Place the crosshair in the location of the desired first corner; then hit `1` to place the first corner of a new rectangle.
  - Place the crosshair in the location of the desired second corner; then hit `2` to place the second corner.

  Action `1` creates a new highlight rectangle consisting of just one block. Action `2` never creates a new block but only sets/resets the second corner of the most recent rectangle.

- Define a highlight rectangle in terms of two variable groups defined by suffixes:
  - Place the crosshair such that the x-coordinate is in the desired horizontal variable group and the y-coordinate in the desired vertical variable group.
  - Hit `3` to create the highlight rectangle.

  As a special case, this allows a highlight square to become a highlight rectangle by letting the x- and y-variable groups be the same, as in Figure 6.4.

- Pan and zoom to snap the view and the highlight rectangle to each other:
  - Place the crosshair in the highlight rectangle to be snapped.
  - Either hit `4` to snap, preserving the aspect ratio.
  - Or hit `5` to snap, distorting the aspect ratio, unless the rectangle is a square.

  If the crosshair is not placed in a highlight rectangle, the most recent one will be used. Note that the squares in a blockplot always remain squares, even if the aspect ratio of the plot has been distorted. Changing the aspect ratio has the consequence that the squares can no longer fill their cells because they have become rectangles.

- Any number of highlight rectangles can coexist. Remove them selectively as follows:
  - Place the crosshair anywhere in a highlight rectangle to be removed.
  - Hit `0` to remove it.

6.4.7 Reference Variables

A recurrent issue when using the AN is that some variables are often of persistent interest. In autism phenotype data, for example, a recurrent theme is to check up on age, gender, and site association (potential confounders) while examining associations within and between various *autism instruments* such as ADOS, ADI, and RBS. To spare users the distraction of hopping back and forth across the multi-hundred square table, the AN implements a notion of *reference variables*, that is, variables that never disappear from view. The AN keeps them tucked in the left and the bottom of the blockplot. The manner in which reference variables present themselves is shown in Figure 6.10. The mechanism for selecting reference variables is by first selecting them with highlight strips (Section 6.4.5), and then hitting

- `R` to turn the strip variables into reference variables.
- `r` to toggle on and off the display of the selected reference variables.

The disentangling of the two actions allows users to keep marking up strips without changing the earlier selected reference variables.

In Figure 6.10, the y-reference variables are `sz.sorted_sites.FAM` and `family.ID`, and their associations with the x-variables are shown in the horizontal band at the bottom. Similarly, the x-reference variables are `age_a_ados_p1.CDV`, `sex_p1.CDV`, `ethnicity_p1.CDV`, and `ados_module_p1.CDV`, and their associations with the y-variables are shown in the vertical band on the left. In the bottom-left corner (the intersection of the reference bands) are shown the associations between x- and y-reference variables.

6.4.8 Searching Variables

Another recurrent issue with analyzing large numbers of variables is simply finding variables. For example,

- Find a variable whose name one remembers partly, but not exactly.
- Find a set of variables whose names share a meaningful syllable.

In the context of autism, for example, it might be of interest to find all variables related to anxiety across all instruments; it would then be sensible to search for all variables that contain the phoneme `anx` in their name. This type of problem can be solved in the AN with a blend of text search and menu selection. We address here the problem of locating one variable and panning to it. To this end, hit,

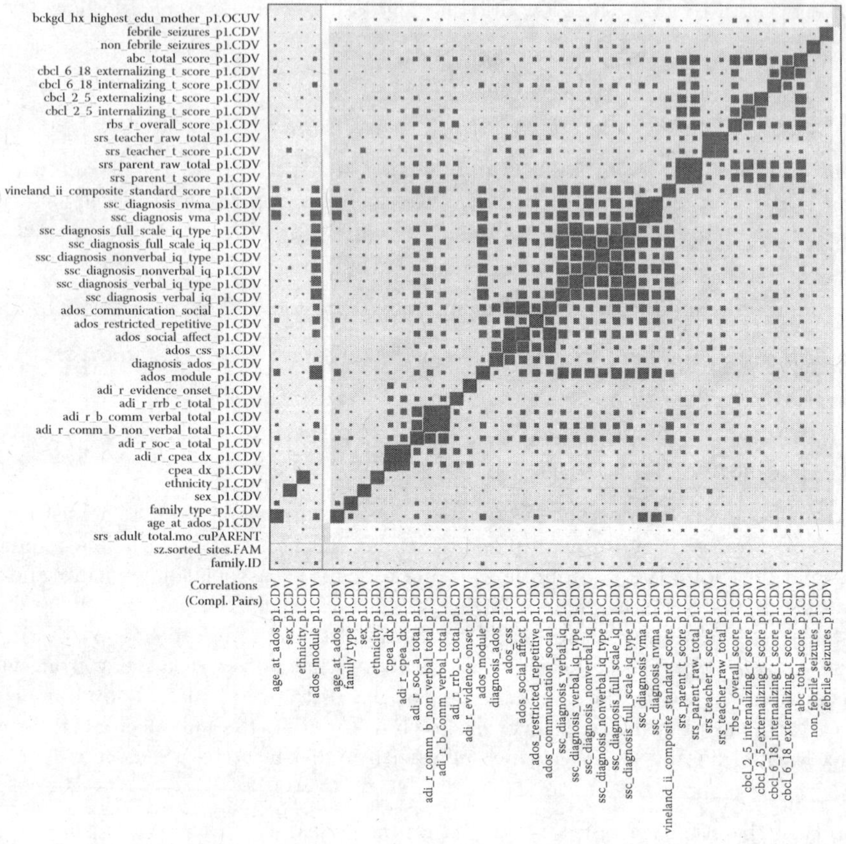

FIGURE 6.10
Reference variables shown in the left and bottom bands. Whenever the user zooms and pans the blockplot, these variables stay in place and show their associations with the variables from the rest of the blockplot.

- `H` to locate a variable on the x-axis.
- `V` to locate a variable on the y-axis.
- `@` to locate a variable on both the x- and y-axes.

In each case, a dialog box pops up where a search string or regular expression can be entered. On hitting `<Return>` or `OK`, a menu appears with the list of variables that contains the search string or matches the regular expression (according to R's `grep()` function). The user is then asked to select one of the offered variables, upon which the AN pans to the variable (depending on `H`, `V`, or `@`) on the x- or the y-axes or both, marks it with a vertical or horizontal highlight strip or both, and places the crosshair on it. (see Figure 6.11).

Search can be bypassed by not entering a search string at all. The menu shows then the complete list of all variables with scrolling.

6.4.9 Lenses: Scatterplots and Barplots/Histograms

We think of barplots, histograms, and scatterplots as lenses into the blocks, each of which represents a pair (x, y) of variables. Taking the pair *under the lens* means looking at

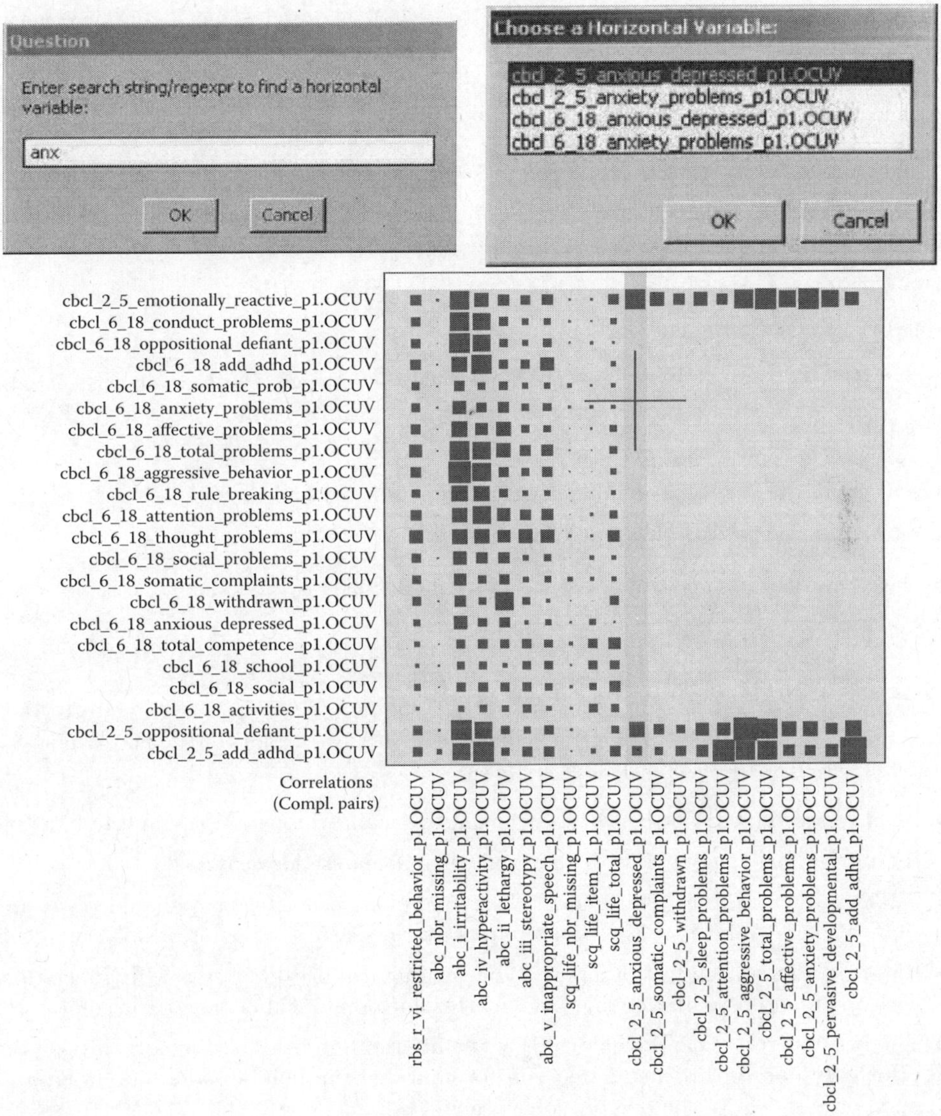

FIGURE 6.11
Text search with `H` for horizontal variables containing `anx`, followed by selection of `cbcl_2_5_anxious_depressed_p1.OCUV`. The view pans horizontally to the selected variable, marks it with a vertical highlight strip, and places the crosshair on it.

the association (and the marginal distribution) in greater detail; see Section 6.3.5. The mechanics are as follows: Hit

- `x` to see in a separate window (Figure 6.7) a scatterplot and barplots/histograms of the two variables marked by the crosshair cursor.
- `y` to switch the x–y roles of the variables.
- `l` to toggle showing a *line*, that is, a smooth if x is quantitative, and a trace of y-means of the x-groups if x is categorical.

Important: The lens window is passive and does not accept interactive input. One must expose the blockplot master window to continue with AN interactions.

These lenses have a simple history mechanism in that the consecutive x–y variable names are collected in a list that can be traversed and edited: Hit

- `PgUp` to take one step back in the history.
- `PgDn` to take one step forward in the history.
- `Home` to jump to the beginning of the history.
- `End` to jump to the end of the history (the present).
- `Delete` to delete the current lens from the history.

Finally, there is a separate lens mechanism with its own window that shows all pairwise scatterplots of the variables currently in highlight strips. An example is shown in Figure 6.8. As to the mechanics, hit

- `z` to create the scatterplot matrix with independently scaled axes.
- `Z` to create the scatterplot matrix with identically scaled axes.

The latter option is sometimes useful when all variables live on the same scale but have somewhat different ranges.

6.4.10 Color Brushing in Scatterplots

Often one would like to focus on groups of cases in the scatterplots of the lens window. This can be achieved with color brushing as follows:

- Hit `s` to see the current lens scatterplot in the main window, replacing the blockplot.
- Hit `r` to fix one corner of a brush at the current mouse location.
- Left-depress and drag the mouse: The rectangular brushing area should open up and change shape. Whenever the brush moves over a scatterplot point, it will change color.
- Right-depress and drag the mouse: The rectangular brushing area will translate along with the mouse. Again, moving over scatterplot points will change their color.
- The brushing color can be changed by cycling through a series of colors, hitting `S`. The color gray does not paint; it is useful for counting the points under the brush as their number is shown in the bottom-left corner.
- Hit `s` to return to the blockplot in the main window.

Thus, hitting `s` toggles between blockplot and scatterplot in the main window. After each brushing operation, the lens scatterplot will follow suit and color its points to match those in the main window.

6.4.11 Linear Adjustment

Another recurrent task in large tables is what we may call *adjustment*. The phrase *adjusting for* x has many synonyms: *accounting for* x, *controlling for* x, *correcting for* x, *adjusting for* x, and holding *x fixed* or *conditioning on* x. Technically most correct is the last expression: we are often interested in the conditional association between variables y and z given (holding fixed) a variable x, as measured, for example, by the conditional correlation $r(y, z|x)$. In the context of the autism phenotype, one may be interested in adjusting for age and/or gender. In practice, particularly in large-p problems, there is rarely sufficient data to truly estimate conditional distributions;* hence, one makes the simplifying assumption that all associations are linear with constant conditional variances (homoscedasticity).† In that case, adjustment of y for x amounts to a linear regression and forming residuals, that is, *residualizing* or *partialling out* is done by subtracting the equation fitted with linear regression: $y_{\cdot x} = y - (b_0 + b_1 x)$. As a consequence, $r(y_{\cdot x}, x) = 0$, that is, by forming $y_{\cdot x}$ one removes from y the linear association with x. This type of linear adjustment generalizes to multiple x variables by residualizing with regard to a multiple linear regression.

In the AN implementation of linear adjustment, one has to select a set of *independent* x-variables, called *adjustors*, and a set of *dependent* y-variables, called the *adjustees*. Often the set of adjustors is small, possibly just one variable such as age, whereas the set of adjustees can be large, for example, all items and summary scales of an autism phenotype instrument

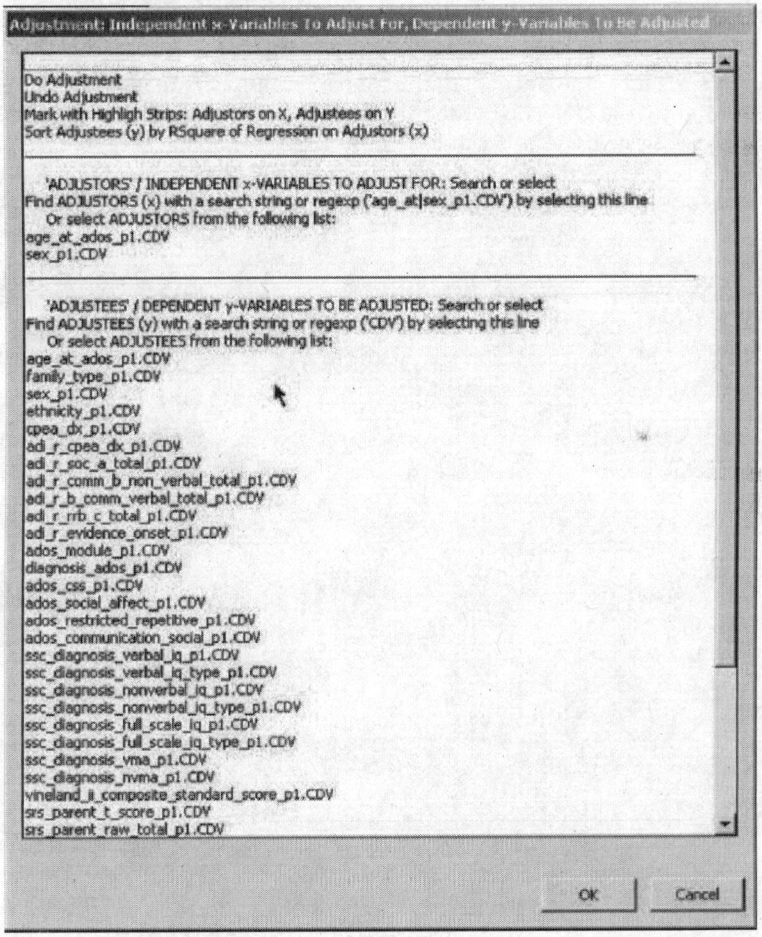

FIGURE 6.12
Screenshot of the adjustment menu. As shown, it enables adjustment of the `srs` variables for `age_at_ados_p1.CDV` and `sex_p1.CDV`.

*Natural exceptions do exist: If we analyze females and males separate, for example, we study gender-conditional associations.

†Both assumptions may be wrong, but some form of adjustment, even if flawed, is often more informative than remaining with raw variables.

such as the *Social Responsiveness Scale* (SRS). The selection mechanisms are the same for both adjustors and adjustees: text search or regular expression matching, followed by menu selection, similar to Section 6.4.8, but here the menu selection allows multiple choices. The mechanics are as follows: Hit

- `A` to call up a large menu that forms the interface for all adjustment operations.

An example is shown in Figure 6.12. Initially, the list of adjustors and adjustees will be empty, so both need to be populated with text searches that require a dialog initiated by selecting the lines `Find ADJUSTORS...` and `Find ADJUSTEES...` in sequence. Figure 6.12 shows the state after having matched the regular expression `age_at|sex_p1.CDV` for adjustors and searched the string `CDV` for adjustees.

Finally, after selection of adjustors and adjustees is completed, the user may select the top line of the menu to actually `Do Adjustment`. Each raw adjustee will then be replaced by its residuals obtained from the regression onto the adjustors. (To undo adjustment, select the second line from the Adjustment dialog, `Undo Adjustment`.)

To assist the visual examination of adjustment results, one may want to select the third line from the top of the menu in order to highlight the adjustors among the x-variables and the adjustees among the y-variables (`Mark with Highlight Strips...`). Turning them further into reference variables (Section 6.4.7) by hitting `R`, we obtain Figure 6.13. As it should be, the correlations between the two adjustors on the x-axis and the many adjustees

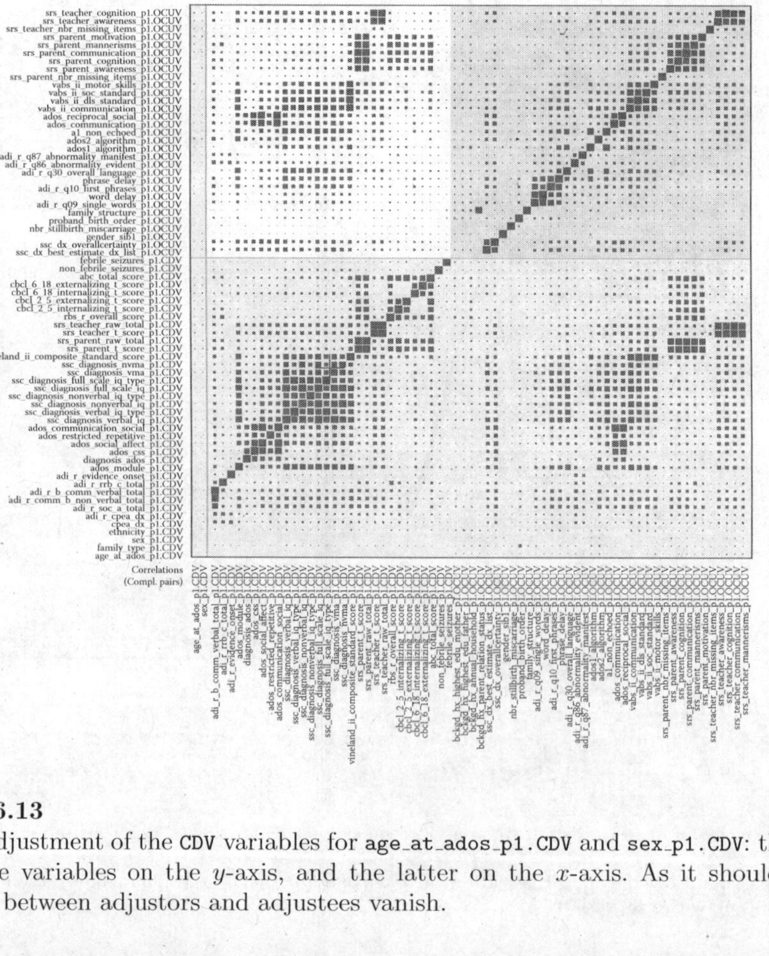

FIGURE 6.13
Results of adjustment of the `CDV` variables for `age_at_ados_p1.CDV` and `sex_p1.CDV`: the former are reference variables on the y-axis, and the latter on the x-axis. As it should be, the correlations between adjustors and adjustees vanish.

on the y-axis vanish. The correlations of the adjustees with other variables may now be of renewed interest because they are free of age and gender *effects*, which would invite a search of the correlations in the horizontal band of the adjustees.

A word of caution is that adjustment of a y-variable is done using only cases for which there are no missing values among the adjustors and obviously the adjustee is not missing either. Thus, the underlying set of cases may have been inadvertently decreased. It is therefore good advice to check the missing pairs patterns with either `ctrl-M` or `ctrl-N` (Section 6.4.4) or by looking at scatterplots (Section 6.4.9).

Having done adjustment of variables, one often wonders how much of it was done and to which variable. To answer this question, select the fourth line from the Adjustment

FIGURE 6.14
List of adjustees/y-variables sorted according to the R^2 values from the regressions onto the adjustors/x-variables.

dialog (`Sort Adjustees...`): The result is a sorted list of the adjustees according to the R^2 values from the regression of the adjustees/y-variables onto the adjustors/x-variables. See Figure 6.14 for an example.

6.4.12 Future of AN

The functionality described here reflects the 2015 implementation of the AN. Changes to the AN are planned, the major one being a redesign to give the lens windows interactive responsiveness as well. Currently all interaction is funneled throught the blockplot window, even if the actions affect the lens window.

Other obvious functionality is still missing, above all sorting of variables, manual and algorithmic. A limited set of sorting operations may be added in a future version of the AN. If readers of this chapter and users of the AN have further suggestions, the authors would appreciate hearing.

Appendix A: Versatility of Correlation Analysis

We return to the apparent limitations of correlations as measures of association, which was left as a loose end in the Section 6.2. We address the objections that (1) correlations are measures of linear association only, (2) correlations reflect bivariate association only, and (3) correlations apply to quantitative variables only. Toward this end, we make the following observations and recommendations:

1. Although it is true that correlation is strictly speaking a measure of linear association among quantitative variables, it is also a fact that correlation is useful as a measure of monotone association in general, even when it is nonlinear. As long as the association is roughly monotone, correlation will be positive when the association is increasing and negative when it is decreasing. Admittedly, correlation is not an optimal measure of nonlinear monotone association, but it is still a useful one, in particular in the large-p problem. Finally, if gross nonlinearity is discovered, it is always possible to replace a variable X with a nonlinear transform $f(X)$ [often $\log(X)$] so its association with other variables becomes more linear.*
2. The objection that correlations only reflect bivariate association is factually correct but practically not very relevant. In practical data analysis, it is too contrived to entertain the possibility that, for example, there exists association among three variables, but there exists no monotone association among each pair of variables.† In general, one follows the principle that lower-order association is more likely than higher-order association; hence, pairwise association is more likely than true interaction among three variables. Therefore, data analysts look first for groups of variables that are linked by pairwise association, and thereafter they may examine whether these variables *also* exhibit higher-order association. Note, however, that even multivariate methods such as principal components

* Linearity of association is not a simple concept. For one thing, it is asymmetric: if Y is linearly associated with X, it does not follow that X is linearly associated with Y. The reason is that the definition of linear association, $\mathrm{E}[Y|X] = \beta_0 + \beta_1 X$, is not symmetric in X and Y. Linearity of association in both directions holds only for certain *nice* distributions such as bivariate Gaussians. A counterexampls is as follows: Let X be *uniformly* distributed on an interval and $Y = \beta_0 + \beta_1 X + \epsilon$ with independent Gaussian ϵ, then Y is linearly associated with X by construction, yet X is *not* linearly associated with Y.

† An example would be three variables jointly uniformly distributed on the surface of a two-sphere in three-space.

analysis (PCA) do not detect true higher-order interaction because they, too, rely on correlations only. Finally, we are not asserting that simple correlation analysis should be the end of data analysis, but it should certainly be near the beginning in the large-p problems envisioned here, namely, in the analysis of relatively noisy data as they arise in many social science and medical contexts.*

3. The final objection we consider is that correlations do not apply to categorical variables. This objection can be refuted with very practical advice on how to make categorical data quantitative and how to interpret the meaning of the resulting correlations. We discuss several cases in turn:

   a. If a categorical variable X is *ordinal* (its categories have a natural order), it is common practice to simply number the categories in order and use the resulting integer variable as a quantitative variable. The resulting correlations will be able to reflect monotone association with other variables that may be expressed by saying "the higher categories of X tend to be associated with higher/lower values/categories of other variables." An obvious objection is that the equi-spaced integers may not be a good quantification of the categories. If this is a serious concern worth some effort, one may want to look into optimal scoring procedures [see, e.g., De Leeuw and van Rijckevorsel (1980) and Gifi (1990)]. The idea behind these methods is to estimate new scores for the categorical variables by making them as linearly associated as possible through optimization of the fit of a joint PCA.

   b. If a categorical variable X is *binary*, it is common practice to numerically code its two categories with the values 0 and 1, thereby creating a so-called *dummy variable*. This practice is pervasive in the analysis of variance (ANOVA), but its usefulness is lesser known in multivariate analysis which is our concern. The interpretation of correlations with dummy variables is highly interesting as it solves two seemingly different association problems:

      i. First-order association between a binary variable X and a quantitative variable Y means that there exists a difference between the two means of Y in the two groups denoted by X. As it turns out, the correlation of a dummy variable X with a quantitative variable Y is mathematically equivalent to forming the t-statistic for a two-sample comparison of the two means of Y in the two categories of X ($t \propto r/(1-r^2)^{1/2}$). Even more, the statistical test for a zero correlation is virtually identical to the t-test for equality of the two means. Thus, two sample mean comparisons can be subsumed under correlation analysis.

      ii. Association between two binary variables means that their 2×2 table shows dependence. This situation is usually addressed with Fisher's exact test of independence. It turns out, however, that Fisher's exact test is equivalent to testing the correlation between the dummy variables, the only discrepancy being that the normal approximation used to calculate the p-value of a correlation is just that, an approximation, although an adequate one in most cases.

   c. If a categorical variable X is truly *nominal* with more than two values, that is, neither binary nor ordinal, we may again follow the lead of ANOVA and replace X with a collection of dummy variables, one per category. For example,

* In other large-p problems, the variables may be so highly structured that they become intrinsically low dimensional, as, for example, in the analysis of libraries of registered images where each variable corresponds to a pixel location and its values consist of intensities at that location across the images. The problem here is not to locate groups of variables with association but to describe the manifold formed by the images in very high-dimensional pixel space. A sensible approach in this case would be nonlinear dimension reduction.

if in a medical context data are collected in multiple sites, it will be of interest to see whether substantive variables in some sites are systematically different from other sites. It is then useful to introduce dummy variables for the sites and examine their correlations with the substantive variables. A significant correlation indicates a significant mean difference at that site compared to the other sites.

This discussion shows that categorical variables can be fruitfully included in correlation analysis, with either numerical coding of ordinal variables or dummy coding of binary and nominal variables.

This concludes our discussion of the versatility of correlation analysis.

Appendix B: Creating and Programming AN Instances

To create a new instance of an AN for a given dataset, use the following R statement:

```
a.n <- a.nav.create(datamatrix)
```

where `datamatrix` is a numeric matrix, not a dataframe. The new AN instance `a.n` can be run with the following R statement:

```
a.nav.run(a.n)
```

These steps are completely general and may be useful for arbitrary numeric data matrices with up to about 2000 variables.

Table B.1 shows a template for forming potentially useful instances of ANs that display large numbers of SSC phenotype variables. As written the statement would produce an AN on the order of 3000 variables.

AN's are implemented not as lists but as *environments*, a relatively little known data structure among most R users. Environments have some interesting properties. One can look inside an AN with the R idiom

```
with(a.n, objects())
```

in order to list the AN internal variables inside the AN instance `a.n`. Assignments and any other kind of programming of the internal state variables can be achieved the same way. For example, if one desires a change of color of highlight strips to *mistyrose*, one can achieve this with the following:

```
with(a.n, { strips.col <- "mistyrose";  a.nav.blockplot() })
```

The call to `a.nav.blockplot()` redisplays the blockplot with the new paramater setting. Changing the blockplot glyph from square to diamond is achieved with

```
with(a.n, {blot.pch <- 18;  a.nav.blockplot() })
```

and reversing the color convention from "blue = positive" to "red = positive" in the style of heatmaps is done with

```
with(a.n, { blot.col.pos <- 2;  blot.col.neg <- 4;  a.nav.blockplot() })
```

Note, however, that this affects only blockplots, not heatmaps, the latter requiring computation of a color scale, not just a binary color decision. Still, there is plenty of opportunity for playfulness by experimenting with display parameters. A more sophisticated example concerns changing the power transformation that maps correlations to glyph sizes:

```
with(a.n, {blot.pow <- .7; a.nav.cors.trans(); a.nav.blockplot() })
```

In addition to redisplay with `a.nav.blockplot()`, this also requires recomputation of the display table with `a.nav.cors.trans()`.

TABLE B.1

Template for joining large numbers of SSC tables and creating an AN for them.

```
a.n <- a.nav.create(cbind(
    "family.ID"=as.numeric(v.families),
    v.sites,  v.srs.bg,  v.individual,
    v.family,  v.parent.race,  v.parent.common,
    v.proband.cdv, v.proband.ocuv,  v.sibling.s1, v.sibling.s2,
    v.ados.common,
    v.ados.1, v.ados.1.raw, v.ados.2, v.ados.2.raw,
    v.ados.3, v.ados.3.raw, v.ados.4, v.ados.4.raw,
    v.adi.r.diagnostic, v.adi.r.pca, v.adi.r,
    v.adi.r.dum, v.adi.r.loss,
    v.ssc.diagnosis,
    v.vineland.ii.p1, v.vineland.ii.s1,
    v.cbcl.2.5.p1,  v.cbcl.2.5.s1,
    v.cbcl.6.18.p1, v.cbcl.6.18.s1,
    v.abc, v.abc.raw,  v.rbs.r, v.rbs.r.raw,
    v.srs.parent.p1,   v.srs.parent.recode.p1,
    v.srs.teacher.p1,  v.srs.teacher.recode.p1,
    v.srs.parent.s1,   v.srs.parent.recode.s1,
    v.srs.teacher.s1,  v.srs.teacher.recode.s1,
    v.srs.adult.fa,    v.srs.adult.recode.fa,
    v.srs.adult.mo,    v.srs.adult.recode.mo,
    v.bapq.fa, v.bapq.recode.fa, v.bapq.mo, v.bapq.recode.mo,
    v.fhi.interviewer.fa, v.fhi.interviewer.mo,
    v.scq.current.p1, v.scq.life.p1,
    v.scq.current.s1, v.scq.life.s1,
    v.ctopp.nr,  v.purdue.pegboard,  v.dcdq,  v.ppvt,
    v.das.ii.early.years, v.das.ii.school.age,
    v.ctrf.2.5, v.trf.6.18,
    v.ssc.med.hx.v2.autoimmune.disorders, v.ssc.med.hx.v2.birth.defects,
    v.ssc.med.hx.v2.chronic.illnesses,    v.ssc.med.hx.v2.diet.medication.sleep,
    v.ssc.med.hx.v2.genetic.disorders,    v.ssc.med.hx.v2.labor.delivery.birth.feeding,
    v.ssc.med.hx.v2.language.disorders,
    v.ssc.med.hx.v2.medical.history.child.1, v.ssc.med.hx.v2.medical.history.child.2,
    v.ssc.med.hx.v2.medical.history.child.3,
    v.ssc.med.hx.v2.medications.drugs.mother,
    v.ssc.med.hx.v2.neurological.conditions,
    v.ssc.med.hx.v2.other.developmental.disorders, v.ssc.med.hx.v2.pdd,
    v.ssc.med.hx.v2.pregnancy.history, v.ssc.med.hx.v2.pregnancy.illness.vaccinations,
    v.ssc.psuh.fa,     vv.ssc.psuh.mo,
    v.temperature.form.raw
    ), remove=T )
```

Readers should make a selection from this template as the full collection creates a data matrix with about 3000 variables.

R environments represent one of the few data types that disobeys the functional programming paradigm that is otherwise fundamental to R. As a consequence, assignment of an AN does not allocate a new copy but passes a reference instead. In particular, the R statement

```
b.n <- a.n
```

creates a variable `b.n` that will be a reference to the same environment as the variable `a.n`. Hence, the two statements

```
a.nav.run(a.n)
a.nav.run(b.n)
```

will run off the same AN instance. They have identical effects in the sense that interactive operations affect the same instance.

Acknowledgments

This work was partially supported by a grant from the Simons Foundation (SFARI award #121221 to A.M.K.). We appreciate obtaining access to the phenotypic data on SFARI Base (https://base.sfari.org). Partial support was also provided by the National Science Foundation Grant DMS-1007689 to A.B.

References

J. Bertin. *Semiology of Graphics*. Madison, WI: University of Wisconsin Press, 1983.

W. S. Cleveland. *The Elements of Graphing Data*. Pacific Grove, CA: Wadsworth & Brooks/Cole, 1985.

J. De Leeuw and J. van Rijckevorsel. HOMALS and PRINCALS—Some generalizations of principal components analysis. In E. Diday et al., editors, *Data Analysis and Informatics II*, pp. 231–242. Amsterdam, the Netherlands: Elsevier Science Publishers, 1980.

M. Friendly. Corrgrams: Exploratory displays of correlation matrices. *The American Statistician*, 56(4):316–324, 2002.

A. Gifi. *Nonlinear Multivariate Analysis*. New York: John Wiley & Sons, 1990.

M. Hills. On looking at large correlation matrices. *Biometrika*, 56(2):249–253, 1969.

H. Hofmann. Exploring categorical data: Interactive mosaic plots. *Metrika*, 51(1):11–26, 2000.

D. J. Murdoch and E. D. Chow. A graphical display of large correlation matrices. *The American Statistician*, 50(2):178–180, 1996.

A. Pilhoefer and A. Unwin. New approaches in visualization of categorical data: R package extracat. *Journal of Statistical Software*, 53(7):1–25, 2013.

S. S. Stevens. On the psychophysical law. *The Psychological Review*, 64(3):153–181, 1957.

S. S. Stevens. *Psychophysics*. New York: John Wiley & Sons, 1975.

S. S. Stevens and E. H. Galanter. Ratio scales and category scales for a dozen perceptual continua. *Journal of Experimental Psychology*, 54(6):377–411, 1957.

H. Wickham, H. Hofmann, and D. Cook. Exploring cluster analysis. http://www.had.co.nz/model-vis/clusters.pdf, 2006.

Part III

Efficient Algorithms

7

High-Dimensional Computational Geometry

Alexandr Andoni

CONTENTS

7.1 Introduction 105
7.2 Dimension Reduction 106
7.3 Space Partitions 107
7.3.1 From LSH to NNS 108
7.3.2 LSH Families 109
7.3.2.1 Bit Sampling (For Hamming Distance) 110
7.3.2.2 Grid Partitioning (For ℓ_1 Distance) 110
7.3.2.3 Random Projection (For Euclidean and ℓ_p Distances) 110
7.3.2.4 Ball Carving (For Euclidean Distance) 110
7.3.2.5 Min-Hash and Sim-Hash 111
7.3.3 Optimality of LSH 111
7.3.4 Data-Dependent Space Partitions 111
7.3.5 The ℓ_∞ Norm 112
7.4 Embeddings 112
7.4.1 Embeddings of Norms 113
7.4.2 Embeddings of Specialized Metrics 113
7.5 Sketching 115
7.5.1 Sketch Constructions 116
7.6 Small Dimension 117
7.7 Conclusion 117
References 118

7.1 Introduction

Consider the following common *similarity search* scenario. We are given a new image, and we need to determine whether it is similar to some image in the existing database, preprocessed beforehand. How do we capture the notion of *similar*? The standard approach is to use a suitable *distance metric*. For example, we can represent a 20×20-pixel image as a 400-dimensional vector, one coordinate per pixel. Then we can measure the (dis)similarity using the Euclidean distance in $\mathbb{R}^{400}$.

This problem, called nearest neighbor search (NNS), admits a straightforward solution—scanning the entire database—but it is prohibitive for databases of modern sizes. Instead, it is imperative to obtain a solution with run-time that is *sublinear* in the database size. The bad news is that this problem suffers from the *curse of dimensionality*: all solutions degrade exponentially fast with the dimension. In fact, the problem is not believed to have such sublinear solutions. The good news is that vast improvements are possible in both theory and practice, once we settle for *approximate* answers. In practice, approximate answers prove to be sufficient even if one looks for *exact* answers: for many natural datasets there are only few entries that are close to being an optimal answer (false positives), and thus we can efficiently filter them.

The above is just an example of how high-dimensional geometry emerges in *big data* questions. In general, the geometry is not necessarily Euclidean, and indeed many interesting questions appear for distances such as Hamming, earthmover distance, and edit distance (Levenshtein distance), to name just a few. This *geometric perspective* confers a number of benefits. First, it brings in our geometric intuition to argue about sets of objects as sets of points. Second, geometric perspective allows us to bring in some powerful tools from the areas such as metric embeddings and functional analysis.

In this chapter, we survey the techniques of the high-dimensional computational geometry through the prism of the NNS problem. From a broader perspective, NNS is just one example of the questions arising when dealing with massive datasets. Yet these questions often benefit from common solution concepts that already surface when considering the NNS problem. In fact, oftentimes, NNS itself serves as a building block for the solutions of the other questions. Hence, we focus on NNS to have a consistent storyline.

We will start by looking at the aforementioned setting: high-dimensional Euclidean space, denoted by $\mathbb{R}^d$ where d is the dimension. This is perhaps the most basic high-dimensional setting. In general, we expect to see a trade-off between the complexity of the geometric structure and the algorithmic efficiency. We now give the exact definition of the approximate nearest neighbor problem.

DEFINITION 7.1 **c-approximate nearest neighbor** *Given a set P of n points in a d-dimensional space $\mathbb{R}^d$, and approximation factor $c > 1$, construct a data structure such that, given any query point q, the data structure returns some point p such that $\mathbf{d}(q,p) \leq c \cdot \min_{p^* \in P} \mathbf{d}(q, p^*)$.*

7.2 Dimension Reduction

If high dimensionality presents a problem, why not reduce it? Indeed, the *high-dimensional geometry 101* technique is to map the points into a space of smaller dimension k, while preserving the distances. The most classic result is the Johnson–Lindenstrauss (JL) lemma [66]. It says that a projection onto a *random* k-dimensional subspace suffices, provided k, is large enough.

LEMMA 7.1 **JL [66]** *Let A be the projection onto a random k-dimensional subspace of $\mathbb{R}^d$, scaled by $\sqrt{1/k}$. Then, for any fixed $\epsilon > 0$, and points $x, y \in \mathbb{R}^d$, we have that*

$$\Pr_A\left[\tfrac{\|Ax-Ay\|}{\|x-y\|} \in (1-\epsilon, 1+\epsilon)\right] \geq 1 - e^{-\Omega(\epsilon^2 k)}.$$

An important consequence is that we can argue about distances among a set of n points. In particular, setting $k = \Theta(C\epsilon^{-2}\log n)$, we obtain the probability of preserving a fixed distance as high as $1 - 1/n^C$, for arbitrary large constant C. By union bound over the n^2 vectors, pairwise differences of the n points are preserved with probability at least $1-n^{-C+2}$. In fact, this is the most common usage of the lemma.

Another crucial aspect of the above map is that it is *oblivious*, that is, independent of the set of points. The alternative, a *nonoblivious* map, would have to first look at the n points before constructing the actual map A. The advantage of an oblivious map is that we can apply it to a new point (sometimes called *out-of-sample extension*).

These properties are already enough to speed up NNS. Indeed, we can pick a projection A as above, and then store points Ap, where $p \in P$ for a given dataset P. On query q, we compute the projection Aq, and then select the point p that minimizes $\|Aq - Ap\|$. The correctness of the algorithm is guaranteed by the JL lemma (applied to the point-set $P \cup \{q\}$). The run-time of the query procedure is $O(nk) + O(dk)$ for $k = O(\epsilon^{-2} \log n)$. Note that the second term corresponds to computing the projection Aq. The query time is an improvement over the naïve $O(nd)$ bound for large d.

Following the original JL lemma, many natural extensions arose. Below are a few that have drawn a particular attention in the theoretical computer science literature:

- Can we improve the target dimension k?

  In general, the answer is no. Jayram and Woodruff [63] show any oblivious map must use dimension $k = \Omega(\epsilon^{-2} \log n)$. Even for nonoblivious maps, Alon [5] shows that $k = \Omega\left(((1/\epsilon^2)/(\log 1/\epsilon)) \log n\right)$ is required. See also [77].

  However, such dimension reduction may be possible for a point-set with *additional structure*. For example, if the point-set lies on a line (in $\mathbb{R}^d$), a much smaller k will suffice. We give an example in Section 7.6.

- Are there dimension reductions for other geometric concepts besides distances?

  It turns out that the JL lemma may be used for other concepts, such as preserving l-flats (for $l \ll k$) or volumes of l-tuples of points [79]. In general, such applications require a higher target dimension k.

- Are there dimension reductions for other spaces besides Euclidean?

  In general, the answer is no. For example, even for the Manhattan ℓ_1 space, it has been proved that dimension reduction for n points, preserving distances up to factor $c > 1$, must use $n^{\Omega(1/c^2)}$ dimensions [25]. More generally, Johnson and Naor [68] show that any space satisfying JL-like dimension reduction must be close to an Euclidean space.

  However, there is an alternative concept for dimension reduction that can be applied to spaces such as ℓ_1, as we will see in Section 7.5.

- Can we choose a more efficient map? For example, can we compute Ap faster than in $O(dk)$ time?

  Early results show alternative ways to choose A. For example, we can take A to have each entry to be from a Gaussian distribution independent, identically distributed (i.i.d.) [42,60], or even random ± 1 [2].

  More surprisingly, we can pick A's such that the computation of the map Ap takes time $\ll kd$. Such techniques, called *fast JL transform*, are often based on a (fast) Hadamard transform. In particular, the first such construction from [3] shows that we can set $A = PHD$, where D is a (random) diagonal matrix, H is the Hadamard transform, and P is a (random) sparse projection matrix. Another approach is also to use a carefully designed *sparse* matrix A [40]. See also [4,69,72,85].

7.3 Space Partitions

Back to the NNS problem, how can we obtain a *sublinear* query time? Note that even with the dimension reduction, the query time of the NNS algorithm from above is linear in n. The next important concept in high-dimensional geometry is space partitions, represented via a hash function $h : \mathbb{R}^d \to U$ for some discrete set U. These lead to sublinear time solutions as we will see next.

What properties would we need from such hash functions? We would like that *close* pairs of points collide (are in the same part), whereas *far* pairs of points do not collide (are in different parts). Whereas such a strong guarantee is impossible (think of the points near one of the perimeters of a part), it becomes attainable in a randomized sense. This leads to the notion of *locality-sensitive hash (LSH) functions*, defined as follows.

DEFINITION 7.2 **LSH** *For a positive real $r > 0$ and $c > 1$, a distribution $\mathcal{H}$ over hash functions $g : \mathbb{R}^d \to U$ is called (r, cr, P_1, P_2)-sensitive if for any two points $p, q \in \mathbb{R}^d$, we have the following:*

- *If $\|p - q\| \leq r$, then $\Pr_{h\in\mathcal{H}}[h(q) = h(p)] \geq P_1$.*
- *If $\|p - q\| \geq cr$, then $\Pr_{h\in\mathcal{H}}[h(q) = h(p)] \leq P_2$.*

In order for an LSH family to be useful, it has to satisfy $P_1 > P_2$.

Note that the definition is designed for a fixed *scale* of distances, that is, we care only about distances $\leq r$ (*close*) versus distances $\geq cr$ (*far*). We can use LSH to solve a threshold version of the nearest neighbor problem, called r-near neighbor problem, and defined as follows:

DEFINITION 7.3 **c-approximate r-near neighbor** *Fix some threshold $r > 0$ and approximation factor $c > 1$. Construct a data structure on a point-set P of n points in a d-dimensional space $\mathbb{R}^d$, such that, given any query point q, if P contains a some point p^* within distance r of q, the data structure reports some point $p \in P$ at distance at most cr from q, with probability at least* 0.9.

We can use an algorithm for the near neighbor problem to solve the nearest neighbor problem as well [53]. Hence we will focus on the former, the near neighbor problem, in the rest of the section.

7.3.1 From LSH to NNS

An LSH family $\mathcal{H}$ can be used to design an efficient algorithm for approximate near neighbor search. The algorithm essentially is one (or more) hash table(s). To build one hash table, we choose a hash function $h \in \mathcal{H}$ and hash each point $p \in P$ into the bucket $h(p)$. Because the total number of buckets may be large, we retain only the nonempty buckets by resorting to (standard) hashing* of the values $h(p)$.

To process a query q, we look up the bucket $h(q)$ and report the first cr-near neighbor found there. Note that, if there exists some r-near neighbor p, then with probability at least P_1, it is present in the bucket $h(q)$, and hence some point is reported. In general, the bucket contains other points as well.

Thus, one hash table achieves a probability of success of P_1, while using $O(n)$ space. We can increase the probability of success to, say, 0.9 by using $L = O(1/P_1)$ independent hash tables, each with its own hash function chosen i.i.d. from $\mathcal{H}$.

Note that, for one hash table, the query run-time depends on the number of far points that collide with the query q. There are at most $P_2 n$ such points in expectation. The overall query time is composed of two terms: (1) $L = O(1/P_1)$ computations of a hash function

*See [35] for more details on hashing.

$h \subset \mathcal{H}$ and (2) $O(P_2 n \cdot L)$ distance computations (in expectation). Hence, it is enough to obtain $P_2 = 1/n$. We will usually think of a hash function computation as taking $O(d)$ time, comparable to the time for distance computation.

Thus, the main LSH performance question becomes: what is the highest P_1 achievable for $P_2 \leq 1/n$? Usually, we obtain such LSH family by amplifying a *base* family. In particular, given a *base* (r, cr, p_1, p_2)-sensitive family $\mathcal{H}$, we can construct a new family $\mathcal{G}$ of hash functions $g = (h_1, \ldots, h_k)$, where $h_i \in \mathcal{H}$ independently. The new family $\mathcal{G}$ is (r, cr, P_1, P_2) sensitive, where $P_1 = p_1^k$ and $P_2 = p_2^k$. For $k = \left\lceil \log_{1/p_2} n \right\rceil$, we obtain $P_2 = p_2^k \leq 1/n$ as desired. At the same time, $P_1 = p_1^k \geq p_1^{\log_{1/p_2} n + 1} = n^{-\rho} \cdot p_1$, where $\rho = (\log 1/p_1)/(\log 1/p_2)$. Note that ρ is invariant to the *amplification process*, that is, this LSH parameter of the amplified family $\mathcal{G}$ is equal to the one of the base family $\mathcal{H}$.

The parameter $\rho = (\log 1/P_1)/(\log 1/P_2)$ is thus the main measure of quality of an LSH family, or, equivalently a (randomized) space partitioning. We summarize the above in the following theorem, proved in the work of Indyk and Motwani [60] who introduced the LSH scheme. We also sketch the entire algorithm in Figure 7.1.

Theorem 7.1 *Fix $d, n \geq 1$, threshold $r \geq 0$, and approximation $c \geq 1$. Suppose there exist some (r, cr, P_1, P_2)-sensitive LSH family. Then there exists an algorithm for the c-approximate r-near neighbor problem using $O(n^{1+\rho}/P_1 + nd)$ storage and preprocessing time. The query time is composed of $O(n^\rho/P_1 \cdot \log_{1/P_2} n)$ computations of a hash function and $O(n^\rho/P_1)$ distance computations.*

Because the query time includes the time to evaluate a hash function from the LSH family, it depends on the actual choice of the LSH family. Furthermore, the stated space bound does not include the space to store the description of the hash functions (which is typically smaller than the other terms).

7.3.2 LSH Families

To complete the algorithm, we need to construct some actual LSH families. There is a number of various LSH families proposed over years. As mentioned above, the main quality parameter is ρ (as a function of c). The second important parameter is the run-time to evaluate a hash function. We present a few important families below, and refer to [12] for a more comprehensive survey of the LSH families.

Preprocessing:

(1) Choose L functions g_i, $i = 1, \ldots, L$, by setting $g_i = (h_{i,1}, h_{i,2}, \ldots, h_{i,k})$, where $h_{i,1}, \ldots, h_{i,k}$ are chosen at random from the LSH family $\mathcal{H}$.

(2) Construct L hash tables, where, for each $j = 1, \ldots, L$, the jth hash table contains the dataset points hashed using the function g_j.

Query algorithm for a query point q:

For each $i = 1, 2, \ldots, L$:

(1) Retrieve the points from the bucket $g_i(q)$ in the ith hash table.

(2) For each of the retrieved point, compute the distance from q to it. If the point is a correct answer, report it and stop.

FIGURE 7.1
Preprocessing and query algorithms based on LSH. For an (r, cr, p_1, p_2)-sensitive family $\mathcal{H}$, we set $k = \left\lceil \log_{1/p_2} n \right\rceil$ and $L = O(n^\rho/p_1)$, where $\rho = (\log 1/p_1)/(\log 1/p_2)$.

7.3.2.1 Bit Sampling (For Hamming Distance)

This is the first (and simplest) LSH family that was introduced in [60]. In this case, the family $\mathcal{H}$ contains all projections of the input point on one of the coordinates, that is, all functions h_i from $\{0,1\}^d$ to $\{0,1\}$ such that $h_i(p) = p_i$, for $i = 1 \ldots d$. A random hash function $h \in \mathcal{H}$ returns a random coordinate of p (note that different applications of h return the *same* coordinate of the argument). The amplified hash function g will return k random coordinates of the argument.

To see that the family $\mathcal{H}$ is locality sensitive with nontrivial parameters, observe that the probability $\Pr_{\mathcal{H}}[h(p) = h(q)]$ is equal to the fraction of coordinates on which p and q agree. Therefore, $P_1 = 1 - r/d$, whereas $P_2 = 1 - cr/d$. One then obtains $\rho = 1/c$ in this case.

7.3.2.2 Grid Partitioning (For ℓ_1 Distance)

First pick a random vector $w \in \mathbb{R}^d$ by choosing each coordinate from a Gamma distribution with expectation r, namely the distribution is $\frac{x}{r^2}e^{-x/r}$ [10,88]. Then pick a vector $s \in \mathbb{R}^d$ where each coordinate s_i is random from $[0, w_i]$. The hash function is $h(x) = (\lfloor (x_1 - s_1)/(w_1) \rfloor, \ldots, \lfloor (x_d - s_d)/(w_d) \rfloor)$. The space partition is obtained by shifting the space randomly and then imposing a regular grid with sidelengths $w_1, \ldots, w_d$. This family yields $\rho = 1/c$ as well. (One can also use a grid with equal side lengths, achieving a slightly worse ρ.)

7.3.2.3 Random Projection (For Euclidean and ℓ_p Distances)

Pick a random projection of $\mathbb{R}^d$ onto a one-dimensional line and chop the line into segments of length w, shifted by a random value $s \in [0, w)$ [43]. Formally, $h(x) = (\lfloor (r \cdot x + s)/w \rfloor$, where $r \in \mathbb{R}^d$ is the projection vector with each coordinate r_i drawn from the Gaussian distribution. The exponent ρ drops strictly below $1/c$ for some (carefully chosen) finite value of w. This LSH family is very useful in practice (see, e.g., [7]).
A generalization of this approach to ℓ_p norms for any $p \in [0, 2)$ is possible as well; this is done by picking the vector r from the p-*stable distribution* [43].

7.3.2.4 Ball Carving (For Euclidean Distance)

This LSH family achieves the best possible ρ for the Euclidean space [11,12]. It can be viewed as a higher dimensional version of the above method.

We construct a hash function h as follows: project the input point x onto a random t-dimensional subspace S. We would now like to partition $\mathbb{R}^t$ *nicely.* It would be natural to partition $\mathbb{R}^t$ using a grid, but it does not achieve a better ρ. This is because this process roughly corresponds to hashing using concatenation of several one-dimensional functions (as above). Because the LSH algorithms perform such concatenation (amplification) anyway, grid partitioning does not result in any improvement.

Instead we partition $\mathbb{R}^t$ into *balls,* instead of cubes as before. Because this is impossible for $t \geq 2$, we approximate such a partition by *carving out balls* (see also [29]). Namely, we create a sequence of balls $B_1, B_2, \ldots$, each of radius w, with centers chosen independently *at random.* Each ball B_i then defines a cell, containing points $B_i \setminus \cup_{j<i} B_j$.

To complete the construction, we need to take care of the following issue: locating a cell containing a given point could require enumeration of all balls, which would take an unbounded amount of time. Instead, one can simulate the above procedure by replacing each ball by a *grid of balls.* It is not difficult to observe that a finite (albeit exponential in t) number of such grids suffices to cover all points in $\mathbb{R}^t$.

The parameter t is determined by a trade-off between the value of $\rho = 1/c^2 + O\left[(\log t)/(\sqrt{t})\right]$ and the time to compute the hash function, which is $t^{O(t)}$.

7.3.2.5 Min-Hash and Sim-Hash

Finally, we present two classic constructions of hash functions that were designed for a *similarity* measure, rather than a distance.

Min-hash is a family sensitive with respect to the Jaccard coefficient [26,27]. Jaccard coefficient between two sets $A, B \subset U$ is defined as $s(A, B) = \frac{|A \cap B|}{|A \cup B|}$. Here, we pick a random permutation π on the ground universe U and define $h_\pi(A) = \min\{\pi(a) \mid a \in A\}$. It is not hard to prove that the probability of collision is $\Pr_\pi[h_\pi(A) = h_\pi(B)] = s(A, B)$.

Sim-hash is a family sensitive with respect to the angle between two vectors $x, y \in \mathbb{R}^d$, namely, $\theta(x, y) = \arccos\left[\frac{x \cdot y}{\|x\| \cdot \|y\|}\right]$ [28]. Similar to [49], we pick a random unit-length vector $u \in \mathbb{R}^d$ and define $h_u(x) = \text{sign}(u \cdot x)$. The hash function can also be viewed as partitioning the space into two half-spaces by a randomly chosen hyperplane. The probability of collision of two vectors is $\Pr_u[h_u(x) = h_u(y)] = 1 - \theta(x, y)/\pi$.

7.3.3 Optimality of LSH

Earlier, we saw that we can obtain exponent $\rho = 1/c$ for the Hamming and Manhattan spaces, and $\rho = 1/c^2$ for the Euclidean space. Can we achieve even better LSH families?

It turns out that these values are the best possible LSH exponents ρ. Definition 7.2 is purely geometric, and hence, one can use functional analytic tools to prove lower bounds on the exponent ρ. This is precisely what [82,86] proved. Below we reproduce the tight bound from [86].

THEOREM 7.2 **[86]** *Fix dimension $d \geq 1$, and approximation $c > 1$. Suppose $\mathcal{H}$ is an (r, cr, P_1, P_2)-sensitive family for the Hamming space, where $P_2 > 2^{-o(d)}$. Then $\rho \geq 1/c - o(1)$.*

Similarly, any LSH family for the Euclidean space has $\rho \geq 1/c^2 - o(1)$.

Note that we assume that P_2 is sufficiently large. Such a condition seems necessary. Otherwise, we can construct a *ball carving* LSH family with $w = cr/2$, achieving $P_2 = 0$, and hence $\rho = 0$. However, we then obtain a prohibitively low $P_1 < 2^{-\Omega(d)}$, implying a query run-time of $2^{\Omega(d)}$. The restriction on P_2 precludes such infeasible families.

7.3.4 Data-Dependent Space Partitions

The above LSH lower bound suggests that the story line of space partitions should be by and large complete: we know space partitions with the best possible quality ρ. Yet, it turns out that we can obtain space partitions with better values of ρ, by stepping outside the LSH framework (Definition 7.2).

In particular, we can get qualitatively better partitions if the partitions are *data dependent* [15,19]. Data-dependent hashing is a family $\mathcal{H}$ that chooses a random hash function h dependent on the given dataset P. As before, such a family yields a near neighbor data structure with the query time dominated by n^ρ hash function evaluations, for the similarly defined exponent ρ. As before, we want a hash function which we can efficiently *evaluate* on a new (query) point q. Otherwise, we could take h to be the Voronoi diagram: $h(q)$ returns the identity of the closest point $p \in D$. Such a function has the ideal $P_1 = 1$ and $P_2 = 0$, but it takes $\Omega(n)$ time to evaluate and is thus useless.

In [19], the data-dependent hashing for the Euclidean space achieves

$$\rho = \frac{1}{2c^2 - 1} + o(1)$$

for which hash function evaluation takes $2^{o(d)}$ time. This improves over the best possible LSH exponent $\rho = 1/c^2 + o(1)$ (*ball carving* LSH from above). Similarly, for the Hamming space, the new approach yields $\rho = [1/(2c - 1)] + o(1)$, improving over the best possible LSH exponent $\rho = 1/c$ (*bit sampling* LSH).

It is important to note that this improvement is for *worst-case* datasets. To put this into perspective, if one were to assume that the dataset has some *special structure*, it would be more natural to expect speedups with data-dependent hashing (e.g., by adapting to the special structure, perhaps implicitly). However, in the worst-case setting, there is no assumed structure to adapt to.

Nonetheless one can wonder whether we can obtain even better hashing assuming some additional structure in the dataset. Indeed, in practice, there is a number of NNS algorithms that design hash codes that depend on the dataset, but most have no guarantees: correctness or performance. A formidable open question is to try to understand the disparity of the data-independent methods (which are often theoretically optimal) and the data-dependent methods (often with better performance); see [39, page 77]. Some further work along these lines was done in [1,41,93].

Finally, let us observe that data-dependent space partitions come with a price tag: they are *not dynamic*. In particular, oftentimes, we need to insert and delete points from the dataset. Standard (data-independent) hashing handles this effortlessly: we can easily add and remove points from the hash table. However, if the hash function depends on the dataset, it may become inadequate once we remove/insert a large part of the dataset. In particular, it may loose its LSH properties. Hence, further work is necessary to make such data structures dynamic.

7.3.5 The ℓ_∞ Norm

The ℓ_∞ norm admits a particularly intriguing NNS solution, also based on space partitions. Although it has no LSH, the algorithm of [55] achieves an approximation of $O(\log \log d)$ for d-dimensional ℓ_∞, with polynomial space. The algorithm can be seen as a data-dependent space partition, organized as a tree. In contrast to the previous hashing approaches, this algorithm has a couple intriguing differences. First, it contains just one tree, constructed deterministically. Second, some dataset points are stored in a few buckets: essentially, a point p is stored in each bucket B for which there exists a (query) point q which is at distance $\leq$ from p and hashes to B. The query algorithm just hashes the query point once to the corresponding bucket and retrieves a near neighbor from that bucket.

7.4 Embeddings

So far we have discussed about techniques for the ℓ_p distances, such as the Manhattan or Euclidean space. How about other, more complex distances? A natural approach is to *reduce* the new distances to the ones we know how to handle, such as the above distances. *Embeddings* provide such a generic reduction, mapping one distance space into another. This purely geometric (functional analytic) concept is useful for many computational problems.

Definition 7.4 *Consider some metric (M, d_M) and a host metric (H, d_H). The map $\phi : M \to H$ is called an embedding of M into H if there exist constants $\alpha, D > 0$ such that for any $x, y \in M$ we have that:*

$$d_M(x, y) \leq \alpha \cdot d_H[\phi(x), \phi(y)] \leq D \cdot d_M(x, y).$$

The factor D is called the distortion (approximation). A randomized embedding *is a randomized map ϕ where the above inequality holds with probability $1 - \delta$ for every fixed x, y, and some $\delta > 0$.*

To see why this is useful, suppose we want to solve NNS under some new metric M (we give some examples below). If we manage to map M into, say, ℓ_1 with distortion D, then we can use the NNS under ℓ_1 to solve NNS under M with approximation, say, $2D$. We need to ensure also that the map is efficiently computable, but this is often a secondary concern. The main question is: what is the best possible distortion D we can achieve?

The JL lemma 7.1 is a classic example of a (randomized) embedding: it maps a high-dimensional Euclidean $\mathbb{R}^d$ space into the lower dimensional $\mathbb{R}^k$, the *host.*

We present a few other classic and illustrative embeddings in Sections 7.4.1 and 7.4.2. A more complete (if only slightly outdated) survey can be also found in [56,59]. Also there is an influential list of open problems in the area in [81].

We also remark that there are other important types of embedding. A very important one is one where we want to embed a finite set of points $P \subset M$. This is usually not as useful for the NNS application because we do not have an *out-of-sample extension*: that is, we do not know how to compute the embedding of the query point $q \notin P$, which is given after the embedding on P is constructed. (See also the discussion in Section 7.7.) Another type is *nearest neighbor preserving* embedding, where the map merely preserves the distance to the (approximate) nearest neighbor within a dataset. Examples of such mapping were given in [54,58].

7.4.1 Embeddings of Norms

Some classic embeddings are those concerning embedding of an ℓ_p norm into some other ℓ_q. We list a few relevant ones as follows.

- ℓ_2 embeds into ℓ_1 isometrically [44,48] (i.e., with distortion $D = 1$). In fact, a $(1+\epsilon$ distortion) map follows from a variant of the JL embedding from Section 7.2: $\phi(x) = \frac{1}{m}Ax$, where A is an $m \times n$ matrix with entries drawn from the Gaussian distribution. This is the standard way to reduce problems under ℓ_2 to problems under ℓ_1 (e.g., in [60] for NNS).

- Hamming space $\{0,1\}^d$ embeds into the square of ℓ_2 isometrically [78]. The latter is the space $\mathbb{R}^d$ where we compute the *distances* as $\mathbf{d}(x,y) = \sum_{i=1}^{d}(x_i - y_i)^2$. Although this is not a metric, it is useful nonetheless: for example, we can use the Euclidean NNS for it. This is a standard way to reduce the Hamming space to ℓ_2 and is the one explaining the tight connection between ρ's for the Hamming and ℓ_2 spaces from Section 7.3.

- ℓ_1^d isometrically embeds into ℓ_∞^m for $m = 2^d$ (see also [80]). The map $\phi(x)$ has a coordinate for each bit vector $b \in \{0,1\}^d$ and is defined as $\phi(x)_b = \sum_i (-1)^{b_i} x_i$. This may be used, for example, for computing the diameter of an n-point set in ℓ_1^d. Although the naïve algorithm takes $\Omega(n^2)$ time to compute the diameter of a point-set, this time is only linear for a point-set in ℓ_∞^m. Specifically, the diameter of a point-set P is just $\max_{i\in[m]}(\max_{p\in P} p_i - \min_{p\in P} p_i)$, a linear-time computation. Thus, this embedding allows us to solve the ℓ_1^d diameter problem in $O(n2^d)$ time.

- Any n-point metric X embeds into ℓ_∞ of dimension $d = n$. The map ϕ has a coordinate for each $x \in Y$ and is defined as $\phi(y)_x = d_X(x,y)$. Thus, ℓ_∞ is *universal* in that it contains any other metric, given a sufficiently high dimension.

7.4.2 Embeddings of Specialized Metrics

Many applications often give rise to metrics that are more complex than the norms from above. We look to embed them into *simpler* metrics, for which we have known algorithms.

The latter metrics include ℓ_1, ℓ_2, and ℓ_∞ (for which we have, say, NNS algorithms by the results from Section 7.3). It turns out that ℓ_1 is a particularly useful host for the following reasons: First, because ℓ_2 embeds into ℓ_1, the latter can accommodate more metrics. Second, many important metrics in fact already have some ℓ_1 *structure* in them.

A powerful aspect is that we can also prove *impossibility* results, termed *non embeddability,* like we did for LSH. A classic example is the proof that any embedding of the Hamming cube $\{0,1\}^d$ into ℓ_2 (of any dimension) requires $\Omega(\sqrt{d})$ distortion [45].

Below we define a few notorious examples of metrics amenable to the embeddings approach. Table 7.1 presents the positive and negative results on embedding these metrics into ℓ_1.

- *Edit distance* (Levenstein distance) is defined for two strings of length d as the minimum number of insertions/deletions/substitutions to transform one string into the other. Edit distance is a basic notion for measuring the degree of misalignment in various structures, and thus plays a central role in several fields, such as bioinformatics or natural language processing sequences. Edit distance on nonrepetitive strings is called *Ulam distance.*

  It is not hard to note that both the edit and Ulam distances contain a copy of Hamming cube of dimension $d^{\Omega(1)}$ (i.e., we can embed the latter into the former with constant distortion). Hence, it is natural to look for embeddings into ℓ_1. Note that asking how well does edit distance embed into the Hamming metric is philosophically equivalent to the question: how much complexity do the insertions/deletions add to the Hamming distance, where we are allowed substitutions only.

- *Earthmover distance* (EMD) is defined on *sets of points* in some metric $(X, \mathbf{d}_X)$. For two sets $A, B \subset X$ of the same size, the earthmover distance is the minimum cost matching between A and B [where the cost of matching a to b is $\mathsf{d}_X(a, b)$]. Most common examples of the *base metric* X are the plane $[d]^2$ and the high-dimensional cube $\{0,1\}^d$. Both have applications in the image vision literature; see, for example, [90] and [50,51].

  Again, because we can embed ℓ_1 into EMD (even over a line), it is natural to target ℓ_1 as the host norm for EMD.

- *Hausdoff distance* is also defined over subsets of a *base metric* $(X, \mathbf{d}_X)$. For two sets $A, B \subset X$, the Hausdoff distance is the minimum between $\max_{a\in A} \min_{b\in B} d_X(a, b)$ and its symmetric version $\max_{b\in B} \min_{a\in A} d_X(a, b)$. This distance is useful in image vision for comparing geometric shapes of points.

TABLE 7.1
Distortion for embedding of various metrics into ℓ_1

Metric	Upper Bound	Lower Bound
Edit distance on $\{0,1\}^d$	$2^{O(\sqrt{\log d \log\log d})}$ [87]	$\Omega(\log d)$ [8,16,71,74]
Ulam distance	$O(\log d)$ [30]	$\Omega(\log d / \log\log d)$ [16]
Block edit distance, edit distance with moves	$O(\log d \log^* d)$ [36–38,83]	—
EMD over $[d]^2$	$O(\log d)$ [28,61,84]	$\Omega(\sqrt{\log d})$ [84]
EMD over $\{0,1\}^t$ (for sets of size s)	$O(\log s \log t)$ [13]	$\Omega(\log s)$ [71]

The Hausdoff metric contains a copy of ℓ_∞, and hence, it is a natural host space. A few such embeddings into ℓ_∞, for different types of metrics X is shown in [47].

Are there even better host spaces? ℓ_∞ is another natural target, especially that it contains any other metric. However, as a host, ℓ_∞ often requires prohibitively high dimension: even embedding the Hamming cube $\{0,1\}^d$ into ℓ_∞ requires dimension exponential in d (see arguments from [67, Chapter 1, Section 8]). Hence, new candidates are needed.

It turns out that the *mixture* of norms is a qualitatively better host. Let us define what we mean by mixture first. The norm $\ell_p^d(\ell_q^k)$ is the space of $d \times k$ matrices, where we compute the norm by first taking ℓ_q norm of each row, and then take the ℓ_p norm of the resulting d-dimensional vector. The strength of such mixed norms has been shown in [14], who showed that the aforementioned Ulam metric over length-d strings (raised to power 0.9) embeds into $\ell_2[\ell_\infty(\ell_1)]$, with dimensions bounded polynomially in d. The distortion of the embedding is *constant*. By contrast, embedding into any of the component spaces provably requires super-constant distortion (see, e.g., Table 7.1 and [67, Chapter 1, Section 8]).

7.5 Sketching

A generalization of the embedding is the notion of *sketching*. Sketching can be thought of as a very weak embedding into a *computational* space, where the *host distance* is an arbitrary computation (e.g., not restricted to be a metric). The main parameter is now the *size* of the sketch, which can be thought of as *host dimension*. Sketches address the most basic, decision version of the distance estimation problem, termed the *distance threshold estimation problem* (DTEP) [91]. The goal of DTEP is to distinguish *close pairs* versus *far pairs* with some probability (similar to the Definition 7.3 of near neighbor problem).

Definition 7.5 *Fix some metric (M, d_M), approximation $D \geq 1$, threshold $r > 0$, failure probability $\delta \in [0, 1/3]$, and size $s \in \mathbb{N}$. The map $\phi : M \to \{0,1\}^s$ is called a* sketch *of M if there exists a referee algorithm $\mathcal{R} : \{0,1\}^s \times \{0,1\}^s \to \{0,1\}$, such that for any $x, y \in M$, the algorithm $\mathcal{R}$ can distinguish between $d_M(x, y) \leq r$ (close pair) versus $d_M(x, y) > Dr$ (far pair), with probability $1 - \delta$.*

Sketching is useful in many applications, including the NNS problem. In particular, we can use a sketch of size s (for, say, $\delta = 0.1$) to construct an NNS data structure with space $n^{O(s)}$. The query time is $O(\log n)$ times the time to evaluate ϕ on the query point. Indeed, from the basic sketch, we can also construct an *amplified sketch*, which has $O(s \log n)$ size and failure probability at most $1 - 1/n^2$: keep $k = O(\log n)$ independent copies of the basic sketch, with the referee algorithm taking the majority vote of those for the k sketches. For a given query point q, this amplified sketch, termed $\phi^k(q)$, is sufficient to determine the approximate near neighbor in an n-point dataset P with probability at least $1 - 1/n$: run the referee algorithm on $\langle \phi^k(q), \phi^k(p) \rangle$ for each $p \in P$. Because this procedure uses only the sketch $\phi^k(q)$, of size ks, we can construct an index for each possible ks-bit input, storing the solution. Overall, we obtain a data structure with $2^{ks} = n^{O(s)}$ space.

Sketches have many applications beyond NNS, including in data-streaming algorithms and compressed sensing, in part by providing an alternative notion of dimension reduction (as we will see later). More recently, it has found uses to speed up algorithms, for example, in numerical linear algebra [95].

Some of these applications use another important variant of sketches, where M is a norm, and we define $\phi : M \to \mathbb{R}^s$ to be a linear map. In this case, we think of s as the number of measurements, as in the compressed sensing literature. Such a linear sketch has the advantage to being easy to update: because $\phi(x + a) = \phi(x) + \phi(a)$, where x is the *current vector*, and a is an *update vector*. As such, it has many applications in streaming.

7.5.1 Sketch Constructions

The first and most useful constructions are for the Euclidean and Hamming spaces. Again, the JL dimension reduction for ℓ_2 already gives a sketch. In particular, dimension reduction is a linear sketch into $s = O[(1/\epsilon^2)\log 1/\delta]$ dimensions for $D = 1 + \epsilon$ approximation (see also [6]).

Most interestingly, ℓ_1 admits a similar linear sketch, to give us a weaker notion of dimension reduction for ℓ_1. The sketch is $\phi(p) = (1/k)Ap$, in which A is a $k \times d$ matrix in which each entry is drawn i.i.d. from the Cauchy distribution [58]. The referee algorithm, on inputs $\phi(p), \phi(q)$, then computes the *median* value of absolute values of the coordinates of $\phi(p) - \phi(q)$. Note that this is different from aforementioned dimension reduction, which can be thought of a sketch with the referee algorithm that computes $\|\phi(p) - \phi(q)\|$. The median operation is what makes this *host space* nonmetric.

LSH is also a sketch, with a special property that the referee algorithm just checks for the equality of the two arguments. Although Definition 7.2 of LSH does not immediately imply a size bound, one can easily notice that an LSH function leads to a sketch of size dependent on P_1 and P_2 only. Rather than describing that, we give a direct sketch construction for the Hamming space.

For the Hamming space, Indyk and Motwani [60] and Kushilevitz et al. [76] show a sketch achieving a size of $s = O[(1/\epsilon^2)\log 1/\delta]$ *bits*, for approximation $D = 1 + \epsilon$. The sketch is a modification of the bit sampling LSH from Section 7.3.2. For fixed threshold $r \leq d/2$, the coordinate $i \in [s]$ of the map $\phi(p)$ is simply defined as the exclusive-or of $k = \lceil d/r \rceil$ randomly chosen bits from p. The referee algorithm for inputs $\phi(p), \phi(q)$ just computes the Hamming distance between $\phi(p)$ and $\phi(q)$: the output is *close pair* iff this fraction is less than a certain threshold.

This sketch plays a very central role for a few reasons. First, it also implies a similar sketch for ℓ_2 of constant size. Second, all sketches of constant size for other metrics M are essentially obtained via a two-step process: first embed M into the Hamming space, and then apply the above sketch. Third, recent results suggest that, at least for *norms*, this approach is the only one in town for obtaining constant size sketches [18].

Nonetheless, there exist other methods to obtain sketches with a nontrivial size, namely, sublinear in the dimension of the input. For example, for the Ulam metric, one can obtain a sketch of $\text{polylog}^{O(1)} d$ size and constant approximation [14]. For EMD metric, the best sketch achieves size d^ϵ for $O(1/\epsilon)$ approximation [9]. There are also methods for obtaining sketches for arbitrary mixed norms [17,65].

Finally, an important aspect of the sketch definition is that we can prove impossibility results for them. Sketching lower bounds usually follow via *communication complexity* arguments [75] for the following communication game. Two players, called Alice and Bob, each have an input point x and y, respectively, and they need to solve the DTEP problem. For this, Alice and Bob each send a message of length s to the referee, who is to decide on the problem. It is easy to see that lower bounds on communication complexity of this game imply sketching lower bounds.

For example, one can prove that the Hamming sketch from above is optimal [62,64,94]. Many other lower bounds have seen been proven. Interestingly, in light of the sketch for ℓ_1, lower bounds on sketching complexity often imply nonembeddability statements as well (see, e.g., [16]).

7.6 Small Dimension

Yet another approach to high-dimensional questions is to assume that the dataset has an additional structure, for example, is *intrinsically low dimensional.* Such assumptions are motivated by the fact that, in many datasets, the data are really explained by a few relevant parameters, and the other parameters are just derivates of those. The simplest such example is when a d-dimensional dataset lies inside a low-dimensional subspace $S \subset \mathbb{R}^d$, of dimension $k \ll d$. In such cases, we would like to obtain solutions with a performance as if the dimension is effectively k. If k is small, we may be able to afford solutions that have exponential dependence on k (e.g., $(1/\epsilon)^{O(k)}$ for $1+\epsilon$ approximation).

Although the above subspace assumption may be too naïve, there are other, more realistic definitions. Particular attention has been drawn to the notion of *doubling dimension*, defined for a dataset P as follows: Let λ be the smallest integer such that for any $p \in P$ and radius r, the set of points that are within r of p can be covered by at most λ balls of radius $r/2$. The doubling dimension is then $\log \lambda$. It is easy to check that d-dimensional ℓ_2 and ℓ_1 spaces have doubling dimension $O(d)$. The notion, introduced in [32,52], has been inspired by the notion of Assouad constant [22]. Some NNS algorithms designed with this notion in mind include [24,73] and others. For example, Indyk and Naor [54] showed that, given a point-set with a doubling dimension k, one can use JL lemma to project it into dimension $m = O(k/\epsilon^2 \cdot \log 1/\epsilon)$ only, sufficient for preserving the approximate nearest neighbor.

Other notions of *intrinsic dimension* include Karger–Ruhl dimension [70], smooth manifolds [23,34], and others [1,31,33,41,46,54].

7.7 Conclusion

As mentioned in the beginning of the chapter, the focus is on techniques for high-dimensional geometry, in particular as applied to the NNS problem.

Many of the same techniques apply in other contexts. For example, some other computational problems in the realm of high-dimensional geometry include the closest pair problem, or variants of clustering. A number of such problems admit efficient solutions based on efficient NNS problem, or the aforementioned techniques directly (see, [57] for examples). For instance, consider the closest pair problem: given a set of n points, we are to find the closest pair inside it. We can solve the problem using NNS: Just construct an NNS data structure, and then query each point to find its closest match. In fact, until recently, this has been the fastest way to solve the (approximate) closest pair problem. Valiant [92] showed how to obtain faster solutions for a *random dataset*, exploiting faster matrix multiplication methods.

Still, there are other important high-dimensional geometry topics left uncovered here. The most prominent such topic is that of embedding *finite metrics* into ℓ_1 or other simple *host spaces*. Introduced to theoretical computer science in the seminal paper of [78], such embeddings have had a big impact on the design of approximation algorithms such as the sparsest cut problem [20,21,89]. We refer to the survey [59] for more details.

References

1. Amirali Abdullah, Alexandr Andoni, Ravindran Kannan, and Robert Krauthgamer. Spectral approaches to nearest neighbor search. In *Proceedings of the Symposium on Foundations of Computer Science*, Philadelphia, PA, 2014.

2. Dimitris Achlioptas. Database-friendly random projections: Johnson-Lindenstrauss with binary coins. *J. Comput. Syst. Sci.*, 66(4):671–687, 2003. (Special issue on PODS 2001 [Santa Barbara, CA].)

3. Nir Ailon and Bernard Chazelle. The fast Johnson–Lindenstrauss transform and approximate nearest neighbors. *SIAM J. Comput.*, 39(1):302–322, 2009.

4. Nir Ailon and Edo Liberty. An almost optimal unrestricted fast Johnson-Lindenstrauss transform. *ACM Trans. Algor.*, 9(3):21, 2013. (Previously in *SODA'11*.)

5. Noga Alon. Problems and results in extremal combinatorics I. *Discrete Math.*, 273: 31–53, 2003.

6. Noga Alon, Yossi Matias, and Mario Szegedy. The space complexity of approximating the frequency moments. *J. Comput. Syst. Sci.*, 58:137–147, 1999. (Previously appeared in *STOC'96*.)

7. Alexandr Andoni, Mayur Datar, Nicole Immorlica, Piotr Indyk, and Vahab Mirrokni. Locality-sensitive hashing scheme based on p-stable distributions. *Nearest Neighbor Methods for Learning and Vision: Theory and Practice*, Neural Processing Information Series. MIT Press, Cambridge, MA, 2006.

8. Alexandr Andoni, Michel Deza, Anupam Gupta, Piotr Indyk, and Sofya Raskhodnikova. Lower bounds for embedding edit distance into normed spaces. In *Proceedings of the ACM-SIAM Symposium on Discrete Algorithms*, pp. 523–526, 2003.

9. Alexandr Andoni, Khanh Do Ba, Piotr Indyk, and David Woodruff. Efficient sketches for earth-mover distance, with applications. In *Proceedings of the Symposium on Foundations of Computer Science*, 2009.

10. Alexandr Andoni and Piotr Indyk. Efficient algorithms for substring near neighbor problem. In *Proceedings of the ACM-SIAM Symposium on Discrete Algorithms*, pp. 1203–1212, 2006.

11. Alexandr Andoni and Piotr Indyk. Near-optimal hashing algorithms for approximate nearest neighbor in high dimensions. In *Proceedings of the Symposium on Foundations of Computer Science*, pp. 459–468, 2006.

12. Alexandr Andoni and Piotr Indyk. Near-optimal hashing algorithms for approximate nearest neighbor in high dimensions. *Commun. ACM*, 51(1):117–122, 2008.

13. Alexandr Andoni, Piotr Indyk, and Robert Krauthgamer. Earth mover distance over high-dimensional spaces. In *Proceedings of the ACM-SIAM Symposium on Discrete Algorithms*, pp. 343–352, 2008. (Previously ECCC Report TR07-048.)

14. Alexandr Andoni, Piotr Indyk, and Robert Krauthgamer. Overcoming the ℓ_1 non-embeddability barrier: Algorithms for product metrics. In *Proceedings of the ACM-SIAM Symposium on Discrete Algorithms*, pp. 865–874, 2009.

15. Alexandr Andoni, Piotr Indyk, Huy L. Nguyen, and Ilya Razenshteyn. Beyond locality-sensitive hashing. In *Proceedings of the ACM-SIAM Symposium on Discrete Algorithms*, 2014. Full version at http://arxiv.org/abs/1306.1547.

16. Alexandr Andoni and Robert Krauthgamer. The computational hardness of estimating edit distance. *SIAM J. Comput. (SICOMP)*, 39(6):2398–2429, 2010. (Previously in *FOCS'07*.)

17. Alexandr Andoni, Robert Krauthgamer, and Krzysztof Onak. Streaming algorithms from precision sampling. In *Proceedings of the Symposium on Foundations of Computer Science*, 2011. Full version at http://arxiv.org/abs/1011.1263.

18. Alexandr Andoni, Robert Krauthgamer, and Ilya Razenshteyn. Sampling and embedding are equivalent for norms. In *Proceedings of the Symposium on Theory of Computing*, 2015. Full version at http://arxiv.org/abs/1411.2577.

19. Alexandr Andoni and Ilya Razenshteyn. Optimal data-dependent hashing for approximate near neighbors. In *Proceedings of the Symposium on Theory of Computing*, 2015. Full version at http://arxiv.org/abs/1501.01062.

20. Sanjeev Arora, James R. Lee, and Assaf Naor. Euclidean distortion and the sparsest cut. In *Proceedings of the Symposium on Theory of Computing*, pp. 553–562, 2005.

21. Sanjeev Arora, Satish Rao, and Umesh Vazirani. Expander flows, geometric embeddings, and graph partitionings. In *Proceedings of the Symposium on Theory of Computing*, pp. 222–231, 2004.

22. Patrice Assouad. Plongements lipschitziens dans $\mathbf{R}^n$. *Bull. Soc. Math. France*, 111(4): 429–448, 1983.

23. Richard G. Baraniuk and Michael B. Wakin. Random projections of smooth manifolds. In *Foundations of Computational Mathematics*, pp. 941–944, 2006.

24. Alina Beygelzimer, Sham Kakade, and John Langford. Cover trees for nearest neighbor. In *Proceedings of the 23rd International Conference on Machine Learning*, pp. 97–104, 2006.

25. Bo Brinkman and Moses Charikar. On the impossibility of dimension reduction in L1. *J. ACM*, 52(5):766–788, 2005.

26. Andrei Broder. On the resemblance and containment of documents. In *Proceedings of Compression and Complexity of Sequences*, pp. 21–29, 1997.

27. Andrei Broder, Steve Glassman, Mark Manasse, and Geoffrey Zweig. Syntactic clustering of the web. In *Proceedings of the 6th International World Wide Web Conference*, pp. 391–404, 1997.

28. Moses Charikar. Similarity estimation techniques from rounding. In *Proceedings of the Symposium on Theory of Computing*, pp. 380–388, 2002.

29. Moses Charikar, Chandra Chekuri, Ashish Goel, Sudipto Guha, and Serge Plotkin. Approximating a finite metric by a small number of tree metrics. In *Proceedings of the Symposium on Foundations of Computer Science*, 1998.

30. Moses Charikar and Robert Krauthgamer. Embedding the Ulam metric into ℓ_1. *Theory Comput.*, 2(11):207–224, 2006.

31. Edgar Chávez, Gonzalo Navarro, Rricardo Baeza-Yates, and José L. Marroquin. Searching in metric spaces. *ACM Comput. Surv.*, 33(3):273–321, September 2001.

32. Ken Clarkson. Nearest neighbor queries in metric spaces. *Discrete Comput. Geom.*, 22(1):63–93, 1999. (Previously in *SoCG97.*)

33. Kenneth L. Clarkson. Nearest-neighbor searching and metric space dimensions. In Gregory Shakhnarovich, Trevor Darrell, and Piotr Indyk, editors, *Nearest-Neighbor Methods for Learning and Vision: Theory and Practice*, pp. 15–59. MIT Press, Cambridge, MA, 2006.

34. Kenneth L. Clarkson. Tighter bounds for random projections of manifolds. In *Proceedings of the ACM Symposium on Computational Geometry*, 2008.

35. Thomas H. Cormen, Charles E. Leiserson, Ronald L. Rivest, and Clifford Stein. *Introduction to Algorithms*, 2nd ed. MIT Press, Cambridge, MA, 2001.

36. Graham Cormode. Sequence distance embeddings. PhD Thesis, University of Warwick, Coventry, 2003.

37. Graham Cormode and S. Muthukrishnan. The string edit distance matching problem with moves. *ACM Trans. Algor.*, 3(1), 2007. (Previously in *SODA'02.*)

38. Graham Cormode, Mike Paterson, Suleyman C. Sahinalp, and Uzi Vishkin. Communication complexity of document exchange. In *Proceedings of the ACM-SIAM Symposium on Discrete Algorithms*, pp. 197–206, 2000.

39. National Research Council. *Frontiers in Massive Data Analysis.* The National Academies Press, Washington, DC, 2013.

40. Anirban Dasgupta, Ravi Kumar, and Tamás Sarlós. A sparse Johnson Lindenstrauss transform. In *Proceedings of the Symposium on Theory of Computing*, pp. 341–350, 2010.

41. Sanjoy Dasgupta and Yoav Freund. Random projection trees and low dimensional manifolds. In *Proceedings of the 40th Annual ACM Symposium on Theory of Computing*, pp. 537–546. ACM, 2008.

42. Sanjoy Dasgupta and Anupam Gupta. An elementary proof of the Johnson–Lindenstrauss lemma. ICSI Technical Report TR-99-006, Berkeley, CA, 1999.

43. Mayur Datar, Nicole Immorlica, Piotr Indyk, and Vahab Mirrokni. Locality-sensitive hashing scheme based on p-stable distributions. In *Proceedings of the ACM Symposium on Computational Geometry*, 2004.

44. Aryeh Dvoretzky. A theorem on convex bodies and applications to banach spaces. *Proc. Natl. Acad. Sci. USA.*, 45:223–226, 1959.

45. Per Enflo. On the nonexistence of uniform homeomorphisms between L_p-spaces. *Ark. Mat.*, 8:103–105, 1969.

46. Christos Faloutsos and Ibrahim Kamel. Relaxing the uniformity and independence assumptions using the concept of fractal dimension. *J. Comput. Syst. Sci.*, 55(2): 229–240, 1997.

47. Martin Farach-Colton and Piotr Indyk. Approximate nearest neighbor algorithms for hausdorff metrics via embeddings. In *Proceedings of the Symposium on Foundations of Computer Science*, 1999.

48. Tadeusz Figiel, Joram Lindenstrauss, and Vitali D. Milman. The dimension of almost spherical sections of convex bodies. *Acta Math.*, 139:53–94, 1977.

49. Michel X. Goemans and David P. Williamson. Improved approximation algorithms for maximum cut and satisfiability problems using semidefinite programming. *J. ACM*, 42:1115–1145, 1995.

50. Kristen Grauman and Trevor Darrell. The pyramid match kernel: Discriminative classification with sets of image features. In *Proceedings of the IEEE International Conference on Computer Vision*, Beijing, China, October 2005.

51. Kristen Grauman and Trevor Darrell. Approximate correspondences in high dimensions. In *Proceedings of Advances in Neural Information Processing Systems*, 2006.

52. Anupam Gupta, Robert Krauthgamer, and James R. Lee. Bounded geometries, fractals, and low-distortion embeddings. In *44th Symposium on Foundations of Computer Science*, pp. 534–543, 2003.

53. Sariel Har-Peled, Piotr Indyk, and Rajeev Motwani. Approximate nearest neighbor: Towards removing the curse of dimensionality. *Theory Comput.*, 1(8):321–350, 2012.

54. Piotr Indyk and Assaf Naor. Nearest neighbor preserving embeddings. *ACM Trans. Algor.*, 2007.

55. Piotr Indyk. On approximate nearest neighbors in non-Euclidean spaces. In *Proceedings of the Symposium on Foundations of Computer Science*, pp. 148–155, 1998.

56. Piotr Indyk. Algorithmic aspects of geometric embeddings (tutorial). In *Proceedings of the Symposium on Foundations of Computer Science*, pp. 10–33, 2001.

57. Piotr Indyk. High-dimensional computational geometry. PhD Thesis. Department of Computer Science, Stanford University, Stanford, CA, 2001.

58. Piotr Indyk. Stable distributions, pseudorandom generators, embeddings and data stream computation. *J. ACM*, 53(3):307–323, 2006. (Previously appeared in *FOCS'00*.)

59. Piotr Indyk and Jiří Matoušek. Low distortion embeddings of finite metric spaces. In *CRC Handbook of Discrete and Computational Geometry*, 2003.

60. Piotr Indyk and Rajeev Motwani. Approximate nearest neighbor: Towards removing the curse of dimensionality. In *Proceedings of the Symposium on Theory of Computing*, pp. 604–613, 1998.

61. Piotr Indyk and Nitin Thaper. Fast color image retrieval via embeddings. In *Workshop on Statistical and Computational Theories of Vision (at ICCV)*, 2003.

62. Piotr Indyk and David Woodruff. Tight lower bounds for the distinct elements problem. In *Proceedings of the Symposium on Foundations of Computer Science*, pp. 283–290, 2003.

63. Thathachar S. Jayram and David P. Woodruff. Optimal bounds for Johnson-Lindenstrauss transforms and streaming problems with subconstant error. *ACM Trans. Algor.*, 9(3):26, 2013. (Previously in *SODA'11*.)

64. Thathachar S. Jayram, Ravi Kumar, and D. Sivakumar. The one-way communication complexity of hamming distance. *Theory Comput.*, 4(1):129–135, 2008.

65. Thathachar S. Jayram and David Woodruff. The data stream space complexity of cascaded norms. In *Proceedings of the Symposium on Foundations of Computer Science*, 2009.

66. William B. Johnson and Joram Lindenstrauss. Extensions of lipshitz mapping into hilbert space. *Contemp. Math.*, 26:189–206, 1984.

67. William B. Johnson and Joram Lindenstrauss, editors. *Handbook of the Geometry of Banach Spaces*, Vol. I. North-Holland Publishing Co., Amsterdam, the Netherlands, 2001.

68. William B. Johnson and Assaf Naor. The Johnson–Lindenstrauss lemma almost characterizes Hilbert space, but not quite. *Discrete Comput. Geom.*, 43(3):542–553, 2010. (Previously in *SODA'09*.)

69. Daniel M. Kane and Jelani Nelson. Sparser Johnson-Lindenstrauss transforms. *J. ACM*, 61(1):4, 2014. (Previosly in *SODA'12*.)

70. David R. Karger and Matthias Ruhl. Finding nearest neighbors in growth-restricted metrics. In *Proceedings of the Symposium on Theory of Computing*, 2002.

71. Subhash Khot and Assaf Naor. Nonembeddability theorems via Fourier analysis. *Math. Ann.*, 334(4):821–852, 2006. (Preliminary version appeared in *FOCS'05*.)

72. Felix Krahmer and Rachel Ward. New and improved Johnson-Lindenstrauss embeddings via the restricted isometry property. *SIAM J. Math. Anal.*, 43(3):1269–1281, 2011.

73. Robert Krauthgamer and James R. Lee. Navigating nets: Simple algorithms for proximity search. In *Proceedings of the ACM-SIAM Symposium on Discrete Algorithms*, 2004.

74. Robert Krauthgamer and Yuval Rabani. Improved lower bounds for embeddings into L_1. In *Proceedings of the ACM-SIAM Symposium on Discrete Algorithms*, pp. 1010–1017, 2006.

75. Eyal Kushilevitz and Noam Nisan. *Communication Complexity*. Cambridge University Press, New York, 1997.

76. Eyal Kushilevitz, Rafail Ostrovsky, and Yuval Rabani. Efficient search for approximate nearest neighbor in high dimensional spaces. *SIAM J. Comput.*, 30(2):457–474, 2000. (Preliminary version appeared in *STOC'98*.)

77. Kasper Green Larsen and Jelani Nelson. The Johnson–Lindenstrauss lemma is optimal for linear dimensionality reduction. arXiv preprint arXiv:1411.2404, 2014.

78. Nathan Linial, Eran London, and Yuri Rabinovich. The geometry of graphs and some of its algorithmic applications. In *Proceedings of the Symposium on Foundations of Computer Science*, pp. 577–591, 1994.

79. Avner Magen. Dimensionality reductions in ℓ_2 that preserve volumes and distance to affine spaces. *Discrete Comput. Geom.*, 38(1):139–153, July 2007. (Preliminary version appeared in *RANDOM'02.*)

80. Jiří Matoušek. On the distortion required for embedding finite metric spaces into normed spaces. *Israel J. Math.*, 93:333–344, 1996.

81. Jiří Matoušek and Assaf Naor. Open problems on embeddings of finite metric spaces. August 2011. Available at http://kam.mff.cuni.cz/ matousek/metrop.ps.gz.

82. Rajeev Motwani, Assaf Naor, and Rina Panigrahy. Lower bounds on locality sensitive hashing. In *Proceedings of the ACM Symposium on Computational Geometry*, pp. 253–262, 2006.

83. S. Muthukrishnan and Cenk Sahinalp. Approximate nearest neighbors and sequence comparison with block operations. In *Proceedings of the Symposium on Theory of Computing*, pp. 416–424, 2000.

84. Assaf Naor and Gideon Schechtman. Planar earthmover is not in L_1. *SIAM J. Comput. (SICOMP)*, 37(3):804–826, 2007. (An extended abstract appeared in *FOCS'06.*)

85. Jelani Nelson, Eric Price, and Mary Wootters. New constructions of RIP matrices with fast multiplication and fewer rows. In *Proceedings of the 25th Annual ACM-SIAM Symposium on Discrete Algorithms*, pp. 1515–1528, Portland, OR, January 5–7, 2014.

86. Ryan O'Donnell, Yi Wu, and Yuan Zhou. Optimal lower bounds for locality sensitive hashing (except when q is tiny). *Trans. Comput. Theory*, 6(1):5, 2014.

87. Rafail Ostrovsky and Yuval Rabani. Low distortion embedding for edit distance. *J. ACM*, 54(5), 2007. (Preliminary version appeared in *STOC'05.*)

88. Ali Rahimi and Benjamin Recht. Random features for large-scale kernel machines. In *Proceedings of Advances in Neural Information Processing Systems*, 2007.

89. Satish Rao. Small distortion and volume preserving embeddings for planar and Euclidean metrics. In *Proceedings of the 15th Annual Symposium on Computational Geometry*, pp. 300–306. ACM, New York, 1999.

90. Yossi Rubner, Carlo Tomasi, and Leonidas J. Guibas. The earth mover's distance as a metric for image retrieval. *Int. J. Comput. Vision*, 40(2):99–121, 2000.

91. Michael Saks and Xiaodong Sun. Space lower bounds for distance approximation in the data stream model. In *Proceedings of the Symposium on Theory of Computing*, pp. 360–369, 2002.

92. Gregory Valiant. Finding correlations in subquadratic time, with applications to learning parities and juntas with noise. In *Proceedings of the Symposium on Foundations of Computer Science*, 2012.

93. Nakul Verma, Samory Kpotufe, and Sanjoy Dasgupta. Which spatial partition trees are adaptive to intrinsic dimension? In *Proceedings of the 25th Conference on Uncertainty in Artificial Intelligence*, pp. 565–574, 2009.

94. David Woodruff. Optimal space lower bounds for all frequency moments. In *Proceedings of the ACM-SIAM Symposium on Discrete Algorithms*, pp. 167–175, 2004.

95. David P. Woodruff. Sketching as a tool for numerical linear algebra. *Found. Trends Theor. Comput. Sci.*, 10:1–157, 2014.

8

IRLBA: Fast Partial Singular Value Decomposition Method

James Baglama

CONTENTS

8.1 Introduction 125
8.2 GKLB Procedure 126
8.3 Augmented Lanczos Bidiagonalization Method 128
8.4 Numerical Performance 132
8.5 Conclusion 132
Appendix 133
References 134

8.1 Introduction

Approximation to some of the largest singular values and associated vectors (largest singular triplets) of very large rectangular matrices is essential in many areas of data analysis, for example, dimension reduction, data mining, data visualization, and detection of patterns. Furthermore, the statistical procedure principal component analysis has a direct relationship to the singular value decomposition (SVD) [16,26,31]. The importance of computing the singular triplets of very large matrices has spurred numerous computational methods in the literature; see, for example, [1,3,4,6,9,12–15,18,20,22,24,27,29,30] and references therein.

In 2005, Baglama and Reichel [1] developed a method, implicitly restarted Lanczos bidiagonalization algorithm (IRLBA), that is well suited for computing some of the largest (and smallest) singular triplets of extremely large rectangular matrices. The development of this routine is based on a long history of methods in eigenvalue and singular value computation. The foundation is based on the commonly used Golub–Kahan–Lanczos bidiagonalization (GKLB) procedure [9], which is described in detail in Section 8.2. However, the pivotal structure of the IRLBA comes from exploiting the mathematical equivalence of two eigenvalue routines and extending them to a restarted GKLB procedure. In 1992, Sorensen [28] developed a powerful eigenvalue computation method for very large eigenvalue problems, which is often referred to as the *implicitly restarted Arnoldi method* (IRAM). The IRAM was later implemented in the popular eigenvalue software package ARPACK [22]. Morgan [25] showed that the IRAM can be implemented by augmenting the Krylov subspace basis vectors by certain vectors. Such an implementation can be less sensitive to propagated round-off errors than the IRAM. Wu and Simon [33] described an eigenvalue method called the *thick-restarted Lanczos tridiagonalization*, which is simple to implement and mathematically equivalent to the symmetric IRAM. Harnessing these connections led to the development of the IRLBA, a simple, powerful, and computationally fast partial SVD method.

Shortly after developing the IRLBA, Baglama and Reichel [3] extended the method to work with the block form of the GKLB procedure [10] and published MATLAB® computer codes `irlba` and `irlbablk` [2]. Block methods are advantageous when computing multiple or clustered singular values and can utilize Level 3 BLAS matrix–matrix products. Also, block methods are favorable when matrices are so large that they have to be retrieved from disk when matrix–vector products with them are to be evaluated. However, there are added complexities to a block method, for example, linear dependence of blocks and block size. We will not discuss block methods in this chapter.

Recently, additional software packages for the IRLBA were developed in the programming languages R and Python. Lewis [23] developed `The irlba Package` in the open source statistical programming language R and Kane and Lewis [17] created `irlbpy`, an implementation of the IRLBA in Python for Numpy. See Section 8.4 for examples demonstrating the performance of the software implementations.

Baglama and Reichel [1] developed two strategies: augmentation with Ritz vectors `irlba(R)` for finding the largest (and smallest) singular triplets and augmentation with harmonic Ritz vectors `irlba(H)` for finding the smallest singular triplets. When seeking to compute the smallest singular triplets of a matrix, augmentation by harmonic Ritz vectors, `irlba(H)`, often yielded faster convergence. This method will not be described in this chapter since our focus is in the context of large data and on computing the largest singular triplets; therefore, we refer the reader to [1] for details on `irlba(H)`. In this chapter, we will refer to `irlba(R)` as IRLBA.

8.2 GKLB Procedure

Let $A \in \mathbb{R}^{\ell \times n}$ be a large sparse matrix. We may assume that $\ell \geq n$, because otherwise we replace the matrix by its transpose. Let $u_i \in \mathbb{R}^{\ell}$ and $v_i \in \mathbb{R}^n$ denote the left and right singular vectors of A associated with the singular value σ_i. Define $U_n = [u_1, u_2, \ldots, u_n] \in \mathbb{R}^{\ell \times n}$ and $V_n = [v_1, v_2, \ldots, v_n] \in \mathbb{R}^{n \times n}$ with orthonormal columns, as well as $\Sigma_n = \text{diag}[\sigma_1, \sigma_2, \ldots, \sigma_n] \in \mathbb{R}^{n \times n}$. Then

$$AV_n = U_n\Sigma_n \quad \text{and} \quad A^T U_n = V_n \Sigma_n \tag{8.1}$$

are the SVD of A and A^T, respectively. We assume the singular values are ordered,

$$\sigma_1 \geq \sigma_2 \geq \ldots \geq \sigma_n \geq 0, \tag{8.2}$$

and refer to $\{\sigma_i, u_i, v_i\}$ as a singular triplet of A.

We are interested in approximating the k largest singular triplets $\{\sigma_i, u_i, v_i\}_{i=1}^{k}$. Let the matrices $U_k \in \mathbb{R}^{\ell \times k}$ and $V_k \in \mathbb{R}^{n \times k}$ consist of the first k columns of the matrices U_n and V_n in the SVD (Equation 8.1) of A, and introduce $\Sigma_k = \text{diag}[\sigma_1, \ldots, \sigma_k] \in \mathbb{R}^{k \times k}$. Then, analogously to Equation 8.1, we have the partial SVD

$$AV_k = U_k\Sigma_k \quad \text{and} \quad A^T U_k = V_k \Sigma_k. \tag{8.3}$$

The approximations to Equation 8.3 can be obtained from projections onto Krylov subspaces

$$\begin{aligned} \mathcal{K}_m(A^TA, p_1) &= \text{span}\{p_1, A^TAp_1, (A^TA)^2p_1, \ldots, (A^TA)^{m-1}p_1\}, \\ \mathcal{K}_m(AA^T, q_1) &= \text{span}\{q_1, AA^Tq_1, (AA^T)^2q_1, \ldots, (AA^T)^{m-1}q_1\}, \end{aligned} \tag{8.4}$$

with initial vectors p_1 and $q_1 = Ap_1/\|Ap_1\|$, respectively. Throughout this discussion, $\|\cdot\|$ denotes the Euclidean vector norm as well as the associated induced matrix norm.

Generically, the GKLB procedure for $m \ll \min\{\ell, n\}$ determines orthonormal bases $\{p_1, p_2, \ldots, p_m\}$ and $\{q_1, q_2, \ldots, q_m\}$ for the Krylov subspaces (Equation 8.4). The GKLB procedure is well-suited for large matrices since the routine only requires the evaluation of matrix–vector products with A and A^T. The steps of the GKLB procedure is presented in the GKLB algorithm. A matrix interpretation at step m of the computations of the GKLB algorithm yields the partial GKLB decomposition,

$$\begin{aligned} AP_m &= Q_m B_m \\ A^T Q_m &= P_m B_m^T + r_m e_m^T \end{aligned} \tag{8.5}$$

where the matrices $P_m = [p_1, \ldots, p_m] \in \mathbb{R}^{n \times m}$ and $Q_m = [q_1, \ldots, q_m] \in \mathbb{R}^{\ell \times m}$ have orthonormal columns, the residual vector $r_m \in \mathbb{R}^n$ satisfies $P_m^T r_m = 0$, and e_m is the mth axis vector of appropriate dimension. Further,

$$B_m = \begin{pmatrix} \alpha_1 & \beta_1 & & & & 0 \\ & \alpha_2 & \beta_2 & & & \\ & & \alpha_3 & \beta_3 & & \\ & & & \ddots & \ddots & \\ & & & & \ddots & \beta_{m-1} \\ 0 & & & & & \alpha_m \end{pmatrix} \in \mathbb{R}^{m \times m} \tag{8.6}$$

is an upper bidiagonal matrix.

Algorithm 8.1 GKLB PROCEDURE

Input: $A \in \mathbb{R}^{\ell \times n}$*: large rectangular matrix,*
$p_1 \in \mathbb{R}^n$ *: initial vector of unit length,*
m *: number of bidiagonalization steps.*

Output: $P_m := [p_1, p_2, \ldots, p_m] \in \mathbb{R}^{n \times m}$ *: matrix with orthonormal columns,*
$Q_m := [q_1, q_2, \ldots, q_m] \in \mathbb{R}^{\ell \times m}$ *: matrix with orthonormal columns,*
$B_m \in \mathbb{R}^{m \times m}$ *: upper bidiagonal matrix (8.6) with entries* α_j *and* β_j*,*
$r_m \in \mathbb{R}^n$ *: residual vector.*

1. $P_1 := p_1;\ q_1 := Ap_1;$
2. $\alpha_1 := \|q_1\|;\ q_1 := q_1/\alpha_1;\ Q_1 := q_1;$
3. for $j = 1 : m$
  4. $r_j := A^T q_j - \alpha_j p_j;$
  5. Reorthogonalization: $r_j := r_j - P_j(P_j^T r_j);$
  6. if $j < m$ *then*
    7. $\beta_j := \|r_j\|;\ p_{j+1} := r_j/\beta_j;\ P_{j+1} := [P_j, p_{j+1}];$
    8. $q_{j+1} := Ap_{j+1} - \beta_j q_j;$
    9. Reorthogonalization: $q_{j+1} := q_{j+1} - Q_j(Q_j^T q_{j+1});$
    10. $\alpha_{j+1} := \|q_{j+1}\|;\ q_{j+1} := q_{j+1}/\alpha_{j+1};\ Q_{j+1} := [Q_j, q_{j+1}];$
  11. endif
12. endfor

The GKLB algorithm only requires matrix vector products with the matrices A and A^T, and the input matrix A can be replaced with functions that evaluate these products. To avoid loss of orthogonality due to finite precision arithmetic, reorthogonalization is performed in lines 5 and 9 of the GKLB algorithm, and the reader is referred to the reorthogonalization strategies discussed in the literature, for example, [19,27,33]. We do remark that Simon and Zha [27] observed that when matrix A is not very ill-conditioned, only the columns of one of the matrices P_m or Q_m need to be reorthogonalized, which reduces the computational cost considerably when $\ell \gg n$.

The number of bidiagonalization steps $m \ll \min\{\ell, n\}$ is assumed to be small enough, so that the partial GKLB decomposition (Equation 8.5) with the stated properties exists and $m > k$ so that an approximation to Equation 8.3 can be determined. We assume that GKLB algorithm does not terminate early, that is, all $\alpha_j > 0$ and $\beta_j > 0$ for $1 \leq j \leq m$; see [1] for a detailed discussion on early termination.

Analogously to Equation 8.1, let $u_i^{(B)} \in \mathbb{R}^m$ and $v_i^{(B)} \in \mathbb{R}^m$ denote the left and right singular vectors of B_m associated with the singular value $\sigma_i^{(B)}$. Define $U_m^{(B)} = [u_1^{(B)}, u_2^{(B)}, \ldots, u_m^{(B)}] \in \mathbb{R}^{m\times m}$ and $V_m^{(B)} = [v_1^{(B)}, v_2^{(B)}, \ldots, v_m^{(B)}] \in \mathbb{R}^{m\times m}$ with orthonormal columns, as well as $\Sigma_m^{(B)} = \mathrm{diag}[\sigma_1^{(B)}, \sigma_2^{(B)}, \ldots, \sigma_m^{(B)}] \in \mathbb{R}^{m\times m}$. Then

$$B_m V_m^{(B)} = U_m^{(B)} \Sigma_m^{(B)} \quad \text{and} \quad B_m^T U_m^{(B)} = V_m^{(B)} \Sigma_m^{(B)} \tag{8.7}$$

are the SVD of B_m and B_m^T, respectively. We assume the singular values of B_m are ordered in the same manner as Equation 8.2.

Notice from Equations 8.5 and 8.7 that

$$\begin{aligned} AP_m v_i^{(B)} - \sigma_i^{(B)} Q_m u_i^{(B)} &= 0 \\ A^T Q_m u_i^{(B)} - \sigma_i^{(B)} P_m v_i^{(B)} &= \left(e_m^T Q_m u_i^{(B)}\right) r_m. \end{aligned} \tag{8.8}$$

Using Equation 8.8, we see that approximations to the singular triplets $\{\sigma_i, u_i, v_i\}$ of A can be obtained from the triplets $\{\sigma_i^{(B)}, Q_m u_i^{(B)}, P_m v_i^{(B)}\}$. The criteria for accepting the triplet $\{\sigma_i^{(B)}, Q_m u_i^{(B)}, P_m v_i^{(B)}\}$ as an approximation are obtained from the second equation of Equation 8.8:

$$\|A^T Q_m u_i^{(B)} - \sigma_i^{(B)} P_m v_i^{(B)}\| = |e_m^T Q_m u_i^{(B)}| \cdot \|r_m\|. \tag{8.9}$$

The singular triplet is accepted as an approximate singular triplet of A when the residual error (Equation 8.9) is smaller than a prescribed tolerance, that is, when

$$|e_m^T Q_m u_i^{(B)}| \cdot \|r_m\| \leq \delta \|A\|, \tag{8.10}$$

for a user-specified value of δ. The value of $\|A\|$ in the bound (Equation 8.10) is easily approximated by the singular value of largest magnitude of the bidiagonal matrix B_m. This computation is of low cost, using successive approximations during iterations leading to a fairly good estimate of $\|A\|$.

Typically, $|e_m^T Q_m u_i^{(B)}| \cdot \|r_m\|$ does not become smaller than a prescribed tolerance for modest values of m. Prohibitive storage requirements of the basis vectors along with the computational cost prevents increasing m to get better approximations. Therefore, $m > k$ is kept of modest size and a restarted algorithm is used.

8.3 Augmented Lanczos Bidiagonalization Method

An efficient method for restarting in the context of eigenvalue problems was proposed by Sorensen [28]. This method can be thought of as a curtailed QR algorithm and requires the user to select a strategy for choosing a sequence of Krylov subspaces via a shift selection used to determine the invariant subspace; see [28] for details. The recursion formulas in [28] have been adapted to the GKLB method first by Björck et al. [7] in 1994 to solve ill-posed problems and then by Kokiopoulou et al. [18]. The shifts are taken from the spectrum of

$A^T A$ and are applied through a bugle and chase algorithm. However, this implementation is prone to round-off errors (see [5,32]); therefore, a mathematically equivalent implementation less prone to round-off errors was developed.

The relationship to the symmetric eigenvalue problems is obtained from the connection to the Lanczos tridiagonal decomposition of the symmetric matrix $A^T A$ by multiplying the first equation in Equation 8.5 from the left side by A^T:

$$A^T A P_m \quad = \quad P_m B_m^T B_m + \alpha_m r_m e_m^T. \tag{8.11}$$

Since B_m is upper triangular, this yields a valid Lanczos tridiagonal decomposition, where $B_m^T B_m$ is an $m \times m$ symmetric tridiagonal matrix. The eigenvalues and eigenvectors of $B_m^T B_m$, referred to as *Ritz values and vectors*, can be used to approximate the eigenvalues and eigenvectors of $A^T A$; see for example [11, Section 9.1.2] for a discussion on Lanczos tridiagonalization. Equation 8.11 provides a matrix representation of the Lanczos tridiagonal decomposition method for creating an orthogonal basis for $\mathcal{K}_m(A^T A, p_1)$ in Equation 8.4. Wu and Simon's [33] mathematically equivalent approach to the symmetric IRAM of Sorensen [28] is to augment $\mathcal{K}_{m-k}(A^T A, p_{k+1})$ with Ritz vectors of $B_m^T B_m$:

$$\tilde{P}_k := \left[P_m v_1^{(B)}, \ldots, P_m v_k^{(B)}\right] \in \mathbb{R}^{n \times k} \tag{8.12}$$

where $p_{k+1} = r_m / \|r_m\|$ and start the Lanczos tridiagonal method with the orthogonal matrix

$$\tilde{P}_{k+1} := \left[P_m v_1^{(B)}, \ldots, P_m v_k^{(B)}, p\right] \in \mathbb{R}^{n \times (k+1)}. \tag{8.13}$$

Because of the relationship between the GKLB decomposition (Equation 8.5) and the Lanczos decomposition (Equation 8.11), we can extend the idea of Wu and Simon [33] to the GKLB method.

Multiplying the matrix (Equation 8.13) from the left by A and using Equation 8.8 yields

$$A\tilde{P}_{k+1} = [\tilde{Q}_k, Ap_{k+1}] \begin{bmatrix} \sigma_1^{(B)} & & & 0 \\ & \ddots & & \\ & & \sigma_k^{(B)} & \\ 0 & & & 1 \end{bmatrix}, \tag{8.14}$$

where

$$\tilde{Q}_k := \left[Q_m u_1^{(B)}, \ldots, Q_m u_k^{(B)}\right] \in \mathbb{R}^{\ell \times k}. \tag{8.15}$$

The matrix, $[\tilde{Q}_k, Ap_{k+1}]$, in Equation 8.14 does not have orthogonal columns since

$$(Ap_{k+1})^T Q_m u_i^{(B)} = \rho_i \tag{8.16}$$

where $\rho_i = (e_m^T Q_m u_i^{(B)}) \cdot \|r_m\|$. Using Equation 8.16, an orthonormal vector q_{k+1} can be created

$$q_{k+1} = \frac{\left(Ap_{k+1} - \sum_{i=1}^{k} \rho_i Q_m u_i^{(B)}\right)}{\alpha_{k+1}} \tag{8.17}$$

with $\alpha_{k+1} = \|q_{k+1}\|$, yielding the orthogonal matrix

$$\tilde{Q}_{k+1} := \left[Q_m u_1^{(B)}, \ldots, Q_m u_k^{(B)}, q_{k+1}\right] \in \mathbb{R}^{\ell \times (k+1)}. \tag{8.18}$$

Equations 8.8, 8.13, 8.16, and 8.18 then yield

$$A\tilde{P}_{k+1} = \tilde{Q}_{k+1}\tilde{B}_{k+1} \tag{8.19}$$

where

$$\tilde{B}_{k+1} := \begin{bmatrix} \sigma_1^{(B)} & & 0 & \rho_1 \\ & \ddots & & \vdots \\ & & \sigma_k^{(B)} & \rho_k \\ 0 & & & \alpha_{k+1} \end{bmatrix} \in \mathbb{R}^{(k+1)\times(k+1)} \tag{8.20}$$

which can be thought of as augmenting $\mathcal{K}_{m-k}(A^TA, p_{k+1})$ with Equation 8.12 and $\mathcal{K}_{m-k}(AA^T, q_{k+1})$ with Equation 8.15. The next vector p_{k+2} can now be obtained normally from the GKLB algorithm, since

$$A^T\tilde{Q}_{k+1} = [\tilde{P}_{k+1}, A^Tq_{k+1}]\begin{bmatrix} \tilde{B}_{k+1} & e_{k+1} \end{bmatrix}^T \tag{8.21}$$

and $(A^Tq_{k+1})^TP_mv_i^{(B)} = 0$ for $1 \le i \le m$. The GKLB algorithm will set $p_{k+2} = (A^Tq_{k+1} - \alpha_{k+1}p_{k+1})/\beta_{k+1}$ with $\beta_{k+1} = \|p_{k+2}\|$ yielding

$$A^T\tilde{Q}_{k+1} = [\tilde{P}_{k+1}, p_{k+2}]\begin{bmatrix} \tilde{B}_{k+1} & \beta_{k+1}e_{k+1} \end{bmatrix}^T. \tag{8.22}$$

Thus, after continuing $m - k$ steps of the GKLB algorithm, we have analogous to Equation 8.5 the modified GKLB (MGKLB) decomposition:

$$\begin{array}{rcl} A\tilde{P}_m & = & \tilde{Q}_m\tilde{B}_m \\ A^T\tilde{Q}_m & = & \tilde{P}_m\tilde{B}_m^T + r_me_m^T \end{array}, \tag{8.23}$$

where

$$\tilde{B}_m = \begin{bmatrix} \tilde{B}_{k+1} & \beta_{k+1} & & 0 \\ & \alpha_{k+2} & \ddots & \\ & & \ddots & \beta_{m-1} \\ 0 & & & \alpha_m \end{bmatrix}, \tag{8.24}$$

$\tilde{P}_m = [\tilde{P}_k, p_{k+1}, \ldots, p_m] \in \mathbb{R}^{n\times m}$ and $\tilde{Q}_m = [\tilde{Q}_k, q_{k+1}, \ldots, q_m] \in \mathbb{R}^{\ell\times m}$ have orthonormal columns, the residual vector $r_m \in \mathbb{R}^n$ satisfies $\tilde{P}_m^Tr_m = 0$. Notice that the first k columns of Equation 8.23 satisfy Equation 8.8. The following MGKLB algorithm implements the modification of the GKLB algorithm that was described above.

Algorithm 8.2 MODIFIED GKLB

Input: $A \in \mathbb{R}^{\ell\times n}$: *large rectangular matrix,*
k : *number of augmenting vectors,*
m : *maximum size of MGKLB decomposition (8.23),*
$\tilde{P}_{k+1} := [P_mv_1^{(B)}, \ldots, P_mv_k^{(B)}, p_{k+1}] \in \mathbb{R}^{n\times(k+1)}$ *orthogonal matrix (8.13),*
$\tilde{Q}_k := [Q_mu_1^{(B)}, \ldots, Q_mu_k^{(B)}] \in \mathbb{R}^{\ell\times k}$ *orthogonal matrix (8.14),*

$$\tilde{B}_{k+1} := \begin{bmatrix} \sigma_1^{(B)} & & 0 & \rho_1 \\ & \ddots & & \vdots \\ & & \sigma_k^{(B)} & \rho_k \\ 0 & & & \alpha_{k+1} \end{bmatrix} \in \mathbb{R}^{(k+1)\times(k+1)} \in \mathbb{R}^{(k+1)\times(k+1)} \text{ (8.20).}$$

Output: $\tilde{P}_m := [\tilde{P}_{k+1}, p_{k+2}, \ldots, p_m] \in \mathbb{R}^{n\times m}$: *matrix with orthonormal columns,*
$\tilde{Q}_m := [\tilde{Q}_k, q_{k+1}, \ldots, q_m] \in \mathbb{R}^{\ell\times m}$: *matrix with orthonormal columns,*
$\tilde{B}_m \in \mathbb{R}^{m\times m}$: *matrix (8.24),*
$r_m \in \mathbb{R}^n$: *residual vector.*

1. $q_{k+1} := Ap_{k+1}$;
2. $q_{k+1} := q_{k+1} - \sum_{i=1}^{k} \rho_i Q_m u_i^{(B)}$; $\alpha_{k+1} := \|q_{k+1}\|$; $\tilde{Q}_{k+1} := [\tilde{Q}_k, q_{k+1}]$;
3. *for* $j = k+1 : m$
   4. $r_j := A^T q_j - \alpha_j p_j$;
   5. *Reorthogonalization:* $r_j := r_j - \tilde{P}_j(\tilde{P}_j^T r_j)$;
   6. *if* $j < m$ *then*
      7. $\beta_j := \|r_j\|$; $p_{j+1} := r_j/\beta_j$; $\tilde{P}_{j+1} := [\tilde{P}_j, p_{j+1}]$;
      8. $q_{j+1} := Ap_{j+1} - \beta_j q_j$;
      9. *Reorthogonalization:* $q_{j+1} := q_{j+1} - \tilde{Q}_j(\tilde{Q}_j^T q_{j+1})$;
      10. $\alpha_{j+1} := \|q_{j+1}\|$; $q_{j+1} := q_{j+1}/\alpha_{j+1}$; $\tilde{Q}_{j+1} := [\tilde{Q}_j, q_{j+1}]$;
   11. *endif*
12. *endfor*

The MGKLB algorithm can also be used in place of the GKLB algorithm when $k = 0$, where the input matrix $\tilde{P}_{k+1} := p_{k+1}$. We now describe the algorithm for computing the largest singular triplets by augmenting the GKLB method with Ritz vectors, the implicitly restarted Lanczos bidiagonalization algorithm augmented with Ritz vectors (IRLBA). The IRLBA is a simplification of the actual computations carried out. For instance, the number of augmented vectors used at each restart typically is larger than the number of desired singular triplets. It was observed in [5,20,21] that a shift too close to a desired singular value caused dampening of the associated desired singular vector and hence slowed down convergence considerably. To overcome this problem in this context, we can augment by $k + ak$ (instead of k) singular triples, where ak is chosen by user, typically 2 or 3, such that $k + ak \leq m - 3$. The term -3 secures that at least 3 orthogonalization steps can be carried out between restarts. See [5] for a heuristic strategy on adjusting ak in the context of implicitly shifted GKLB method for least square problems. A similar heuristic strategy can be used for augmentation.

Algorithm 8.3 Implicitly Restarted Lanczos Bidiagonalization Algorithm Augmented with Ritz Vectors

Input: $A \in \mathbb{R}^{\ell\times n}$,
$p_1 \in \mathbb{R}^n$: *initial vector of unit length,*
m : *number of bidiagonalization steps,*
k : *number of desired singular triplets,*
δ : *tolerance for accepting computed approximate singular triple, cf. (8.10).*

Output: Computed set of approximate singular triples $\{\sigma_j, u_j, v_j\}_{j=1}^{k}$ *of A.*

1. *Compute partial GKLB decomposition (8.5) using GKLB Algorithm or MGKLB Algorithm with* $k = 0$.
2. *Compute the singular value decomposition (8.7) of* B_m.
3. *Check convergence: If all k desired singular triplets satisfy (8.10) then exit.*
4. *Determine the matrices* $\tilde{P}_{k+1}$, $\tilde{Q}_k$ *and* $\tilde{B}_{k+1}$, *by (8.13) (8.14), and (8.20), respectively.*
5. *Compute partial MGKLB decomposition (8.23) using MGKLB Algorithm.*
6. *Goto 2.*

8.4 Numerical Performance

A simple MATLAB code, `irlbar`, that implements IRLBA is given in the Appendix. For a full MATLAB implementation of IRLBA, see [2]. The speed of IRLBA is significant and can be seen by the following straightforward example. Consider, the $1,977,885 \times 109,900$ Rucci1 matrix in the Florida Sparse Matrix Collection [8]. The matrix group Rucci contains matrices for least-squares problems and can be downloaded using the University of Florida's Sparse Matrix Collection program `UFget`. The MATLAB code `irlbar` was more than three times as fast as MATLAB's internal `svds` for computing the six largest singular triplets of the Rucci1 matrix within the same tolerance, 10^{-5}. Speed was measured with MATLAB's `tic` and `toc` in version 8.3.0.532 (R2014a) on an iMac with 32 GB memory and 3.5 Ghz Intel processor.

Anecdotal evidence of performance of the IRLBA in the statistical programming language R was done by Bryan Lewis [23]. Lewis used IRLBA to compute the five largest singular triplets on the Netflix training dataset ($480,189 \times 17,770$ matrix) in a few minutes on a laptop; see http://illposed.net/irlba.html for details.

The software implementations of IRLBA have existed for some time now in both MATLAB [2] and R [23]. Recently Kane and Lewis [17] created the `irlbpy` package for Python, a pip-installable open-source implementation of the IRLBA that is available from Github at https://github.com/bwlewis/irlbpy. The `irlbpy` package is compatible with dense and sparse data, accepting either numpy 2D arrays or matrices, or scipy sparse matrices as input. The performance of `irlbpy`, the IRLBA augmented with Ritz vector, is demonstrated in the graphs in Figure 8.1. The benchmarks in Figure 8.1 were performed on a MacBook Pro with a quad-core 2.7 GHz Intel Core i7 with 16 GB of 1600 MHz DDR3 RAM running Python version 2.7.3, Numpy version 1.7.0, and SciPy version 0.12.0. All matrices were square and randomly generated. Elements in the graphs in Figure 8.1 represent the order of the matrices. These graphs show that in practice, when searching for the largest singular triplets, IRLBA scales linearly with the size of the data, which gives it a tremendous advantage over the traditional SVD methods. The IRLBA is particularly well suited to problems when m and n are not too different, which are often the most computationally challenging ones. All examples in Figure 8.1 can be found at https://github.com/bwlewis/irlbpy.

8.5 Conclusion

This chapter provides an overview of the IRLBA method augmented with Ritz vectors developed in 2005 by Baglama and Reichel [1] and shows that the method is well suited for finding the largest singular triplets of very large matrices. The method can easily be implemented in a variety of programming languages and is computationally fast when compared to similar methods. We thank Michael Kane and Bryan Lewis for all of their work in this book and with the software implementations of IRLBA.

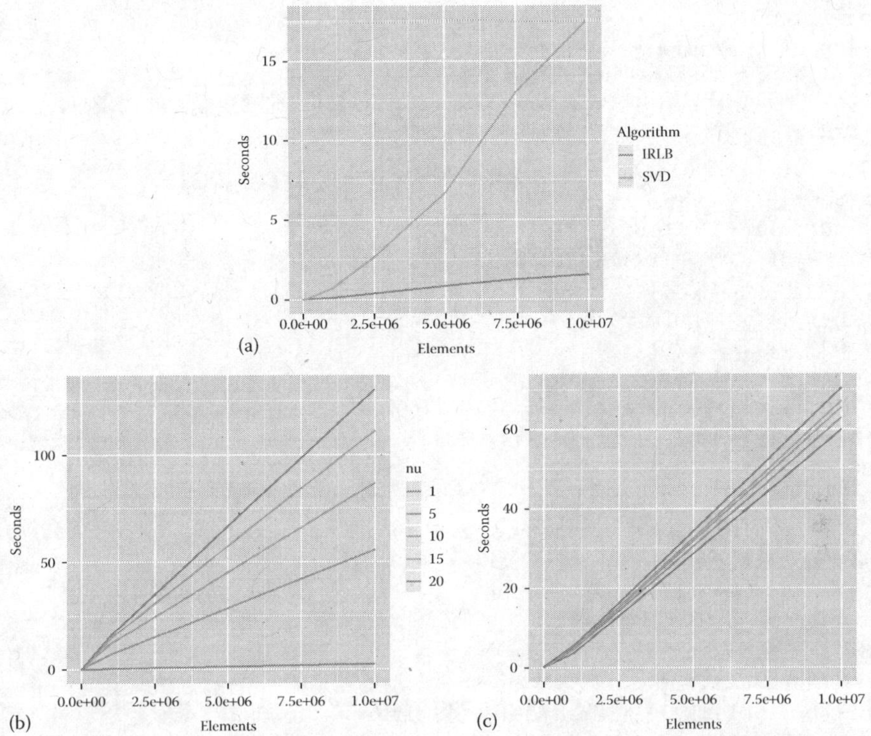

FIGURE 8.1
(a) Performance comparison of the irlbpy and the Python numpy implementation of the SVD calculating the 10 largest singular triplets of square random matrices. (b) The CPU time required for irlbpy on dense square random matrices for specified values of nu (the number of singular vectors). (c) The CPU time required for irlbpy on sparse square random matrices for specified values of nu (the number of singular vectors).

Appendix

```
function [U,S,V] = irlbar(A)
% Sample MATLAB code for IRLBA Augmentation Ritz.
% Complete MATLAB code: http://www.netlib.org/numeralgo/na26.tgz
% Handbook of Big Data
% IRLBA: Fast Partial Singular Value Decomposition
% Author: James Baglama
m = 20; k = 6; ak = 3; Smax = 1; J = 1; delta = 1d-5;
P = randn(size(A,2),1);
```

```
for iter=1:1000
  P(:,J) = P(:,J)/norm(P(:,J));
  Q(:,J) = A*P(:,J);
  if J > 1, Q(:,J) = Q(:,J) - Q(:,1:J-1)*B(1:J-1,J);  end
  B(J,J) = norm(Q(:,J));
  Q(:,J) = Q(:,J)/B(J,J);
  for i=J:m
    r = (Q(:,i)'*A)' - B(i,i)*P(:,i);
    r = r - P(:,1:i)*(r'*P(:,1:i))';
    if i < m
        B(i,i+1) = norm(r);
        P(:,i+1) = r/B(i,i+1);
        Q(:,i+1) = A*P(:,i+1) - B(i,i+1)*Q(:,i);
        B(i+1,i+1) = norm(Q(:,i+1));
        Q(:,i+1) = Q(:,i+1)/B(i+1,i+1);
    end
  end
  [U,S,V] = svd(B); Smax = max(Smax,S(1,1));
  rnorm = norm(r);
  P(:,1:k+ak) = P*V(:,1:k+ak);
  Q(:,1:k+ak) = Q*U(:,1:k+ak);
  S = S(1:k+ak,1:k+ak);
  rho  = rnorm*U(m,1:k+ak);
  if max(abs(rho(1:k))) < Smax*delta || iter == 1000
      V =  P(:,1:k); U = Q(:,1:k); S = S(1:k,1:k);
      return;
  end
  B = [S, rho'];
  J = k+ak+1;
  P(:,J)= r/rnorm;
end
```

References

1. James Baglama and Lothar Reichel. Augmented implicitly restarted Lanczos bidiagonalization methods. *SIAM Journal on Scientific Computing*, 27(1):19–42, 2005.

2. James Baglama and Lothar Reichel. Primer for the Matlab functions IRLBA and IRLBABLK. Available online. http://www.netlib.org/numeralgo/na26.tgz, 2006.

3. James Baglama and Lothar Reichel. Restarted block Lanczos bidiagonalization methods. *Numerical Algorithms*, 43(3):251–272, 2006.

4. James Baglama and Lothar Reichel. An implicitly restarted block Lanczos bidiagonalization method using leja shifts. *BIT Numerical Mathematics*, 53(2):285–310, 2013.

5. James Baglama and Daniel Richmond. Implicitly restarting the LSQR algorithm. *Electronic Transactions on Numerical Analysis*, 42:85–105, 2014.

6. Michael Berry. Computing the sparse singular value decomposition via SVDPACK. In Gene Golub, Mitchell Luskin, and Anne Greenbaum (eds.), *Recent Advances in Iterative Methods*, pp. 13–29. Springer, New York, 1994.

7. Åke Björck, Eric Grimme, and Paul Van Dooren. An implicit shift bidiagonalization algorithm for ill-posed systems. *BIT Numerical Mathematics*, 34(4):510–534, 1994.

8. Timothy Davis and Yifan Hu. The University of Florida sparse matrix collection. *ACM Transactions on Mathematical Software (TOMS)*, 38(1):1, 2011.

9. Gene Golub and William Kahan. Calculating the singular values and pseudo-inverse of a matrix. *Journal of the Society for Industrial & Applied Mathematics, Series B: Numerical Analysis*, 2(2):205–224, 1965.

10. Gene Golub, Franklin Luk, and Michael Overton. A block Lanczos method for computing the singular values and corresponding singular vectors of a matrix. *ACM Transactions on Mathematical Software* (*TOMS*), 7(2):149–169, 1981.

11. Gene Golub and Charles Van Loan. *Matrix Computations*, 3 edition. Johns Hopkins University Press, Baltimore, MD, 1996.

12. Michiel Hochstenbach. A Jacobi–Davidson type SVD method. *SIAM Journal on Scientific Computing*, 23(2):606–628, 2001.

13. Michiel Hochstenbach. Harmonic and refined extraction methods for the singular value problem, with applications in least squares problems. *BIT Numerical Mathematics*, 44(4):721–754, 2004.

14. Zhongxiao Jia and Datian Niu. An implicitly restarted refined bidiagonalization Lanczos method for computing a partial singular value decomposition. *SIAM Journal on Matrix Analysis and Applications*, 25(1):246–265, 2003.

15. Zhongxiao Jia and Datian Niu. A refined harmonic Lanczos bidiagonalization method and an implicitly restarted algorithm for computing the smallest singular triplets of large matrices. *SIAM Journal on Scientific Computing*, 32(2):714–744, 2010.

16. Ian Jolliffe. *Principal Component Analysis*, 2 edition. Springer, New York, 2002.

17. Michael Kane and Bryan Lewis. irlby: Truncated SVD by implicitly restarted Lanczos bidiagonalization for Python numpy. Available online. https://github.com/bwlewis/irlbpy/tree/master/doc/scipy2013, 2013.

18. Effrosyni Kokiopoulou, Constantine Bekas, and Efstratios Gallopoulos. Computing smallest singular triplets with implicitly restarted Lanczos bidiagonalization. *Applied Numerical Mathematics*, 49(1):39–61, 2004.

19. Rasmus Munk Larsen. Lanczos bidiagonalization with partial reorthogonalization. *DAIMI Report Series*, 27(537), 1998.

20. Rasmus Munk Larsen. Propack-software for large and sparse SVD calculations. Available online. http://sun. stanford. edu/rmunk/PROPACK, 2004.

21. Richard Lehoucq. Implicitly restarted Arnoldi methods and subspace iteration. *SIAM Journal on Matrix Analysis and Applications*, 23(2):551–562, 2001.

22. Richard Lehoucq, Danny Sorensen, and Chao Yang. *ARPACK Users' Guide: Solution of Large-Scale Eigenvalue Problems with Implicitly Restarted Arnoldi Methods*, Vol. 6. SIAM, Philadelphia, PA, 1998.

23. Bryan Lewis. IRLBA: Fast partial SVD by implicitly-restarted Lanczos bidiagonalization. R package version 1.0.3. Available online. http://rforge.net/irlba/, 2009.

24. Edo Liberty, Franco Woolfe, Per-Gunnar Martinsson, Vladimir Rokhlin, and Mark Tygert. Randomized algorithms for the low-rank approximation of matrices. *Proceedings of the National Academy of Sciences USA*, 104(51):20167–20172, 2007.

25. Ronald Morgan. On restarting the Arnoldi method for large nonsymmetric eigenvalue problems. *Mathematics of Computation of the American Mathematical Society*, 65(215):1213–1230, 1996.

26. Jonathon Shlens. A tutorial on principal component analysis. arXiv preprint arXiv:1404.1100, 2014.

27. Horst Simon and Hongyuan Zha. Low-rank matrix approximation using the Lanczos bidiagonalization process with applications. *SIAM Journal on Scientific Computing*, 21(6):2257–2274, 2000.

28. Danny Sorensen. Implicit application of polynomial filters in ak-step Arnoldi method. *SIAM Journal on Matrix Analysis and Applications*, 13(1):357–385, 1992.

29. Martin Stoll. A Krylov–Schur approach to the truncated SVD. *Linear Algebra and its Applications*, 436(8):2795–2806, 2012.

30. Sabine Van Huffel. Partial singular value decomposition algorithm. *Journal of Computational and Applied Mathematics*, 33(1):105–112, 1990.

31. Michael Wall, Andreas Rechtsteiner, and Luis Rocha. Singular value decomposition and principal component analysis. In Daniel Berrar, Werner Dubitzky, and Martin Granzow (eds.), *A Practical Approach to Microarray Data Analysis*, pp. 91–109. Springer, New York, 2003.

32. David Watkins. *The Matrix Eigenvalue Problem: GR and Krylov Subspace Methods*. SIAM, Philadelphia, PA, 2007.

33. Kesheng Wu and Horst Simon. Thick-restart Lanczos method for large symmetric eigenvalue problems. *SIAM Journal on Matrix Analysis and Applications*, 22(2): 602–616, 2000.

9

Structural Properties Underlying High-Quality Randomized Numerical Linear Algebra Algorithms

Michael W. Mahoney and Petros Drineas

CONTENTS

9.1 Introduction ... 137
9.2 Overview ... 138
9.3 Our Main Technical Result ... 140
9.3.1 Statement of the Main Technical Result ... 140
9.3.2 Popular Special Case ... 141
9.3.3 Proof of the Main Technical Result ... 142
9.4 Applications of Our Main Technical Result ... 143
9.4.1 CSSP: Theory ... 143
9.4.2 CSSP: Data Analysis and Machine Learning ... 145
9.4.3 Random Projections for Low-Rank Matrix Approximations ... 146
9.4.4 Improved Results for Nyström-Based Machine Learning ... 148
9.5 Conclusions ... 149
Acknowledgments ... 149
References ... 150

9.1 Introduction

In recent years, the amount of data that has been generated and recorded has grown enormously, and data are now seen to be at the heart of modern economic activity, innovation, and growth. See, for example, the report by the McKinsey Global Institute [51], which identifies ways in which Big Data have transformed the modern world, as well as the report by the National Research Council [19], which discusses reasons for and technical challenges in massive data analysis. In many cases, these so-called Big Data are modeled as matrices, basically since an $m \times n$ matrix A provides a natural mathematical structure with which to encode information about m objects, each of which is described by n features. As a result, while linear algebra algorithms have been of interest for decades in areas such as numerical linear algebra (NLA) and scientific computing, in recent years, there has been renewed interest in developing matrix algorithms that are appropriate for the analysis of large datasets that are represented in the form of matrices. For example, tools such as the singular value decomposition (SVD) and the related principal components analysis (PCA) [38] permit the low-rank approximation of a matrix, and they have have had a profound impact in diverse areas of science and engineering. They have also been studied extensively in large-scale machine learning and data analysis applications, in settings ranging from web search engines and social network analysis to the analysis of astronomical and biological data.

Importantly, the structural and noise properties of matrices that arise in machine learning and data analysis applications are typically very different than those of matrices that arise in scientific computing and NLA. This has led researchers to revisit traditional problems in light of new requirements and to consider novel algorithmic approaches to many traditional matrix problems. One of the more remarkable trends in recent years is a new paradigm that arose in theoretical computer science (TCS) and that involves the use of randomization as a computational resource for the design and analysis of algorithms for fundamental matrix problems. Randomized NLA (RandNLA) is the interdisciplinary research area that exploits randomization as a computational resource to develop improved algorithms for large-scale linear algebra problems, for example, matrix multiplication, linear regression, and low-rank matrix approximation [49]. In this chapter, we will discuss RandNLA, highlighting how many of the most interesting RandNLA developments for problems related to improved low-rank matrix approximation boil down to exploiting a particular structural property of Euclidean vector spaces. This structural property is of interest in and of itself (for researchers interested in linear algebra *per se*), but it is also of interest more generally (for researchers interested in *using* linear algebra) since it highlights strong connections between algorithms for many seemingly unrelated matrix problems.

9.2 Overview

As background, we note that early work in RandNLA focused on low-rank approximation problems and led to results that were primarily of theoretical interest in idealized models of data access [23–25,34,57,63]. An overview of RandNLA for readers not familiar with the area has recently been provided [49]. Subsequent work on very overdetermined linear regression problems, for example, least-squares regression problems with an input matrix $A \in \mathbb{R}^{m \times n}$, with $m \gg n$, led to several remarkable successes for RandNLA: theoretical results for worst-case inputs for the running time in the RAM model that improve upon the 200-year old Gaussian elimination [17,26,31,53,56]; high-quality implementations that are competitive with or better than traditional deterministic implementations, for example, as provided by LAPACK, on a single machine [2,18,62]; and high-quality implementations in parallel and distributed environments on up to terabyte-sized input matrices [16,54,55,70,71].

As has been described in detail, for example, in [49], both the more theoretical and the more applied successes of RandNLA for these very overdetermined linear regression problems were achieved by using, implicitly or explicitly, the so-called statistical leverage scores of the tall input matrix A.* In some cases, the use of leverage scores was explicit, in that one used exact or approximate leverage scores to construct a nonuniform importance sampling probability distribution with respect to which to sample rows from the input matrix, thereby constructing a data-aware subspace embedding [26,28]. In other cases, the use of leverage scores was implicit, in that one performed a random projection, thereby implementing a data-oblivious subspace embedding [31,68].† In both cases, the improved

*The statistical leverage scores of a tall matrix $A \in \mathbb{R}^{m \times n}$ with $m \gg n$ are equal to the diagonal elements of the projection matrix onto the column span of A [14,48,50]. Thus, they capture a subtle but important structural property of the Euclidean vector space from which the data were drawn.

†Random projections can be applied in more general metric spaces, but in a Euclidean vector space, a random projection essentially amounts to rotating to a random basis, where the leverage scores are uniform and thus where uniform sampling can be applied [49].

theoretical and practical results for overdetermined linear regression problems were obtained by coupling the original, rather theoretical, RandNLA ideas more closely with structural properties of the input data [49].

In parallel with these successes on overdetermined regression problems, there have also been several impressive successes on applying RandNLA methods to a wide range of seemingly different low-rank matrix approximation problems.[‡] For example, consider the following problems (which are described in more detail in Section 9.4):

- The column subset selection problem (CSSP), in which one seeks to select the most informative subset of exactly k columns from a matrix.
- The problem of using random projections to approximate low-rank matrix approximations faster than traditional SVD-based or QR-based deterministic methods for worst-case input matrices and/or for inputs that are typical in scientific computing applications.
- The problem of developing improved Nyström-based low-rank matrix approximations of symmetric positive definite matrices.
- The problem of developing improved machine learning and data analysis methods to identify interesting features in the data (feature selection).

These problems often arise in very different research areas, and they are—at least superficially—quite different. Relatedly, it can be difficult to tell what—if anything—improved algorithms for one problem mean for the possibility of improved algorithms for the others.

In this chapter, we highlight and discuss a particular deterministic structural property of Euclidean vector spaces that underlies the recent improvements in RandNLA algorithms for all of the above low-rank matrix approximation problems.[§] (See Lemma 9.1 for a statement of this result.) This structural property characterizes the interaction between the singular subspaces of the input matrix A and *any* (deterministic or randomized) *sketching* matrix. In particular, this structural property is deterministic, in the sense that it is a statement about the (fixed) input data A and not the (randomized) algorithm. Moreover, it holds for arbitrary matrices A, that is, matrices that have an arbitrarily large number of columns and rows and not necessarily just tall-and-thin or short-and-fat matrices A, as was the case in the over or under-determined least-squares problems. The structural property thus applies most directly to problems where one is interested in low-rank approximation with respect to a low-rank space of dimension $k \ll \min\{m, n\}$.

In RandNLA, the sketching matrix is typically either a matrix representing the operation of sampling columns or rows from the input matrix, or a matrix representing the random projection operation. In that case, this structural property has an interpretation in terms of how the sampling or projection operation interacts with the subspaces defined by the top and bottom part of the spectrum of A. We emphasize, however, that this structural property holds more generally: in particular, it holds for *any* (deterministic or randomized) *sketching* matrix and thus it is a property of independent interest. For example, while it is outside the scope of this chapter to discuss in detail, one can easily imagine using this property to

[‡]By *low-rank matrix approximation problems*, we informally mean problems where the input is a general matrix $A \in \mathbb{R}^{m \times n}$, where both m and n are large, and a rank parameter $k \ll \min\{m, n\}$; the output is a low-rank approximation to A, not necessarily the optimal one, that is computed via the SVD.

[§]Although this structural property is central to all of the above problems, its role is typically obscured, since it is often secondary to the main result of interest in a given paper, and thus it is hidden deep within the analysis of each of the superficially different methods that use it. This property was first introduced by Boutsidis et al. [10] in the context of the CSSP, it was subsequently used by Halko et al. [44] to simplify the description of several related random projection algorithms, and it was then used—typically knowingly, but sometimes unknowingly—by many researchers working on these and other problems.

derandomize RandNLA algorithms or to develop other deterministic matrix algorithms for these and related matrix problems or to develop improved heuristics in machine learning and data analysis applications. In the remainder of this chapter, we highlight this structural property, stating and presenting an analysis of a more general version of it than has been previously available. We also describe how it is used in several of the recent improvements to various RandNLA algorithms for low-rank matrix approximation problems.

9.3 Our Main Technical Result

In this section, we state and prove our main technical result. This technical result is a structural condition that characterizes the interaction between the singular subspaces of the input matrix A and *any* deterministic or randomized *sketching* matrix.

9.3.1 Statement of the Main Technical Result

Recall that, given a matrix $A \in \mathbb{R}^{m\times n}$, many RandNLA algorithms seek to construct a *sketch* of A by post-multiplying A by some *sketching* matrix $Z \in \mathbb{R}^{n\times r}$, where r is much smaller than n. (For example, Z could represent the action of random sampling or random projection.) Thus, the resulting matrix $AZ \in \mathbb{R}^{m\times r}$ is matrix that is much smaller than the original matrix A, and the interesting question is what kind of approximation guarantees does it offer for A.

A common approach is to explore how well AZ spans the principal subspace of A, and one metric of accuracy is the error matrix, $A - P_{AZ}A$, where $P_{AZ}A$ is the projection of A onto the subspace spanned by the columns of AZ. Formally,

$$P_{AZ} = (AZ)(AZ)^{+} = U_{AZ}U_{AZ}^{T}.$$

Recall that $X^{+} \in \mathbb{R}^{n\times m}$ is the Moore–Penrose pseudoinverse of any matrix $X \in \mathbb{R}^{m\times n}$, and that it can be computed via the SVD of X; see [38] for details. Similarly, $U_{AZ} \in \mathbb{R}^{m\times \rho}$ is the matrix of the left singular vectors of AZ, where ρ is the rank of AZ. The following structural result offers a means to bound any unitarily invariant norm of the error matrix $A - P_{AZ}A$.

Lemma 9.1 *Given $A \in \mathbb{R}^{m\times n}$, let $Y \in \mathbb{R}^{n\times k}$ be any matrix such that $Y^TY = I_k$. Let $Z \in \mathbb{R}^{n\times r}$ $(r \geq k)$ be any matrix such that Y^TZ and AY have full rank. Then, for any unitarily invariant norm ξ, we have that*

$$\|A - P_{AZ}A\|_{\xi} \leq \left\|A - AYY^{T}\right\|_{\xi} + \left\|\left(A - AYY^{T}\right)Z(Y^{T}Z)^{+}\right\|_{\xi}. \tag{9.1}$$

Three comments about this lemma, one regarding Z, one regarding Y, and one regarding the interaction between Z and Y, are in order.

- Lemma 9.1 holds for any matrix Z, regardless of whether Z is constructed deterministically or randomly. In the context of RandNLA, typical constructions of Z would represent a random sampling or random projection operation.

- The orthogonal matrix Y in the above lemma is also arbitrary. In the context of RandNLA, one can think of Y either as $Y = V_k$, where $V_k \in \mathbb{R}^{n\times k}$ is the matrix of the top k right singular vectors of A, or as some other orthogonal matrix that approximates V_k; however, Lemma 9.1 holds more generally.

- As stated in Lemma 9.1, Y must satisfy two conditions: the matrix Y^TZ must have full rank, equal to k, since $r \geq k$, and the matrix AY must also have full rank, again equal to k. If $Y = V_k$, then the constraint that AY must have full rank is trivially satisfied, assuming that A has rank at least k. Additionally, the sampling and random projection approaches that are used in high-quality RandNLA algorithms with sufficiently large values of r guarantee that the rank condition on Y^TZ is satisfied [26,49]. More generally, though, one could perform an *a posteriori* check that these two conditions hold.

9.3.2 Popular Special Case

Before providing a proof of this structural result, we will now consider a popular special case of Lemma 9.1. To do so, we will let $Y = V_k \in \mathbb{R}^{n\times k}$, namely the orthogonal matrix of the top k right singular vectors of A. (Actually, any orthogonal matrix spanning that same subspace would do in this discussion.) For notational convenience, we will let $V_{k,\perp}\mathbb{R}^{n\times(\rho-k)}$ (respectively, $\Sigma_{k,\perp} \in \mathbb{R}^{(n-\rho)\times(n-\rho)}$) be the matrix of the bottom $\rho - k$ right singular vectors (respectively, singular values) of A. Let $A_k \in \mathbb{R}^{m\times n}$ be the best rank k approximation to A as computed by the SVD. It is well known that

$$A_k = AV_kV_k^T$$

Assuming that V_k^TZ has full rank, then Lemma 9.1 implies that

$$\|A - P_{AZ}A\|_{\xi} \leq \|A - A_k\|_{\xi} + \left\|(A - A_k)\, Z\left(V_k^TZ\right)^+\right\|_{\xi}$$

Note here that

$$A - A_k = U_{k,\perp}\Sigma_{k,\perp}V_{k,\perp}^T$$

and if we drop, using unitary invariance, the matrix $U_{k,\perp}$ from the second norm at the right-hand side of the above inequality, then we get

$$\|A - P_{AZ}A\|_{\xi} \leq \|A - A_k\|_{\xi} + \left\|\Sigma_{k,\perp}\left(V_{k,\perp}^TZ\right)\left(V_k^TZ\right)^+\right\|_{\xi}$$

For the special case of $\xi \in \{2, F\}$, this is exactly the structural condition underlying the randomized low-rank projection algorithms of [44] that was first introduced in the context of the CSSP [10]. We summarize the above discussion in the following lemma.

Lemma 9.2 *Given $A \in \mathbb{R}^{m\times n}$, let $V_k \in \mathbb{R}^{n\times k}$ be the matrix of the top k right singular vectors of A. Let $Z \in \mathbb{R}^{n\times r}$ ($r \geq k$) be any matrix such that Y^TZ has full rank. Then, for any unitarily invariant norm ξ,*

$$\|A - P_{AZ}A\|_{\xi} \leq \|A - A_k\|_{\xi} + \left\|\Sigma_{k,\perp}\left(V_{k,\perp}^TZ\right)\left(V_k^TZ\right)^+\right\|_{\xi} \qquad (9.2)$$

Equation 9.2 immediately suggests a proof strategy for bounding the error RandNLA algorithms for low-rank matrix approximation: identify a sketching matrix Z such that V_k^TZ has full rank; at the same time, bound the relevant norms of $\left(V_k^TZ\right)^+$ and $V_{k,\perp}Z$.

Lemma 9.1 generalizes the prior use of Lemma 9.2 in several important ways:

- First, it is not necessary to focus on random sampling matrices or random projection matrices, but instead, we consider arbitrary sketching matrices Z. This was actually implicit in the analysis of the original version of Lemma 9.2 [10], but it seems worth making that explicit here. It does, however, require the extra condition that AZ also has full rank.

- Second, it is not necessary to focus on V_k and so we consider the more general case of any arbitrary orthogonal matrix $Y \in \mathbb{R}^{n\times k}$ instead of V_k.
- Third, it is not necessary to focus on the spectral or Frobenius norm, as it is straightforward to prove this result for any unitarily invariant matrix norm.

9.3.3 Proof of the Main Technical Result

This proof of Lemma 9.1 follows our previous proof of Lemma 9.2 from [10], simplifying it and generalizing it at appropriate places. We start by noting that

$$\|A - P_{AZ}A\|_\xi = \left\|A - (AZ)\,(AZ)^+\,A\right\|_\xi \tag{9.3}$$

Then, for any unitarily invariant norm ξ [45],

$$(AZ)^+A = \arg\min_{X\in R^{r\times n}} \|A - (AZ)\,X\|_\xi$$

This implies that in Equation 9.3, we can replace $(AZ)^+\,A$ with any other $r\times n$ matrix and the equality with an inequality. In particular, we replace $(AZ)^+\,A$ with $\left(AYY^TZ\right)^+\,AYY^T$, where AYY^T is a rank-k approximation to A (not necessarily the best rank-k approximation to A):

$$\begin{aligned}\|A - P_{AZ}A\|_\xi &= \left\|A - AZ\,(AZ)^+\,A\right\|_\xi \\ &\leq \left\|A - AZ\left(AYY^TZ\right)^+\,AYY^T\right\|_\xi\end{aligned}$$

This suboptimal choice for X is essentially the *heart* of our proof: it allows us to manipulate and further decompose the error term, thus making the remainder of the analysis feasible. Use $A = A - AYY^T + AYY^T$ and the triangle inequality to get

$$\begin{aligned}&\|A - P_{AZ}A\|_\xi \\ &\leq \left\|A - AYY^T + AYY^T - (A{-}AYY^T{+}AYY^T)\,Z\left(AYY^TZ\right)^+\,AYY^T\right\|_\xi \\ &\leq \|A - AYY^T\|_\xi + \|AYY^T - AYY^TZ(AYY^TZ)^+AYY^T\|_\xi \\ &+ \|(A - AYY^T)\,Z(AYY^TZ)^+AYY^T\|_\xi\end{aligned}$$

We now prove that the second term in the last inequality is equal to zero. Indeed,

$$\begin{aligned}&\|AYY^T - AYY^TZ(AYY^TZ)^+AYY^T\|_\xi \\ &= \|AYY^T - AYY^TZ(Y^TZ)^+(AY)^+AYY^T\|_\xi \\ &= \|AYY^T - AYY^T\|_\xi = 0\end{aligned} \tag{9.4}$$

In Equation 9.4, we replaced $\left(AYY^TZ\right)^+$ by $\left(Y^TZ\right)^+(AY)^+$, using the fact that both matrices Y^TZ and AY have full rank. The fact that both matrices have full rank also implies

$$Y^TZ\left(Y^TZ\right)^+ = I_k \quad\text{and}\quad (AY)^+\,AY = I_k$$

which concludes the derivation. Using the same manipulations and dropping Y^T using unitary invariance, we get

$$\|(A - AYY^T)\,Z(AYY^TZ)^+AYY^T\|_\xi = \|(A - AYY^T)\,Z(Y^TZ)^+\|_\xi$$

which concludes the proof.

9.4 Applications of Our Main Technical Result

In this section, we discuss several settings where exploiting the structural result highlighted in Lemma 9.1 results in improved analyses of RandNLA algorithms for low-rank matrix approximation problems.

9.4.1 CSSP: Theory

The special case of Lemma 9.2 corresponding to the spectral and Frobenius norm was first identified and established in our prior work on the CSSP [10]. The CSSP is the problem of choosing the *best* (in a sense that we will make precise shortly) set of r columns from an $m \times n$ matrix A. Given the importance of the CSSP in both NLA and TCS applications of RandNLA; here we will describe in some detail the role of Equation 9.1 in this context, as well as the related work. In the next section, we will describe applied aspects of the CSSP.

First of all, the CSSP can be formally defined as follows: given a matrix $A \in \mathbb{R}^{m \times n}$, one seeks a matrix $C \in \mathbb{R}^{m \times r}$ consisting of r columns of A such that

$$\left\|A - CC^{+}A\right\|_{\xi}$$

is minimized. While one could use any norm to measure the error $A - CC^{+}A$, the most common choices are $\xi = 2$ or $\xi = F$. Most of the early work on CSSP in the NLA literature focused on error bounds of the form

$$\left\|A - CC^{+}A\right\|_{\xi} \leq \alpha \left\|A - A_k\right\|_{\xi}$$

where A_k is the best rank k approximation to A. The objective was to make the multiplicative error factor α as small as possible. In this setting, the choice of r is critical, and almost all early work focused on $r = k$, namely the setting where *exactly* k columns of A are chosen in order to approximate the best rank-k approximation to the matrix. The first result in this domain goes back to Golub in the 1960s [37]. It was quickly followed by numerous papers in the NLA community studying algorithms and bounds for the CSSP, with a primary focus on the spectral norm ($\xi = 2$). Almost all the early papers analyzed deterministic, greedy approaches for the CSSP, including the landmark work by Gu and Eisenstat [41], which provided essentially optimal algorithms (in terms of α) for the spectral norm variant of the CSSP.

The work of [8,10] was the first attempt to design a randomized algorithm for both the spectral and the Frobenius norm version of the CSSP. The fundamental contribution of [8,10] was an early, simple version of the structural result of Equation 9.1, which allowed us to combine in a nontrivial way deterministic and randomized methods from the NLA and TCS communities for the CSSP. More specifically, Algorithm 9.1 (see also Section 9.4.2, where we will discuss this algorithm from a more applied perspective) is a two-phase approach that was proposed in order to identify k columns of A to be included in C: first, sample $O(k \log k)$ columns of A with respect to the leverage scores, a highly informative probability distribution over the columns of A that biases the sampling process toward important columns; second, using deterministic column subset selection algorithms, choose *exactly* k columns out of the $O(k \log k)$ columns sampled in the first phase. Deriving the error bounds for the proposed two-phase approach was done by bounding the second term of Equation 9.1 as follows: first, one bounds the relevant norm of $\left(A - YY^{T}A\right) Z$, where Y was equal to V_k and Z was a sampling matrix encoding both the randomized and the deterministic phase of the proposed algorithm; then, a lower bound on the smallest singular value of the matrix $Y^{+}Z$ was also proven. The latter bound was derived by properties of the leverage

Algorithm 9.1 A two-stage algorithm for the CSSP.

Input: $A \in \mathbb{R}^{m \times n}$, integer $k \ll \min\{m, n\}$.
Output: $C \in \mathbb{R}^{m \times k}$ with k columns of A.

1. **Randomized Stage:**
   - Let $V_k \in \mathbb{R}^{n \times k}$ be *any* orthogonal basis spanning the top-k right singular subspace of A.
   - Compute the sampling probabilities p_i for all $i = 1 \ldots n$:
   $$p_i = \frac{1}{k} \left\| \left(V_k^T\right)^{(i)} \right\|_2^2, \tag{9.5}$$
   where $\left(V_k^T\right)^{(i)}$ denotes the ith column of V_k^T as a column vector.
   - Randomly select and rescale $c = O(k \log k)$ columns of V_k^T according to these probabilities.
2. **Deterministic Stage:**
   - Let $\tilde{V}^T$ be the $k \times c$ non-orthogonal matrix consisting of the down-sampled and rescaled columns of V_k^T.
   - Run a deterministic QR algorithm on $\tilde{V}^T$ to select exactly k columns of $\tilde{V}^T$.
   - Return the corresponding columns of A.

score sampling as well as by properties of the deterministic column selection algorithm applied in the second phase. Submultiplicativity of unitarily invariant norms was finally used to conclude the proof. The work of [8,10] provided a major improvement on previous bounds for the Frobenius norm error of the CSSP, showing that the proposed randomized algorithm achieves $\alpha = O(k \log^{1/2} k)$ with constant probability. Prior work had exponential dependencies on k.

The above bound motivated Deshpande and Rademacher [20] to look at the CSSP using the so-called volume sampling approach. They designed and analyzed an approximation algorithm that guaranteed $\alpha = \sqrt{k+1}$ for the Frobenius norm, running in time $O(knm^3 \log m)$. This algorithm matched a lower bound for the CSSP presented in [21]. It is worth noting that [20] also presented faster versions of the above algorithm. The current state-of-the-art approach (in terms of speed) appeared in the work of [42], who presented a randomized algorithm that runs in $O\left(knm^2\right)$ time and guarantees $\alpha = \sqrt{k+1}$, with constant probability. Neither of these papers use the inequality that we discuss here. It would be interesting to understand how one could leverage structural results in order to prove the above bounds.

We now consider the relaxation of the CSSP, where r is allowed to be greater than k. In this framework, when $r = \Omega(k \log k/\epsilon)$, relative-error approximations, namely approximations where $\alpha = 1 + \epsilon$, are known. For example, [29,30] presented the first result that achieved such a bound, using random sampling of the columns of A according to the Euclidean norms of the rows of V_k, which are the leverage scores that we mentioned earlier in this chapter. More specifically, a $(1 + \epsilon)$-approximation was proven by setting

$r = \Omega\left(k\epsilon^{-2}\log\left(k\epsilon^{-1}\right)\right)$. Subsequently, [63] argued that the same technique gives a $(1+\epsilon)$-approximation using $r = \Omega\left(k\log k + k\epsilon^{-1}\right)$ columns, and this improved the running time by essentially computing approximations to the singular vectors of A. It is precisely in this context that the matrix Y of Equation 9.1 would be useful, since it would allow us to work with approximation to the singular vectors of A. While neither of these papers used the structural result of Equation 9.1 explicitly, they both implicitly had to follow similar derivations. As a matter of fact, Equation 9.1 could be a starting point for both papers [29,63] and with little additional work could result in constant factor approximations. However, in order to get relative error bounds, additional care and more technical details are necessary. A long line of work followed [29,63] showing alternative algorithms, often with improved running times, that achieve comparable relative error bounds [22,32,33,65].

A major open question on the CSSP was whether one could derive meaningful error bounds for values of r that are larger than k but smaller than $O(k\log k)$. Toward that end, the first major breakthrough allowing sampling of fewer than $O(k\log k)$ columns appeared in [6,7], where it was proven that by setting $r = 2k/\epsilon$ (up to lower order terms), one can achieve relative error approximations to the CSSP. Once more, structural inequalities along the lines of Equation 9.1 were at the forefront, combined with a novel column selection procedure invented by Batson et al. [3]. Using the structural inequality *per se* would only result in a constant factor approximation, but an additional adaptive sampling step guaranteed the required relative error approximation. Followup work by Guruswami and Sinop [42] presented algorithms based on volume sampling that set $r = k/\epsilon$ (up to lower order terms), thus exactly matching known lower bounds for the CSSP when $r > k$. The running time of all these algorithms is at least linear in the dimensions of the input matrix, but recent progress on subspace preserving embeddings that run in input sparsity time has removed this dependency. We refer the interested reader to [17,53,56] for RandNLA algorithms that run in input sparsity time, plus lower order terms.

9.4.2 CSSP: Data Analysis and Machine Learning

The CSSP algorithm of [10] has also been applied in several machine learning and data analysis applications; for example, see [9,11,12,46,59,60]. In this section, we informally describe our experiences when using such approaches in data analysis and machine learning tasks. Our objective here is to provide some insight as to what is going on *under the hood* with this method as well as provide some speculation to justify its success in applications.

Recall Algorithm 9.1, our two-stage hybrid algorithm for the CSSP [10], and note that both the original choice of columns in the first phase, and the application of the QR algorithm in the second phase involve the matrix V_k^T rather than the matrix A itself. In words, V_k^T is the matrix defining the relevant nonuniformity structure over the columns of A [30,50]. The analysis of this algorithm (a large part of which boiled down to the proof of Lemma 9.2) makes critical use of exact or approximate versions of the importance sampling probabilities given in Equation 9.5. These are a generalization of the concept of *statistical leverage scores*; see [49,50] as well as [14,15,66] for a detailed discussion. Here, we note informally that leverage scores capture a notion of *outlierness or* the extent to which data points are *spread out or* the *influence* of data points in low-rank and least-squares approximation problems.

Observe that the second stage of Algorithm 9.1 involves a QR computation. It is critical to the success of this algorithm to apply this QR procedure on the randomly sampled version of V_k^T, that is, the matrix defining the worst-case nonuniformity structure in A, rather than on A itself. We have also observed the importance of this empirically. To understand this, recall that an important aspect of different QR algorithms is how they make the so-called pivot rule decisions about which columns to keep [39]; recall also that such decisions can be tricky when the columns in the matrix that is input to the QR algorithm are not orthogonal or spread out in similarly *nice* ways (e.g., when it is the case that two columns are approximately, but not exactly, collinear). With this in mind, here are several empirical observations we have made that shed light on the inner workings of the CSSP algorithm and its usefulness in applications.

- Since the QR decomposition can be used to solve directly the CSSP, we investigated several alternative algorithms for the QR decomposition; we also compared each QR alternative to the CSSP using that version of QR in the second phase. An initial observation was that *off-the-shelf* implementations of alternative algorithms for the QR decomposition behave quite differently—for example, some versions such as the low-rank revealing QR algorithm of [13] tend to perform much better than other versions such as the qrxp algorithm of [4,5]. Although not surprising to NLA practitioners, this observation indicates that *off-the-shelf* implementations in large-scale data applications should be used carefully. A second, less obvious, observation is that preprocessing with the randomized first phase tends to improve worse-performing variants of QR more than better variants. Part of this is simply due to the fact that the worse-performing variants have more room to improve, but part of this is also due to the fact that more sophisticated versions of QR tend to make elaborate pivot rule decisions. This sophistication is relatively less important after the randomized phase has selected columns that are already spread out and biased toward the important or outlying directions.

- To understand better the role of randomness in the algorithm, we also investigated the effect of applying algorithms for the QR decomposition directly on V_k^T (without running the randomized phase first) and then keeping the corresponding columns of A. Interestingly, with this *preprocessing*, we tended to get better columns than if we ran QR decomposition algorithms directly on the original matrix A. Again, the interpretation seems to be that, since the norms of the columns of V_k^T define the relevant nonuniformity structure of A, working directly with those columns tends to avoid (even in traditional deterministic settings) situations where pivot rules fail to choose good columns.

- Of course, we also observed that randomization further improves the results, assuming that care is taken in choosing the rank parameter k and the sampling parameter c. In practice, the choice of k should be viewed as a *model selection* question. By choosing $c = k, 1.5k, 2k, \ldots$, we often observed a *sweet spot*, in a bias-variance sense, as a function of increasing c. That is, for a fixed k, the behavior of the deterministic QR algorithms improves by choosing somewhat more than k columns, but that improvement is degraded by choosing too many columns in the randomized phase.

9.4.3 Random Projections for Low-Rank Matrix Approximations

There has been massive interest recently in implementing random projection algorithms for use in scientific computing applications. One thing that has enabled this is that the structural condition identified in Lemma 9.2 makes it easier to parameterize RandNLA algorithms in terms more familiar to the NLA and scientific computing communities (and thus this was a very important step in the development of practically useful RandNLA methods for low-rank matrix approximation.) To see how this relates to our main technical result, consider the following basic random projection algorithm. Given a matrix $A \in \mathbb{R}^{m \times n}$ and a rank parameter:

- Construct an $n \times \ell$, with $\ell = O(k/\epsilon)$, structured random projection matrix Ω, for example, uniformly sample a few rows from a randomized Hadamard transform (see, e.g., [31] for a precise definition of the randomized Hadamard transform).
- Return $B = A\Omega$.

This algorithm, which amounts to choosing uniformly at random a small number ℓ of columns in a randomly rotated basis, was introduced in [63], where it is proven that

$$\|A - P_{B_k}A\|_F \leq (1+\epsilon)\|A - P_{U_k}A\|_F \tag{9.6}$$

where $P_{B_k}A$ is the projection of A onto the best rank-k approximation of B, holds with high probability. This bound, which is the random projection analog of the relative-error CUR matrix approximations of [30,50], provides a bound only on the reconstruction error of the top part of the spectrum of the input matrix. Additionally, it necessitates sampling a relatively large number of columns $\ell = O(k/\epsilon)$.

In many practical applications, for example, when providing high-quality numerical implementations, it is preferable to parameterize the problem in order to choose some number $\ell = k + p$ columns, where p is a modest additive oversampling factor, for example, p is equal to 10 or 20 or k. When attempting to be this aggressive at minimizing the size of the sample, the choice of the oversampling factor p is quite sensitive to the input. That is, whereas the bound of Equation 9.6 holds for any worst-case input, here the proper choice for the oversampling factor p could depend on the matrix dimensions, the decay properties of the spectrum, and the particular choice made for the random projection matrix [43,44,47,52,61,69].

To deal with these issues, the best numerical implementations of RandNLA algorithms for low-rank matrix approximation, and those that obtain the strongest results in terms of minimizing p, take advantage of Lemma 9.2 in a somewhat different way than was originally used in the analysis of the CSSP. For example, rather than choosing $O(k \log k)$ dimensions and then filtering them through *exactly* k dimensions, one can choose some number ℓ of dimensions and project onto a k'-dimensional subspace, where $k < k' \leq \ell$, while exploiting Lemma 9.2 to bound the error, as appropriate for the computational environment at hand [44].

Consider, for example, the following random projection algorithm. Given $A \in \mathbb{R}^{m \times n}$, a rank parameter k, and an oversampling factor p:

- Set $\ell = k + p$.
- Construct an $n \times \ell$ random projection matrix Ω, either with i.i.d. Gaussian entries or in the form of a structured random projection such as uniformly sampling a few rows from a randomized Hadamard transform.
- Return $B = A\Omega$.

Although this approach is quite similar to the algorithms of [58,63], algorithms parameterized in this form were first introduced in [47,52,69], where a suite of bounds of the form

$$\|A - Z\|_2 \lesssim 10\sqrt{\ell \min\{m,n\}}\,\|A - A_k\|_2$$

were shown to hold with high probability. Here, Z is a rank-k-or-greater matrix, easily constructed from B. Such results can be used to obtain the so-called *interpolative decomposition*, a variant of the basic CSSP with explicit numerical conditioning properties, and [47,52,69] also provided *a posteriori* error estimates that are useful in situations where one wants to choose the rank parameter k to be the numerical rank, as opposed to *a priori* specifying k as part of the input. Such *a priori* choices were more common in TCS algorithms for the same problem that predated the aforementioned approach.

Consider, in addition, how the following random projection algorithm addresses the issue that the decay properties of the spectrum can be important when it is of interest to aggressively minimize the oversampling parameter p. Given a matrix $A \in \mathbb{R}^{m \times n}$, a rank parameter k, an oversampling factor p, and an iteration parameter q:

- Set $\ell = k + p$.
- Construct an $n \times \ell$ random projection matrix Ω, either with i.i.d. Gaussian entries or in the form of a structured random projection such as uniformly sampling a few rows from a randomized Hadamard transform.
- Return $B = (AA^T)^q A\Omega$.

This algorithm, as well as a numerically stable variant of it, was introduced in [61], where it was shown that bounds of the form

$$\|A - Z\|_2 \lesssim \left(10\sqrt{\ell \min\{m, n\}}\right)^{1/(4q+2)} \|A - A_k\|_2$$

hold with high probability. Again, Z is a rank-k-or-greater matrix easily constructed from B; this bound should be compared with the bound of the previous algorithm. Basically, this random projection algorithm modifies the previous algorithm by coupling a form of the power iteration method within the random projection step and, in many cases, it leads to improved performance [44,61].

In their review, [44] used Lemma 9.2 to clarify and simplify these and other prior random projection methods. (Subsequent work, e.g., that of [40] which develops RandNLA algorithms within the subspace iteration framework, has continued to use Lemma 9.2 in somewhat different ways.) Lemma 9.2 was explicitly reproven (with squares in the norms) in [44], using a proof based on the perturbation theory of orthogonal projectors, thus providing an elegant alternative to the original proof of the inequality. Our inequality in Lemma 9.2 was an essential ingredient of their work, allowing the authors of [44] to bound the performance of their algorithms based on the relationship between the singular vectors corresponding to the large singular values of A and their counterparts corresponding to the small singular values of A. As the authors of [44] observe, "when a substantial proportion of the mass of A appears in the small singular values, the constructed basis may have low accuracy. Conversely, when the large singular values dominate, it is much easier to identify a good low-rank basis." Our main inequality, originally developed within the context of the CSSP, precisely quantifies this tradeoff in a strong sense, and it serves as a starting point and foundation for the RandNLA theory reviewed in [44].

9.4.4 Improved Results for Nyström-Based Machine Learning

Symmetric positive semi-definite (SPSD) matrices are of interest in many applications, in particular for the so-called kernel-based machine learning methods [64]. In many situations, matrices of interest are moderately well approximated by low-rank matrices, and in many of these cases, one is interested in the so-called Nyström-based low-rank matrix approximation [27,36,67]. These are low-rank matrix approximations that are expressed in terms of actual columns and rows, that is, they are essentially CSSP methods for SPSD matrices that preserve the SPSD property. A challenge here is that, while CSSP methods provide high-quality bounds for general matrices, it is difficult to preserve the SPSD property and thus extend these to provide high-quality SPSD low-rank approximation of SPSD matrices. Indeed, early work on Nyström methods was either heuristic [67] or provided rigorous but weak worst-case theory [27].

A qualitative improvement in this area occurred with Gittens and Mahoney [36], which used a result from Gittens [35] to preserve the SPSD property, while working with leverage-based column sampling and related random projection methods. A critical component of the analysis of [36] involved providing structural decompositions, which are variants of Lemma 9.2 for SPSD matrices for the spectral, Frobenius, and trace norms. Subsequent to this, Anderson et al. [1] introduced the so-called spectral gap error bound method to provide still finer results in a common case: when one performs a very modest amount of oversampling for input kernel matrices that *do not have* a large spectral gap, but that *do have* a spectrum that decays rapidly. The analysis of [1] used a result from Gu [40] that extended Lemma 9.2 by providing an analogous structural statement when one is interested in splitting the matrix into three parts: the top, middle, and bottom (rather than just top and bottom) parts of the spectrum. In each of these cases, increasingly finer results are derived for several related problems by exploiting structural properties having to do with the interaction of sampling/projection operators in the RandNLA algorithms with various parts of the vector space defined by the input matrix.

9.5 Conclusions

The interdisciplinary history of RandNLA has seen a gradual movement toward providing increasingly finer bounds for a range of low-rank (and other) matrix problems. In this chapter, we have highlighted, described, and extended a deterministic structural result underlying many state-of-the-art RandNLA algorithms for low-rank matrix approximation problems. A general theme in this development is that this is accomplished by using general algorithmic and statistical tools and specializing them to account for the fine-scale structure of the Euclidean vector space defined by the data matrix. For example, while a vanilla application of the Johnson–Lindenstrauss lemma, which is applicable to vectors in general metric spaces, leads to interesting results (e.g., additive-error bounds on the top part of the spectrum of the matrix being approximated), much stronger results (e.g., relative-error bounds, the CSSP results that first introduced the predecessor of Lemma 9.1, as well as the other results we have reviewed here) can be obtained by exploiting the vector space structure of the Euclidean spaces defined by the top and bottom parts of the spectrum of A.

A challenge in interdisciplinary research areas such as RandNLA is that algorithms solving seemingly different problems use similar structural results in various ways. At the same time, diverse research areas study those problems from many different perspectives. As a result, highlighting structural commonalities is rare and such structural results usually get *buried* deep inside the technical analysis of the proposed methods. Highlighting the central role of such structural results is important, especially as RandNLA methods are increasingly being applied to data analysis tasks in applications ranging from genetics [46, 59,60] to astronomy [73] and mass spectrometry imaging [72], and as RandNLA algorithms are increasingly being implemented in large-scale parallel and distributed computational environments [54,55,70,71].

Acknowledgments

MWM acknowledges the Army Research Office, the Defense Advanced Research Projects Agency XDATA and GRAPHS programs, and the Department of Energy for providing partial support for this work. PD acknowledges the National Science Foundation for providing partial support for this work via IIS-1319280, CCF-1016501, and DMS-1008983.

References

1. D. G. Anderson, S. S. Du, M. W. Mahoney, C. Melgaard, K. Wu, and M. Gu. Spectral gap error bounds for improving CUR matrix decomposition and the Nyström method. In *Proceedings of the 18th International Workshop on Artificial Intelligence and Statistics*, pp. 19–27, 2015.

2. H. Avron, P. Maymounkov, and S. Toledo. Blendenpik: Supercharging LAPACK's least-squares solver. *SIAM Journal on Scientific Computing*, 32:1217–1236, 2010.

3. J. D. Batson, D. A. Spielman, and N. Srivastava. Twice-Ramanujan sparsifiers. In *Proceedings of the 41st Annual ACM Symposium on Theory of Computing*, pp. 255–262, 2009.

4. C. H. Bischof and G. Quintana-Ortí. Algorithm 782: Codes for rank-revealing QR factorizations of dense matrices. *ACM Transactions on Mathematical Software*, 24(2):254–257, 1998.

5. C. H. Bischof and G. Quintana-Ortí. Computing rank-revealing QR factorizations of dense matrices. *ACM Transactions on Mathematical Software*, 24(2):226–253, 1998.

6. C. Boutsidis, P. Drineas, and M. Magdon-Ismail. Near-optimal column-based matrix reconstruction. In *Proceedings of the 52nd Annual IEEE Symposium on Foundations of Computer Science*, pp. 305–314, 2011.

7. C. Boutsidis, P. Drineas, and M. Magdon-Ismail. Near-optimal column-based matrix reconstruction. *SIAM Journal on Computing*, 43(2):687–717, 2014.

8. C. Boutsidis, M. W. Mahoney, and P. Drineas. An improved approximation algorithm for the column subset selection problem. Technical report. Preprint: arXiv:0812.4293, 2008.

9. C. Boutsidis, M. W. Mahoney, and P. Drineas. Unsupervised feature selection for principal components analysis. In *Proceedings of the 14th Annual ACM SIGKDD Conference*, pp. 61–69, 2008.

10. C. Boutsidis, M. W. Mahoney, and P. Drineas. An improved approximation algorithm for the column subset selection problem. In *Proceedings of the 20th Annual ACM-SIAM Symposium on Discrete Algorithms*, pp. 968–977, 2009.

11. C. Boutsidis, M. W. Mahoney, and P. Drineas. Unsupervised feature selection for the *k*-means clustering problem. In *Annual Advances in Neural Information Processing Systems 22: Proceedings of the 2009 Conference*, 2009.

12. C. Boutsidis, A. Zouzias, M. W. Mahoney, and P. Drineas. Randomized dimensionality reduction for k-means clustering. *IEEE Transactions on Information Theory*, 61(2):1045–1062, 2015.

13. T. F. Chan and P.C. Hansen. Low-rank revealing QR factorizations. *Numerical Linear Algebra with Applications*, 1:33–44, 1994.

14. S. Chatterjee and A. S. Hadi. Influential observations, high leverage points, and outliers in linear regression. *Statistical Science*, 1(3):379–393, 1986.

15. S. Chatterjee and A. S. Hadi. *Sensitivity Analysis in Linear Regression*. John Wiley & Sons, New York, 1988.

16. K. L. Clarkson, P. Drineas, M. Magdon-Ismail, M. W. Mahoney, X. Meng, and D. P. Woodruff. The fast Cauchy transform and faster robust linear regression. In *Proceedings of the 24th Annual ACM-SIAM Symposium on Discrete Algorithms*, pp. 466–477, 2013.

17. K. L. Clarkson and D. P. Woodruff. Low rank approximation and regression in input sparsity time. In *Proceedings of the 45th Annual ACM Symposium on Theory of Computing*, pp. 81–90, 2013.

18. E. S. Coakley, V. Rokhlin, and M. Tygert. A fast randomized algorithm for orthogonal projection. *SIAM Journal on Scientific Computing*, 33(2):849–868, 2011.

19. National Research Council. *Frontiers in Massive Data Analysis*. National Academies Press, Washington, DC, 2013.

20. A. Deshpande and L. Rademacher. Efficient volume sampling for row/column subset selection. In *Proceedings of the 51st Annual IEEE Symposium on Foundations of Computer Science*, pp. 329–338, 2010.

21. A. Deshpande, L. Rademacher, S. Vempala, and G. Wang. Matrix approximation and projective clustering via volume sampling. In *Proceedings of the 17th Annual ACM-SIAM Symposium on Discrete Algorithms*, pp. 1117–1126, 2006.

22. A. Deshpande and S. Vempala. Adaptive sampling and fast low-rank matrix approximation. In *Proceedings of the 10th International Workshop on Randomization and Computation*, pp. 292–303, 2006.

23. P. Drineas, R. Kannan, and M. W. Mahoney. Fast Monte Carlo algorithms for matrices I: Approximating matrix multiplication. *SIAM Journal on Computing*, 36:132–157, 2006.

24. P. Drineas, R. Kannan, and M. W. Mahoney. Fast Monte Carlo algorithms for matrices II: Computing a low-rank approximation to a matrix. *SIAM Journal on Computing*, 36:158–183, 2006.

25. P. Drineas, R. Kannan, and M. W. Mahoney. Fast Monte Carlo algorithms for matrices III: Computing a compressed approximate matrix decomposition. *SIAM Journal on Computing*, 36:184–206, 2006.

26. P. Drineas, M. Magdon-Ismail, M. W. Mahoney, and D. P. Woodruff. Fast approximation of matrix coherence and statistical leverage. *Journal of Machine Learning Research*, 13:3475–3506, 2012.

27. P. Drineas and M. W. Mahoney. On the Nyström method for approximating a Gram matrix for improved kernel-based learning. *Journal of Machine Learning Research*, 6:2153–2175, 2005.

28. P. Drineas, M. W. Mahoney, and S. Muthukrishnan. Sampling algorithms for ℓ_2 regression and applications. In *Proceedings of the 17th Annual ACM-SIAM Symposium on Discrete Algorithms*, pp. 1127–1136, 2006.

29. P. Drineas, M. W. Mahoney, and S. Muthukrishnan. Subspace sampling and relative-error matrix approximation: Column-based methods. In *Proceedings of the 10th International Workshop on Randomization and Computation*, pp. 316–326, 2006.

30. P. Drineas, M. W. Mahoney, and S. Muthukrishnan. Relative-error CUR matrix decompositions. *SIAM Journal on Matrix Analysis and Applications*, 30:844–881, 2008.

31. P. Drineas, M. W. Mahoney, S. Muthukrishnan, and T. Sarlós. Faster least squares approximation. *Numerische Mathematik*, 117(2):219–249, 2010.

32. D. Feldman and M. Langberg. A unified framework for approximating and clustering data. In *Proceedings of the 43rd Annual ACM Symposium on Theory of Computing*, pp. 569–578, 2011.

33. D. Feldman, M. Monemizadeh, C. Sohler, and D. P. Woodruff. Coresets and sketches for high dimensional subspace approximation problems. In *Proceedings of the 21st Annual ACM-SIAM Symposium on Discrete Algorithms*, pp. 630–649, 2010.

34. A. Frieze, R. Kannan, and S. Vempala. Fast Monte-Carlo algorithms for finding low-rank approximations. In *Proceedings of the 39th Annual IEEE Symposium on Foundations of Computer Science*, pp. 370–378, 1998.

35. A. Gittens. The spectral norm error of the naive Nyström extension. Technical report. Preprint: arXiv:1110.5305, 2011.

36. A. Gittens and M. W. Mahoney. Revisiting the Nyström method for improved large-scale machine learning. Technical report. Preprint: arXiv:1303.1849, 2013.

37. G. H. Golub. Numerical methods for solving linear least squares problems. *Numerische Mathematik*, 7:206–216, 1965.

38. G. H. Golub and C. F. Van Loan. *Matrix Computations.* Johns Hopkins University Press, Baltimore, MD, 1989.

39. G. H. Golub and C. F. Van Loan. *Matrix Computations.* Johns Hopkins University Press, Baltimore, MD, 1996.

40. M. Gu. Subspace iteration randomization and singular value problems. Technical report. Preprint: arXiv:1408.2208, 2014.

41. M. Gu and S. C. Eisenstat. Efficient algorithms for computing a strong rank-revealing QR factorization. *SIAM Journal on Scientific Computing*, 17:848–869, 1996.

42. V. Guruswami and A. K. Sinop. Optimal column-based low-rank matrix reconstruction. In *Proceedings of the 23rd Annual ACM-SIAM Symposium on Discrete Algorithms*, pp. 1207–1214, 2012.

43. N. Halko, P.-G. Martinsson, Y. Shkolnisky, and M. Tygert. An algorithm for the principal component analysis of large data sets. Technical report. Preprint: arXiv:1007.5510, 2010.

44. N. Halko, P.-G. Martinsson, and J. A. Tropp. Finding structure with randomness: Probabilistic algorithms for constructing approximate matrix decompositions. *SIAM Review*, 53(2):217–288, 2011.

45. R.A. Horn and C.R. Johnson. *Matrix Analysis.* Cambridge University Press, New York, 1985.

46. A. Javed, P. Drineas, M. W. Mahoney, and P. Paschou. Efficient genomewide selection of PCA-correlated tSNPs for genotype imputation. *Annals of Human Genetics*, 75(6): 707–722, 2011.

47. E. Liberty, F. Woolfe, P.-G. Martinsson, V. Rokhlin, and M. Tygert. Randomized algorithms for the low-rank approximation of matrices. *Proceedings of the National Academy of Sciences of the United States of America*, 104(51):20167–20172, 2007.

48. P. Ma, M. W. Mahoney, and B. Yu. A statistical perspective on algorithmic leveraging. *Journal of Machine Learning Research*, 32(1):91–99, 2014.

49. M. W. Mahoney. Randomized algorithms for matrices and data. In *Foundations and Trends in Machine Learning*. NOW Publishers, Boston, MA, 2011.

50. M. W. Mahoney and P. Drineas. CUR matrix decompositions for improved data analysis. *Proceedings of the National Academy of Sciences of the United States of America*, 106:697–702, 2009.

51. J. Manyika, M. Chui, B. Brown, J. Bughin, R. Dobbs, C. Roxburgh, and A. H. Byers. Big data: The next frontier for innovation, competition, and productivity. Technical report, McKinsey Global Institute, 2011.

52. P.-G. Martinsson, V. Rokhlin, and M. Tygert. A randomized algorithm for the decomposition of matrices. *Applied and Computational Harmonic Analysis*, 30:47–68, 2011.

53. X. Meng and M. W. Mahoney. Low-distortion subspace embeddings in input-sparsity time and applications to robust linear regression. In *Proceedings of the 45th Annual ACM Symposium on Theory of Computing*, pp. 91–100, 2013.

54. X. Meng and M. W. Mahoney. Robust regression on MapReduce. In *Proceedings of the 30th International Conference on Machine Learning*, 2013.

55. X. Meng, M. A. Saunders, and M. W. Mahoney. LSRN: A parallel iterative solver for strongly over- or under-determined systems. *SIAM Journal on Scientific Computing*, 36(2):C95–C118, 2014.

56. J. Nelson and N. L. Huy. OSNAP: Faster numerical linear algebra algorithms via sparser subspace embeddings. In *Proceedings of the 54th Annual IEEE Symposium on Foundations of Computer Science*, pp. 117–126, 2013.

57. C. H. Papadimitriou, P. Raghavan, H. Tamaki, and S. Vempala. Latent semantic indexing: A probabilistic analysis. In *Proceedings of the 17th ACM Symposium on Principles of Database Systems*, pp. 159–168, 1998.

58. C. H. Papadimitriou, P. Raghavan, H. Tamaki, and S. Vempala. Latent semantic indexing: A probabilistic analysis. *Journal of Computer and System Sciences*, 61(2): 217–235, 2000.

59. P. Paschou, J. Lewis, A. Javed, and P. Drineas. Ancestry informative markers for fine-scale individual assignment to worldwide populations. *Journal of Medical Genetics*, doi:10.1136/jmg.2010.078212, 2010.

60. P. Paschou, E. Ziv, E. G. Burchard, S. Choudhry, W. Rodriguez-Cintron, M. W. Mahoney, and P. Drineas. PCA-correlated SNPs for structure identification in worldwide human populations. *PLoS Genetics*, 3:1672–1686, 2007.

61. V. Rokhlin, A. Szlam, and M. Tygert. A randomized algorithm for principal component analysis. *SIAM Journal on Matrix Analysis and Applications*, 31(3):1100–1124, 2009.

62. V. Rokhlin and M. Tygert. A fast randomized algorithm for overdetermined linear least-squares regression. *Proceedings of the National Academy of Sciences of the United States of America*, 105(36):13212–13217, 2008.

63. T. Sarlós. Improved approximation algorithms for large matrices via random projections. In *Proceedings of the 47th Annual IEEE Symposium on Foundations of Computer Science*, pp. 143–152, 2006.

64. B. Schölkopf and A. J. Smola. *Learning with Kernels: Support Vector Machines, Regularization, Optimization, and Beyond.* MIT Press, Cambridge, MA, 2001.

65. N. D. Shyamalkumar and K. Varadarajan. Efficient subspace approximation algorithms. In *Proceedings of the 18th Annual ACM-SIAM Symposium on Discrete Algorithms*, pp. 532–540, 2007.

66. P. F. Velleman and R. E. Welsch. Efficient computing of regression diagnostics. *The American Statistician*, 35(4):234–242, 1981.

67. C. K. I. Williams and M. Seeger. Using the Nyström method to speed up kernel machines. In *Annual Advances in Neural Information Processing Systems 13: Proceedings of the 2000 Conference*, pp. 682–688, 2001.

68. D. P. Woodruff. Sketching as a tool for numerical linear algebra. In *Foundations and Trends in Theoretical Computer Science.* NOW Publishers, Boston, MA, 2014.

69. F. Woolfe, E. Liberty, V. Rokhlin, and M. Tygert. A fast randomized algorithm for the approximation of matrices. *Applied and Computational Harmonic Analysis*, 25(3): 335–366, 2008.

70. J. Yang, X. Meng, and M. W. Mahoney. Quantile regression for large-scale applications. *SIAM Journal on Scientific Computing*, 36:S78–S110, 2014.

71. J. Yang, X. Meng, and M. W. Mahoney. Implementing randomized matrix algorithms in parallel and distributed environments. Technical report. Preprint: arXiv:1502.03032, 2015.

72. J. Yang, O. Rubel, Prabhat, M. W. Mahoney, and B. P. Bowen. Identifying important ions and positions in mass spectrometry imaging data using CUR matrix decompositions. *Analytical Chemistry*, 87(9):4658–4666, 2015.

73. C.-W. Yip, M. W. Mahoney, A. S. Szalay, I. Csabai, T. Budavari, R. F. G. Wyse, and L. Dobos. Objective identification of informative wavelength regions in galaxy spectra. *The Astronomical Journal*, 147(110):15, 2014.

10

Something for (Almost) Nothing: New Advances in Sublinear-Time Algorithms

Ronitt Rubinfeld and Eric Blais

CONTENTS

10.1 Introduction 155
10.1.1 Clustering: An Illustrative Example 156
10.2 Testing Properties of Point Sets 157
10.2.1 Clustering 157
10.2.2 Surface Area 158
10.3 Testing Properties of Graphs 159
10.3.1 Diameter 159
10.3.2 Vertex Cover 160
10.4 Testing Properties of Functions 160
10.4.1 Feature Selection 161
10.4.2 Model Selection 161
10.4.3 Data Quality 162
10.4.3.1 Lipschitz Property 162
10.4.3.2 Monotonicity 163
10.4.4 Alternative Query and Sampling Models 163
10.5 Other Topics 164
References 164

10.1 Introduction

What computational problems can we solve when we only have time to look at a tiny fraction of the data? This general question has been studied from many different angles in statistics. More recently, with the recent proliferation of massive datasets, it has also become a central question in computer science as well. Essentially, all of the research on this question starts with a simple observation: Except for a very small number of special cases, the only problems that can be solved in this very restrictive setting are those that admit *approximate* solutions.

In this chapter, we focus on a formalization of approximate solutions that has been widely studied in an area of theoretical computer science known as *property testing.* Let X denote the underlying dataset, and consider the setting where this dataset represents a combinatorial object. Let P be any property of this type of combinatorial object. We say that X is ϵ-*close* to having property P if we can modify at most an ϵ fraction of X to obtain the description X' of an object that does have property P; otherwise, we say that X

is ϵ-*far* from having the property. A randomized algorithm A is an ϵ-*tester* for P if it can distinguish with large constant probability* between datasets that represent objects with the property P from those that are ϵ-far from having the same property. (The algorithm A is free to output anything on inputs that do not have the property P but are also not ϵ-far from having this property; it is this leeway that will enable property testers to be so efficient.)

There is a close connection between property testing and the general parameter estimation. Let X be a dataset and $\theta = \theta(X)$ be any parameter of this dataset. For every threshold t, we can define the property of having $\theta \leq t$. If we have an efficient algorithm for testing this property, we can also use it to efficiently obtain an estimate $\widehat{\theta}$ that is close to θ in the sense that $\widehat{\theta} \leq \theta$ and the underlying object X is ϵ-close to another dataset X' with $\theta(X') = \widehat{\theta}$. Note that this notion of closeness is very different from the notions usually considered in parameter estimation; instead of determining it as a function $L(\theta, \widehat{\theta})$ of the true and estimated values of the parameter itself, here the quality of the estimate is a function of the underlying dataset.

10.1.1 Clustering: An Illustrative Example

Let X be a set of n points in $\mathbb{R}^d$. A fundamental question is how well the points in X can be clustered. This question can be formalized as follows. Let $r > 0$ be a fixed radius, and let θ_r be the minimum number of clusters of radius r that are required to capture all the points in X. The problem of determining θ_r exactly is NP-hard, as is the problem of estimating its value up to any constant factor [20,23,40]. But Alon et al. [1] show that the closely related problem of distinguishing datasets that can be clustered into at most k clusters of radius r from those that are far from having this property can be solved in time that is *independent* of the number of points in X.†

Theorem 10.1 [1] *There is an algorithm that examines at most $\widetilde{O}(\frac{k \cdot d}{\epsilon})$ points in X and with large probability (i) accepts if the points in X can be grouped into at most k clusters of radius r and (ii) rejects if no subset of $(1 - \epsilon)n$ points in X can be grouped into k clusters.*

The testing algorithm for clustering can be used to obtain an efficient estimator of the clustering parameter θ_r in the following sense.

Corollary 10.1. *There is an algorithm that examines at most $\widetilde{O}((\theta_r \cdot d)/\epsilon)$ points in X and returns a value $\widehat{\theta}_r$ such that with large probability $\widehat{\theta}_r \leq \theta_r$ and all but at most ϵn points in X can be partitioned into $\widehat{\theta}_r$ clusters of radius r.*

We reiterate that, unlike in the standard parameter estimation setting, we have no guarantee on the closeness of θ_r and the estimate $\widehat{\theta}_r$ returned by the algorithm. Instead, we are guaranteed that *most* of the points can be clustered in $\widehat{\theta}_r$ clusters. This notion of approximation has a number of advantages.

---

*That is, with probability $1 - \delta$ for some fixed constant $\delta < (1/2)$. With standard techniques, the success probability of a tester can easily be boosted to any arbitrary amount, so throughout this chapter, we will simply fix δ to be a small enough constant, say, $\delta = (1/3)$ and write *with large constant probability* to mean with probability $1 - \delta$.

†Here and throughout the rest of the chapter, running times are in the model where samples or queries to X are completed in a constant amount of time. We will also use the tilde notation $\widetilde{O}(m)$ to hide polylog factors in m for clarity of presentation.

First, it is robust to noise. Adding a small number of outlier points can have a significant impact on the clustering parameter θ_r of a dataset. However, since the algorithm only examines a constant number of points, with high probability, it does not observe any of the outliers and so these noisy points do not affect the estimator. Furthermore, many of the property testing algorithms can be made robust to higher noise rates, so that even if outliers are observed, they do not affect the result by much. Similarly, the algorithm is appropriate when the underlying dataset is constantly changing; the same robustness means that the estimate changes smoothly as points are added and removed from the dataset.

A second advantage is that it leads to *extremely* efficient algorithms. The algorithms are so efficient that they can be used as a preprocessing step, even in situations where more accurate estimates of the clustering parameter are required. This is the case, for example, in settings where we are interested in learning how well the data can be clustered; here, the testing algorithm can be used in a preprocessing step to quickly identify point sets that are not even close to being clusterable into a reasonable number of clusters. In the case that the preprocessing algorithm identifies such a point set, alternative learning algorithms can be applied to those datasets instead.

The study of property testing was initiated in [6,26,55] and has been extremely active ever since. In the rest of this chapter, we highlight some of the properties of point sets, graphs, and functions that can be tested efficiently. Our goal is simply to provide a glimpse of the results that can be obtained with the tools that have been developed in this research area. More detailed discussions on these topics can be found in many other more comprehensive surveys [12,24,34,50–54].

10.2 Testing Properties of Point Sets

A common machine learning problem involves extracting structural information from a set X of points. As we have already seen in the introduction, sublinear-time algorithms can be used to efficiently perform preprocessing tasks for these problems. In fact, these algorithms have been shown to be useful in testing properties of both finite sets of points and (implicit representations of) infinite sets of points. To illustrate the former, we revisit the clustering problem in a bit more detail; for the latter, we show how sublinear-time algorithms can be used to estimate the surface area of continuous sets.

10.2.1 Clustering

Let us return to the problem of clustering points. To illustrate the variety of formalizations of this problem that are efficiently testable, let us now consider the setting where X is a set of points in a general metric space and we bound the *diameter* of the clusters (i.e., the maximum distance between any two points in the cluster) by some parameter d.

We can test if X can be clustered into at most k clusters of diameter d very efficiently in the following way.

Theorem 10.2 [1] *Let X be a set of points in a metric space. There is an algorithm that queries $O((k \log k)/\epsilon)$ points in X and with large constant probability (i) accepts if X can be clustered into k clusters of diameter d and (ii) rejects if we cannot cluster the points into k clusters of diameter $2d$ even if we remove an ϵ fraction of the points in X.*

The algorithm that achieves the bound in Theorem 10.1 maintains a set of cluster centers by repeatedly picking a sample point that is not covered by previously chosen cluster centers. If more than k cluster centers are chosen by this process, then the algorithm rejects, otherwise it accepts. The work of [1] shows that this simple algorithm satisfies the theorem's requirements. Note that if the point set cannot be clustered into k clusters of diameter d, but can be clustered into k clusters of diameter $2d$ if less than ϵ fraction of the points are thrown out, then it is OK for the algorithm to either accept or reject.

In many situations, we might know that the points are not clusterable into k clusters, but would still like to know if a very large fraction of the points can be clustered into k clusters. Note that our standard definition of property testers is of no use in this *tolerant* version of the clustering problem. The tolerant problem is in general more difficult, but several tolerant clustering problems can also be solved with sublinear-time algorithms [12,48]. For example, there is a tolerant analog of Theorem 10.2.

Theorem 10.3 [48] *Given* $0 < \epsilon_1 < \epsilon_2 < 1$. *Let* X *be a set of points in a metric space. There is an algorithm that queries at most* $\tilde{O}(k/(\epsilon_2 - \epsilon_1)^2)$ *points in* X, *and with large constant probability (i) accepts if at least* $(1 - \epsilon_1)$ *fraction of* X *can be clustered into k clusters of diameter d, and (ii) rejects if we cannot cluster more than* $(1 - \epsilon_2)$ *fraction of the points into* k *clusters of diameter* $2d$.

For more variants of the clustering problem considered in the property testing framework, see, for example, [1,11,12,41,48].

10.2.2 Surface Area

The property testing framework can also be applied to settings where the dataset represents a subset of a continuous space. Let $S \subseteq [0,1]^n$ be a subset of the unit n-dimensional hypercube, and consider any representation X of this subset for which algorithms can query an input $x \in [0,1]^n$ and observe whether $x \in S$ or not.

A fundamental parameter of the set S is its *surface area*, defined by $\mathrm{surf}(S) = \lim_{\delta \to 0} \left|\partial S^{(\delta/2)}\right| / \delta$, where $\partial S^{(\delta/2)} \subseteq [0,1]^n$ is the set of points at distance at most $\delta/2$ from the boundary of S. In the one-dimensional case, $S \subseteq [0,1]$ is a union of intervals and $\mathrm{surf}(S)$ corresponds to the number of disjoint intervals in S. And when $n = 2$, $\mathrm{surf}(S)$ corresponds to the perimeter of the set S.

Since the surface area of a set S can always be increased by an arbitrary amount while modifying S itself on a set of measure 0, it is impossible to estimate the surface area of S within any additive or multiplicative factor with any finite (or even countable) number of queries. We can, however, test whether S has small surface area with a small number of queries.

Theorem 10.4 [42] *Fix any* $0 < \alpha < 1$. *There is an algorithm that queries at most* $O(1/\epsilon)$ *points and with large probability (i) accepts* S *when it has surface area at most* α, *and (ii) rejects* S *when every set* S' *that differs from* S *on at most an* ϵ *measure has surface area* $\mathrm{surf}(S') > \alpha$.

Neeman's theorem [42] was obtained by improving the original analysis of an algorithm due to Kothari et al. [32], who were in turn building on previous work of Kearns and Ron [31] and Balcan et al. [3]. The algorithm itself works in a way that is conceptually similar to Buffon's classic needle problem: It drops a (virtual) needle onto the space $[0,1]^n$ and queries the two endpoints of the needles. If exactly one of those endpoints is in S, then we know that the needle crossed the boundary of S. Computing the probability of this event gives us a measure of the noise sensitivity of S, and connections between the surface area and noise sensitivity then lead to the proof of correctness of the algorithm.

10.3 Testing Properties of Graphs

The setting in which the underlying dataset X represents a graph G is particularly well suited for the design of sublinear-time algorithms. In this section, we explore two problems—a connectivity problem and an optimization problem—to illustrate what sublinear-time algorithms can do.

10.3.1 Diameter

The famous *small world* theory states that in any social group, every two members of the group are connected to each other via a short chain of acquaintances [13]. In particular, the *six degrees of separation* theory posits that everyone on Earth is connected by a chain of acquaintances of length at most 6. (See [16] for an introduction to these and many other interesting topics on graphs.) How efficiently can we test the small world theory on a given social network?

The study of the small world theory can be formalized in terms of the diameter of graphs. Let G be a graph where each person in the social group corresponds to a vertex, and an edge is placed between vertices that correspond to people that know each other. The *diameter* of G is the maximum distance between any two vertices in the graph. We can test whether the small world theory holds for the social group represented by G by testing whether the diameter of this graph is small. Parnas and Ron have shown that we can perform this task in the property testing framework with a number of queries that is *independent* of the size of the graph.

Theorem 10.5 [46] *Let G be a graph with maximum degree d. There is an algorithm that queries $\tilde{O}(\epsilon^{-3})$ edges in G and with large probability (1) accepts if G has diameter at most D and (2) rejects if every subgraph G' obtained by removing at most an ϵ fraction of the vertices in G has diameter greater than $2D$.*

This result should look at least a little surprising at first glance: With a number of queries that is sublinear in n, we cannot even determine the distance between any two fixed vertices v, w in G. Therefore, any algorithm for testing the diameter of a graph must instead test G for some other global property that distinguishes graphs with diameter D from those that are far from having diameter $2D$. That is what the algorithm in [46] does. Specifically, the algorithm estimates the *expansion* of G by sampling several start vertices, performing $O(1/\epsilon)$ steps of a breadth-first search from each of these vertices, and estimating the size of the neighborhoods around the vertices that have been sampled.

The algorithm for testing small-diameter graphs can also be used to estimate the diameter θ_{diam} of a graph G.

Corollary 10.2. *Let G be a graph with n vertices and maximum degree d. For every $\gamma > 1$, there is an algorithm that queries at most $\tilde{O}(\epsilon^{-3} \log_\gamma \theta_{\text{diam}})$ edges of G and outputs an estimate $\widehat{\theta}_{\text{diam}}$ such that with large probability $\widehat{\theta}_{\text{diam}} \leq \theta_{\text{diam}}$ and every subgraph G' with at least $(1-\epsilon)n$ nodes has diameter at least $\widehat{\theta}_{\text{diam}}/2\gamma$.*

Sublinear-time algorithms for several variants of the diameter task, including tolerant versions, have been considered in [7,46].

10.3.2 Vertex Cover

A *vertex cover* of the graph $G = (V, E)$ is a subset $V' \subseteq V$ such that every edge in E is adjacent to some vertex in V'. Let $\theta_{VC} = \theta_{VC}(G)$ denote the size of the minimum vertex cover of G. While the vertex cover problem is NP-complete [30], there is a linear-time algorithm that always outputs an estimate $\widehat{\theta}_{VC}$ that is at most twice as large as the true value of the minimum vertex cover of G. (This algorithm was independently discovered by Gavril and Yannakakis. See, e.g., [45] for the details.)

When the input graph G has maximum degree at most d, Parnas and Ron [47] have shown that there is an algorithm that can approximate θ_{VC} even more efficiently. Specifically, for every $\epsilon > 0$, there is an algorithm that returns an estimate $\widehat{\theta}_{VC}$ that satisfies $\theta_{VC} \leq \widehat{\theta}_{VC} \leq 2\theta_{VC} + \epsilon|V|$ and that runs in time that depends only on d and ϵ, but *not* on the size of the graph G. This result has since been sharpened, yielding the following testing algorithm.

Theorem 10.6 [44] *There is an $\tilde{O}(d) \cdot \mathrm{poly}(1/\epsilon)$ time algorithm which on input a graph $G = (V, E)$ of average degree d and a parameter ϵ, outputs an estimate $\widehat{\theta}_{VC}$ which with large constant probability satisfies $\theta_{VC} \leq \widehat{\theta}_{VC} \leq 2\theta_{VC} + \epsilon|V|$.*

The original vertex cover estimator of Parnas and Ron [47] was obtained by establishing and exploiting a fundamental connection between distributed computation and sublinear-time algorithms: If there is a k-round distributed computation for a graph problem where the degree of the input graph is bounded by d, then—since the output of a particular node can depend only on nodes that are within a radius of at most k—the distributed computation can be simulated in sequential time $d^{O(k)}$. This connection has since become an important and widely used source of techniques in the design of sublinear-time algorithms. In recent years, distributed computation has made great strides in finding *local distributed algorithms*, which are algorithms that run in $O(1)$ rounds [33]. Such algorithms have been found for approximate vertex cover, approximate matching, approximated packing, and covering problems [18,19,36,47]. All of these algorithms can be turned into sublinear-time algorithms, which estimate the corresponding parameter of the input graph.

The later improvements that led to Theorem 10.6 were obtained by a different technique introduced by Nguyen and Onak [43]. They showed that greedy algorithms can be simulated in a local fashion. This connection has also proven to be very influential in the design of sublinear-time algorithms, leading to the design of algorithms for the approximate vertex cover, approximate matching, approximate set cover, and approximated packing and covering problems [28,36–38,43,44,49,56].

10.4 Testing Properties of Functions

The last setting we consider is the one where the dataset represents a function $f : \mathcal{X}_1 \times \cdots \times \mathcal{X}_n \to \mathcal{Y}$ mapping n features to some value in a (finite or infinite) set $\mathcal{Y}$. (We will be particularly interested in the situation where $\mathcal{X}_1 = \cdots = \mathcal{X}_n = \mathcal{Y} = \{0, 1\}$, in which case $f : \{0, 1\}^n \to \{0, 1\}$ is a Boolean function.) A common task in this scenario is the (supervised) machine learning problem, where f is a target function, and the learning algorithm attempts to identify a hypothesis function h that is close to f while observing the value of $f(x_1, \ldots, x_n)$ (i.e., the label of the example $(x_1, \ldots, x_n)$) on as few inputs as possible. In the following subsections, we examine some sublinear-time algorithms that prove to be particularly useful for this general problem.

10.4.1 Feature Selection

One of the preliminary tasks when learning functions over rich feature sets is to identify the set of features that are relevant. A corresponding parameter estimation task is to determine the number of relevant features for a given target function. This task has been formalized in the property testing framework as the *junta testing* problem.

The function $f : \{0,1\}^n \to \{0,1\}$ is a k-junta if there is a set $J \subseteq [n]$ of at most k coordinates such that the value of $f(x)$ is completely determined by the values $\{x_i\}_{i \in J}$. The coordinates in the minimal set J that satisfies this condition are called *relevant* to f; the remaining coordinates are *irrelevant.* Fischer et al. [21] showed that we can test whether f is a k-junta with algorithms that have a running time that is *independent* of the total number n of coordinates. This result was further sharpened in [4,5], yielding the following result.

Theorem 10.7 [5] *There is an algorithm that queries the value of $f : \{0,1\}^n \to \{0,1\}$ on $\tilde{O}(k/\epsilon)$ inputs and with large constant probability (i) accepts when f is a k-junta, and (ii) rejects when f is ϵ-far from k-juntas.*

With the same reduction that we have already seen with the parameter estimation tasks for point sets and graphs, we can use the junta testing algorithm to obtain a good estimate of the number θ_{junta} of relevant features for a given function.

Corollary 10.3. *There is an algorithm that queries the value of $f : \{0,1\}^n \to \{0,1\}$ on $\tilde{O}(\theta_{\text{junta}}/\epsilon)$ inputs and returns an estimate $\widehat{\theta}_{\text{junta}}$ such that with large probability $\widehat{\theta}_{\text{junta}} \leq \theta_{\text{junta}}$ and f is ϵ-close to being a $\widehat{\theta}_{\text{junta}}$-junta.*

The same result also applies to the much more general setting where $f : \mathcal{X}_1 \times \cdots \times \mathcal{X}_n \to \mathcal{Y}$ is a function mapping n-tuples where each attribute comes from any finite set and where $\mathcal{Y}$ is an arbitrary range. See [5] for details.

10.4.2 Model Selection

Another ubiquitous preliminary task in machine learning is determining which is the right learning algorithm to use for a given target function. This problem is known as *model selection.* The model selection task is often completed by using domain-specific knowledge (e.g., by using algorithms that have successfully learned similar functions in the past), but sublinear-time algorithms can also provide useful tools for this task when such knowledge is not available.

Consider, for example, the algorithms for learning decision tree representations of Boolean functions. A decision tree is a full binary tree with indices in $[n]$ associated with each internal node, the labels $0, 1$ associated with the two edges that connect an internal node with its two children, and a Boolean value associated with each leaf. Every input $x \in \{0,1\}^n$ determines a unique path from the root to one of the leaves in a decision tree by following the edge labeled with x_i from an internal node labeled with i, and the function $f_T : \{0,1\}^n \to \{0,1\}$ corresponds to a decision tree T if for every input $x \in \{0,1\}^n$, the leaf reached by x is labeled with $f_T(x)$. The *size* of a decision tree is the number of nodes it contains, and the *decision tree (size) complexity* of a function is the size of the smallest decision tree that represents it. Decision tree learning algorithms are most appropriate for functions with small decision tree complexity. As Diakonikolas et al. [14] showed, we can test whether a function has small decision tree complexity with a number of queries that is independent of the total number n of features. Chakraborty et al. [9] later improved the query complexity to obtain the following tight bounds on its query complexity.

Theorem 10.8 [9] *Fix $s \geq 1$ and $\epsilon > 0$. There is an algorithm that queries the value of $f : \{0,1\}^n \to \{0,1\}$ on $\widetilde{O}(s/\epsilon^2)$ inputs and with large constant probability (i) accepts if f has decision tree complexity at most s, and (ii) rejects if f is ϵ-far from having decision tree complexity s.*

Diakonikolas et al. [14] obtained the first result on testing small decision tree complexity by introducing a new technique called *testing by implicit learning*. The idea of this technique is that for many classes of functions, there are extremely efficient algorithms for learning the high-level structure of the function without identifying which are the relevant features. In the case of functions with small decision tree complexity, this means that we can learn the shape of the decision tree that represents the target function—but not the labels associated with each node in the tree—with a running time that is independent of n. This technique is quite powerful, and it has been used to test many other properties as well, including the circuit complexity, minimum DNF size complexity, and Fourier degree of Boolean functions.

The same algorithms can also be used to provide good estimates $\widehat{\theta}_{\mathrm{DT}}$ of the decision tree complexity θ_{DT} of Boolean functions.

Corollary 10.4. *There is an algorithm that queries the value of $f : \{0,1\}^n \to \{0,1\}$ on $\widetilde{O}(\theta_{\mathrm{DT}}/\epsilon^2)$ inputs and returns an estimate $\widehat{\theta}_{\mathrm{DT}}$ such that with large probability $\widehat{\theta}_{\mathrm{DT}} \leq \theta_{\mathrm{DT}}$ and f is ϵ-close to being representable with a decision tree of size $\widehat{\theta}_{\mathrm{DT}}$.*

There are also other models that can be tested very efficiently using completely different techniques. For example, another well-known learning model is that of *linear threshold functions* (or halfspaces). The function $f : \{0,1\}^n \to \{0,1\}$ is a linear threshold function if there are real-valued weights $w_1, \ldots, w_n$ and a threshold $t \in \mathbb{R}$ such that for every $x \in \{0,1\}^n$, $f(x) = \mathrm{sign}(\sum_{i=1}^{n} w_i x_i - t)$. Matulef et al. [39] showed that we can test whether a function is a linear threshold function using a constant number of queries.

Theorem 10.9 [39] *Fix $\epsilon > 0$. There is an algorithm that queries the value of $f : \{0,1\}^n \to \{0,1\}$ on $\mathrm{poly}(1/\epsilon)$ inputs and with large constant probability (i) accepts if f is a linear threshold function, and (ii) rejects if f is ϵ-far from being a linear threshold function.*

10.4.3 Data Quality

Collected data is notorious for being very noisy, and, in particular, containing entries that are erroneous for various reasons. Can we estimate the quality of a dataset? Here are some instances in which sublinear algorithms can be of assistance.

10.4.3.1 Lipschitz Property

One common property of many datasets is a controlled rate of change. For example, a sensor measuring the ambient temperature will not observe extreme fluctuations within short time scales. However, in noisy datasets, the noisy entries often break this property. So one test we can do on a dataset to evaluate its quality is whether it has this property.

Formally, the property of having a bounded rate of change is known as the *Lipschitz* property. The function $f : \{1, \ldots, n\} \to \mathbb{R}$ is t-Lipschitz for some $t \geq 0$ if for every $x, x' \in [n]$, we have $|f(x) - f(x')| \leq t \cdot |x - x'|$. As Jha and Raskhodnikova showed [29], we can test whether a function is Lipschitz with sublinear-time algorithms.

Theorem 10.10 [29] *Fix any $t > 0$. There is an algorithm that queries $f : \{1, 2, \ldots, n\} \to \mathbb{R}$ on $O((1/\epsilon)/\log n)$ inputs and with large constant probability (i) accepts f when it is t-Lipschitz, and (ii) rejects f when it is ϵ-far from t-Lipschitz.*

One natural idea for testing the Lipschitz property of a function f may be to select some neighboring indices $i, i+1 \in [n]$, verifying that $|f(i) - f(i+1)| \leq t$, and repeating this test some number of times. This idea, however, will not work: A function that has a single, enormous jump in value will appear to be Lipschitz on any pair that does not cross the jump, even though it is very far from Lipschitz. Jha and Raskhodnikova bypass this possible barrier by considering a completely different testing algorithm, based on the monotonicity testing algorithms we describe below. They also show how the algorithm can be extended to test the Lipschitz property for functions over many other domains as well.

10.4.3.2 Monotonicity

A second property that is common to many types of non-noisy datasets is *monotonicity*. For example, data that represents the cumulative flow that has passed through a sensor will be a non-decreasing monotone sequence. Formally, $f : [n] \to \mathbb{R}$ is *monotone* if $f(1) \leq f(2) \leq \cdots \leq f(n)$. We can also test the monotonicity of a function with a sublinear-time algorithm.

Theorem 10.11 [17] *There is an algorithm that queries $f : \{1, 2, \ldots, n\} \to \mathbb{R}$ on $O((1/\epsilon) \log n)$ inputs and with large constant probability (i) accepts f when it is monotone, and (ii) rejects f when it is ϵ-far from monotone.*

As was the case with the Lipschitz-testing problem, the idea of choosing neighboring pairs $i, i+1 \in [n]$ and verifying $f(i) \leq f(i+1)$ does not lead to a valid sublinear-time algorithm for testing monotonicity. Another natural idea is to choose m elements uniformly at random from $[n]$, call them $i_1 \leq \ldots \leq i_m \in [n]$ and verify that $f(i_1) \leq \cdots \leq f(i_m)$. This approach *does* lead to a sublinear-time algorithm, but one that is not nearly as efficient as the one which gives the bound in Theorem 10.11. It can be shown that this approach requires $\Omega(\sqrt{n})$ queries to correctly reject all the functions that are far from monotone. Ergün et al. [17] obtained an exponentially more efficient monotonicity tester by taking a completely different approach in which the tester simulates a binary search. It chooses $i \in [n]$ uniformly at random, queries $f(i)$, and then searches for the value $f(i)$ in the sequence $f(1), \ldots, f(n)$ under the assumption that f is monotone. When f is indeed monotone, this binary search correctly leads to i. Interestingly, for *any* function that is far from monotone, this binary search simulation will identify a witness of non-monotonicity (i.e., a pair $i < j \in [n]$ of indices for which $f(i) > f(j)$) with reasonably large probability.

There are also sublinear-time algorithms for testing the monotonicity of functions over many other domains. For some of the results in this direction, see [8,10,15,22,25].

10.4.4 Alternative Query and Sampling Models

The results described in this section have all been in the setting where the algorithm can query the value of the target function on any inputs of its choosing. This setting corresponds to the *membership query model* in machine learning. For many applications in machine learning, however, the membership query model is unrealistic and algorithms must operate in more restrictive query models. Two alternative query models have received particular attention in the machine learning community: The (passive) *sampling* model and the *active query* model. In the sampling model, the inputs on which the algorithm observes the value of the target function are drawn at random from some fixed distribution. In the active query model, a larger number of inputs are drawn from some distribution over the function's domain, and the algorithm can query the value of the target function on any of the points that were drawn.

Many efficient learning algorithms have been devised for both the sampling and active query models. Similarly, sublinear-time algorithms have been introduced to test fundamental properties of Boolean functions (and other combinatorial objects) in the sampling and active query models as well. For example, linear-threshold functions can be tested with a sublinear number of samples or active queries.

Theorem 10.12 [3] *Fix $\epsilon > 0$. There is an algorithm that observes the value of $f : \mathbb{R}^n \to \{0,1\}$ on $\tilde{O}(\sqrt{n}) \cdot \text{poly}(1/\epsilon)$ inputs drawn independently at random from the n-dimensional standard normal distribution and with large constant probability (i) accepts if f is a linear threshold function, and (ii) rejects if f is ϵ-far from being a linear threshold function.*

For more on sublinear-time algorithms and on their limitations in the sampling and active query models, see [2,3,26,27].

10.5 Other Topics

A related area of study is how to understand properties underlying a distribution over a very large domain, when given access to samples from that distribution. This is a scenario that is well studied in statistics, information theory, database algorithms, and machine learning algorithms. For example, it may be important to understand whether the distribution has certain properties, such as being close to uniform, Gaussian, high entropy, or independent. It may also be important to learn parameters of the distribution, or to learn a concise representation of an approximation to the distribution. Recently, surprising bounds on the sample complexity of these problems have been achieved. Although we do not mention these problems in any further detail in this chapter, we point the reader to the surveys of [35,53] and to Chapter 15 by Ilias Diakonikolas in this book.

References

1. N. Alon, S. Dar, M. Parnas, and D. Ron. Testing of clustering. *SIAM Journal of Discrete Mathematics*, 16(3):393–417, 2003.

2. N. Alon, R. Hod, and A. Weinstein. On active and passive testing. *CoRR*, http://arxiv.org/abs/1307.7364, 2013.

3. M. Balcan, E. Blais, A. Blum, and L. Yang. Active property testing. In *Proceedings of the 53rd Annual IEEE Symposium on Foundations of Computer Science*, pp. 21–30, New Brunswick, NJ, 2012.

4. E. Blais. Improved bounds for testing juntas. In *APPROX-RANDOM '08*, pp. 317–330, Springer, Cambridge, MA, 2008.

5. E. Blais. Testing juntas nearly optimally. In *Proceedings of the 41st Annual ACM Symposium on the Theory of Computing*, pp. 151–158, ACM, Bethesda, MD, 2009.

6. M. Blum, M. Luby, and R. Rubinfeld. Self-testing/correcting with applications to numerical problems. *Journal of Computer and System Sciences*, 47:549–595, 1993. (Earlier version in STOC'90.)

7. A. Campagna, A. Guo, and R. Rubinfeld. Local reconstructors and tolerant testers for connectivity and diameter. In *APPROX-RANDOM*, pp. 411–424, Springer, Berkeley, CA, 2013.

8. D. Chakrabarty and C. Seshadhri. A o(n) monotonicity tester for boolean functions over the hypercube. In *STOC*, pp. 411–418, ACM, Palo Alto, CA, 2013.

9. S. Chakraborty, D. García-Soriano, and A. Matsliah. Efficient sample extractors for juntas with applications. In *Automata, Languages and Programming: 38th International Colloquium*, pp. 545–556, Springer, Zurich, Switzerland, 2011.

10. X. Chen, R. A. Servedio, and L. Tan. New algorithms and lower bounds for monotonicity testing. In *55th IEEE Annual Symposium on Foundations of Computer Science*, pp. 286–295. Philadelphia, PA, October 18–21, 2014,

11. A. Czumaj and C. Sohler. Abstract combinatorial programs and efficient property testers. *SIAM Journal on Computing*, 34(3):580–615, 2005.

12. A. Czumaj and C. Sohler. Sublinear-time algorithms. *Bulletin of the EATCS*, 89:23–47, 2006.

13. I. de Sola Pool and M. Kochen. Contacts and influence. *Social Networks*, 1(1):5–51, 1979.

14. I. Diakonikolas, H. Lee, K. Matulef, K. Onak, R. Rubinfeld, R. Servedio, and A. Wan. Testing for concise representations. In *Proceedings of the 48th Annual IEEE Symposium on Foundations of Computer Science*, pp. 549–558, IEEE, Providence, RI, 2007.

15. Y. Dodis, O. Goldreich, E. Lehman, S. Raskhodnikova, D. Ron, and A. Samorodnitsky. Improved testing algorithms for monotonocity. In *Proceedings of RANDOM*, pp. 97–108, Springer, Berkeley, CA, 1999.

16. D. A. Easley and J. M. Kleinberg. *Networks, Crowds, and Markets – Reasoning About a Highly Connected World*. Cambridge University Press, New York, 2010.

17. F. Ergün, S. Kannan, S. R. Kumar, R. Rubinfeld, and M. Viswanathan. Spot-checkers. *JCSS*, 60(3):717–751, 2000.

18. G. Even, M. Medina, and D. Ron. Best of two local models: Local centralized and local distributed algorithms. arXiv preprint arXiv:1402.3796, 2014.

19. G. Even, M. Medina, and D. Ron. Distributed maximum matching in bounded degree graphs. arXiv preprint arXiv:1407.7882, 2014.

20. T. Feder and D. H. Greene. Optimal algorithms for approximate clustering. In *Proceedings of the 20th Annual ACM Symposium on Theory of Computing*, May 2–4, 1988, Chicago, IL, pp. 434–444, 1988.

21. E. Fischer, G. Kindler, D. Ron, S. Safra, and A. Samorodnitsky. Testing juntas. *Journal of Computer and System Sciences*, 68(4):753–787, 2004.

22. E. Fischer, E. Lehman, I. Newman, S. Raskhodnikova, R. Rubinfeld, and A. Samrodnitsky. Monotonicity testing over general poset domains. In *Proceedings of*

the 34th Annual ACM Symposium on the Theory of Computing, pp. 474–483, ACM, Montreal, Canada, 2002.

23. R. J. Fowler, M. S. Paterson, and S. L. Tanimoto. Optimal packing and covering in the plane are np-complete. *IPL*, pp. 434–444, 1981.

24. O. Goldreich. Combinatorial property testing – A survey. In *Randomization Methods in Algorithm Design*, pp. 45–60, AMS, Princeton, NJ, 1998.

25. O. Goldreich, S. Goldwasser, E. Lehman, D. Ron, and A. Samordinsky. Testing monotonicity. *Combinatorica*, 20(3):301–337, 2000.

26. O. Goldreich, S. Goldwasser, and D. Ron. Property testing and its connection to learning and approximation. *Journal of the ACM*, 45:653–750, 1998.

27. O. Goldreich and D. Ron. On sample-based testers. In *Proceedings of the 6th Innovations in Theoretical Computer Science*, pp. 337–345, ACM, Rehovot, Israel, 2015.

28. A. Hassidim, Y. Mansour, and S. Vardi. Local computation mechanism design. In *Proceedings of the 15th ACM Conference on Economics and Computation*, pp. 601–616. ACM, Palo Alto, CA, 2014.

29. M. Jha and S. Raskhodnikova. Testing and reconstruction of lipschitz functions with applications to data privacy. *Journal on Computing*, 42(2):700–731, 2013.

30. R. M. Karp. Reducibility among combinatorial problems. In *Proceedings of a Symposium on the Complexity of Computer Computations*, pp. 85–103. March 20–22, 1972, IBM Thomas J. Watson Research Center, Yorktown Heights, NY, 1972.

31. M. J. Kearns and D. Ron. Testing problems with sublearning sample complexity. *Journal of Computer and System Sciences*, 61(3):428–456, 2000.

32. P. Kothari, A. Nayyeri, R. O'Donnell, and C. Wu. Testing surface area. In *Proceedings of the 25th ACM-SIAM Symposium on Discrete Algorithms*, pp. 1204–1214, SIAM, Portland, OR, 2014.

33. F. Kuhn, T. Moscibroda, and R. Wattenhofer. Local computation: Lower and upper bounds. *CoRR*, http://arxiv.org/abs/1011.5470, 2010.

34. R. Kumar and R. Rubinfeld. Algorithms column: Sublinear-time algorithms. *SIGACT News*, 34:57–67, 2003.

35. R. Kumar and R. Rubinfeld. Sublinear time algorithms. *SIGACT News*, 34:57–67, 2003.

36. R. Levi, R. Rubinfeld, and A. Yodpinyanee. Local computation algorithms for graphs of non-constant degrees. arXiv preprint arXiv:1502.04022, 2015.

37. Y. Mansour, A. Rubinstein, S. Vardi, and N. Xie. Converting online algorithms to local computation algorithms. In *Automata, Languages, and Programming*, pp. 653–664. Springer, Warwick, 2012.

38. Y. Mansour and S. Vardi. A local computation approximation scheme to maximum matching. In *Approximation, Randomization, and Combinatorial Optimization: Algorithms and Techniques*, pp. 260–273. Springer, Berkeley, CA, 2013.

39. K. Matulef, R. O'Donnell, R. Rubinfeld, and R. A. Servedio. Testing halfspaces. *SIAM Journal on Computing*, 39(5):2004–2047, 2010.

40. N. Megiddo and E. Zemel. An $O(n \log n)$ randomizing algorithm for the weighted euclidean 1-center problem. *Journal of Algorithms*, 7(3):358–368, 1986.

41. N. Mishra, D. Oblinger, and L. Pitt. Sublinear time approximate clustering. In *Proceedings of the 12th Annual ACM-SIAM Symposium on Discrete Algorithms*, pp. 439–447. Society for Industrial and Applied Mathematics Philadelphia, PA, 2001.

42. J. Neeman. Testing surface area with arbitrary accuracy. In *Proceedings of the 46th Annual ACM Symposium on the Theory of Computing*, pp. 393–397, ACM, New York, 2014.

43. H. N. Nguyen and K. Onak. Constant-time approximation algorithms via local improvements. In *Proceedings of the 49th Annual IEEE Symposium on Foundations of Computer Science*, pp. 327–336, IEEE, Philadelphia, PA, 2008.

44. K. Onak, D. Ron, M. Rosen, and R. Rubinfeld. A near-optimal sublinear-time algorithm for approximating the minimum vertex cover size. In *Proceedings of the 23rd Annual ACM-SIAM Symposium on Discrete Algorithms*, pp. 1123–1131. SIAM, Kyoto, Japan, 2012.

45. C. Papadimitriou and K. Steiglitz. *Combinatorial Optimization: Algorithms and Complexity.* Dover Publications, Mineola, NY, 1998.

46. M. Parnas and D. Ron. Testing the diameter of graphs. *Random Structures and Algorithms*, 20(2):165–183, 2002.

47. M. Parnas and D. Ron. Approximating the minimum vertex cover in sublinear time and a connection to distributed algorithms. *Theoretical Computer Science*, 381(1–3): 183–196, 2007.

48. M. Parnas, D. Ron, and R. Rubinfeld. Tolerant property testing and distance approximation. *Journal of Computer and System Sciences*, 72(6):1012–1042, 2006.

49. O. Reingold and S. Vardi. New techniques and tighter bounds for local computation algorithms. arXiv preprint arXiv:1404.5398, 2014.

50. D. Ron. Property testing. In S. Rajasekaran, P. M. Pardalos, J. H. Reif, and J. Rolim (eds.), *Handbook on Randomization*, Vol. II, pp. 597–649, Springer, 2001.

51. D. Ron. Property testing: A learning theory perspective. *Foundations and Trends in Machine Learning*, 3:307–402, 2008.

52. R. Rubinfeld. Sublinear time algorithms. In *Proceedings of the International Congress of Mathematicians*, Vol. 3, pp. 1095–1111, AMS, Madrid, Spain, 2006.

53. R. Rubinfeld. Taming big probability distributions. *ACM Crossroads*, 19(1):24–28, 2012.

54. R. Rubinfeld and A. Shapira. Sublinear time algorithms. *SIAM Journal of Discrete Mathematics*, 25(4):1562–1588, 2011.

55. R. Rubinfeld and M. Sudan. Robust characterizations of polynomials with applications to program testing. *SIAM Journal on Computing*, 25:252–271, 1996.

56. Y. Yoshida, Y. Yamamoto, and H. Ito. An improved constant-time approximation algorithm for maximum matchings. In *Proceedings of the 41st Annual ACM Symposium on the Theory of Computing*, pp. 225–234, ACM, Bethesda, MD, 2009.

Part IV

Graph Approaches

11

Networks

Elizabeth L. Ogburn and Alexander Volfovsky

CONTENTS

11.1 Introduction 171
11.2 Network Models 173
11.2.1 Erdos–Renyi–Gilbert Model 173
11.2.2 Stochastic Blockmodel 174
11.2.3 General Latent Space Model 176
11.2.4 Testing for Network Structure 177
11.2.4.1 Bickel and Sarkar (2013) Main Result 177
11.2.4.2 Volfovsky and Hoff (2014) Main Result 177
11.3 Observations Sampled from Network Nodes 178
11.3.1 Terminology and Notation 179
11.3.2 Experiments in Networks 179
11.3.2.1 Fisherian Hypothesis Testing 180
11.3.2.2 Estimation of Causal Effects in Randomized Experiments on Networks 181
11.3.3 Observational Studies 182
11.3.3.1 Peer Effects 182
11.3.3.2 Instrumental Variable Methods 183
11.3.3.3 Dependence 184
11.3.3.4 Targeted Maximum Loss-Based Estimation for Causal Effects in Networks 185
11.4 Discussion and Future Directions 185
References 186

11.1 Introduction

Networks are collections of objects (*nodes* or *vertices*) and pairwise relations (ties or edges) between them. Formally, a graph G is a mathematical object composed of two sets: the vertex set $V = \{1, \ldots, n\}$ lists the nodes in the graph and the edge set $E = \{(i, j) : i \sim j\}$ lists all of the pairwise connections among the nodes. Here $\sim$ defines the relationship between nodes. The set E can encode binary or weighted relationships and directed or undirected relationships. A common and more concise representation of a network is given by the $n \times n$ adjacency matrix A, where entry a_{ij} represents the directed relationship from object i to object j. Most often in statistics, networks are assumed to be unweighted and undirected, resulting in adjacency matrices that are symmetric and binary: $a_{ij} = a_{ji}$ is an indicator of whether i and j share an edge. A pair of nodes is known as a *dyad*; a network with n nodes has $\binom{n}{2}$ distinct dyads, and in an undirected graph, this is also the total number of possible edges. The *degree* of a node is its number *neighbors*, or nodes with which it shares an edge. In a directed network, each node has an in-degree and an out-degree; in an undirected network, these are by definition the same. Some types of networks, such as family trees and street maps, have been used for centuries to efficiently represent relationships among objects (i.e., people and locations, respectively), but the genesis of the mathematical study of networks and their topology (*graph theory*) is usually attributed to Euler's 1741 Seven Bridges of Königsberg (Euler, 1741).

Beginning with Euler's seminal paper and continuing through the middle of the twentieth century, the formal study of networks or graphs was the exclusive domain of deterministic sciences such as mathematics, chemistry, and physics; its primary objectives were the description of properties of a given, fixed graph, for example, the number of edges, paths, or loops of a graph or taxonomies of various kinds of subgraphs. Random graph theory was first introduced by the mathematicians Erdos and Renyi (1959). A random graph is simply a random variable whose sample space is a collection of graphs. It can be characterized by a probability distribution over the sample space of graphs or by the graph-generating mechanism that produces said probability distribution. Random graph theory has become a vibrant area of research in statistics: random graph models have been used to describe and analyze gene networks, brain networks, social networks, economic interactions, the formation of international treaties and alliances, and many other phenomena across myriad disciplines. Common to all of these disparate applications is a focus on quantifying similarities and differences among local and global topological features of different networks. A random graph model indexes a probability distribution over graphs with parameters, often having topological interpretations; the parameters can be estimated using an observed network as data. Parameter estimates and model fit statistics are then used to characterize the topological features of the graph. We describe some such models and estimating procedures in Section 11.2.

Over the past 5–10 years, interest has grown in a complementary but quite different area of network research, namely the study of causal effects in social networks. Here, the network itself is not causal, but edges in the network represent the opportunity for one person to influence another. Learning about the causal effects that people may have on their social contacts concerns outcomes and covariates sampled from network nodes—outcomes superimposed over an underlying network topology—rather than features of the network topology. A small but growing body of literature attempts to learn about *peer effects* (also called *induction* or *contagion*) using network data (e.g., Christakis and Fowler, 2007, 2008, 2010): these are the causal effects that one individual's outcome can have on the outcomes of his or her social contacts. A canonical example is infectious disease outcomes, where one individual's disease status effects his or her contacts' disease statuses. *Interference* or *spillover* effects are related but distinct causal effects that are also of interest in network settings; these are the causal effects that one individual's treatment or exposure can have on his or her contacts' outcomes. For example, vaccinating an individual against an infectious disease is likely to have a protective effect on his or her contacts' disease statuses.

Simple randomized experiments that facilitate causal inference in many settings cannot be applied to the study of contagion or interference in social networks. This is because the individual subjects (nodes) who would be independently randomized in classical settings do not furnish independent outcomes in the network setting. In Section 11.3, we describe recent methodological advances toward causal inference using network data. Before that, in Section 11.2, we describe some current work on probabilistic network generating models. While it is possible to be relatively complete in our survey of the literature on causal inference for outcomes sampled from social network nodes, the literature on network generating models is vast, and we limit our focus to models that we believe to be appropriate for modeling social networks and that we see as potential tools for furthering the project of causal inference using social network data.

Networks are inarguably examples of *big data*, but just how big they are is an open question. Big data often points to large sample sizes and/or high dimensionality. Networks can manifest both kinds of bigness, with a tradeoff between them. On the one hand, a network can be seen as a single observation of a complex, high-dimensional object, in which case sample size is small but dimensionality is high. On the other hand, a network can be seen as comprising a sample of size on the order of the number of nodes or the number of edges. In this case, sample size is large but complexity and dimensionality are less than they would be if the entire network were considered to be a single observation. In reality, the effective sample size for any given network is likely to lie somewhere between 1 and the number of nodes or edges. We are aware of only one published paper that directly tackles the question of sample size for network models: Kolaczyk and Krivitsky (2011) relate sample size to asymptotic rates of convergence of maximum likelihood estimates under certain model assumptions. A notion of sample size undergirds any statistical inference procedure, and most of the models we describe below inherently treat the individual edges or nodes as units of observation rather than the entire network. In some cases, this approach ignores key structure and complexity in the network and results in inferences that are likely to be invalid. We do not explicitly focus on issues of sample size and complexity in this chapter, but note that the tradeoff between network-as-single-complex-object and network-as-large-sample is a crucial and understudied component of statistics for network data.

11.2 Network Models

Different network models are designed to capture different levels of structure and variability in a network. We discuss three models in increasing order of complexity: the Erdos–Renyi–Gilbert model, the stochastic blockmodel and the latent space model. For each of these three models, we describe the parameters and properties of the model and, where appropriate, propose estimation and testing procedures to fit the model to observed network data. For more extensive surveys of the literature on random graph models, see Goldenberg et al. (2010) and Kolaczyk (2009).

11.2.1 Erdos–Renyi–Gilbert Model

The first random graph model, developed simultaneously by Paul Erdos and Alfred Renyi and by Edgar Gilbert, considers a random graph G with a fixed number of nodes $n = |V|$ and a fixed number of undirected edges $e = |E|$ that are selected at random from the pool of $\binom{n}{2}$ possible edges. This induces a uniform distribution over the space of graphs with n nodes and e edges (Erdos and Renyi, 1959; Gilbert, 1959). A slight variation on this model fixes n but only specifies e as the expected number of edges in an independent sample—that is, the probability of any particular edge is given by $p = e/\binom{n}{2}$, so that e is the expected but not necessarily exact number of realized edges. Under both of these formulations, the primary objects of interest are functions of p and n; therefore, these models collapse all of the possible complexity in a network into two parameters and provide only a high-level overview of the network.

Much of the early work on the Erdos–Renyi–Gilbert model concentrated on its asymptotic behavior. One of the most celebrated results describes a phase change in the structure of Erdos–Renyi–Gilbert random graphs as a function of expected degree $\lambda = pn$, namely the almost sure emergence of a giant component as $n \to \infty$ when λ converges to a constant greater than 1. A giant component is a connected component (a subgraph in which all nodes are connected to one another by paths) that contains a strictly positive fraction of the nodes. According to the phase change results, all other components are *small* in the sense that none of them contain more than $\mathcal{O}(\log n)$ nodes. If λ converges to a constant smaller than 1, then almost surely all components are *small* in this sense. Finally, for $\lambda = 1$, the largest component is almost surely $\mathcal{O}(n^{2/3})$ (Durrett, 2007). While this is a simplistic model for real-world networks, the emergence of the giant component is of practical importance when performing inference.

Perhaps the most significant criticism of this model is that real-world networks generally do not exhibit constant expected degrees across nodes; power law degree distributions (Barabási and Albert, 1999; Albert and Barabási, 2002), and departures from those (Clauset et al., 2009) are thought to be especially common. A natural extension of the Erdos–Renyi–Gilbert model, allowing for a power-law and other degree distributions, partitions the nodes into groups having different expected degrees, essentially interpolating several different Erdos–Renyi–Gilbert graphs (Watts and Strogatz, 1998). However, these models can become unwieldy; for example, efficiently generating a simple graph with a user-specified degree distribution requires sequential importance sampling (Blitzstein and Diaconis, 2011). Additionally, as we will see in Section 11.2.3, nonconstant degree distributions can be accommodated very intuitively by the latent space model.

A sample from an undirected Erdos–Renyi–Gilbert model with $n = 20$ nodes and edge probability $p = .25$ is displayed in the first panel of Figure 11.1. The expected degree for each node in the graph is $np = 4$; the observed average degree is 5.5. Estimation of the probability of edge formation under this model is straightforward via the binomial likelihood $p^e(1-p)^{\binom{n}{2}-e}$, where e is the observed number of edges, and in this case $\hat{p} = .289$. The simplicity of this model and estimation procedure make it extremely appealing for inference when we cannot observe the full network, as the marginal distribution of any subgraph is easily computed, but the lack of any structure on the nodes and their degrees ensures that this model a simplification of reality in most cases.

11.2.2 Stochastic Blockmodel

A higher level of model complexity is achieved by the *stochastic blockmodel* (Holland et al., 1983; Nowicki and Snijders, 2001; Wang and Wong, 1987), which recognizes that a given

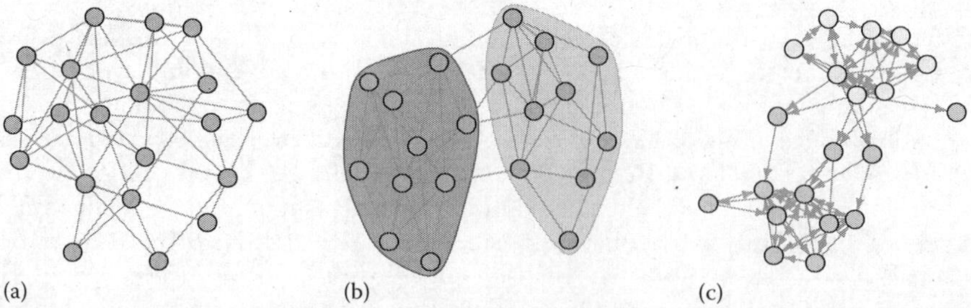

FIGURE 11.1
Networks generated using the three models described in Section 11.2. They are: (a) an Erdos–Renyi–Gilbert graph with $p = 1/2$; (b) a stochastic blockmodel with probability matrix $P = \begin{pmatrix} 0.5 & 0.2 \\ 0.2 & 0.4 \end{pmatrix}$; and (c) a directed latent space model based on the latent variable $s_{ij} = \alpha_i + \alpha_i\alpha_j + \epsilon_{ij}$ where $\alpha_i, \epsilon_{ij} \overset{\text{iid}}{\sim} \text{normal}(0, 1)$.

network node is more likely to be connected to some nodes than to others (e.g., because it is more similar to some nodes than to others). This is codified in the assumption that the n nodes in a network are separated into $k < n$ nonoverlapping groups and the relationship between any two nodes depends only on their group memberships. Nodes that belong to the same group are stochastically equivalent—that is, probability distributions over their edges are identical. The Erdos–Renyi–Gilbert model is a special case of a stochastic blockmodel with $k = 1$. By introducing structure in the form of multiple groups of nodes, the stochastic blockmodel captures an additional level of complexity and relaxes the assumption of identical expected degree across all nodes. While this model is not generally compatible with power law degree distributions, it is very flexible.

The parameter of a stochastic blockmodel is a $k \times k$ probability matrix P, where entry p_{ij} is the probability that a node in group i is connected by an edge to a node in group j. Edges can be directed or undirected. The main constraint on P is that every entry is between 0 and 1. While $p_{ij} = 0$ or $= 1$ may be plausible, many estimation procedures make the assumption that p_{ij} is bounded away from 0 and 1. For undirected networks, an additional assumption is that the matrix P is symmetric (or simply upper triangular), while for directed networks, this requirement can be relaxed. In the middle panel of Figure 11.1, we see an undirected network simulated from a two block stochastic blockmodel where the probability of edges within each block is greater than that between the blocks. Additionally, one of the blocks has a higher probability of within group edges than the other.

The color coding in the figure clearly demarcates the two groups in the stochastic blockmodel and it is easy to see that each of the groups can be viewed marginally as an Erdos–Renyi–Gilbert graph. Given the group labels, we can perform inference as in the Erdos–Renyi–Gilbert case, treating each class of edges (within each group and between each pair of groups) individually to estimate the entries of P. However, we rarely know group membership *a priori*, making estimation of the stochastic blockmodel parameters much more complicated, since the group labels must be inferred. There are two main approaches to this estimation process. The first is a model-driven approach in which group membership is a well-defined parameter to be estimated jointly with the elements of P; this approach can be viewed as a special case of the latent space model (see Section 11.2.3), where the multiplicative latent effects are k dimensional vectors with a single nonzero entry. The second approach is a heuristic approach involving spectral clustering. Given the number of clusters or blocks, k, and an adjacency matrix A, the first step is to find the k eigenvectors corresponding to the k largest eigenvalues (in absolute value; Rohe et al., 2011) of the graph Laplacian L $(= D^{1/2}AD^{1/2}$, where $D_{ii} = \sum_j a_{ij})$. Treating the rows of the concatenated $n \times k$ matrix of eigenvectors as samples in $\mathbb{R}^k$, the next step is to run a k-means algorithm to cluster the rows into k nonoverlapping sets. These sets estimate the groups of the underlying stochastic blockmodel, and Rohe et al. (2011) provide bounds on the number of nodes that will be assigned to the wrong cluster under conditions on the expected average degree as well as the number of clusters. The power of their result lies in the fact that they allow the number of clusters to grow with sample size. Choi et al. (2012) developed similar results for a model-based approach to clustering in stochastic blockmodels. After clustering, estimation of P is straightforward.

It has recently been shown that stochastic blockmodels can provide a good approximation to a general class of exchangeable graph models characterized by a graphon: a function mapping the unit square to the unit interval and representing the limiting probability of edges in a graph (Airoldi et al., 2013). This suggests that, given the relatively weak assumption of an exchangeable graph model, a stochastic blockmodel approximation may lead to approximately valid inference. In other words, despite the simplicity of the stochastic blockmodel and the fact that the only structure it models is at the group level, it captures enough structure to closely approximate a large class of exchangeable random graph models.

Extensions to the stochastic blockmodel include mixed membership models (Airoldi et al., 2008) and degree corrected stochastic blockmodels, which induce power law distributions on the degrees (Karrer and Newman, 2011).

11.2.3 General Latent Space Model

A final level of complexity is afforded by the *general latent space model.* Under this model, the nodes of a network are embedded into a low-dimensional latent space, usually Euclidean, and the probability of an edge between any two nodes is a function of their latent positions. For example, in the *latent distance model*, the probability of a tie increases as the (Euclidean) distance between the latent positions decreases (Hoff et al., 2002). This captures both reciprocity and transitivity in the formation of network edges: since distances are symmetric, if the probability of an edge between i and j is high, then the probability of an edge between j and i will also be high, and the triangle inequality suggests that if i and j are close and j and t are close, then i and t are going to be close. Reciprocity and transitivity are properties that are thought to be important in real-world networks but are impossible to incorporate into the Erdos–Renyi–Gilbert model or the stochastic blockmodel. The inherent symmetry of the distance model rules out the possibility that certain nodes have a greater affinity for ties than others, and to circumvent this limitation, the general latent space model allows for asymmetric functions of the latent positions as well as for node- and dyad-specific covariates to affect the probability of tie formation. An example of a latent space model with additive and multiplicative functions of the latent positions as well as such covariates is described in detail below.

Consider an $n \times n$ asymmetric adjacency matrix A, representing a directed graph, and let X be an $n \times n \times p$ array of observed characteristics. Each $n \times n$ slice of X is either constant in the rows (representing a fixed effect that contributes to the propensity to send ties in the network, or *sender effect*); constant in the columns (representing a fixed effect that contributes to the propensity to receive ties in the network, or *receiver effect*); or neither, representing dyadic effects. We can model a_{ij} as the indicator $1_{s_{ij}>0}$ that $s_{ij} > 0$, where $s_{ij} = X_{ij\cdot}\theta + \alpha_i + \beta_j + u_i^t v_j + \epsilon_{ij}$, $X_{ij\cdot}$ is the p-dimensional vector of covariates associated with the relationship between nodes i and j, α_i is an additive sender effect, β_j is an additive receiver effect, and $u_i^t v_j$ is a multiplicative effect (as it is the projection of u_i in the direction of v_j in the latent space) that captures similarity between nodes i and j (Hoff, 2005). This model is a generalization of the social relations model of Warner et al. (1979). Reciprocity can be introduced into the model by allowing for the error terms $(\epsilon_{ij}, \epsilon_{ji})$ to be correlated. Here $X_{ij\cdot}$ might include sender-specific information, receiver-specific information, or dyadic information. The additive latent effects α_i and β_j contain information about the affinity of nodes i and j to send and receive ties in general, while the multiplicative effect $u_i^t v_j$ contains the information on the latent similarity of the two nodes. In particular, if the nodes are close in the latent space ($u_i^t v_j > 0$), then the probability of a tie is increased and if they are far apart ($u_i^t v_j < 0$), then it is decreased.

The third panel of Figure 11.1 displays a directed network generated from the latent class model described above (without covariates and with a one-dimensional latent space). The two sets of nodes are colored according to the sign of α_i. The emergence of the two clusters is due to the multiplicative effect $\alpha_i\alpha_j$: ties are more likely between individuals for whom the signs of α_i match. This demonstrates the ability of this model to capture stochastic blockmodel behavior. Each node has its own probability of sending a tie to another node, which allows for much greater flexibility than the blockmodel. The yellow nodes send out more ties to the blue nodes than they receive from the blue nodes, due to the additional additive effect of α_i in the model as nodes with $\alpha_i > 0$ have a higher probability of sending out ties.

General latent space models can be fit to data from a real network via a Markov chain Monte Carlo algorithm (Hoff, 2005). A salient advantage of these models is their ability to model restrictions on the sampling design according to which data from a network is collected. For example, when collecting information about friendship networks in a survey setting, researchers often ask individuals to name their top five friends. This type of network sampling scheme is known as the *fixed rank nominations* scheme and is explored in detail in Hoff et al. (2013). When this sampling design is ignored, estimation of effects on the probability of edge formation is imprecise, potentially leading to incorrect inference. The ability to account for restrictions on the sampling design makes this general class of models potentially promising for causal inference using data from partially observed networks.

11.2.4 Testing for Network Structure

All three models described above make assumptions about the similarity among nodes in a network, allowing for stochastic equivalence, homophily or both (Hoff, 2007). Recent work by Bickel and Sarkar (2013) and Volfovsky and Hoff (2014) proposes two different testing procedures for the amount of similarity among nodes in a relational dataset. These tests can inform of the validity of the assumptions underlying the three models described above; rejecting the null hypothesis can be seen as an indication that the data exhibit more complexity than the null model allows. Bickel and Sarkar (2013) leverage Tracy–Widom theory to develop a hypothesis test for the null hypothesis that the graph comes from an Erdos–Renyi–Gilbert model (rejection of the null suggests the presence of blocks or clusters, as in the stochastic blockmodel), while Volfovsky and Hoff (2014) develop a test for correlation among the rows and columns of a relational data matrix within the context of the normal model (defined below) and provide an extension to the latent space model for networks that informs the choice of dimension of the latent space.

11.2.4.1 Bickel and Sarkar (2013) Main Result

Let A be the adjacency matrix of an Erdos–Renyi random graph with parameter p and let $\hat{p}$ be the estimate of p. For the centered and scaled adjacency matrix,

$$\tilde{A}' = \frac{A - (n\hat{p}11^t - \hat{p}I)}{\sqrt{(n-1)\hat{p}(1-\hat{p})}}$$

the limiting distribution of the leading eigenvalue, $\lambda_1(\tilde{A}')$ is given by

$$n^{2/3}(\lambda_1(\tilde{A}') - 2) \xrightarrow{d} \text{Tracy–Widom}$$

Given this limiting distribution, it is now easy to construct a test for the null hypothesis that a graph is generated from an Erdos–Renyi model with parameter p. Bickel and Sarkar (2013) propose using this test to recursively find the blocks of the stochastic blockmodel of Section 11.2.2. In particular, if the test rejects the null hypothesis, then the algorithm splits the graph into two blocks and recurses the test on each block.

11.2.4.2 Volfovsky and Hoff (2014) Main Result

Let S be an $n \times n$ random matrix distributed according to the matrix normal distribution with zero mean matrix and Kronecker covariance structure $\Sigma_{\text{col}} \otimes \Sigma_{\text{row}}$. If the entries of S represent a weighted relationship between actors i and j in a network, then the identities $\text{E}[ZZ^t] = \Sigma_{\text{row}}\text{tr}(\Sigma_{\text{col}})$ and $\text{E}[S^tS] = \Sigma_{\text{col}}\text{tr}(\Sigma_{\text{row}})$ suggest the interpretation of Σ_{row} and

Σ_{col} as the covariance of the network nodes as senders and as receivers, respectively. Under the normal model, using a single sample matrix, we can construct a likelihood ratio test for row and column dependenc under this model. This is because both under the null hypothesis that Σ_{row} and Σ_{col} are diagonal positive definite and under the alternative hypothesis that Σ_{row} and Σ_{col} are positive definite, the matrix normal likelihood is bounded for a single matrix S.

To connect this test to binary networks we make use of the latent model of Section 11.2.3. Consider a graph with adjacency matrix A where the probability of an edge is modeled as a function of latent multiplicative sender and receiver effects, $u_i, v_j \in \mathbb{R}^R$ using the probit link: $\Pr(a_{ij} = 1) = \Phi(\gamma + u_i^t v_j)$. Writing this model in the latent variable formulation we write $a_{ij} = 1_{[s_{ij} > -\gamma]}$, where $s_{ij} = u_i^t v_j + \epsilon_{ij}$. The $n \times R$ matrices U and V formed by stacking the vectors u_i, $i = 1, ..., n$ and v_j, $j = 1, ..., n$, describe the row and column heterogeneity in S, respectively, since $\text{E}[SS^t] = U(V^tV)U^t + I$ and $\text{E}[S^tS] = V(U^tU)V^t + I$. The main challenge here is choosing the appropriate rank R to use for the model. This can be achieved by performing the likelihood ratio test described above on the latent scale for a sequence of ranks. When the test stops rejecting the null of no dependence among the nodes, it means that the latent vectors capture all of the dependence between senders and between receivers present in A. The above-described likelihood ratio test can be applied on the latent scale. Since latent space models are best fit using Bayesian methodology (Hoff, 2005, 2008), we can easily construct a posterior predictive p-value using the techniques described in Thompson and Geyer (2007).

Testing procedures have been recently developed for more complicated models: Yang et al. (2014) proposed a novel test for a graphon, a limit object for random graphs. The models described in this section carry with them the underlying assumption of infinite exchangeability, that is, that the finite networks being modeled comprise subsamples of an infinite graph where the nodes can be relabeled without affecting the joint distribution of the graph. In a recent work, Volfovsky and Airoldi (2014) demonstrated that distributions that satisfy the substantially weaker assumption of finite exchangeability are close in total variation distance to the distribution of graphs satisfying the stronger assumption. This suggests that inference made under the stronger assumption is likely to be appropriate even when only the weaker assumption holds.

11.3 Observations Sampled from Network Nodes

In most of the literature on networks, the network itself is the object of study: features of network topology and probability models for edge formation, node addition, and network generation. But situations abound in which the network can be thought of as a nuisance parameter and interest is instead in the behavior and attributes of the network nodes. For social networks, which are our focus here, we might be interested in how behaviors spread from one person to their social contacts, how attributes cluster among network nodes, or how one person's randomly assigned treatment might affect their social contacts' outcomes. The underlying network gives important structure to the data—network ties represent opportunities for contagion or correlation—but interest is in the effects, not the determinants, of the network topology. Research methods for analyzing data on outcomes sampled from a single network is nascent and remains underdeveloped. In what follows we describe recent work in this area and conclude with a description of open problems. Most of the research in this area assumes that the network is fixed and known.

11.3.1 Terminology and Notation

In this section, we will use the terms *nodes, subjects,* and *individuals* interchangeably. This is a slight abuse of the term *node* but should cause no confusion as we are not concerned with network topology except insofar as it informs relations among the subjects and the observations they furnish. Let Y_i represent an outcome for node/subject i and let Z_i be a treatment or exposure for individual i. Sometimes, we will index the outcomes with time, that is, Y_i^t is the outcome for subject i at time t. If we have observed n subjects, $\mathbf{Y}$ is an n-dimensional vector of outcomes for subjects 1 through n, possibly indexed by time, and $\mathbf{Z}$ is an n-dimensional vector of exposures or treatments for subjects 1 through n.

Questions about the influence one subject has on the outcome of another subject are inherently questions about causal effects, which are defined in terms of potential or counterfactual outcomes (see, e.g., Hernan, 2004; Rubin, 2005). In general, a unit-level potential outcome, $Y_i(z)$, is defined as the outcome that we would have observed for subject i if we could have intervened to set that subject's treatment or exposure Z_i to value z, where z is in the support of Z. But social networks represent a paradigmatic opportunity for *interference*: one subject's exposure may affect not only his own outcome but also the outcomes of his social contacts and possibly other subjects. This means that the traditional unit-level potential outcomes are not well defined. Instead, $Y_i(\mathbf{z})$ is the outcome that we would have observed if we could have set the vector of exposures for the entire population, $\mathbf{Z}$, to $\mathbf{z} = (z_1, ..., z_n)$, where for each i, z_i is in the support of Z. In the presence of interference, there are many types of causal effects that might be of interest. Unit-level causal effects isolate the effect of a subject's own exposure on his outcome. These effects are usually defined either holding other subjects' exposures constant or averaging over possible exposure distributions for other subjects. *Spillover effects* quantify the effect on subject i's outcome of other subjects' exposures. For a binary treatment, the contrast $\sum_{i=1}^{n} E[Y_i(\mathbf{1}) - Y_i(\mathbf{0})]$ is often of interest. This is the difference in average potential outcomes in a world in which every subject is assigned to treatment compared to a world in which every subject is assigned to control. Eckles et al. (2014) call this particular estimand the average treatment effect (ATE); however, to differentiate this estimand from the ATE defined in the absence of interference, we will adopt the terminology of Halloran and Struchiner (1995) and refer to $\sum_{i=1}^{n} E[Y_i(\mathbf{1}) - Y_i(\mathbf{0})]$ as the *overall ATE*. See Ogburn and VanderWeele (2014a) and references therein for further discussion of causal effects in the presence of interference and of the distinction between interference and contagion.

We distinguish between interference, which is present when one subject's treatment or exposure may affect others' outcomes, and *peer effects* or *contagion*, which are present when one subject's outcome may influence or transmit to other subjects (Ogburn and VanderWeele, 2014a). In the literature on peer effects, an *ego* is defined as a subject whose outcome we are interested in studying and the ego's *alters* are the ego's neighbors, that is, subjects who share an edge with the ego in the underlying network. A peer effect is a causal effect on an ego's outcome at time t of his alter's outcome at time s for some $s < t$.

11.3.2 Experiments in Networks

The design of randomized experiments in networks, when subjects and their treatments may not be independent, is an area of recent but increasing interest. Without attempting to be exhaustive, this section reviews what we consider to be the most important threads in this line of research.

Experiments are difficult for two reasons: interference, which may make it impossible to simultaneously observe the treatment condition (e.g., every subject is treated) for some units and the control condition (e.g., no subject is treated) for others, and dependence among observations, which makes the estimation of standard errors difficult. Fisherian randomization-based inference can circumvent the problem of dependence, as described in Sections 11.3.2.1 and 11.3.2.2. Other randomization-based approaches assume that the only source of dependence is interference, and therefore that observations are independent conditional on treatment. There are two approaches to dealing with the challenge of interference in the randomization literature: assumptions on the limits of interference and attempts to minimize bias due to interference. Both are discussed below.

11.3.2.1 Fisherian Hypothesis Testing

Most of the work on inference about outcomes sampled from network nodes concerns randomized experiments. But there is an important distinction to be made between inference from randomized experiments and the specific case of *Fisherian randomization-based inference*, pioneered by Fisher (1922) and applied to network-like settings by Rosenbaum (2007) and Bowers et al. (2013). Fisherian randomization-based inference is founded on the very intuitive notion that, under the null hypothesis of no effect of treatment on any subject (sometimes called the *sharp null hypothesis* to distinguish it from other null hypotheses that may be of interest), the treated and control groups are random samples from the same underlying distribution. Fisherian randomization-based inference treats outcomes as fixed and treatment assignments as random variables: quantities that depend on the vector of treatment assignments are the only random variables in this paradigm. Therefore, dependence among outcomes is a nonissue.

In an influential paper, Rosenbaum (2007) proposed the use of *distribution-free statistics* (statistics whose distribution under the null hypothesis can be determined *a priori*, without reference to the data) to perform hypothesis tests and derive confidence intervals in the presence of interference. The Mann–Whitney statistic, for example, takes all pairs consisting of one treated and one untreated subject and counts the number of times that the treated subject had a greater outcome than the untreated subject. The null distribution of this statistic is known *a priori* and does not depend on any aspect of the data-generating distribution of the outcomes; it is therefore agnostic to any dependence among the outcomes. After deriving the null distribution for such a statistic, one can compare the observed distribution of the statistic to the null distribution to perform a hypothesis test and to derive confidence intervals for the magnitude of the departure from the null hypothesis in the event that it is rejected.

A slightly different version of randomization-based inference is developed by Bowers et al. (2013). Under the null hypothesis, that is, supposing that we are observing outcomes in the world in which the null is true, we can generate the randomization-based null distribution of any test statistic by enumerating all of the possible treatment assignment permutations and recalculating the test statistic for each one. For example, suppose we have a network with four nodes and our experiment dictates assigning half to treatment. Our test statistic is the difference in mean outcomes among the treated compared to the controls. The null distribution of this statistic is comprised of six equiprobable realizations of the mean difference: $[(Y_1+Y_2)/2]-[(Y_3+Y_4)/2]$, $[(Y_3+Y_4)/2]-[(Y_1+Y_2)/2]$, $[(Y_1+Y_3)/2]-[(Y_2+Y_4)/2]$, $[(Y_2+Y_4)/2]-[(Y_1+Y_3)/2]$, $[(Y_1+Y_4)/2]-[(Y_2+Y_3)/2]$, and $[(Y_2+Y_3)/2]-[(Y_1+Y_4)/2]$, corresponding to the six possible permutations of the treatment assignment vector. If, in reality, subjects 1 and 2 were assigned to treatment and 3 and 4 to control, then the observed test statistic is the first in the list above—the mean outcome among treated minus the mean outcome among controls. We can compare the observed test statistic to the statistic's null distribution and ask the question "how likely was this value to have occurred by chance, assuming that the null hypothesis is true?"

Of course, Bowers et al. (2013) consider settings considerably more complex than the simple example above. Specifically, they propose testing any parametric model $\mathcal{H}(y_i(\mathbf{z}); \beta, \tau) = y_i(\mathbf{0})$ that maps one subject's potential outcome under an arbitrary treatment assignment vector $\mathbf{z}$ to the same subject's potential outcome under treatment assignment $\mathbf{0}$, that is under the assignment in which no subject receives treatment. The two parameters β and τ index the effect of subject i's own treatment and the spillover effect of others' treatments, respectively, on subject i's outcome. Assuming the correct parametric form for the model, the true values of the parameters β and τ are those for which $\{\mathcal{H}(y_i(\mathbf{z}); \beta, \tau) : i \text{ treated}\}$ and $\{\mathcal{H}(y_i(\mathbf{z}); \beta, \tau) : i \text{ control}\}$ are both collections of estimates of $Y(\mathbf{0})$ and are therefore random samples from the same underlying distribution. The authors propose tests for this using the Komolgorov–Smirnov test statistic, which is a nonparametric comparison of the probability distribution of the estimated potential outcomes $Y(\mathbf{0})$ between the treated and control groups. They derive p-values and confidence intervals for β and τ, which facilitate testing specific hypotheses about unit-level and spillover effects of treatment.

11.3.2.2 Estimation of Causal Effects in Randomized Experiments on Networks

Fisherian randomization-based inference, described in Section 11.3.2.1, permits hypothesis testing but not the estimation of causal effects. A few recent papers have taken on the challenge of estimating spillover effects and the ATE of a randomized treatment in the presence of interference.

Toulis and Kao (2013) discussed estimation of the spillover effect of having k of one's neighbors assigned to treatment compared to the null condition of having no treated neighbors. They call the state of having k-treated neighbors *k-exposure*. Estimation of the effect of k-exposure is challenging in part because, if nodes are randomized independently to treatment and control, there may be no nodes with k-treated neighbors and/or no nodes with no treated neighbors. Define V_k to be the set of all nodes with at least k neighbors, that is, the set of nodes eligible *a priori* to be exposed or unexposed to k-exposure. Toulis and Kao (2013) proposed a randomization scheme, *insulated neighbors randomization*, that randomly selects some portion *shared neighbors* (nodes that are neighbors of at least two nodes in V_k) to be assigned to control before sequentially assigning eligible nodes in V_k to either k-exposure or to the null condition. Assigning nodes to the exposure or null conditions rather than to treatment or control ensures that these conditions will be observed in the data. However, assigning a node to be in one condition or the other determines the treatment assignments of that node's neighbors and may eliminate or reduce the possibility of finding other nodes with unassigned neighbors, that is, nodes that can be randomized in the next step of the algorithm. Assigning some portion of shared neighbors to control in a first step increases the number of nodes available to be randomized during the next steps of the algorithm.

Ugander et al. (2013) and Eckles et al. (2014) focused on estimation of the overall ATE (defined above, Section 11.3.1). These two papers propose and elaborate on a new method of randomization, *graph cluster randomization*, that assigns clusters of adjacent nodes to treatment or control. The informal rationale is that, for nodes in the center of the cluster, the world looks like one in which the entire network is assigned to either treatment or control. Therefore, for these nodes, the observed outcome should be equal to or close to the potential outcome that we would have observed if we had assigned the entire network, instead of just the cluster, to either treatment or control. Ugander et al. (2013) assumes that various local exposure conditions for subject i (e.g., i and all of i's neighbors are treated or i and $x\%$ of i's neighbors are treated) result in an observed outcome for subject i that is precisely equal to the potential outcome we would have observed for subject i if every subject had been treated. The overall ATE can then be estimated by comparing nodes with these exposure conditions to nodes with the prespecified null exposure conditions (e.g., the node and none of its neighbors are treated). The authors derive Horwitz–Thompson estimators of the ATE under this class of assumptions and using graph cluster randomization. Graph cluster randomization reduces the variance of standard Horwitz–Thompson estimators with respect to naive randomization schemes, in which nodes are randomly assigned to treatment conditions independently of their neighbors, because it increases the probability of observing nodes who are in the prespecified exposure conditions of interest.

Eckles et al. (2014) relax the assumption that local exposure conditions result in observed outcomes that are identical to the potential outcome had the entire network been assigned the same condition; instead, they investigate conditions under which graph cluster randomization will reduce bias in the estimated overall ATE compared to naive randomization when that assumption does not hold. Specifically, they describe a data-generating process in which one subject's treatment affects his or her own outcome, which in turn affects his neighbors' outcomes, then the neighbors' outcomes can affect their neighbors' outcomes, and so on. This is an example of *interference by contagion* (Ogburn and VanderWeele 2014a). Under this model, every node's outcome can be affected by every other node's treatment assignment, but the effect of one node's treatment on another's outcome is likely to decay with network distance. Intuitively, if i and all of i's neighbors are treated, then the observed value Y_i is closer to $Y_i(\mathbf{Z} = \mathbf{1})$ than it would have been if some or none of its neighbors had been treated. Eckles et al. (2014) formalize this intuition and prove that graph cluster randomization reduces bias compared to independent randomization. They also explore bias-variance tradeoffs: larger clusters result in observed conditions that are closer (so to speak) to the desired counterfactual world in which the entire network had the same treatment assignment; larger clusters also result in fewer units to be randomized and therefore in larger variance of Horwitz–Thompson estimators. See Eckles et al. (2014) for details and recommendations.

Two related and recent methods bear brief mentioning: Choi (2014) proposed a method for detecting clustering of outcomes that would be consistent with spillover from one subject to another and is highly robust to misspecification of the network topology. Aronow and Samii (2013) proposed a method for estimating unit-level and spillover effects of randomized treatments in relatively sparse networks. Their method is based on an *exposure model*, similar to the model $\mathcal{H}(y_i(\mathbf{z}); \beta, \tau) = y_i(\mathbf{0})$ of Bowers et al. (2013), and the exposure conditions of Ugander et al. (2013), which partitions the space of all potential outcomes $Y_i(\mathbf{z})$ into equivalence classes.

11.3.3 Observational Studies

In many settings randomization is not feasible. It may be unethical to randomize individuals to conditions that are known to be harmful, or impossible to randomize them to conditions that are more complex than a simple treatment assignment. When randomization is not possible, we rely on observational data to provide information about treatment effects and peer effects.

11.3.3.1 Peer Effects

A growing body of research regresses an ego's outcome at time t on the outcome of one of his alters at time $t-1$ using generalized linear models (GLMs) and, for longitudinal data, generalized estimating equations (GEEs), reporting the coefficients on the alters' outcomes as estimates of peer effects (Ali and Dwyer, 2009; Cacioppo et al., 2009; Christakis and Fowler, 2007, 2008, 2013; Fowler and Christakis, 2008; Lazer et al., 2010; Rosenquist et al., 2010). This work has come under two major lines of criticism. First, there is the problem of adequate control for confounding when trying to tease apart homophily and peer influence (Cohen-Cole and Fletcher, 2008; Lyons, 2011; Manski, 1993, 2013; Noel and Nyhan, 2011; Shalizi and Thomas, 2011; VanderWeele, 2011). Homophily is the tendency of people who share similar characteristics to adjacent in a social network (to be friends, to be related to one another, to work in the same company, etc.), and, like peer influence, it manifests as correlated outcomes among nodes that are close to one another in the network. Christakis and Fowler (2007, 2008, 2010, 2013) proposed controlling for homophily by including the alter's and the ego's past outcomes in their regression models, however Shalizi and Thomas (2011) demonstrated that this does not suffice to control for homophily on unobserved characteristics. In general, unless every covariate affecting friendship formation is observed and controlled for, it is not possible to differentiate between homophily and peer influence without strong parametric assumptions, and possibly not even then (Shalizi and Thomas, 2011).

An orthogonal line of criticism of the GLM/GEE approach to assessing peer influence is that these classes of models are intended for independent observations, while observations sampled from a social network are likely to be dependent (Lyons, 2011; VanderWeele et al., 2012). Indeed, the very hypothesis of peer effects entails dependence among observations. When a statistical procedure is grounded in the assumption of independence, while in fact observations are positively correlated (as we would expect them to be for contagious outcomes in a social network), then the resulting standard errors and statistical inference will be anticonservative. In some cases the assumption of independence may hold under the null hypothesis of no peer effects (VanderWeele et al., 2012), but it is unknown whether tests that rely on this fact have any power under the alternative hypothesis to detect the presence of the causal effects of interest (Shalizi, 2012).

Although problematic in myriad ways, using GLMs and GEEs to regress an ego's outcome on his alters' lagged outcomes is the most widespread and, until recently, the only proposal for estimating peer effects using social network data. Below we discuss two refinements to these methods (one addresses the *reflection problem* and the other addresses the problem of dependence) and a new proposal that avoids the methodological issues that plague the use of GLMs and GEEs but that requires a very rich set of observations over time and over network nodes.

11.3.3.2 Instrumental Variable Methods

O'Malley et al. (2014) proposed an instrumental variable (IV) solution to the problem of disentangling peer effects from homophily. An instrument is a random variable, V, that affects exposure but has no effect on the outcome conditional on exposure. When the exposure—outcome relation suffers from unmeasured confounding but an instrument can be found that is not confounded with the outcome, IV methods can be used to recover valid estimates of the causal effect of the exposure on the outcome. In this case, there is unmeasured confounding of the relation between an alter's outcome at time $t-1$ and an ego's outcome at time t whenever there is homophily on unmeasured traits. We refer the reader to Angrist et al. (1996), Angrist and Pischke (2008), Greenland (2000), and Pearl (2000) for accessible reviews of IV methods.

O'Malley et al. (2014) propose using a gene that is known to be associated with the outcome of interest as an instrument. In their paper, they focus on perhaps the most highly publicized claim of peer effects, namely that there are significant peer effects of body mass index (BMI) and obesity (Christakis and Fowler, 2007). If there is a gene that affects BMI but that does not affect other homophilous traits, then that gene is a valid instrument for the effect of an alter's BMI on his ego's BMI. The gene affects the ego's BMI only through the alter's manifest BMI (and it is independent of the ego's BMI conditional on the alter's BMI), and there is unlikely to be any confounding, measured or unmeasured, of the relation between an alter's gene and the ego's BMI.

There are two challenges to this approach. First, the power to detect peer effects is dependent in part upon the strength of the instrument—exposure relation which, for genetic instruments, is often weak. Indeed, O'Malley et al. (2014) reported low power for their data analyses. Second, in order to assess peer effects at more than a single time point (i.e., the average effect of the alter's outcomes on the ego's outcomes up to that time point), multiple instruments are required. O'Malley et al. (2014) suggest using a single gene interacted with age to capture time-varying gene expression, but this could further attenuate the instrument—exposure relation and this method is not valid unless the effect of the gene on the outcome really does vary with time; if the gene-by-age interactions are highly collinear then they will fail to act as differentiated instruments for different time points.

11.3.3.3 Dependence

To deal with the problem of dependent observations in the estimation of peer effects, Ogburn and VanderWeele (2014b) proposed analyzing a subsample of alter-ego pairs that are mutually independent conditional on carefully chosen observations on intermediate nodes in the network. Testing and estimation of peer effects can then proceed using GLMs or GEEs, conditional on the appropriate set of observations. Ogburn and VanderWeele (2014b) focus on two specific types of peer effects that are of interest in the context of infectious diseases, but their main idea is quite general. We briefly describe their method in the context of a toy example.

Consider the network of five nodes in a *bow tie* formation depicted in Figure 11.2. If the only dependence among observations sampled from nodes one through five is due to peer effects, and if these effects cannot be transmitted more than once per unit of time, then $\left(Y_1^{t-1}, Y_2^t\right)$ is independent of (Y_4^{t-1}, Y_5^t) conditional on $(Y_3^{t-1}, Y_3^{t-2}, ..., Y_3^0)$. Then, we can use standard statistical models to regress Y_5^t on Y_4^{t-1} and Y_1^{t-1} on Y_2^t, conditioning on the appropriate observations. In some cases conditioning on Y_3^{t-1} or on a summary of $(Y_3^{t-1}, Y_3^{t-2}, ..., Y_3^0)$ may suffice. The requisite conditioning event could change the interpretation of the causal effect of interest (i.e., the conditional causal effect may be different from the unconditional causal effect); in these cases we can perform hypothesis tests about the unconditional causal effects but not estimate them. In other cases, conditioning does not change the interpretation and estimation and testing are both feasible.

The conditional inference proposal of Ogburn and VanderWeele (2014b) suffers from low power both because it requires subsampling from the original network, resulting in a diminished sample size, and because when the conditional and unconditional causal effects differ the former is generally biased towards the null value relative to the latter. This direction of bias is what permits valid hypothesis tests in the conditional models, but it also results in reduced power. However, this proposal is first step in the ongoing endeavor to

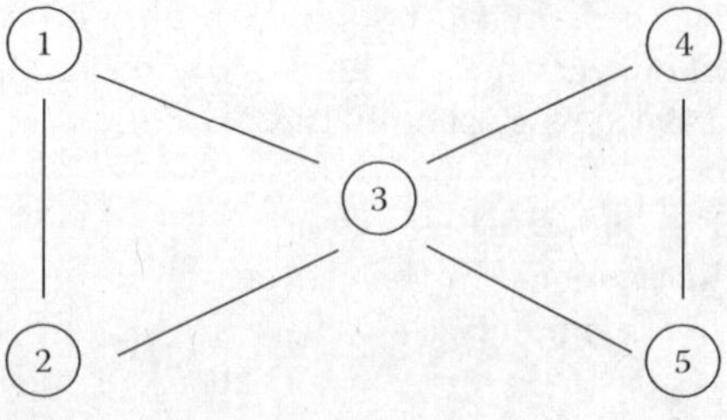

FIGURE 11.2
Bow tie network.

develop methods for valid inference using data collected from a single network. Furthermore, it sheds light on the issues of model misspecification and invalid standard errors for which other proposals to use GLMs and GEEs to assess peer effects have been criticized.

11.3.3.4 Targeted Maximum Loss-Based Estimation for Causal Effects in Networks

Building upon important work by Mark van der Laan on causal inference for nonindependent units (van der Laan, 2014), van der Laan et al. (forthcoming) propose targeted minimum loss-based estimation (TMLE) of average unit-level treatment effects in the presence of interference, of average spillover effects as defined by user-specified exposure functions, of peer effects, and of changes to the network itself (i.e., addition and/or removal of edges). Specifically, they propose semiparametric efficient estimators for $E\left[\frac{1}{n}\sum_{i=1}^{n} Y_i(\mathbf{z})\right]$, the expected average potential outcome under exposure regime $\mathbf{Z} = \mathbf{z}$, where the definition of Z_i is broadened to include any variable that precedes the outcome Y_i. It could include a list of edges emanating from node i, previously occurring outcomes for the alters of node i, or manipulated or observed exposure or treatment variables of node i itself or of the alters of node i. A large class of causal effects can be estimated as the difference of $E\left[\frac{1}{n}\sum_{i=1}^{n} Y_i(\mathbf{z})\right]$ and $E\left[\frac{1}{n}\sum_{i=1}^{n} Y_i(\mathbf{z}')\right]$ for exposures $\mathbf{z}$ and $\mathbf{z}'$ of interest. These estimators can also handle longitudinal data, that is, estimation of $E\left[\frac{1}{n}\sum_{i=1}^{n} Y_i^t(\bar{\mathbf{z}}^t)\right]$, where Y_i^t is the outcome for individual i at time t and $\bar{\mathbf{Z}}^t$ is the collection of vectors $\left(\bar{\mathbf{Z}}^1, ..., \bar{\mathbf{Z}}^{t-1}\right)$.

The details of TMLE are beyond the scope of this chapter but we refer the reader to van der Laan and Rose (2011) for an introduction. For the purposes of comparison to the other methods described above, it suffices to understand that the estimators in question are based on the efficient influence function for the observed data functional that, under some assumptions, identifies the causal estimand $E\left[\frac{1}{n}\sum_{i=1}^{n} Y_i(\mathbf{z})\right]$. The assumptions required for identification are strong and require observation of a rich data structure, which may not always be feasible, affordable, or practical. When these assumptions are met and the mean counterfactual outcome is identified, the proposed estimation procedure is optimal and principled. While the other methods can be seen as somewhat ad hoc attempts to overcome suboptimal data, this is an optimal approach for very rich data.

Specifically, van der Laan et al. (forthcoming) make two strong conditional independence assumptions in addition to the usual assumption of no unmeasured confounders: first, that at time t, node i is independent of all other nodes conditional on all the data from time $t-1$, and second, that at time t, node i is independent of all data from time $t-1$ conditional on his alters' data from time $t-1$. Essentially, these two assumptions imply that any dependence of one node on another is due to information transmitting at discrete times along one edge at a time and that the network (and all data on every node) is observed at least as frequently as information can be transmitted. Although these assumptions are strong, they are to some extent under the researcher's control; meeting them is partially a matter of the richness of the data and therefore of study design and/or resources. The additional assumptions required for the consistency and asymptotic normality of the estimators are relatively weak; these methods can account for the presence of a small number of highly connected and highly influential nodes and for a model of asymptotic growth in which the number of edges per node grows (slowly) with n.

11.4 Discussion and Future Directions

The preceding two sections comprise an overview of state-of-the-art approaches to network modeling and to causal inference using observations sampled from a fixed network. Unfortunately, in many scenarios, the network is only partially observed or is observed with noise, so treating it as fixed and known (as most of the methods in Section 11.3 do) may be inappropriate. This makes the already-difficult project of causal inference even more challenging. The naive approach to causal inference using incomplete network data would be to impute missing data in a first step and then to proceed with causal inference as if the data estimated in the first step were fixed and known. The primary downside of this procedure is that it does not incorporate the uncertainty from the network fitting into the uncertainty about the causal effects; a procedure that performs both tasks simultaneously is highly desirable.

In Lunagomez and Airoldi (2014), the authors tackle the problem of jointly modeling the sampling mechanism for causal inference as well as the underlying network on which the data was collected. The model selected for the network in this chapter is the simple Erdos–Renyi model that depends on a single parameter p. Since the network is not fully observed under the sampling scheme discussed in this chapter (respondent-driven sampling), the network model is chosen to accommodate marginalizing out the missing network information in a Bayesian framework. The use of a simple network model makes computation tractable, but the framework proposed by Lunagomez and Airoldi (2014) can theoretically be relaxed to incorporate any network model.

An alternative approach could be based on the proposal of Fosdick and Hoff (2013). While these authors do not discuss estimation of causal effects, their procedure for the joint modeling of network and nodal attributes can be adapted to a model-based causal analysis. In particular, the authors leverage Section 11.2.3 to first test for a relationship between nodal attributes Y_i and the latent position vector $\text{lat}_i = (a_i, b_i, U_{i\cdot}, V_{i\cdot})$ and, when evidence for such a relationship is found, to jointly model the vector (Y_i, lat_i). Considering the nodal attributes as potential outcomes and writing $(Y_i(0), Y_i(1), \text{lat}_i)$, it should in principle be possible to jointly model the full data vector using the same Markov chain Monte Carlo procedure as in Fosdick and Hoff (2013).

Without fully observing the network it is difficult to precisely define, let alone to estimate, the causal effects discussed in Section 11.3. Jointly modeling network topology, to account for missing data or subsampling, and causal effects for observations sampled from network nodes, is one of the most important and challenging areas for future research. The work of Lunagomez and Airoldi (2014) and Fosdick and Hoff (2013) point toward powerful and promising solutions, but much work remains to be done.

References

E.M. Airoldi, D.M. Blei, S.E. Fienberg, and E.P. Xing. Mixed membership stochastic blockmodels. *The Journal of Machine Learning Research*, 9:1981–2014, 2008.

E.M. Airoldi, T.B. Costa, and S.H. Chan. Stochastic blockmodel approximation of a graphon: Theory and consistent estimation. In *Advances in Neural Information Processing Systems*, pp. 692–700, 2013.

R. Albert and A.-L. Barabási. Statistical mechanics of complex networks. *Reviews of Modern Physics*, 74(1):47, 2002.

M.M. Ali and D.S. Dwyer. Estimating peer effects in adolescent smoking behavior: A longitudinal analysis. *Journal of Adolescent Health*, 45(4):402–408, 2009.

J.D. Angrist, G.W. Imbens, and D.B. Rubin. Identification of causal effects using instrumental variables. *Journal of the American Statistical Association*, 91(434):444–455, 1996.

J.D. Angrist and J.-S. Pischke. *Mostly Harmless Econometrics: An Empiricist's Companion*. Princeton University Press, Princeton, NJ, 2008.

P.M. Aronow and C. Samii. Estimating average causal effects under general interference. Technical report, http://arxiv.org/abs/1305.6156, 2013.

A.-L. Barabási and R. Albert. Emergence of scaling in random networks. *Science*, 286(5439): 509–512, 1999.

P.J. Bickel and P. Sarkar. Hypothesis testing for automated community detection in networks. arXiv preprint arXiv:1311.2694, 2013.

J. Blitzstein and P. Diaconis. A sequential importance sampling algorithm for generating random graphs with prescribed degrees. *Internet Mathematics*, 6(4):489–522, 2011.

J. Bowers, M.M. Fredrickson, and C. Panagopoulos. Reasoning about interference between units: A general framework. *Political Analysis*, 21(1):97–124, 2013.

J.T. Cacioppo, J.H. Fowler, and N.A. Christakis. Alone in the crowd: The structure and spread of loneliness in a large social network. *Journal of Personality and Social Psychology*, 97(6):977, 2009.

D.S. Choi. Estimation of monotone treatment effects in network experiments. arXiv preprint arXiv:1408.4102, 2014.

D.S. Choi, P.J. Wolfe, and E.M. Airoldi. Stochastic blockmodels with a growing number of classes. *Biometrika*, 99(2):273–284, 2012.

N.A. Christakis and J.H. Fowler. The spread of obesity in a large social network over 32 years. *New England Journal of Medicine*, 357(4):370–379, 2007.

N.A. Christakis and J.H. Fowler. The collective dynamics of smoking in a large social network. *New England Journal of Medicine*, 358(21):2249–2258, 2008.

N.A. Christakis and J.H. Fowler. Social network sensors for early detection of contagious outbreaks. *PLoS One*, 5(9):e12948, 2010.

N.A. Christakis and J.H. Fowler. Social contagion theory: Examining dynamic social networks and human behavior. *Statistics in Medicine*, 32(4):556–577, 2013.

A. Clauset, C.R. Shalizi, and M.E.J. Newman. Power-law distributions in empirical data. *SIAM Review*, 51(4):661–703, 2009.

E. Cohen-Cole and J.M. Fletcher. Is obesity contagious? Social networks vs. environmental factors in the obesity epidemic. *Journal of Health Economics*, 27(5):1382–1387, 2008.

R. Durrett. *Random Graph Dynamics*, vol. 200. Cambridge University Press, Cambridge, New York, 2007.

D. Eckles, B. Karrer, and J. Ugander. Design and analysis of experiments in networks: Reducing bias from interference. arXiv preprint arXiv:1404.7530, 2014.

P. Erdos and A. Renyi. On random graphs I. *Publicationes Mathematicae Debrecen*, 6: 290–297, 1959.

L. Euler. Solutio problematis ad geometriam situs pertinentis. *Commentarii Academiae Scientiarum Petropolitanae*, 8:128–140, 1741.

R.A. Fisher. On the mathematical foundations of theoretical statistics. In *Philosophical Transactions of the Royal Society of London. Series A, Containing Papers of a Mathematical or Physical Character*, pp. 309–368, 1922.

B.K. Fosdick and P.D. Hoff. Testing and modeling dependencies between a network and nodal attributes. arXiv preprint arXiv:1306.4708, 2013.

J.H. Fowler and N.A. Christakis. Estimating peer effects on health in social networks: A response to Cohen-Cole and Fletcher; Trogdon, Nonnemaker, Pais. *Journal of Health Economics*, 27(5):1400, 2008.

E.N. Gilbert. Random graphs. *The Annals of Mathematical Statistics*, 30:1141–1144, 1959.

A. Goldenberg, A.X. Zheng, S.E. Fienberg, and E.M. Airoldi. A survey of statistical network models. *Foundations and Trends® in Machine Learning*, 2(2):129–233, 2010.

S. Greenland. An introduction to instrumental variables for epidemiologists. *International Journal of Epidemiology*, 29(4):722–729, 2000.

M.E. Halloran and C.J. Struchiner. Causal inference in infectious diseases. *Epidemiology*, 6 (2):142–151, 1995.

M.A. Hernan. A definition of causal effect for epidemiological research. *Journal of Epidemiology and Community Health*, 58(4):265–271, 2004.

P. Hoff, B. Fosdick, A. Volfovsky, and K. Stovel. Likelihoods for fixed rank nomination networks. *Network Science*, 1(03):253–277, 2013.

P.D. Hoff. Bilinear mixed-effects models for dyadic data. *Journal of the American Statistical Association*, 100(469):286–295, 2005.

P.D. Hoff. Discussion of "Model-based clustering for social networks," by Handcock, Raftery and Tantrum. *Journal of the Royal Statistical Society, Series A*, 170(2):339, 2007.

P.D. Hoff. Modeling homophily and stochastic equivalence in symmetric relational data. In J.C. Platt, D. Koller, Y. Singer, and S. Roweis (eds.), *Advances in Neural Information Processing Systems 20*, pp. 657–664. MIT Press, Cambridge, MA, 2008. http://cran.r-project.org/web/packages/eigenmodel/.

P.D. Hoff, A.E. Raftery, and M.S. Handcock. Latent space approaches to social network analysis. *Journal of the American Statistical Association*, 97(460):1090–1098, 2002.

P.W. Holland, K.B. Laskey, and S. Leinhardt. Stochastic blockmodels: First steps. *Social Networks*, 5(2):109–137, 1983.

B. Karrer and M.E.J. Newman. Stochastic blockmodels and community structure in networks. *Physical Review E*, 83(1):016107, 2011.

E.D. Kolaczyk. *Statistical Analysis of Network Data*. Springer, New York, 2009.

E.D. Kolaczyk and P.N. Krivitsky. On the question of effective sample size in network modeling. arXiv preprint arXiv:1112.0840, 2011.

D. Lazer, B. Rubineau, C. Chetkovich, N. Katz, and M. Neblo. The coevolution of networks and political attitudes. *Political Communication*, 27(3):248–274, 2010.

S. Lunagomez and E. Airoldi. Bayesian inference from non-ignorable network sampling designs. arXiv preprint arXiv:1401.4718, 2014.

R. Lyons. The spread of evidence-poor medicine via flawed social-network analysis. *Statistics, Politics, and Policy*, 2(1), 2011.

C.F. Manski. Identification of endogenous social effects: The reflection problem. *The Review of Economic Studies*, 60(3):531–542, 1993.

C.F. Manski. Identification of treatment response with social interactions. *The Econometrics Journal*, 16(1):S1–S23, 2013.

H. Noel and B. Nyhan. The unfriending problem: The consequences of homophily in friendship retention for causal estimates of social influence. *Social Networks*, 33(3): 211–218, 2011.

K. Nowicki and T.A.B. Snijders. Estimation and prediction for stochastic blockstructures. *Journal of the American Statistical Association*, 96(455):1077–1087, 2001.

E.L. Ogburn and T.J. VanderWeele. Causal diagrams for interference. *Statistical Science*, 29(4):559–578, 2014a.

E.L. Ogburn and T.J. VanderWeele. Vaccines, contagion, and social networks. arXiv preprint arXiv:1403.1241, 2014b.

A.J. O'Malley, F. Elwert, J.N. Rosenquist, A.M. Zaslavsky, and N.A. Christakis. Estimating peer effects in longitudinal dyadic data using instrumental variables. *Biometrics*, 70(3):506–515, 2014.

J. Pearl. *Causality: Models, Reasoning and Inference*, vol. 29. Cambridge University Press, New York, 2000.

K. Rohe, S. Chatterjee, and B. Yu. Spectral clustering and the high-dimensional stochastic blockmodel. *The Annals of Statistics*, 39(4):1878–1915, 2011.

P.R. Rosenbaum. Interference between units in randomized experiments. *Journal of the American Statistical Association*, 102(477):191–200, 2007.

J.N. Rosenquist, J. Murabito, J.H. Fowler, and N.A. Christakis. The spread of alcohol consumption behavior in a large social network. *Annals of Internal Medicine*, 152(7): 426–433, 2010.

D.B. Rubin. Causal inference using potential outcomes. *Journal of the American Statistical Association*, 100(469), 2005.

C.R. Shalizi. Comment on "why and when 'flawed' social network analyses still yield valid tests of no contagion." *Statistics, Politics, and Policy*, 3(1):1–3, 2012.

C.R. Shalizi and A.C. Thomas. Homophily and contagion are generically confounded in observational social network studies. *Sociological Methods & Research*, 40(2):211–239, 2011.

E.A. Thompson and C.J. Geyer. Fuzzy p-values in latent variable problems. *Biometrika*, 94 (1):49–60, 2007.

P. Toulis and E. Kao. Estimation of causal peer influence effects. In *Proceedings of the 30th International Conference on Machine Learning*, pp. 1489–1497, 2013.

J. Ugander, B. Karrer, L. Backstrom, and J. Kleinberg. Graph cluster randomization: Network exposure to multiple universes. In *Proceedings of the 19th ACM SIGKDD International Conference on Knowledge Discovery and Data Mining*, pp. 329–337. ACM, 2013.

M.J. van der Laan. Causal inference for a population of causally connected units. *Journal of Causal Inference*, 2(1):13–74, 2014.

M.J. van der Laan, E.L. Ogburn, and I. Diaz. Causal inference for social networks. (forthcoming).

M.J. van der Laan and S. Rose. *Targeted Learning: Causal Inference for Observational and Experimental Data*. Springer, New York, 2011.

T.J. VanderWeele. Sensitivity analysis for contagion effects in social networks. *Sociological Methods & Research*, 40(2):240–255, 2011.

T.J. VanderWeele, E.L. Ogburn, and E.J. Tchetgen Tchetgen. Why and when "flawed" social network analyses still yield valid tests of no contagion. *Statistics, Politics, and Policy*, 3(1):1–11, 2012.

A. Volfovsky and E. Airoldi. Characterization of finite group invariant distributions. arXiv preprint arXiv:1407.6092, 2014.

A. Volfovsky and P.D. Hoff. Testing for nodal dependence in relational data matrices. *Journal of the American Statistical Association*, 2014.

Y.J. Wang and G.Y. Wong. Stochastic blockmodels for directed graphs. *Journal of the American Statistical Association*, 82(397):8–19, 1987.

R.M. Warner, D.A. Kenny, and M. Stoto. A new round robin analysis of variance for social interaction data. *Journal of Personality and Social Psychology*, 37(10):1742, 1979.

D.J. Watts and S.H. Strogatz. Collective dynamics of "small-world" networks. *Nature*, 393 (6684):440–442, 1998.

J.J. Yang, Q. Han, and E.M. Airoldi. Nonparametric estimation and testing of exchangeable graph models. In *Proceedings of the 17th International Conference on Artificial Intelligence and Statistics*, pp. 1060–1067, 2014.

12

Mining Large Graphs

David F. Gleich and Michael W. Mahoney

CONTENTS

12.1 Introduction 192
12.1.1 Scope and Overview 192
12.2 Preliminaries 193
12.2.1 Graph Representations 193
12.2.2 Graph Mining Tasks 194
12.2.3 Classification of Large Graphs 195
12.2.4 Large Graph Mining Systems 197
12.2.5 Sources for Data 197
12.3 Canonical Types of Large-Scale Graph Mining Methods 198
12.3.1 Geodesic Neighborhood-Based Graph Mining 198
12.3.2 Diffusion Neighborhood-Based Graph Mining 199
12.3.3 Generalized Matrix-Vector Products Graph Mining 199
12.4 Mining with Geodesic Neighborhoods 199
12.4.1 Single Neighborhoods 199
12.4.2 All Neighborhoods 200
12.4.3 Complexities with Power-Law Graphs 200
12.5 Mining with Diffusion Neighborhoods 201
12.5.1 ACL Push Methods 203
12.5.2 Random Walks with Restart 203
12.6 Mining with Generalized Matrix-Vector Products 204
12.6.1 Algorithms with Standard Matrix-Vector Products 205
12.6.2 Algorithms with Semi-Ring Matrix-Vector Products 205
12.6.3 General Updates 207
12.6.4 Edge-Oriented Updates 207
12.6.5 Complexities with Power-Law Graphs 208
12.6.6 Implementations in SQL 208
12.7 Limitations and Tradeoffs in Mining Large Graph 208
12.7.1 Graph Drawing 209
12.7.2 Viral Propagation 210
12.7.3 Communities and Modularity 211
12.7.3.1 Preliminaries 211
12.7.3.2 Modularity Definition 212
12.7.3.3 Modularity as a Cut Measure 212
12.8 Large Graph Mining in the Future 214
12.8.1 Mining with Streaming Procedures 214
12.8.2 Mining with Generalized Matrix–Matrix Products 214

Acknowledgments 215
References 215

12.1 Introduction

Graphs provide a general representation or data model for many types of data, where pair-wise relationships are known or thought to be particularly important.* Thus, it should not be surprising that interest in graph mining has grown with the recent interest in *big data*. Much of the big data generated and analyzed involves pair-wise relationships among a set of entities. For example, in e-commerce applications such as with Amazon's product database, customers are related to products through their purchasing activities; on the web, web pages are related through hypertext linking relationships; on social networks such as Facebook, individuals are related through their friendships; and so on. Similarly, in scientific applications, research articles are related through citations; proteins are related through metabolic pathways, co-expression, and regulatory network effects within a cell; materials are related through models of their crystalline structure; and so on.

While many graphs are small, many large graphs are now extremely LARGE. For example, in early 2008, Google announced that it had indexed over one trillion URLs on the internet, corresponding to a graph with over one trillion nodes [1]; in 2012, the Facebook friendship network spanned 721 million individuals and had 137 billion links [2]; phone companies process a few trillion calls a year [3]; the human brain has around 100 billion neurons and 100 trillion neuronal connections [4]; one of the largest reported graph experiments involved 4.4 trillion nodes and around 70 trillion edges in a synthetic experiment that required one petabyte of storage space [5]; and one of the largest reported experiments with a real-world graph involved over 1.5 trillion edges [6].

Given the ubiquity, size, and importance of graphs in many application areas, it should come as no surprise that large graph mining serves numerous roles within the large-scale data analysis ecosystem. For example, it can help us learn new things about the world, including both the chemical and biological sciences [7,8] as well as results in the social and economic sciences such as the Facebook study that showed that any two people in the(ir) world can be connected through approximately four intermediate individuals [2]. Alternatively, large graph mining produces similar information for recommendation, suggestion, and prediction from messy data [9,10]; it can also tell us how to optimize a data infrastructure to improve response time [11]; and it can tell us when and how our data are anomalous [12].

12.1.1 Scope and Overview

In this chapter, we will provide an overview of several topics in the general area of mining large graphs. This is a large and complicated area. Thus, rather than attempting to be comprehensive, we will instead focus on what seems to us to be particularly interesting or underappreciated algorithmic developments that will in upcoming years provide the basis for an improved understanding of the properties of moderately large to very large informatics graphs. There are many reviews and overviews for the interested reader to learn more about graph mining; see, for example, [13,14]. An important theme in our chapter is that large graphs are often very different than small graphs and thus intuitions from small graphs

*In the simplest case, a graph $G = (V, E)$ consists of a set V of vertices or nodes and a set E of edges, where each edge consists of an undirected pairs of nodes. Of course, in many applications one is interested in graphs that have weighted or directed edges, are time-varying, have additional meta-information associated with the nodes or edges, and so on.

often simply do not hold for large graphs. A second important theme is that, depending on the size of the graph, different classes of algorithms may be more or less appropriate. Thus, we will concern ourselves primarily with *what* is (and is not) even possible in large graph mining; we'll describe *why* one might (or might not) be interested in performing particular graph mining tasks that are possible; and we will provide brief comments on *how* to make a large graph mining task work on a large distributed system such as MapReduce cluster or a Spark cluster. Throughout, we'll highlight some of the common challenges, we'll discuss the heuristics and procedures used to overcome these challenges, and we'll describe how some of these procedures are useful outside the domain for which they were originally developed.* At several points, we will also highlight the relationships between seemingly distinct methods and unexpected, often implicit, properties of large-scale graph algorithms.

12.2 Preliminaries

When data is† represented as a graph, the objects underlying the relationships are called *nodes* or *vertices*, and the relationships are called *edges*, *links*, or *arcs*. For instance, if we are considering a dataset representing web pages and the links from one page to another, then the vertices represent the web pages and the edges represent those links between pages. The result is a directed graph because edges between pages need not be reciprocal. Thus, the idea with representing the data as a graph is that we can abstract the details of a particular domain away into the formation of a graph. Then we can take a domain-specific question, such as "How do I understand phone calling patterns?," and we can rephrase that as a question about the vertices and edges in the graph that is used to model the data.

Let us note that there are often many ways to turn a set of data into a graph. There could be multiple types of possible edges corresponding to different types of relationships among the objects. This is common in what is known as semantic graph analysis and semantic graph mining. Determining what edges to use from such a graph is a fascinating problem that can often have a dramatic effect on the result and/or the scalability of an algorithm. In order to keep our discussion contained, however, we will assume that the underlying graph has been constructed in such a way that the graph mining tasks we discuss make sense on the final graph. Having a non-superficial understanding of what graph mining algorithms actually do and why they might or might not be useful often provides excellent guidance on choosing nodes/edges to include or exclude in the graph construction process.

12.2.1 Graph Representations

The canonical graph we analyze is $G = (V, E)$, where V is the set of vertices and E is the set of edges. We will use n to denote the number of vertices. We assume that the number of edges is $O(n)$ as well, and we will use this for complexity results. If we wish to be specific, the number of edges will be $|E|$. Graphs can be either directed or undirected, although some algorithms may not make sense on both types.

*We have attempted in this preliminary work to strike a balance between providing accurate intuition about our perspective on large graph mining and precise formal statements. In the main text, we skew toward accurate intuition, and in some cases, we provide additional technical caveats for the experts in the footnotes.

†Or *are*—aside from the linguistic issue, one of the challenges in developing graph algorithms is that graphs can be used to represent a single data point as well as many data points. For example, there is $N = 1$ web graph out there, but graphs are also used to represent correlations and similarities between many different data points, each of which is represented by a feature vector. Different research areas think about these issues in very different ways.

While for tiny graphs, for example, graphs containing fewer than several thousand nodes, one can take a *bird's eye* view and think about the entire graph since, for example, it can be stored in processor cache, for larger graphs, it is important to worry about how the data are structured to determine how algorithms run. We need to discuss two important representations of graphs that have a large impact on what is and is not possible with large graph mining.

Edge list. The edge list is simply a list of pairs of vertices in the graph, one pair for each edge. Edges can appear in any order. There is no index, so checking whether or not an edge exists requires a linear scan over all edges. This might also be distributed among many machines. Edge lists are common in graphs created based on translating data from sources such as log files into relationships.

Adjacency list. Given a vertex, its adjacency list is the set of neighbors for that vertex. An adjacency list representation allows us to query for this set of neighbors in a time that we will consider constant.* Adjacency lists are common when graphs are an explicit component of the original data model.

The adjacency list is the most flexible format because it can always serve as an edge list through a simple in-place transformation. In comparison, although building the adjacency list representation from an edge list is a linear-time operation, it may involve an expensive amount of data movement within a distributed environment.†

12.2.2 Graph Mining Tasks

We will use the following representative problems/algorithms to help frame our discussion below.

Random walk steps. A random walk in a graph moves from vertex to vertex by randomly choosing a neighbor. For most adjacency list representations, one step of a random walk is a constant time operation.‡ Running millions of random walk steps given in an adjacency list representation of a large graph is easy,§ and these steps can be used to extract a small region of a massive graph nearby that seed [16,17].

Connected components. Determining the connected components of a graph is a fundamental step in most large graph mining pipelines. On an adjacency list, this can be done using breadth-first search in $O(n)$ time and memory. On an edge list, this can also be done in $O(n)$ time and memory, assuming that the diameter of the graph does not grow with the size of the graph, by using semi-ring iterations [18] that we will discuss in Section 12.6.

PageRank. PageRank [16] is one of a host of graph centrality measures [19] that give information to address the question "What are the most important nodes in my graph?" See [20] for a long list of examples of where it has been successfully used to analyze large graphs. Just as with connected components, it takes $O(n)$ time and memory to compute PageRank, in either the adjacency list representation or edge list representation. Computing PageRank is one of the most common primitives used to test large graph analysis frameworks (e.g., [21–23]).

*Various implementations and systems we consider may not truly guarantee *constant time* access to the neighborhood set of vertices, for example, it may be $O(\log n)$, or be constant in some loosely amortized sense, but this is still a useful approximation for the purposes of distinguishing access patterns for algorithms in large graph mining.

†This data movement is a great fit for Google's MapReduce system.

‡This is not always guaranteed because selecting a random neighbor may be an $O(d)$ operation, where d is the degree of the node, depending on the implementation details.

§Current research efforts are devoted to running random walks with restarts for millions of seeds concurrently on edge list representations of massive graphs [15].

Effective diameter. The effective diameter of a graph is the length of the longest path necessary to connect 90% of the possible node pairs.* Understanding this value guides our intuition about short paths between nodes. Generating an accurate estimate of the effective diameter is possible in $O(n)$ time and memory using a simple algorithm with a sophisticated analysis [24,25].

Extremal eigenvalues. There are a variety of matrix structures associated with a graph. One of the most common is the adjacency matrix, denoted $\mathbf{A}$, where $A_{i,j} = 1$ if there is an edge between vertices i and j and $A_{i,j} = 0$ otherwise.† Another common matrix is the normalized Laplacian, denoted $\mathcal{L}$, where $\mathcal{L}_{i,i} = 1$ and $\mathcal{L}_{i,j} = 1/\sqrt{\text{degree}(i) \cdot \text{degree}(j)}$ if there is an edge between i and j, and $\mathcal{L}_{i,j} = 0$ otherwise. The largest and smallest eigenvalues and eigenvectors of the adjacency or normalized Laplacian matrix of a graph reveal a host of graph properties, from a network centrality score known as *eigenvector centrality* to the Fiedler vector that indicates good ways of splitting a graph into pieces [26,27]. The best algorithms for these problems use the ARPACK software [28], which includes sophisticated techniques to lock eigenvalues and vectors after they have converged. This method would require something like $O(nk \log n)$ time and memory to compute reasonable estimates of the extremal k eigenvalues and eigenvectors.‡

Triangle counting. Triangles, or triples of vertices (i, j, k) where all are connected, have a variety of uses in large graph mining. For instance, counting the triangles incident to a node helps indicate the tendency of the graph to have interesting groups, and thus feature in many link prediction, recommendation systems, and anomaly detections schemes. Given a sparse graph (such that there are order n edges), computing the triangles takes $O(n\sqrt{n})$ work and memory.

All-pairs problems. Explicit all-pairs computations (shortest paths, commute times, and graph kernels [29]) on graphs are generally infeasible for large graphs. Sometimes, there are algorithms that enable fast (near constant-time) queries of any given distance pair or the closest k-nodes query; and there is a class of algorithms that generate so-called Nyström approximations of these distances that yields near-constant time queries. Finding exact scalable methods for these problems is one of the open challenges in large graph mining.

There are of course many other things that could be computed, for example, the δ-hyperbolicity properties of a graph with an $\Theta(n^4)$ algorithm [30]; however, these are many of the most representative problems/algorithms in which graph miners are interested. See Table 12.1 for a brief summary.

12.2.3 Classification of Large Graphs

We now classify large graphs based on their size. As always with a classification, this is only a rough guide that aids our intuition about some natural boundaries in how properties of graph mining change with size. We will use the previous list of tasks from Section 12.2.2

*The diameter of a graph is the length of the longest shortest path to connect all pairs of nodes that have a valid path between them. This measure is not reliable/robust, as many graphs contain a small number of outlier pieces that increase the diameter a lot. Clearly, the exact percentile is entirely arbitrary, but choosing 90% is common. A parameter-less alternative is the average distance in the graph.

†Formally, all matrices associated with a graph require a mapping of the vertices to the indicates 1 to n; however, many implementations of algorithms with matrices on graphs need not create this mapping explicitly. Instead, the algorithm can use the natural vertices identifiers with the implicit understanding that the algorithm is equivalent to some ordering of the vertices.

‡This bound is not at all precise, but a fully precise bound is not a useful guide to practice; this statement represents a working intuition for how long it takes compared to other ideas.

TABLE 12.1
Several common graph primitives and their time and memory complexity.

Random walk with restart	$O(1)$ time and $O(1)$ memory
Connected components	$O(n)$ time and memory
PageRank	$O(n)$ time and memory
Extremal eigenvalues	$O(n \log n)$ time and memory
Triangle counting	$O(n\sqrt{n})$ time and memory
All-pairs shortest paths	$O(n^3)$ time and $O(n^2)$ memory

to provide context for what is and is not possible as graphs get larger. Again, let n be the number of vertices in the graph. Also, recall that realistic graphs are typically *extremely* sparse, for example, roughly tens to at most hundreds of edges per node on average; thus, the number of nodes and the number of edges are both $O(n)$.

Small graphs (under 10k vertices). For the purposes of this chapter, a small graph has fewer than 10,000 vertices. At this size, standard algorithms run easily. For instance, computing all-pairs, shortest paths takes $O(n^3)$ time and $O(n^2)$ memory. This is not a problem for any modern computer.*

A large small graph (10k–1M vertices). Moving beyond small graphs reveals a regime of what we will call *large small* graphs. These are graphs where $O(n^2)$ time algorithms are possible, but $O(n^2)$ memory algorithms become prohibitive or impossible.† We consider these graphs more strongly associated with small graphs though, because there are many tasks, such as diameter computations, that can be done exactly on these graphs, with some additional time. Two differences are worth noting: (1) the most important properties of graphs in this regime (and larger) are very different than the properties of small graphs [33], and (2) even if quadratic time computations are possible, they can be challenging, and they can become prohibitive if they are used in an exploratory data analysis mode or as part of a large cross-validation computation. Thus, some of the algorithms we will discuss for larger graphs can be used fruitfully in these situations.

Small large graphs (1M–100M vertices). This chapter is about large graph mining, and in many ways the transition between small and large graphs occurs around one million vertices. For instance, with a graph of five million vertices, algorithms that do $O(n^2)$ computations are generally infeasible without specialized computing resources. That said, with appropriate considerations being given to computational issues, graphs with between 1M and 100M vertices are reasonably easy to mine with fairly sophisticated techniques given modest computing resources. The basic reason for this is the extreme sparsity of real-world networks. Real-world graphs in this size regime typically have an average degree between 5 and 100. Thus, even a large real-world graph would have at most a few billion edges. This would consume a few gigabytes of memory and could easily be tackled on a modern laptop or desktop computer with 32 Gb of memory. For instance, computing a PageRank vector on a graph with 60M vertices takes a few minutes on a modern laptop. We view this regime attractively, as it elicits many of the algorithmic and statistical challenges of mining

*That being said, this does not mean that the naïve cubic algorithm is best, for example, faster algorithms that have been developed for much larger graphs can implicitly regularize against noise in the graph [31,32]. Thus, they might be better even for rather small graphs, even when more expensive computations are possible.

†On large distributed high performance computers, algorithms with $O(n^2)$ memory and $O(n^3)$ computation are possible on such graphs; however, these systems are not commonly used to mine graphs in this size range.

much larger graphs, without the programming and databases and systems overhead issues of working with even larger problems.

Large graphs (100M–10B vertices). With a few hundred million or even a few billion vertices, the complexity of running even simple graph algorithms increases. However, in this regime, even the largest public networks will fit into main memory on large shared memory systems with around 1TB of main memory.* This was the motivation of the Ligra project [23]. Also, the effective diameter computations on the Facebook networks with 70B edges were done on a single shared memory machine [2].

LARGE graphs (over 10B vertices). With over 10 billion vertices, even shared memory systems are unable to cope with the scale of the networks. The particular number defining this threshold will no doubt become outdated at some point, but there are and will continue to be sufficiently massive networks, where shared memory machines no longer work and specialized distributed techniques are required. This is the case, for instance, with the entire web graph. Note that while global mining, tasks may require a distributed memory computer, it is often possible to extract far smaller subsets of these LARGE graphs that are only large and can be easily handled on a shared memory computer.† The types of problems that we can expect to solve on extremely LARGE graphs are only very simple things such as triangles, connected components, PageRank, and label propagation [5,6].

12.2.4 Large Graph Mining Systems

Mining large graphs can be done with custom software developed for each task. However, there are now a number of graph mining systems (and there continue to be more that are being developed) that hope to make the process easier. These systems abstract standard details away and provide a higher-level interface to manipulate algorithms running on a graph. Three relevant properties of such systems are as follows:

Batch or online. A batch system must process the entire graph for any task, whereas an online system provides access to arbitrary regions of the graph more quickly.

Adjacency or edge list. A system that allows adjacency access enables us to get *all* neighbors of a given node. A system that allows edge list access only gives us a set of edges.

Distributed or centralized. If the graph mining system is distributed, then systems can only access local regions of the graph that are stored on a given machine, and the data that are needed to understand the remainder of the graph may be remote and difficult to access; a centralized system has a more holistic view of the graph.

For instance, a MapReduce graph processing system is a batch, distributed system that provides either edge list [34,35] or adjacency access [36]; GraphLab [22] is a distributed, online, adjacency system; and Ligra [23] is an online, adjacency list, centralized system.

12.2.5 Sources for Data

One of the vexing questions that often arises is: "Where do I get data to test my graph algorithm?" Here, we highlight a few sources.

Stanford Network Analysis Project
https://snap.stanford.edu/data/index.html

*It may be faster to work with them on distributed systems, but our point is that shared memory implementations are possible and far easier than distributed implementations.

†This is likely the best strategy for most of those who are interested in non trivial analytics on LARGE graphs.

This website has a variety of social network data up to a few billion edges.* There is also a host of metadata associated with the networks there, including some ground-truth data for real-world communities in large networks.

Laboratory for Web Algorithmics
http://law.di.unimi.it/datasets.php
The Laboratory for Web Algorithmics group at the University of Milano maintains datasets for use with their graph compression library. They have a variety of web graphs and social networks up to a few billion edges.

Web Graphs: ClueWeb and Common Crawl
http://www.lemurproject.org/clueweb12/webgraph.php/
http://webdatacommons.org/hyperlinkgraph/
Both the ClueWeb group and Common Crawl groups maintain web graphs from their web crawling and web search engine projects. The most recent of these has 3.5 billion vertices and 128 billion edges.† The link graph is freely available while access to the entire crawl information, including the page text, requires purchasing access (ClueWeb) or may be access via Amazon's public datasets (Common Crawl).

University of Florida Sparse Matrix collection
http://www.cise.ufl.edu/research/sparse/matrices/
There is a close relationship between sparse matrices and graph theory through the adjacency (or Laplacian) matrix. The Florida sparse matrix repository contains many adjacency matrices for many real-world graphs. These range in size from a few thousand vertices up to hundreds of millions of edges. For instance, the datasets from the recent DIMACS challenge on graph partitioning [37] are all contained in this repository. Many of these datasets come from much more structured scientific computing applications.

12.3 Canonical Types of Large-Scale Graph Mining Methods

There are three canonical types of large-scale graph mining methods that cover the vast majority of use cases and algorithms. At root, these methods describe data access patterns and depending on the implementation details (some of which we will discuss in the next few sections), they can be used to implement a wide range of graph algorithms for a wide range of graph problems.

12.3.1 Geodesic Neighborhood-Based Graph Mining

Geodesic neighborhood-based computations involve a vertex, its neighboring vertices, and the edges among them. They are among the easiest to scale to large graphs, and they support a surprising variety of different applications, for example, anomaly detection [12]. These methods are typically very *easy* to scale to large graphs when working simultaneously with all of the vertices. To determine whether or not an algorithm that uses this primitive will scale to even larger graphs, the main issue is the size of the highest degree node. Two

*Detailed empirical results for these and many other informatics graphs have been reported previously [33].

†Web graphs require special treatment in terms of number of nodes due to the presence of a crawling frontier.

examples of tasks that can be accomplished with geodesic neighborhood-based graph mining are the triangle counting and computing extremal eigenvalues of all neighborhoods.

12.3.2 Diffusion Neighborhood-Based Graph Mining

Diffusion neighborhood-based computations can be thought of as a *softer* or *fuzzy* version of geodesic neighborhood-based computations.* They can be used to answer questions such as "What does the region of this graph look like around this specific object?" These methods are also *easy* to scale to massive graphs because they do *not* need to explore the entire graph. For example, random walks with restart are an instance of this idea.† One should think of running these diffusion neighborhoods on only $O(\log n)$ or $O(\sqrt{n})$ of the nodes instead of on all nodes.

12.3.3 Generalized Matrix-Vector Products Graph Mining

The bulk of our chapter will focus on what is possible with large graph mining that must use the entire graph. Because such graphs have billions or trillions of edges, nearly linear-time algorithms are the only algorithms that can run on such massive graphs. Despite this limitation, there are a tremendous number of useful mining tasks that can be done in near linear time. For instance, we can compute an accurate estimate of the effective diameter of a graph in near linear time, which is what Facebook used to determine that there are roughly four degrees of separation between individuals [2]. Thus, effective diameter, extremal eigenvalues, PageRank, connected components, and host of other ideas [38] are all instances of generalized matrix-vector product graph mining. The importance of this primitive is frequently suggested in the literature for scalable graph algorithms [18,35]. There is a problem with high-degree nodes with large neighborhoods (think of Barack Obama on Twitter, or a molecule like water in a cell that interacts with a huge number of other molecules) for straightforward use of this type of mining, but there are many ideas about how to address this challenge [22,39].

12.4 Mining with Geodesic Neighborhoods

A geodesic neighborhood of a vertex is the induced subgraph of a vertex v and all of its neighbors within r-steps. A surprisingly wide and useful set of graph mining tasks are possible by analyzing these geodesic neighborhoods.

12.4.1 Single Neighborhoods

Perhaps the simplest large graph mining task involves the one-step geodesic neighborhood of a single node called the *target*. This is useful for visualizing a small piece of a large network to build intuition about that target node. In the context of social networks, this one-step neighborhood is also called the *egonet*. We can then perform a variety of analyses on that neighborhood to understand its role. Common examples of target nodes are suspicious

*In a slightly more precise sense, these are spectral-based, or diffusion-based, relaxations of vertex neighborhood methods.

†There is a way to reduce this task to the previous geodesic primitive, but the examples in subsequent sections show that the two scenarios have a different flavor, and they can lead to very different results in practice.

individuals in a social network and curious proteins and metabolites in biological networks. A single neighborhood can also reveal structural holes predicted by social theory [40].

Implementation. Any mining task that depends on a single neighborhood is well-suited to systems that permit fast neighbor access through the adjacency list. Note that getting a single neighborhood would require two passes over an edge-list or adjacency-list representation stored in a file or in a batch system. Thus, single neighborhood queries are inefficient in such systems.

12.4.2 All Neighborhoods

A richer class of graph mining tasks involve using *all* of the one-step geodesic neighborhoods, that is, the one-step geodesic neighborhood of all of the nodes. For example, consider the task of counting the number of triangles of a massive network. Each triangle in the network is an edge in a one-step neighborhood that does not involve the target node. Thus, by measuring properties of all neighborhoods, we can compute the number of triangles each vertex is associated with as well as the clustering coefficients. More complex all-neighborhoods analysis also enables various types of graph summaries and motif detection.

Implementation. A computation involving all neighborhoods is easy to parallelize by recognizing that each individual neighborhood computation is independent. Forming some of the local neighborhood may be expensive, although this work can be balanced in a variety of standard ways.

Approximations. Forming all of the one-step neighborhoods takes work that scales as $O(n\sqrt{n})$ for sparse graphs—see the discussion in Section 12.2. As graphs become LARGE, even this level of computation is not feasible. Streaming computations are an active research area that provides an alternative (see Section 12.8.1).

Example: Oddball anomaly detection. One example of how neighborhood mining works in practice is given by the so-called Oddball anomaly detection method [12]. The goal of this graph mining task is to find anomalous nodes in a network. To do this, one can compute the following statistics for each local neighborhood graph:

- The number of vertices of the neighborhood,
- The number of edges of the neighborhood,
- The total weight of the neighborhood (for weighted graphs),
- The largest eigenvalue of the adjacency matrix for the neighborhood.

The result of each analysis is a single real-valued number that is a feature of the node having to do with the vertex neighborhood. Thus, the overall result is a set of four features associated with each vertex.* Oddball then applies an outlier detection method to this four-dimensional dataset, and it is able to distinguish a variety of types of anomalous nodes on the Twitter network [12].

12.4.3 Complexities with Power-Law Graphs

One of the challenges that arises when doing all-neighborhoods analysis of real-world networks is the highly skewed distribution of vertex degrees. These networks possess

*That is, this method involves associating a feature vector with each node, where the labels of the feature vector provide information about the node and its place in the graph.

a few vertices of extremely high degree. Constructing and manipulating these vertex neighborhoods then becomes challenging. For instance, on the Twitter network, there are nodes with millions of neighbors such as President Obama around the time of his reelection in 2012. Performing local analysis of this neighborhood itself becomes a large graph mining task. This same problem manifests itself in a variety of different ways. For batch computations in MapReduce, it is called the curse of the last reducer [41]. There are no entirely satisfying, general solutions to these skewed degree problems, and it is a fundamental challenge for large-scale machine learning and data analysis more generally. Strategies to handle them include using additional computational resources for these high-degree nodes such as large shared memory systems [23] or vertex and edge splitting frameworks [22].

12.5 Mining with Diffusion Neighborhoods

The use of graph diffusions in graph mining is typically a formalization of the following idea:

Importance flows from a source node along edges of the graph to target nodes.

The mechanics of how the diffusion behaves on an edge of the graph determines the particular type of diffusion. Well known examples are

- The PageRank diffusion [16]
- The Katz diffusion [42]
- The heat kernel diffusion [29,43]
- The truncated random walk diffusion [44]

These diffusions, and many minor variations, are frequently invented and reinvented under a host of different names [45]: in biology networks, for instance, a PageRank diffusion may also be called an *information diffusion* [46]; spectral methods and local spectral methods implement variants of this idea [31]; diffusion-based information is also known as *guilt by association* [47]; and so on.

A diffusion neighborhood can be thought of as a soft or fuzzy version of a geodesic distance-based neighborhood. It is a neighborhood that, intuitively, follows the *shape* of the graph instead of following the geodesic distance.* We illustrate the difference on a simple example in Figure 12.1. These diffusion neighborhoods are commonly used for large graph mining because they can be computed extremely quickly. For instance, it is possible to compute the diffusion neighborhood of a random node in the Clueweb12 dataset (with 60B edges) on a modest server that costs less than $7500 within a second or two. Importantly, just as with a geodesic distance neighborhood, finding these diffusion neighborhoods can be done without exploring the entire graph.

Although there is a formal mathematical setting for diffusions, here we maintain an informal discussion.† Suppose that source of a diffusion is only a single node u in the graph.

*In some cases, one can make a precise connection with notions of diffusion distance or resistance distance, and in other cases the connection is only informal.

†The majority of this section applies to all types of diffusion neighborhoods using adaptations of the ideas to the nature of those diffusions [49–52].

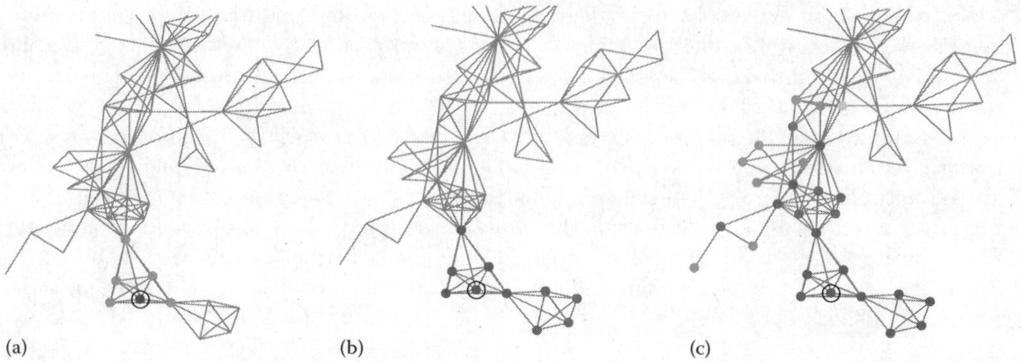

FIGURE 12.1
An illustration (a) of a geodesic neighborhood in Newman's netscience graph [48] around the circled node, with neighbors colored yellow. Diffusion neighborhoods: (b) small diffusion neighborhood and (c) larger diffusion neighborhood of the circled node for comparison; nodes are colored based on their diffusion value, red is large and orange and yellow are smaller. Note that the diffusion neighborhood does not extend beyond the natural borders in the graph.

Then the PageRank diffusion models where dye (or heat or mass or ...) is injected at u and flows under the following dynamics:

1. At a node, the dye is evenly divided among all neighbors of u.
2. Along each edge, only β of the dye survives transmission.

This type of diffusion is often thought to be appropriate for modeling how a scarce resource such as attention, importance, influence, or association could flow in a graph, where each edge is partially uncertain. A diffusion neighborhood is then the region of the graph where the values of the diffusion, or some normalized value of the diffusion, exceed a threshold. Using a small value for the threshold will select a large region of the graph, whereas using a large value will select a small region of the graph. In Figure 12.1, we illustrate two different diffusion neighborhoods on a small network by varying the threshold used to create them.

Diffusion neighborhoods are one of the most scalable primitives in large graph mining, and they can be used to support a large variety of tasks. Similarly to a geodesic neighborhood of a vertex being easy to compute, so too, given adjacency access, the diffusion neighborhood is easy to compute in the same setting. One can use the following two related strategies:

1. The Andersen–Chung–Lang (ACL) push procedure (Section 12.5.1).
2. The random walks with restart method (Section 12.5.2).

Before describing these methods, we first review a small number of the many applications of diffusion neighborhood ideas.

Example: Guilt-by-association mining. In guilt-by-association mining, the graph describes relationships in some type of connected system where one believes there to be a functional connection between nodes. This type of mining is commonly used with biological networks where connections are putative relationships between biological objects (species, genes, drugs, etc.) or with social networks where the edges are potential influence links. In biology, diffusion neighborhoods answer the question: "What might I be missing if I'm interested in a particular node?" The result is a set of predictions about what should be predicted based on a diffusion from a particular node [46,47,53].

Example: Semi-supervised learning. Semi-supervised learning is closely related to guilt-by-association mining. The general idea is the same, but the setup changes slightly. As a canonical example, consider a large graph with a few labeled nodes. One often believes that the labels should remain relatively smoothly varying over the edges, and so the semi-supervised learning problem is to propagate the small set of known labels through the rest of the graph [54]. A diffusion neighborhood mining scheme produces what should be a high-precision set where the label applies. Note that we must use the scalable strategies listed below to propagate the diffusion through the network; straightforward techniques and naïve implementations often do not scale.

Example: Local community detection. Communities in large graphs are sets of vertices that are in some sense internally cohesive and/or separate from other vertices.* Diffusion neighborhoods are an important component of many community detection methods [31,33].† These methods identify a community around a seed node by propagating a diffusion and then truncating it to a high-quality set of nodes through a procedure called sweep cut. Repeating this process for multiple nodes can yield high-quality overlapping communities [58] on small large (as well as small and large) graphs.

12.5.1 ACL Push Methods

The ACL push method is a scalable method to propagate, or evaluate, a diffusion, given a seed node or set of seed nodes [31].‡ It maintains a list of vertices where the diffusion propagation needs to be updated and a set of diffusion values. At each step, it picks a node and acquires the update, then *pushes* the influence of the update to the node's neighbors. (Hence the name.) The algorithm ends once all remaining updates are below a threshold. The result is a set of diffusion values on a small set of nodes. When push is used for community detection, one can use these values to generate a set that satisfies a worst-case approximation bound guaranteeing the set returned by the algorithm is not too far away from the best possible.§

Implementation. Given adjacency access, it is possible to scale this method to arbitrary sized graphs as the method needs to access the adjacency information for a constant number of nodes. Also, a variety of graph mining systems support updating a diffusion only on the *needs-to-be-updated* set [22,23,60].

12.5.2 Random Walks with Restart

One alternative to using the ACL push procedure is to employ a Monte Carlo approach. Diffusions are associated with random-walk processes and we can simply simulate the random walk to propagate the diffusion [17,61,62]. Tracking where the random walk moves in the graph provides most of the information on the diffusion, and a few thousand random walks provide acceptable accuracy in many cases [61,62].

Implementation. Implementation with adjacency access is trivial, as it simply involves a sequence of neighborhood queries that constitute a random walk. The situation is different for implementations without neighborhood access. If the graph is stored in a manner that does not permit efficient neighborhood access, then any of the techniques in the next section

---

*It would require another chapter to discuss communities in large networks in appropriate depth [33, 55,56].

†In particular, spectral algorithms that are commonly used to detect communities have strong connections with diffusion-based neighborhood methods [57].

‡Variants and extensions exist for a host of other diffusions [49,50,59].

§This is done with a sweep cut procedure and uses a localized instance of a Cheeger inequality.

on generalized matrix-vector products will work. However, these are often inefficient. It may take 20–100 *passes* over the graph in order to evaluate the diffusion from a single seed. Diffusion neighborhoods are usually computed for multiple seeds (usually between 10 and 10,000), and recent research gives a few strategies to compute these random walks simultaneously [15].

12.6 Mining with Generalized Matrix-Vector Products

Generalized matrix-vector products are one of the most flexible and scalable ways to mine large graphs [18,35]. As the name suggests, these methods emerge from a generalized notion of a matrix-vector product on generalizations of the adjacency matrix of a graph. Scalable methods for matrix-vector products date back to the dawn of computing [63], and their use with generalized matrix-vector products was recognized early [64]. All of these methods and algorithms apply to batch systems rather than online systems.*

A matrix-vector product $\mathbf{y} = \mathbf{A}\mathbf{x}$ with the adjacency matrix of a graph expresses the computational primitive:

$$y_v = \sum_{u \in N(v)} x_u, \tag{12.1}$$

where $N(v)$ is the neighbor set of node v. If $\mathbf{A}$ represents a directed graph, then matrix-vector products with $\mathbf{A}$ sum over the out-neighbors of v, whereas matrix-vector products with $\mathbf{A}^T$ sum over the in-neighbors of v. In a more general sense, a matrix-vector product can be seen as a special case of the following computational primitive.

$$\text{Update vertex } v\text{'s data based on a function } f \text{ of its neighbors data} \tag{12.2}$$

The standard matrix-vector product uses summation as the function. Iterative sequences of these operations, with different functions, compute connected components, single-source shortest paths, label propagation, effective diameters, and distance histograms, as we will see shortly. Operations such as minimum spanning trees [18], maximum weight matchings [65], and message passing methods [66] fit into the same framework as well.

Graph system support. The generalized matrix-vector product idea is incorporated in a few different software libraries under a different guise. Pregel expresses this concept through the idea of a vertex and edge programming interface [21]. Both GraphLab and Ligra adopt this same type of vertex and edge programming [22,23]. These vertex and edge programs specify the aggregation operation on v as well as the information transmitted from u to v. Pegasus makes the matrix-vector interpretation explicit [35], as does Combinatorial BLAS [67].

Two types of functions. We will consider two classes of function f. The first class is a *reduction operation*, which is a generalization of the summation operation. Reduction operations are associative functions of their data. That is, we can apply f to a subset of the neighbor information and then later integrate that with the rest of the information. The second class is just a *general function* f that can do anything with the neighbor information. One simple example related to what we will see below is computing the *median* value of all neighbors. This is not associative and depends on the entire set of elements. This distinction is important as various optimizations employed by graph systems, such as the vertex-splitting in GraphLab [22], only work for reduction functions.

*A standard use case is to use the result of a batch generalized matrix-vector product algorithm to enable or accelerate an online operation. For instance, compute recommendations using generalized matrix-vector products and store some results for online queries.

12.6.1 Algorithms with Standard Matrix-Vector Products

Even the standard matrix-vector product is a key to many large graph mining methods. We give two examples below.

Implementation. A parallel matrix-vector product is easy to implement on a centralized graph system as each vertex runs its own update equation independently. (This assumes that all updates are independent, as they are in all of the following examples.) Distributed implementations require a means to *move* data along the edges of the graph. These are often precomputed at the start of a procedure given the current data distribution, or maintained with some type of distributed hash-table. Matrix-vector products can easily work with adjacency or edge-list information, which makes them a highly flexible graph mining primitive.

Example: PageRank. The global PageRank vector is the result of a diffusion—with seeds *everywhere* in the graph. This yields information about the important nodes from *all* vertices. It is usually computed on a directed graph using the iteration:

$$\textbf{Initialize: } x_v^{(\text{start})} = 1, \qquad \textbf{Iterate: } x_v^{(\text{next})} = \alpha \sum_{u \in N^{\text{in}}(v)} x_u^{(\text{cur})}/d_v + 1,$$

where $N^{\text{in}}(v)$ is the set of in-neighbors. This is just a small adjustment to the standard matrix-vector product above. Usually α is taken to be 0.85,* and 20 or 30 iterations suffice for most purposes for this value of α.

Example: Extremal eigenvalues and approximate number of triangles. The extremal eigenvalues and eigenvectors of the adjacency matrix and normalized Laplacian matrix can be provided by the ARPACK software [28], and its parallel PARPACK variant [68], or through simple subspace iterative methods. The key to all of these ideas is to perform a sequence of matrix-vector products with the adjacency or Laplacian matrix. Extremal eigenvalues of the adjacency matrix provide an accurate estimate of the total number of triangles in a graph at the cost of a few matrix-vector products [69]. The extremal eigenvectors of the normalized Laplacian matrix indicate good ways to split the graph into pieces [26,27].

12.6.2 Algorithms with Semi-Ring Matrix-Vector Products

Our first generalization of matrix-vector products involves changing what *addition* and *multiplication* by using a semi-ring.†,‡ We use $\oplus$ and $\otimes$ to denote the *changed* addition and multiplication operations to distinguish them from the usual operations. A classic example of this case is the *min-plus* semi-ring, where we set $a \oplus b = \min(a, b)$ and $a \otimes b = a + b$. Each of these new operations has their own set of *identity elements*, just like adding 0 and

*Note, though, that α really is just a regularization parameter, and so its value should be chosen according to a model selection rule. See [20] for a discussion on values of α.

†More formally, a semi-ring is a set that is closed under two binary operations: $\otimes$ and $\oplus$ along with their respective identity elements: ①, the multiplicative identity element and ⓪, the additive identity element. These operations must be associative and distributive.

‡This generalization may seem peculiar to readers who have not seen it before. It is similar to the usual matrix-vector product in that it can be formally written in the same way. Relatedly, if communication is a more precious resource than computation, then algorithms that communicate in similar ways—which is what writing algorithms in terms of primitives such as matrix-vector multiplication is essentially doing—can potentially provide more sophisticated computation (than the usual *multiply, then sum* that the usual matrix-vector product performs) at little or no additional time cost. This is the case, and considering algorithms that can be expressed in this way, that is, as matrix-vector products with non-standard semi-ring matrix-vector multiplication, that is, is *much* more powerful than considering just the usual matrix-vector product.

multiplying by 1 do not change the answer. The identity elements in *min-plus* are ⓪ $= \infty$ and ① $= 0$. Note that using the *min-plus* semi-ring means that we continue to work with numbers, but just change the way these numbers are manipulated by these operations.

A wide variety of classic graph algorithms can be expressed as generalized matrix-vector products using a semi-ring. This idea is more fully explored in the edited volume: *Graph Algorithms in the Language of Linear Algebra* [18]. Note that for a general matrix and vector $\mathbf{A}$ and $\mathbf{x}$ the matrix-vector $\mathbf{y} = \mathbf{Ax}$ produces the element-wise computation:

$$y_i = A_{i,1} \times x_1 + A_{i,2} \times x_2 + \cdots + A_{i,n} \times x_n.$$

The idea with a semi-ring generalized matrix-vector product is that we replace all of these algebraic operations with their semi-ring counterparts:

$$y_i = A_{i,1} \otimes x_1 \oplus A_{i,2} \otimes x_2 \oplus \cdots \oplus A_{i,n} \otimes x_n.$$

Implementation. Implementations of these semi-ring iterative algorithms work just like the implementations of the standard matrix-vector products described above. The only difference is that the actual operations involved change. Note that the semi-ring methods are all *reduction functions* applied to the neighbor data because semi-rings are guaranteed to be associative.

Example: Single-source shortest paths. In fact, using the *min-plus* algebra we can encode the solution of a single-source shortest path computation.* Recall that this operation involves computing the shortest path distance from a source vertex s to all other vertices v. Let $A_{v,u}$ be the distance between vertex v and u, $A_{v,u} =$ ⓪ if they are not connected and $A_{v,v} =$ ① otherwise. Consider the iteration:

$$\textbf{Initialize}: \quad x_v^{(\text{start})} = \begin{cases} ① & v = s \\ ⓪ & v \neq s, \end{cases}$$

$$\textbf{Iterate}: \quad x_v^{(\text{next})} = A_{v,1} \otimes x_1^{(\text{cur})} \oplus A_{v,1} \otimes x_2^{(\text{cur})} \oplus \cdots \oplus A_{v,1} \otimes x_n^{(\text{cur})}$$

$$x_v^{(\text{next})} = \min_{u \in N(v) \cup \{v\}} \left[A_{v,u} + x_u^{(\text{cur})} \right].$$

At each iteration, we find the shortest path to all vertices that are one link further than each previous step. This iteration is closely related to Dijkstra's algorithm without a priority queue.

Example: Connected components. There is also a *min-times* semi-ring, where $a \oplus b = \min(a, b)$ and $a \otimes b = a \times b$ (the regular multiplication operation). Here, ① $= 1$ and ⓪ $= \infty$. Let $A_{v,u} =$ ① if v and u have an edge, $A_{v,u} =$ ⓪ otherwise, and let $A_{v,v} =$ ①. Using this semi-ring, we can compute the connected components of a graph:

$$\textbf{Initialize}: \quad x_v^{(\text{start})} = \text{unique id for } v$$

$$\textbf{Iterate}: \quad x_v^{(\text{next})} = A_{v,1} \otimes x_1^{(\text{cur})} \oplus A_{v,1} \otimes x_2^{(\text{cur})} \oplus \cdots \oplus A_{v,1} \otimes x_n^{(\text{cur})}$$

$$x_v^{(\text{next})} = \min_{u \in N(v) \cup \{v\}} \left[x_u^{(\text{cur})} \right].$$

Once the values do not change in an iteration, all vertices in the same connected component will have the same value on their vertex. If the vertices are labeled 1 to n, then using those labels suffice for the unique ids.

*This can also be used to compute a breadth-first search as well.

12.6.3 General Updates

The most general of the generalized matrix-vector product operations apply arbitrary functions to the neighbor data. For instance, in the example we will see with label propagation clustering, each neighbor sends labels to a vertex v and the vertex takes the *most frequent* incoming label. This operation is not a reduction as it depends on all of the neighboring data, which eliminates some opportunities to optimize intermediate data transfer.* Each of the three examples we will see use different functions, but the unifying theme of these operations is that each step is an instance of Equation 12.2 for some function f. Consequently, all of the parallelization, distribution, and system support is identical between all of these operations.

Implementation. These operations are easy to implement both for adjacency and edge list access in centralized or distributed settings. Getting the information between neighbors, that is, the communication, is the difficult step. In distributed settings, there may be a great deal of data movement required and optimizing this is an active area of research.

Example: Label propagation for clusters and communities. Label propagation is a method to divide a graph into small clusters or communities [70] that has been used to optimize distributions of graph vertices to processors [11] and to optimize the ordering of vertices in adjacency matrices [71]. It works by giving each vertex a unique id (like in the connected components algorithm) and then having vertices iteratively assume the id of the most frequently seen label in their neighborhood (where ties are broken arbitrarily). As we already explained, this is an instance of a generalized matrix-vector product. A few iterations of this procedure suffice for most graphs. The output depends strongly on how ties break and a host of other implementation details.

Example: Distance histograms and average distance. A distance histogram of a network shows the number of vertex pairs separated by k links. It is a key component to the effective diameter computation and also the average distance. Recall that the effective diameter is the smallest k such that (say) 90% of all pairs are connected by k links. If these computations are done exactly, we need one shortest-path computation from each node in the graph, which has a terrible complexity. However, the distance histogram and the neighborhood function of a node can both be approximated, with high accuracy, using generalized matrix-vector products. The essential idea is the Flajolet–Martin count sketch [72] and the HyperLogLog counter [73] to *approximate* the number of vertices at distance exactly k from each vertex. Both of these approximations maintain a small amount of data associated with each vertex. This information is aggregated in a specific way at each vertex to update the approximation.† The aggregation is formally a reduction, and so this method can take advantage of those optimizations. These techniques have been demonstrated on Large graphs with almost 100 billion edges.

12.6.4 Edge-Oriented Updates

We have described these generalized matrix-vector products as updating quantities at each vertex. There is no limitation to vertex-oriented updates only. The same ideas apply edge-oriented updates by viewing them as generalized matrix-vector products with the *line-graph* or *dual-graph* of the input graph. In the dual graph, we replace each edge with a vertex and connect each new vertex to the vertices that represent all adjacent edges.

---

*In MapReduce environments, one example of this optimization is the use of local combiners to reduce the number of key-value pairs sent to the reducers.

†The specifics of the algorithm are not our focus here, see [25] for a modern description.

12.6.5 Complexities with Power-Law Graphs

Power-law, or highly skewed, degree distribution pose problems for efficient implementations of generalized matrix-vector products at scale. The PowerGraph extension of GraphLab [22] contains a number of ideas to improve performance with formal reductions and power-law graphs based on vertex splitting ideas that create virtual *copies* of vertices with lower degree. These large degree vertices, however, tend not to prohibit implementations of these ideas on large graphs and only make them slower.

12.6.6 Implementations in SQL

Generalized matrix-vector products are possible to implement even in traditional database systems that implement SQL [74]. Using a distributed SQL database such as Greenplum will evaluate these tasks with reasonable efficiency even for large graphs. As an example, here we illustrate how to perform the generalized matrix-vector product for connected components in SQL. The graph is stored as a table that provides edge-list access.* The columns head and tail indicate the start and end of each edge. The initial vector is stored as a table with a vertex id and the unique id associated with it (which could be the same).

```
edges : id | head | tail
x : id | comp
```

In the iteration, we create the vector $x^{(\text{next})}$ from x:

```
CREATE TABLE xnext AS (
  SELECT e.tail AS id, MIN(x.comp) AS comp
  FROM edges e INNER JOIN x ON e.head = x.id
  GROUP BY e.tail );
```

This query takes the graph structure, joins it with the vector such that each component of the table x is mapped to the head of each edge. Then we group them by the tail of each edge and take the *MIN* function over all components. This is exactly what the iteration in the connected components example did.

12.7 Limitations and Tradeoffs in Mining Large Graph

In many cases, individuals who employ graph mining tools want to obtain some sort of qualitative understanding of or insight into their data. This soft and subtle goal differs in important ways from simply using the graph to obtain better prediction accuracy in some well-defined downstream machine learning task. In particular, it can differ from the use of the algorithms and techniques we have focused on in the previous sections, for example, when those algorithms are used as black-box components in larger analytics frameworks such as various machine learning pipelines that are increasingly common. A common temptation in this setting is to use the intuition obtained from mining small graph, assuming or hoping that the intuition thereby obtained is relevant or useful for much larger graphs. *In general, it is not.* Using intuition obtained from small graphs can lead to qualitatively incorrect understanding of the behavior and properties of larger graphs; it can lead to qualitatively incorrect understanding of the behavior of algorithms that run on larger graphs.

*We assume that the graph structure is undirected, so both edges (u, v) and (v, u) are stored, and that each vertex has a self-loop.

At root, the reason that our intuition fails in larger graphs is that—for typical informatic graphs—the *local* structure of a large graph is distinct from and qualitatively different than its *global* structure.* A small subgraph of size roughly 100 vertices *is* a global structure in a graph with only 1000 vertices; however, it is a local structure in a graph with millions of vertices. As typical graphs get larger and larger, much of the local structure does not change or grow [33,57]; instead, one simply observes more and more varied pockets of local structure. Hence one aspect of our point: a fundamental difference between small graph mining and large graph mining is that for large graphs, the global structure of the graph (think of the *whole graph*) and its local structure (think of *vertex neighborhoods*) are very different, while, for small graphs, these two types of structures are much more similar.

Moreover, in a large realistic graph, these local structures connect up with each other in ways that are nearly random/quasirandom, or just slightly better than random/quasirandom. A good example of this to keep in mind is the case of community detection, as first described in [33] and as elaborated upon in [57]. The result of those exhaustive empirical investigations was that large real-world graphs do *not* have *good* large communities. This is very different than working with graphs of a few thousand nodes, where good clusters and communities of size 5%–25% of the graph do exist. As the graphs get larger and larger, the good clusters/communities stay roughly of the same size. Thus, if we insist on finding good communities then we may find hundreds or thousands of good small communities in graphs with millions or more of nodes, but we won't find good large communities. That being said, in a large realistic graph, there certainly are large groups of nodes (think 10% of the graph size) with *better than random* community structure (for example, [11,58]); and there certainly are large groups of nodes (again, think 10% of the graph size) with slightly better community quality score (for whatever score is implicitly or explicitly being optimized by the community detection algorithm that one decides to run) than the community quality score that an arbitrary 10% of the nodes of the graph would have; there are many methods that find these latter structures.

In the remainder of this section, we illustrate three examples in which the qualitative difference between large graphs and small graphs manifests and our natural small graph intuition fails: graph drawing, *viral* propagation, and modularity-based communities.

12.7.1 Graph Drawing

Perhaps the pictorially most vivid illustration of the difference between small graphs and large graphs is with respect to visualization and graph drawing. There is no shortage of graph layout ideas that proclaim to visualize *large graphs* [75,76]. While graph layout algorithms are often able to find interesting and useful structures in graphs with around 1000 vertices, they almost universally fail at finding any useful or interesting structure in graphs with more than 10,000 vertices.† The reason for this is that graph drawing algorithms attempt to show both the local and global structure simultaneously by seeking an arrangement of vertices that respects the local edge structure for all edges in the graph. This is not possible for graphs with strong expander-like properties [33,57]. Relatedly, as we will explain shortly in terms of communities, there is surprisingly little global structure to be found.

A better strategy for large graphs is to use summary features to reveal the graph structure. This is essentially how the oddball anomaly detection method works [12]. Each vertex is summarized with a few small local features. The result is a set of

*Informally, by local structure, we mean, for example, the properties of a single node and its nearest neighbors, while by global structure, we mean the properties of the graph as a whole or that involve a constant fraction of the nodes of the graph.

†These *failures* can be quite beautiful, though, from an artistic point of view.

less-artistic-but-more-informative scatter plots that show multivariate relationships among the vertices. Anomalies are revealed because they are outliers in the space of local features. Hive plots of networks are an attempt to make these multivariate plots reveal some of the correlation structure among these attributes on the edges [78].

12.7.2 Viral Propagation

Another qualitative goal in large graph mining is to understand the spread of information within a network. This is often called *viral propagation* due to its relationship with how a virus spreads through a population. This is also a property that is fundamentally different between large graphs and small graphs. Consider the two graphs from Figure 12.2. For each graph, we place three *seed* nodes in these graphs, and we look at how far information would spread from these seeds to the rest of the graph in three steps.* The results of this simple experiment are in Figure 12.3, and it too illustrates this difference between small and large graphs. In small graphs, each of the viral propagations from the source nodes find their own little region of the graph; each region can be meaningfully interpreted, and there is only a very little overlap between different regions. In the large graph, the viral propagations quickly spread and intersect and overlap throughout the graph. This qualitative difference is of fundamental importance, and is not limited to our relatively-simple notion of information propagation; instead, it also holds much more generally for more complex diffusions [57, Figures 12 and 13].

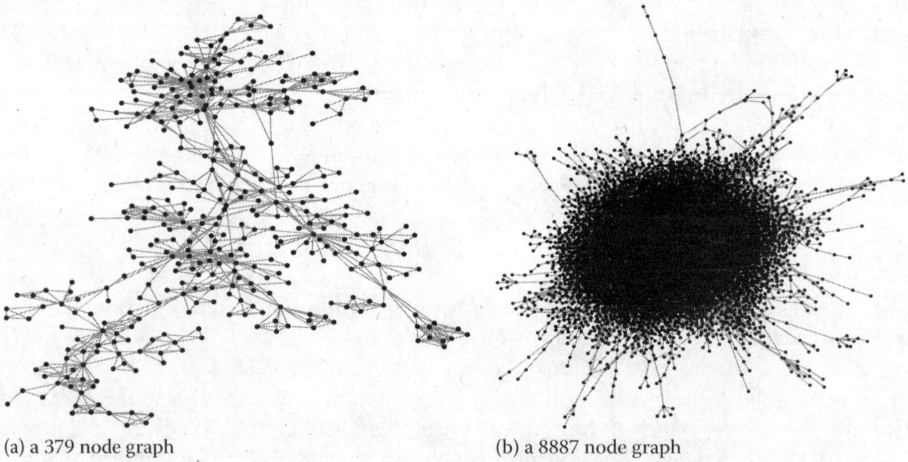

(a) a 379 node graph (b) a 8887 node graph

FIGURE 12.2
Graph drawing for a small and large graph. The small graph drawing (a) shows considerable local structure and reveals some overall topology of the relationships (the graph is Newman's network science collaborators [48]). The large graph drawing (b) shows what is affectionately called a *hairball* and does not reveal any meaningful structure (the graph is a human protein–protein interaction network [77]). The failure of graph drawing to show any meaningful structure in large networks is an example of how we should not draw intuition from small graphs when mining large graphs.

*Here, we are looking at the three-step geodesic neighborhoods of each of the three seeds, but we observe similar results with diffusion-based dynamics and other dynamics.

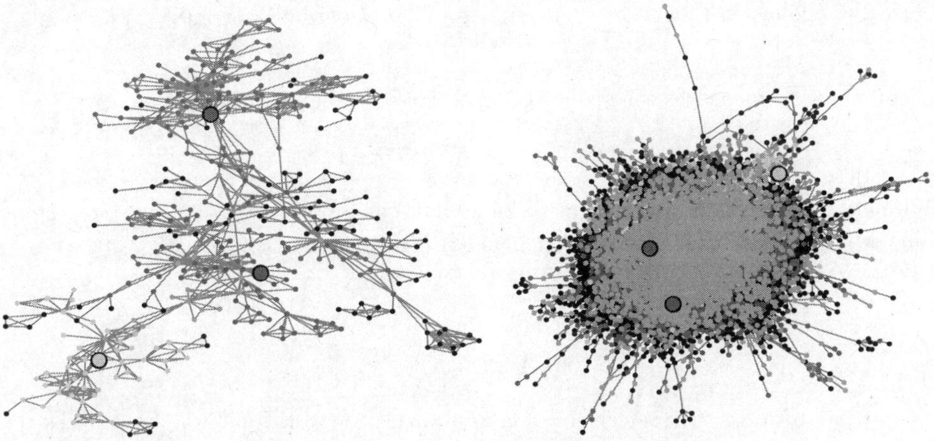

(a) a 379 node graph (b) an 8887 node graph

FIGURE 12.3
Here, we illustrate three steps of geodesic propagation in a small graph (a) and a larger graph (b). The propagations start from three nodes (the big red, yellow, and blue ones). Green nodes are overlaps among the yellow and blue propagations. These figures show that in large graphs, propagations and diffusions quickly spread everywhere, whereas in small graphs, propagations and diffusions stay somewhat isolated. (We did not draw all edges in [b] which causes some colored nodes to appear out of *nowhere* in the *arms* of the figure.) The qualitatively different connectivity properties between large and small graphs is an example of how we should not draw intuition from small graphs when mining large graphs.

12.7.3 Communities and Modularity

Community detection is, for many, the holy grail of graph mining. Communities, or clusters, are thought to reveal or hint at deeper structures and deeper design principles that help to understand or explain a graph. Most people start off by saying that communities are sets of nodes that in some sense have more and/or better connections internally than with the remainder of the graph. Conductance is probably the combinatorial quantity that most-closely captures the intuition underlying this bicriteria [33,55,57]. Another popular community quality metric is known as modularity [79]. Here, we discuss what the modularity objective is and what structures the modularity objective finds in small graphs and in large graphs. As we will see, the types of structures that the modularity objective finds in small versus large graphs are qualitatively different.

12.7.3.1 Preliminaries

For a set of vertices $S \subseteq V$, we use $\bar{S}$ to denote its complement. The volume of a set is a very simple measure of how much vertex information is in that set:

$$\mathrm{vol}(S) = \sum_{i \in S} d_i,$$

where d_i is the degree of node i. We follow the convention $\mathrm{vol}(G) = \mathrm{vol}(V)$ to denote the total volume of the graph. The *edges* function counts the number of edges between subsets of vertices and counts *both* edges:

$$\text{edges}(S,T) = \sum_{i\in S, j\in T} A_{i,j} \qquad \text{and} \qquad \text{edges}(S) = \text{edges}(S,S).$$

The cut function measures the size of the interface between S and $\bar{S}$:

$$\text{cut}(S) = \text{edges}(S,\bar{S}) = \text{cut}(\bar{S}). \tag{12.3}$$

The function cut(S) is often thought to be a trivial or uninteresting measure for the cluster quality of a set S since it often returns singletons, even for graphs that clearly have good clusters. Note that we have the following relationships:

$$\begin{aligned} \text{edges}(S) &= \text{vol}(S) - \text{edges}(S,\bar{S}) = \text{vol}(S) - \text{cut}(S), \\ \text{vol}(S) &= \text{vol}(G) - \text{vol}(\bar{S}). \end{aligned}$$

We use a partition to represent a set of communities. A partition $\mathcal{P}$ of the vertices consists of disjoint subsets of vertices:

$$\mathcal{P} = \{S_1, \ldots, S_k\} \qquad S_i \cap S_j = \emptyset : i \neq j \qquad \bigcup_j S_j = V.$$

12.7.3.2 Modularity Definition

The modularity score for a vertex partition of a graph quantifies how well each group in the partition reflects the structure of an idealized *module* or community of the graph. The analogy comes from an engineering standpoint: a good component or independent module of a complex system should have an internal structure that is nonrandom. The same analogy is thought to apply to a community: a good community should have more internal structure than purely random connections. The modularity score Q of a subset of vertices S codifies this intuition:

$$Q(S) = \frac{1}{\text{vol}(G)}\left(\text{edges}(S) - \frac{1}{\text{vol}(G)}\text{vol}(S)^2\right). \tag{12.4}$$

The term $(1/\text{vol}(G))\,\text{vol}(S)^2$ is the *expected* number of edges among vertices in S, assuming that edges are randomly distributed with the probability of an arbitrary edge (i,j) proportional to $d_i d_j$. Thus, modularity should be *large* when we find a set of vertices that looks non-random. The modularity score of a partition of the graph is then defined to be the sum of modularity scores for its constituent pieces:

$$Q(\mathcal{P}) = \sum_{S\in\mathcal{P}} Q(S).$$

12.7.3.3 Modularity as a Cut Measure

Here, we will reformulate the modularity functions $Q(S)$ and $Q(\mathcal{P})$ in terms of the cut function of Equation 12.3,* and we will describe the implications of this reformulation for finding good communities in small versus large graphs.

*The following material was originally derived in collaboration with Ali Pinar at Sandia National Laboratories. He graciously allowed us to include the material with only an acknowledgment.

Consider, first, two-way partitions. For convenience's sake, let $\nu = 1/\operatorname{vol}(G)$. Note that then:

$$Q(S) = \nu(\underbrace{\operatorname{vol}(S) - \operatorname{cut}(S)}_{=\operatorname{edges}(S)} - \nu \operatorname{vol}(S) \underbrace{(\operatorname{vol}(G) - \operatorname{vol}(\bar{S}))}_{=\operatorname{vol}(S)})$$
$$= \nu(\nu \operatorname{vol}(S) \operatorname{vol}(\bar{S}) - \operatorname{cut}(S)).$$

From this, we have that $Q(S) = Q(\bar{S})$ because $\operatorname{cut}(S) = \operatorname{cut}(\bar{S})$. Consider the modularity of a two-way partition and observe*:

$$\begin{aligned}
Q(\mathcal{P}_2) &= \frac{1}{2}[Q(S) + Q(\bar{S}) + Q(S) + Q(\bar{S})] \\
&= \frac{\nu}{2}(\operatorname{edges}(S) - \nu \operatorname{vol}(S)^2 + \operatorname{edges}(\bar{S}) - \nu \operatorname{vol}(\bar{S})^2 \\
&\quad + 2\nu \operatorname{vol}(S) \operatorname{vol}(\bar{S}) - 2 \operatorname{cut}(S)) \\
&= \frac{\nu}{2}\left(\operatorname{vol}(S) + \operatorname{vol}(\bar{S}) - 4 \operatorname{cut}(S) + \nu(\operatorname{vol}(S) - \operatorname{vol}(\bar{S}))^2\right).
\end{aligned}$$

Hence,

$$Q(S) = \frac{1}{4} - \frac{\nu}{4}\left(4 \operatorname{cut}(S) + \nu(\operatorname{vol}(S) - \operatorname{vol}(\bar{S}))^2\right).$$

From this formulation of the objective we conclude the following theorem.

Theorem 12.1 *The best two way modularity partition corresponds to finding a subset S that minimizes* $\operatorname{cut}(S) + \nu/4(\operatorname{vol}(S) - \operatorname{vol}(\bar{S}))^2$.

In words, a two-way modularity partition is a minimum cut problem with a size constraint in terms of total volume. The constraint or bias toward having $\operatorname{vol}(S) = \operatorname{vol}(\bar{S})$ is extremely strong, however, and thus there is a very strong bias toward finding very well-balanced clusters. This is true whether or not those clusters satisfy the intuitive bicriteria that communities should be set of nodes that have more and/or better connections internally than with the remainder of the graph.

Consider, next, multi-way partitions and we see that the generalization of modularity to multi-way partitions is equally illuminating:

$$Q(\mathcal{P}) = \sum_{S \in \mathcal{P}} Q(S) = \frac{|\mathcal{P}|}{4} - \frac{\nu}{4} \sum_{S \in \mathcal{P}} \left[4 \operatorname{cut}(S) + \nu(\operatorname{vol}(S) - \operatorname{vol}(\bar{S}))^2\right],$$

where $|\mathcal{P}|$ is the number of partitions. An equivalent formulation helps to make the magnitude of the terms more clear:

$$\operatorname{vol}(G) Q(\mathcal{P}) = |\mathcal{P}| \frac{\operatorname{vol}(G)}{4} - \sum_{S \in \mathcal{P}} \left[\operatorname{cut}(S) + (\nu/4)(\operatorname{vol}(S) - \operatorname{vol}(\bar{S}))^2\right],$$

In other words, when considering a multi-way partitioning problem with the modularity objective, adding a new community yields a bonus of $\operatorname{vol}(G)/4$, whereas the cost of this addition is proportional to the cut and the difference in volume. More concretely, optimal modularity partitions for the multi-way partitioning problem will provide a strong bias toward finding many clusters of roughly equal size, whether or not those clusters satisfy the intuitive bicriteria of being community-like, unless there are extremely good cuts in the network.

*This result is derived in a slightly convoluted way, but we have yet to devise a more concise proof.

Thus, in small graphs, such as those on the left of Figures 12.2 and 12.3 that lead to a nice visualization, Equation 12.4 empirically captures the bicriteria that communities are sets of nodes that have more and/or better connections internally than with the remainder of the graph. In large graphs, however, this is typically not the case, and it is not the case for reasons that are fundamental to the structure of the modularity objective. There are applications in which it is of interest to find large clusters that, while not being particularly good, are slightly better than other clusters that are worse, and in those cases using modularity or another objective that provides an extremely strong bias toward finding well-balanced clusters might be appropriate. It is, however, very different than the intuition one obtains by applying the modularity objective on small graphs.

12.8 Large Graph Mining in the Future

Large graph mining is a growing field, and there are many excellent ideas we cannot discuss in depth. We will conclude this chapter by highlighting two active research areas that are particularly exciting for their prospect to impact our mining capabilities in future years.

12.8.1 Mining with Streaming Procedures

Streaming procedures for graphs take input as a stream of edge insertions or edge deletions and must maintain an accurate or approximate representation of some aspect of the entire graph at any point of time. For instance, a simple measure might be the number of edges. These methods become complex because edges may be repeatedly inserted or deleted, but the count should not reflect these duplicate operations. Graph streams are highly related to batch methods for edge-list structures, and *variants of streaming algorithms may be the best algorithm to run even when the entire graph is available in memory.** For instance, it is possible to compute accurate estimates of graph motif counts on graph streams [80]. We expect these procedures to be useful for rapid graph summarization methods. And there are a host of recent results on the opportunities of graph streaming procedures [81]. As highlighted in that survey, a weakness in the graph streaming literature is that streaming algorithms tend to require undirected graphs. Most large graphs are directed.

12.8.2 Mining with Generalized Matrix–Matrix Products

Generalizations of matrix–matrix products are a challenging class of graph mining computations that apply to many *all-pairs* problems. All-pairs shortest paths and all-pairs commute time are two different methods to calculate *distances* between all pairs of vertices in a graph. Shortest paths operate on the graph structure exactly and use geodesic distance. Commute times are distances based on the expected time for a random walk to visit a distant node and return. Graph kernels are a more general setting for commute times that enable a variety of notions of distance and affinity [29]. All of these schemes are intractable to compute exactly for large graphs as the output information is $O(n^2)$. However, there are algorithms that enable fast (near constant-time) queries of any given distance pair or the closest k-nodes query. Moreover, there is a class of algorithms that generate so-called Nyström approximations of these distances that yield near-constant time queries. Finding

*The algorithmic-statistical issues underlying this observation are analogous to those underlying our empirical and theoretical results showing that the ACL push method is often the method of choice even for rather small graphs where more expensive diffusion-based procedures are certainly possible to perform.

scalable methods for these problems is one of the open challenges in large graph mining, and the research landscape of these methods is filled with approximations and estimations. For example, one of the best methods for link prediction in social networks are based on the *Katz matrix*, which is the result of a sequence of matrix-matrix products [82]. These products were approximated in order to make the computation efficient.

Acknowledgments

DGF would like to acknowledge the NSF through award CCF-1149756 for providing partial support. MWM would like to acknowledge the Army Research Office, the Defense Advanced Research Projects Agency XDATA and GRAPHS programs, and the Department of Energy for providing partial support for this work.

References

1. Jesse Alpert and Nissan Hajaj. We knew the web was big .... Official Google Blog. Available online https://googleblog.blogspot.in/2008/07/we-knew-web-was-big.html, July 2008. Accessed on July 11, 2009.

2. Lars Backstrom, Paolo Boldi, Marco Rosa, Johan Ugander, and Sebastiano Vigna. Four degrees of separation. In *Proceedings of the 4th Annual ACM Web Science Conference*, pp. 33–42. ACM, New York, 2012.

3. Chris Strohm and Timothy R. Homan. NSA spying row in Congress ushers in debate over Big Data. *Bloomberg News*, July 25, 2013.

4. Carl Zimmer. 100 trillion connections: New efforts probe and map the brain's detailed architecture. *Scientific American*, 304:58–63, 2011.

5. Paul Burkhardt and Chris Waring. An NSA big graph experiment. Technical Report NSA-RD-2013-056002v1, U.S. National Security Agency, 2013.

6. Eduardo Fleury, Silvio Lattanzi, and Vahab Mirrokni. ASYMP: Fault-tolerant graph mining via asynchronous message passing, 2015. (Under submission.)

7. Richard L. Martin, Berend Smit, and Maciej Haranczyk. Addressing challenges of identifying geometrically diverse sets of crystalline porous materials. *Journal of Chemical Information and Modeling*, 52(2):308–318, 2012.

8. Ulrich Stelzl, Uwe Worm, Maciej Lalowski, Christian Haenig, Felix H. Brembeck, Heike Goehler, Martin Stroedicke et al. A human protein-protein interaction network: A resource for annotating the proteome. *Cell*, 122(6):957–968, 2005.

9. Paolo Boldi, Francesco Bonchi, Carlos Castillo, Debora Donato, Aristides Gionis, and Sebastiano Vigna. The query-flow graph: Model and applications. In *Proceedings of the 17th ACM Conference on Information and Knowledge Management*, pp. 609–618. ACM, New York, 2008.

10. Alessandro Epasto, Jon Feldman, Silvio Lattanzi, Stefano Leonardi, and Vahab Mirrokni. Reduce and aggregate: Similarity ranking in multi-categorical bipartite

graphs. In *Proceedings of the 23rd International Conference on World Wide Web*, pp. 349–360. ACM, New York, 2014.

11. Johan Ugander and Lars Backstrom. Balanced label propagation for partitioning massive graphs. In *Proceedings of the 6th ACM International Conference on Web Search and Data Mining*, pp. 507–516. ACM, New York, 2013.

12. Leman Akoglu, Mary McGlohon, and Christos Faloutsos. Oddball: Spotting anomalies in weighted graphs. In Mohammed Zaki, Jeffrey Yu, B. Ravindran, and Vikram Pudi (eds.), *Advances in Knowledge Discovery and Data Mining*, volume 6119 of *Lecture Notes in Computer Science*, pp. 410–421. Springer, Berlin, Germany, 2010.

13. Deepayan Chakrabarti and Christos Faloutsos. Graph mining: Laws, generators, and algorithms. *ACM Computing Surveys*, 38(1):2, 2006.

14. Stefan Bornholdt and Heinz G. Schuster (eds.). *Handbook of Graphs and Networks: From the Genome to the Internet.* John Wiley & Sons, Weinheim, Germany, 2003.

15. Bahman Bahmani, Kaushik Chakrabarti, and Dong Xin. Fast personalized PageRank on MapReduce. In *Proceedings of the International Conference on Management of Data*, pp. 973–984. ACM, New York, 2011.

16. Lawrence Page, Sergey Brin, Rajeev Motwani, and Terry Winograd. The PageRank citation ranking: Bringing order to the web. Technical Report 1999-66, Stanford University, November 1999.

17. Jia-Yu Pan, Hyung-Jeong Yang, Christos Faloutsos, and Pinar Duygulu. Automatic multimedia cross-modal correlation discovery. In *Proceedings of the 10th ACM SIGKDD International Conference on Knowledge Discovery and Data Mining*, pp. 653–658. ACM, New York, 2004.

18. Jeremy V. Kepner and John Gilbert. *Graph Algorithms in the Language of Linear Algebra.* SIAM, Philadelphia, PA, 2011.

19. Dirk Koschützki, Katharina A. Lehmann, Leon Peeters, Stefan Richter, Dagmar Tenfelde-Podehl, and Oliver Zlotowski. Centrality indicies. In Ulrik Brandes and Thomas Erlebach (eds.), *Network Analysis: Methodological Foundations*, volume 3418 of *Lecture Notes in Computer Science*, Chapter 3, pp. 16–61. Springer, Berlin, Germany, 2005.

20. David F. Gleich. PageRank beyond the web. *SIAM Review*, 57(3):321–363, August 2015.

21. Grzegorz Malewicz, Matthew H. Austern, Aart J.C. Bik, James C. Dehnert, Ilan Horn, Naty Leiser, and Grzegorz Czajkowski. Pregel: A system for large-scale graph processing. In *Proceedings of the ACM SIGMOD International Conference on Management of Data*, pp. 135–146. ACM, New York, 2010.

22. Joseph E. Gonzalez, Yucheng Low, Haijie Gu, Danny Bickson, and Carlos Guestrin. Powergraph: Distributed graph-parallel computation on natural graphs. In *Presented as Part of the 10th USENIX Symposium on Operating Systems Design and Implementation*, pp. 17–30. USENIX, Hollywood, CA, 2012.

23. Julian Shun and Guy E. Blelloch. Ligra: A lightweight graph processing framework for shared memory. *SIGPLAN Notices*, 48(8):135–146, February 2013.

24. Christopher R. Palmer, Phillip B. Gibbons, and Christos Faloutsos. ANF: A fast and scalable tool for data mining in massive graphs. In *Proceedings of the 8th ACM SIGKDD*

International Conference on Knowledge Discovery and Data Mining, pp. 81–90. ACM, New York, 2002.

25. Paolo Boldi, Marco Rosa, and Sebastiano Vigna. HyperANF: Approximating the neighbourhood function of very large graphs on a budget. In *Proceedings of the 20th International Conference on World Wide Web*, pp. 625–634. ACM, New York, 2011.

26. Milena Mihail. Conductance and convergence of Markov chains-a combinatorial treatment of expanders. In *30th Annual Symposium on Foundations of Computer Science*, pp. 526–531. IEEE, Research Triangle Park, NC, October 30–November 1, 1989.

27. Miroslav Fiedler. Algebraic connectivity of graphs. *Czechoslovak Mathematical Journal*, 23(98):298–305, 1973.

28. Richard B. Lehoucq, Danny C. Sorensen, and Chao Yang. *ARPACK User's Guide: Solution of Large Scale Eigenvalue Problems by Implicitly Restarted Arnoldi Methods.* SIAM Publications, Philadelphia, PA, October 1997.

29. Risi I. Kondor and John D. Lafferty. Diffusion kernels on graphs and other discrete input spaces. In *Proceedings of the 19th International Conference on Machine Learning*, pp. 315–322. Morgan Kaufmann Publishers, San Francisco, CA, 2002.

30. Aaron B. Adcock, Blair D. Sullivan, Oscar R. Hernandez, and Michael W. Mahoney. Evaluating OpenMP tasking at scale for the computation of graph hyperbolicity. In *Proceedings of the 9th IWOMP*, pp. 71–83. Springer, Berlin, Germany, 2013.

31. Reid Andersen, Fan Chung, and Kevin Lang. Local graph partitioning using PageRank vectors. In *Proceedings of the 47th Annual IEEE Symposium on Foundations of Computer Science*, pp. 475–486. IEEE, Berkeley, CA, 2006.

32. David F. Gleich and Michael M. Mahoney. Anti-differentiating approximation algorithms: A case study with min-cuts, spectral, and flow. In *Proceedings of the International Conference on Machine Learning*, pp. 1018–1025, 2014.

33. Jure Leskovec, Kevin J. Lang, Anirban Dasgupta, and Michael W. Mahoney. Community structure in large networks: Natural cluster sizes and the absence of large well-defined clusters. *Internet Mathematics*, 6(1):29–123, 2009.

34. Jonathan Cohen. Graph twiddling in a MapReduce world. *Computing in Science and Engineering*, 11(4):29–41, 2009.

35. U Kang, Duen H. Chau, and Christos Faloutsos. PEGASUS: A peta-scale graph mining system implementation and observations. In *9th IEEE International Conference on Data Mining*, pp. 229–238, IEEE, Miami, FL, December 2009.

36. Jimmy Lin and Chris Dyer. *Data-Intensive Text Processing with MapReduce*. Morgan & Claypool, San Rafael, CA, 2010.

37. David A. Bader, Henning Meyerhenke, Peter Sanders, and Dorothea Wagner (eds.), *Graph Partitioning and Graph Clustering. 10th DIMACS Implementation Challenge Workshop*, volume 588 of *Contemporary Mathematics*. American Mathematical Society, Providence, RI, 2013.

38. Michael W. Mahoney, Lorenzo Orecchia, and Nisheeth K. Vishnoi. A local spectral method for graphs: With applications to improving graph partitions and exploring data graphs locally. *Journal of Machine Learning Research*, 13:2339–2365, August 2012.

39. U. Kang and Christos Faloutsos. Beyond 'caveman communities': Hubs and spokes for graph compression and mining. In *Proceedings of the IEEE 11th International Conference on Data Mining*, pp. 300–309. IEEE, Washington, DC, 2011.

40. Ronald Burt. *Structural Holes: The Social Structure of Competition.* Harvard University Press, Cambridge, MA, 1995.

41. Siddharth Suri and Sergei Vassilvitskii. Counting triangles and the curse of the last reducer. In *Proceedings of the 20th International Conference on World Wide Web*, pp. 607–614. ACM, New York, 2011.

42. Leo Katz. A new status index derived from sociometric analysis. *Psychometrika*, 18(1):39–43, March 1953.

43. Fan Chung. The heat kernel as the PageRank of a graph. *Proceedings of the National Academy of Sciences USA*, 104(50):19735–19740, December 2007.

44. Daniel A. Spielman and Shang-Hua Teng. A local clustering algorithm for massive graphs and its application to nearly-linear time graph partitioning. arXiv: cs.DS: 0809.3232, 2008.

45. Frank Lin and William Cohen. Power iteration clustering. In *Proceedings of the 27th International Conference on Machine Learning*, 2010.

46. Andreas M. Lisewski and Olivier Lichtarge. Untangling complex networks: Risk minimization in financial markets through accessible spin glass ground states. *Physica A: Statistical Mechanics and its Applications*, 389(16):3250–3253, 2010.

47. Danai Koutra, Tai-You Ke, U. Kang, Duen Horng Chau, Hsing-Kuo Kenneth Pao, and Christos Faloutsos. Unifying guilt-by-association approaches: Theorems and fast algorithms. In *ECML/PKDD*, pp. 245–260, Springer, Berlin, Germany, 2011.

48. Mark E. J. Newman. Finding community structure in networks using the eigenvectors of matrices. *Physical Review E*, 74(3):036104, September 2006.

49. Francesco Bonchi, Pooya Esfandiar, David F. Gleich, Chen Greif, and Laks V.S. Lakshmanan. Fast matrix computations for pairwise and columnwise commute times and Katz scores. *Internet Mathematics*, 8(1–2):73–112, 2012.

50. Rumi Ghosh, Shang-hua Teng, Kristina Lerman, and Xiaoran Yan. The interplay between dynamics and networks: Centrality, communities, and Cheeger inequality. In *Proceedings of the 20th ACM SIGKDD International Conference on Knowledge Discovery and Data Mining*, pp. 1406–1415. ACM, New York, 2014.

51. Sebastiano Vigna. Spectral ranking. arXiv: cs.IR:0912.0238, 2009.

52. Ricardo Baeza-Yates, Paolo Boldi, and Carlos Castillo. Generalizing PageRank: Damping functions for link-based ranking algorithms. In *Proceedings of the 29th Annual International ACM SIGIR Conference on Research and Development in Information Retrieval*, pp. 308–315. ACM, Seattle, WA, August 2006.

53. Julie L. Morrison, Rainer Breitling, Desmond J. Higham, and David R. Gilbert. GeneRank: Using search engine technology for the analysis of microarray experiments. *BMC Bioinformatics*, 6(1):233, 2005.

54. Dengyong Zhou, Olivier Bousquet, Thomas N. Lal, Jason Weston, and Bernhard Schölkopf. Learning with local and global consistency. In *NIPS*, pp. 321–328, 2003.

55. Satu E. Schaeffer. Graph clustering. *Computer Science Review*, 1(1):27–64, 2007.

56. Jierui Xie, Stephen Kelley, and Boleslaw K. Szymanski. Overlapping community detection in networks: The state-of-the-art and comparative study. *ACM Computing Surveys*, 45(4):43:1–43:35, August 2013.

57. Lucas G. S. Jeub, Prakash Balachandran, Mason A. Porter, Peter J. Mucha, and Michael W. Mahoney. Think locally, act locally: Detection of small, medium-sized, and large communities in large networks. *Physical Review E*, 91:012821, January 2015.

58. Joyce J. Whang, David F. Gleich, and Inderjit S. Dhillon. Overlapping community detection using seed set expansion. In *Proceedings of the 22nd ACM International Conference on Conference on Information and Knowledge Management*, pp. 2099–2108. ACM, New York, October 2013.

59. Kyle Kloster and David F. Gleich. Heat kernel based community detection. In *Proceedings of the 20th ACM SIGKDD International Conference on Knowledge Discovery and Data Mining*, pp. 1386–1395. ACM, New York, 2014.

60. Donald Nguyen, Andrew Lenharth, and Keshav Pingali. A lightweight infrastructure for graph analytics. In *Proceedings of the 24th ACM Symposium on Operating Systems Principles*, pp. 456–471. ACM, New York, 2013.

61. K. Avrachenkov, N. Litvak, D. Nemirovsky, and N. Osipova. Monte carlo methods in PageRank computation: When one iteration is sufficient. *SIAM Journal on Numerical Analysis*, 45(2):890–904, February 2007.

62. Christian Borgs, Michael Brautbar, Jennifer Chayes, and Shang-Hua Teng. Multi-scale matrix sampling and sublinear-time PageRank computation. *Internet Mathematics*, Available online http://dx.doi.org/10.1080/15427951.2013.802752. Accessed on October 23, 2015. 2013.

63. Stephen R. Troyer. Sparse matrix multiplication. Technical Report ILLIAC IV Document Number 191, University of Illinois, Urbana-Champagne, 1968.

64. B. A. Carré. An algebra for network routing problems. *IMA Journal of Applied Mathematics*, 7(3):273–294, 1971.

65. M. Bayati, D. Shah, and M. Sharma. Max-product for maximum weight matching: Convergence, correctness, and LP duality. *IEEE Transactions on Information Theory*, 54(3):1241–1251, March 2008.

66. Pan Zhang and Cristopher Moore. Scalable detection of statistically significant communities and hierarchies, using message passing for modularity. *Proceedings of the National Academy of Sciences USA*, 111(51):18144–18149, 2014.

67. Aydn Buluç and John R. Gilbert. The Combinatorial BLAS: Design, implementation, and applications. *International Journal of High Performance Computing Applications*, 25(4):496–509, November 2011.

68. K. J. Maschhoff and D. C. Sorensen. P_ARPACK: An efficient portable large scale eigenvalue package for distributed memory parallel architectures. In *Proceedings of the 3rd International Workshop on Applied Parallel Computing, Industrial Computation and Optimization*, volume 1184 of *LNCS*, pp. 478–486. Springer, London, 1996.

69. C.E. Tsourakakis. Fast counting of triangles in large real networks without counting: Algorithms and laws. In *Proceedings of the 8th IEEE International Conference on Data Mining*, pp. 608–617. ICDM, Pisa, Italy, December 2008.

70. Usha N. Raghavan, Réka Albert, and Soundar Kumara. Near linear time algorithm to detect community structures in large-scale networks. *Physical Review E*, 76:036106, September 2007.

71. Paolo Boldi, Marco Rosa, Massimo Santini, and Sebastiano Vigna. Layered label propagation: A multiresolution coordinate-free ordering for compressing social networks. In *Proceedings of the 20th WWW2011*, pp. 587–596, ACM, New York, March 2011.

72. Philippe Flajolet and G. Nigel Martin. Probabilistic counting algorithms for data base applications. *Journal of Computer and System Sciences*, 31(2):182–209, September 1985.

73. Philippe Flajolet, Éric Fusy, Olivier Gandouet, and Frédéric Meunier. HyperLogLog: The analysis of a near-optimal cardinality estimation algorithm. In *Conference on Analysis of Algorithms*, pp. 127–146, DMTCS, Nancy, France, 2007.

74. Jeffrey Cohen, Brian Dolan, Mark Dunlap, Joseph M. Hellerstein, and Caleb Welton. MAD skills: New analysis practices for Big Data. *Proceedings of the VLDB Endowment*, 2(2):1481–1492, August 2009.

75. A. T. Adai, S. V. Date, S. Wieland, and E. M. Marcotte. LGL: Creating a map of protein function with an algorithm for visualizing very large biological networks. *Journal of Molecular Biology*, 340(1):179–190, June 2004.

76. Shawn Martin, W. Michael Brown, Richard Klavans, and Kevin W. Boyack. OpenOrd: an open-source toolbox for large graph layout. *Proceedings of SPIE*, 7868:786806–786806-11, 2011.

77. Gunnar Klau. A new graph-based method for pairwise global network alignment. *BMC Bioinformatics*, 10(Suppl 1):S59, January 2009.

78. Martin Krzywinski, Inanc Birol, Steven J.M. Jones, and Marco A. Marra. Hive plots–rational approach to visualizing networks. *Briefings in Bioinformatics*, 13(5):627–644, 2012.

79. M. E. J. Newman and M. Girvan. Finding and evaluating community structure in networks. *Physical Review E*, 69(2):026113, Februery 2004.

80. Madhav Jha, Comandur Seshadhri, and Ali Pinar. A space efficient streaming algorithm for triangle counting using the birthday paradox. In *Proceedings of the 19th ACM SIGKDD International Conference on Knowledge Discovery and Data Mining*, pp. 589–597. ACM, New York, 2013.

81. Andrew McGregor. Graph stream algorithms: A survey. *SIGMOD Record*, 43(1):9–20, May 2014.

82. Xin Sui, Tsung-Hsien Lee, Joyce J. Whang, Berkant Savas, Saral Jain, Keshav Pingali, and Inderjit Dhillon. Parallel clustered low-rank approximation of graphs and its application to link prediction. In Hironori Kasahara and Keiji Kimura (eds.), *Languages and Compilers for Parallel Computing*, volume 7760 of *Lecture Notes in Computer Science*, pp. 76–95. Springer, Berlin, Germany, 2013.

Part V

Model Fitting and Regularization

13

Estimator and Model Selection Using Cross-Validation

Iván Díaz

CONTENTS

13.1 Introduction 223
13.2 Classification of Chemicals 227
13.3 Estimation of the Prediction Error 227
 13.3.1 Cross-Validation with Correlated Units 228
13.4 Discrete Model Selection 228
13.5 Model Stacking and Super Learning 231
 13.5.1 Assessing the Prediction Error of a Stacked Predictor 232
13.6 Asymptotic Results for the Cross-Validated Estimator Selector and the Cross-Validated Risk 233
 13.6.1 Asymptotic Optimality of the Cross-Validation Selector for Prediction 233
 13.6.2 Asymptotic Inference for the Cross-Validated Risk Estimator 235
Appendix A: R Code 237
Appendix B: Description of the Variables of the Example in Section 13.2 238
References 239

13.1 Introduction

Suppose we observe an independent and identically distributed sample $Z_1, \ldots, Z_n$ of random variables with distribution P_0, and assume that P_0 is an element of a statistical model $\mathcal{M}$. Suppose also that nothing is known about P_0, so that $\mathcal{M}$ represents the nonparametric model. Statistical and machine learning are concerned with drawing inferences about target parameters η_0 of the distribution P_0. The types of parameters discussed in this chapter are typically functions η_0 of z, which can be represented as the minimizer of the expectation of a loss function. Specifically, we consider parameters that may be defined as

$$\eta_0 = \arg\min_{\eta \in \mathcal{F}} \int L(z, \eta)\, dP_0(z), \tag{13.1}$$

where $\mathcal{F}$ is a space of functions of z and L is a loss function of interest. The choice of space $\mathcal{F}$ and loss function L explicitly defines the estimation problem. Below we discuss some examples of parameters that may be defined as in Equation 13.1.

Example 1. *Prediction.* Consider a random vector $Z = (X, Y)$, where Y is an outcome of interest and X is a p-dimensional vector of covariates. A key problem in statistics and artificial intelligence is that of predicting the values of the random variable Y, given $X = x$ is observed. In this case, the parameter of interest η_0 may be defined as Equation 13.1, where $\mathcal{F}$ is an appropriately defined space of functions of x and L is an appropriately chosen loss function.

The space $\mathcal{F}$ must satisfy constraints imposed on the parameter η_0. For example, if the range of Y in the interval (a, b), so is the range of $\eta_0(x)$ and the functions $\eta(x)$ in $\mathcal{F}$ must also have range (a, b). Analogously, if Y is binary, $\mathcal{F}$ must be the space of functions taking values on $[0, 1]$.

Common choices for the loss function are the squared error and the absolute error:

$$L(z,\eta) = \begin{cases} (y - \eta(x))^2 \\ |y - \eta(x)| \end{cases}$$

The mean squared-error loss function yields $\eta_0(x)$, which is equal to the regression function $E(Y|X = x) = \int y\, dP_0(y|X = x)$, whereas the absolute error loss function yields $\eta_0(x)$, which is equal to the conditional median of Y given $X = x$.

Example 2. *Conditional Density Estimation.* As in the previous example, assume that Y is a continuous outcome and X is a p-dimensional vector of covariates, but we are now interested in estimating the density of Y conditional on $X = x$, denoted by $\eta_0(y|x)$. In this case, $\mathcal{F}$ is the space of all nonnegative functions η of y and x satisfying $\int \eta(y|x)dy = 1$. A common choice for the loss function is the negative log-likelihood:

$$L(z,\eta) = -\log \eta(y|x)$$

If Y is a binary random variable, its conditional density is uniquely identified by the conditional expectation. Thus, prediction and density estimation are equivalent problems. For binary Y, both the negative log-likelihood and the mean squared error are appropriate loss functions.

Example 3. *Estimation of the Dose–Response Curve.* In addition to Y and X, consider a continuous treatment variable T, and assume that we are interested in estimating the function $\eta_0(t) = E\{E(Y|T = t, X)\}$, where the outer expectation is taken with respect to the marginal distribution of X with $T = t$ fixed. Under certain untestable assumptions (cf. positivity and no unmeasured confounders), $\eta_0(t)$ can be interpreted as the expected outcome that would be observed in a hypothetical world in which $P(T = t) = 1$. This interpretation gives $\eta_0(t)$ the name *dose–response curve.*

The dose–response curve may also be defined as $\eta_0 = \arg\min_{\eta \in \mathcal{F}} \int L(z,\eta)\, dP_0(z)$, where $\mathcal{F}$ is an appropriately defined space of functions of t. A possible choice for the loss function is

$$L(z,\eta) = \frac{(y - \eta(t))^2}{g_0(t|x)}$$

where $g_0(t|x)$ denotes the conditional density of T given $X = x$, evaluated at $T = t$. Although other choices of loss function are available, this choice suffices for illustration purposes. In particular, note that, compared to the previous problems, this loss function depends on the generally unknown density $g_0(t|x)$. In this example, g_0 is a so-called *nuisance parameter*: a parameter whose estimation is necessary but which is not the target parameter itself. In this case, we favor the notation $L_{g_0}(z, \eta)$, to acknowledge the dependence of L on an unknown parameter g_0.

The most common problem in data analysis applications is the prediction problem described in Example 1. Throughout this chapter we focus on this example to illustrate all the relevant concepts, treating two different but related problems. In the first problem, *estimator or model selection*, the aim is to find an optimal estimator among a given class of estimators, where optimality is with respect to the minimal prediction risk. In the second problem, *estimator performance assessment*, the aim is to estimate the risk as a measure of generalization error of the estimator, that is, a measure of the ability of the estimator to correctly predict the units out of the sample. These two problems are discussed in more detail in Sections 13.6.1 and 13.6.2, respectively.

We discuss a model selection approach involving the following steps:

Step 1. Define the parameter of interest using formulation (Equation 13.1). In particular, this involves choosing a loss function of interest.

Step 2. Propose a finite collection $\mathcal{L} = \{\hat{\eta}_k : k = 1, \ldots, K_n\}$ of candidate estimators for η. We call this collection a *library*.

For illustration, consider Example 1. Each candidate estimator $\hat{\eta}_k$ is seen as an algorithm that takes a training sample $\mathcal{T} = \{Z_i : i = 1, \ldots, n\}$ as an input and outputs as an estimated function $\hat{\eta}_k(x)$. The literature in machine and statistical learning provides us with a wealth of algorithms that may be used in this step. Examples include algorithms based on regression trees (e.g., random forests [RFs], classification and regression trees, Bayesian classification and regression trees), algorithms based on smoothing (e.g., generalized additive models, local polynomial regression, multivariate adaptive regression splines), and others (e.g., support vector machines [SVM] and neural networks). Note that we have allowed the number of algorithms K_n to be indexed by n.

Step 3. Construct an estimate $\hat{R}(\hat{\eta}_k)$ of the risk

$$R_0(\hat{\eta}_k) = \int L(z, \hat{\eta}_k) dP_0(z)$$

and define the estimator of η_0 as $\hat{\eta}_{\hat{k}}$, where

$$\hat{k} = \arg \min_{k \in \{1, \ldots, K_n\}} \hat{R}(\hat{\eta}_k)$$

The second step of this process relies on the statistical and machine learning literature to build a rich library of candidate estimators. Fortunately, outcome prediction has been extensively studied and a large variety of estimation algorithms exist. However, other problems such as dose–response curve estimation have not enjoyed as much attention from the data science community. In such problems, the proposal of a rich library of candidate estimators may be a more difficult task.

Construction of the estimator $\hat{R}(\hat{\eta}_k)$ in the third step poses some challenges, because the dataset $\mathcal{T}$ must be used both to train the algorithm $\hat{\eta}_k$ and to assess its performance. As an example of these challenges, consider a naïve risk estimator, given by the empirical risk $\frac{1}{n}\sum_{i=1}^{n} L(\hat{\eta}_k, Z_i)$, which suffers from various drawbacks. First, unless the candidates in the library $\mathcal{L}$ consider very small spaces $\mathcal{F}$ (e.g., logistic regression or exponential families in regression and density estimation), a selector based on the empirical risk may result in highly variable and possibly ill-defined estimators (cf. overfitting and curse of dimensionality). In addition, in terms of prediction assessment, the empirical risk estimator is usually an underestimate. This is a well-recognized problem arising as a consequence of evaluating the performance of the prediction algorithm on the same data that were used to train it. Other classical model selection approaches such as Akaike's information criterion or the Bayesian information criterion also fail to account for the fact that prediction methods are usually data driven [1].

As a solution to the above problems, statistical and machine learning methods have shifted towards data-splitting techniques. The main idea is to split the data so that the training and assessment datasets are independent. Some of the most well-known data-splitting techniques are as follows:

- *Multifold cross-validation.* A number of folds J is chosen, and the data are randomly partitioned in J subsamples. Each of J times, a different subsample is left out, and the algorithm is trained in the remaining portion of the sample. Units in the left-out subsample are posteriorly used to assess the performance of the algorithm through computation of the loss function. These individual performance measures are averaged across units and subsamples to construct the risk estimate.
- *Leave-one-out cross-validation.* This is multifold cross-validation with $J = n$. The algorithm is trained n times. Each time, unit $i \in \{1, \ldots, n\}$ is excluded from the training dataset, and it is used to assess the performance of the algorithm. The performance measures (loss function) across units i are averaged to construct the risk estimate. This method has various practical and theoretical disadvantages. First, it can be computationally intensive because the estimator needs to be trained n times. Second, the theoretical results presented in Section 13.6 below require that the size of the validation sample converges to infinity, and therefore do not cover leave-one-out cross-validation.
- *Bootstrap resampling.* Draw a number J of bootstrap samples (samples of size n drawn with replacement). Train the algorithm in each bootstrap sample, and assess its performance in the left-out portion of the data (i.e., the data that were not included in the bootstrap sample). Average the performance measures across units and bootstrap samples to obtain an estimate of the risk. For large sample sizes, the proportion of units in the validation set may be approximated as $(1 - 1/n)^n \approx \mathrm{e}^{-1} \approx 0.368$.
- *Monte Carlo resampling.* For some predetermined sample size m, draw J subsamples of size m without replacement. Train the algorithm J times using only the m units in each subsample, and assess its performance using the left-out $n - m$ units. Average the performance measures across units and samples to obtain an estimate of the risk.

For conciseness of presentation, we focus on multifold cross-validation and refer to it simply as cross-validation. The remaining of the chapter is organized as follows. In Section 13.2, we briefly describe an applied example that will serve to illustrate the methods. In Section 13.3, we describe estimation of the risk R_0 of an estimator $\hat{\eta}$ using cross-validation. Section 13.4 describes a model selection algorithm using a library $\mathcal{L}$ with finite number of candidates. In Section 13.5, we discuss an estimator in which the library $\mathcal{L}$ is allowed to have infinite candidates indexed by an Euclidean parameter. In Section 13.6, we present two key theoretical results: (1) a convergence result guaranteeing that the cross-validation selector is guaranteed to choose the algorithm in the library that is closest to the true value η_0, where the notion of distance is given by the chosen loss function, as the sample size n increases; and (2) asymptotic linearity result that may be used to compute confidence intervals and test hypotheses about the risk of a given algorithm. We illustrate most concepts using the `SuperLearner` library in R, and provide the code in Appendix A at the end of the chapter.

13.2 Classification of Chemicals

Throughout the chapter we use the quantitative structure-activity relationship (QSAR) biodegradation dataset to illustrate the methods in a binary regression problem, using the library `SuperLearner` in R. The QSAR dataset was built in the Milano Chemometrics and QSAR Research Group, and is available online at the UC Irvine Machine Learning Repository [3]. The dataset contains measures on 41 biodegradation experimental values of 1055 chemicals, collected from the webpage of the National Institute of Technology and Evaluation of Japan. The aim is to develop classification models to discriminate ready (356) and not ready (699) biodegradable molecules. A description of the variables may be found in Appendix B.

13.3 Estimation of the Prediction Error

In this section, we consider a single estimator $\hat{\eta}$ and drop the index k from the notation. Estimates $\hat{\eta}$ of η_0 are usually obtained by training an algorithm on an i.i.d. sample $Z_1, \ldots, Z_n$ of the random variable Z. The objective of this section is to construct an estimate of the prediction error of $\hat{\eta}$. To do this, we view the estimator $\hat{\eta}$ as an algorithm that takes as input a given dataset and outputs a predictive function $\hat{\eta}(x)$ that may be evaluated at any value x.

Consider the following cross-validation setup. Let $\mathcal{V}_1, \ldots, \mathcal{V}_J$ denote a random partition of the index set $\{1, \ldots, n\}$ into J validation sets of approximately the same size, that is, $\mathcal{V}_j \subset \{1, \ldots, n\}$; $\bigcup_{j=1}^{J} \mathcal{V}_j = \{1, \ldots, n\}$; and $\mathcal{V}_j \cap \mathcal{V}_{j'} = \emptyset$. In addition, for each j, the associated training sample is given by $\mathcal{T}_j = \{1, \ldots, n\} \setminus \mathcal{V}_j$. Denote by $\hat{\eta}_{\mathcal{T}_j}$ the prediction function obtained by training the algorithm using only data in the sample $\mathcal{T}_j$. The cross-validated prediction error of an estimated function $\hat{\eta}$ is defined as

$$\hat{R}(\hat{\eta}) = \frac{1}{J} \sum_{j=1}^{J} \frac{1}{|\mathcal{V}_j|} \sum_{i \in \mathcal{V}_j} L(Z_i, \hat{\eta}_{\mathcal{T}_j}) \tag{13.2}$$

Figure 13.1 provides a schematic explanation of the steps involved in the cross-validated estimation of the risk assuming $n = 15$ and $J = 5$. The data are assumed ordered at random.

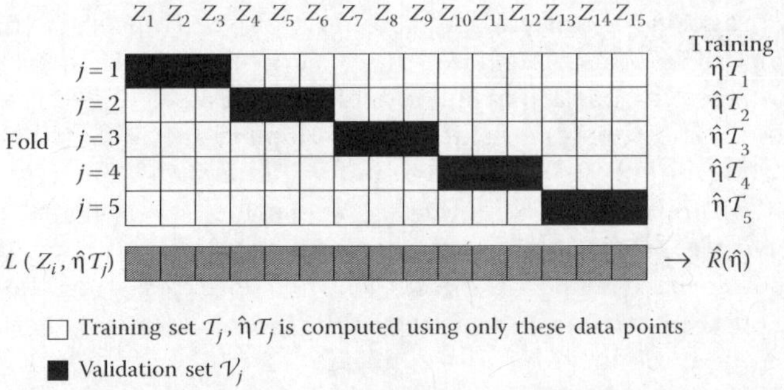

FIGURE 13.1
Cross-validated estimation of the risk assuming $n = 15$ and $J = 5$.

First, the algorithm is trained J times, using only data in $\mathcal{T}_j$ each time. Then, for each j, the performance of $\hat{\eta}_{\mathcal{T}_j}$ is evaluated on all the units i in the left-out portion of the sample, $\mathcal{V}_j$. Lastly, the performance measures $L(Z_i, \hat{\eta}_{\mathcal{T}_j})$ are averaged across units in $\mathcal{V}_j$, and across sample splits j, giving $\hat{R}(\hat{\eta})$.

Intuitively, $\hat{R}(\hat{\eta})$ is a good measure of the risk of $\hat{\eta}$ because, unlike the empirical risk, it incorporates the randomness in $\hat{\eta}$ by considering a sample $\hat{\eta}_{\mathcal{T}_j} : j = 1, \ldots, J$, instead of a fixed $\hat{\eta}$ trained using all the sample. In addition, the performance of the estimator is assessed based on data outside the training set, therefore providing an honest assessment of predictive power.

13.3.1 Cross-Validation with Correlated Units

In various applications, the data may not be assumed independently distributed. Such is the case, for example, of longitudinal studies in the medical sciences in which the objective is to predict the health status of a patient at a given time point, conditional on his health status and covariates in the previous time point. Specifically, consider an observation unit (e.g., a patient) i, with $t = 1, \ldots, m_i$ measurements for each unit (e.g., index t may represent geographical locations, measurement times, etc.). Denote by $X_i = (X_{i1}, X_{i2}, \ldots, X_{im_i})$ the covariate vector and by $Y_i = (Y_{i1}, Y_{i2}, \ldots, Y_{im_i})$ the outcome vector for unit i. Each X_{it} may be a covariate vector itself, containing observations recorded at time t but also at previous times, for example at the most recent past $t-1$. In this case, the correct assumption is that $Z_i = (X_i, Y_i) : i = 1, \ldots, n$ are an i.i.d sample of a random variable $Z \sim P_0$. The predictive function, given by $\eta_0(x, t) = E(Y_t | X_t = x)$, may be estimated using the same type of predictive algorithms discussed above, adding to the explanatory variables a time variable containing the index t.

However, note that these data are independent across the index i, but not the index t. As a result, the optimality properties of cross-validation presented in Section 13.6 will only hold if cross-validation is performed on the index set $\{i : i = 1, \ldots, n\}$. This is an important clarification to prevent cross-validation users from naïvely cross-validating on the index set $\{(i, t) : i = 1, \ldots, n; t = 1, \ldots, m_i\}$, that is, once a unit i is chosen to belong to a validation dataset $\mathcal{V}_j$, all its observations $(i, t) : t = 1, \ldots, m_i$ must also be in $\mathcal{V}_j$.

13.4 Discrete Model Selection

An important step of the model selection approach outlined in the introduction of the chapter involves proposing a collection of estimation algorithms $\mathcal{L} = \{\hat{\eta}_k : j = 1, \ldots, K_n\}$. Some of these algorithms may be based on a subject-matter expert's knowledge (e.g., previous studies suggesting particular functional forms, knowledge of the physical nature of a phenomenon, etc.), some may be flexible data-adaptive methods (of which the statistical and machine learning literature have developed a large variety involving varying degrees of flexibility and computational complexity), and some other algorithms may represent a researcher's favorite prediction tool, or simply standard practice. For example, in a regression problem, it may be known to a subject-matter expert that the relation between a given predictor and the outcome is logarithmic. In that case, a parametric model including a logarithmic term may be included in the library.

Our aim is to construct a candidate selector based on predictive power. This aim may be achieved by defining the estimator as the candidate in the library with the smallest the prediction error estimate $\hat{R}(\hat{\eta}_k)$. That is, the selector is defined as

$$\hat{k} = \arg\min_k \hat{R}(\hat{\eta}_k) \tag{13.3}$$

which is referred to as the *discrete super learner* in [5]. Its corresponding predictive function is given by $\hat{\eta}_{DSL} = \hat{\eta}_{\hat{k}}$, that is, the predictive function of the algorithm with the smallest prediction risk.

For example, consider the problem described in Section 13.2, where we consider the following library of candidate estimators (we give only brief and intuitive descriptions of each algorithm; complete discussions may be found in most modern statistical learning textbooks).

- *Logistic regression with main terms* (*generalized linear model* [*GLM*]). This prediction method represents standard practice in fields such as epidemiology. The main idea is to estimate the coefficients β_j in the parametrization

$$\operatorname{logit} \eta_0(x) = \beta_0 + \sum_{j=1}^{41} \beta_j x_j$$

  where $\operatorname{logit}(p) = \log(p/(1-p))$.

- *Generalized additive model* (*GAM*). The main idea of a GAM is to extend the GLM by considering a model where the predictors enter nonlinearly in the equation. That is, consider the following model:

$$\operatorname{logit} \eta_0(x) = \beta_0 + \sum_{j=1}^{41} \beta_j f_j(x_j)$$

  where the functions f_j are assumed smooth but otherwise unspecified and are typically estimated using smoothing techniques such as cubic splines or local polynomial regression.

- *SVM.* In its simplest form (linear), an SVM is a classifier that separates the X space using a hyperplane, in a way such that the points Y in each of two categories $\{0, 1\}$ are maximally separated. The intuition behind the prediction method is best explained with a figure; a toy example for two-dimensional X and binary Y with perfect separation is presented in Figure 13.2.

- *RF.* This is a prediction algorithm that runs many classification trees. To obtain the probability $\hat{\eta}(x)$, the vector x is run down each of the trees in the forests, and the

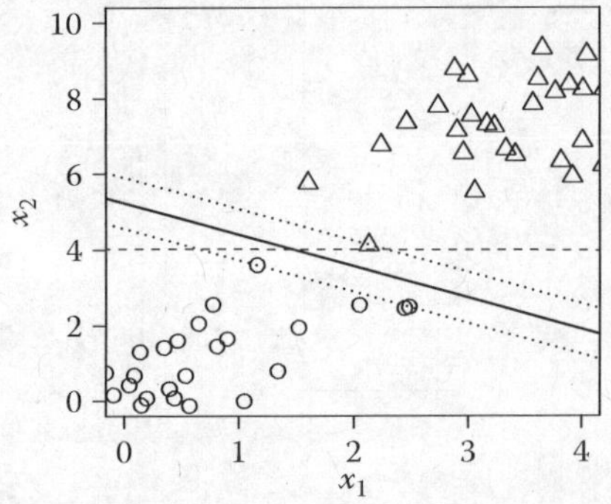

FIGURE 13.2
SVM illustration. The shape of the points defines the categories, the solid and dotted lines represent the SVM maximum separation margin. The dashed line provides suboptimal separation.

classification results are averaged. Each tree is grown by running a classification tree on $q \ll p$ randomly selected variables on a bootstrap sample from the original data. Each tree is grown to the largest extent possible.

- *Multivariate adaptive regression splines (MARS)*. The predictor is built as

$$\eta_0(x) = \beta_0 + \sum_{s=1}^{S} \beta_j B_s(x)$$

  where each B_s is a basis function and S is a tuning parameter. The basis functions take the form of hinge functions $\max(0, x_j - c_j)$ or $\max(0, c_j - x_j)$, where c_j is a tuning parameter called *knot*. Basis functions may also take the form of the product of two or more hinge functions. The MARS predictor is built in a forward–backward fashion, by adding and deleting terms to minimize the sum of squared errors.

- *Mean*. For comparison, we add the most naïve prediction algorithm: $\hat{\eta}(x) = \bar{Y}$.

The cross-validated risk $\hat{R}(\hat{\eta}_k)$ of each of these algorithms applied to our illustrating example is presented in Table 13.4, and may be computed using the `SuperLearner` package in R (code available in Appendix A), which uses the mean squared-error function. These estimated risks indicate that the best predictor for this dataset, among the candidates studied, is the RF.

Figure 13.3 shows the receiver operating characteristic (ROC) curves computed with cross-validated and non-cross-validated predictions. The area under the curve (AUC) is also

TABLE 13.1
Cross-validated risk for each algorithm applied to classification of chemicals.

GLM	GAM	SVM	RF	MARS	Mean
0.1003	0.0985	0.1021	0.0933	0.1154	0.224

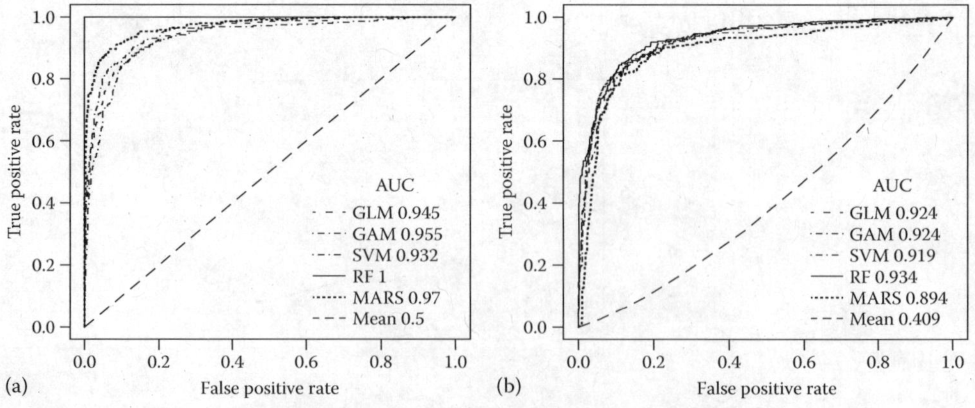

FIGURE 13.3
ROC curve and AUC for each prediction method. (a) Complete sample prediction. (b) Cross-validated prediction.

displayed as a performance measure: an area of 1 indicates perfect prediction, whereas an area of 0.5 indicates that the predictor is not better than a coin toss. This graph illustrates the importance of using cross-validation. Consider first the ROC curves in Figure 13.3a. In this graph, the RF seems to perfectly fit the data, arising suspicion for overfitting and poor generalization power. Meanwhile, MARS seems to be the best performing algorithm. Figure 13.3b shows the ROC computed with cross-validated predictions. Note that, according to Figure 13.3b, the conclusions obtained from Figure 13.3a are wrong. The RF has the best generalization power, whereas the generalization power of the MARS is the poorest among all the algorithms considered.

13.5 Model Stacking and Super Learning

In the previous section, we described an algorithm that may be used to select a unique estimator from a discrete library of candidate algorithms. In this section, we improve discrete model selection by using an ensemble model that combines the predictions of all the models in the discrete candidate library. The main idea behind the super learner (or more generally a stacked predictor) is to use a parametrization $\hat{\eta}_\alpha$ to combine the predictors $\hat{\eta}_k$. Examples of this parametrization include

$$\hat{\eta}_\alpha(z) = \begin{cases} \sum_{k=1}^{K} \alpha_k \hat{\eta}_k(z) \\ \operatorname{expit}\left(\sum_{k=1}^{K} \alpha_k \operatorname{logit}(\hat{\eta}_k(z)) \right) \end{cases}$$

where expit is its inverse of the logit function. The first parametrization is often referred to as a linear model, whereas the second one is referred to as a logistic model, and is often used for binary regression. In the linear model, one may decide to restrict the values α_k to the set of positive weights summing up to one. This constraint on the α parameters would be particularly relevant for estimation of a conditional density function, because it would guarantee that the final estimate is a proper density function.

For simplicity, we focus on parametric models for the ensemble model. In principle, however, any prediction method could be used to combine the predictors in the discrete library.

In this formulation, the optimal selection problem may be equivalently framed as selection of the optimal weights α in a library of candidate estimators given by $\mathcal{L} = \{\hat{\eta}_\alpha(z) : \alpha\}$. It can be seen that the library used for the discrete super learner of the previous section is a subset of this library where $\alpha_k \in \{0, 1\}$. Selection of a candidate estimator in this library is carried out in a similar fashion to discrete model selection, but the optimization is performed in an infinite set as opposed to a finite one. The super learning predictive function is thus defined as $\hat{\eta}_{SL} = \hat{\eta}_{\hat{\alpha}}$, where the selector equals

$$\hat{\alpha} = \arg\min_{\alpha} \hat{R}(\hat{\eta}_\alpha) \tag{13.4}$$

The optimization in Equation 13.4 is often a convex optimization problem that can be readily solved using standard software. In particular, computing $\hat{\alpha}$ involves only one additional step compared to the discrete selection algorithm of the previous section. As an example, consider the regression problem with a continuous outcome and note that

$$\begin{aligned} L(Z_i, \hat{\eta}_{\alpha,\mathcal{T}_j}) &= \left(Y_i - \alpha_k \hat{\eta}_{k,\mathcal{T}_j}(X_i)\right)^2 \\ &= \left(Y_i - \sum_{k=1}^{K_n} \alpha_k H_{k,i}\right)^2 \end{aligned}$$

where we have introduced a set of variables $H_k : k = 1, \ldots, K_n$, computed, for unit i, as $H_{k,i} = \hat{\eta}_{\alpha,\mathcal{T}_j}(X_{k,i})$. The cross-validated risk is equal to

$$\begin{aligned} \hat{R}(\hat{\eta}_\alpha) &= \frac{1}{J}\sum_{j=1}^{J} \frac{1}{|\mathcal{V}_j|} \sum_{i \in \mathcal{V}_j} L(Z_i, \hat{\eta}_{\alpha,\mathcal{T}_j}) \\ &= \frac{1}{n}\sum_{i=1}^{n} \left(Y_i - \sum_{k=1}^{K_n} \alpha_k H_{k,i}\right)^2 \end{aligned}$$

Thus, computation of $\hat{\alpha}$ in Equation 13.4 is reduced to computation of the ordinary least-squares estimator of a regression of Y with predictors $H_k : k = 1, \ldots, K_n$. Note that the variables H_k must also be computed to evaluate the discrete super learner of the previous section. As a result, computation of the super learner involves running only one additional regression, compared to the discrete super learner. This optimization problem under a constraint on the parameter space such as restricting the values α_k to the set of positive weights summing up to one is implemented in the `SuperLearner` package in R. In our chemical classification example, the weights of each algorithm in the super learner are given in Table 13.2.

Note that the RF gets more than half the weight in the predictor, in agreement with the results from the discrete super learner of the previous section.

13.5.1 Assessing the Prediction Error of a Stacked Predictor

As with any prediction method, the considerations presented in Section 13.3 about over fitting apply to a stacked predictor such as the super learner. Consequently, cross-validation provides the correct tool to assess the performance of the super learner. The cross-validated prediction error is thus given by

$$\hat{R}(\hat{\eta}_{\mathrm{SL}}) = \frac{1}{J}\sum_{j=1}^{K} \frac{1}{|\mathcal{V}_j|} \sum_{i \in \mathcal{V}_j} L(Z_i, \hat{\eta}_{\mathrm{SL},\mathcal{T}_j})$$

where $\eta_{\mathrm{SL},\mathcal{T}_j}$ is the super learner trained using only data in $\mathcal{T}_j$. Note that training $\hat{\eta}_{\mathrm{SL},\mathcal{T}_j}$ involves further splitting of $\mathcal{T}_j$ in validation and training subsamples, which results in larger computation times for the risk of the super learner. In our chemical classification data, we obtain the results presented in Table 13.3, using the function `CV.SuperLearner` from the package `SuperLearner` (code in Appendix A).

TABLE 13.2
Weights of each prediction algorithm in the chemical classification data.

GLM	GAM	SVM	RF	MARS	Mean
0.0000	0.2641	0.0109	0.5514	0.1736	0.0000

TABLE 13.3
Cross-validated risk for each algorithm, including the super learner, applied to classification of chemicals.

SL	DSL	GLM	GAM	SVM	RF	MARS	Mean
0.0887	0.0931	0.0991	0.0976	0.1022	0.0931	0.1094	0.2239

These estimated risks are slightly different from those in Table 13.4. This randomness is caused by the different validation splits used in each analysis, and generally do not cause an important amount of variability. For certain datasets and cross-validation splits, it is possible that the super learner is outperformed by the discrete super learner (or, equivalently, by one of the candidates in the library). In such cases, the difference between both is expected to vanish as the sample size increases, as we argue in Section 13.6 below. In our applications, we have never observed the difference to be practically relevant in favor of the discrete super learner.

13.6 Asymptotic Results for the Cross-Validated Estimator Selector and the Cross-Validated Risk

In this section, we discuss the conditions for obtaining asymptotic optimality of the cross-validation selector. The benchmark used is an optimal selector that uses the true, unknown data generating distribution P_0 to assess the risk of the predictor. We present two different results, both originally proven in [2]. First, we discuss the conditions under which the cross-validation selector converges to the optimal benchmark. Second, we present asymptotic formulas for standard errors and confidence intervals for the cross-validated risk estimate $\hat{R}(\hat{\eta})$, based on the asymptotic linearity of the cross-validated risk.

We focus on asymptotic optimality of the discrete super learner, but the results also apply to the super learner with parametric family for the ensemble learner. To start, let us define some relevant quantities:

- The *conditional risk* is the risk of an estimator assessed using the true distribution P_0 (or, equivalently, using an infinite validation dataset):

$$R_0(\hat{\eta}_k) = \frac{1}{J}\sum_{j=1}^{J}\int L(z, \hat{\eta}_{k,\mathcal{T}_j})dP_0(z)$$

- The *optimal risk* is the conditional risk achieved with the true function η_0 and is defined as

$$R_0(\eta_0) = \int L(z, \eta_0)dP_0(z)$$

- The *oracle selector* is the estimation algorithm that would be selected using the conditional risk:

$$\tilde{k} = \arg\min_k R_0(\hat{\eta}_k)$$

13.6.1 Asymptotic Optimality of the Cross-Validation Selector for Prediction

Theorem 1 of 2 establishes that, under the following conditions:

i. The loss function is the quadratic loss function $L(Z, \eta) = (Y - \eta(X))^2$,

ii. $P(|Y| \leq M) = 1$ for some $M < \infty$,

iii. $P(\sup_{k,X} |\hat{\eta}_k(X)| \leq M) = 1$,

iv. $(\log(K_n))/(n(R_0(\hat{\eta}_{\tilde{k}}) - R_0(\eta_0))) \xrightarrow{P} 0$ as $n \to \infty$, where $\xrightarrow{P}$ denotes convergence in probability,

we have that

$$\frac{R_0(\hat{\eta}_{\hat{k}}) - R_0(\eta_0)}{R_0(\hat{\eta}_{\tilde{k}}) - R_0(\eta_0)} \xrightarrow{P} 1 \qquad \text{and} \qquad \frac{E[R_0(\hat{\eta}_{\hat{k}})] - R_0(\eta_0)}{E[R_0(\hat{\eta}_{\tilde{k}})] - R_0(\eta_0)} \to 1$$

The proof of the result may be consulted in the original research article, along other useful convergences and inequalities.

This is a very important result establishing the asymptotic optimality of cross-validation model selection for prediction, in the sense that a selector based on cross-validation is asymptotically equivalent to an optimal oracle selector based on the risk under the true, unknown data generating distribution P_0.

In practice, assumptions (ii) and (iii) imply that the outcome must be bounded (i.e., it may not take on arbitrarily large values), and, perhaps most importantly, that each of the predictors of the library must respect its bounds. In addition, assumption (iv) is satisfied if the risk difference $R_0(\hat{\eta}_{\tilde{k}}) - R_0(\eta_0)$ is bounded in probability and the ratio $\log(K_n)/n$ converges to zero in probability.

We now illustrate the implication of these asymptotic results with a simulated example.

Simulation setup: Let $X = (X_1, X_2, X_3)$ and Y be drawn from the joint distribution implied by the conditional distributions

$$\begin{aligned} X_1 &\sim N(0,1) \\ X_2|X_1 &\sim N(\sin(X_1), 1) \\ X_3|X_2, X_1 &\sim N(X_1X_2, |X_1|) \\ Y|X_3, X_2, X_1 &\sim Ber\{\text{expit}(\cos(X_1)|X_2| + X_3^2X_1 - \exp(X_3))\} \end{aligned}$$

where $Ber\{p\}$ is the Bernoulli distribution with probability p. Consider three of the algorithms of Section 13.4: the GLM, GAM, and MARS, and the sample sizes n = 100, 500, 1,000, 5,000, 10,000. In addition, consider a validation sample of size $n = 10^7$, used to approximate the true risks $R_0(\hat{\eta}_k)$ (i.e., approximate integrals with respect to the measure P_0). For each sample size, we draw 500 samples. We then use each of these samples to compute the selector $\hat{k}$ and use the validation sample of size 10^7 to approximate $R_0(\hat{\eta}_k) : k = 1, 2, 3$, which includes $R_0(\hat{\eta}_{\hat{k}})$. We proceed to compute $R_0(\hat{\eta}_{\tilde{k}})$ as $\min_k R_0(\hat{\eta}_k)$, and average the results across 500 samples to approximate $E[R_0(\hat{\eta}_{\hat{k}})]$ and $E[R_0(\hat{\eta}_{\tilde{k}})]$.

Simulation results: Figure 13.4 shows the ratios of the expected risk differences

$$\frac{E[R_0(\hat{\eta}_{\hat{k}})] - R_0(\eta_0)}{E[R_0(\hat{\eta}_{\tilde{k}})] - R_0(\eta_0)} \tag{13.5}$$

which, as predicted by theory, can be seen converging to 1.

In addition, Table 13.4 shows an approximation to the joint distribution of $\tilde{k}$ and $\hat{k}$ for different sample sizes in the simulation described above. Each entry of the table is the probability that a given algorithm is chosen as $\hat{k}$ and $\tilde{k}$. These probabilities are approximated by computing $\hat{k}$ and $\tilde{k}$ for each of the 500 samples and counting the number of times that each algorithm is selected. Note that both selectors converge to the MARS as the sample size increases.

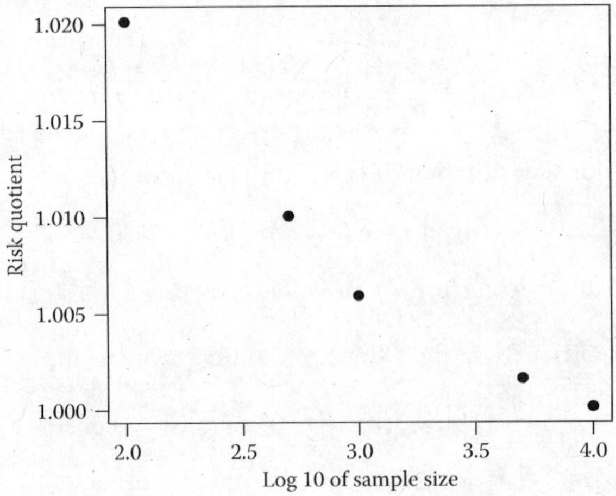

FIGURE 13.4
Risk difference ratio in Equation 13.5 for different sample sizes

TABLE 13.4
Simulated joint distribution of $\hat{k}$ and $\tilde{k}$ for different sample sizes.

		$\tilde{k}$		
n	$\hat{k}$	**MARS**	**GAM**	**GLM**
	MARS	0.004	0.080	0.008
100	GAM	0.016	0.582	0.022
	GLM	0.020	0.244	0.024
	MARS	0.142	0.200	0.000
500	GAM	0.296	0.362	0.000
	GLM	0.000	0.000	0.000
	MARS	0.762	0.064	0.000
1,000	GAM	0.148	0.026	0.000
	GLM	0.000	0.000	0.000
	MARS	0.996	0.002	0.000
5,000	GAM	0.000	0.002	0.000
	GLM	0.000	0.000	0.000
	MARS	0.998	0.000	0.000
10,000	GAM	0.002	0.000	0.000
	GLM	0.000	0.000	0.000

13.6.2 Asymptotic Inference for the Cross-Validated Risk Estimator

In addition to selecting an optimal algorithm, estimation of the risk may be an objective in itself. We approach this problem as a statistical estimation problem and consider the asymptotic distribution of the statistics involved so that standard errors and confidence intervals for the risk estimate may be computed. For the cross-validated risk estimator discussed, such standard errors and confidence intervals may be based on the Gaussian asymptotic distribution of the estimator. For a general estimator $\hat{\eta}$, Dudoit and van der

Laan [2] showed that

$$\hat{R}(\hat{\eta}) - R_0(\hat{\eta}) = \frac{1}{n}\sum_{i=1}^{n}(L(Z_i, \eta^\star) - R_0(\eta^\star)) + o_P(1/\sqrt{n}) \tag{13.6}$$

where $\eta^\star$ is a fixed limiting function of the algorithm $\hat{\eta}$, in the sense that

$$\sqrt{n}||L(z, \hat{\eta}) - L(z, \eta^\star)||_{P_0} = o_P(1) \tag{13.7}$$

assuming that this limit exists. Here we have denoted $||f||^2_{P_0} = \int f^2(z)dP_0(z)$, for a function f of z.

In particular, Equation 13.6 and the central limit theorem imply that

$$\sqrt{n}(\hat{R}(\hat{\eta}) - R_0(\hat{\eta})) \xrightarrow{d} N(0, \sigma^2) \tag{13.8}$$

where $\sigma^2 = \text{var}\{L(Z, \eta^\star) - R_0(\eta^\star)\}$. This result may be used to construct a $(1-\alpha)100\%$ confidence level interval for the conditional (on the sample) parameter $R_0(\hat{\eta})$ as

$$\hat{R}(\hat{\eta}) \pm z_{\alpha/2}\frac{\hat{\sigma}}{\sqrt{n}}$$

where

$$\hat{\sigma}^2 = \frac{1}{J}\sum_{j=1}^{J}\frac{1}{|\mathcal{V}_j|}\sum_{i\in\mathcal{V}_j}(L(Z_i, \hat{\eta}_{\mathcal{T}_j}) - \hat{R}(\hat{\eta}))^2$$

and z_α is such that $P(X > z_\alpha) = \alpha$, for a standard Gaussian random variable X. In general, this cross-validated estimator of the variance should be preferred to its non-cross-validated version, as the latter may not be appropriate to use with data-adaptive estimators $\hat{\eta}$. In our working example, the estimated standard error $\hat{\sigma}_k/\sqrt{n}$ associated to the risks of Table 13.3 are given in Table 13.5.

The asymptotic linearity result given in Equation 13.6 has other additional useful implications. For example, the joint distribution of the vector $\hat{R} = (\hat{R}(\hat{\eta}_1), \ldots, \hat{R}(\hat{\eta}_{K_n}))$ of estimated risks may be obtained as

$$\sqrt{n}(\hat{R} - R_0) \xrightarrow{d} N(0, \Sigma)$$

where $\hat{R}_0 = (R_0(\hat{\eta}_1), \ldots, R_0(\hat{\eta}_{K_n}))$ and Σ is a matrix with (k, l)th element equal to

$$\sigma_{kl} = \text{cov}\{L(Z, \eta_k^\star), L(Z, \eta_l^\star)\}$$

An important application of this result is testing whether two predictors have the same conditional risk $R_0(\hat{\eta})$. For example, define $\theta = R_0(\hat{\eta}_{\text{SL}}) - R_0(\hat{\eta}_{DSL})$ and assume that we want to test the hypothesis

$$H_0 : \theta = 0 \quad \text{vs} \quad H_1 : \theta \neq 0$$

TABLE 13.5
Estimated risks and standard deviations in the chemical classification example.

	SL	DSL	GLM	GAM	SVM	RF	MARS	Mean
$\hat{R}(\hat{\eta}_k)$	0.0887	0.0931	0.0991	0.0976	0.1022	0.0931	0.1094	0.2239
$\hat{\sigma}_k$	0.0108	0.0105	0.0114	0.0115	0.0107	0.0105	0.0126	0.0001

of whether the super learner and the discrete super learner provide the same conditional risk. According to Equation 13.6, the statistic $T = \hat{R}(\hat{\eta}_{\text{SL}}) - \hat{R}(\hat{\eta}_{DSL})$ satisfies

$$\sqrt{n}(T - \theta) \xrightarrow{d} N(0, \tau^2)$$

where

$$\tau^2 = \text{var}\{L(Z, \eta^\star_{\text{SL}}) - L(Z, \eta^\star_{DL})\}$$

Here $\eta^\star_{\text{SL}}$ and $\eta^\star_{DSL}$ are the limits of the super learner and the discrete super learner defined as in Equation 13.7.

The hypothesis H_0 may be rejected at the α level if $\sqrt{n}|T|/\hat{\tau} > z_\alpha$, where $\hat{\tau}^2$ is the cross-validated estimate of the variance τ^2,

$$\hat{\tau}^2 = \frac{1}{J}\sum_{j=1}^{J}\frac{1}{|\mathcal{V}_j|}\sum_{i\in\mathcal{V}_j}(L(Z_i, \hat{\eta}_{SL,\mathcal{T}_j}) - L(Z_i, \hat{\eta}_{DSL,\mathcal{T}_j}) - \hat{R}(\hat{\eta}_{\text{SL}}) + \hat{R}(\hat{\eta}_{DSL}))^2$$

In our chemical classification example, the statistic $\sqrt{n}|T|/\hat{\tau}$ equals 2.1841, which yields a rejection of the hypothesis of equality of the conditional risks at level 0.05. The conditional (on the sample) 95% confidence interval for the risk difference θ is equal to $(-0.0083, -0.0004)$.

Appendix A: R Code

```
## read data
data <- read.table('http://archive.ics.uci.edu/ml/
                    machine-learning-databases/00254/biodeg.csv', sep=';')

## prepare outcome and covariates
X <- data[, -42]
Y <- data[,  42]
Y <- (Y=='RB')*1

## load package and create library
require('SuperLearner')
L  <- c('SL.glm', 'SL.gam', 'SL.svm', 'SL.randomForest', 'SL.earth', 'SL.mean')

## super learner
SL <- SuperLearner(Y, X, SL.library = L, family=binomial(), cvControl=list(V=20))

## cross-validation of the super learner
CVSL <- CV.SuperLearner(Y, X, SL.library = L, family=binomial())

## estimate of the standard deviation of the risk of the discrete super learner
RDSL <- var(CVSL$discreteSL.predict - summary(CVSL)$Table[2,2])

## estimate of the standard deviation of the risk of the super learner
RSL <- var(CVSL$SL.predict - summary(CVSL)$Table[1,2])

## estimate of the standard deviation of the risk of the candidates in teh library
RS  <- diag(var(t(t(CVSL$library.predict) - summary(CVSL)$Table[-c(1,2),2])))

## statistic for hypothesis test
T <- -diff(summary(CVSL)$Table[1:2,2])
tau <- sqrt(var(CVSL$SL.predict  - CVSL$discreteSL.predict))

## test
abs(T) > qnorm(0.975) * tau / sqrt(dim(data)[1])
```

Appendix B: Description of the Variables of the Example in Section 13.2

The 42 variables in the dataset are, in order of appearance:

1. SpMax_L: Leading eigenvalue from Laplace matrix
2. J_Dz(e): Balaban-like index from Barysz matrix weighted by Sanderson electronegativity
3. nHM: Number of heavy atoms
4. F01[N-N]: Frequency of N-N at topological distance 1
5. F04[C-N]: Frequency of C-N at topological distance 4
6. NssssC: Number of atoms of type ssssC
7. nCb-: Number of substituted benzene C(sp2)
8. C%: Percentage of C atoms
9. nCp: Number of terminal primary C(sp3)
10. nO: Number of oxygen atoms
11. F03[C-N]: Frequency of C-N at topological distance 3
12. SdssC: Sum of dssC E-states
13. HyWi_B(m): Hyper–Wiener-like index (log function) from Burden matrix weighted by mass
14. LOC: Lopping centric index
15. SM6_L: Spectral moment of order 6 from Laplace matrix
16. F03[C-O]: Frequency of C-O at topological distance 3
17. Me: Mean atomic Sanderson electronegativity (scaled on carbon atom)
18. Mi: Mean first ionization potential (scaled on carbon atom)
19. nN-N: Number of N hydrazines
20. nArNO2: Number of nitro groups (aromatic)
21. nCRX3: Number of CRX3
22. SpPosA_B(p): Normalized spectral positive sum from Burden matrix weighted by polarizability
23. nCIR: Number of circuits
24. B01[C-Br]: Presence/absence of C-Br at topological distance 1
25. B03[C-Cl]: Presence/absence of C-Cl at topological distance 3
26. N-073: Ar2NH/Ar3N/Ar2N-Al / R..N..R

27. SpMax_A: Leading eigenvalue from adjacency matrix (Lovasz–Pelikan index)
28. Psi_i_1d: Intrinsic state pseudoconnectivity index-type 1d
29. B04[C-Br]: Presence/absence of C-Br at topological distance 4
30. SdO: Sum of dO E-states
31. TI2_L: Second Mohar index from Laplace matrix
32. nCrt: Number of ring tertiary C(sp3)
33. C-026: R–CX–R
34. F02[C-N]: Frequency of C-N at topological distance 2
35. nHDon: Number of donor atoms for H-bonds (N and O)
36. SpMax_B(m): Leading eigenvalue from Burden matrix weighted by mass
37. Psi_i_A: Intrinsic state pseudoconnectivity index-type S average
38. nN: Number of nitrogen atoms
39. SM6_B(m): Spectral moment of order 6 from Burden matrix weighted by mass
40. nArCOOR: Number of esters (aromatic)
41. nX: Number of halogen atoms
42. experimental class: ready biodegradable (RB) and not ready biodegradable (NRB)

References

1. L. Breiman. The little bootstrap and other methods for dimensionality selection in regression: x-fixed prediction error. *J. Am. Stat. Assoc.*, 87(419):738–754, 1992.
2. S. Dudoit and M. J. van der Laan. Asymptotics of cross-validated risk estimation in estimator selection and performance assessment. *Stat. Methodol.*, 2(2):131–154, 2005.
3. M. Lichman. UCI machine learning repository, School of Information and Computer Science, University of California, Irvine, CA, http://archive.ics.uci.edu/ml, 2013.
4. K. Mansouri, T. Ringsted, D. Ballabio, R. Todeschini, and V. Consonni. Quantitative structureactivity relationship models for ready biodegradability of chemicals. *J. Chem. Inf. Model.*, 53(4):867–878, 2013.
5. M. J. van der Laan, E. Polley, and A. Hubbard. Super learner. *Stat. Appl. Genetics Mol. Biol.*, 6:25, 2007.

14

Stochastic Gradient Methods for Principled Estimation with Large Datasets

Panos Toulis and Edoardo M. Airoldi

CONTENTS

14.1 Introduction 241
14.1.1 Outline 245
14.2 Stochastic Approximation 245
14.2.1 Sakrison's Recursive Estimation Method 246
14.3 Estimation with Stochastic Gradient Methods 247
14.3.1 Bias and Variance 247
14.3.2 Stability 248
14.3.3 Choice of Learning Rate Sequence 249
14.3.4 Efficient Computation of Implicit Methods 250
14.3.5 Extensions 251
14.3.5.1 Second-Order Methods 251
14.3.5.2 Averaging 252
14.3.5.3 Monte Carlo Stochastic Gradient Descent 253
14.4 Other Applications 254
14.4.1 Online EM Algorithm 254
14.4.2 MCMC Sampling 256
14.4.3 Reinforcement Learning 257
14.4.4 Deep Learning 258
14.5 Glossary 259
References 259

14.1 Introduction

Parameter estimation by optimization of an objective function, such as maximum-likelihood and maximum a posteriori, is a fundamental idea in statistics and machine learning (Fisher, 1922, Lehmann and Casella, 2003, Hastie et al., 2011). However, widely used optimization-based estimation algorithms, such as Fisher scoring, the Expectation-Maximization (EM) algorithm, and iteratively reweighted least squares (Fisher, 1925, Dempster et al., 1977, Green, 1984), are not scalable to modern datasets with hundreds of millions of data points and hundreds or thousands of covariates (National Research Council, 2013).

To illustrate, let us consider the problem of estimating the true parameter value $\theta_\star \in \mathbb{R}^p$ from an i.i.d. sample $D = \{X_n, Y_n\}$, for $n = 1, 2, \ldots, N$; $X_n \in \mathbb{R}^p$ is the covariate vector and $Y_n \in \mathbb{R}^d$ is the outcome distributed conditionally on X_n according to the known distribution f and unknown model parameters $\theta_\star$,

$$Y_n | X_n \sim f(\cdot; X_n, \theta_\star)$$

We assume that the data points (X_n, Y_n) are observed in sequence (streaming data). The log-likelihood, $\log f(Y; X, \theta)$, as a function of the parameter value θ given a data point (X, Y), will be denoted by $\ell(\theta; Y, X)$; for brevity, we define $\ell(\theta; D) = \sum_{n=1}^{N} \ell(\theta; X_n, Y_n)$ as the complete data log-likelihood.

Traditional estimation methods are typically iterative and have a running time complexity that ranges between $O(Np^3)$ and $O(Np)$ in worst cases and best cases, respectively. Newton–Raphson methods, for instance, update an estimate θ_{n-1} of the parameters through the recursion

$$\theta_n = \theta_{n-1} - H_{n-1}^{-1} \nabla \ell(\theta_{n-1}; D) \tag{14.1}$$

where $H_n = \nabla\nabla\ell(\theta_n; D)$ is the $p \times p$ Hessian matrix of the complete data log-likelihood. The matrix inversion and the likelihood computation over the dataset D imply complexity $O(Np^{2+\epsilon})$, which makes the algorithm unsuited for estimation with large datasets. Fisher scoring replaces the Hessian matrix in Equation 14.1 with its expected value over a data point (X_n, Y_n), that is, it uses the Fisher information matrix $\mathcal{I}(\theta) = -\mathbb{E}\left(\nabla\nabla\ell(\theta; X_n, Y_n)\right)$. The advantage of this method is that a steady increase in the likelihood is possible because the difference

$$\ell(\theta + \epsilon\Delta\theta; D) - \ell(\theta; D) \approx \epsilon\, \ell(\theta; D)^\intercal \mathcal{I}(\theta)^{-1} \ell(\theta; D) + O(\epsilon^2)$$

can be made positive for an appropriately small value $\epsilon > 0$, because $\mathcal{I}(\theta)$ is positive definite. However, Fisher scoring is computationally comparable to Newton–Raphson's, and thus it is also unsuited for estimation with large datasets. Other general estimation algorithms, such as EM or iteratively reweighted least squares (Green, 1984), have similar computational constraints.

Quasi-Newton methods are a powerful alternative that is widely used in practice. In quasi-Newton methods, the Hessian in the Newton–Raphson algorithm is approximated by a low-rank matrix that is updated at each iteration as new values of the gradient become available. This yields an algorithm with complexity $O(Np^2)$ or $O(Np)$ in certain favorable cases (Hennig and Kiefel, 2013).

However, estimation with large datasets requires complexity that scales linearly with N, the number of data points, but sublinearly with p, the number of parameters. The first requirement on N seems hard to overcome, because each data point carries information for $\theta_\star$ by the i.i.d. data assumption. Therefore, gracious scaling with p is necessary.

Such computational requirements have recently sparked interest in procedures that utilize only *first-order* information, that is, methods that utilize only the gradient function. A prominent procedure that fits this description is *stochastic gradient descent* (SGD), defined through the iteration

$$\theta_n^{\text{sgd}} = \theta_{n-1}^{\text{sgd}} + a_n \nabla \ell(\theta_{n-1}^{\text{sgd}}; X_n, Y_n) \tag{14.2}$$

We will refer to Equation 14.2 as SGD with *explicit updates* or *explicit SGD* for short, because the next iterate θ_n^{sgd} can be computed immediately after the new data point (X_n, Y_n) is observed. The sequence $a_n > 0$ is known as the *learning rate* sequence, typically defined such that $na_n \to \alpha > 0$, as $n \to \infty$. The parameter $\alpha > 0$ is the *learning rate parameter*, and it is crucial for the convergence and stability of explicit SGD.

From a computational perspective, the SGD procedure (Equation 14.2) is appealing because the expensive inversion of $p \times p$ matrices, as in Newton–Raphson, is replaced by a single sequence of scalars $a_n > 0$. Furthermore, the log-likelihood is evaluated at a single data point (X_n, Y_n), and not on the entire dataset D.

From a theoretical perspective, the explicit SGD procedure is justified because Equation 14.2 is a special case of the stochastic approximation method of Robbins and Monro (1951). By the theory of stochastic approximation, explicit SGD converges to a point θ_∞ that satisfies $\mathbb{E}(\nabla\ell(\theta_\infty; X, Y)) = 0$; under typical regularity conditions, θ_∞ is exactly the true parameter value $\theta_\star$. As a recursive statistical estimation method, explicit SGD was first proposed by Sakrison (1965) in a simple second-order form, that is, using the Fisher information matrix in iteration (Equation 14.2); the simplicity of SGD has also made it very popular in optimization and machine learning with large datasets (Le Cun and Bottou, 2004, Zhang, 2004, Spall, 2005).*

However, the remarkable simplicity of explicit SGD comes at a price, as the SGD procedure requires careful tuning of the learning rate parameter α. For small values of α, the iterates θ_n^{sgd} will converge very slowly to $\theta_\star$ (large bias), whereas for large values of α, the iterates θ_n^{sgd} will either have a large asymptotic variance (with respect to random data D) or even diverge numerically. In large datasets with many parameters (large p), the balance between bias, variance, and stability is very delicate, and nearly impossible to achieve without appropriately modifying Equation 14.2.

Interestingly, the simple modification of explicit SGD defined through the iteration

$$\theta_n^{\text{im}} = \theta_{n-1}^{\text{im}} + a_n \nabla\ell(\theta_n^{\text{im}}; X_n, Y_n) \tag{14.3}$$

can resolve its stability issue virtually at no cost. We will refer to Equation 14.3 as *implicit stochastic gradient descent* or *implicit SGD* for short (Toulis et al., 2014, Toulis and Airoldi, 2015b). Equation 14.3 is implicit because the next iterate θ_n^{im} appears on both sides of the equation. This equation is a p-dimensional fixed-point equation, which is generally hard to solve. However, for a large family of statistical models, it can be reduced to a one-dimensional fixed-point equation. We discuss computational issues of implicit SGD in Section 14.3.4.

The first intuition for implicit SGD is obtained using a Taylor expansion of the implicit update (Equation 14.3). In particular, assuming a common point $\theta_{n-1}^{\text{sgd}} = \theta_{n-1}^{\text{im}} = \theta$, a Taylor expansion of Equation 14.3 around θ_{n-1}^{im} implies

$$\Delta\theta_n^{\text{im}} = \left(\mathbb{I} + a_n \hat{\mathcal{I}}(\theta; X_n, Y_n)\right)^{-1} \Delta\theta_n^{\text{sgd}} + O(a_n^2) \tag{14.4}$$

where

$\Delta\theta_n = \theta_n - \theta_{n-1}$ for both explicit and implicit methods
$\hat{\mathcal{I}}(\theta; X_n, Y_n) = -\nabla\nabla\ell(\theta; X_n, Y_n)$ is the observed Fisher information matrix
$\mathbb{I}$ is the $p \times p$ identity matrix

Thus, implicit SGD uses updates that are a *shrinked* version of the explicit ones. The shrinkage factor in Equation 14.4 depends on the observed information up to the nth data point and is similar to shrinkage in ridge regression.

Naturally, implicit SGD has also a Bayesian interpretation. In particular, if the log-likelihood is continuously differentiable, then the update in Equation 14.3 is equivalent to the update

$$\theta_n^{\text{im}} = \arg\max_{\theta \in \mathbb{R}^p} \left\{ a_n \ell(\theta; X_n, Y_n) - \frac{1}{2}||\theta - \theta_{n-1}^{\text{im}}||^2 \right\} \tag{14.5}$$

*Recursive estimation methods using stochastic approximation were originally developed for problems with streaming data. However, these methods are more broadly applicable to estimation with a static dataset. Asymptotically, these two scenarios are equivalent, with the estimates converging to the true parameter value $\theta_\star$. Estimates with a static dataset (i.e., with a finite sample) converge instead to the point that minimizes some predefined empirical loss, for example, based on the likelihood.

The iterate θ_n^{im} from Equation 14.5 is the posterior mode of the following Bayesian model:

$$\begin{aligned} \theta|\theta_{n-1}^{\text{im}} &\sim \mathcal{N}(\theta_{n-1}^{\text{im}}, a_n \mathbb{I}) \\ Y_n|X_n, \theta &\sim f(\cdot; X_n, \theta) \end{aligned} \tag{14.6}$$

where $\mathcal{N}$ denotes the normal distribution. Therefore, the learning rate a_n relates to the information received after n data points have been observed, and encodes our trust on the current estimate θ_{n-1}^{im}. The Bayesian formulation (Equation 14.6) demonstrates the flexibility of implicit SGD. For example, depending on the parameter space of $\theta_\star$, the Bayesian model in Equation 14.6 could be different; for instance, if $\theta_\star$ was a scale parameter, then the normal distribution could be replaced by an inverse chi-squared distribution. Furthermore, instead of $a_n\mathbb{I}$ as the prior variance, it would be statistically efficient to use the Fisher information matrix $(1/n)\mathcal{I}(\theta_{n-1}^{\text{im}})^{-1}$, completely analogous to Sakrison's method—we discuss these ideas in Section 14.3.5.1.

There is also a tight connection of Equation 14.5 to *proximal methods* in optimization. For example, if we replaced the stochastic component $\ell(\theta; X_n, Y_n)$ in Equation 14.5 with the complete data log-likelihood $\ell(\theta; D)$, then Equation 14.5 would be essentially the proximal point algorithm of Rockafellar (1976) that applies to deterministic settings. This algorithm is known for its numerical stability, and has been generalized through the idea of splitting algorithms (Lions and Mercier, 1979); see Parikh and Boyd (2013) for a comprehensive review. The convergence of proximal methods with a stochastic component, as in Equation 14.5, has been analyzed recently—under various forms and assumptions—by Bertsekas (2011), Ryu and Boyd (2014), and Rosasco et al. (2014). From a statistical perspective, Toulis and Airoldi (2015a) derived the asymptotic variance of θ_n^{sgd} and θ_n^{im} as estimators of $\theta_\star$, and provided an algorithm to efficiently compute Equation 14.5 for the family of generalized linear models—we show a generalization of this result in Section 14.3.4. In the online learning literature, regret analyses of implicit methods have been given by Kivinen et al. (2006) and Kulis and Bartlett (2010). Further intuitions for proximal methods (Equation 14.5) have been given by Krakowski et al. (2007) and Nemirovski et al. (2009), who showed that proximal methods can fit better in the geometry of the parameter space. Finally, (Toulis et al., 2015) derived a stochastic approximation framework that encompasses stochastic proximal methods, and showed that it retains the asymptotic properties of the framework of Robbins and Monro, but is significantly more robust in the non-asymptotic regime.

Arguably, the normalized least mean squares (NLMS) filter (Nagumo and Noda, 1967) was the first statistical model that used an implicit update as in Equation 14.3 and was shown to be robust to input noise (Slock, 1993). Two other recent stochastic proximal methods are Prox-SVRG (Xiao and Zhang, 2014) and Prox-SAG (Schmidt et al., 2013, section 6). The main idea in both methods is to replace the gradient in Equation 14.5 with an estimate of the full gradient averaged over all data points that has the same expectation with the gradient of Equation 14.3 but smaller variance. Because of their operational complexity, we will not discuss these methods further. Instead, in Section 14.3.5.1, we will discuss a related proximal method, namely AdaGrad (Duchi et al., 2011), that maintains one learning rate for each parameter component and updates these learning rates as new data points are observed.

Example 14.1 *Consider the linear normal model, $Y_n|X_n \sim \mathcal{N}(X_n^\intercal\theta_\star, 1)$. The log-likelihood for this model is $\ell(\theta; X_n, Y_n) = -\frac{1}{2}(Y_n - X_n^\intercal\theta_\star)^2$. Therefore, the explicit SGD procedure will be*

$$\theta_n^{\text{sgd}} = \theta_{n-1}^{\text{sgd}} + a_n(Y_n - X_n^\intercal\theta_{n-1}^{\text{sgd}})X_n = (\mathbb{I} - a_n X_n X_n^\intercal)\theta_{n-1}^{\text{sgd}} + a_n Y_n X_n \tag{14.7}$$

Equation 14.7 is known as the least mean squares filter (LMS) in signal processing, or as the Widrow–Hoff algorithm (Widrow and Hoff, 1960), *and it is a special case of explicit SGD.*

The stability problems of explicit SGD become apparent by inspection of Equation 14.7; a misspecification of a_n can lead to a poor next iterate θ_n^{sgd}, for example, when $\mathbb{I} - a_n X_n X_n^{\intercal}$ has large negative eigenvalues—we discuss these issues in Section 14.3.2.

The implicit SGD procedure for the linear model is

$$\begin{aligned}\theta_n^{\mathrm{im}} &= \theta_{n-1}^{\mathrm{im}} + a_n(Y_n - X_n^{\intercal}\theta_n^{\mathrm{im}})X_n \Rightarrow \\ \theta_n^{\mathrm{im}} &= (\mathbb{I} + a_n X_n X_n^{\intercal})^{-1}\theta_{n-1}^{\mathrm{im}} + a_n(\mathbb{I} + a_n X_n X_n^{\intercal})^{-1} Y_n X_n \end{aligned} \tag{14.8}$$

Equation 14.8 is known as the NLMS filter in signal processing (Nagumo and Noda, 1967). *In contrast to explicit SGD, the implicit iterate θ_n^{im} is a weighted average between the previous iterate $\theta_{n-1}^{\mathrm{im}}$ and the new observation $Y_n X_n$, which is now stable to misspecifications of the learning rate a_n.*

14.1.1 Outline

The structure of this chapter is as follows. In Section 14.2, we give an overview of the Robbins–Monro procedure and Sakrison's recursive estimation method, which provide the theoretical basis for SGD methods. In Section 14.3, we introduce a simple generalization of explicit and implicit SGD, and we analyze them as *statistical estimation procedures* for the model parameters $\theta_\star$ after n data points have been observed. In Section 14.3.1, we give results on the frequentist statistical properties of SGD estimators, that is, their asymptotic bias and variance across multiple realizations of the dataset D. We then leverage these results to study optimal learning rate sequences a_n (Section 14.3.3), the loss of statistical information in SGD, and numerical stability (Section 14.3.2). In Section 14.3.5, we illustrate three extensions of the SGD methods, in particular: (1) second-order SGD methods (Section 14.3.5.1), which adaptively approximate the Fisher information matrix; (2) averaged SGD methods, which use larger learning rates together with averaging of the iterates; and (3) Monte Carlo SGD methods, which can be applied when the log-likelihood cannot be efficiently computed. In Section 14.4, we review applications of SGD in statistics and machine learning, namely, online EM, Markov chain Monte Carlo (MCMC) posterior sampling, reinforcement learning, and deep learning.

14.2 Stochastic Approximation

Consider a random variable $H(\theta)$ that depends on parameter θ; for simplicity, assume that $H(\theta)$ and θ are real numbers. The regression function, $h(\theta) = \mathbb{E}(H(\theta))$, is decreasing but possibly unknown. Robbins and Monro (1951) considered the problem of finding the unique point $\theta_\star$ for which $h(\theta_\star) = 0$. They devised a procedure, known as *the Robbins–Monro procedure*, in which an estimate θ_{n-1} of $\theta_\star$ is utilized to sample one new data point $H(\theta_{n-1})$; by definition, $\mathbb{E}(H(\theta_{n-1}) | \theta_{n-1}) = h(\theta_{n-1})$. The estimate is then updated according to the following rule:

$$\theta_n = \theta_{n-1} + a_n H(\theta_{n-1}) \tag{14.9}$$

The scalar $a_n > 0$ is the *learning rate* and should decay to zero, but not too fast to guarantee convergence. Robbins and Monro (1951) proved that $\mathbb{E}\left((\theta_n - \theta_\star)^2\right) \to 0$, if

a. $\mathbb{E}\left(H(\theta)^2 | \theta\right) < \infty$, for any θ, and

b. $\sum_{i=1}^{\infty} a_i = \infty$ and $\sum_{i=1}^{\infty} a_i^2 < \infty$.

Extensions to multiple dimensions were soon given by Blum (1954). The necessary conditions for convergence in such cases are the negative definiteness of the Jacobian of h, or that H is the stochastic gradient of a function with unique zero (Wei, 1987, Ruppert, 1988b, section 4).

The original proof of Robbins and Monro (1951) is technical but the main idea is straightforward. Let $b_n \triangleq \mathbb{E}\left((\theta_n - \theta_\star)^2\right)$ denote the squared error of the iterates in Equation 14.9; then from iteration (Equation 14.9), it follows:

$$b_n = b_{n-1} + 2a_n \mathbb{E}\left((\theta_{n-1} - \theta_\star)h(\theta_{n-1})\right) + a_n^2 \mathbb{E}\left(H(\theta_{n-1})^2\right)$$

In the neighborhood of $\theta_\star$, we assume that $h(\theta_{n-1}) \approx h'(\theta_\star)(\theta_{n-1} - \theta_\star)$, and thus

$$b_n = (1 + 2a_n h'(\theta_\star))b_{n-1} + a_n^2 \mathbb{E}\left(H(\theta_{n-1})^2\right) \tag{14.10}$$

For a learning rate $a_n = \alpha/n$, using typical techniques in stochastic approximation (Chung, 1954), we can derive from Equation 14.10 that $b_n \to 0$. Furthermore, $nb_n \to \alpha^2\sigma^2(2\alpha|h'(\theta_\star)| - 1)^{-1}$, where $\sigma^2 \triangleq \mathbb{E}\left(H(\theta_\star)^2\right)$, as shown by several authors (Chung, 1954, Sacks, 1958, Fabian, 1968). Clearly, the learning rate parameter α is critical for the performance of the Robbins–Monro procedure. Its optimal value is $\alpha_\star = 1/h'(\theta_\star)$, which requires knowledge of the true parameter value $\theta_\star$ and the slope of h at that point. This optimality result inspired an important line of research on *adaptive* stochastic approximation methods, such as the Venter process (Venter, 1967), in which quantities that are important for the convergence and efficiency of iterates θ_n (e.g., the quantity $h'(\theta_\star)$) are being estimated as the stochastic approximation proceeds.

14.2.1 Sakrison's Recursive Estimation Method

Although initially motivated by sequential experiment design, the Robbins–Monro procedure was soon modified for statistical estimation. Similar to the estimation setup in Section 14.1, Sakrison (1965) was interested in estimating the parameters $\theta_\star$ of a model that generated i.i.d. observations (X_n, Y_n), in a way that is computationally and statistically efficient. Sakrison first recognized that one could set $H(\theta) \triangleq \nabla \log \ell(\theta; X_n, Y_n)$ in the Robbins–Monro procedure (Equation 14.9), and use the identity $\mathbb{E}\left(\nabla\ell(\theta_\star; X_n, Y_n)\right) = 0$ to show why the procedure will converge to the true parameter value $\theta_\star$. Sakrison's *recursive estimation method* was essentially the first *explicit* SGD method proposed in the literature:

$$\theta_n = \theta_{n-1} + a_n \mathcal{I}(\theta_{n-1})^{-1} \nabla\ell(\theta_{n-1}; X_n, Y_n) \tag{14.11}$$

where a_n is a learning rate sequence that satisfies the Robbins–Monro conditions in Section 14.2. The SGD procedure (Equation 14.11) is *second order*, because it uses the Fisher information matrix in addition to the log-likelihood gradient. By the theory of stochastic approximation, $\theta_n \to \theta_\star$, and thus $\mathcal{I}(\theta_n) \to \mathcal{I}(\theta_\star)$. Sakrison (1965) proved that $n\mathbb{E}\left(||\theta_n - \theta_\star||^2\right) \to \text{trace}(\mathcal{I}(\theta_\star)^{-1})$, which indicates that estimation of $\theta_\star$ is asymptotically optimal, that is, it achieves the minimum variance of the maximum-likelihood estimator. However, Sakrison's method is not computationally efficient, as it requires an expensive matrix inversion at every iteration. Still, it reveals that the estimation of the Fisher information matrix is essential for optimal SGD. Adaptive second-order methods leverage this insight to approximate the Fisher information matrix and improve upon first-order SGD methods.

14.3 Estimation with Stochastic Gradient Methods

We slightly generalize the SGD methods in Section 14.1 through the definitions

$$\theta_n^{\text{sgd}} = \theta_{n-1}^{\text{sgd}} + a_n C \nabla \ell(\theta_{n-1}^{\text{sgd}}; X_n, Y_n) \tag{14.12}$$

$$\theta_n^{\text{im}} = \theta_{n-1}^{\text{im}} + a_n C \nabla \ell(\theta_n^{\text{im}}; X_n, Y_n) \tag{14.13}$$

where C is symmetric and positive definite, and commutes with $\mathcal{I}(\theta_\star)$; adaptive second-order methods where C is updated at every iteration are discussed in Section 14.3.5.1. The iterate θ_n^{sgd} is the explicit SGD estimator of $\theta_\star$ after the nth data point has been observed; similarly, θ_n^{im} is the implicit SGD estimator of $\theta_\star$. The total number of data points, denoted by N, will be assumed to be practically infinite. We will then compare the asymptotic variance of those estimators with the variance of the maximum-likelihood estimator on n data points, which, under typical regularity conditions, has variance $\frac{1}{n}\mathcal{I}(\theta_\star)^{-1}$. The evaluation is done from a frequentist perspective, that is, across multiple realizations of the dataset up to n data points $D = \{(X_1, Y_1), (X_2, Y_2), \ldots, (X_n, Y_n)\}$, under the same model f and true parameter value $\theta_\star$.*

Typically, both SGD methods have two phases, namely the *exploration phase* and the *convergence phase* (Amari, 1998, Bottou and Murata, 2002). In the exploration phase, the iterates approach $\theta_\star$, whereas in the convergence phase, they jitter around $\theta_\star$ within a ball of slowly decreasing radius. We will overview a typical analysis of SGD in the final convergence phase, where a Taylor approximation in the neighborhood of $\theta_\star$ is assumed accurate (Murata, 1998, Toulis et al., 2014). In particular, let $\mu(\theta) = \mathbb{E}(\nabla \ell(\theta; X_n, Y_n))$, and assume

$$\mu(\theta_n) = \mu(\theta_\star) + J_\mu(\theta_\star)(\theta_n - \theta_\star) + o(a_n) \tag{14.14}$$

where:

J_μ is the Jacobian of the function $\mu(\cdot)$
$o(a_n)$ denotes a vector sequence with norms of order $o(a_n)$

Under typical regularity conditions, $\mu(\theta_\star) = 0$ and $J_\mu(\theta_\star) = -\mathcal{I}(\theta_\star)$ (Lehmann and Casella, 1998).

14.3.1 Bias and Variance

Denote the biases of the two SGD methods with $\mathrm{E}(\theta_n^{\text{sgd}} - \theta_\star) \triangleq b_n^{\text{sgd}}$ and $\mathrm{E}(\theta_n^{\text{im}} - \theta_\star) \triangleq b_n^{\text{im}}$. Then, by taking expectations in Equations 14.12 and 14.13, we obtain the recursions

$$b_n^{\text{sgd}} = (\mathbb{I} - a_n C \mathcal{I}(\theta_\star))\, b_{n-1}^{\text{sgd}} + o(a_n) \tag{14.15}$$

$$b_n^{\text{im}} = (\mathbb{I} + a_n C \mathcal{I}(\theta_\star))^{-1}\, b_{n-1}^{\text{im}} + o(a_n) \tag{14.16}$$

We observe that convergence—the rate at which the two methods become unbiased in the limit—differs in the two SGD methods. The explicit SGD method converges faster than the implicit one because $||(\mathbb{I} - a_n C\mathcal{I}(\theta_\star))|| < ||(\mathbb{I} + a_n C\mathcal{I}(\theta_\star))^{-1}||$, for sufficiently large n, but the rates become equal in the limit as $a_n \to 0$. However, the implicit method compensates by being more stable in the specification of the learning rate sequence and the

*This is an important distinction because, traditionally, the focus in optimization has been to obtain fast convergence to a parameter value that minimizes the empirical loss, for example, the maximum-likelihood. From a statistical viewpoint, under variability of the data, there is a tradeoff between convergence to an estimator and the estimator's asymptotic variance (Le Cun and Bottou, 2004).

condition matrix C. Loosely speaking, the bias b_n^{im} cannot be much worse than b_{n-1}^{im} because $(\mathbb{I} + a_n C\mathcal{I}(\theta_\star))^{-1}$ is a contraction matrix, for any choice of $a_n > 0$. Exact nonasymptotic derivations for the bias of explicit SGD are given by Moulines and Bach (2011), and for the bias of implicit SGD by Toulis and Airoldi (2015a).

Regarding statistical efficiency, Toulis et al. (2014) showed that, if $(2C\mathcal{I}(\theta_\star) - \mathbb{I}/\alpha)$ is positive definite, it holds that

$$n\text{Var}(\theta_n^{\text{sgd}}) \to \alpha^2(2\alpha C\mathcal{I}(\theta_\star) - \mathbb{I})^{-1}C\mathcal{I}(\theta_\star)C^\intercal$$
$$n\text{Var}(\theta_n^{\text{im}}) \to \alpha^2(2\alpha C\mathcal{I}(\theta_\star) - \mathbb{I})^{-1}C\mathcal{I}(\theta_\star)C^\intercal \tag{14.17}$$

where $\alpha = \lim_{n\to\infty} na_n$ is the learning rate parameter of SGD, as defined in Section 14.1. Therefore, both SGD methods have the same asymptotic efficiency, which depends on the learning rate parameter α and the Fisher information matrix $\mathcal{I}(\theta_\star)$. Intuitively, the term $(2\alpha C\mathcal{I}(\theta_\star) - \mathbb{I})^{-1}$ in Equation 14.17 is a factor that shows how much information is lost by the SGD methods. For example, setting $C = \mathcal{I}(\theta_\star)^{-1}$ and $\alpha = 1$, implies $(2\alpha C\mathcal{I}(\theta_\star) - \mathbb{I})^{-1} = \mathbb{I}$, and the asymptotic variance for both estimators is $(1/n)\mathcal{I}(\theta_\star)^{-1}$, that is, it is the minimum variance attainable by the maximum-likelihood estimator. This is exactly Sakrison's result presented in Section 14.2.1.

Asymptotic variance results similar to Equation 14.17, but not in the context of model estimation, were first studied in the stochastic approximation literature by Chung (1954), Sacks (1958), and followed by Fabian (1968) and several other authors (see also Ljung et al., 1992, parts I, II), where more general formulas are possible using a Lyapunov equation.

14.3.2 Stability

Stability has been a well-known issue for explicit SGD (Gardner, 1984, Amari et al., 1997). In practice, the main problem is that the learning rate sequence a_n needs to agree with the eigenvalues of the Fisher information matrix $\mathcal{I}(\theta_\star)$. To see this, let us simplify Equations 14.15 and 14.16 by dropping the remainder terms $o(a_n)$. It follows that

$$b_n^{\text{sgd}} = (\mathbb{I} - a_n C\mathcal{I}(\theta_\star))b_{n-1}^{\text{sgd}} = P_1^n b_0$$
$$b_n^{\text{im}} = (\mathbb{I} + a_n C\mathcal{I}(\theta_\star))^{-1}b_{n-1}^{\text{im}} = Q_1^n b_0 \tag{14.18}$$

where $P_1^n = \prod_{i=1}^n(\mathbb{I} - a_i C\mathcal{I}(\theta_\star))$, $Q_1^n = \prod_{i=1}^n(\mathbb{I} + a_i C\mathcal{I}(\theta_\star))^{-1}$, and b_0 denotes the initial bias of the two procedures from a common starting point θ_0. The matrices P_1^n and Q_1^n describe how fast the initial bias b_0 decays for both SGD methods. For small-to-moderate n, the two matrices critically affect the stability of SGD methods. For simplicity, we compare those matrices assuming rate $a_n = \alpha/n$ and a fixed condition matrix $C = \mathbb{I}$.

Under such assumptions, the eigenvalues of P_1^n can be calculated as $\lambda_i' = \prod_{j=1}^n(1 - \alpha\lambda_i/j) = O(n^{-\alpha\lambda_i})$, for $0 < \alpha\lambda_i < 1$, where λ_i are the eigenvalues of the Fisher information matrix $\mathcal{I}(\theta_\star)$. Thus, the magnitude of P_1^n will be dominated by $\lambda_{\max}$, the maximum eigenvalue of $\mathcal{I}(\theta_\star)$, and the rate of convergence to zero will be dominated by $\lambda_{\min}$, the minimum eigenvalue of $\mathcal{I}(\theta_\star)$. For stable eigenvalues λ_i', the terms in the aforementioned product need to be less than 1; therefore, it is desirable that $|1 - \alpha\lambda_{\max}| \leq 1 \Rightarrow \alpha \leq 2/\lambda_{\max}$. For statistical efficiency, it is desirable that $(2\alpha\mathcal{I}(\theta_\star) - \mathbb{I})$ is positive definite, as shown in Equation 14.17, and so $\alpha > 1/(2\lambda_{\min})$. In high-dimensional settings, the conditions for stability and efficiency are hard to satisfy simultaneously, because $\lambda_{\max}$ is usually much larger than $\lambda_{\min}$. Thus, in explicit SGD, a small learning rate can guarantee stability, but this comes at a price in convergence, which will be at the order of $O(n^{-\alpha\lambda_{\min}})$. On the other hand, a large learning rate increases the convergence rate but it comes at a price in stability.

In stark contrast, the implicit procedure is *unconditionally stable*. The eigenvalues of Q_1^n are $\lambda_i' = \prod_{j=1}^{n} 1/(1+\alpha\lambda_i/j) = O(n^{-\alpha\lambda_i})$, and thus are guaranteed to be less than 1 for any choice of the learning rate parameter α, because $(1+\alpha\lambda_i/j)^{-1} < 1$, for every i and $\alpha > 0$. The critical difference with explicit SGD is that it is no longer required to have a small α for stability because the eigenvalues of Q_1^n are always less than 1.

Based on this analysis, the magnitude of P_1^n can become arbitrarily large, and thus explicit SGD is likely to numerically diverge. In contrast, Q_1^n is guaranteed to be bounded and so, under any misspecification of the learning rate parameter, implicit SGD is guaranteed to remain bounded. The instability of explicit SGD is well known and requires careful work to be avoided in practice. In the following section, we focus on the related task of selecting the learning rate sequence.

14.3.3 Choice of Learning Rate Sequence

An interesting observation about the asymptotic variance results (Equation 14.17) is that, for any choice of the learning rate parameter α, it holds that

$$\alpha^2(2\alpha C\mathcal{I}(\theta_\star) - I)^{-1}C\mathcal{I}(\theta_\star)C^\intercal \geq \mathcal{I}(\theta_\star)^{-1} \tag{14.19}$$

where $A \geq B$ indicates that $A - B$ is nonnegative definite for two matrices A and B. Hence, both SGD methods incur an information loss when compared to the maximum-likelihood estimator, and the loss can be quantified exactly through Equation 14.17. Such information loss can be avoided if we set $C = \mathcal{I}(\theta_\star)^{-1}$ and $\alpha = 1$.* However, this requires knowledge of the Fisher information matrix on the true parameters $\theta_\star$, which are unknown. The Venter process (Venter, 1967) was the first method to follow an adaptive approach to estimate the Fisher matrix, and was later analyzed and extended by several other authors (Fabian, 1973, Lai and Robbins, 1979, Amari et al., 2000, Bottou and Le Cun, 2005). Adaptive methods that perform an approximation of the matrix $\mathcal{I}(\theta_\star)$ (e.g., through a quasi-Newton scheme) have recently been applied with considerable success (Schraudolph et al., 2007, Bordes et al., 2009); we review such methods in Section 14.3.5.1.

However, an efficiency loss is generally unavoidable in first-order SGD, that is, when $C = \mathbb{I}$. In such cases, there is no loss only when the eigenvalues λ_i of the Fisher information matrix are identical. When those eigenvalues are distinct, one reasonable way to set the learning rate parameter α is to minimize the trace of the asymptotic variance matrix in Equation 14.17, that is, solve

$$\hat{\alpha} = \arg\min_{\alpha} \sum_i \frac{\alpha^2\lambda_i}{(2\alpha\lambda_i - 1)} \tag{14.20}$$

under the constraint that $\alpha > 1/(2\lambda_{\min})$, thus making an undesirable but necessary compromise for convergence in all parameter components. However, the eigenvalues λ_i are unknown in practice and need to be estimated from the data. This problem has received significant attention recently and several methods exist (see Karoui, 2008, and references within).

Several more options for setting the learning rate are available, due to a voluminous amount of research literature on learning rate sequences for stochastic approximation and SGD. In general, the learning rate for explicit SGD should be of the form $a_n = \alpha(\alpha\beta + n)^{-1}$. Parameter α controls the asymptotic variance (see Equation 14.17), and a reasonable choice

*Equivalently, we could have a sequence of matrices C_n that converges to $\mathcal{I}(\theta_\star)^{-1}$, as in Sakrison's procedure (Sakrison, 1965).

is the solution of Equation 14.20, which requires estimates of the eigenvalues of the Fisher information matrix $\mathcal{I}(\theta_\star)$. A simpler choice is to use $\alpha = 1/\lambda_{\min}$, where $\lambda_{\min}$ is the minimum eigenvalue of $\mathcal{I}(\theta_\star)$; the value $1/\lambda_{\min}$ is an approximate solution of Equation 14.20 with good empirical performance (Xu, 2011, Toulis et al., 2014). Parameter β is used to stabilize explicit SGD. In particular, it normalizes the learning rate to account for the variance of the stochastic gradient $\text{Var}\left(\nabla\ell(\theta_n; X_n, Y_n)\right) = \mathcal{I}(\theta_\star) + O(a_n)$, for points near $\theta_\star$. One reasonable value is $\beta = \text{trace}(\mathcal{I}(\theta_\star))$, which can be estimated easily by summing norms of the score function, that is, $\hat{\beta} = \sum_{i=1}^{n} ||\nabla\ell(\theta_{i-1}; X_i, Y_i)||^2$. This idea is extended to multiple dimensions by Amari et al. (2000), Duchi et al. (2011) and Schaul et al. (2012); we discuss further in Section 14.3.5.1.

For implicit SGD, a learning rate sequence $a_n = \alpha(\alpha+n)^{-1}$ works well in practice (Toulis et al., 2014). As before, α controls statistical efficiency, and we can set $\alpha = 1/\lambda_{\min}$, as in explicit SGD. The additional stability term β of explicit SGD is unnecessary in implicit SGD because the implicit method performs an indirect normalization of the learning rate—this is similar to shrinkage described in Equation 14.4.

Eventually, tuning the learning rate sequence depends on problem-specific considerations, and there is a considerable variety of sequences that have been employed in practice (George and Powell, 2006, Schaul et al., 2012). Principled design of learning rates in first-order SGD remains an important research topic; for example, recent work has investigated variance reduction techniques (Johnson and Zhang, 2013, Wang et al., 2013), or even constant learning rates for least-squares models (Bach and Moulines, 2013). Second-order methods that essentially maintain multiple learning rates, one for each parameter component, are discussed in Section 14.3.5.1.

14.3.4 Efficient Computation of Implicit Methods

The update in implicit SGD (Equation 14.3) is a p-dimensional fixed-point equation, which is generally hard to solve. However, in many statistical models, Equation 14.3 can be reduced to a one-dimensional fixed-point equation, which can be computed very fast using a numerical root-finding method.

Consider a linear statistical model where $\ell(\theta; X_n, Y_n)$ depends on θ only through the linear term $X_n^\intercal\theta$. A large family of models satisfy this condition: generalized linear models, generalized additive models, proportional hazards, etc. We denote $\ell(\theta; X_n, Y_n) = g_n(X_n^\intercal\theta)$, where we suppressed the dependence of g on X_n, Y_n in the subscript n. Then, $\nabla\ell(\theta; X_n, Y_n) = g_n'(X_n^\intercal\theta)X_n$, and therefore the direction of the gradient of the log-likelihood is parameter free. It follows that the implicit procedure can be written as

$$\theta_n^{\text{im}} = \theta_{n-1}^{\text{im}} + a_n\lambda_n\nabla\ell(\theta_{n-1}^{\text{im}}; X_n, Y_n) \tag{14.21}$$

where the gradient is now calculated at the previous estimate θ_{n-1}^{im} and λ_n is an appropriate scaling. We now derive λ_n by combining the definition of implicit SGD (Equations 14.3 and 14.21):

$$\begin{aligned} \theta_{n-1}^{\text{im}} + a_n\lambda_n\nabla\ell(\theta_{n-1}^{\text{im}}; X_n, Y_n) &= \theta_{n-1}^{\text{im}} + a_n\nabla\ell(\theta_n^{\text{im}}; X_n, Y_n) \Rightarrow \\ \lambda_n g_n'(X_n^\intercal\theta_{n-1}^{\text{im}}) &= g_n'(X_n^\intercal\theta_n^{\text{im}}) \end{aligned} \tag{14.22}$$

Using Equation 14.21 in 14.22, we get

$$\lambda_n = \frac{g_n'\left(X_n^\intercal\theta_{n-1}^{\text{im}} + a_n\lambda_n||X_n||^2 g_n'(X_n^\intercal\theta_{n-1}^{\text{im}})\right)}{g_n'(X_n^\intercal\theta_{n-1}^{\text{im}})} \tag{14.23}$$

Equation 14.23 is a one-dimensional fixed-point equation with respect to λ_n. Thus, the implicit iterate θ_n^{im} of Equation 14.3 can be efficiently computed by first obtaining λ_n from

Equation 14.23, and then using Equation 14.21. Narrow search bounds for Equation 14.23 are usually available; see, for example, algorithm 1 by Toulis et al. (2014) for implicit SGD on generalized linear models and algorithm 2 by Tran et al. (2015b) for implicit SGD on the Cox proportional hazards model. Fast implementation of implicit SGD methods are included in the `sgd` R package (Tran et al., 2015a,b).

14.3.5 Extensions

Here, we illustrate three extensions of the SGD methods: second-order SGD methods, which adaptively approximate the Fisher information matrix; averaged SGD methods, which use larger learning rates together with averaging of the iterates; and Monte Carlo SGD, which can be applied when the log-likelihood cannot be efficiently computed.

14.3.5.1 Second-Order Methods

Sakrison's recursive estimation method (Equation 14.11) is the archetype of second-order SGD, but it requires prior knowledge of the Fisher information matrix $\mathcal{I}(\theta_\star)$. Several methods aim to recursively estimate the Fisher information matrix and use those estimates within the main procedure of estimating $\theta_\star$; such methods are known as *adaptive*. Early adaptive methods in stochastic approximation were given by Nevelson and Khasminskiĭ (1973), Wei (1987), and Spall (2000); translated into an SGD procedure, such methods recursively estimate $\mathcal{I}(\theta_\star)$ by fixing a covariate value X_n, perturbing the parameter estimate θ_{n-1}—for example, by taking $\theta_{n-1} \pm \epsilon u$, where $\epsilon > 0$ is a small constant and u is a basis vector—and then sampling outcome Y_n, given the fixed covariate and parameter values. While such methods are very useful when one has control over the data generation process as, for example, in sequential experiment design, they are impractical for modern estimation tasks with large datasets.

A simple and effective approach to recursively estimate $\mathcal{I}(\theta_\star)$ was developed by Amari et al. (2000). The idea is to estimate $\mathcal{I}(\theta_\star)$ through a separate stochastic approximation procedure and use the estimate $\hat{\mathcal{I}}$ in the procedure for $\theta_\star$ as follows:

$$\begin{aligned} \hat{\mathcal{I}}_n &= (1 - c_n)\hat{\mathcal{I}}_{n-1} + c_n \nabla\ell(\theta_{n-1}; X_n, Y_n)\nabla\ell(\theta_{n-1}; X_n, Y_n)^\intercal \\ \theta_n &= \theta_{n-1} + a_n \hat{\mathcal{I}}_n^{-1} \nabla\ell(\theta_{n-1}; X_n, Y_n) \end{aligned} \tag{14.24}$$

Inversion of the estimate $\hat{\mathcal{I}}_n$ is relatively cheap through the Sherman–Morrison formula. This scheme, however, introduces the additional problem of determining the sequence c_n in Equation 14.24. Amari et al. (2000) advocated for a small constant $c_n = c > 0$ determined through computer simulations.

An alternative approach based on quasi-Newton methods was developed by Bordes et al. (2009). Their method, termed *SGD-QN*, approximated the Fisher information matrix through a *secant condition* as in the original BFGS algorithm (Broyden, 1965). The secant condition in SGD-QN is

$$\theta_n - \theta_{n-1} \approx \hat{\mathcal{I}}_{n-1}^{-1}\left[\nabla\ell(\theta_n; X_n, Y_n) - \nabla\ell(\theta_{n-1}; X_n, Y_n)\right] \triangleq \hat{\mathcal{I}}_{n-1}^{-1}\Delta\ell_n \tag{14.25}$$

where $\hat{\mathcal{I}}_n$ are kept diagonal. If L_n denotes the diagonal matrix with the ith diagonal element $L_{ii} = (\theta_{n,i} - \theta_{n-1,i})/\Delta\ell_{n,i}$, then the update for $\hat{\mathcal{I}}_n$ is

$$\hat{\mathcal{I}}_n \leftarrow \hat{\mathcal{I}}_{n-1} + \frac{2}{r}(L_n - \hat{\mathcal{I}}_{n-1}) \tag{14.26}$$

whereas the update for θ_n is similar to Equation 14.24. The parameter r is controlled internally in the algorithm, and counts the number of times the update (Equation 14.26) has been performed.

Another notable method is *AdaGrad* (Duchi et al., 2011), which maintains multiple learning rates using gradient information only. In one popular variant of the method, AdaGrad keeps a $p \times p$ diagonal matrix of learning rates A_n that is updated at every iteration; on observing data (X_n, Y_n), AdaGrad updates A_n as follows:

$$A_n = A_{n-1} + \text{diag}(\nabla \ell(\theta_{n-1}; X_n, Y_n) \nabla \ell(\theta_{n-1}; X_n, Y_n)^\intercal) \tag{14.27}$$

where $\text{diag}(\cdot)$ is the diagonal matrix with the same diagonal as its matrix argument. Estimation with AdaGrad proceeds through the iteration

$$\theta_n = \theta_{n-1} + \alpha A_n^{-1/2} \nabla \ell(\theta_{n-1}; X_n, Y_n) \tag{14.28}$$

where $\alpha > 0$ is shared among all parameter components. The original motivation for AdaGrad stems from proximal methods in optimization, but there is a statistical intuition why the update (Equation 14.28) is reasonable. In many dimensions, where some parameter components affect outcomes less frequently than others, AdaGrad *estimates* the information that has *actually* been received for each component. A conservative estimate of this information is provided by the elements of A_n in Equation 14.27, which is justified because, under typical conditions, $\mathbb{E}\left(\nabla \ell(\theta; X_n, Y_n) \nabla \ell(\theta; X_n, Y_n)^\intercal\right) = \mathcal{I}(\theta)$.

In fact, Toulis and Airoldi (2014) showed that the asymptotic variance of AdaGrad satisfies

$$\sqrt{n}\text{Var}(\theta_n) \to \frac{\alpha}{2} \text{diag}(\mathcal{I}(\theta_\star))^{-1/2}.$$

The asymptotic variance of AdaGrad has rate $O(1/\sqrt{n})$, which indicates significant loss of information. However, this rate is attained *regardless* of the specification of the learning rate parameter α. In contrast, as shown in Section 14.3.1, first-order SGD procedures require $(2\alpha\mathcal{I}(\theta_\star) - \mathbb{I})$ to be positive-definite in order to achieve the $O(1/n)$ rate, but the rate can be significantly worse if this condition is not met. For instance, Nemirovski et al. (2009) give an example of misspecification of α, where the rate of first-order explicit SGD is $O(n^{-\epsilon})$, and $\epsilon > 0$ is positive but arbitrarily small.

All the second-order methods presented so far are explicit; however, they can have straightforward variants using implicit updates. For example, in the method of Amari et al. (2000), one can use the implicit update

$$\theta_n = \theta_{n-1} + a_n \hat{\mathcal{I}}_n^{-1} \nabla \ell(\theta_n; X_n, Y_n) \tag{14.29}$$

instead of the explicit one in Equation 14.24. The solution of Equation 14.29 does not present additional challenges, compared to Section 14.3.4, because inverses of the estimates $\hat{\mathcal{I}}_n$ are easy to compute.

14.3.5.2 Averaging

In certain models, second-order methods can be avoided and still statistical efficiency can be achieved through a combination of larger learning rates a_n with averaging of the iterates θ_n. The corresponding SGD procedure is usually referred to as *averaged SGD*, or *ASGD* for short.* Averaging in stochastic approximation was studied independently by Ruppert (1988a) and Bather (1989), who proposed similar averaging schemes. If we use the notation

*The acronym ASGD is also used in machine learning to denote *asynchronous* SGD, that is, a variant of SGD that can be parallelized on multiple machines. We will not consider this variant here.

of Section 14.2, Ruppert (1988a) considered the following modification of the Robbins–Monro procedure (Equation 14.9):

$$\theta_n = \theta_{n-1} + a_n H(\theta_{n-1})$$
$$\bar{\theta}_n = \frac{1}{n}\sum_{i=1}^{n}\theta_i \tag{14.30}$$

where $a_n = \alpha n^{-c}$, $1/2 < c < 1$, and $\bar{\theta}_n$ are considered the estimates of $\theta_\star$, instead of θ_n. Under certain conditions, Ruppert (1988a) showed that $n\mathrm{Var}(\bar{\theta}_n) \to \sigma^2/h'(\theta_\star)^2$, where $\sigma^2 = \mathrm{Var}\,(H(\theta)|\,\theta = \theta_\star)$. Therefore, $\bar{\theta}_n$ achieves the minimum variance that is possible according to the analysis in Section 14.2.

Ruppert (1988a) gives a nice statistical intuition on why averaging with larger learning rates implies statistical efficiency. First, write $H(\theta_n) = h(\theta_n) + \varepsilon_n$, where ε_n are zero-mean independent random variables with finite variance. By solving the Equation 14.9, we get

$$\theta_n - \theta_\star = \sum_{i=1}^{n}\gamma_{in} a_i \varepsilon_i + o(1) \tag{14.31}$$

where $\gamma_{in} = \exp\{-A(n) + A(i)\}$, $A(m) = K\sum_{j=1}^{m} a_j$ is the function of partial sums, and K is a constant. Ruppert (1988a) shows that Equation 14.31 can be rewritten as

$$\theta_n - \theta_\star = a_n \sum_{i=b(n)}^{n}\gamma_{in}\varepsilon_i + o(1) \tag{14.32}$$

where $b(n) = \lfloor n - n^c \log n \rfloor$ and $\lfloor\cdot\rfloor$ is the positive integer floor function. When $a_n = a/n$, Ruppert (1988a) shows that $b(n) = O(1)$ and $\theta_n - \theta_\star$ is the weighted average over all noise variables ε_n. In this case, there is significant autocorrelation in the series θ_n and averaging actually can make things worse. However, when $a_n = \alpha n^{-c}$, for $1/2 < c < 1$, $\theta_n - \theta_\star$ is a weighted average of only $O(n^c \log n)$ noise variables. In this case, the iterates $\theta_{\lfloor p_1 n \rfloor}$ and $\theta_{\lfloor p_2 n \rfloor}$, for $0 < p_1 < p_2 < 1$, are asymptotically uncorrelated, and thus averaging improves estimation efficiency.

Polyak and Juditsky (1992) derive further significant results for averaged SGD, showing in particular that ASGD can be asymptotically efficient as second-order SGD under certain conditions (e.g., strong convexity of the expected log-likelihood). In fact, ASGD is usually referred to as the *Polyak–Ruppert averaging scheme.* Adoption of averaging schemes for statistical estimation has been slow but steady over the years (Zhang, 2004, Nemirovski et al., 2009, Bottou, 2010, Cappé, 2011). One practical reason is that a bad selection of the learning rate sequence can cause ASGD to converge more slowly than classical explicit SGD (Xu, 2011). Such problems can be avoided by using implicit SGD with averaging because implicit methods can afford larger learning rates that can speed up convergence. At the same time using implicit updates in Equation 14.30 still maintains asymptotic efficiency (Toulis et al., 2015b).

14.3.5.3 Monte Carlo Stochastic Gradient Descent

A key requirement for the application of SGD procedures is that the likelihood is easy to evaluate. However, this is not possible in many situations, for example, when the likelihood is only known up to a normalizing constant. In such cases, Equations 14.12 and 14.13 cannot be applied directly because $\nabla\ell(\theta; X, Y) = S(X,Y) - Z(\theta)$, and while S is easy to compute, Z is hard to compute as it entails a multidimensional integral.

However, if sampling from the model is feasible, then a variant of explicit SGD, termed *Monte Carlo SGD* (Toulis and Airoldi, 2015a), can be constructed to take advantage of the identity $\mathbb{E}(\nabla\ell(\theta_\star; X, Y)) = 0$, which implies $\mathbb{E}(S(X,Y)) = Z(\theta_\star)$. Starting from an estimate θ_0^{mc}, we iterate the following steps for $n = 1, 2, \ldots$:

1. Observe covariate X_n and outcome Y_n; compute $S_n \triangleq S(X_n, Y_n)$.

2. Get m samples $\widetilde{Y}_{n,i}|X_n, \theta_{n-1}^{\text{mc}} \sim f(\cdot; X_n, \theta_{n-1}^{\text{mc}})$, for $i = 1, 2, \ldots, m$.

3. Compute statistic $\widetilde{S}_{n-1} \triangleq (1/m)\sum_{i=1}^{m} S(X_n, \widetilde{Y}_{n,i})$.

4. Update estimate θ_{n-1}^{mc} through

$$\theta_n^{\text{mc}} = \theta_{n-1}^{\text{mc}} + a_n C(S_n - \widetilde{S}_{n-1}) \tag{14.33}$$

This method is valid under typical assumptions of stochastic approximation theory because it converges to a point $\theta_\infty^{\text{mc}}$ such that $\mathbb{E}\left(S(X, \widetilde{Y})|\theta_\infty^{\text{mc}}\right) = \mathbb{E}(S(X,Y)) = Z(\theta_\star)$, and thus $\mathbb{E}(\nabla\ell(\theta_\infty^{\text{mc}}, X, Y)) = 0$ as required. Furthermore, the asymptotic variance of estimates of Monte Carlo SGD satisfies

$$n\text{Var}(\theta_n^{\text{mc}}) \to (1 + 1/m) \cdot \alpha^2(2\alpha C\mathcal{I}(\theta_\star) - I)^{-1} C\mathcal{I}(\theta_\star)C^\intercal \tag{14.34}$$

which exceeds the variance of the typical explicit (or implicit) SGD estimator in Equation 14.17 by a factor of $(1 + 1/m)$.

In its current form, Monte Carlo SGD (Equation 14.33) is only explicit; an implicit version would require to sample data from the next iterate, which is technically challenging. Still, an *approximate* implicit implementation of Monte Carlo SGD is possible through shrinkage, for example, through shrinking θ_n^{mc} by a factor $(\mathbb{I} + a_n\mathcal{I}(\theta_n^{\text{mc}}))^{-1}$ or more easily by $(1 + a_n\text{trace}(\mathcal{I}(\theta_n^{\text{mc}})))^{-1}$.

Theoretically, Monte Carlo SGD is based on *sampling-controlled* stochastic approximation methods (Dupuis and Simha, 1991), in which the usual regression function of the Robbins–Monro procedure (Equation 14.9) is only accessible through sampling, for example, through MCMC. Convergence in such settings is subtle because it depends on the ergodicity of the underlying Markov chain (Younes, 1999). Finally, when perfect sampling from the underlying model is not possible, we may use samples $\widetilde{S}_n$ that are obtained by a handful of MCMC steps, even before the chain has converged. This is the idea of *contrastive divergence algorithm*, which we briefly discuss in Section 14.4.4.

14.4 Other Applications

In this section, we will review additional applications of stochastic approximation and SGD, giving a preference to breadth over depth.

14.4.1 Online EM Algorithm

The EM algorithm (Dempster et al., 1977) is a numerically stable procedure to compute the maximum-likelihood estimator in latent variable models. Slightly changing the notation of previous sections, let X_n denote the latent variable, Y_n denote the outcome distributed conditional on X_n, and assume model parameters $\theta_\star$. Also, let $f_{\text{com}}(X_n, Y_n; \theta)$ and $f_{\text{obs}}(Y_n; \theta)$ denote, respectively, the complete data and observed data densities; similarly,

ℓ_{com} and ℓ_{obs} denote the respective log-likelihoods. For simplicity, we will assume that f_{com} is an exponential family model in the natural parameterization, that is,

$$f_{\text{com}}(X_n, Y_n; \theta) = \exp\{S(X_n, Y_n)^\intercal \theta_\star - A(\theta_\star) + B(X_n, Y_n)\} \tag{14.35}$$

for appropriate functions S, A, and B. The Fisher information matrix of complete data for parameter value θ is denoted by $\mathcal{I}_{\text{com}}(\theta) = -\mathbb{E}(\nabla\nabla\ell_{\text{com}}(\theta; X_n, Y_n))$; similarly, the Fisher information matrix of observed data is denoted by $\mathcal{I}_{\text{obs}}(\theta) = -\mathbb{E}(\nabla\nabla\ell_{\text{obs}}(\theta; Y_n))$. Furthermore, we assume a finite dataset, where $\mathbf{Y} = (Y_1, \ldots, Y_N)$ denotes all observed data and $\mathbf{X} = (X_1, \ldots, X_N)$ denotes all missing data.

The classical EM algorithm proceeds by iterating the following steps:

$$Q(\theta, \theta_{n-1}; \mathbf{Y}) = \mathbb{E}(\ell_{\text{com}}(\theta; \mathbf{X}, \mathbf{Y}) | \theta_{n-1}, \mathbf{Y}) \qquad \textbf{E-step} \tag{14.36}$$

$$\theta_n = \arg\max_\theta Q(\theta, \theta_{n-1}; \mathbf{Y}) \qquad \textbf{M-step} \tag{14.37}$$

Dempster et al. (1977) showed that the EM algorithm converges to the maximum-likelihood estimator $\hat{\theta} = \arg\max_\theta \ell_{\text{obs}}(\theta; \mathbf{Y})$, and that EM is an ascent algorithm, that is, the likelihood is strictly increasing at each iteration. Despite this highly desirable numerical stability, the EM algorithm is impractical for estimation with large datasets because it involves expensive operations, both in the expectation and maximization steps, that need to performed on the entire set of N data points.

To speed up the EM algorithm, Titterington (1984) considered a procedure defined through the iteration

$$\theta_n = \theta_{n-1} + a_n \mathcal{I}_{\text{com}}(\theta_{n-1})^{-1} \nabla \ell_{\text{obs}}(\theta_{n-1}; Y_n) \tag{14.38}$$

This procedure is essentially Sakrison's recursive estimation method described in Section 14.2.1, appropriately modified to use the Fisher information matrix of observed data. In the univariate case, Titterington (1984) applied Fabian's theorem (Fabian, 1968) to show that the estimate in Equation 14.38 satisfies $\sqrt{n}(\theta_n - \theta_\star) \sim \mathcal{N}(0, \mathcal{I}_{\text{com}}(\theta_\star)^{-2}\mathcal{I}_{\text{obs}}(\theta_\star))/(2\mathcal{I}_{\text{obs}}(\theta_\star)\mathcal{I}_{\text{com}}(\theta_\star)^{-1} - 1)$. Thus, as in the classical EM algorithm, the efficiency of Titterington's method (Equation 14.38) depends on the fraction of missing information. Notably, Lange (1995) considered single Newton–Raphson steps in the M-step of the EM algorithm, and derived a procedure that is similar to Equation 14.38.

However, the procedure 14.38 is essentially an explicit stochastic gradient method, and, unlike EM, it can have serious stability and convergence problems. In the exponential family model (Equation 14.35), Nowlan (1991) considered the first true *online* EM algorithm as follows:

$$\begin{aligned} S_n &= (1-\alpha)S_{n-1} + \alpha\mathbb{E}(S(X_n, Y_n) | \theta_{n-1}, Y_n) && \textbf{E-step} \\ \theta_n &= \arg\max_\theta \ell_{\text{com}}(\theta; S_n) && \textbf{M-step} \end{aligned} \tag{14.39}$$

where $\alpha \in (0, 1)$. In words, algorithm 14.39 starts from some initial sufficient statistic S_0 and then uses stochastic approximation with a constant step-size α to update it. The maximization step is identical to that of classical EM, and it is more stable than procedure 14.38 because, as iterations proceed, S_n accumulates information over the entire dataset. A variant of Nowlan's method with a decreasing step-size was later developed by Sato and Ishii (2000) as follows:

$$\begin{aligned} S_n &= (1-a_n)S_{n-1} + a_n\mathbb{E}(S(X_n, Y_n) | \theta_{n-1}, Y_n) && \textbf{E-step} \\ \theta_n &= \arg\max_\theta \ell_{\text{com}}(\theta; S_n) && \textbf{M-step} \end{aligned} \tag{14.40}$$

By the theory of stochastic approximation, procedure 14.40 converges to the observed data maximum-likelihood estimate $\hat{\theta}$. In contrast, procedure 14.39 will not converge with a constant α; it will rather reach a point in the vicinity of $\hat{\theta}$ more rapidly than Equation 14.40 and then oscillate around $\hat{\theta}$. Further online EM algorithms have been developed by several authors (Neal and Hinton, 1998, Cappé and Moulines, 2009). Examples of a growing body of applications of such methods can be found in works by Neal and Hinton (1998), Sato and Ishii (2000), Liu et al. (2006), and Cappé (2011).

14.4.2 MCMC Sampling

As before, we need to slightly extend our notation to a Bayesian setting. Let θ denote model parameters with an assumed prior distribution $\pi(\theta)$. A common task in Bayesian inference is to sample from the posterior distribution $f(\theta|\mathbf{Y}) \propto \pi(\theta)f(\mathbf{Y}|\theta)$, given N observed data points $\mathbf{Y} = \{Y_1, \ldots, Y_N\}$.

The Hamiltonian Monte Carlo (HMC) (Neal, 2011) is an MCMC method in which auxiliary parameters p are introduced to improve sampling from $f(\theta|\mathbf{Y})$. In the augmented parameter space, we consider a function $H(\theta, p) = U(\theta) + K(p) \in \mathbb{R}^+$, where $U(\theta) = -\log f(\theta|\mathbf{Y})$ and $K(p) = (1/2)p^\intercal M p$, M being positive definite. Next, we consider the density

$$h(\theta, p|\mathbf{Y}) = \exp\{-H(\theta, p)\} = \exp\{-U(\theta) - K(p)\} = f(\theta|\mathbf{Y}) \times \mathcal{N}(p, M^{-1})$$

In this parameterization, the variables p are independent of θ. Assuming an initial state (θ_0, p_0), sampling with HMC proceeds in iterations indexed by $n = 1, \ldots$, as follows:

1. Sample $p^* \sim \mathcal{N}(0, M^{-1})$.

2. Using *Hamiltonian dynamics*, compute $(\theta_n, p_n) = \text{ODE}(\theta_{n-1}, p^*)$.

3. Perform a Metropolis–Hastings step for the proposed transition $(\theta_{n-1}, p^*) \to (\theta_n, p_n)$ with acceptance probability $\min[1, \exp(-H(\theta_n, p_n) + H(\theta_{n-1}, p^*))]$.

Step 2 is the key idea in HMC. The parameters (θ, p) are mapped to a physical system, where θ is the position of the system and p is the momentum. The potential of the physical system is $U(\theta)$ and its kinetic energy is $K(p)$. Function H is known as the *Hamiltonian*. The Hamiltonian dynamics refer to a set of ordinary differential equations (ODE) that govern the movement of the system, and thus determine the future values of (θ, p) given a pair of current values. Being a closed physical system, the Hamiltonian of the system, $H(\theta, p) = U(\theta) + K(p)$, is constant. Thus, in Step 3 of HMC it holds that $-H(\theta_n, p_n) + H(\theta_{n-1}, p^*) = 0$, and thus the acceptance probability is 1, assuming that the solution of the ODE is exact. This is a significant improvement over generic Metropolis–Hastings, where it is usually hard to achieve high acceptance probabilities.

A special case of HMC, known as *Langevin dynamics* (Girolami and Calderhead, 2011), defines the sampling iterations as follows:

$$\begin{aligned} \eta_n &\sim \mathcal{N}(0, \epsilon I) \\ \theta_n &= \theta_{n-1} + \frac{\epsilon}{2}(\nabla \log \pi(\theta_{n-1}) + \nabla \log f(\mathbf{Y}|\theta_{n-1})) + \eta_n \end{aligned} \tag{14.41}$$

The sampling procedure 14.41 follows from HMC by a numerical solution of the ODE in Step 2 of the algorithm using the *leapfrog* method (Neal, 2011). Parameter $\epsilon > 0$ in Equation 14.41 determines the size of the leapfrog in the numerical solution of Hamiltonian differential equations.

Welling and Teh (2011) studied a simple modification of Langevin dynamics (Equation 14.41) using a stochastic gradient as follows:

$$\eta_n \sim \mathcal{N}(0, \epsilon_n) \cdot$$
$$\theta_n = \theta_{n-1} + \frac{\epsilon_n}{2}(\nabla \log \pi(\theta_{n-1}) + (N/b) \sum_{i \in \text{batch}} \nabla \log f(Y_i|\theta_{n-1})) + \eta_n \tag{14.42}$$

The step sizes $\epsilon_n > 0$ satisfy the typical Robbins–Monro requirements, that is, $\sum \epsilon_i = \infty$ and $\sum \epsilon_i^2 < \infty$. Procedure 14.42 is using stochastic gradients averaged over a *batch* of b data points, a technique usually employed in SGD to reduce noise in stochastic gradients. Sato and Nakagawa (2014) proved that procedure 14.42 converges to the true posterior $f(\theta|\mathbf{Y})$ using an elegant theory of stochastic calculus. Sampling through stochastic gradient Langevin dynamics has since generated a lot of related work in posterior sampling for large datasets, and it is still a rapidly expanding research area with contributions from various disciplines (Hoffman et al., 2013, Korattikara et al., 2014, Pillai and Smith, 2014).

14.4.3 Reinforcement Learning

Reinforcement learning is the multidisciplinary study of how autonomous agents perceive, learn, and interact with their environment (Bertsekas and Tsitsiklis, 1995). Typically, it is assumed that time t proceeds in discrete steps, and at every step an *agent* is at state $x_t \in \mathcal{X}$, where $\mathcal{X}$ is the state space. On entering a state x_t, two things happen. First, an agent receives a probabilistic *reward* $R(x_t) \in \mathbb{R}$, and, second, the agent takes an *action* $a \in \mathcal{A}$, where $\mathcal{A}$ denotes the action space. This action is determined by the agent's *policy*, which is a function $\pi : \mathcal{X} \to \mathcal{A}$, mapping a state to an action. Nature then decides a *transition* to state x_{t+1} according to a probability that is unknown to the agent.

One important task in reinforcement learning is to estimate the *value function* $V^\pi(x)$, which quantifies the expected value of a specific state $x \in \mathcal{X}$ with respect to policy π, defined as

$$V^\pi(x) = \mathbb{E}(R(x)) + \gamma \mathbb{E}(R(x_1)) + \gamma^2 \mathbb{E}(R(x_2)) + \cdots \tag{14.43}$$

where:

x_t denotes the state that will be reached starting at x after t transitions
$\gamma \in (0, 1)$ is a parameter that discounts future rewards

Uncertainty in $R(x_t)$ includes the uncertainty of the state x_t because of the stochasticity in state transitions, and the uncertainty from the reward distribution. Thus, $V^\pi(x)$ admits a recursive definition as follows:

$$V^\pi(x) = \mathbb{E}(R(x)) + \gamma \mathbb{E}(V^\pi(x_1)) \tag{14.44}$$

When the state is a high-dimensional vector, one popular approach is to use a linear approximation for $V(x)$, such that $V(x) = \theta_\star^\intercal \phi(x)$, where $\phi(x)$ maps a state to a *feature space* with fewer dimensions and $\theta_\star$ is a vector of fixed parameters. If the agent is at state x_t, then the recursive equation (Equation 14.44) can be rewritten as

$$\mathbb{E}(R(x_t) - (\theta_\star^\intercal \phi_t - \gamma \theta_\star^\intercal \phi_{t+1})|\, \phi_t) = 0 \tag{14.45}$$

where we set $\phi_t = \phi(x_t)$ for notational convenience. Similar to SGD, this suggests a stochastic approximation method to estimate $\theta_\star$ through the following iteration:

$$\theta_{t+1} = \theta_t + a_t \left[R(x_t) - (\theta_t^\intercal \phi_t - \gamma \theta_t^\intercal \phi_{t+1})\right] \phi_t \tag{14.46}$$

where a_t is a learning rate sequence that satisfies the Robbins–Monro conditions of Section 14.2. Procedure 14.46 is known as the *temporal differences* (TD) learning algorithm (Sutton, 1988). Implicit versions of this algorithm have recently emerged to solve the known stability issues of the classical TD algorithm (Wang and Bertsekas, 2013, Tamar et al., 2014). For example, Tamar et al. (2014) consider computing the term $\theta_t^\intercal \phi_t$ at the future iterate, the resulting *implicit* TD algorithm being defined as

$$\theta_{t+1} = (I + a_t \phi_t \phi_t^\intercal)^{-1} [\theta_t + a_t(R(x_t) + \gamma \theta_t^\intercal \phi_{t+1})\phi_t] \tag{14.47}$$

Similar to implicit SGD, iteration 14.47 stabilizes the TD iteration 14.46. With the advent of online multiagent markets, methods and applications in reinforcement learning have been receiving a renewed stream of research effort (Gosavi, 2009).

14.4.4 Deep Learning

Deep learning is the task of estimating parameters of statistical models that can be represented by multiple layers of nonlinear operations, such as neural networks (Bengio, 2009). Such models, also referred to as *deep architectures*, consist of *units* that can perform a basic prediction task, and are grouped in layers such that the output of one layer forms the input of another layer that sits directly on top. Furthermore, the models are usually augmented with *latent units* that are defined to represent structured quantities of interest, such as edges or shapes in an image.

One basic building block of deep architectures is the Restricted Boltzmann Machine (RBM). The complete-data density for one data point (X, Y) of the states of hidden and observed input units, respectively, is given by

$$f(X, Y; \theta) = \frac{\exp\{-b'Y - c'x - X'WY\}}{Z(\theta)} \tag{14.48}$$

where $\theta = (b, c, W)$ are the model parameters, and the function $Z(\theta) = \sum_{X,Y} \exp\{-b'Y - c'x - X'WY\}$, also known as the partition function, acts as the normalizing constant. Furthermore, the sample spaces for X and Y are discrete (e.g., binary) and finite. The observed-data density is thus $f(Y; \theta) = \sum_X f(X, Y; \theta)$. Let $H(X, Y; \theta) = b'Y + c'x + X'WY$, such that $f(X, Y; \theta) = (e^{-H(X,Y;\theta)})/(Z(\theta))$. Also consider the observed data $\mathbf{Y} = \{Y_1, Y_2, \ldots, Y_N\}$ and missing data $\mathbf{X} = \{X_1, X_2, \ldots, X_n\}$.

Through simple algebra, one can obtain the gradient of the log-likelihood of observed data in the following convenient form:

$$\nabla \ell(\theta; \mathbf{Y}) = -\left[\mathbb{E}\left(\nabla H(\mathbf{X}, \mathbf{Y}; \theta)\right) - \mathbb{E}\left(\nabla H(\mathbf{X}, \mathbf{Y}; \theta) | \, \mathbf{Y}\right)\right] \tag{14.49}$$

where $H(\mathbf{X}, \mathbf{Y}; \theta) = \sum_{n=1}^{N} H(X_n, Y_n; \theta)$. In practical situations, the data points (X_n, Y_n) are binary. Therefore, the conditional distribution of the missing data $X_n|Y_n$ is readily available through a logistic regression model, and thus the second term of Equation 14.49 is easy to sample from. Similarly, $Y_n|X_n$ is easy to sample from. However, the first term in Equation 14.49 requires sampling from the joint distribution of the complete data $(\mathbf{X}, \mathbf{Y})$, which conceptually is easy to do using the aforementioned conditionals and a Gibbs sampling scheme (Geman and Geman, 1984). However, the domain for both $\mathbf{X}$ and $\mathbf{Y}$ is typically very large, for example, it comprises thousands or millions of units, and thus a full Gibbs on the joint distribution is impossible.

The method of *contrastive divergence* (Hinton, 2002, Carreira-Perpinan and Hinton, 2005) has been applied for training such models with considerable success. The algorithm proceeds as follows for steps $i = 1, 2, \ldots$:

1. Sample one state $Y^{(i)}$ from the empirical distribution of observed data $\mathbf{Y}$.
2. Sample $X^{(i)}|Y^{(i)}$, that is, the hidden state.
3. Sample $Y^{(i,\text{new})}|X^{(i)}$.
4. Sample $X^{(i,\text{new})}|Y^{(i,\text{new})}$.
5. Evaluate the gradient (Equation 14.49) using $(X^{(i)}, Y^{(i)})$ for the second term and the sample $(X^{(i,\text{new})}, Y^{(i,\text{new})})$ for the first term.
6. Update the parameters in θ using constant-step-size SGD and the estimated gradient from Step 5.

In other words, contrastive divergence attempts to estimate $\nabla\ell(\theta; \mathbf{Y})$ in Equation 14.49. This estimation is biased because $(X^{(i,\text{new})}, Y^{(i,\text{new})})$ is assumed to be from the exact joint distribution of (X, Y); however, they are single Gibbs iterations starting from the observed and imputed data $(X^{(i)}, Y^{(i)})$, respectively. In theory, Steps 3 and 4 could be repeated k times; for example, if $k \to \infty$ the sampling distribution of $(X^{(i,\text{new})}, Y^{(i,\text{new})})$ would be the exact joint distribution of (X, Y), leading to unbiased estimation of $\nabla\ell(\theta; \mathbf{Y})$ of Equation 14.49. Surprisingly, it has been empirically observed that $k = 1$ is enough for good performance in many learning tasks (Hinton, 2002, Taylor et al., 2006, Salakhutdinov et al., 2007, Bengio, 2009, Bengio and Delalleau, 2009), which is a testament to the power and flexibility of stochastic gradient methods.

14.5 Glossary

SGD: Stochastic gradient descent.

References

Amari, S.-I. (1998). Natural gradient works efficiently in learning. *Neural Computation*, 10(2):251–276.

Amari, S.-I., Chen, T.-P., and Cichocki, A. (1997). Stability analysis of learning algorithms for blind source separation. *Neural Networks*, 10(8):1345–1351.

Amari, S.-I., Park, H., and Fukumizu, K. (2000). Adaptive method of realizing natural gradient learning for multilayer perceptrons. *Neural Computation*, 12(6):1399–1409.

Bach, F. and Moulines, E. (2013). Non-strongly-convex smooth stochastic approximation with convergence rate $o(1/n)$. In *Advances in Neural Information Processing Systems*, pp. 773–781.

Bather, J. (1989). *Stochastic Approximation: A Generalisation of the Robbins-Monro Procedure*, volume 89. Mathematical Sciences Institute, Cornell University, Ithaca, NY.

Bengio, Y. (2009). Learning deep architectures for AI. *Foundations and Trends in Machine Learning*, 2(1):1–127.

Bengio, Y. and Delalleau, O. (2009). Justifying and generalizing contrastive divergence. *Neural Computation*, 21(6):1601–1621.

Bertsekas, D. P. (2011). Incremental proximal methods for large scale convex optimization. *Mathematical Programming*, 129(2):163–195.

Bertsekas, D. P. and Tsitsiklis, J. N. (1995). Neuro-dynamic programming: An overview. In *Proceedings of the 34th IEEE Conference on Decision and Control*, volume 1, pp. 560–564. IEEE, New Orleans, LA.

Blum, J. R. (1954). Multidimensional stochastic approximation methods. *The Annals of Mathematical Statistics*, 25:737–744.

Bordes, A., Bottou, L., and Gallinari, P. (2009). SGD-QN: Careful quasi-Newton stochastic gradient descent. *The Journal of Machine Learning Research*, 10:1737–1754.

Bottou, L. (2010). Large-scale machine learning with stochastic gradient descent. In Lechevallier, Y. and Saporta, G. (eds.), *Proceedings of COMPSTAT*, pp. 177–186. Springer, Berlin, Germany.

Bottou, L. and Le Cun, Y. (2005). Online learning for very large datasets. *Applied Stochastic Models in Business and Industry*, 21(2):137–151.

Bottou, L. and Murata, N. (2002). Stochastic approximations and efficient learning. *The Handbook of Brain Theory and Neural Networks*, 2nd edition. The MIT Press, Cambridge, MA.

Broyden, C. G. (1965). A class of methods for solving nonlinear simultaneous equations. *Mathematics of Computation*, 19:577–593.

Cappé, O. (2011). Online EM algorithm for Hidden Markov models. *Journal of Computational and Graphical Statistics*, 20(3):728–749.

Cappé, O. and Moulines, E. (2009). Online Expectation–Maximization algorithm for latent data models. *Journal of the Royal Statistical Society: Series B (Statistical Methodology)*, 71(3):593–613.

Carreira-Perpinan, M. A. and Hinton, G. E. (2005). On contrastive divergence learning. In Cowell, R. and Ghahramani, Z. (eds.), *Proceedings of the 10th International Workshop on Artificial Intelligence and Statistics*, pp. 33–40. The Society for Artificial Intelligence and Statistics.

Chung, K. L. (1954). On a stochastic approximation method. *The Annals of Mathematical Statistics*, 25:463–483.

Dempster, A., Laird, N., and Rubin, D. (1977). Maximum likelihood from incomplete data via the EM algorithm. *Journal of the Royal Statistical Society, Series B*, 39:1–38.

Duchi, J., Hazan, E., and Singer, Y. (2011). Adaptive subgradient methods for online learning and stochastic optimization. *The Journal of Machine Learning Research*, 12:2121–2159.

Dupuis, P. and Simha, R. (1991). On sampling controlled stochastic approximation. *IEEE Transactions on Automatic Control*, 36(8):915–924.

Fabian, V. (1968). On asymptotic normality in stochastic approximation. *The Annals of Mathematical Statistics*, 39:1327–1332.

Fabian, V. (1973). Asymptotically efficient stochastic approximation: The RM case. *Annals of Statistics*, 1:486–495.

Fisher, R. A. (1922). On the mathematical foundations of theoretical statistics. *Philosophical Transactions of the Royal Society of London. Series A, Containing Papers of a Mathematical or Physical Character*, 222:309–368.

Fisher, R. A. (1925). *Statistical Methods for Research Workers.* Oliver and Boyd, Edinburgh, Scotland.

Gardner, W. A. (1984). Learning characteristics of stochastic gradient descent algorithms: A general study, analysis, and critique. *Signal Processing*, 6(2):113–133.

Geman, S. and Geman, D. (1984). Stochastic relaxation, Gibbs distributions, and the Bayesian restoration of images. *IEEE Transactions on Pattern Analysis and Machine Intelligence*, (6):721–741.

George, A. P. and Powell, W. B. (2006). Adaptive stepsizes for recursive estimation with applications in approximate dynamic programming. *Machine Learning*, 65(1):167–198.

Girolami, M. and Calderhead, B. (2011). Riemann manifold Langevin and Hamiltonian Monte Carlo methods. *Journal of the Royal Statistical Society: Series B (Statistical Methodology)*, 73(2):123–214.

Gosavi, A. (2009). Reinforcement learning: A tutorial survey and recent advances. *INFORMS Journal on Computing*, 21(2):178–192.

Green, P. J. (1984). Iteratively reweighted least squares for maximum likelihood estimation, and some robust and resistant alternatives. *Journal of the Royal Statistical Society. Series B (Methodological)*, 46:149–192.

Hastie, T., Tibshirani, R., and Friedman, J. (2011). *The Elements of Statistical Learning: Data Mining, Inference, and Prediction*, 2nd edition. Springer, New York.

Hennig, P. and Kiefel, M. (2013). Quasi-newton methods: A new direction. *The Journal of Machine Learning Research*, 14(1):843–865.

Hinton, G. E. (2002). Training products of experts by minimizing contrastive divergence. *Neural Computation*, 14(8):1771–1800.

Hoffman, M. D., Blei, D. M., Wang, C., and Paisley, J. (2013). Stochastic variational inference. *The Journal of Machine Learning Research*, 14(1):1303–1347.

Johnson, R. and Zhang, T. (2013). Accelerating stochastic gradient descent using predictive variance reduction. In Burges, C. J. C., Bottou, L., Welling, M., Ghahramani, Z., and Weinberger K. Q. (eds.), *Advances in Neural Information Processing Systems*, Curran Associates, Inc., pp. 315–323.

Karoui, N. E. (2008). Spectrum estimation for large dimensional covariance matrices using random matrix theory. *Annals of Statistics*, 36(6):2757–2790.

Kivinen, J., Warmuth, M. K., and Hassibi, B. (2006). The p-norm generalization of the LMS algorithm for adaptive filtering. *IEEE Transactions on Signal Processing*, 54(5): 1782–1793.

Korattikara, A., Chen, Y., and Welling, M. (2014). Austerity in MCMC land: Cutting the Metropolis-Hastings budget. In *Proceedings of the 31st International Conference on Machine Learning*, pp. 181–189.

Krakowski, K. A., Mahony, R. E., Williamson, R. C., and Warmuth, M. K. (2007). A geometric view of non-linear online stochastic gradient descent. *Author Website*.

Kulis, B. and Bartlett, P. L. (2010). Implicit online learning. In *Proceedings of the 27th International Conference on Machine Learning*, pp. 575–582.

Lai, T. L. and Robbins, H. (1979). Adaptive design and stochastic approximation. *Annals of Statistics*, 7:1196–1221.

Lange, K. (1995). A gradient algorithm locally equivalent to the EM algorithm. *Journal of the Royal Statistical Society. Series B (Methodological)*, Wiley, 57(2):425–437.

Le Cun, L. B. Y. and Bottou, L. (2004). Large scale online learning. *Advances in Neural Information Processing Systems*, 16:217–224.

Lehmann, E. L. and Casella, G. (1998). *Theory of Point Estimation*, volume 31. Springer, New York.

Lehmann, E. L. and Casella, G. (2003). *Theory of Point Estimation*, 2nd edition. Springer, New York.

Lions, P.-L. and Mercier, B. (1979). Splitting algorithms for the sum of two nonlinear operators. *SIAM Journal on Numerical Analysis*, 16(6):964–979.

Liu, Z., Almhana, J., Choulakian, V., and McGorman, R. (2006). Online EM algorithm for mixture with application to internet traffic modeling. *Computational Statistics & Data Analysis*, 50(4):1052–1071.

Ljung, L., Pflug, G., and Walk, H. (1992). *Stochastic Approximation and Optimization of Random Systems*, volume 17. Springer Basel AG, Basel, Switzerland.

Moulines, E. and Bach, F. R. (2011). Non-asymptotic analysis of stochastic approximation algorithms for machine learning. In *Advances in Neural Information Processing Systems*, pp. 451–459.

Murata, N. (1998). A statistical study of online learning. *Online Learning and Neural Networks*. Cambridge University Press, Cambridge.

Nagumo, J.-I. and Noda, A. (1967). A learning method for system identification. *IEEE Transactions on Automatic Control*, 12(3):282–287.

National Research Council (2013). *Frontiers in Massive Data Analysis*. National Academies Press, Washington, DC.

Neal, R. (2011). MCMC using Hamiltonian dynamics. *Handbook of Markov Chain Monte Carlo*, volume 2, pp. 113–162. Chapman & Hall/CRC Press, Boca Raton, FL.

Neal, R. M. and Hinton, G. E. (1998). A view of the EM algorithm that justifies incremental, sparse, and other variants. In Jordan, M. I. (ed.), *Learning in Graphical Models*, pp. 355–368. Springer, Cambridge, MA.

Nemirovski, A., Juditsky, A., Lan, G., and Shapiro, A. (2009). Robust stochastic approximation approach to stochastic programming. *SIAM Journal on Optimization*, 19(4):1574–1609.

Nevelson, M. B. and Khasminskiĭ, R. Z. (1973). *Stochastic Approximation and Recursive Estimation*, volume 47. American Mathematical Society, Providence, RI.

Nowlan, S. J. (1991). Soft competitive adaptation: Neural network learning algorithms based on fitting statistical mixtures, Carnegie Mellon University, Pittsburgh, PA.

Parikh, N. and Boyd, S. (2013). Proximal algorithms. *Foundations and Trends in Optimization*, 1(3):123–231.

Pillai, N. S. and Smith, A. (2014). Ergodicity of approximate MCMC chains with applications to large datasets. arXiv preprint: arXiv:1405.0182.

Polyak, B. T. and Juditsky, A. B. (1992). Acceleration of stochastic approximation by averaging. *SIAM Journal on Control and Optimization*, 30(4):838–855.

Robbins, H. and Monro, S. (1951). A stochastic approximation method. *The Annals of Mathematical Statistics*, 22:400–407.

Rockafellar, R. T. (1976). Monotone operators and the proximal point algorithm. *SIAM Journal on Control and Optimization*, 14(5):877–898.

Rosasco, L., Villa, S., and Vũ, B. C. (2014). Convergence of stochastic proximal gradient algorithm. arXiv preprint: arXiv:1403.5074.

Ruppert, D. (1988a). Efficient estimations from a slowly convergent robbins-monro process. Technical report, Cornell University Operations Research and Industrial Engineering, Ithaca, NY.

Ruppert, D. (1988b). Stochastic approximation. Technical report, Cornell University Operations Research and Industrial Engineering, Ithaca, NY.

Ryu, E. K. and Boyd, S. (2014). Stochastic proximal iteration: A non-asymptotic improvement upon stochastic gradient descent. *Author website, early draft.*

Sacks, J. (1958). Asymptotic distribution of stochastic approximation procedures. *The Annals of Mathematical Statistics*, 29(2):373–405.

Sakrison, D. J. (1965). Efficient recursive estimation; application to estimating the parameters of a covariance function. *International Journal of Engineering Science*, 3(4):461–483.

Salakhutdinov, R., Mnih, A., and Hinton, G. (2007). Restricted Boltzmann machines for collaborative filtering. In *Proceedings of the 24th International Conference on Machine Learning*, pp. 791–798. ACM, New York.

Sato, I. and Nakagawa, H. (2014). Approximation analysis of stochastic gradient Langevin Dynamics by using Fokker-Planck equation and Ito process. *JMLR W&CP*, 32(1): 982–990.

Sato, M.-A. and Ishii, S. (2000). Online EM algorithm for the normalized Gaussian network. *Neural Computation*, 12(2):407–432.

Schaul, T., Zhang, S., and LeCun, Y. (2012). No more pesky learning rates. In *Proceedings of the 30th International Conference on Machine Learning*, pp. 343–351.

Schmidt, M., Le Roux, N., and Bach, F. (2013). Minimizing finite sums with the stochastic average gradient. Technical report, HAL 00860051.

Schraudolph, N., Yu, J., and Günter, S. (2007). A stochastic quasi-Newton method for online convex optimization. In *Proceedings of the 11th International Conference on Artificial Intelligence and Statistics*, pp. 436–443.

Slock, D. T. (1993). On the convergence behavior of the LMS and the normalized LMS algorithms. *IEEE Transactions on Signal Processing*, 41(9):2811–2825.

Spall, J. C. (2000). Adaptive stochastic approximation by the simultaneous perturbation method. *IEEE Transactions on Automatic Control*, 45(10):1839–1853.

Spall, J. C. (2005). *Introduction to Stochastic Search and Optimization: Estimation, Simulation, and Control*, volume 65. John Wiley & Sons, Hoboken, NJ.

Sutton, R. S. (1988). Learning to predict by the methods of temporal differences. *Machine Learning*, 3(1):9–44.

Tamar, A., Toulis, P., Mannor, S., and Airoldi, E. M. (2014). Implicit temporal differences. In *Neural Information Processing Systems, Workshop on Large-Scale Reinforcement Learning*.

Taylor, G. W., Hinton, G. E., and Roweis, S. T. (2006). Modeling human motion using binary latent variables. In *Advances in Neural Information Processing Systems*, pp. 1345–1352.

Titterington, D. M. (1984). Recursive parameter estimation using incomplete data. *Journal of the Royal Statistical Society. Series B (Methodological)*, 46:257–267.

Toulis, P. and Airoldi, E. M. (2015a). Implicit stochastic gradient descent. arXiv preprint: arXiv:1408.2923.

Toulis, P. and Airoldi, E. M. (2015b). Scalable estimation strategies based on stochastic approximations: Classical results and new insights. *Statistics and Computing*, 25(4): 781–795.

Toulis, P., Rennie, J., and Airoldi, E. M. (2014). Statistical analysis of stochastic gradient methods for generalized linear models. *JMLR W&CP*, 32(1):667–675.

Toulis, P. and Airoldi, E. (2015a). Implicit stochastic approximation. arXiv:1510.00967.

Toulis, P., Tran, D., and Airoldi, E. M. (2015b). Towards stability and optimality in stochastic gradient descent. arXiv:1505.02417.

Tran, D., Lan, T., Toulis, P., and Airoldi, E. M. (2015a). *Stochastic Gradient Descent for Scalable Estimation.* R package version 0.1.

Tran, D., Toulis, P., and Airoldi, E. M. (2015b). Stochastic gradient descent methods for estimation with large data sets. arXiv preprint: arXiv:1509.06459.

Venter, J. (1967). An extension of the Robbins-Monro procedure. *The Annals of Mathematical Statistics*, 38:181–190.

Wang, C., Chen, X., Smola, A., and Xing, E. (2013). Variance reduction for stochastic gradient optimization. In *Advances in Neural Information Processing Systems*, pp. 181–189.

Wang, M. and Bertsekas, D. P. (2013). Stabilization of stochastic iterative methods for singular and nearly singular linear systems. *Mathematics of Operations Research*, 39(1): 1–30.

Wei, C. (1987). Multivariate adaptive stochastic approximation. *Annals of Statistics*, 15:1115–1130.

Welling, M. and Teh, Y. W. (2011). Bayesian learning via stochastic gradient Langevin dynamics. In *Proceedings of the 28th International Conference on Machine Learning*, pp. 681–688.

Widrow, B. and Hoff, M. E. (1960). Adaptive switching circuits. *IRE WESCON Convention Record*, 4:96–104. (Defense Technical Information Center.)

Xiao, L. and Zhang, T. (2014). A proximal stochastic gradient method with progressive variance reduction. *SIAM Journal on Optimization*, 24:2057–2075.

Xu, W. (2011). Towards optimal one pass large scale learning with averaged stochastic gradient descent. arXiv:1107.2490.

Younes, L. (1999). On the convergence of markovian stochastic algorithms with rapidly decreasing ergodicity rates. *Stochastics*, 65(3–4):177–228.

Zhang, T. (2004). Solving large scale linear prediction problems using stochastic gradient descent algorithms. In *Proceedings of the 21st International Conference on Machine Learning*, p. 116. ACM, New York.

15

Learning Structured Distributions

Ilias Diakonikolas

CONTENTS

15.1 Introduction 267
15.2 Historical Background 268
15.3 Definitions and Preliminaries 269
15.4 Types of Structured Distributions 270
15.4.1 Shape-Constrained Distributions 270
15.4.2 Aggregation of Structured Distributions 271
15.5 The Cover Method and Sample Bounds 271
15.6 Learning Univariate Structured Distributions 273
15.6.1 Learning Monotone Distributions 274
15.6.2 Agnostically Learning Histograms 275
15.6.2.1 Applications to Learning Structured Distributions 276
15.6.3 Agnostically Learning Piecewise Polynomials 276
15.6.3.1 Applications to Learning Structured Distributions 276
15.7 Learning Multivariate Structured Distributions 277
15.8 Conclusions and Future Directions 279
References 279

15.1 Introduction

Discovering a hidden structure in data is one of the cornerstones of modern data analysis. Because of the diversity and complexity of modern datasets, this is a very challenging task and the role of efficient algorithms is of paramount importance in this context. The majority of available datasets are in raw and unstructured form, consisting of example points without corresponding labels. A large class of unlabeled datasets can be modeled as samples from a probability distribution over a very large domain. An important goal in the exploration of these datasets is understanding the underlying distributions.

Estimating distributions from samples is a paradigmatic and fundamental unsupervised learning problem that has been studied in statistics since the late nineteenth century, starting with the pioneering work of Pearson [55]. During the past couple of decades, there has been a large body of work in computer science on this topic with a focus on *computational efficiency.*

The area of distribution estimation is well motivated in its own right and has seen a recent surge of research activity, in part due to the ubiquity of structured distributions in the natural and social sciences. Such structural properties of distributions are sometimes direct consequences of the underlying application problem or they are a plausible explanation of the model under investigation.

In this chapter, we give a survey of both classical and modern techniques for distribution estimation with a focus on recent algorithmic ideas developed in theoretical computer science. These ideas have led to computationally and statistically efficient algorithms for learning broad families of models. For the sake of concreteness, we illustrate these ideas with specific examples. Finally, we highlight outstanding challenges and research directions for future work.

15.2 Historical Background

The construction of an estimate of an unknown probability density function (pdf) based on observed data is a classical problem in statistics with a rich history and extensive literature (see, e.g., [4,26,27,58,60]). A number of generic methods have been proposed in the mathematical statistics literature, including histograms, kernels, nearest neighbor estimators, orthogonal series estimators, maximum likelihood, and more. The reader is referred to [44] for a survey of these techniques.

The oldest and most natural estimator is the histogram, first introduced by Pearson [55]. Given a number of samples (observations) from a pdf, the method partitions the domain into a number of bins and outputs the empirical density that is constant within each bin. It should be emphasized that the number of bins to be used and the width and location of each bin are unspecified by the method. The problem of finding the optimal number and location of the bins to minimize the error is an inherently algorithmic question, because the ultimate goal is to obtain learning algorithms that are computationally efficient.

Suppose that we are given a number of samples from a density that we believe is from (or very close to) a given family $\mathcal{C}$, for example, it is a mixture of a small number of Gaussian distributions. Our goal is to estimate the target distribution in a precise, well-defined way. There are three different goals in this context.

1. In *nonproper* learning (density estimation) the goal is to output an approximation to the target density without any constraints on its representation. That is, the output distribution is not necessarily a member of the family $\mathcal{C}$.

2. In *proper* learning the goal is to output a density in $\mathcal{C}$ that is a good approximation to the target density.

3. In *parameter* learning the goal is to identify the parameters of the target distribution, for example, the mixing weights and the parameters of the components up to a desired accuracy. (The notion of parameter learning is well defined for parametric classes $\mathcal{C}$.)

Note that nonproper learning and proper learning are equivalent in terms of sample size, given any (nonproper) hypothesis we can do a brute-force search to find its closest density in $\mathcal{C}$. However, it is not clear whether this computation can be performed efficiently.

We remark that the task of parameter learning is possible only under certain separation assumptions on the components. Even under such assumptions, it can be a more demanding task than proper learning. In particular, it is possible that two distinct distributions in $\mathcal{C}$, whose parameters are far from each other give rise to densities that are close to each other. Moreover, parameter learning strongly relies on the assumption that there is no noise in the data, and hence it may not be meaningful in many realistic settings. These facts motivate the study of proper learning algorithms in the noisy setting.

The focus of this chapter is on general techniques and efficient algorithms for density estimation and proper learning. Because of the space constraints, we do not elaborate on the algorithmic methods used for the problem of parameter learning.

The structure of this chapter is as follows: after some basic definitions (Section 15.3), in Section 15.4, we give a classification of the types of distribution families studied in the literature. In Section 15.5, we describe a classical method from statistics to efficiently select from a given a set of candidate hypothesis distributions. Section 15.6 describes recent algorithmic ideas from theoretical computer science to learn structured univariate densities. Section 15.7 discusses the challenging case of high-dimensional distributions. We conclude with some future directions in Section 15.8.

15.3 Definitions and Preliminaries

We consider a standard notion of learning an unknown probability distribution from samples [46], which is a natural analog of Valiant's well-known probably approximately correct (PAC) model for learning Boolean functions [67] to the unsupervised setting of learning an unknown probability distribution. We remark that our definition is essentially equivalent to the notion of minimax rate of convergence in statistics [27].

Given access to independent draws from an unknown pdf p, the goal is to approximate p in a certain well-defined sense. More specifically, the goal of a learning algorithm is to output a hypothesis distribution h that is *close* to the target distribution p. One can choose various metrics to measure the distance between distributions. Throughout this chapter, we measure the closeness between distributions using the *statistical distance* or total variation distance. The *statistical distance* between two densities $p, q : \Omega \to \mathbb{R}_+$ is defined as

$$d_{\mathrm{TV}}(p,q) = \frac{1}{2}\|p-q\|_1 = \frac{1}{2}\int_{\Omega} |p(x) - q(x)|dx$$

(When Ω is discrete the above integral is replaced by a sum.)

A distribution learning problem is defined by a class $\mathcal{C}$ of probability distributions over a domain Ω. The domain Ω may be discrete, for example, $\Omega = [n] := \{1, \ldots, n\}$, or continuous, for example, $\Omega = \mathbb{R}$, one-dimensional or high-dimensional. In the *noiseless* setting, we are promised that $p \in \mathcal{C}$ and the goal is to construct a hypothesis h such that with probability at least $9/10$* the total variation distance $d_{\mathrm{TV}}(h,p)$ between h and p is at most ϵ, where $\epsilon > 0$ is the accuracy parameter.

The *noisy* or *agnostic* model captures the situation of having adversarial noise in the data. In this setting, we do not make any assumptions about the target density p and the goal is to find a hypothesis h that is almost as accurate as the *best* approximation of p by any distribution in $\mathcal{C}$. Formally, given $\epsilon > 0$ and sample access to a target distribution p, the goal of an *agnostic learning algorithm for* $\mathcal{C}$ is to compute a hypothesis distribution h such that, with probability at least $9/10$, it holds

$$d_{\mathrm{TV}}(h,p) \leq \alpha \cdot \mathrm{opt}_{\mathcal{C}}(p) + \epsilon$$

*We note that, using standard techniques, the confidence probability can be boosted to $1 - \delta$, for any $\delta > 0$, with a multiplicative overhead of $O(\log(1/\delta))$ in the sample size.

where $\mathrm{opt}_{\mathcal{C}}(p) := \inf_{q \in \mathcal{C}} d_{\mathrm{TV}}(q, p)$, that is, $\mathrm{opt}_{\mathcal{C}}(p)$ is the statistical distance between p and the closest distribution to it in $\mathcal{C}$ and $\alpha \geq 1$ is a universal constant.

We will use the following two standard metrics to measure the performance of a learning algorithm: (1) the *sample complexity*, that is, the number of samples drawn by the algorithm, and (2) the *computational complexity*, that is, the worst-case running time of the algorithm. An algorithm is statistically efficient if its sample complexity is information-theoretically optimal, and it is computationally efficient if its computational complexity is polynomial in its sample complexity. The *gold standard* is a statistically efficient algorithm whose computational complexity is linear in its sample size.

As mentioned in the introduction, proper and nonproper learning of any class $\mathcal{C}$ are equivalent in terms of sample complexity, but not necessarily equivalent in terms of computational complexity. We also remark that, for broad classes of distributions $\mathcal{C}$, agnostic learning and noiseless learning are equivalent in terms of sample complexity. However, designing computationally efficient agnostic learning algorithms is, in general, a much more challenging task.

15.4 Types of Structured Distributions

In this section, we provide a broad categorization of the most common types of structured distributions that have been considered in the statistics and computer science literatures. We also briefly summarize a few standard methods to learn such distributions in statistics.

In the following sections, we will describe a set of algorithmic techniques that lead to provably efficient learning algorithms for most of these distribution families.

15.4.1 Shape-Constrained Distributions

For distributions over $\mathbb{R}^d$ (or a discrete d-dimensional subset, e.g., $[n]^d$), a very natural type of structure to consider is some sort of *shape constraint* on the pdf defining the distribution.

Statistical research in this area started in the 1950s and the reader is referred to [4] for a summary of the early work. Most of the literature has focused on one-dimensional distributions, with a few exceptions during the past decade. Various structural restrictions have been studied over the years, starting from monotonicity, unimodality, convexity, and concavity [6,7,9,12,35,38,39,41,45,56,70], and more recently focusing on structural restrictions such as log-concavity and k-monotonicity [1–3,32,37,49,69]. The reader is referred to [40] for a recent book on the subject.

The most common method used in statistics to address shape-constrained inference problems is the maximum likelihood estimator (MLE) and its variants. The challenge is to analyze the performance of the MLE in this context. It turns out that for several univariate learning problems of this sort the MLE performs quite well in terms of statistical efficiency. While the MLE is very popular and quite natural, there exist natural inference problems (see, e.g., [10]) where it performs poorly in terms of statistical and computational efficiency, as well as noise tolerance.

A related line of work in mathematical statistics [28–30,47,48] uses nonlinear estimators based on wavelet techniques to learn continuous distributions whose densities satisfy various smoothness constraints, such as Triebel and Besov-type smoothness. We remark that the focus of these works is on the statistical efficiency of the proposed estimators and not on computational complexity.

15.4.2 Aggregation of Structured Distributions

Aggregations of structured random variables are very popular as they can model many rich phenomena. Two prominent examples of this sort are mixture models and sums of simple random variables. Mixtures of structured distributions have received much attention in statistics [51,57,64] and, more recently, in theoretical computer science [19,54].

We remark that early statistical work on mixture models focuses on parameter learning. In practice, this problem is typically handled with nonconvex heuristics such as the expectation–maximization (EM) algorithm. Recent algorithmic techniques rely on the moment problem and tensor decomposition. However, such algorithms lead to sample complexities that are inherently exponential in the number of components.

Learning sums of simple random variables has received recent attention in the computer science literature [20,22]. Such distributions have various applications in areas such as survey sampling, case-control studies, and survival analysis (see, e.g., [16] for the case of sums of indicators).

15.5 The Cover Method and Sample Bounds

The first fundamental question that arises in the context of learning an unknown probability distribution is information-theoretic:

What is the minimum sample size that is necessary and sufficient to learn an unknown $p \in \mathcal{C}$ up to total variation distance ϵ?

While this question has been extensively investigated in statistics, information theory, and, more recently, computer science, the information-theoretically optimal sample size is not yet understood, even for some relatively simple families of distributions. It turns out that the optimal sample complexity depends on the structure of the underlying density class in a subtle way.

In this section, we describe a general powerful method that yields nearly tight upper bounds on the sample complexity of learning. The method, which we term the *cover method*, is classical in statistics and information theory and has its roots in early work of A. N. Kolmogorov. The high-level idea is to analyze the structure of the metric space $\mathcal{C}$ under total variation distance. The method postulates that the structure of this metric space characterizes the sample complexity of learning. To describe the method in detail we introduce some basic terminology.

Let $(\mathcal{X}, d)$ be a metric space. Given $\delta > 0$, a subset $\mathcal{Y} \subseteq \mathcal{X}$ is said to be a *δ-cover of $\mathcal{X}$* with respect to the metric $d : \mathcal{X}^2 \to \mathbb{R}_+$ if for every $\mathbf{x} \in \mathcal{X}$ there exists some $\mathbf{y} \in \mathcal{Y}$ such that $d(\mathbf{x}, \mathbf{y}) \leq \delta$. There may exist many δ-covers of $\mathcal{X}$, but one is typically interested in those with minimum cardinality. The *δ-covering number* of $(\mathcal{X}, d)$ is the minimum cardinality of any δ-cover of $\mathcal{X}$. Intuitively, the covering number captures the *size* of the metric space.

Covering numbers—and their logarithms, known as *metric entropy* numbers—were first defined by Kolmogorov in the 1950s and have since played a central role in a number of areas, including approximation theory, geometric functional analysis (see, e.g., [8,31,53] and [11,33,50,52]), information theory, statistics, and machine learning (see, e.g., [5,42,43,73,74] and [27,65,68]).

In the context of distribution learning, the cover method is summarized in the following theorem.

Theorem 15.1. *Let $\mathcal{C}$ be an arbitrary family of distributions and $\epsilon > 0$. Let $\mathcal{C}_\epsilon \subseteq \mathcal{C}$ be an ϵ-cover of $\mathcal{C}$ of cardinality N. Then there is an algorithm that uses $O(\epsilon^{-2} \log N)$ samples from an unknown distribution $p \in \mathcal{C}$ and, with probability at least $9/10$, outputs a distribution $h \in \mathcal{C}_\epsilon$ that satisfies $d_{\mathrm{TV}}(h, p) \leq 6\epsilon$.*

An equivalent version of Theorem 15.1 (with a slightly different terminology) was given by Yatracos [74] (see also Chapter 7 of [27] for a detailed discussion). The above statement appears as Lemma C.1 in [23].

As we explain in detail below, the algorithm implicit in the above theorem is *not* computationally efficient in general. Indeed, even assuming that we have an explicit construction of a minimal size ϵ-cover, the algorithm takes time at least $\Omega(N/\epsilon^2)$—that is, *exponential* in its sample size.

We point out that the cover method can serve as a very useful tool in the design of computationally efficient learning algorithms. Indeed, many algorithms in the literature work by constructing a *small* set S of candidate hypotheses with the guarantee that at least one of them is close to the target distribution. The cover method can be used as a postprocessing step to efficiently select an appropriate candidate in the set S. This simple idea has been used in the design of fast proper learning algorithms for various natural classes of distributions, including sums of independent integer random variables [20,22], Gaussian mixtures [24,63], and other high-dimensional distributions [25].

We now provide a brief intuitive explanation of the argument in [23] establishing Theorem 15.1. (The corresponding proof of [27,74] is quite similar.) Given a description of the cover $\mathcal{C}_\epsilon$, the algorithm performs a tournament between the distributions in $\mathcal{C}_\epsilon$, by running a hypothesis testing routine for every pair of distributions in $\mathcal{C}_\epsilon$. The obvious implementation of this tournament takes time $\Omega(N^2/\epsilon^2)$. Recent algorithmic work [24,63] has improved this to nearly linear in N, namely $O(N \log N/\epsilon^2)$. However, this running time bound is still exponential in the sample complexity of the algorithm.

The hypothesis testing routine can be viewed as a simple *competition* between two candidate hypothesis distributions. If at least one of the two candidate hypotheses is close to the target distribution p, then with high probability over the samples drawn from p the hypothesis testing routine selects as winner a candidate that is close to p. The algorithm outputs a distribution in the cover $\mathcal{C}_\epsilon$ that was never a loser (that is, won or tied against all other distributions in the cover). We remark that the analysis of the algorithm is elementary, relying only on the Chernoff bound and the union bound.

Another important property of the cover method is its noise tolerance. It generalizes naturally yielding an agnostic learning algorithm with the same sample complexity. More specifically, for an arbitrary target distribution p with $\mathrm{opt}_{\mathcal{C}}(p) = \inf_{q \in \mathcal{C}} d_{\mathrm{TV}}(q, p)$, the tournament-based algorithm makes $O(\epsilon^{-2} \log N)$ i.i.d. draws from p and outputs a hypothesis h in $\mathcal{C}_\epsilon$ satisfying $d_{\mathrm{TV}}(h, p) \leq O(\mathrm{opt}_{\mathcal{C}}(p) + \epsilon)$. The reader is referred to Chapter 7.3 of [27] for an explicit proof of this fact.

The sample upper bound of $O(\epsilon^{-2} \log N)$ cannot be improved in general, in the sense that there exist distribution families, where it is information-theoretically optimal up to constant factors. In fact, Yang and Barron [73] showed that for many smooth nonparametric classes the metric entropy number characterizes the sample complexity of learning. We note, however, that metric entropy does not provide a characterization in general. There exist distribution families, where the $O(\epsilon^{-2} \log N)$ sample upper bound is suboptimal.

As a simple example, consider the set of all *singleton* distributions over $[n]$, that is, the class contains n distinct distributions each supported on a single point of the domain. It is easy to see that Theorem 15.1 gives a sample upper bound of $O(\epsilon^{-2} \log n)$ for this case, while one sample suffices to uniquely specify the target distribution. For a more natural example, consider the class of Poisson binomial distributions (PBDs), that is, sums $\sum_{i=1}^{n} X_i$ of n mutually independent Bernoulli random variables, $X_1, \ldots, X_n$. It is not difficult to show that the covering number of the set of PBDs is $\Omega(n/\epsilon)$. Hence, Theorem 15.1 cannot give an upper bound better than $\widetilde{\Omega}(\epsilon^{-2}) \cdot \log n$. On the other hand, a sample upper bound of $\widetilde{O}(\epsilon^{-2})$ was recently obtained in [22]. These examples raise the following natural question.

Open Problem 15.1. *Is there a* complexity measure *of a distribution class* $\mathcal{C}$ *that* characterizes *the sample complexity of learning* $\mathcal{C}$*?*

We recall that the Vapnik–Chervonenkis dimension of a class of Boolean functions plays such a role in Valiant's PAC model [66], that is, it tightly characterizes the number of examples that are required to PAC learn an arbitrary function from the class.

15.6 Learning Univariate Structured Distributions

In this section, we consider the problem of nonproper learning of an unknown univariate probability distribution, that is, a distribution with a density function $p : \Omega \to \mathbb{R}_+$, where the sample space Ω is a subset of the real line. We focus on two basic cases: (1) $\Omega = [n]$, where the set $[n]$ is viewed as an ordered set and (2) $\Omega = [a, b]$ with $a \leq b \in \mathbb{R}$. Given a family $\mathcal{C}$ of univariate distributions, can we design a sample-optimal and computationally efficient learning algorithm for $\mathcal{C}$? Can we achieve this goal in the more challenging agnostic setting? It turns out that the answer to both questions turns out to be *yes* for broad classes of structured families $\mathcal{C}$.

If the target distribution is arbitrary, the learning problem is well understood. More specifically, suppose that the class $\mathcal{C}$ of target distributions is the set of all distributions over $[n]$. It is a folklore fact that $\Theta(n/\epsilon^2)$ samples are necessary and sufficient for learning within the total variation distance ϵ in this case. The underlying algorithm is also straightforward, that is, output the empirical distribution. For distributions over very large domains, a linear dependence on n is of course impractical, both from running time and sample complexity perspective.

For continuous distributions the learning problem is not solvable without any assumptions. Indeed, learning an arbitrary distribution over $[0, 1]$ to any constant accuracy $\epsilon < 1$ requires infinitely many samples. This follows, for example, from the aforementioned discrete lower bound for $n \to \infty$. Hence, it is important to focus our attention on structured distribution families.

In the main part of this section, we describe recent work from theoretical computer science that yields sample-optimal and computationally efficient algorithms for learning broad classes of structured distributions. The main idea of the approach is that the *existence* of good piecewise polynomial approximations for a family $\mathcal{C}$ can be leveraged for the design of efficient learning algorithms for $\mathcal{C}$. The approach is inspired and motivated by classical results in statistics and combines a variety of techniques from algorithms, probability, and approximation theory.

Piecewise polynomials (splines) have been extensively used in statistics as tools for inference tasks, including density estimation, see, for example, [61,62,71,72]. We remark that splines in statistics have been used in the context of the MLE, which is very different than the aforementioned approach. Moreover, the degree of the splines used in statistical literature is typically bounded by a small constant.

In Section 15.6.1, we describe classical work in statistics on learning monotone densities that served as an inspiration for the piecewise polynomial approach. In Section 15.6.2, we describe how to use piecewise constant approximations for learning and argue why it is insufficient for some cases. Finally, in Section 15.6.3, we describe the general approach in detail.

15.6.1 Learning Monotone Distributions

Monotonicity is arguably one of the simplest shape constraints. Learning a monotone density was one of the first problems studied in this context by Grenander [38]. We present a result by Birgé [6,7], who gave a sample-optimal and computationally efficient algorithm for this problem. More specifically, Birgé showed the following.

Theorem 15.2 [6,7] *Fix $L, H > 0$; let $\mathcal{M}$ be the set of nonincreasing densities $p : [0, L] \to [0, H]$. There is a computationally efficient algorithm that given $m = O((1/\epsilon^3)\log(1 + H \cdot L))$ samples from an arbitrary $p \in \mathcal{M}$ outputs a hypothesis h satisfying $d_{\mathrm{TV}}(h, p) \leq \epsilon$ with probability at least 9/10. Moreover, $\Omega((1/\epsilon^3)\log(1 + H \cdot L))$ samples are information-theoretically necessary for this problem.*

An adaptation of the above theorem holds for monotone distributions over $[n]$, yielding an efficient algorithm with optimal sample complexity of $O((1/\epsilon^3)\log n)$ for the discrete setting as well.

To sketch the proof of this theorem, we will need a few definitions. Given m independent samples $s_1, \ldots, s_m$, drawn from a density $p : \Omega \to \mathbb{R}_+$, the *empirical distribution* $\widehat{p}_m$ is the discrete distribution supported on $\{s_1, \ldots, s_m\}$ defined as follows: for all $z \in \Omega$, $\widehat{p}_m(z) = |\{j \in [m] \mid s_j = z\}|/m$.

For a measurable function $f : I \to \mathbb{R}_+$ and $A \subseteq I$, we will denote $f(A) = \int_A f(x)dx$.

Definition 15.1. A function $f : I \to \mathbb{R}$ is called a *t-histogram* if it is piecewise constant with at most t interval pieces. For a function $f : I \to \mathbb{R}$ and an interval partition $\{I_1, \ldots, I_t\}$ of the domain, the *flattened version* $\bar{f}$ of f is the t-histogram defined by $\bar{f}(x) = f(I_j)/|I_j|$ for all $x \in I_j$.

Birgé's algorithm works as follows [7]: it partitions the domain into a set of intervals and outputs the flattened empirical distribution on those intervals. Its correctness relies on an approximation lemma that he proves.

Lemma 15.1 [7] *Fix $L, H > 0$. There exists a partition of $[0, H]$ into $t = O((1/\epsilon)\log(1 + H \cdot L))$ intervals such that for any $p \in \mathcal{M}$ it holds $d_{\mathrm{TV}}(\bar{p}, p) \leq \epsilon$.*

An analog of the lemma holds for discrete monotone distributions over $[n]$ establishing a bound of $t = O((1/\epsilon)\log n)$ on the number of intervals.

Note that the interval decomposition of the lemma is *oblivious*, in the sense that it does not depend on the underlying monotone density. This is a very strong guarantee that facilitates the learning algorithm. Indeed, given the guarantee of the lemma, the algorithm is straightforward. The monotone learning problem is *reduced* to the problem of learning a distribution over a known finite support of cardinality $t = O((1/\epsilon)\log(1 + H \cdot L))$.

In summary, one can break Birgé's approach in two conceptual steps:

- Prove that any monotone distribution is ϵ-close in total variation distance to a t-histogram distribution, where the parameter t is small.
- Agnostically learn the target distribution using the class of t-histogram distributions as a hypothesis class.

This scheme is quite general and can be applied to any structured distribution class as long as there exists a good piecewise constant approximation. In general, such a histogram approximation may not be fixed for all distributions in the family. Indeed, this is the case for most natural families of distributions. To handle this case, we need an agnostic learning algorithm for t-histogram distributions with an *unknown* partition.

15.6.2 Agnostically Learning Histograms

In this section, we study the problem of agnostically learning t-histogram distributions with an unknown partition. Formally, given a bound t on the number of intervals, we want to design a computationally efficient algorithm that uses an optimal sample size and approximates the target distribution nearly as accurately as the best t-histogram. As sketched in the previous section, such an algorithm would have several applications in learning classes of shape-restricted densities.

Denote by $\mathcal{H}_t$ the family of t-histogram distributions over $[0, 1]$.* The first step is to determine the optimal sample complexity of the learning problem. It is easy to see that $\Omega(t/\epsilon^2)$ is a lower bound and simple arguments can be used to get an upper bound of $\tilde{O}(t/\epsilon^2)$ using the cover method described in Section 15.5.

The problem of agnostically learning t-histogram distributions with $\tilde{O}(t/\epsilon^2)$ samples and poly(t/ϵ) time† is algorithmically nontrivial. If one is willing to relax the sample size to $O(t/\epsilon^3)$, it is easy to obtain a computationally efficient algorithm [13,21]. The first efficient algorithm with near-optimal-sample complexity was obtained in [14] and is based on dynamic programming.

To sketch the algorithm in [14] we will need a more general metric between distributions that generalizes the total variation distance. Fix a family of subsets $\mathcal{A}$ over $[0, 1]$. We define the $\mathcal{A}$-*distance* between p and q by $\|p - q\|_{\mathcal{A}} := \max_{A \in \mathcal{A}} |p(A) - q(A)|$. (Note that if $\mathcal{A}$ is the set of all measurable subsets of the domain, the $\mathcal{A}$-distance is identical to the total variation distance.) The *Vapnik–Chervonenkis (VC)-dimension* of $\mathcal{A}$ is the maximum size of a subset $X \subseteq [0, 1]$ that is shattered by $\mathcal{A}$ (a set X is shattered by $\mathcal{A}$, if for every $Y \subseteq X$ some $A \in \mathcal{A}$ satisfies $A \cap X = Y$).

The VC inequality. Fix a family of subsets $\mathcal{A}$ over $[n]$ of VC-dimension d. The *VC inequality* is the following result from empirical process theory:

Theorem 15.3 [27, p. 31] *Let $\widehat{p}_m$ be an empirical distribution of m samples from p. Let $\mathcal{A}$ be a family of subsets of VC-dimension d. Then*

$$\mathbb{E}\left[\|p - \widehat{p}_m\|_{\mathcal{A}}\right] \leq O(\sqrt{d/m})$$

In other words, for $m = \Omega(d/\epsilon^2)$, with probability 9/10, the empirical distribution $\widehat{p}_m$ will be ϵ-close to p in $\mathcal{A}$-distance. We remark that this sample bound is asymptotically optimal (up to a constant factor) for all values of d and ϵ.

Let $\mathcal{A}_k$ be the collection of all subsets of the domain that can be expressed as unions of at most k (disjoint) intervals. The intuition is that the collection $\mathcal{A}_{2t}$ characterizes t-histograms in a precise way. Consider the following algorithm for agnostically learning a distribution p.

1. Draw $m = \Theta(t/\epsilon^2)$ samples from p.
2. Output the distribution $h \in \mathcal{H}_t$ that minimizes the quantity $\|h - \widehat{p}_m\|_{\mathcal{A}_k}$ (up to an additive error $\gamma = O(\epsilon)$).

*We choose the domain to be $[0, 1]$ for simplicity. All the results that we will describe extend straightforwardly to distributions over any interval or over a discrete set.

†We use the notation poly(x), $x \in \mathbb{R}_+$, to denote a function that is bounded from above by a fixed degree polynomial in x.

It is not difficult to show that this is an agnostic learning algorithm for $\mathcal{H}_t$. The main observation needed for the proof is that the $\mathcal{A}_{2t}$ distance between two t-histograms is identical to their total variation distance.

The algorithm in [14] uses a dynamic programming approach to efficiently perform step (2) above, and its analysis relies on the VC inequality. More recently, a near-linear time algorithm, that is, an algorithm with running time $\tilde{O}(t/\epsilon^2)$, was developed in [15].

15.6.2.1 Applications to Learning Structured Distributions

The aforementioned agnostic learning algorithm has been used as the key algorithmic ingredient to learn various classes of structured distributions. An additional ingredient needed is a structural approximation result stating that for the underlying distribution family $\mathcal{C}$ there exists an ϵ-approximation by t-histograms for an appropriately small value of the parameter t. For example, by using the structural approximation results of [13], one obtains near-sample-optimal and near-linear time estimators for various well-studied classes including multimodal densities, monotone hazard rate (MHR) distributions, and others.

However, there exist distribution families where the approach of approximating by histograms *provably* leads to suboptimal sample complexity. A prominent such example is the class of log-concave distributions. This motivates the more general approach of approximating by piecewise polynomials.

15.6.3 Agnostically Learning Piecewise Polynomials

We say that a distribution q over $[0,1]$ is a *t-piecewise degree-d distribution* if there is a partition of $[0,1]$ into t disjoint intervals $I_1, \ldots, I_t$ such that $q(x) = q_j(x)$ for all $x \in I_j$, where each of $q_1, \ldots, q_t$ is a univariate polynomial of degree at most d. Let $\mathcal{P}_{t,d}$ denote the class of all t-piecewise degree-d pdf over $[0,1]$. We have the following theorem.

Theorem 15.4 [14] *Let p be any pdf over $[0,1]$. There is an algorithm that, given t, d, ϵ, and $\tilde{O}(t(d+1)/\epsilon^2)$ samples from p, runs in time* $\mathrm{poly}(t, d+1, 1/\epsilon)$ *and with high-probability outputs an $O(t)$-piecewise degree-d hypothesis h such that $d_{\mathrm{TV}}(p,h) \le O(\mathrm{opt}_{t,d}) + \epsilon$, where* $\mathrm{opt}_{t,d} := \inf_{r \in \mathcal{P}_{t,d}} d_{\mathrm{TV}}(p,r)$ *is the error of the best t-piecewise degree-d distribution for p.*

It is shown in [14] that the number of samples used by the aforementioned algorithm is information-theoretically optimal in all three parameters up to logarithmic factors.

The high-level approach to prove this theorem is similar to the one described in the previous paragraph for the case of histograms. Let $\mathcal{A}_k$ be the collection of all subsets of the domain that can be expressed as unions of at most $k = 2t(d+1)$ intervals. The intuition is that the collection $\mathcal{A}_k$ characterizes piecewise polynomials with t pieces and degree d. Similarly, the following is an agnostic learning algorithm for p.

1. Draw $m = \Theta(t(d+1)/\epsilon^2)$ samples from p.
2. Output $h \in \mathcal{P}_{t,d}$ that minimizes the quantity $\|h - \widehat{p}_m\|_{\mathcal{A}_k}$ (up to an additive error $\gamma = O(\epsilon)$).

We remark that the optimization problem in step 2 is nonconvex. However, it has sufficient structure so that (an appropriately relaxed version of) it can be solved in polynomial time by a combination of convex programming and dynamic programming.

15.6.3.1 Applications to Learning Structured Distributions

Theorem 15.4 yields near-sample-optimal and computationally efficient estimators for a very broad class of structured distribution families, including arbitrary mixtures of natural distribution families, such as multimodal, concave, convex, log-concave, MHR, sums of indicators, and others. Given a class $\mathcal{C}$ that we want to learn, we have the following general approach:

- Prove that any distribution in $\mathcal{C}$ is ϵ-close in total variation distance to a t-piecewise degree-d distribution, for appropriate values of t and d.
- Agnostically learn the target distribution using the class of t-piecewise degree-d distributions.

We emphasize that there are many combinations of (t, d) that guarantee an ϵ-approximation. To minimize the sample complexity of the learning algorithm in the second step, one would like to use the values that minimize the product $t(d+1)$. This is, of course, an approximation theory problem that depends on the structure of the family $\mathcal{C}$.

For example, if $\mathcal{C}$ is the class of log-concave distributions, the optimal t-histogram ϵ-approximation requires $\tilde{\Theta}(1/\epsilon)$ intervals. This leads to an algorithm with sample complexity $\tilde{\Theta}(1/\epsilon^3)$. On the other hand, it can be shown that any log-concave distribution has a piecewise *linear* ϵ-approximation with $\tilde{\Theta}(1/\epsilon^{1/2})$ intervals, which gives us a $\tilde{\Theta}(1/\epsilon^{5/2})$ sample algorithm. Perhaps surprisingly, this cannot be improved using higher degrees as one can show a sample lower bound of $\Omega(1/\epsilon^{5/2})$.

As a second example, let $\mathcal{C}$ be the class of k-mixtures of Gaussians in one dimension. By approximating these functions by piecewise polynomials of degree $O(\log(1/\epsilon))$, we obtain an efficient agnostic algorithm using $\tilde{O}(k/\epsilon^2)$ samples. This sample bound is optimal up to logarithmic factors. It should be noted that this is the first computationally efficient and sample near-optimal algorithm for this problem.

It should be emphasized that the algorithm of [14] is theoretically efficient (polynomial time), but it may be relatively slow for real applications with large datasets. This prompts the following question: Is the full algorithmic power of convex programming and dynamic programming necessary to achieve this level of sample efficiency? Ideally one would like a simple combinatorial algorithm for these estimation tasks that runs in near-linear time. This is an interesting open problem of significant practical interest.

Open Problem 15.2. *Is there a sample-optimal and linear time algorithm for agnostically learning piecewise polynomial distributions?*

Note that the aforementioned approach leads to *nonproper* learning algorithms. In many settings, for example, for latent variable models, obtaining proper learning algorithms is important for the underlying application. In particular, we pose the following concrete open problem.

Open Problem 15.3. *Is there a* $\mathrm{poly}(k, 1/\epsilon)$ *time algorithm for* properly *learning k-mixtures of simple parametric classes?*

15.7 Learning Multivariate Structured Distributions

The problem of learning an unknown structured density over $\mathbb{R}^d$, $d > 1$, has been studied in statistics and machine learning in many settings. We refer the reader to a relatively recent survey on multidimensional density estimation [59] with a focus on sample complexity.

Despite intense research efforts, our understanding of the high-dimensional setting is still quite limited. There are two regimes of interest: (1) the dimension d is small, that is, a fixed constant independent of the problem size, and (2) the dimension d is large, that is, part of the input.

For low-dimensional settings, one may be able to handle learning problems whose sample complexity (and hence, running time) is exponential in d. For some natural distribution families such an exponential dependence is inherent, for example, for high-dimensional arbitrary log-concave densities. Recent statistical research on the topic attempts to determine tight upper and lower bounds on the minimax rate of convergence [17,18] in the context of the MLE. From a computer science perspective, the goal for these settings is the same: design an algorithm with information-theoretic optimal sample size and polynomial running time.

For high-dimensional settings, problems that inherently require sample complexity exponentially in d are considered intractable. Interestingly enough, a wide variety of natural and important high-dimensional estimation problems have sample complexity polynomial (or even linear) in the dimension. The bottleneck for such problems is to design computationally efficient algorithms. Circumventing the curse of dimensionality is one of the most challenging research directions in distribution learning.

During the past couple of decades, several natural high-dimensional learning problems have been studied in the theoretical computer science literature. In a few prominent cases, theoretically efficient algorithms have been discovered. Two examples include the development of computationally efficient algorithms for learning mixtures of a constant number of high-dimensional Gaussian distributions [54], and a constant number of discrete product distributions [34,36]. We remark that both of these algorithms are based on the method of moments and are in fact proper. These algorithms represent important progress in our theoretical understanding of these challenging and important problems. However, while they run in polynomial time, the exponents in their running time are quite high. Both algorithms [34,54] run in time $(d/\epsilon)^{f(k)}$, where d is the dimension and k is the number of components in the mixture. Hence, there is still a lot of ground to be covered in our understanding of these questions.

At this point, we would like to highlight a fundamental high-dimensional problem that has received significant attention in statistics, but no nontrivial algorithm is known to date. A *t-piece d-dimensional histogram* is a pdf p over the domain $[0,1]^d$ of the following sort: the domain $[0,1]^d$ is partitioned into t axis-aligned hyper-rectangles $R_1, \ldots, R_t$, and the distribution p is piecewise constant over each rectangle R_i. It follows from Theorem 15.3 that $O(td/\epsilon^2)$ samples information-theoretically suffice to learn such distributions (even agnostically). However, no algorithm with subexponential running time is known. A major goal is to answer the following question.

Open Problem 15.4. *Is there a* poly$(d, t, 1/\epsilon)$ *time algorithm for learning t-piece d-dimensional histograms?*

Another fundamental gap in our understanding concerns mixtures of high-dimensional Gaussians. Recall that there exists a learning algorithm for k-mixtures of d-dimensional Gaussians that runs in time $(d/\epsilon)^{f(k)}$ [54]. The learning algorithm follows from the corresponding parameter learning algorithm. For the parameter learning setting, however, the exponential dependence on k is inherent in the sample complexity of the problem (hence, also in the running time) even for $d = 1$. However, no such information-theoretic barrier exists for the problem of density estimation. This motivates the following problem.

Open Problem 15.5. *Is there a* poly$(d, k, 1/\epsilon)$ *time algorithm for learning a mixture of k d-dimensional Gaussians?*

Analogous questions can be asked for various mixture models and more general latent variable models.

15.8 Conclusions and Future Directions

In this chapter, we gave a biased survey of the distribution learning literature from a computer science perspective, that is, with an explicit focus on the computational efficiency of our estimators. We presented recent work in theoretical computer science on the design of sample-optimal and computationally efficient estimators. Many important questions remain open, and the interplay between algorithms and statistics is crucial to their resolution. We conclude this chapter with two important research directions.

One of the most important challenges in statistical learning is handling data that are corrupted by noise. In most cases, the difficulty is not information-theoretic but rather computational. Many popular algorithms (e.g., MLE) are not tolerant to even a small amount of noise in the data. A fundamental gap in our understanding concerns high-dimensional problems.

Research Direction 15.1. *Develop computationally efficient* agnostic *learning algorithms for high-dimensional distribution learning problems.*

A concrete problem is that of learning a binary product distribution with adversarial noise. This problem is, of course, straightforward in the noiseless setting; however, it becomes very challenging in the presence of even a small constant fraction of noisy observations. A more challenging open problem is agnostically learning mixture models, for example, for two high-dimensional Gaussians or even binary product distributions.

Overall, the body of work on statistical estimation has focused on worst-case instances both in terms of algorithms and lower bounds. A natural goal is to go beyond worst-case analysis and design algorithms that provably perform near optimally on *every* input.

Research Direction 15.2. *Develop* instance-by-instance optimal *algorithms for distribution learning problems.*

We believe that progress in this direction will lead to efficient algorithms that perform very well in practice.

References

1. F. Balabdaoui, K. Rufibach, and J. A. Wellner. Limit distribution theory for maximum likelihood estimation of a log-concave density. *Annals of Statistics*, 37(3):1299–1331, 2009.

2. F. Balabdaoui and J. A. Wellner. Estimation of a k-monotone density: Limit distribution theory and the spline connection. *Annals of Statistics*, 35(6):2536–2564, 2007.

3. F. Balabdaoui and J. A. Wellner. Estimation of a k-monotone density: Characterizations, consistency and minimax lower bounds. *Statistica Neerlandica*, 64(1):45–70, 2010.

4. R. E. Barlow, D. J. Bartholomew, J. M. Bremner, and H. D. Brunk. *Statistical Inference under Order Restrictions.* Wiley, New York, 1972.

5. L. Birgé. On estimating a density using Hellinger distance and some other strange facts. *Probability Theory and Related Fields*, 71(2):271–291, 1986.

6. L. Birgé. Estimating a density under order restrictions: Nonasymptotic minimax risk. *Annals of Statistics*, 15(3):995–1012, 1987.

7. L. Birgé. On the risk of histograms for estimating decreasing densities. *Annals of Statistics*, 15(3):1013–1022, 1987.

8. R. Blei, F. Gao, and W. V. Li. Metric entropy of high dimensional distributions. *Proceedings of the American Mathematical Society* (*AMS*), 135(12):4009–4018, 2007.

9. H. D. Brunk. On the estimation of parameters restricted by inequalities. *The Annals of Mathematical Statistics*, 29(2):437–454, 1958.

10. L. Le Cam. Maximum likelihood: An introduction. *International Statistical Review*, 58:153–171, 1990.

11. B. Carl and I. Stephani. *Entropy, Compactness and the Approximation of Operators*, volume 98 of Cambridge Tracts in Mathematics. Cambridge University Press, Cambridge, 1990.

12. K. S. Chan and H. Tong. Testing for multimodality with dependent data. *Biometrika*, 91(1):113–123, 2004.

13. S. Chan, I. Diakonikolas, R. Servedio, and X. Sun. Learning mixtures of structured distributions over discrete domains. In *SODA*, pp. 1380–1394, 2013.

14. S. Chan, I. Diakonikolas, R. Servedio, and X. Sun. Efficient density estimation via piecewise polynomial approximation. In *STOC*, pp. 604–613, 2014.

15. S. Chan, I. Diakonikolas, R. Servedio, and X. Sun. Near-optimal density estimation in near-linear time using variable-width histograms. In *NIPS*, pp. 1844–1852, 2014.

16. S. X. Chen and J. S. Liu. Statistical applications of the Poisson-Binomial and conditional Bernoulli distributions. *Statistica Sinica*, 7:875–892, 1997.

17. M. Cule and R. Samworth. Maximum likelihood estimation of a multi-dimensional log-concave density. *Journal of the Royal Statistical Society: Series B* (*Statistical Methodology*), 72:545–607, 2010.

18. M. Cule and R. Samworth. Theoretical properties of the log-concave maximum likelihood estimator of a multidimensional density. *Electronic Journal of Statistics*, 4:254–270, 2010.

19. S. Dasgupta. Learning mixtures of Gaussians. In *Proceedings of the 40th Annual Symposium on Foundations of Computer Science*, pp. 634–644, 1999.

20. C. Daskalakis, I. Diakonikolas, R. O'Donnell, R. A. Servedio, and L. Tan. Learning sums of independent integer random variables. In *FOCS*, pp. 217–226, 2013.

21. C. Daskalakis, I. Diakonikolas, and R. A. Servedio. Learning k-modal distributions via testing. In *SODA*, pp. 1371–1385, 2012.

22. C. Daskalakis, I. Diakonikolas, and R. A. Servedio. Learning Poisson binomial distributions. In *STOC*, pp. 709–728, 2012.

23. C. Daskalakis, I. Diakonikolas, and R. A. Servedio. Learning k-modal distributions via testing. *Theory of Computing*, 10(20):535–570, 2014.

24. C. Daskalakis and G. Kamath. Faster and sample near-optimal algorithms for proper learning mixtures of gaussians. In *Proceedings of The 27th Conference on Learning Theory*, pp. 1183–1213, 2014.

25. A. De, I. Diakonikolas, and R. Servedio. Learning from satisfying assignments. In *Proceedings of the 26th Annual ACM-SIAM Symposium on Discrete Algorithms*, pp. 478–497, 2015.

26. L. Devroye and L. Györfi. *Nonparametric Density Estimation: The* L_1 *View.* Wiley, 1985.

27. L. Devroye and G. Lugosi. *Combinatorial Methods in Density Estimation.* Springer Series in Statistics, Springer, New York, 2001.

28. D. L. Donoho and I. M. Johnstone. Minimax estimation via wavelet shrinkage. *Annals of Statistics*, 26(3):879–921, 1998.

29. D. L. Donoho, I. M. Johnstone, G. Kerkyacharian, and D. Picard. Wavelet shrinkage: Asymptopia. *Journal of the Royal Statistical Society, Series. B*, 371–394, 1995.

30. D. L. Donoho, I. M. Johnstone, G. Kerkyacharian, and D. Picard. Density estimation by wavelet thresholding. *Annals of Statistics*, 24(2):508–539, 1996.

31. R. M Dudley. Metric entropy of some classes of sets with differentiable boundaries. *Journal of Approximation Theory*, 10(3):227–236, 1974.

32. L. Dumbgen and K. Rufibach. Maximum likelihood estimation of a log-concave density and its distribution function: Basic properties and uniform consistency. *Bernoulli*, 15(1):40–68, 2009.

33. D. E. Edmunds and H. Triebel. *Function Spaces, Entropy Numbers, Differential Operators*, volume 120 of Cambridge Tracts in Mathematics. Cambridge University Press, Cambridge, 1996.

34. J. Feldman, R. O'Donnell, and R. A. Servedio. Learning mixtures of product distributions over discrete domains. *SIAM Journal on Computing*, 37(5):1536–1564, 2008.

35. A.-L. Fougères. Estimation de densités unimodales. *Canadian Journal of Statistics*, 25:375–387, 1997.

36. Y. Freund and Y. Mansour. Estimating a mixture of two product distributions. In *Proceedings of the 12th Annual Conference on Computational Learning Theory*, pp. 183–192, 1999.

37. F. Gao and J. A. Wellner. On the rate of convergence of the maximum likelihood estimator of a k-monotone density. *Science in China Series A: Mathematics*, 52: 1525–1538, 2009.

38. U. Grenander. On the theory of mortality measurement. *Skandinavisk Aktuarietidskrift*, 39:125–153, 1956.

39. P. Groeneboom. Estimating a monotone density. In *Proceedings of the Berkeley Conference in Honor of Jerzy Neyman and Jack Kiefer*, pp. 539–555, 1985.

40. P. Groeneboom and G. Jongbloed. *Nonparametric Estimation under Shape Constraints: Estimators, Algorithms and Asymptotics.* Cambridge University Press, 2014.

41. D. L. Hanson and G. Pledger. Consistency in concave regression. *Annals of Statistics*, 4(6):1038–1050, 1976.

42. R. Hasminskii and I. Ibragimov. On density estimation in the view of Kolmogorov's ideas in approximation theory. *Annals of Statistics*, 18(3):999–1010, 1990.

43. D. Haussler and M. Opper. Mutual information, metric entropy and cumulative relative entropy risk. *Annals of Statistics*, 25(6):2451–2492, 1997.

44. A. J. Izenman. Recent developments in nonparametric density estimation. *Journal of the American Statistical Association*, 86(413):205–224, 1991.

45. H. K. Jankowski and J. A. Wellner. Estimation of a discrete monotone density. *Electronic Journal of Statistics*, 3:1567–1605, 2009.

46. M. Kearns, Y. Mansour, D. Ron, R. Rubinfeld, R. Schapire, and L. Sellie. On the learnability of discrete distributions. In *Proceedings of the 26th STOC*, pp. 273–282, 1994.

47. G. Kerkyacharian and D. Picard. Density estimation in Besov spaces. *Statistics & Probability Letters*, 13(1):15–24, 1992.

48. G. Kerkyacharian, D. Picard, and K. Tribouley. Lp adaptive density estimation. *Bernoulli*, 2(3):229–247, 1996.

49. R. Koenker and I. Mizera. Quasi-concave density estimation. *Annals of Statistics*, 38(5):2998–3027, 2010.

50. A. N. Kolmogorov and V. M. Tihomirov. ε-entropy and ε-capacity of sets in function spaces. *Uspekhi Matematicheskikh Nauk*, 14:3–86, 1959.

51. B. Lindsay. *Mixture Models: Theory, Geometry and Applications*. Institute for Mathematical Statistics, Hayward, CA, 1995.

52. G. G. Lorentz. Metric entropy and approximation. *Bulletin of the American Mathematical Society*, 72:903–937, 1966.

53. Y. Makovoz. On the Kolmogorov complexity of functions of finite smoothness. *Journal of Complexity*, 2(2):121–130, 1986.

54. A. Moitra and G. Valiant. Settling the polynomial learnability of mixtures of Gaussians. In *FOCS*, pp. 93–102, 2010.

55. K. Pearson. Contributions to the mathematical theory of evolution. ii. Skew variation in homogeneous material. *Philosophical Transactions of the Royal Society of London*, 186:343–414, 1895.

56. B. L. S. Prakasa Rao. Estimation of a unimodal density. *Sankhya Series A*, 31:23–36, 1969.

57. R. A. Redner and H. F. Walker. Mixture densities, maximum likelihood and the EM algorithm. *SIAM Review*, 26:195–202, 1984.

58. D. W. Scott. *Multivariate Density Estimation: Theory, Practice and Visualization*. Wiley, New York, 1992.

59. D. W. Scott and S. R. Sain. *Multidimensional Density Estimation*. volume 24 of Handbook of Statistics, pp. 229–261, 2005.

60. B. W. Silverman. *Density Estimation.* Chapman & Hall, London, 1986.

61. C. J. Stone. The use of polynomial splines and their tensor products in multivariate function estimation. *Annals of Statistics*, 22(1):118–171, 1994.

62. C. J. Stone, M. H. Hansen, C. Kooperberg, and Y. K. Truong. Polynomial splines and their tensor products in extended linear modeling: 1994 Wald memorial lecture. *Annals of Statistics*, 25(4):1371–1470, 1997.

63. A. T. Suresh, A. Orlitsky, J. Acharya, and A. Jafarpour. Near-optimal-sample estimators for spherical gaussian mixtures. In *Advances in Neural Information Processing Systems*, pp. 1395–1403, 2014.

64. D. M. Titterington, A. F. M. Smith, and U. E. Makov. *Statistical Analysis of Finite Mixture Distributions.* Wiley, 1985.

65. A. B. Tsybakov. *Introduction to Nonparametric Estimation.* Springer, 2008.

66. L. Valiant. A theory of the learnable. *Communications of the ACM*, 27(11):1134–1142, 1984.

67. L. G. Valiant. A theory of the learnable. In *Proceedings of the 16th Annual ACM Symposium on Theory of Computing*, pp. 436–445. ACM Press, New York, 1984.

68. A. W. van der Vaart and J. A. Wellner. *Weak Convergence and Empirical Processes.* Springer Series in Statistics. Springer-Verlag, New York, 1996. (With applications to statistics.)

69. G. Walther. Inference and modeling with log-concave distributions. *Statistical Science*, 24(3):319–327, 2009.

70. E. J. Wegman. Maximum likelihood estimation of a unimodal density. I. and II. *The Annals of Mathematical Statistics*, 41:457–471, 2169–2174, 1970.

71. E. J. Wegman and I. W. Wright. Splines in statistics. *Journal of the American Statistical Association*, 78(382):351–365, 1983.

72. R. Willett and R. D. Nowak. Multiscale poisson intensity and density estimation. *IEEE Transactions on Information Theory*, 53(9):3171–3187, 2007.

73. Y. Yang and A. Barron. Information-theoretic determination of minimax rates of convergence. *Annals of Statistics*, 27(5):1564–1599, 1999.

74. Y. G. Yatracos. Rates of convergence of minimum distance estimators and Kolmogorov's entropy. *Annals of Statistics*, 13:768–774, 1985.

16

Penalized Estimation in Complex Models

Jacob Bien and Daniela Witten

CONTENTS

16.1 Introduction 285
16.2 Loss Functions 287
16.2.1 Linear Regression 287
16.2.2 Matrix Completion 287
16.2.3 Precision Matrix Estimation 288
16.3 Structure-Inducing Convex Penalties 288
16.3.1 The Lasso 288
16.3.2 The Group Lasso 290
16.3.3 The Nuclear Norm 291
16.4 Algorithms 291
16.4.1 Blockwise Coordinate Descent 292
16.4.2 Proximal Gradient Method 293
16.4.3 Alternating Direction Method of Multipliers 294
16.5 Applications 295
16.5.1 Multivariate Regression with the Group Lasso 295
16.5.2 Matrix Completion with the Nuclear Norm 296
16.5.3 Graphical Models with the Lasso 297
16.6 Discussion 298
Acknowledgments 299
References 299

16.1 Introduction

In recent years, both the popular press and the scientific community have been focused on the potential of Big Data. The phrase has been used to refer to the very large amounts of data that are now being routinely collected by e-commerce sites, molecular biologists, sociologists, credit card companies, astrophysicists, and more. As computing becomes less expensive (and, in some cases, as experimental technologies make it possible to measure a growing number of features), the scale of data being collected across a broad range of fields will continue to increase at a rapid clip.

From the perspective of a classical statistician, more data are typically better data. After all, most classical statistical methods and results rely on the assumption that the sample size is extremely large. If Big Data were only characterized by enormous sample sizes, then its challenges would be purely *computational* in nature. However, two aspects inherent to much of today's Big Data lead to *statistical* challenges:

1. While the sample size might be large, the number of features for which measurements are available is often much larger. For instance, a web search company might track every single query made by each of its users. In this setting, the number of users (the sample size) is huge, but the number of possible queries (the set of features) is orders of magnitude larger. Similarly, in biology, new technologies have made it possible to obtain a detailed molecular snapshot of the activity of a tissue sample or even a single cell; however, this snapshot is expensive and so typically the sample size is quite small relative to the number of molecular measurements that are obtained. These examples are *high dimensional* and there are many more features than observations.
2. When faced with old-fashioned small data, statisticians often seek to answer very simple questions, such as *Is this parameter nonzero?* and *Is X correlated with Y?* However, on the basis of Big Data, we often ask far more complex questions, such as *Which of these 1,000,000 parameters are nonzero?* and *What are the conditional dependence relationships among these 30,000 features?*

In essence, people ask very complex questions on the basis of Big Data; answering these questions leads to statistical challenges. Because so much data are available and so many features have been measured, we become ambitious and seek to fit very complex models. However, this level of complexity often cannot be supported by the available sample size, leading to a host of problems, such as overfitting. Even seemingly simple tasks—such as fitting a linear model to predict a response on the basis of a set of features—can be quite challenging with Big Data.

In the classical statistical setting, we often estimate a parameter vector $\boldsymbol{\theta}$ as the minimizer of some loss function $\mathcal{L}(\boldsymbol{\theta})$, which might be the negative log-likelihood of the data under some model. In the context of Big Data, reducing the complexity of the parameter space is of paramount importance. We can do this by making an assumption about the *structure* of $\boldsymbol{\theta}$—for instance, that it is *sparse* or *low-rank*—and selecting a penalty function $\mathcal{P}$ that encourages this structure in $\boldsymbol{\theta}$. We can then estimate $\boldsymbol{\theta}$ as $\hat{\boldsymbol{\theta}}$, a minimizer of

$$\underset{\boldsymbol{\theta}}{\text{minimize}} \left\{ \mathcal{L}(\boldsymbol{\theta}) + \lambda \mathcal{P}(\boldsymbol{\theta}) \right\}, \tag{16.1}$$

where λ is a nonnegative tuning parameter that controls the tradeoff between the loss function (which encourages the parameter estimate to fit the data) and the penalty function (which encourages the parameter estimate to conform to our structural assumptions). For a suitably chosen penalty function $\mathcal{P}$, Equation 16.1 can overcome some of the problems associated with the complexity of the parameter space, thereby yielding a good estimate of $\boldsymbol{\theta}$. This makes Equation 16.1 a valuable framework when working with Big Data.

Typically, the loss function $\mathcal{L}$ is convex. If the penalty function $\mathcal{P}$ is also chosen to be convex, then Equation 16.1 is a convex optimization problem. This means that every local optimum is a global optimum and that we have access to a sophisticated set of tools for finding the minimizer of Equation 16.1 (Boyd and Vandenberghe, 2004). This is particularly important in the context of Big Data, for which efficient algorithms and implementations are critical.

In this chapter, we will explore the *loss + penalty* framework given in Equation 16.1 in the setting, where both $\mathcal{L}$ and $\mathcal{P}$ are convex functions. We will consider three motivating examples: linear regression, matrix completion, and Gaussian graphical modeling. In Section 16.2, we will explore the convex loss functions associated with these motivating examples. In Section 16.3, we will introduce some convex penalty functions that can be used to induce particular types of structure in the parameters. We will explore three algorithms for solving convex optimization problems in Section 16.4 and will apply them to our three motivating examples in Section 16.5. Finally, we close with a discussion in Section 16.6.

In this chapter, we will *not* consider the theoretical aspects of the estimators obtained via the *loss + penalty* framework discussed here. For a very thorough exposition of these theoretical considerations, we refer the interested reader to Bühlmann and van de Geer (2011).

We use the following notational conventions. Random variables and random vectors are capitalized (e.g., A), fixed scalars are in lowercase (e.g., a), fixed vectors are in lowercase bold (e.g., $\mathbf{a}$), and matrices are in capital bold (e.g., $\mathbf{A}$). For a matrix $\mathbf{A}$, $\mathbf{A}_j$ denotes its jth column and A_{ij} denotes its (i, j)th element. The notation $\mathbf{diag}(a_i)$ indicates a diagonal matrix with elements $a_1, \ldots, a_p$ on the diagonal.

We typically will use Latin letters to represent the data and Greek letters to represent parameters and optimization variables. We will use $\boldsymbol{\theta}$ as the optimization variable for a generic optimization problem, as in Equation 16.1. The solution to an optimization problem with optimization variable $\boldsymbol{\theta}$ will be denoted using a hat, that is, $\hat{\boldsymbol{\theta}}$. In the special cases of linear regression, matrix completion, and the Gaussian graphical model, we will represent the parameters using $\boldsymbol{\beta}$, $\boldsymbol{\Gamma}$, and $\boldsymbol{\Omega}$, respectively.

16.2 Loss Functions

In this chapter, we consider convex loss functions, which arise quite often in the context of complex statistical models. Often the loss function is motivated as the negative log-likelihood for the data, under some distributional assumptions. Here, we describe three convex loss functions that arise in Big Data applications. These will serve as illustrative examples throughout this chapter.

16.2.1 Linear Regression

Consider the model

$$Y = X^T \boldsymbol{\beta} + \epsilon,$$

where Y is a response variable, $X = (X_1, \ldots, X_p)^T$ is a p-vector of features, $\boldsymbol{\beta} = (\beta_1, \ldots, \beta_p)^T$ is a p-dimensional parameter vector, and ϵ is a noise term. Our goal is to estimate the elements of $\boldsymbol{\beta}$ on the basis of n independent observations of X and Y.

Let $\mathbf{X}$ denote the $n \times p$ data matrix and $\mathbf{y}$ denote the response vector of length n. The *squared-error* loss function takes the form

$$\mathcal{L}(\boldsymbol{\beta}) = \frac{1}{2}\|\mathbf{y} - \mathbf{X}\boldsymbol{\beta}\|_2^2. \tag{16.2}$$

Minimizing Equation 16.2 leads to the standard least-squares estimator for $\boldsymbol{\beta}$.

16.2.2 Matrix Completion

Suppose that we have an $m \times n$ data matrix $\mathbf{X}$, which is a noisy observation of some unknown matrix $\boldsymbol{\Gamma}$. That is,

$$\mathbf{X} = \boldsymbol{\Gamma} + \mathcal{E},$$

where $\mathcal{E}$ is an $m \times n$ matrix of independent noise terms. Consider the task of estimating $\boldsymbol{\Gamma}$ in the setting where *only a subset of the elements of* $\mathbf{X}$ *are observed*. We let $\mathcal{O} \subseteq \{1, \ldots, m\} \times \{1, \ldots, n\}$ denote the set of indices of the elements of $\mathbf{X}$ that are observed. This is known as the *matrix completion problem* and has been extensively investigated in the context of user recommendation systems (Cai et al., 2010; Mazumder et al., 2010).

We could try to estimate $\mathbf{\Gamma}$ in this setting by minimizing the loss function

$$\mathcal{L}(\mathbf{\Gamma}) = \frac{1}{2} \sum_{(i,j)\in\mathcal{O}} (X_{ij} - \Gamma_{ij})^2 \tag{16.3}$$

with respect to $\mathbf{\Gamma}$. Unfortunately, the solution $\hat{\mathbf{\Gamma}}$ is trivial and not useful: $\hat{\Gamma}_{ij}$ equals X_{ij} for $(i,j) \in \mathcal{O}$ and can take on any value for $(i,j) \notin \mathcal{O}$. In effect, the problem is that the parameter space is too complex given the available data (the elements of the matrix $\mathbf{X}$ that are in the set $\mathcal{O}$).

We will see in Section 16.5 that if we are willing to make certain assumptions about the structure of $\mathbf{\Gamma}$—and if we encode those structural assumptions via an appropriate convex penalty—then the loss function (Equation 16.3) can be successfully used to estimate the matrix $\mathbf{\Gamma}$.

16.2.3 Precision Matrix Estimation

Consider a p-dimensional multivariate normal random vector,

$$X = (X_1, \ldots, X_p)^T \sim N_p(\boldsymbol{\mu}, \boldsymbol{\Sigma}),$$

where $\mu_j = \mathbb{E}[X_j]$ and $\sigma_{jk} = \text{Cov}(X_j, X_k)$. Classical statistical theory tells us that a zero element of the precision matrix, $\boldsymbol{\Omega} = \boldsymbol{\Sigma}^{-1}$, corresponds to a pair of random variables that are conditionally independent—that is, independent given the other $p-2$ random variables (see, e.g., Mardia et al. 1979). Therefore, the set of conditional dependence relationships, referred to as a *graphical model*, is given by the sparsity pattern of $\boldsymbol{\Omega}$ (see, e.g., Koller and Friedman 2009).

Let $\mathbf{X}$ denote an $n \times p$ data matrix, for which the rows represent n independent draws from the random vector X. Then a natural loss function takes the form

$$\mathcal{L}(\boldsymbol{\Omega}) = -\text{logdet}\boldsymbol{\Omega} + \text{trace}(\mathbf{S}\boldsymbol{\Omega}), \tag{16.4}$$

where $\mathbf{S}$ is the empirical covariance matrix of $\mathbf{X}$. The loss function (Equation 16.4) is convex in $\boldsymbol{\Omega}$; notably, it is *not* convex in $\boldsymbol{\Sigma}$.

16.3 Structure-Inducing Convex Penalties

In this section, we introduce three convex penalties that induce three very simple types of structure. The *lasso* induces sparsity on the elements of a vector; the *group lasso* induces sparsity on groups of elements of a vector; and the *nuclear norm* induces sparsity on the singular values of a matrix. Although we discuss only these three penalties in detail, in Table 16.1, we demonstrate the breadth of structures attainable through convex penalties.

16.3.1 The Lasso

In the setting of Section 16.2.1, suppose that we wish to perform linear regression in such a way that no more than k of the elements of $\boldsymbol{\beta}$ are estimated to be nonzero. That is, rather than minimizing the loss function (16.2) with respect to $\boldsymbol{\beta}$, we could consider the problem

$$\underset{\boldsymbol{\beta}}{\text{minimize}} \left\{ \frac{1}{2} \|\mathbf{y} - \mathbf{X}\boldsymbol{\beta}\|_2^2 \right\} \text{ subject to } \|\boldsymbol{\beta}\|_0 \leq k. \tag{16.5}$$

TABLE 16.1
Examples of convex penalties from the recent literature.

Name	Structure	Example	References
Lasso	Sparsity	$\hat{\beta}_j = 0$	Tibshirani (1996)
Group lasso (GL)	Group sparsity	$\hat{\beta}_g = 0$	Yuan and Lin (2007a)
Hierarchical GL	Hierarchical sparsity	$\hat{\beta}_g = 0 \Longrightarrow \hat{\beta}_h = 0$	Zhao et al. (2009)
Overlapping GL	Zero unions	$\hat{\beta}_{g \cup h} = 0$	Jenatton et al. (2011)
Latent overlapping GL	Nonzero unions	$\hat{\beta}_{g \cup h} \neq 0$	Obozinski et al. (2011a)
Fused lasso	Sparse differences	$\hat{\beta}_j = \hat{\beta}_{j+1}$	Tibshirani et al. (2005)
ℓ_1 trend filtering	Sparse discrete derivatives	$\hat{\beta}_j - \hat{\beta}_{j-1} = \hat{\beta}_{j+1} - \hat{\beta}_j$	Kim et al. (2009); Tibshirani (2014)
Isotonic lasso	Monotonicity	$\hat{\beta}_j \leq \hat{\beta}_{j+1}$	Tibshirani et al. (2011)
OSCAR	Clustered coefficients	$\hat{\beta}_j = \hat{\beta}_k$	Bondell and Reich (2008)
Nuclear norm	Low rank	$\sigma_j(\hat{\Omega}) = 0$	Fazel (2002)
Group fusion	Identical vectors	$\hat{\beta} = \hat{\gamma}$	Hocking et al. (2011), among others
Generalized lasso	Sparse linear combinations	$\mathrm{d}^T \hat{\beta} = 0$	Tibshirani and Taylor (2011); She (2010)

Note: For each penalty, a description of the structure induced and a reference are provided.

Here $\|\boldsymbol{\beta}\|_0$ denotes the ℓ_0 *norm*, or the cardinality (number of nonzero elements) of $\boldsymbol{\beta}$. Equation 16.5 is known as *best-subsets regression.*

Unfortunately, the ℓ_0 norm is nonconvex and Equation 16.5 cannot be efficiently solved, when p is large. To address this problem, we can replace the ℓ_0 norm with an ℓ_1 norm, to get a convex relaxation of the above problem:

$$\underset{\boldsymbol{\beta}}{\text{minimize}} \left\{ \frac{1}{2} \|\mathbf{y} - \mathbf{X}\boldsymbol{\beta}\|_2^2 \right\} \text{ subject to } \sum_{j=1}^{p} |\beta_j| \leq c. \tag{16.6}$$

For small values of c, the value of $\boldsymbol{\beta}$ that minimizes Equation 16.6 will tend to be sparse—that is, to have elements exactly equal to zero. Equation 16.6 is equivalent to (Boyd and Vandenberghe, 2004)

$$\underset{\boldsymbol{\beta}}{\text{minimize}} \left\{ \frac{1}{2} \|\mathbf{y} - \mathbf{X}\boldsymbol{\beta}\|_2^2 + \lambda \sum_{j=1}^{p} |\beta_j| \right\}, \tag{16.7}$$

where λ is some nonnegative tuning parameter. Roughly speaking, as λ increases, the solution $\hat{\boldsymbol{\beta}}$ to Equation 16.7 will tend to become sparser.

The penalty function in Equation 16.7, $\mathcal{P}(\boldsymbol{\beta}) = \sum_{j=1}^{p} |\beta_j|$, is known as a *lasso* (or ℓ_1) penalty (Tibshirani, 1996). It has been extensively explored in combination with a number of loss functions for a variety of problems, such as linear regression, generalized linear modeling (Friedman et al., 2010), survival analysis (Tibshirani, 1997), graphical modeling (Yuan and Lin, 2007b), and more (Tibshirani, 2011). We will apply it to graphical modeling in Section 16.5.3.

To better understand the ℓ_1 penalty, we consider its use with a very simple loss function,

$$\underset{\boldsymbol{\beta}}{\text{minimize}} \left\{ \frac{1}{2}\|\mathbf{y} - \boldsymbol{\beta}\|_2^2 + \lambda \sum_{j=1}^{p} |\beta_j| \right\}. \tag{16.8}$$

It can be shown that $\hat{\boldsymbol{\beta}}$, the solution to Equation 16.8, has the form

$$\hat{\beta}_j = \mathcal{S}(y_j, \lambda) = \begin{cases} y_j - \lambda & \text{if } y_j > \lambda \\ 0 & \text{if } -\lambda \leq y_j \leq \lambda \\ y_j + \lambda & \text{if } y_j < -\lambda, \end{cases} \tag{16.9}$$

where $\mathcal{S}$ is the *soft-thresholding operator*. Inspection of Equation 16.9 sheds some light on the fact that an ℓ_1 penalty can result in a sparse solution when λ is large.

16.3.2 The Group Lasso

Consider again the linear regression setting of Section 16.2.1. Suppose that $\boldsymbol{\beta}$ is naturally partitioned into G groups, $\boldsymbol{\beta} = (\boldsymbol{\beta}_1^T, \ldots, \boldsymbol{\beta}_G^T)^T$, and we wish to obtain an estimate of $\boldsymbol{\beta}$ such that for each $g = 1, \ldots, G$, the subvector $\boldsymbol{\beta}_g$ is either entirely zero or entirely nonzero. To achieve this, we can apply a *group lasso* (or ℓ_2 norm) penalty (Yuan and Lin, 2007a) of the form

$$\mathcal{P}(\boldsymbol{\beta}) = \sum_{g=1}^{G} \|\boldsymbol{\beta}_g\|_2. \tag{16.10}$$

The group lasso penalty encourages the coefficients $\boldsymbol{\beta}_g$ within the gth group to be entirely zero ($\boldsymbol{\beta}_g = \mathbf{0}$) or entirely nonzero. In practice, one typically uses a weighted version of the penalty, $\mathcal{P}(\boldsymbol{\beta}) = \sum_{g=1}^{G} w_g \|\boldsymbol{\beta}_g\|_2$, where w_g is the square root of the number of elements in group g, but to simplify the exposition in this chapter we take $w_g = 1$ throughout.

A number of extensions to the group lasso have been proposed, for instance to accommodate overlapping groups (Jacob et al., 2009; Jenatton et al., 2011) and to induce sparsity within the groups (Simon et al., 2013b). We explore the use of the group lasso in the context of multivariate linear regression in Section 16.5.1.

It is instructive to consider a very simple optimization problem involving a group lasso penalty,

$$\underset{\boldsymbol{\beta}}{\text{minimize}} \left\{ \frac{1}{2}\|\mathbf{y} - \boldsymbol{\beta}\|_2^2 + \lambda \sum_{g=1}^{G} \|\boldsymbol{\beta}_g\|_2 \right\}. \tag{16.11}$$

It can be seen that for the gth group, the solution to Equation 16.11 takes the form

$$\hat{\boldsymbol{\beta}}_g = \begin{cases} \mathbf{y}_g (1 - \lambda/\|\mathbf{y}_g\|_2) & \text{if } \|\mathbf{y}_g\|_2 > \lambda \\ \mathbf{0} & \text{if } \|\mathbf{y}_g\|_2 \leq \lambda, \end{cases} \tag{16.12}$$

where $\mathbf{y} = (\mathbf{y}_1^T, \ldots, \mathbf{y}_G^T)^T$. From Equation 16.12 it is clear that the group lasso yields group sparsity: $\hat{\boldsymbol{\beta}}_g$ will be either entirely zero or entirely nonzero (assuming that all elements of $\mathbf{y}_g$ are nonzero).

In a setting with exactly one feature per group (i.e., $G = p$), the group lasso and lasso penalties are identical. In this case, Equations 16.8 and 16.9 are identical to Equations 16.11 and 16.12.

16.3.3 The Nuclear Norm

The convex penalties in Sections 16.3.1 and 16.3.2 were applied to a vector. We now consider a penalty that is applied to a matrix. The *nuclear norm* of an $m \times n$ matrix $\mathbf{\Gamma}$ takes the form

$$\mathcal{P}(\mathbf{\Gamma}) = \|\mathbf{\Gamma}\|_* = \sum_{j=1}^{m} \sigma_j(\mathbf{\Gamma}), \tag{16.13}$$

where $\sigma_1(\mathbf{\Gamma}), \ldots, \sigma_m(\mathbf{\Gamma})$ are the singular values of $\mathbf{\Gamma}$ (here we have assumed that $m \leq n$ so that $\mathbf{\Gamma}$ has no more than m nonzero singular values). The nuclear norm can be interpreted as the ℓ_1 norm of the singular values of the matrix $\mathbf{\Gamma}$ and it encourages sparsity in the singular values. Equivalently, it encourages the matrix $\mathbf{\Gamma}$ to have low rank.

The nuclear norm is convex (Fazel, 2002) and is of growing interest in the statistical community in a variety of contexts, including matrix completion (Candès and Recht, 2009; Cai et al., 2010; Mazumder et al., 2010), multivariate regression (Yuan et al., 2007), and graphical modeling in the presence of latent variables (Chandrasekaran et al., 2012; Ma et al., 2013). We explore its use in the context of matrix completion in Section 16.5.2.

We now consider a very simple optimization problem involving the nuclear norm,

$$\underset{\mathbf{\Gamma}}{\text{minimize}} \left\{ \frac{1}{2} \|\mathbf{X} - \mathbf{\Gamma}\|_F^2 + \lambda \|\mathbf{\Gamma}\|_* \right\}, \tag{16.14}$$

where $\|\cdot\|_F^2$ denotes the squared Frobenius norm—that is, the sum of squared elements—of a matrix. Let $\mathbf{Udiag}(\sigma_j)\mathbf{V}^T$ denote the singular value decomposition of the matrix $\mathbf{X}$. Then, the solution to Equation 16.14 takes the form

$$\hat{\mathbf{\Gamma}} = \mathbf{Udiag}\left(\mathcal{S}(\sigma_j, \lambda)\right) \mathbf{V}^T, \tag{16.15}$$

where $\mathcal{S}$ is the soft-thresholding operator seen in Equation 16.9 (see, e.g., Mazumder et al., 2010).

16.4 Algorithms

When applied to a convex loss function and a convex penalty function, the *loss + penalty* framework (Equation 16.1) allows us to formulate an estimator as the solution to a convex optimization problem. Such problems have the very attractive property that any local optimum is also a global optimum. Furthermore, we can make use of a rich literature of convex optimization methods with guaranteed convergence results and excellent practical performance (Boyd and Vandenberghe, 2004).

In particular, the convex optimization problems that arise in the context of large-scale statistical modeling typically involve a nondifferentiable objective. In what follows, we will assume that the loss function is differentiable and that the penalty function is not.* In this section, we describe three general approaches for minimizing nondifferentiable convex functions. All three methods involve breaking down the original optimization problem into smaller subproblems that are easier to solve. As we introduce each approach, we will describe

*In the examples in Section 16.3, the penalty functions are nondifferentiable. We assume in what follows that the loss function is differentiable, though that need not be the case in general (e.g., the *hinge loss* in support vector machines is nondifferentiable, Hastie et al., 2009).

the characteristics of problems for which it is well suited. An example of each approach is presented in Section 16.5.

In most applications, the tuning parameter λ in Equation 16.1 is not known *a priori*. For certain specific loss functions and penalties, solutions for *all* $\lambda \geq 0$ have been worked out (Osborne et al., 2000; Efron et al., 2004; Tibshirani and Taylor, 2011). However, typically we simply solve Equation 16.1 along a finite grid of λ values. In such cases, it is computationally advantageous to initialize the algorithm, for each value of λ, using the solution for a nearby λ value; this is known as a *warm start*. For certain loss functions and penalties, information from nearby λ values can be used to exclude certain parameters from consideration, thereby reducing the effective size of the problem (El Ghaoui et al., 2012; Tibshirani et al., 2012; Wang et al., 2013; Xiang et al., 2014).

16.4.1 Blockwise Coordinate Descent

Suppose that $\mathcal{L}(\theta)$ is convex and differentiable, and that $\mathcal{P}(\theta)$ is convex and *separable*, in the sense that it can be written as $\sum_{k=1}^{K} \mathcal{P}_k(\theta_k)$, where $\theta = (\theta_1^T, \ldots, \theta_K^T)^T$ is a partition of the vector θ into K blocks. In *blockwise coordinate descent* (BCD), we cycle through these K blocks, minimizing the objective with respect to each block in turn while holding all others fixed.

The full BCD algorithm is presented in Algorithm 16.1. Note that in this algorithm the BCD updates are done sequentially. Therefore, the blocks with indices preceding k have already been updated, whereas the others have not.*

Algorithm 16.1 BCD Algorithm for a Separable Penalty $\sum_{k=1}^{K} \mathcal{P}_k(\theta_k)$

Input: $\theta^{(0)}$, $t = 1$.
repeat
  for $k = 1, \ldots, K$ **do**
    $\theta_k^{(t)} \in \arg\min_{\theta_k} \left\{ \mathcal{L}(\theta_1^{(t)}, \ldots, \theta_{k-1}^{(t)}, \theta_k, \theta_{k+1}^{(t-1)}, \ldots, \theta_K^{(t-1)}) + \lambda \mathcal{P}_k(\theta_k) \right\}$
  end
  $t \leftarrow t + 1$
until *convergence;*

Tseng (2001) shows that under some mild technical conditions, every cluster point of the iterates of BCD is a minimizer of Equation 16.1. The key assumption is that the nondifferentiable part of the objective is separable.

For many common penalties, the block coordinate update in Algorithm 16.1 can be solved in closed form. For example, for the lasso with squared-error loss (Equation 16.7), we take each coordinate as its own block, with $\mathcal{P}_j(\beta_j) = |\beta_j|$. Then the block coordinate update takes the form

$$\beta_j^{(t)} \in \arg\min_{\beta_j} \left\{ \frac{1}{2} \|\mathbf{r}^{-j} - \beta_j \mathbf{X}_j\|_2^2 + \lambda |\beta_j| \right\},$$

where $\mathbf{r}^{-j} = \mathbf{y} - \sum_{k:k<j} \mathbf{X}_k \beta_k^{(t)} - \sum_{k:k>j} \mathbf{X}_k \beta_k^{(t-1)}$ denotes the jth partial residual. This problem is efficiently solved in closed form via the soft-thresholding operator (Equation 16.9):

$$\beta_j^{(t)} \leftarrow \mathcal{S}(\mathbf{X}_j^T \mathbf{r}^{-j}, \lambda) / \|\mathbf{X}_j\|^2.$$

*In Algorithm 16.1, we use "$\in$" as the objective may not have a unique minimizer.

For BCD, as with other methods, using warm starts can reduce the number of iterations required to achieve convergence. Furthermore, blocks that are set to zero in the solution for a given value of λ typically remain zero for nearby values of λ. Friedman et al. (2010) use this information to avoid updating all of the blocks in every cycle of the BCD algorithm, thus speeding up the run time per iteration.

As presented in Algorithm 16.1, the BCD algorithm cycles through the blocks $k = 1, \ldots, K, 1, \ldots, K, \ldots$ until convergence. However, other choices are also possible.

16.4.2 Proximal Gradient Method

In BCD, we make use of the fact that minimizing the objective over one block of variables at a time can be much easier than a joint minimization over all blocks simultaneously. In the *proximal gradient method* (PGM), also known as *generalized gradient descent*, we again replace the original problem with a series of easier problems, this time by simplifying the loss function.

As motivation, suppose that we are interested in minimizing $\mathcal{L}(\boldsymbol{\theta})$ with respect to $\boldsymbol{\theta}$ in the absence of a penalty. Because $\mathcal{L}$ is convex and differentiable, we can apply *gradient descent*. The tth iteration takes the form

$$\boldsymbol{\theta}^{(t)} \leftarrow \boldsymbol{\theta}^{(t-1)} - s\nabla\mathcal{L}(\boldsymbol{\theta}^{(t-1)}),$$

where s is a suitably chosen step size (or sequence of step sizes, in which case s depends on t).

However, if $\mathcal{P}$ is nondifferentiable, then gradient descent cannot be applied to Equation 16.1 because the gradient of the objective does not exist. PGM, presented in Algorithm 16.2, generalizes gradient descent to this setting.

Algorithm 16.2 PGM Algorithm with Fixed Step Size $s \leq 1/L$

Input: $\boldsymbol{\theta}^{(0)}$, step size s, $t = 1$.
repeat
  $\boldsymbol{\theta}^{(t)} \leftarrow \text{Prox}_{s\lambda\mathcal{P}(\cdot)}\left(\boldsymbol{\theta}^{(t-1)} - s\nabla\mathcal{L}(\boldsymbol{\theta}^{(t-1)})\right)$
  $t \leftarrow t+1$
until *convergence;*

The key ingredient in Algorithm 16.2 is the function $\text{Prox}_{s\lambda\mathcal{P}(\cdot)}$, which is the *proximal operator* of the function $s\lambda\mathcal{P}(\cdot)$. It is defined as

$$\text{Prox}_{s\lambda\mathcal{P}(\cdot)}(\tilde{\boldsymbol{\theta}}) = \arg\min_{\boldsymbol{\theta}} \left\{\frac{1}{2}\|\boldsymbol{\theta} - \tilde{\boldsymbol{\theta}}\|_2^2 + s\lambda\mathcal{P}(\boldsymbol{\theta})\right\}. \tag{16.16}$$

The objective of Equation 16.16 is of the *loss + penalty* form, but with a very simple loss function. Because this loss function is strongly convex, the minimum is attained at a unique point. For many penalties, $\text{Prox}_{s\lambda\mathcal{P}(\cdot)}(\tilde{\boldsymbol{\theta}})$ can be evaluated very simply. For example, Equations 16.9, 16.12, and 16.15 are the proximal operators for the lasso, group lasso, and nuclear norm penalties, respectively.

Let us assume that $\nabla\mathcal{L}(\boldsymbol{\theta})$ is Lipschitz continuous with Lipschitz constant L. If we choose a step size $s \leq 1/L$, then PGM is guaranteed to converge.* In particular, after t iterations (with fixed step size $s = 1/L$),

$$\left(\mathcal{L}(\boldsymbol{\theta}^{(t)}) + \lambda\mathcal{P}(\boldsymbol{\theta}^{(t)})\right) - \left(\mathcal{L}(\hat{\boldsymbol{\theta}}) + \lambda\mathcal{P}(\hat{\boldsymbol{\theta}})\right) \leq \frac{L\|\boldsymbol{\theta}^{(0)} - \hat{\boldsymbol{\theta}}\|^2}{2t}, \tag{16.17}$$

*Lipschitz continuity of $\nabla\mathcal{L}$ is a requirement for PGM to converge. However, if the Lipschitz constant L is unknown, then a line search scheme can be used instead of using a fixed step size.

where $\hat{\theta}$ is any global optimum of Equation 16.1. This indicates that halving the left-hand side of Equation 16.17 could potentially require doubling the number of iterations. Furthermore, the $\|\theta^{(0)} - \hat{\theta}\|^2$ term in Equation 16.17 indicates the value of warm starts: if $\|\theta^{(0)} - \hat{\theta}\|^2$ is halved, then the left-hand side of Equation 16.17 may be halved as well.

Equation 16.17 indicates that at the tth iteration of PGM, the difference between the optimal value and the current value of the objective is on the order of $1/t$. Remarkably, a simple and conceptually minor modification to Algorithm 16.2 leads to a convergence rate of $1/t^2$ (Beck and Teboulle, 2009; Nesterov, 2013). Furthermore, when $\mathcal{L}(\theta) + \lambda\mathcal{P}(\theta)$ is strongly convex, then the convergence rates are even better (Nesterov, 2013). See Beck and Teboulle (2009) and Parikh and Boyd (2013) for accessible introductions to PGM.

16.4.3 Alternating Direction Method of Multipliers

The *alternating direction method of multipliers* (ADMM) algorithm dates back to the 1970s (Gabay and Mercier, 1976; Eckstein and Bertsekas, 1992) but was recently popularized in the context of fitting large-scale penalized statistical models by Boyd et al. (2010). Suppose that we have an optimization problem of the form

$$\underset{\theta,\alpha}{\text{minimize}} \{f(\theta) + g(\alpha)\} \text{ subject to } \mathbf{A}\theta + \mathbf{B}\alpha = \mathbf{c}, \tag{16.18}$$

where θ and α are vector-valued optimization variables, $\mathbf{A}$ and $\mathbf{B}$ are constant matrices, $\mathbf{c}$ is a constant vector, and f and g are convex functions. The *augmented Lagrangian* corresponding to this problem takes the form

$$L_\rho(\theta, \alpha, \mathbf{u}) = f(\theta) + g(\alpha) + \mathbf{u}^T(\mathbf{A}\theta + \mathbf{B}\alpha - \mathbf{c}) + (\rho/2)\|\mathbf{A}\theta + \mathbf{B}\alpha - \mathbf{c}\|^2. \tag{16.19}$$

Here, $\mathbf{u}$ is a *dual variable*, and ρ is some positive constant. The ADMM algorithm for this problem is outlined in Algorithm 16.3.

Algorithm 16.3 ADMM Algorithm

Input: $\alpha^{(0)}$, $\mathbf{u}^{(0)}$, $\rho > 0$, $t = 1$.
repeat
  $\theta^{(t)} \in \arg\min_\theta \left\{L_\rho(\theta, \alpha^{(t-1)}, \mathbf{u}^{(t-1)})\right\}$
  $\alpha^{(t)} \in \arg\min_\alpha \left\{L_\rho(\theta^{(t)}, \alpha, \mathbf{u}^{(t-1)})\right\}$
  $\mathbf{u}^{(t)} \leftarrow \mathbf{u}^{(t-1)} + \rho(\mathbf{A}\theta^{(t)} + \mathbf{B}\alpha^{(t)} - \mathbf{c})$
  $t \leftarrow t + 1$
until *convergence;*

Essentially, ADMM provides a simple way to decouple the f and g functions in the optimization problem (Equation 16.18). In Algorithm 16.3, the update for θ involves f but not g, and the update for α involves g but not f. ADMM is an attractive choice when the updates for θ and α in Algorithm 16.3 have closed forms. In fact, when both $\mathbf{A}$ and $\mathbf{B}$ are orthogonal matrices, the updates for θ and α involve the proximal operator discussed in Section 16.4.2.

To recast Equation 16.1 into the form of Equation 16.18 so that an ADMM algorithm can be applied, we simply write

$$\underset{\beta,\alpha}{\text{minimize}} \{\mathcal{L}(\beta) + \lambda\mathcal{P}(\alpha)\} \text{ subject to } \beta - \alpha = \mathbf{0}. \tag{16.20}$$

Algorithm 16.3 can then be applied directly. As we will see in Section 16.5, this decoupling of the loss function $\mathcal{L}$ and the penalty function $\mathcal{P}$ can be quite beneficial in cases where both $\mathcal{L}$ and $\mathcal{P}$ are simple but where the coupling between them leads to challenges in optimization.

Convergence of the ADMM algorithm is guaranteed under some mild conditions (Eckstein and Bertsekas, 1992). However, ADMM can be slow in practice, in that many iterations of the updates for $\boldsymbol{\theta}$, $\boldsymbol{\alpha}$, and $\mathbf{u}$ in Algorithm 16.3 may be required for convergence to a reasonable level of accuracy. Strategies for varying the value of the ρ parameter in Equation 16.19 have been proposed to reduce the number of iterations required for convergence (Boyd et al., 2010).

16.5 Applications

In this section, we synthesize the ideas presented thus far by considering three specific applications. In each case, we combine a loss function from Section 16.2, a penalty from Section 16.3, and an algorithm from Section 16.4.

16.5.1 Multivariate Regression with the Group Lasso

Consider a generalization of the linear regression model introduced in Section 16.2.1 to a multivariate response, $Y \in \mathbb{R}^m$:

$$Y = \mathcal{B}X + \epsilon.$$

Here $\mathcal{B}$ is an $m \times p$ matrix of coefficients with each row corresponding to a response variable and $\epsilon \in \mathbb{R}^m$ is a vector of independent noise terms.

Suppose that we observe n independent draws from this model, giving $\mathbf{Y} \in \mathbb{R}^{n \times m}$ and $\mathbf{X} \in \mathbb{R}^{n \times p}$. Then a natural loss function is

$$\mathcal{L}(\mathcal{B}) = \frac{1}{2}\|\mathbf{Y} - \mathbf{X}\mathcal{B}^T\|_F^2. \tag{16.21}$$

By writing $\mathbf{y} = \text{vec}(\mathbf{Y})$ and $\boldsymbol{\beta} = \text{vec}(\mathcal{B}^T)$, we see that this problem can be reexpressed as in Equation 16.2 of Section 16.2.1, with design matrix $\mathbf{I}_m \otimes \mathbf{X}$.

Instead of simply estimating $\mathcal{B}$ as the minimizer of Equation 16.21, which would be equivalent to fitting m separate linear regression models, we can apply a penalty that allows us to borrow strength across the m problems. In machine learning, this sharing of information across related problems is known as multitask learning. For example, if we believe that certain predictors are completely irrelevant to all m responses, then we could impose a group lasso penalty on the columns of $\mathcal{B}$ (Argyriou et al., 2008; Obozinski et al., 2011b),

$$\underset{\mathcal{B}}{\text{minimize}} \left\{ \frac{1}{2}\|\mathbf{Y} - \mathbf{X}\mathcal{B}^T\|_F^2 + \lambda \sum_{j=1}^{p} \|\mathcal{B}_j\|_2 \right\}. \tag{16.22}$$

As a result of this penalty, the coefficient estimates for the jth feature will equal zero in all m regression problems or else will be nonzero in all m regression problems.

Because the penalty in Equation 16.22 is separable across the columns of $\mathcal{B}$, we can apply BCD to solve this problem. In the tth iteration, the block coordinate update for $\mathcal{B}_j$ is given by

$$\mathcal{B}_j^{(t)} \in \arg\min_{\mathcal{B}_j} \left\{ \frac{1}{2}\|\mathbf{R}^{-j} - \mathbf{X}_j\mathcal{B}_j^T\|_F^2 + \lambda\|\mathcal{B}_j\|_2 \right\}, \tag{16.23}$$

where

$$\mathbf{R}^{-j} = \mathbf{Y} - \sum_{k:k<j} \mathbf{X}_k \left(\mathcal{B}_k^{(t)}\right)^T - \sum_{k:k>j} \mathbf{X}_k \left(\mathcal{B}_k^{(t-1)}\right)^T$$

is the jth partial residual matrix. Assume, for ease of notation, that $\|\mathbf{X}_j\|_2 = 1$. After some algebra, one finds that the minimizer of Equation 16.23 is unique and that

$$\mathcal{B}_j^{(t)} = \arg\min_{\mathcal{B}_j} \left\{ \frac{1}{2}\|\mathcal{B}_j - (\mathbf{R}^{-j})^T\mathbf{X}_j\|_2^2 + \lambda\|\mathcal{B}_j\|_2 \right\}.$$

From Equations 16.11 and 16.12, the solution to the above is given by

$$\mathcal{B}_j^{(t)} = \max\left(1 - \frac{\lambda}{\|(\mathbf{R}^{-j})^T\mathbf{X}_j\|_2}, 0\right)(\mathbf{R}^{-j})^T\mathbf{X}_j.$$

Algorithm 16.4 displays the BCD approach to solving Equation 16.22. Further details are provided in Simon et al. (2013a).

Algorithm 16.4 BCD for Multivariate Regression with Group Lasso

Input: $\mathbf{X}$, $\mathbf{Y}$, $\lambda \geq 0$, $\mathcal{B}^{(0)}$, $t = 1$.
repeat
  for $j = 1, \ldots, p$ **do**
    $\mathbf{R}^{-j} \leftarrow \mathbf{Y} - \sum_{k:k<j} \mathbf{X}_k(\mathcal{B}_k^{(t)})^T - \sum_{k:k>j} \mathbf{X}_k(\mathcal{B}_k^{(t-1)})^T$
    $\mathbf{B}_j^{(t)} \leftarrow \max\left(1 - \frac{\lambda}{\|(\mathbf{R}^{-j})^T\mathbf{X}_j\|_2}, 0\right)(\mathbf{R}^{-j})^T\mathbf{X}_j$
  end
  $t \leftarrow t + 1$
until *convergence;*

16.5.2 Matrix Completion with the Nuclear Norm

Consider the matrix completion problem introduced in Section 16.2.2. As noted in that section, without additional assumptions on the structure of $\mathbf{\Gamma}$, the observed entries of $\mathbf{X}$ do not provide any information about the unobserved entries of $\mathbf{\Gamma}$.

A natural structural assumption is that $\mathbf{\Gamma}$ has low rank—that is, a small number of factors explains the variability in $\mathbf{\Gamma}$. Ji and Ye (2009), Cai et al. (2010), Mazumder et al. (2010), Ma et al. (2011), and others combine Equation 16.3 with the nuclear norm penalty introduced in Section 16.3.3 to yield the optimization problem

$$\underset{\mathbf{\Gamma}}{\text{minimize}} \left\{ \frac{1}{2} \sum_{(i,j)\in\mathcal{O}} (X_{ij} - \Gamma_{ij})^2 + \lambda\|\mathbf{\Gamma}\|_* \right\}. \tag{16.24}$$

The nuclear norm penalty is not separable in the sense discussed in Section 16.4.1, and therefore BCD is not a natural choice for solving Equation 16.24. Instead, we apply PGM, as in Ji and Ye (2009). Because

$$\frac{\partial\mathcal{L}}{\partial\Gamma_{ij}} = \begin{cases} \Gamma_{ij} - X_{ij} & \text{if } (i,j) \in \mathcal{O} \\ 0 & \text{otherwise,} \end{cases}$$

it follows that $\nabla\mathcal{L}$ has Lipschitz constant 1. Thus we can take the step size, $s = 1$. Therefore, in the tth iteration, the gradient step takes the form

$$\left[\mathbf{\Gamma}^{(t-1)} - \nabla\mathcal{L}(\mathbf{\Gamma}^{(t-1)})\right]_{ij} = \begin{cases} X_{ij} & \text{if } (i,j) \in \mathcal{O} \\ \Gamma_{ij}^{(t-1)} & \text{if } (i,j) \notin \mathcal{O}. \end{cases} \tag{16.25}$$

Algorithm 16.5 PGM for Matrix Completion

Input: $\mathbf{X}$, $\lambda \geq 0, \mathbf{\Gamma}^{(0)}, t = 1$.
repeat

$$\Theta_{ij} \leftarrow \begin{cases} X_{ij} & \text{if } (i,j) \in \mathcal{O} \\ \Gamma_{ij}^{(t-1)} & \text{if } (i,j) \notin \mathcal{O} \end{cases}$$

$[\mathbf{U}, \mathbf{diag}(\sigma_j), \mathbf{V}] \leftarrow \texttt{SingularValueDecomposition}(\mathbf{\Theta})$

$\mathbf{\Gamma}^{(t)} \leftarrow \mathbf{Udiag}(\mathcal{S}(\sigma_j, \lambda))\mathbf{V}^T$

$t \leftarrow t + 1$

until *convergence;*

Combining this with the nuclear norm proximal operator given in Section 16.3.3 leads to Algorithm 16.5 for solving Equation 16.24.

The repeated singular value decompositions in Algorithm 16.5 are computationally burdensome. Mazumder et al. (2010) observe that $\mathbf{\Gamma}^{(t-1)} - \nabla\mathcal{L}(\mathbf{\Gamma}^{(t-1)})$ in Equation 16.25 is the sum of a sparse matrix and a low-rank matrix and they exploit this structure to perform efficient computations.

16.5.3 Graphical Models with the Lasso

Consider the problem of estimating the conditional dependence relationships among elements of a multivariate normal random vector. As discussed in Section 16.2.3, this amounts to identifying the zero elements of the corresponding precision matrix. We can combine the loss function in Equation 16.4 with an ℓ_1 penalty to arrive at the convex optimization problem

$$\underset{\mathbf{\Omega}}{\text{minimize}} \left\{ -\text{logdet}\mathbf{\Omega} + \text{trace}(\mathbf{S\Omega}) + \lambda \sum_{i,j} |\Omega_{ij}| \right\}. \tag{16.26}$$

The solution to Equation 16.26 serves as an estimate for $\mathbf{\Sigma}^{-1}$. Equation 16.26 is known as the *graphical lasso* and has been studied extensively from a computational (Friedman et al., 2007; d'Aspremont et al., 2008; Yuan, 2008; Boyd et al., 2010; Scheinberg et al., 2010; Hsieh et al., 2011; Witten et al., 2011; Mazumder and Hastie, 2012a; Tran-Dinh et al., 2015) and theoretical (Yuan and Lin, 2007b; Rothman et al., 2008; Ravikumar et al., 2011) perspective. When λ is sufficiently large, the resulting estimate for $\mathbf{\Sigma}^{-1}$ will be sparse, leading to a sparse estimate for the conditional independence graph.

We now consider the problem of solving Equation 16.26. BCD has been used to solve Equation 16.26 (Friedman et al., 2007; d'Aspremont et al., 2008; Mazumder and Hastie, 2012b); however, the resulting algorithm is somewhat complex as each block coordinate update requires solving a lasso problem. By contrast, an ADMM algorithm for Equation 16.26 takes a particularly simple and elegant form (Boyd et al., 2010).

To apply ADMM to solve Equation 16.26, we rewrite the problem as

$$\underset{\mathbf{\Omega}, \tilde{\mathbf{\Omega}}}{\text{minimize}} \left\{ -\text{logdet}\mathbf{\Omega} + \text{trace}(\mathbf{S\Omega}) + \lambda \sum_{i,j} |\tilde{\Omega}_{ij}| \right\} \text{ subject to } \mathbf{\Omega} - \tilde{\mathbf{\Omega}} = \mathbf{0}. \tag{16.27}$$

The augmented Lagrangian (Equation 16.19) then takes the form

$$L_\rho(\mathbf{\Omega}, \tilde{\mathbf{\Omega}}, \mathbf{U}) = -\text{logdet}\mathbf{\Omega} + \text{trace}(\mathbf{S\Omega}) + \lambda \sum_{i,j} |\tilde{\Omega}_{ij}| + \text{trace}(\mathbf{U}^T(\mathbf{\Omega} - \tilde{\mathbf{\Omega}})) + (\rho/2)\|\mathbf{\Omega} - \tilde{\mathbf{\Omega}}\|_F^2.$$

To apply Algorithm 16.3, we need to find the value of $\mathbf{\Omega}$ that minimizes $L_\rho(\mathbf{\Omega}, \tilde{\mathbf{\Omega}}, \mathbf{U})$, with $\tilde{\mathbf{\Omega}}$ and $\mathbf{U}$ held fixed and to find the value of $\tilde{\mathbf{\Omega}}$ that minimizes $L_\rho(\mathbf{\Omega}, \tilde{\mathbf{\Omega}}, \mathbf{U})$, with $\mathbf{\Omega}$ and $\mathbf{U}$ held fixed. Completing the square reveals that the second of these problems entails a simple update involving the soft-thresholding operator (Equation 16.9). To minimize $L_\rho(\mathbf{\Omega}, \tilde{\mathbf{\Omega}}, \mathbf{U})$ with respect to $\mathbf{\Omega}$ with $\tilde{\mathbf{\Omega}}$ and $\mathbf{U}$ held fixed, we note that the solution will satisfy the optimality condition

$$\mathbf{\Omega}^{-1} - \rho\mathbf{\Omega} = \mathbf{S} + \mathbf{U} - \rho\tilde{\mathbf{\Omega}}.$$

This means that the eigenvectors of $\mathbf{\Omega}$ are the same as the eigenvectors of $\mathbf{S} + \mathbf{U} - \rho\tilde{\mathbf{\Omega}}$ and that the eigenvalues of $\mathbf{\Omega}$ are a simple function of the eigenvalues of $\mathbf{S} + \mathbf{U} - \rho\tilde{\mathbf{\Omega}}$. This function, which can be derived via the quadratic formula, takes the form

$$\mathcal{H}(\mathbf{Z}) = \mathbf{V}\mathbf{diag}\left(\frac{-e_i + \sqrt{e_i^2 + 4\rho}}{2\rho}\right)\mathbf{V}^T, \tag{16.28}$$

where $\mathbf{V}\mathbf{diag}(e_i)\mathbf{V}^T$ is the eigendecomposition of (a symmetric matrix) $\mathbf{Z}$. The function $\mathcal{H}$ will be used in Algorithm 16.6.

Details of the ADMM algorithm for solving Equation 16.26 are given in Algorithm 16.6. The updates for $\tilde{\mathbf{\Omega}}$ and $\mathbf{U}$ can be performed in $\mathcal{O}(p^2)$ operations, for $\mathbf{S}$ a $p \times p$ matrix. By contrast, the update for $\mathbf{\Omega}$ requires that we compute the eigen-decomposition of a $p \times p$ matrix; this requires $\mathcal{O}(p^3)$ operations.

Algorithm 16.6 ADMM for the Graphical Lasso

Input: $\mathbf{S} \succeq \mathbf{0}$, $\lambda \geq 0$, $\rho > 0$, $\tilde{\mathbf{\Omega}}^{(0)}$, $\mathbf{U}^{(0)}$, $t = 1$.
repeat
  $\mathbf{\Omega}^{(t)} \leftarrow \mathcal{H}(\mathbf{S} + \mathbf{U}^{(t-1)} - \rho\tilde{\mathbf{\Omega}}^{(t-1)})$ [$\mathcal{H}$ defined in (16.28)]
  $\tilde{\mathbf{\Omega}}^{(t)} \leftarrow \mathcal{S}(\mathbf{U}^{(t-1)} + \rho\mathbf{\Omega}^{(t)}, \lambda)/\rho$ [$\mathcal{S}$ defined in (16.9)]
  $\mathbf{U}^{(t)} \leftarrow \mathbf{U}^{(t-1)} + \rho(\mathbf{\Omega}^{(t)} - \tilde{\mathbf{\Omega}}^{(t)})$
  $t \leftarrow t + 1$
until *convergence;*

16.6 Discussion

The growing scale of modern datasets in research and in industry has opened the door to increasingly ambitious demands of data. It has become routine to fit models that are far more complex than would ever have been imagined previously. In many areas, the increase in the complexity of the models considered is in fact outpacing the growth of the sample sizes. This can lead to severe overfitting, unless problem-specific structural assumptions are built into the estimation procedure.

In this chapter, we have reviewed a powerful framework for making tractable what would otherwise be hopelessly underspecified statistical problems. The key idea is to strike a balance between good model fit to the data (through the loss function) and model simplicity (through the penalty function). This tension between flexibility and simplicity is not a new concept to statisticians, who refer to it as the *bias-variance tradeoff* (see, e.g., Hastie et al. 2009).

Within the *loss + penalty* framework of Equation 16.1, the value of λ is used to control where our estimator $\hat{\theta}$ lies in this tradeoff. When λ is small, we have a highly flexible model, which in the case of insufficient observations could be prone to overfitting. At the other extreme, when λ is large, we get a model that is less sensitive to the data observed, which is beneficial when there are not enough observations to support a more complex model. The optimal choice of the parameter λ depends on many factors that are unknowable to a data analyst. Conceptually, it depends on how much information the data contain about the unknown parameter $\boldsymbol{\theta}$, on the choice of penalty, and on the structure possessed by $\boldsymbol{\theta}$. In practice, cross-validation, AIC, and BIC are often used to select a value of λ (see, e.g., Hastie et al. 2009).

In recent years, the theoretical properties of the solution to Equation 16.1 have been studied extensively. A common thread in this work is that under a certain set of assumptions, if the complexity of the model is allowed to grow faster than the sample size, then penalized estimators can work reliably in settings where the classical unpenalized versions fail completely. Many authors have analyzed Equation 16.1 in the context of specific loss functions and specific penalties (see Bühlmann and van de Geer 2011 and references therein for a comprehensive overview of theoretical results). Negahban et al. (2012) consider Equation 16.1 in considerable generality.

Throughout this chapter, we have assumed that the loss and penalty functions are convex. As mentioned earlier, convex formulations are attractive from a computational standpoint—we do not have to worry about suboptimality of local minima, and we can apply standard optimization methods, such as those presented in Section 16.4. Beyond this, the convex framework has an advantage in that a solution $\hat{\boldsymbol{\theta}}$ to Equation 16.1 has a simple characterization in terms of a set of optimality conditions (see, e.g., Boyd and Vandenberghe 2004); this facilitates the study of its theoretical properties.

In this chapter, we have ignored a large literature of penalized estimation methods that make use of nonconvex penalties (Fan and Li, 2001; Zhang, 2010). These methods yield estimators that closely match the desired problem structure and that have attractive theoretical properties. However, they pay a price in terms of local minima and difficulties in computation.

In recent years, the success of penalized estimation techniques has led to a rich interplay between the fields of statistics and optimization. For example, Agarwal et al. (2012) revisit the theoretical convergence rate of PGM and show that a faster rate is obtained up to the level of accuracy that is of interest in a statistical context. Another recent line of work studies the tradeoffs between computational efficiency and statistical optimality (Berthet and Rigollet, 2013; Chandrasekaran and Jordan, 2013; Ma and Wu, 2015).

In this chapter, we have presented a flexible toolkit for fitting complex models to large-scale data. As the data continue to grow in scale, so too will the complexity of the questions being asked, and consequently the need for penalized estimation techniques to answer those questions.

Acknowledgments

JB was supported in part by NSF Award DMS-1405746 and DW was supported in part by NSF CAREER Award DMS-1252624.

References

Agarwal, A., Negahban, S. and Wainwright, M. J. (2012), Fast global convergence of gradient methods for high-dimensional statistical recovery, *The Annals of Statistics* **40**(5), 2452–2482.

Argyriou, A., Evgeniou, T. and Pontil, M. (2008), Convex multi-task feature learning, *Machine Learning* **73**(3), 243–272.

Beck, A. and Teboulle, M. (2009), A fast iterative shrinkage-thresholding algorithm for linear inverse problems, *SIAM Journal on Imaging Sciences* **2**(1), 183–202.

Berthet, Q. and Rigollet, P. (2013), Complexity theoretic lower bounds for sparse principal component detection, in: *Conference on Learning Theory*, pp. 1046–1066.

Bondell, H. D. and Reich, B. J. (2008), Simultaneous regression shrinkage, variable selection, and supervised clustering of predictors with OSCAR, *Biometrics* **64**(1), 115–123.

Boyd, S., Parikh, N., Chu, E., Peleato, B. and Eckstein, J. (2010), Distributed optimization and statistical learning via the ADMM, *Foundations and Trends in Machine Learning* **3**(1), 1–122.

Boyd, S. and Vandenberghe, L. (2004), *Convex Optimization*, Cambridge University Press, Cambridge.

Bühlmann, P. and van de Geer, S. (2011), *Statistics for High-Dimensional Data: Methods, Theory and Applications*, Springer, New York.

Cai, J.-F., Candès, E. J. and Shen, Z. (2010), A singular value thresholding algorithm for matrix completion, *SIAM Journal on Optimization* **20**(4), 1956–1982.

Candès, E. J. and Recht, B. (2009), Exact matrix completion via convex optimization, *Foundations of Computational Mathematics* **9**(6), 717–772.

Chandrasekaran, V. and Jordan, M. I. (2013), Computational and statistical tradeoffs via convex relaxation, *Proceedings of the National Academy of Sciences USA* **110**(13), E1181–E1190. http://www.pnas.org/content/110/13/E1181.abstract.

Chandrasekaran, V., Parrilo, P. A. and Willsky, A. S. (2012), Latent variable graphical model selection via convex optimization, *The Annals of Statistics* **40**(4), 1935–1967.

d'Aspremont, A., Banerjee, O. and El Ghaoui, L. (2008), First-order methods for sparse covariance selection, *SIAM Journal on Matrix Analysis and Applications* **30**(1), 56–66.

Eckstein, J. and Bertsekas, D. (1992), On the Douglas-Rachford splitting method and the proximal point algorithm for maximal monotone operators, *Mathematical Programming* **55**(3, Ser. A), 293–318.

Efron, B., Hastie, T., Johnstone, I. and Tibshirani, R. (2004), Least angle regression, *Annals of Statistics* **32**(2), 407–499.

El Ghaoui, L., Viallon, V. and Rabbani, T. (2012), Safe feature elimination in sparse supervised learning, *Pacific Journal of Optimization* **8**(4), 667–698.

Fan, J. and Li, R. (2001), Variable selection via nonconcave penalized likelihood and its oracle properties, *Journal of the American Statistical Association* **96**, 1348–1360.

Fazel, M. (2002), Matrix rank minimization with applications, PhD thesis, Stanford University, Stanford, CA.

Friedman, J., Hastie, T. and Tibshirani, R. (2007), Sparse inverse covariance estimation with the graphical lasso, *Biostatistics* **9**, 432–441.

Friedman, J. H., Hastie, T. and Tibshirani, R. (2010), Regularization paths for generalized linear models via coordinate descent, *Journal of Statistical Software* **33**(1), 1–22.

Gabay, D. and Mercier, B. (1976), A dual algorithm for the solution of nonlinear variational problems via finite element approximation, *Computers & Mathematics with Applications* **2**(1), 17–40.

Hastie, T., Tibshirani, R. and Friedman, J. (2009), *The Elements of Statistical Learning: Data Mining, Inference and Prediction*, Springer, New York.

Hocking, T. D., Joulin, A., Bach, F. et al. (2011), Clusterpath: An algorithm for clustering using convex fusion penalties, in: *28th International Conference on Machine Learning*, Bellevue, WA.

Hsieh, C.-J., Dhillon, I. S., Ravikumar, P. K. and Sustik, M. A. (2011), Sparse inverse covariance matrix estimation using quadratic approximation, in: *Advances in Neural Information Processing Systems*, pp. 2330–2338.

Jacob, L., Obozinski, G. and Vert, J.-P. (2009), Group lasso with overlap and graph lasso, in: *Proceedings of the 26th Annual International Conference on Machine Learning*, ACM, pp. 433–440.

Jenatton, R., Audibert, J.-Y. and Bach, F. (2011), Structured variable selection with sparsity-inducing norms, *The Journal of Machine Learning Research* **12**, 2777–2824.

Ji, S. and Ye, J. (2009), An accelerated gradient method for trace norm minimization, in: *Proceedings of the 26th Annual International Conference on Machine Learning*, ACM, pp. 457–464.

Kim, S.-J., Koh, K., Boyd, S. and Gorinevsky, D. (2009), ℓ_1 trend filtering, *SIAM Review* **51**(2), 339–360.

Koller, D. and Friedman, N. (2009), *Probabilistic Graphical Models: Principles and Techniques*, MIT Press, Cambridge, MA.

Ma, S., Goldfarb, D. and Chen, L. (2011), Fixed point and Bregman iterative methods for matrix rank minimization, *Mathematical Programming* **128**(1–2), 321–353.

Ma, S., Xue, L. and Zou, H. (2013), Alternating direction methods for latent variable Gaussian graphical model selection, *Neural Computation* **25**, 2172–2198.

Ma, Z. and Wu, Y. (2015), Computational barriers in minimax submatrix detection, *Annals of Statistics* **43**, 1089–1116.

Mardia, K., Kent, J. and Bibby, J. (1979), *Multivariate Analysis*, Academic Press, New York.

Mazumder, R. and Hastie, T. (2012a), Exact covariance thresholding into connected components for large-scale graphical lasso, *Journal of Machine Learning Research* **13**, 781–794.

Mazumder, R. and Hastie, T. (2012b), The graphical lasso: New insights and alternatives, *Electronic Journal of Statistics* **6**, 2125–2149.

Mazumder, R., Hastie, T. and Tibshirani, R. (2010), Spectral regularization algorithms for learning large incomplete matrices, *The Journal of Machine Learning Research* **11**, 2287–2322.

Negahban, S. N., Ravikumar, P., Wainwright, M. J. and Yu, B. (2012), A unified framework for high-dimensional analysis of M-estimators with decomposable regularizers, *Statistical Science* **27**(4), 538–557.

Nesterov, Y. (2013), Gradient methods for minimizing composite functions, *Mathematical Programming* **140**(1), 125–161.

Obozinski, G., Jacob, L. and Vert, J. (2011a), Group lasso with overlaps: The latent group lasso approach, arXiv:1110.0413.

Obozinski, G., Wainwright, M. J., Jordan, M. I. et al. (2011b), Support union recovery in high-dimensional multivariate regression, *The Annals of Statistics* **39**(1), 1–47.

Osborne, M., Presnell, B. and Turlach, B. (2000), A new approach to variable selection in least squares problems, *IMA Journal of Numerical Analysis* **20**, 389–404.

Parikh, N. and Boyd, S. (2013), Proximal algorithms, *Foundations and Trends in Optimization* **1**(3), 123–231.

Ravikumar, P., Wainwright, M. J., Raskutti, G. et al. (2011), High-dimensional covariance estimation by minimizing ℓ_1-penalized log-determinant divergence, *Electronic Journal of Statistics* **5**, 935–980.

Rothman, A., Bickel, P., Levina, E. and Zhu, J. (2008), Sparse permutation invariant covariance estimation, *Electronic Journal of Statistics* **2**, 494–515.

Scheinberg, K., Ma, S. and Goldfarb, D. (2010), Sparse inverse covariance selection via alternating linearization methods, in: *Advances in Neural Information Processing Systems*, pp. 2101–2109.

She, Y. (2010), Sparse regression with exact clustering, *Electronic Journal of Statistics* **4**, 1055–1096.

Simon, N., Friedman, J. and Hastie, T. (2013a), A blockwise descent algorithm for group-penalized multiresponse and multinomial regression, arXiv:1311.6529.

Simon, N., Friedman, J., Hastie, T. and Tibshirani, R. (2013b), A sparse-group lasso, *Journal of Computational and Graphical Statistics* **22**(2), 231–245.

Tibshirani, R. (1996), Regression shrinkage and selection via the lasso, *Journal of the Royal Statistical Society: Series B (Statistical Methodology)* **58**, 267–288.

Tibshirani, R. (1997), The lasso method for variable selection in the Cox model, *Statistics in Medicine* **16**, 385–395.

Tibshirani, R. (2011), Regression shrinkage and selection via the lasso: A retrospective, *Journal of the Royal Statistical Society: Series B (Statistical Methodology)* **73**(3), 273–282.

Tibshirani, R., Bien, J., Friedman, J., Hastie, T., Simon, N., Taylor, J. and Tibshirani, R. J. (2012), Strong rules for discarding predictors in lasso-type problems, *Journal of the Royal Statistical Society: Series B (Statistical Methodology)* **74**(2), 245–266.

Tibshirani, R., Saunders, M., Rosset, S., Zhu, J. and Knight, K. (2005), Sparsity and smoothness via the fused lasso, *Journal of the Royal Statistical Society: Series B* **67**, 91–108.

Tibshirani, R. J. (2014), Adaptive piecewise polynomial estimation via trend filtering, *The Annals of Statistics* **42**(1), 285–323.

Tibshirani, R. J., Hoefling, H. and Tibshirani, R. (2011), Nearly-isotonic regression, *Technometrics* **53**(1), 54–61.

Tibshirani, R. J. and Taylor, J. (2011), The solution path of the generalized lasso, *The Annals of Statistics* **39**(3), 1335–1371.

Tran-Dinh, Q., Kyrillidis, A. and Cevher, V. (2015), Composite self-concordant minimization, *The Journal of Machine Learning Research* **16**, 371–416.

Tseng, P. (2001), Convergence of a block coordinate descent method for nondifferentiable minimization, *Journal of Optimization Theory and Applications* **109**(3), 475–494.

Wang, J., Zhou, J., Wonka, P. and Ye, J. (2013), Lasso screening rules via dual polytope projection, in: C. Burges, L. Bottou, M. Welling, Z. Ghahramani and K. Weinberger, eds, *Advances in Neural Information Processing Systems 26*, Curran Associates, pp. 1070–1078.

Witten, D., Friedman, J. and Simon, N. (2011), New insights and faster computations for the graphical lasso, *Journal of Computational and Graphical Statistics* **20(4)**, 892–900.

Xiang, Z. J., Wang, Y. and Ramadge, P. J. (2014), Screening tests for lasso problems, arXiv:1405.4897.

Yuan, M. (2008), Efficient computation of ℓ_1 regularized estimates in Gaussian graphical models, *Journal of Computational and Graphical Statistics* **17(4)**, 809–826.

Yuan, M., Ekici, A., Lu, Z. and Monteiro, R. (2007), Dimension reduction and coefficient estimation in multivariate linear regression, *Journal of the Royal Statistical Society: Series B (Statistical Methodology)* **69**(3), 329–346.

Yuan, M. and Lin, Y. (2007a), Model selection and estimation in regression with grouped variables, *Journal of the Royal Statistical Society, Series B* **68**, 49–67.

Yuan, M. and Lin, Y. (2007b), Model selection and estimation in the Gaussian graphical model, *Biometrika* **94**(10), 19–35.

Zhang, C.-H. (2010), Nearly unbiased variable selection under minimax concave penalty, *The Annals of Statistics* **38**(2), 894–942.

Zhao, P., Rocha, G. and Yu, B. (2009), The composite absolute penalties family for grouped and hierarchical variable selection, *The Annals of Statistics* **37**(6A), 3468–3497.

17

High-Dimensional Regression and Inference

Lukas Meier

CONTENTS

17.1 Introduction 305
17.2 Model Selection and Parameter Estimation 306
17.2.1 Ridge Regression and the Lasso 307
17.3 Extending Classical Inference Procedures 308
17.3.1 Ridge Projection 308
17.3.2 Lasso Projection 309
17.3.3 Extension to Generalized Linear Models 311
17.3.4 Covariance Test 311
17.4 Subsampling, Sample Splitting, and p-Value Aggregation 312
17.4.1 From Selection Frequencies to Stability Selection 312
17.4.2 Sample Splitting and p-Value Aggregation 313
17.5 Hierarchical Approaches 314
17.5.1 Group-Bound Confidence Intervals 316
17.6 Discussion and Outlook 316
References 317

17.1 Introduction

Linear (or generalized) linear models are probably the most widely used statistical analysis tools in all areas of applications. Combined with regularization approaches (see Section 17.2) they can easily handle situations where the number of predictors greatly exceeds the number of observations (high-dimensional data). Despite their structural simplicity, (generalized) linear models often perform very well in such situations. In addition, they can be used as *screening tools*: the selected predictors form the basis for more complex models (e.g., models that include interactions or nonlinear functions).

These properties make (generalized) linear models also potentially attractive in the context of *big data*, where both the number of observations and the number of features (predictors) are very large. As is typical with new technologies, the number of features is growing at a much faster rate than the number of observations. For example, new sensor technology in smartphones offers a very detailed view of the physical activity of a user, while the number of observations (the users) stays more or less constant. In that sense, *big data* is typically also high-dimensional data. Of course, a very large number of observations also call for new efficient algorithms.

While there exist numerous theoretical results regarding estimation and model selection properties of many regularization-based approaches (see, e.g., [4] or [7]), only recently progress has been made regarding the assignment of uncertainty (statistical inference) [13,15,19,21,29,31,32].

We illustrate a (biased) selection of inference procedures and show how they can be applied in R. Our focus is on a fundamental understanding of the methods and on their appropriate application. Therefore, a lot of mathematical details will be skipped.

The rest of this chapter is organized as follows: In Section 17.2, we give a (short) overview of some of the model selection and parameter estimation procedures that are based on regularization. In Section 17.3, we illustrate methods that allow for frequentist inference for regularization approaches in high-dimensional situations, while in Section 17.4, we focus on resampling-based methods. In Section 17.5, we present some hierarchical inference approaches. Parts of this chapter are based on restructured versions of [3] and [5].

17.2 Model Selection and Parameter Estimation

We consider the usual linear regression setup, where we have a response vector $Y = (Y_1, \ldots, Y_n)^T \in \mathbb{R}^n$ and an $n \times p$ design matrix X whose columns (predictors) we denote by $X^{(j)}, j = 1, \ldots, p$. The classical linear regression model is

$$Y = X\beta + E \tag{17.1}$$

where $\beta = (\beta_1, \ldots, \beta_p)^T \in \mathbb{R}^p$ is the coefficient vector and $E = (E_1, \ldots, E_n) \in \mathbb{R}^n$ contains the random errors. Usual assumptions are: E_i i.i.d. $\sim \mathcal{N}(0, \sigma^2)$, that is, the errors are independent and follow a normal distribution with constant variance σ^2. In the classical low-dimensional case ($n \gg p$), the least-squares estimator of model 17.1 is given by

$$\widehat{\beta} = (X^T X)^{-1} X^T Y$$

and tests and confidence intervals for β can be easily derived, see Section 17.3.

The main goal in high-dimensional regression problems ($p \gg n$) is dimensionality reduction, that is, model selection. We denote by

$$S = \{j;\ \beta_j \neq 0\}$$

the active set of the parameter vector β. Moreover, let $s = |S|$ be the cardinality of S. We assume that the underlying true model is sparse, that is, $s < n \ll p$.

The selected (or estimated) model is denoted by $\hat{S} \subseteq \{1, \ldots, p\}$. Ideally, a model selection procedure should be model selection consistent, meaning that $\hat{S} = S$ with high probability. A less stringent criterion is the so-called screening property, where we require that $S \subseteq \hat{S}$ with high probability. This means that we can (possibly dramatically) reduce the predictor space without *missing anything* from the underlying true model.

For $p > n$, the regression model 17.1 is overparametrized. We can always find a parameter vector β that gives a perfect fit to the data. In addition, the model 17.1 is not identifiable because there are always other vectors $\beta^* \in \mathbb{R}^p$ that lead to the same prediction $X\beta = X\beta^*$. In fact, this holds true for any $\beta^* = \beta + \xi$, if $\xi \in \mathbb{R}^p$ lies in the null space of X. Hence, any method will need further assumptions on the design matrix X, see, for example, [28] for the lasso estimator defined in Equation 17.3.

A common approach to do model selection and parameter estimation in high-dimensional regression problems is regularization. In the following, we implicitly assume that the design matrix is suitably centered and scaled.

17.2.1 Ridge Regression and the Lasso

A *classical* regularization estimator is ridge regression [12] that penalizes the ℓ_2-norm of the coefficient vector,

$$\widehat{\beta}_{\text{Ridge}} = \arg\min_{\beta} \left\{ \frac{1}{n}\|Y - X\beta\|_2^2 + \lambda \sum_{j=1}^{p} \beta_j^2 \right\} \tag{17.2}$$

for some tuning parameter $\lambda > 0$, where $\|x\|_2^2 = \sum_{i=1}^{n} x_i^2$ for $x \in \mathbb{R}^n$. The ridge estimator is given by

$$\widehat{\beta}_{\text{Ridge}} = \left(\widehat{\Sigma} + \lambda I_p\right)^{-1} \frac{1}{n} X^T Y$$

where I_p is the p-dimensional identity matrix and

$$\widehat{\Sigma} = \frac{1}{n} X^T X$$

Hence, the ridge estimator is a linear estimator. Note, however, that it is *not* sparse, that is, it *cannot* be used for model selection, but it allows for (unique) parameter estimation in a high-dimensional setting. In addition, $\widehat{\beta}_{\text{Ridge}}$ has the property that it always lies in the row space of X, leading to a potentially large projection bias (if the true coefficient vector β does not lie in the row space of X).

An alternative and more *modern* regularization method is the lasso [27] that penalizes the ℓ_1-norm of the coefficients,

$$\widehat{\beta}_{\text{Lasso}} = \arg\min_{\beta} \left\{ \frac{1}{n}\|Y - X\beta\|_2^2 + \lambda \sum_{j=1}^{p} |\beta_j| \right\} \tag{17.3}$$

There is no closed-form solution available anymore in the general case, but there exist efficient algorithms to solve the optimization problem (Equation 17.3), see [6,8]. Because of the geometry of the ℓ_1-norm, the lasso is a sparse estimator, that is, some components of $\widehat{\beta}_{\text{Lasso}}$ are shrunken exactly to zero, meaning that the lasso simultaneously performs model selection and parameter estimation. A lot of alternatives and extensions have been proposed, see, for example, [11] for an overview. Of course, the lasso is not the only estimator leading to a sparse solution.

Ridge Regression and lasso in R

Both ridge and lasso are available in R, for example, through the function `lm.ridge` in the package `MASS` [30] or the function `glmnet` in the package `glmnet` [8] (among many others). For the lasso, the syntax is as follows:

```
> fit <- glmnet(x, y) ## lasso for various values of lambda
                      ## x: design matrix, y: response vector
> plot(fit) ## plot the whole solution path
> fit.cv <- cv.glmnet(x, y) ## perform cross-validation (cv)
> coef(fit.cv) ## coefficient vector for cv-optimal lambda
```

17.3 Extending Classical Inference Procedures

Classical frequentist inference deals with (individual) testing problems of the form

$$H_{0,j} : \beta_j = 0$$

versus, for example, alternatives $H_{A,j} : \beta_j \neq 0$. Similarly, groupwise (simultaneous) tests

$$H_{0,G} : \beta_j = 0 \text{ for all } j \in G$$

versus $H_{A,G} = H_{0,G}^c$, where $G \subseteq \{1, \ldots, p\}$ is a group (subset) of predictors, can be performed. More informatively, we can always construct the corresponding confidence intervals (regions) by *collecting* all null hypotheses that cannot be rejected by the statistical test at the appropriate significance level.

To perform a test for β_j on some significance level α, we need the (asymptotic) distribution of $\widehat{\beta}_j$ (or a function thereof) under the null hypothesis $H_{0,j}$. For the standard least-squares estimator of the model 17.1, we have

$$\widehat{\beta} \sim \mathcal{N}_p\left(\beta, \sigma^2 (X^T X)^{-1}\right)$$

Therefore,

$$\frac{\widehat{\beta}_j - \beta_j}{\sigma\sqrt{(X^T X)_{jj}^{-1}}} \sim \mathcal{N}(0, 1)$$

if $n \gg p$ and if no model selection is involved (or the t-distribution if we also estimate σ). We will now illustrate some similar results in the high-dimensional situation where $p \gg n$.

17.3.1 Ridge Projection

As the ridge estimator is a linear estimator, the covariance matrix of $\widehat{\beta}_{\text{Ridge}}$ can be easily derived, we denote it by $\sigma^2\Omega$, where Ω is given by

$$\Omega = \frac{1}{n}\left(\widehat{\Sigma} + \lambda I_p\right)^{-1} \widehat{\Sigma} \left(\widehat{\Sigma} + \lambda I_p\right)^{-1}$$

Moreover, let θ be the projection of β on the row space of X, that is,

$$\theta = P_X \beta$$

where P_X is the corresponding projection matrix. Remember that $\widehat{\beta}_{\text{Ridge}}$ is an estimator of θ. Under suitable assumptions on the design matrix X, we can neglect the estimation bias of $\widehat{\beta}_{\text{Ridge}}$ with respect to θ [23], and have

$$\frac{(\widehat{\beta}_{\text{Ridge}} - \theta)}{\sigma} \approx \mathcal{N}_p(0, \Omega)$$

for λ suitably small.

However, we are interested in β and not θ. This means that we have to do an additional correction for the projection bias. Because $\theta = P_X \beta$, we have

$$\frac{\theta_j}{P_{X;jj}} = \beta_j + \sum_{k \neq j} \frac{P_{X;jk}}{P_{X;jj}} \beta_k$$

Therefore, the projection bias corrected ridge estimator is defined as

$$\widehat{b}_j = \frac{\widehat{\beta}_{\text{ridge};j}}{P_{X;jj}} - \sum_{k \neq j} \frac{P_{X;jk}}{P_{X;jj}} \widehat{\beta}_k$$

where $\widehat{\beta}$ is an initial estimator, typically the ordinary lasso (when regressing Y vs. X). Under (mild) assumptions, we have

$$\frac{(\widehat{b}_j - \beta_j)}{\sigma\sqrt{\Omega_{jj}}/P_{X;jj}} \approx Z_j + \Delta_j,\ Z_j \sim \mathcal{N}(0,1) \tag{17.4}$$

for large n (and p) and some nonnegligible Δ_j, see [2] for more details. More generally, we can also derive the (joint) distribution of $\widehat{b} = (\widehat{b}_1, \ldots, \widehat{b}_p)^T$ for doing simultaneous tests.

In practice, we do *not* know the error variance σ^2. We will use a (fully automatic) plug-in estimate based on the scaled lasso [24] as a default value. Note that the estimation of σ in the high-dimensional set-up is non-trivial, see, for example, [22] for a comparison of different approaches.

p-values based on the distribution of Equation 17.4 are *individual* p-values. Multiple-testing correction is possible using standard techniques.

Ridge Projection in R

We use the function `ridge.proj` in the R-package `hdi` [17]. We get a fitted object by calling

```
> fit.ridge <- ridge.proj(x, y)
```

p-values for the (standard) null hypotheses $\beta_j = 0$ are stored in `pval`. Multiple-testing corrected p-values can be found in `pval.corr`. It is also possible to manually adjust the p-values by, for example, applying

```
> p.adjust(fit.ridge$pval, method = "BY")
```

if we are interested in controlling the false-discovery rate according to method `"BY"` that stands for *Benjamini & Yekutieli* [1].

If we want to (simultaneously) test whether $\beta_G = 0$ for $G = \{1, 2, 3\}$, we can get the corresponding p-value by calling

```
> fit.ridge$groupTest(group = 1:3)
```

Individual confidence intervals can be calculated by applying the common extractor function `confint` on the fitted object.

```
> confint(fit.ridge, level = 0.95)
```

17.3.2 Lasso Projection

The lasso estimator is sparse, and even for fixed p, we asymptotically have a point mass at zero [14], making statistical inference difficult (see also the comments in [5]).

The theoretical properties of the ridge estimator were mainly based on its linear form. We were able to write the components of $\widehat{\beta}_{\text{Ridge}}$ as

$$\widehat{\beta}_{\text{Ridge},j} = (Z^{(j)})^T Y$$

for some so-called score vector $Z^{(j)}$. This does not hold true anymore for the lasso estimator. However, for *any* score vector $Z^{(j)}$, we have

$$\mathbb{E}[(Z^{(j)})^T Y] = (Z^{(j)})^T X^{(j)} \beta_j + \sum_{k \neq j} (Z^{(j)})^T X^{(k)} \beta_k$$

A linear but biased estimator of β_j is therefore given by

$$\widehat{b}_j = \frac{(Z^{(j)})^T Y}{(Z^{(j)})^T X^{(j)}}$$

with

$$\mathbb{E}[\widehat{b}_j] = \beta_j + \sum_{k \neq j} P_{jk} \beta_k$$

where

$$P_{jk} = \frac{(Z^{(j)})^T X^{(k)}}{(Z^{(j)})^T X^{(j)}}$$

In the low-dimensional case, we can find a $Z^{(j)}$ that is orthogonal to all $X^{(k)}, k \neq j$, by defining $Z^{(j)}$ as the residuals when regressing $X^{(j)}$ versus $X^{(k)}, k \neq j$ (leading to an unbiased estimator). In fact, this is how the classical OLS estimator can be obtained. This is not possible anymore in the high-dimensional situation. However, we can use a *lasso projection* by defining $Z^{(j)}$ as the residuals of a lasso regression of $X^{(j)}$ versus all other predictor variables $X^{(k)}, k \neq j$, leading to the bias corrected estimator

$$\widehat{b}_j = \frac{(Z^{(j)})^T Y}{(Z^{(j)})^T X^{(j)}} - \sum_{k \neq j} P_{jk} \widehat{\beta}_{\text{Lasso},k}$$

where $\widehat{\beta}_{\text{Lasso}}$ is the lasso estimator when regressing Y versus all predictors in X. In contrast to $\widehat{\beta}_{\text{Lasso}}$, the estimator $\widehat{b}$ is *not* sparse anymore, that is, the lasso estimator got *de-sparsified.* Asymptotic theory is available for the *de-sparsified* estimator. Under suitable regularity conditions, it holds that for large n (and p)

$$\frac{(\widehat{b}_j - \beta_j)}{\sigma\sqrt{\Omega_{jj}}} \approx \mathcal{N}(0, 1)$$

where

$$\Omega_{jj} = \frac{(Z^{(j)})^T Z^{(j)}}{\left((X^{(j)})^T Z^{(j)}\right)^2}$$

and similarly for the multivariate counterpart. See [29] for details, also the uniformity of convergence.

A major drawback of the lasso projection approach is the computation of the p different lasso regressions for the regularized projection step. However, the problem is highly parallelizable by construction.

Lasso Projection in R

We use the function `lasso.proj` in the R-package `hdi`. It shares a very similar interface and output structure with the function `ridge.proj`. We get a fitted object using

```
> fit.lasso <- lasso.proj(x, y)
```

Again, p-values for the (standard) null hypotheses $\beta_j = 0$ are stored in `pval` and their multiple-testing counterparts in `pval.corr`. It is also possible to do simultaneous tests, for example, for $G = \{1, 2, 3\}$,

```
> fit.lasso$groupTest(group = 1:3)
```

and to get the confidence intervals using the function `confint`.

The method can be parallelized by setting the option `parallel = TRUE` (and using a suitable value for `ncores`). In addition, user-defined score vectors can be supplied through the argument `Z`.

17.3.3 Extension to Generalized Linear Models

Conceptually, the presented methods can be extended to generalized linear models by using a weighted squared-error approach [5]. The idea is to first apply a (standard) ℓ_1-penalized maximum likelihood (lasso) estimator and use its solution to construct the corresponding weighted least-squares problem (in the spirit of the iteratively re-weighted least-squares algorithm IRLS). The presented methods can then be applied to the re-weighted problem.

Extensions to Generalized Linear Models in R

Both methods have a `family` argument. If we have a binary outcome Y, we can use

```
> fit.ridge <- ridge.proj(x, y, family = "binomial")
```

to fit a logistic regression model with a binary response `y` using the ridge projection method.

17.3.4 Covariance Test

Another recent method that is also available in R is the so-called covariance test [15] and its extension, the *spacing test* [26] (requiring fewer assumptions and with exact finite sample results). The idea is to do sequential inference along the lasso solution path (similar as in forward stepwise regression) by performing a (conditional) test whenever a predictor enters the path. A heuristic to extend the methods to generalized linear models (GLMs) is available, again through the IRLS approach.

Compared to the previous methods, the covariance test is a *conditional* test. Although theory and more importantly software yield p-values on an individual variable level, interpretation is now different. A p-value is now rather corresponding to a lasso step than to the individual variable entering at the corresponding step; for a new dataset, we might see a different variable at the same step. See also the discussion of [15] and the corresponding rejoinder. An analogous example for this different philosophy can be found in the rejoinder of [15], when trying to determine the test error of the k-step lasso solution by cross-validation, we would run the lasso on different subsets of the dataset and average the observed test errors. A different model (with respect to the selected variables, but not size) is potentially being selected at every cross-validation iteration.

Covariance Test in R

We use the R-package `covTest` [25]. For the linear case, it needs a `lars` object [10] as input.

```
> fit.lars    <- lars(x, y)
> fit.covTest <- covTest(fit.lars, x, y)
```

The p-values are stored in `results`. The call for the GLM situation is very similar

```
> fit.lars.glm     <- lars.glm(x, y, family = "binomial")
> fit.covTest.glm <- covTest(fit.lars.glm, x = x, y = y)
```

17.4 Subsampling, Sample Splitting, and p-Value Aggregation

17.4.1 From Selection Frequencies to Stability Selection

Because sparse estimators have a point mass at zero, it is not straightforward to apply bootstrap or subsampling techniques to do inference or to construct confidence intervals.

Nevertheless, bootstrap techniques have been widely used in model selection problems to assess the *stability* of a selected model. The idea is to focus on those predictors that are still being selected when the dataset is being *reshuffled*. The selection frequency of a predictor (in a total of B samples) can therefore be used as a heuristic measure of its stability.

A theoretical foundation of such an approach can be found in [20]. Assume that we have a model selection procedure that selects (on average) q predictors (for example, by using the q predictors that enter the lasso path first when varying the penalty parameter λ). At every iteration b, we perform the following steps, $b = 1, \ldots, B$, for example, $B = 500$.

1. Draw subsample $I_b^* \subset \{1, \ldots, n\}$ (without replacement) of size $\lfloor n/2 \rfloor$.
2. Apply the model selection procedure to subsampled data leading to $\widehat{S}_b^* = \widehat{S}(I_b^*)$.

This allows us to calculate an empirical selection frequency $\widehat{\pi}_j$ for every predictor $x^{(j)}$, $j = 1, \ldots, p$,

$$\widehat{\pi}_j = \frac{1}{B} \#\{b;\, j \in \widehat{S}_b^*\}$$

For a frequency threshold $1/2 < \pi_{\text{thres}} < 1$, we define our final model as

$$\widehat{S} = \{j;\, \widehat{\pi}_j \geq \pi_{\text{thres}}\}$$

This means that we use those predictors in our final model that are being selected in at least $\pi_{\text{thres}} \times 100\%$ of the subsamples.

Under suitable assumptions, we have control of the expected number of false positives:

$$\mathbb{E}[V] \leq \frac{1}{2\pi_{\text{thres}} - 1} \frac{q^2}{p} \tag{17.5}$$

where $V = |\widehat{S} \cap S^c|$, see [20] for details. If we use

$$q = \sqrt{\alpha p (2\pi_{\text{thres}} - 1)}$$

we can control the familywise error rate at level $\alpha \in (0, 1)$, that is,

$$P(V > 0) \leq \alpha$$

In practice, we typically specify a bound on $\mathbb{E}[V]$ (the expected number of false positives that we are willing to tolerate) and a threshold π_{thres} (e.g., $\pi_{\text{thres}} = 0.75$). Using Equation 17.5 we can then derive the corresponding value of q to ensure control of $\mathbb{E}[V]$.

Stability Selection in R

We use the function `stability` in the R-package `hdi`. If we want to control $\mathbb{E}[V] \leq 1$, we use

```
> fit.stability <- stability(x, y, EV = 1)
```

A default value of $\pi_{\text{thres}} = 0.75$ is being used. The *stable* predictors can be found in `select` and the selection frequency of every predictor in `freq`. By construction, the algorithm is highly parallelizable (use the options `parallel` and `ncores`).

By default, the model selection criterion uses the first q predictors in the lasso path of the linear model (implemented in the function `lasso.firstq`). Extensions to other models (beyond the linear model) are straightforward by setting the argument `model.selector` appropriately. This means that the function can be applied to *any* method that provides an appropriate model selection function.

17.4.2 Sample Splitting and p-Value Aggregation

Other approaches are based on sample splitting [21,31]. The idea is to split the dataset into two (disjoint) parts: the first part is used for model selection where the high-dimensional problem is reduced to a *reasonable* size (e.g., using the lasso). The second part is used for (classical) low-dimensional statistical inference (using the selected model on the first part). The p-values on the second part are *honest* as the two parts of the dataset are disjoint. In more details, the algorithm in [31] works as follows:

1. Partition the sample $\{1, \ldots, n\} = I_1 \cup I_2$ with $I_1 \cap I_2 = \emptyset$ and $|I_1| = \lfloor n/2 \rfloor$ and $|I_2| = n - \lfloor n/2 \rfloor$.
2. Using only I_1, select the variables $\hat{S} \subseteq \{1, \ldots, p\}$. Assume or enforce that $|\hat{S}| \leq |I_1| = \lfloor n/2 \rfloor \leq |I_2|$.
3. Using classical least-squares theory, compute p-values $P_{\text{raw,j}}$ for $H_{0,j}$, for $j \in \hat{S}$ using only I_2. For $j \notin \hat{S}$, assign $P_{\text{raw},j} = 1$.
4. Adjust p-values for multiple testing using Bonferroni correction on the selected model $\hat{S}$ (with $|\hat{S}| \ll p$),

$$P_{\text{corr},j} = \min(P_j \cdot |\hat{S}|, 1)$$

If the selected model $\hat{S}$ contains the true model S, the p-values are correct. For any model selection procedure with the screening property, we therefore (asymptotically) get p-values $P_{\text{corr},j}$ controlling the familywise error rate.

To get reproducible results (that do not depend on a single data split), we can run the sample splitting algorithm B times, for example, $B = 50$ or $B = 100$, yielding B different p-values for every predictor,

$$P^{[1]}_{\text{corr},j}, \ldots, P^{[B]}_{\text{corr},j}, \; j = 1, \ldots, p$$

Clearly, the different p-values corresponding to the same predictor are not independent. Nevertheless, we can aggregate them using an (arbitrary) prespecified γ-quantile, $0 < \gamma < 1$, leading to

$$Q_j(\gamma) = \min\left(\text{emp. } \gamma\text{-quantile}\{P^{[b]}_{\text{corr},j}/\gamma;\ b = 1, \ldots, B\}, 1\right) \tag{17.6}$$

the so-called quantile aggregated p-values, see [21] for details. The price that we have to pay for using a (potentially small) quantile is the factor $1/\gamma$. For example, if we choose the median, we have to multiply all p-values by the factor of 2. This is called the multisample splitting algorithm [21]. It is loosely related to stability selection. For example, for $\gamma = 0.5$, we require a predictor to be selected in at least 50% of the sample splits with a small enough p-value. Moreover, quantile aggregation as defined in Equation 17.6 is a general (conservative) p-value aggregation procedure that works under *arbitrary* dependency structures.

A priori it is not clear how to select the parameter γ. We can even search for the best γ-quantile in a range $(\gamma_{\min}, 1)$, for example, $\gamma_{\min} = 0.05$, leading to the aggregated p-value,

$$P_j = \min\left((1 - \log(\gamma_{\min})) \inf_{\gamma \in (\gamma_{\min}, 1)} Q_j(\gamma), 1\right) \quad j = 1, \ldots, p$$

The price for this additional search is the factor $1 - \log(\gamma_{\min})$. Under suitable assumptions, the p-values P_j are controlling the familywise error rate [21]. The smaller we choose $\gamma_{\min}$, the more susceptible we are again to a specific realization of the B sample splits. Therefore, we should choose a large value of B in situations where γ is small.

Multisample Splitting in R

We use the function `multi.split` in the R-package `hdi`.

```
> fit.multi <- multi.split(x, y)
```

We can use any model for which there is a model selection function (defined in argument `model.selector`) and a *classical* p-value function (argument `classical.fit`). The default uses lasso (with cross-validation) and a linear model fit. Extensions to GLMs and many more models are (from a technical point of view) straightforward.

The p-values are stored in `pval.corr`. Note that by construction the multisample splitting algorithm (only) provides p-values for familywise error control.

Confidence intervals can also be obtained through the function `confint`; however, the level has already to be set in the call of the function `multi.split` (argument `ci.level`).

17.5 Hierarchical Approaches

In most applications we are faced with (strongly) correlated design matrices. Already in the low-dimensional case, two strongly correlated predictors might have large (individual) p-values, while the joint null hypothesis can be clearly rejected. Moreover, too strong correlation in the design matrix might also violate assumptions of the previously discussed methods regarding identifiability. It is therefore desirable to have hierarchical approaches that start at the *global* null hypothesis that tests whether *any* of the predictors has an influence on the response. If yes, one continues to some *finer granularity* depending on the signal strength and the correlation structure of the design matrix. To do so, we can use a hierarchical clustering approach [9], with a distance measure based on the correlation matrix of the design matrix. See Figure 17.1 for an example of a cluster dendrogram (based on the example in R below). We use a *top-down* approach where we start at the root node that corresponds to the global null hypothesis

$$H_{0,G_0} : \beta_{G_0} = 0$$

for $G_0 = \{1, \ldots, p\}$. If we can reject this null hypothesis, we continue testing the corresponding clusters in the next hierarchy level. We stop going down the hierarchy tree as soon as we cannot reject a null hypothesis anymore. Such an approach can be implemented using the previously described methods (or any method that allows for groupwise testing), see, for example, [16,18].

Hierarchical Procedures in R

For both ridge and lasso projection, the fitted object are equipped with a function `clusterGroupTest` that implements a hierarchical testing approach.

```
> fit.ridge <- ridge.proj(x, y)
> out.clust <- fit.ridge$clusterGroupTest()
> plot(out.clust)
```

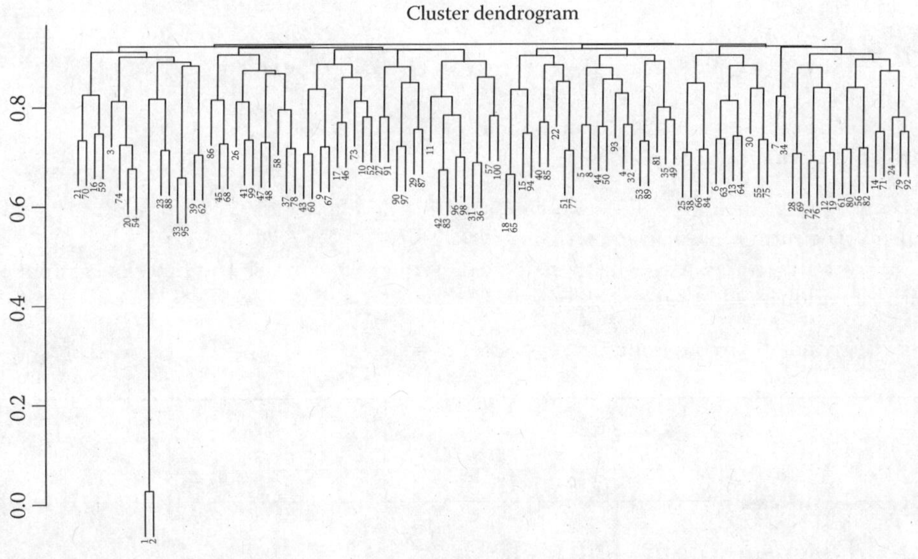

FIGURE 17.1
Cluster dendrogram of the dataset of the R example using a distance measure based on the correlation matrix of the design matrix.

17.5.1 Group-Bound Confidence Intervals

Confidence intervals can also be constructed for groups of parameters. The approach of [19] derives confidence intervals for the ℓ_1-norm

$$\|\beta_G\|_1 = \sum_{j \in G} |\beta_j|$$

for a group of variables $G \subseteq \{1, \ldots, p\}$. If the confidence interval does not cover 0, we can reject the (simultaneous) null hypothesis $H_0 : \beta_G = 0$ on the corresponding significance level. The confidence intervals in [19] are valid without any assumption on the design matrix X (in contrast to the previously discussed methods). Moreover, the method is hierarchical:

- If we cannot reject $H_0 : \beta_G = 0$, none of $H_0 : \beta_{G'}$ for $G' \subseteq G$ can be rejected either.
- On the other hand, if we can reject $H_0 : \beta_G = 0$, we can reject all $H_0 : \beta_{G'}$ for $G' \supseteq G$.

Moreover, the power of the method is unaffected by adding highly correlated predictors to a group. The price that has to be paid is weaker power on an *individual* variable level.

Group-Bound Confidence Intervals in R

We use the function `groupBound` (with user-specified grouping input) and the function `clusterGroupBound` (with automatic hierarchical clustering) in the R-package `hdi`. By default, a coverage level of 0.95 is being used. We illustrate the method on a small simulated dataset.

```
> n <- 100; p <- 100
> set.seed(19)
> x1 <- rnorm(n); x2 <- x1 + 0.25 * rnorm(n)
> cor(x1,x2)
## [1] 0.9724111
> x <- cbind(x1, x2, matrix(rnorm(n * (p - 2)), nrow = n))
> y <- x[,1] + x[,2] + rnorm(n)
> fit.cluster <- clusterGroupBound(x, y)
> plot(fit.cluster)
```

As can be seen in Figure 17.2, we can identify the cluster of the two relevant variables but not the individual variables themselves.

If we want to test a specific (predefined) group, we can use the function `groupBound` with the additional argument `group`.

```
> fit.group <- groupBound(x, y, group = 1:2)
```

17.6 Discussion and Outlook

With the availability of both mathematical theory and implementations in R, frequentist statistical inference in complex high-dimensional datasets is nowadays possible for linear and generalized linear models. While sparsity is an attractive property from an estimation

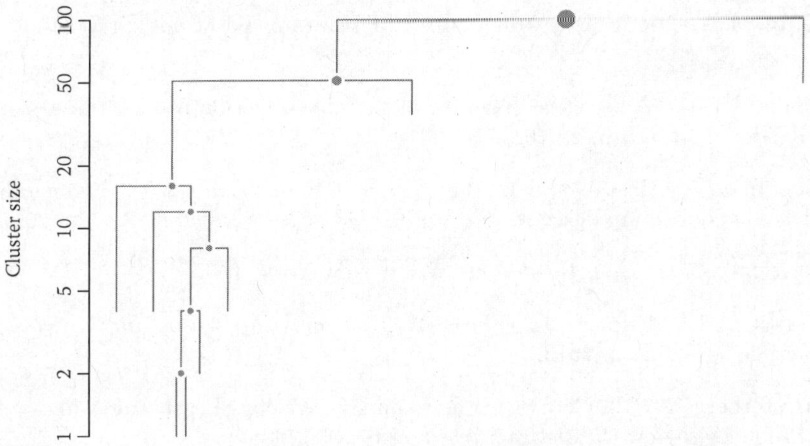

FIGURE 17.2
Visualization of the hierarchical testing procedure. Clusters with a corresponding rejected null hypothesis are labeled with a filled circle. The cluster size is indicated on the y-axis.

point of view, it makes statistical inference inherently more difficult. Hence, nonsparse or desparsified approaches are more suitable from the statistical inference point of view.

Although we have omitted most of the details regarding technical assumptions of the presented methodology (on the sparsity of the coefficient vector, the design matrix, and the error term), we want to point out that they can be difficult or even impossible to check. This makes those methods more attractive that need fewer (or checkable) assumptions. As in a low-dimensional setting, diagnostic tools should be used to check model assumptions carefully for a sound basis of any conclusions drawn from statistical inference. However, appropriate tools are still largely missing.

Moreover, some of the methods (like ridge or lasso projection) call for new computational approaches to handle datasets where the number of observations is very large. Combining these methods with sample splitting might be a suitable approach to handle such situations.

References

1. Y. Benjamini and D. Yekutieli. The control of the false discovery rate in multiple testing under dependency. *Annals of Statistics*, 29(4):1165–1188, 2001.

2. P. Bühlmann. Statistical significance in high-dimensional linear models. *Bernoulli*, 19:1212–1242, 2013.

3. P. Bühlmann, M. Kalisch, and L. Meier. High-dimensional statistics with a view towards applications in biology. *Annual Review of Statistics and Its Applications*, 1:255–278, 2014.

4. P. Bühlmann and S. van de Geer. *Statistics for High-Dimensional Data: Methods, Theory and Applications.* Springer-Verlag, Berlin, Germany, 2011.

5. R. Dezeure, P. Bühlmann, L. Meier, and N. Meinshausen. Confidence intervals, p-values and R-software hdi. arXiv:1408.4026, 2014.

6. B. Efron, T. Hastie, I. Johnstone, and R. Tibshirani. Least angle regression. *Annals of Statistics*, 32(2):407–499, 2004.

7. J. Fan and J. Lv. A selective overview of variable selection in high dimensional feature space. *Statistica Sinica*, 20:101–148, 2010.

8. J. Friedman, T. Hastie, and R. Tibshirani. Regularized paths for generalized linear models via coordinate descent. *Journal of Statistical Software*, 33:1–22, 2010.

9. J. Hartigan. *Clustering Algorithms*. Wiley, New York, 1975.

10. T. Hastie and B. Efron. *LARS: Least Angle Regression, Lasso and Forward Stagewise*. R package version 1.2, 2013.

11. T. Hesterberg, N. H. Choi, L. Meier, and C. Fraley. Least angle and ℓ_1 penalized regression: A review. *Statistics Surveys*, 2:61–93, 2008.

12. A. E. Hoerl and R. W. Kennard. Ridge regression: Biased estimation for nonorthogonal problems. *Technometrics*, 12(1):55–67, 1970.

13. A. Javanmard and A. Montanari. Confidence intervals and hypothesis testing for high-dimensional regression. *Journal of Machine Learning Research*, 15:2869–2909, 2014.

14. K. Knight and W. Fu. Asymptotics of lasso-type estimators. *Annals of Statistics*, 28(5):1356–1378, 2000.

15. R. Lockhart, J. Taylor, R. J. Tibshirani, and R. Tibshirani. A significance test for the lasso. *Annals of Statistics*, 42(2):413–468, 2014.

16. J. Mandozzi and P. Bühlmann. Hierarchical testing in the high-dimensional setting with correlated variables. *Journal of the American Statistical Association*, 2015, doi: 10.1080/01621459.2015.1007209.

17. L. Meier, N. Meinshausen, and R. Dezeure. *HDI: High-Dimensional Inference*. R package version 0.1-2, 2014.

18. N. Meinshausen. Hierarchical testing of variable importance. *Biometrika*, 95(2):265–278, 2008.

19. N. Meinshausen. Group-bound: Condence intervals for groups of variables in sparse high-dimensional regression without assumptions on the design. *Journal of the Royal Statistical Society: Series B (Statistical Methodology)*, 77:923–945, 2015.

20. N. Meinshausen and P. Bühlmann. Stability Selection (with discussion). *Journal of the Royal Statistical Society: Series B (Statistical Methodology)*, 72:417–473, 2010.

21. N. Meinshausen, L. Meier, and P. Bühlmann. P-values for high-dimensional regression. *Journal of the American Statistical Association*, 104:1671–1681, 2009.

22. S. Reid, R. Tibshirani, and J. Friedman. A study of error variance estimation in lasso regression. arXiv:1311.5274, 2013.

23. J. Shao and X. Deng. Estimation in high-dimensional linear models with deterministic design matrices. *Annals of Statistics*, 40(2):812–831, 2012.

24. T. Sun and C.-H. Zhang. Scaled sparse linear regression. *Biometrika*, 99:879–898, 2012.

25. J. Taylor, R. Lockhart, R. J. Tibshirani, and R. Tibshirani. *covTest: Computes covariance test for adaptive linear modelling.* R package version 1.02, 2013.

26. R. J. Tibshirani, J. Taylor, R. Lockhart, and R. Tibshirani. Exact post-selection inference for sequential regression procedures. arXiv:1401.3889, 2015.

27. R. Tibshirani. Regression shrinkage and selection via the lasso. *Journal of the Royal Statistical Society: Series B (Statistical Methodology)*, 58:267–288, 1996.

28. S. van de Geer and P. Bühlmann. On the conditions used to prove oracle results for the lasso. *Electronic Journal of Statistics*, 3:1360–1392, 2009.

29. S. van de Geer, P. Bühlmann, Y. Ritov, and R. Dezeure. On asymptotically optimal confidence regions and tests for high-dimensional models. *Annals of Statistics*, 42(3): 1166–1202, 2014.

30. W. N. Venables and B. D. Ripley. *Modern Applied Statistics with S*, 4th edition. Springer, New York, 2002.

31. L. Wasserman and K. Roeder. High dimensional variable selection. *Annals of Statistics*, 37(5A):2178–2201, 2009.

32. C.-H. Zhang and S. Zhang. Confidence intervals for low dimensional parameters in high dimensional linear models. *Journal of the Royal Statistical Society: Series B (Statistical Methodology)*, 76(1):217–242, 2014.

Part VI

Ensemble Methods

18

Divide and Recombine: Subsemble, Exploiting the Power of Cross-Validation

Stephanie Sapp and Erin LeDell

CONTENTS

18.1 Introduction 323
18.2 Subsemble Ensemble Learning for Big Data 325
18.2.1 The Subsemble Algorithm 325
18.2.2 Oracle Result for Subsemble 327
18.2.3 A Practical Subsemble Implementation 328
18.2.3.1 subsemble R Code Example 329
18.2.4 Performance Benchmarks 330
18.2.4.1 Model Performance 330
18.2.4.2 Computational Performance 331
18.3 Subsembles with Subset Supervision 331
18.3.1 Supervised Subsembles 332
18.3.2 The SRT Subsemble Algorithm 333
18.3.2.1 Constructing and Selecting the Number of Subsets 333
18.3.3 SRT Subsemble in Practice 334
18.4 Concluding Remarks 335
18.5 Glossary 335
References 337

18.1 Introduction

As massive datasets become increasingly common, new scalable approaches to prediction are needed. Given that memory and runtime constraints are common in practice, it is important to develop practical machine learning methods that perform well on big datasets in a fixed computational resource setting. Procedures using subsets from a training set are promising tools for prediction with large-scale datasets [16]. Recent research has focused on developing and evaluating the performance of various subset-based prediction procedures. Subsetting procedures in machine learning construct subsets from the available training data, then train an algorithm on each subset, and finally combine the results across the subsets to form a final prediction. Prediction methods operating on subsets of the training data can take advantage of modern computational resources, because machine learning on subsets can be massively parallelized.

Bagging [1], or bootstrap aggregating, is a classic example of a subsampling prediction procedure. Bagging involves drawing many bootstrap samples of a fixed size, fitting the same underlying algorithm on each bootstrap sample, and obtaining the final prediction by averaging the results across the fits. Bagging can lead to significant model performance gains when used with weak or unstable algorithms such as classification or regression trees. The bootstrap samples are drawn with replacement, so each bootstrap sample of size n contains approximately 63.2% of the unique training examples, while the remainder of the observations contained in the sample are duplicates. Therefore, in bagging, each model is fit using only a subset of the original training observations. The drawback of taking a simple average of the output from the subset fits is that the predictions from each of the fits are weighted equally, regardless of the individual quality of each fit. The performance of a bagged fit can be much better compared to that of a nonbagged algorithm, but a simple average is not necessarily the optimal combination of a set of *base learners.*

An *average mixture* (AVGM) procedure for fitting the parameter of a parametric model has been studied by Zhang et al. [16]. AVGM partitions the full available dataset into disjoint subsets, estimates the parameter within each subset, and finally combines the estimates by simple averaging. Under certain conditions on the population risk, the AVGM can achieve better efficiency than training a parametric model on the full data. A *subsampled average mixture* (SAVGM) procedure, an extension of AVGM, is proposed in [16] and is shown to provide substantial performance benefits over AVGM. As with AVGM, SAVGM partitions the full data into subsets and estimates the parameter within each subset. However, SAVGM also takes a single subsample from each partition, reestimates the parameter on the subsample, and combines the two estimates into a so-called subsample-corrected estimate. The final parameter estimate is obtained by simple averaging of the subsample-corrected estimates from each partition. Both procedures have a theoretical backing; however, the results rely on using parametric models.

An ensemble method for classification with large-scale datasets, using subsets of observations to train algorithms, and combining the classifiers linearly, was implemented and discussed in the case study of [8] at Twitter, Inc.

While not a subset method, *boosting*, formulated in [4], is an example of an ensemble method that differentiates between the quality of each fit in the ensemble. Boosting iterates the process of training a weak learner on the full dataset, then reweighting observations, with higher weights given to poorly classified observations from the previous iteration. However, boosting is not a subset method, because all observations are iteratively reweighted, and thus all observations are needed at each iteration. Boosting is also a sequential algorithm, and hence cannot be parallelized.

Another nonsubset ensemble method that differentiates between the quality of each fit is the *Super Learner* algorithm of [14], which generalizes and establishes the theory for *stacking* procedures developed by Wolpert [15] and extended by Breiman [2]. Super Learner learns the optimal weighted combination of a *base learner library* of candidate base learner algorithms by using cross-validation and a second-level *metalearning* algorithm. Super Learner generalizes stacking by allowing for general loss functions and hence a broader range of estimator combinations.

The *Subsemble* algorithm is a method proposed in [12], for combining results from fitting the same underlying algorithm on different subsets of observations. Subsemble is a form of supervised stacking [2,15] and is similar in nature to the Super Learner algorithm, with the distinction that base learner fits are trained on subsets of the data instead of the full training set. Subsemble can also accommodate multiple base learning algorithms, with each algorithm being fit on each subset. The approach has many benefits and differs from other ensemble methods in a variety of ways.

First, any type of underlying algorithm, parametric or nonparametric, can be used. Instead of simply averaging subset-specific fits, Subsemble differentiates fit quality across the subsets and learns a weighted combination of the subset-specific fits. To evaluate fit quality and determine the weighted combination, Subsemble uses cross-validation, thus, using independent data to train the base learners and learn the weighted combination. Finally, Subsemble has desirable statistical performance and can improve prediction quality on both small and large datasets.

This chapter focuses on the statistical properties and performance of the Subsemble algorithm. We present an oracle result for Subsemble, showing that Subsemble performs as well as the best possible combination of the subset-specific fits. Empirically, it has been shown that Subsemble performs well as a prediction procedure for moderate- and large-sized datasets [12]. Subsemble can, and often does, provide better prediction performance than fitting a single base algorithm on the full available dataset.

18.2 Subsemble Ensemble Learning for Big Data

Let $X \in \mathbb{R}^p$ denote a real-valued vector of covariates and let $Y \in \mathbb{R}$ represent a real-valued outcome value with joint distribution, $P_0(X, Y)$. Assume that a training set consists of n independent and identically distributed observations, $O_i = (X_i, Y_i)$ of $O \sim P_0$. The goal is to learn a function $\hat{f}(X)$ for predicting the outcome, Y, given the input X.

Assume that there is a set of L machine learning algorithms, $\Psi^1, ..., \Psi^L$, where each is indexed by an algorithm class and a specific set of model parameters. These algorithms can be any class of supervised learning algorithms, such as a Random Forest, Support Vector Machine, or a linear model. The *base learner library* can also include copies of the same algorithm, specified by different sets of tuning parameters. Typically, in stacking-based [2,15] ensemble methods, functions, $\hat{\Psi}^1, ..., \hat{\Psi}^L$, are learned by applying base learning algorithms, $\Psi^1, ..., \Psi^L$, to the full training dataset and then combining these fits using a metalearning algorithm, Φ, trained on the cross-validated predicted values from the base learners. Historically, in stacking methods, the metalearning method is often chosen to be some sort of regularized linear model, such as nonnegative least squares (NNLS) [2]; however, a variety of parametric and nonparametric methods can be used to learn the optimal combination output from the base fits. In the Super Learner algorithm, the metalearning algorithm is specified as a method that minimizes the cross-validated risk of some particular *loss function* of interest, such as *negative log-likelihood loss* or *squared-error loss*.

18.2.1 The Subsemble Algorithm

Instead of using the entire dataset to obtain a single fit, $\hat{\Psi}^l$, for each base learner, Subsemble applies algorithm Ψ^l to multiple different subsets of the available observations. The subsets are created by partitioning of the entire training set into J disjoint subsets. The subsets are commonly created randomly and of the same size. With L unique base learners and J subsets, the ensemble then comprises a total of $L \times J$ subset-specific fits, $\hat{\Psi}^l_j$. As in the Super Learner algorithm, Subsemble obtains the optimal combination of the fits by minimizing cross-validated risk through cross-validation.

In stacking algorithms, *V-fold cross-validation* is often used to generate what is called the *level-one* data. The level-one data is the input data to the metalearning algorithm, which is different from the *level-zero* data or the original training dataset. In the Super Learner algorithm, the level-one data consists of the V-fold cross-validated predicted values from each base learning algorithm. With L base learners and a training set of n observations, the level-one data will be an $n \times L$ matrix and serve as the design matrix in the metalearning task.

In the Subsemble algorithm, a modified version of V-fold cross-validation is used to obtain the level-one data. Each of the J subsets is partitioned further into V folds, so that the vth validation fold spans across all J subsets. For each base learning algorithm, Ψ^l, the (j, v)th iteration of the cross-validation process is defined as follows:

1. Train the (j, v)th subset-specific fit, $\hat{\Psi}^l_{j,v}$, by applying Ψ^l to the observations that are in folds $\{1, ..., V\} \setminus v$, but restricted to subset j. The training set used here is a subset of the jth subset and contains $(n(v-1))/Jv$ observations.

2. Using the subset-specific fit, $\hat{\Psi}^l_{j,v}$, predicted values are generated for the entire vth validation fold, including those observations that are not in subset j. The size of the validation set for the (j, v)th iteration is n/V.

This unique version of cross-validation generates predicted values for all n observations in the full training set, while only training on subsets of data. A total of $L \times J$ learner-subset models are cross-validated, resulting in an $n \times (L \times J)$ matrix of level-one data that can be used to train the metalearning algorithm, Φ. A diagram depicting the Subsemble algorithm using a single underlying base learning algorithm, ψ is shown in Figure 18.1.

More formally, we define $P_{n,v}$ as the empirical distribution of the observations not in the vth fold. For each observation i, define $P_{n,v(i)}$ to be the empirical distribution of the observations not in the fold containing observation i. The optimal combination is selected by applying the metalearning algorithm Φ to the following redefined set of n observations: $(\tilde{X}_i, Y_i)$, where $\tilde{X}_i = \{\tilde{X}^l_i\}^L_{l=1}$, and $\tilde{X}^l_i = \{\hat{\Psi}^l_j(P_{n,v(i)})(X_i)\}^J_{j=1}$. That is, for each i, the level-one input vector, $\tilde{X}_i$, consists of the $L \times J$ predicted values obtained by evaluating the $L \times J$ subset-specific estimators trained on the data excluding the $v(i)$th fold at X_i.

The cross-validation process is used only to generate the level-one data, so as a separate task, $L \times J$ final subset-specific fits are trained, using the entire subset j as the training set for each (l, j)th fit. The final Subsemble fit comprises the $L \times J$ subset-specific fits, $\hat{\Psi}^l_j$ and a metalearner fit, $\hat{\Phi}$. Pseudocode for the Subsemble algorithm is shown in Figure 18.2.

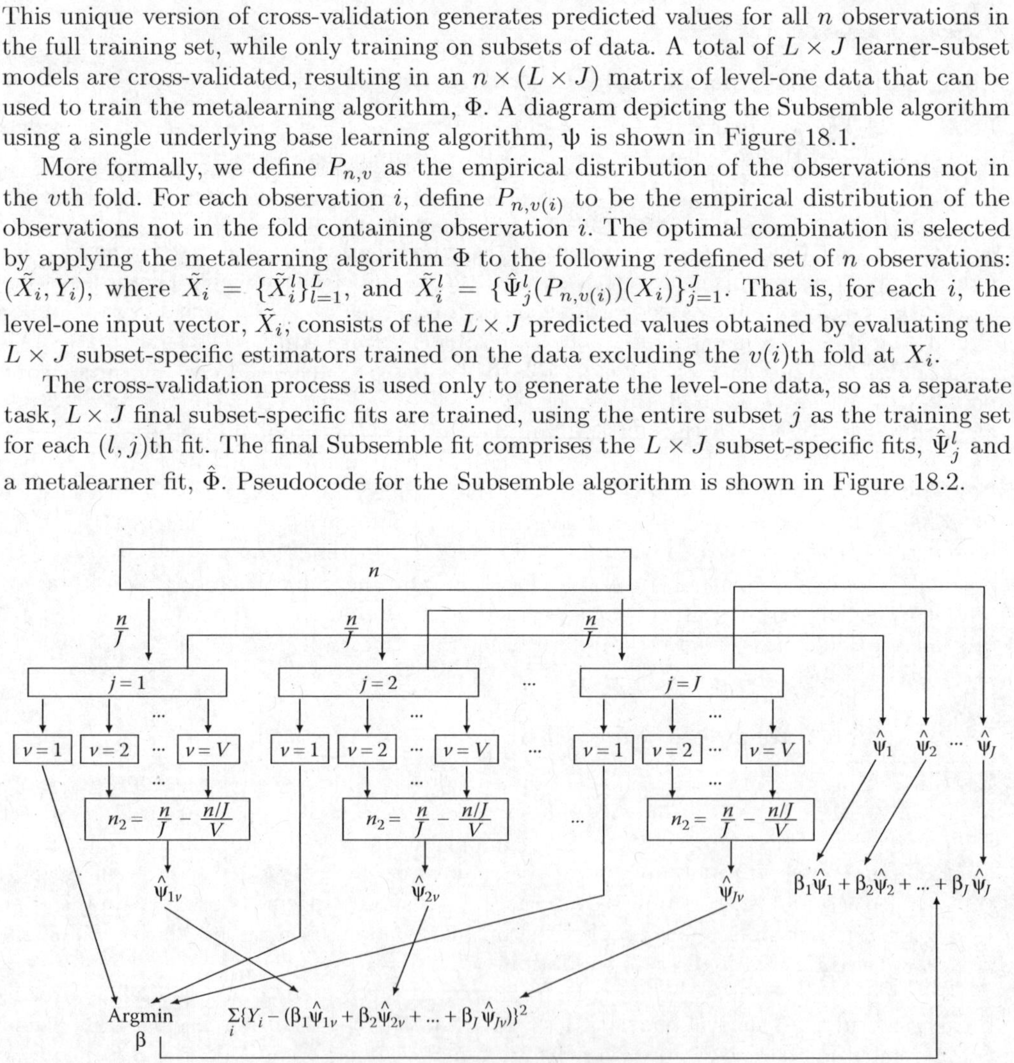

FIGURE 18.1
Diagram of the Subsemble procedure using a single base learner ψ and linear regression as the metalearning algorithm.

Algorithm 18.1 Subsemble

- Assume n observations $(X_i,\ Y_i)$
- Partition the n observations into J disjoint subsets
- Base learning algorithms: $\Psi^1, \ldots, \Psi^L$
- Metalearner algorithm: Φ
- Optimal combination: $\hat{\Phi}(\{\hat{\Psi}^l_1, \ldots, \hat{\Psi}^l_J\}^L_{l=1})$

```
for j ← 1 : J do
    // Create subset-specific base learner fits
    for l ← 1 : L do
        Ψ̂^l_j ← apply Ψ^l to observations i such that i ∈ j
    end for
    // Create V folds
    Randomly partition each subset j into V folds
end for

for v ← 1 : V do
    // CV fits
    for l ← 1 : L do
        Ψ̂^l_{j,v} ← apply Ψ^l to observations i such that i ∈ j, i ∉ v
    end for
    for i : i ∈ v do
        // Predicted values
        X̃_i ← ({Ψ̂^l_{1,v}(X_i), ..., Ψ̂^l_{J,v}(X_i)}^L_{l=1})
    end for
end for

Φ̂ ← apply Φ to training data (Y_i, X̃_i)

Φ̂({Ψ̂^l_1, ..., Ψ̂^l_J}^L_{l=1}) ← final prediction function
```

FIGURE 18.2
Pseudocode for the Subsemble algorithm.

18.2.2 Oracle Result for Subsemble

The following oracle result gives a theoretical guarantee of Subsemble's performance, was proven in [12], and follows directly from the work of [14]. Theorem 18.1 has been extended from the original formulation to allow for L base learners instead of a single base learner. The squared-error loss function is used as an example metalearning algorithm in Theorem 18.1.

Theorem 18.1 *Assume that the metalearner algorithm* $\hat{\Phi} = \hat{\Phi}_\beta$ *is indexed by a finite-dimensional parameter* $\beta \in \mathbf{B}$. *Let* $\mathbf{B}_n$ *be a finite set of values in* $\mathbf{B}$, *with the number of values growing at most polynomial rate in* n. *Assume that there exist bounded sets* $\mathbf{Y} \in \mathbb{R}$ *and Euclidean* $\mathbf{X}$ *such that* $P((Y, X) \in \mathbf{Y} \times \mathbf{X}) = 1$ *and* $P(\hat{\Psi}^l(P_n) \in \mathbf{Y}) = 1$ *for* $l = 1, \ldots, L$.

Define the cross-validation selector of β *as*

$$\beta_n = \arg\min_{\beta \in \mathbf{B}_n} \sum_{i=1}^{n} \left\{ Y_i - \hat{\Phi}_\beta(\tilde{X}_i) \right\}^2$$

and define the oracle selector of β *as*

$$\tilde{\beta}_n = \arg\min_{\beta \in \mathbf{B}_n} \frac{1}{V} \sum_{v=1}^{V} E_0 \left[\left\{ E_0[Y|X] - \hat{\Phi}_\beta(P_{n,v}) \right\}^2 \right]$$

Then, for every $\delta > 0$*, there exists a constant* $C(\delta) < \infty$ *(defined in* [13]*) such that*

$$E \frac{1}{V} \sum_{v=1}^{V} E_0 \left[\left\{ E_0[Y|X] - \hat{\Phi}_{\beta_n}(P_{n,v}) \right\}^2 \right]$$

$$\leq (1+\delta) E \frac{1}{V} \sum_{v=1}^{V} E_0 \left[\left\{ E_0[Y|X] - \hat{\Phi}_{\tilde{\beta}_n}(P_{n,v}) \right\}^2 \right] + C(\delta) \frac{V \log n}{n}$$

As a result, if none of the subset-specific learners converge at a parametric rate, then the oracle selector does not converge at a parametric rate, and the cross-validation estimator $\hat{\Phi}_{\beta_n}$ *is asymptotically equivalent with the oracle estimator* $\hat{\Phi}_{\tilde{\beta}_n}$*. Otherwise, the cross-validation estimator* $\hat{\Phi}_{\beta_n}$ *achieves a near parametric* $(\log n)/n$ *rate.*

Theorem 18.1 tells us that the risk difference, based on squared-error loss, of the Subsemble from the true $E_0[Y|X]$ can be bounded from above by a function of the risk difference of the oracle procedure. Note that the oracle procedure results in the best possible combination of the subset-specific fits, because the oracle procedure selects β to minimize the *true* risk difference. In practice, the underlying algorithm is unlikely to converge at a parametric rate, so it follows that Subsemble performs as well as the best possible combination of subset-specific fits. It has also been shown empirically that Subsembles perform at least as well as and typically better than simple averaging [12] of the subset-specific fits. Because averaging, or bagging, is an example of combining the subset-specific fits, it follows from Theorem 18.1 that the Subsemble algorithm is asymptotically superior than bagging the subset-specific fits.

Note that Theorem 18.1 does not specify how many subsets are best, or how Subsemble's combination of many subset-specific fits will perform relative to fitting a single algorithm, Ψ^l, just once on the full training set. The *Supervised Regression Tree* (*SRT*) *Subsemble* algorithm [11], discussed in Section 18.3, will provide further insight into how to data adaptively select the optimal number of subsets.

18.2.3 A Practical Subsemble Implementation

The Subsemble algorithm offers a practical *divide-and-conquer* approach to supervised ensemble learning with big data. The original training dataset can be partitioned into J disjoint subsets, each of which can reside in memory on one node of a cluster. Assuming that the subsets contain roughly the same number of training examples, the computational burden of training with the full dataset of n observations is reduced to training on a dataset of size n/J. This can greatly reduce both the (per-node) memory and total runtime requirements of the training process, while still allowing each base learning algorithm to see all of the original training samples. Subsemble offers an advantage over approaches that use only a single subset of the data, thereby wasting valuable training data.

The base learners are trained independently of each other, so much of the Subsemble algorithm is embarrassingly parallel in nature. The V-fold cross-validation process of generating the level-one predicted values involves training and testing a total of $L \times J \times V$ models. These models can be trained and evaluated simultaneously, in parallel, across $L \times J \times V$ nodes. After generating the cross-validated level-one data, the metalearning algorithm is trained using this data.

The metalearning step is performed after the cross-validation step, as it uses the level-one data produced by the cross-validation step as input. This step involves training a metalearning algorithm on a design matrix of dimension, $n \times (L \times J)$; however, a subset of the level-one design matrix can be used if prohibited by memory constraints. Alternatively, an online algorithm can be used for a metalearner if the level-one data does not fit into memory.

The final ensemble model will consist of the metalearner fit and $L \times J$ base learner fits. These final base learner fits can be fit in parallel. Alternatively, the $L \times J$ subset-specific fits from any vth iteration of the cross-validation step can be saved instead of fitting $L \times J$ new models; however, these models will be fit using approximately $((V-1)/V)n/J$, instead of n/J, training observations. Therefore, if resources are available, it is preferable to additionally fit the $L \times J$ models (each trained using n/J observations), separate from the cross-validation step. Given appropriate parallel computing resources (at least $L \times J \times V$ cores), the entire ensemble can be trained in parallel in just two or three steps.

A parallelized implementation of the Subsemble algorithm is available in the **subsemble** R package [7]. Support for both multicore and multinode clusters is available in the software. This package currently uses the **SuperLearner** R package's [10] machine learning algorithm wrapper interface to provide access to approximately 30 machine learning algorithms that can be used as base learners. The user can also define their own algorithm wrappers by utilizing the **SuperLearner** wrapper template.

The SRT Subsemble algorithm, discussed in Section 18.3, provides a way to determine the optimal number of subsets. However, in practice, the number of subsets may be determined by the computational infrastructure available to the user. By increasing the number of subsets, the user can re-size the learning problem into a set of computational tasks that fit within specific resource constraints. This is particularly useful if compute nodes are easy to come by, but the memory on each node is limited. The larger the memory (RAM) on each compute node, the bigger your subsets can be.

18.2.3.1 subsemble R Code Example

In this section, we present an R code example that shows the main arguments required to train a Subsemble fit using the **subsemble** R package. The interface for the `subsemble` function should feel familiar to R users who have used other modeling packages in R. The user must specify the base learner library, the metalearning algorithm, and optionally, the number of desired data partitions/subsets.

Algorithm functions (e.g., `"SL.gam"`) from the **SuperLearner** package are used to specify the base learner library and metalearner. Support for other types of base learner and metalearner functions, such as those specified using the **caret** [5] R package, is on the development road map for the **subsemble** package. In contrast to the **SuperLearner** package, the **subsemble** package allows the user to choose any algorithm for the metalearner and does not require the metalearner to be a linear model that minimizes the cross-validated risk of a given loss function. Most machine learning algorithms work by minimizing some loss function (or surrogate loss function), so this functionality is not that different in practice; however it does allow the user to specify a nonparametric metalearning algorithm.

The code example uses a three-learner library consisting of a Generalized Additive Model (`"SL.gam"`), a Support Vector Machine (`"SL.svm.1"`), and Multivariate Adaptive Regression Splines (`"SL.earth"`). The metalearner is specified as a generalized linear model with Lasso regularization (`"SL.glmnet"`). A number of algorithm wrapper functions are included in the **SuperLearner** package. However, the user may want to define nondefault model parameters for a base learner. To illustrate this, one custom base learner (the SVM) is included in the example ensemble. To create a custom wrapper function, the user may pass along any nondefault arguments to the default function wrapper for that algorithm.

```
library("subsemble") # Also loads the SuperLearner package
library("cvAUC") # For model evaluation

# Set up the Subsemble:

# Create one nondefault base learner function to use in the library
SL.svm.1 <- function(..., type.class = "C-classification") {
       SL.svm(..., type.class = type.class)
}

# Base learner functions from SuperLearner package
learner <- c("SL.gam", "SL.svm.1", "SL.earth")
metalearner <- "SL.glmnet" # Metalearner
subsets <- 4  # Number of subsets
```

By default a *cross-product* Subsemble will be created using the `subsemble` function, but this can be modified using the `learnControl` argument. Because four subsets and three base learners are specified by the user, this will result in an ensemble of $4 \times 3 = 12$ subset-specific fits.

```
# Train and evaluate the Subsemble fit:

fit <- subsemble(x = x, y = y, newx = newx,
                 family = binomial(),
                 learner = learner,
                 metalearner = metalearner,
                 subsets = subsets)

# Evaluate model performance on a test set
auc <- cvAUC::AUC(predictions = fit$pred, labels = newy)
```

18.2.4 Performance Benchmarks

This section presents benchmarks of the model performance and runtime of the Subsemble algorithm as implemented in the **subsemble** R package, version 0.0.9. This example uses the same three-algorithm base learner library and metalearner that was specified in the R code example in Section 18.2.3.1.

Binary outcome training datasets with 10 numerical features were simulated using the `twoClassSim` function in the **caret** R package [5]. Training sets of increasing size were generated, and an independent test set of 100,000 observations was used to estimate model performance as measured by area under the ROC curve (AUC). Confidence intervals for the test set AUC estimates were generated using the **cvAUC** R package [6].

18.2.4.1 Model Performance

As shown in Figure 18.3, the performance of the 2-subset and 10-subset Subsemble is comparable to the Super Learner algorithm. In this example, after about 100,000 training observations, the 95% confidence intervals for AUC for the three models overlap. For smaller

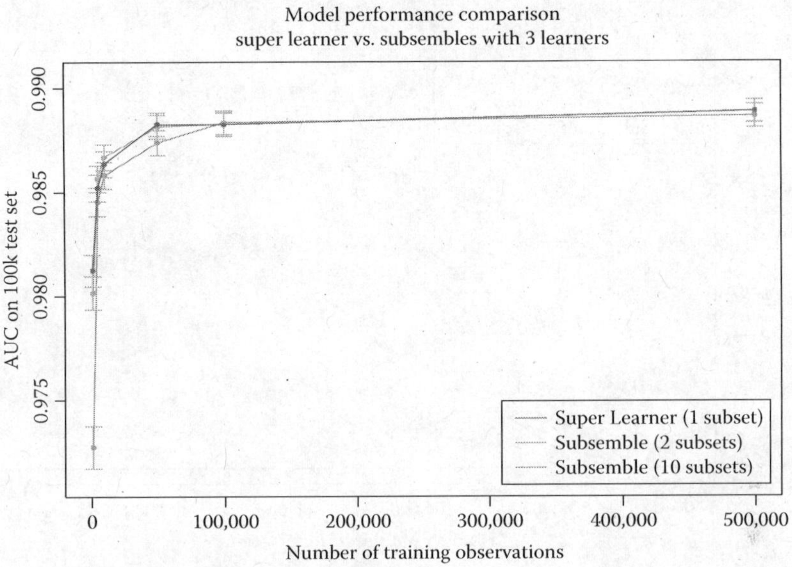

FIGURE 18.3
Model performance for Subsemble and Super Learner for training sets of increasing size.

training sets, Subsemble model performance can dip below Super Learner if too many subsets are used. Once the subsets become too small, they may fail to sufficiently estimate the distribution of the full training set.

18.2.4.2 Computational Performance

These benchmarks were performed on a single *r3.8xlarge* instance on Amazon's Elastic Compute Cloud (EC2) with 32 virtual CPUs and 244 GB of RAM using R version 3.1.1. Both single-threaded and multicore implementations of Subsemble and Super Learner were measured. For this example, there are a total of $3 \times J$ subset-specific fits because three base learners were used in the Subsemble. In the case of $J = 10$, there are 30 subset-specific models that need to be trained, which can be fit all at once on a 32-core machine using the multicore option in the software. Subsembles with a larger number of subsets and base learners can also be trained in parallel on multinode clusters. The cross-validation and base learning tasks are computationally independent tasks, so as long as a big enough cluster is used, the subset-specific models can all be trained at the same time. For maximum efficiency, a cluster with at least $L \times J$ cores should be used. The training time for multicore Subsemble and multicore Super Learner is shown in Figure 18.4 for training sets of increasing size.

18.3 Subsembles with Subset Supervision

Different methods for creating Subsemble's subsets result in different Subsembles, because the performance of the final Subsemble estimator can vary depending on the specific partitioning of the data into subsets. The simplest approach to creating subsets is to

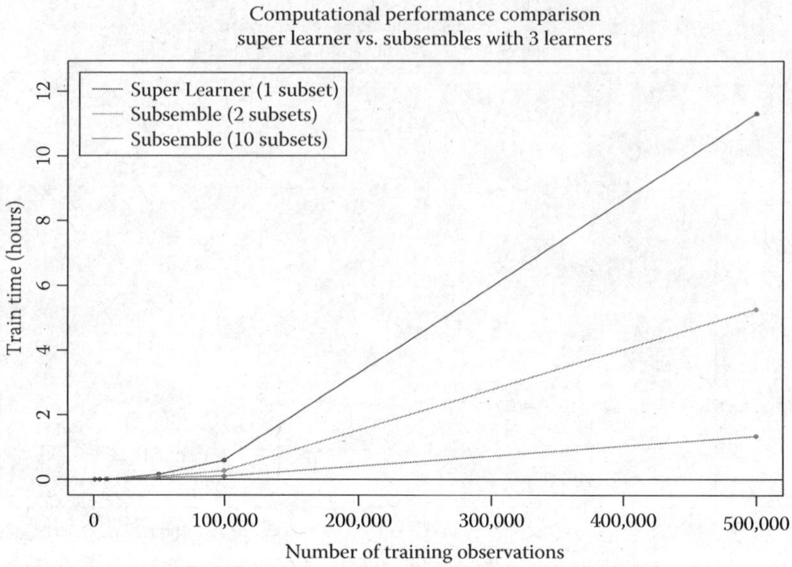

FIGURE 18.4
Training time for Subsemble and Super Learner for training sets of increasing size.

randomly partition the n training observations into J subsets of size n/J; however, this still requires the user to choose a value for J, or to try several values for J.

In this section, we introduce the *Supervised Subsembles* method [11] for partitioning a dataset into the subsets used in Subsemble. Supervised Subsembles create subsets via supervised partitioning of the *covariate space* and use a form of *histogram regression* [9] as the metalearner. We also discuss a practical supervised Subsemble method called *Supervised Regression Tree Subsemble*, or *SRT Subsemble*, which employs *regression trees* to both partition the observations into the subsets used in Subsemble and select the number of subsets to use. In each subsection, we highlight the computational independence properties of these methods that are advantageous for applications involving big data.

18.3.1 Supervised Subsembles

The subsets used in supervised Subsembles are obtained by a supervised partitioning of the covariate space, $\mathcal{X} = \bigcup_{j=1}^{J} S_j$, to create J disjoint subsets $S_1, \ldots, S_J$, such that any given vector of covariates belongs to exactly one of the J subsets. There are many unsupervised methods that can be used to partition the covariate space; however, supervised partitioning methods will create a partitioning that is predictive of the outcome. Given the number of clusters, J, this technique will partition the covariate space; however, it does not directly solve the problem of choosing an optimal value for J.

Compared to randomly selecting the subsets, constructing the subsets to be internally similar, yet distinct from each other, results in locally smoothed subset-specific fits. The added diversity among the subset-specific fits can improve the overall performance of the ensemble. In this case, each subset-specific fit is optimal for a distinct partition of the covariate space. Because a subset-specific fit, $\hat{\Psi}_j^l$, is tailored for the subspace S_j, it will not necessarily be the case that $\hat{\Psi}_j^l$ will be a good predictor for observations belonging to the subspace, $S_{j'}$, where $j \neq j'$.

To account for this, supervised Subsembles use a modified version of histogram regression as the metalearner to combine the subset-specific fits. The usual form of histogram regression, applied to the J subsets $\{S_j\}_{j=1}^J$, produces a local average of the outcome Y within each subset. In contrast, the modified version of histogram regression outputs the associated $\hat{\Psi}_j^l$ for each subset S_j. In addition, this version of histogram regression includes a coefficient and intercept within each subset. Note that while linear regression is used in this chapter as an illustrative example, any algorithm can be used to obtain the overall fit within each subset. The histogram regression metalearning fit, $\hat{\Phi}$, for combining the subset-specific fits is defined as follows:

$$\hat{\Phi}(\hat{\Psi}^1, \ldots, \hat{\Psi}^L)(x) = \sum_{j=1}^{J} \left[I(x \in S_j) \left(\beta_j^0 + \sum_{l=1}^{L} \beta_j^l \hat{\Psi}_j^l(x) \right) \right] \tag{18.1}$$

These supervised Subsembles have the benefit of preserving the subset computational independence. That is, if subsets are known a priori, by keeping the subset assignments fixed, computations on the subsets of the Supervised Subsemble described in this section remain computationally independent across the entire procedure.

To see this, let β_n be the cross-validation selector of β and use the squared-error loss as an example. As shown in [11],

$$\begin{aligned} \beta_n &= \arg\min_{\beta} \sum_{i=1}^{n} \left\{ Y_i - \hat{\Phi}_{\beta}(\tilde{X}_i) \right\}^2 \\ &= \left\{ \arg\min_{\beta_j} \sum_{i: i \in S_j} \left(Y_i - \left[\beta_j^0 + \sum_{l=1}^{L} \beta_j^l \hat{\Psi}_{j,v(i)}^l (X_i) \right] \right)^2 \right\}_{j=1}^{J} \end{aligned}$$

Thus, each term β_j can be estimated by minimizing cross-validated risk using only the data in subset S_j. Unlike when using randomly constructed subsets, supervised subsets remove the requirement of recombining data to produce the final prediction function for the Subsemble algorithm.

18.3.2 The SRT Subsemble Algorithm

SRT Subsemble is a practical supervised Subsemble algorithm that uses regression trees to determine both of the number of subsets, J, and the partitioning of the covariate space.

With large-scale data, reorganizing a dataset into different pieces can be a challenge from an infrastructure perspective. In a cluster setting, this requirement could require copying a large amount of data between nodes. As a result, it is preferable to avoid approaches that split and then recombine data across the existing subsets. After the initial partitioning of the data across nodes, it is more computationally efficient to create additional splits that divide an already existing partition.

18.3.2.1 Constructing and Selecting the Number of Subsets

The Classification and Regression Tree (CART) algorithm [3] recursively partitions the covariate space by creating binary splits of one covariate at a time. Concretely, using the covariate vector $X_i = (X_i^1, \ldots, X_i^K)$, the first iteration of CART selects a covariate X^k, and then creates the best partition of the data based on that covariate. As a metric to measure and select the best covariate split for a continuous outcome, some *splitting criterion* is used. For classification trees, Gini impurity or information gain is often used as a splitting criterion. For regression trees, typically, the split that minimizes the overall sum of squares is selected. For additional details, we refer the reader to [3].

The first iteration of CART creates the first partition of the data based on two regions $S_1^1 = I(X^k \leq c_1)$ and $S_1^2 = I(X^k > c_1)$. Subsequent splits are obtained greedily, by repeating this procedure on each new partition. For example, the second iteration of CART selects a covariate, $X^{k'}$, and partitions S_1^1 into $S_2^1 = I(X^k \leq c_1,\ X^{k'} \leq c_2)$ and $S_2^2 = I(X^k \leq c_1,\ X^{k'} > c_2)$. For a given partitioning, the standard prediction function from CART outputs the local average of the outcome Y within each subset.

To partition the covariate space and select the number of subsets, SRT Subsemble applies CART as follows:

1. Run the CART algorithm on the dataset, resulting in a sequence of nested partitionings of the covariate space. That is, the CART algorithm outputs a sequence of subtrees; a first tree with a single root node, a second tree with two nodes, a third tree with three nodes, and so on, ending with the full tree with M nodes. The m nodes of each mth subtree are treated as a candidate partitioning into m subsets.
2. Next, explore the sequence of M possible partitions (sequence of subtrees) produced by CART, beginning at the root. For each candidate number of subsets $1, \ldots, M$, a supervised Subsemble model is fit. Moreover, with m subsets, create L subset-specific fits, $\hat{\Psi}_j^l$, for each subset $j = 1, \ldots, m$, and create the overall prediction function according to Equation 18.1. Note that CART is used to create the subsets S_j that appear in Equation 18.1.
3. Finally, choose the number of subsets that produce the supervised Subsemble with minimum cross-validated risk.

18.3.3 SRT Subsemble in Practice

SRT Subsemble has desirable computational independence (by subset) and provides a mechanism to learn the optimal number and constituency of the subsets to use in the Subsemble algorithm. Note that as a consequence of this independence, fitting a sequence of Subsembles in a series of subtrees, each subsequent Subsemble only requires computation for the two new nodes at each step. That is, given the Subsemble fit with, say, m subsets, computing the next Subsemble with $m + 1$ subsets only requires computation for the two new nodes formed in the $(m + 1)^{\text{st}}$ split of the tree. This is a result of the fact that the nodes are computationally independent in the SRT Subsemble framework, and also that at each split of the tree, all nodes remain the same, except for the single node in the mth tree (that is split into two new nodes in the $[m + 1]^{\text{st}}$ tree).

There are several choices available for practitioners applying the SRT Subsemble process in practice. These user-selected options allow SRT Subsemble to be quite flexible with options to suit the application at hand. There is no single, best approach; instead the options will be determined based on the application, computational constraints, and desired properties of the estimator.

The first consideration relates to building and exploring the tree. One possibility is to simply build a very large tree (resulting in a full tree with M nodes), build a Subsemble for each subtree, $1, \ldots, M$, and through this process simply locate the Subsemble with the lowest cross-validated risk among the sequence of subtrees outputted by CART. Alternatively, a greedy process can be used. Instead of calculating cross-validated risk for all subtrees of a very large tree, the cross-validated risk can be computed while the tree is being built. That is, after each additional split to the tree, build the associated Subsemble, calculate the associated cross-validated risk, and refrain from making additional splits once some stopping criteria is achieved. As a simple example, the stopping criteria could be an increase of the cross-validated risk.

Second, the user must decide where in the tree to start building Subsembles. The most obvious approach is to start with building a Subsemble at the root node of the tree, meaning the Subsemble is built with only one subset containing all observations. A Subsemble with one subset is equivalent to the Super Learner algorithm [14]. For small to moderate-sized datasets, where computational considerations are of less of a concern, this is a good choice. However, for large-scale datasets, it may be preferable to first split the data into partitions of some desired size, and then begin the Subsemble process on the subsets. This approach would allow the user to take advantage of multiple independent computational resources, because each partition of data could be transferred to a dedicated computational resource (all subsequent computations remain independent from other partitions).

18.4 Concluding Remarks

In this chapter, we presented the Subsemble algorithm, a flexible subset ensemble prediction method. Subsemble partitions a training set into subsets of observations, fits one or more underlying algorithm on each subset, and combines the subset-specific fits through a second-level metalearning algorithm using a unique form of V-fold cross-validation. We provided a theoretical performance guarantee showing that Subsemble performs as well as the best possible combination of the subset-specific fits. Further, we described the practical implementation of the Subsemble algorithm that is available in the **subsemble** R package, and presented performance benchmarks that demonstrate desirable predictive performance with significant runtime improvements as compared with full-data ensembles such as generalized stacking. We described using a supervised partitioning of the covariate space to create Subsemble's subsets. We discussed the computational advantages of this supervised subset creation approach, and described the practical SRT Subsemble algorithm that will construct the covariate partitioning and learn the optimal number of subsets.

18.5 Glossary

Average mixture (AVGM) algorithm: A procedure for estimating a parameter in a parametric model using subsets of training data. Given m different machines and a dataset of size N, partition the data into samples of size $n = N/m$, and distribute n samples to each machine. Then compute the empirical minimizer on each partition of the data and average all the parameter estimates across the machines to obtain a final estimate.

Bagging: Bootstrap aggregating, or bagging, is an ensemble algorithm designed to improve the stability and accuracy of machine learning algorithms used in statistical classification and regression. Bagging is a special case of the model averaging approach.

Base learner: A supervised machine learning algorithm (with a specific set of tuning parameters) used as part of the ensemble.

Base learner library: A set of base learners that make up the ensemble.

Boosting: A boosting algorithm iteratively learns weak classifiers and adds them to a final strong classifier.

Covariate space: The space, $\mathcal{X}$, that the input data, X, is sampled from. For example, $\mathcal{X}$ could be equal to $\mathbb{R}^p$ or $\{0,1\}^p$.

Histogram regression: A prediction method that, given a partitioning of the covariate space into J subsets, models each subset as the average outcome among the training data within that subset.

Level-one data: The independent predictions generated from validation (typically V-fold cross-validation) of the base learners. This data is the input to the metalearner. This is also called the set of *cross-validated predicted values.*

Level-zero data: The original training dataset that is used to train the base learners.

Metalearner: A supervised machine learning algorithm that is used to learn the optimal combination of the base learners. This can also be an optimization method such as nonnegative least squares (NNLS), COBYLA, or L-BFGS-B for finding the optimal linear combination of the base learners.

Negative log-likelihood loss: The negative log of the probability of the data given the model.

Regression trees: A prediction method that recursively partitions the covariate space of the training data. The terminal nodes are modeled using linear regression.

Splitting criterion: In learning a regression tree, the criterion used to determine where to split.

Squared-error loss: The squared-error loss of an estimator measures the average of the squares of the error, or the difference between the estimator and what is estimated.

Subsampled average mixture (SAVGM): A bias-corrected version of the AVGM algorithm with substantially better performance.

Subsemble: Subsemble is a general subset ensemble prediction method that partitions the full dataset into subsets of observations, fits a specified underlying algorithm on each subset, and uses a unique form of V-fold cross-validation to output a prediction function that combines the subset-specific fits. An oracle result provides a theoretical performance guarantee for Subsemble.

Super Learner (SL): Super Learner is an ensemble algorithm, which takes as input a library of supervised learning algorithms and a metalearning algorithm. SL uses cross-validation to data-adaptively select the best way to combine the algorithms. It is general because it can be applied to any loss function $L(\psi)$ or $L_\eta(\psi)$ (and thus corresponding risk $R_0(\psi) = E_0 L(\psi)$), or any risk function, $R_{P_0}(\psi)$. It is optimal in the sense of asymptotic equivalence with oracle selector as implied by oracle inequality. These generality and optimality properties also apply to Subsemble.

Supervised Regression Tree (SRT) Subsemble: A practical supervised Subsemble algorithm that uses regression trees to determine both of the number of subsets, J, and the partitioning of the covariate space.

Stacking: Stacking is a broad class of algorithms that involve training a second-level metalearner to ensemble a group of base learners. For prediction, the Super Learner algorithm is equivalent to generalized stacking.

V-fold cross-validation: Another name for k-fold cross-validation. In k-fold cross-validation, the data is partitioned into k folds, and then a model is trained using the observations from $k-1$ folds. Next, the model is evaluated on the held out set. This is repeated k times and estimates are averaged over the k-folds.

References

1. Leo Breiman. Bagging predictors. *Machine Learning*, 24(2):123–140, 1996.

2. Leo Breiman. Stacked regressions. *Machine Learning*, 24(1):49–64, 1996.

3. Leo Breiman, Jerome Friedman, Richard A. Olshen, and Charles J. Stone. *Classification and Regression Trees*. Wadsworth & Brooks, Monterey, CA, 1984.

4. Yoav Freund and Robert E. Schapire. A decision-theoretic generalization of on-line learning and an application to boosting. *Journal of Computer and System Sciences*, 55:119–139, 1997.

5. Max Kuhn. Contributions from Jed Wing, Steve Weston, Andre Williams, Chris Keefer, Allan Engelhardt, Tony Cooper, Zachary Mayer, and the R Core Team. *caret: Classification and Regression Training*. R package version 6.0-35, 2014.

6. Erin LeDell, Maya Petersen, and Mark van der Laan. *cvAUC: Cross-Validated Area Under the ROC Curve Confidence Intervals*. R package version 1.1.0, 2015.

7. Erin LeDell, Stephanie Sapp, and Mark van der Laan. *subsemble: An Ensemble Method for Combining Subset-Specific Algorithm Fits*. R package version 0.0.8, 2014.

8. Jimmy Lin and Alek Kolcz. Large-scale machine learning at Twitter. In *Proceedings of the ACM SIGMOD International Conference on Management of Data*, pp. 793–804. ACM, New York, 2012.

9. Andrew Nobel. Histogram regression estimation using data-dependent partitions. *The Annals of Statistics*, 24(3):1084–1105, 1996.

10. Eric Polley and Mark van der Laan. *SuperLearner: Super Learner Prediction*. R package version 2.0-14, 2014.

11. Stephanie Sapp and Mark J. van der Laan. A scalable supervised subsemble prediction algorithm. Technical Report 321, Division of Biostatistics Working Paper Series, University of California, Berkeley, CA, April 2014.

12. Stephanie Sapp, Mark J. van der Laan, and John Canny. Subsemble: An ensemble method for combining subset-specific algorithm fits. *Journal of Applied Statistics*, 41(6):1247–1259, 2014.

13. Mark J. van der Laan, Sandrine Dudoit, and Aad W. van der Vaart. The cross-validated adaptive epsilon-net estimator. *Statistics and Decisions*, 24(3):373–395, 2006.

14. Mark J. van der Laan, Eric C. Polley, and Alan E. Hubbard. Super learner. *Statistical Applications in Genetics and Molecular Biology*, 6(1):25, 2007.

15. David H. Wolpert. Stacked generalization. *Neural Networks*, 5(2):241–259, 1992.

16. Yuchen Zhang, John C. Duchi, and Martin J. Wainwright. Communication-efficient algorithms for statistical optimization. *Journal of Machine Learning Research*, 14(1):3321–3363, 2013.

19

Scalable Super Learning

Erin LeDell

CONTENTS

19.1 Introduction 339
19.2 The Super Learner Algorithm 340
19.2.1 Stacking 340
19.2.2 Base Learners 341
19.2.3 Metalearning Algorithm 341
19.2.4 Oracle Properties 342
19.2.5 Comparison to Other Ensemble Learners 343
19.3 Super Learner Software 343
19.3.1 SuperLearner R Package 345
19.3.2 Subsemble R Package 345
19.3.3 H2O Ensemble 346
19.3.3.1 R Code Example 347
19.3.4 Performance Benchmarks 348
19.3.5 Computational Details 349
19.4 Online Super Learning 350
19.4.1 Optimization in Online Learning 350
19.4.2 The OSL Algorithm 351
19.4.3 A Practical Online Super Learner 352
19.5 Super Learner in Practice 352
19.6 Concluding Remarks 353
19.7 Glossary 353
References 355

19.1 Introduction

Super Learning is a generalized loss-based ensemble learning framework that was theoretically validated in [42]. This template for learning is applicable to and currently being used across a wide class of problems including problems involving biased sampling, missingness, and censoring. It can be used to estimate marginal densities, conditional densities, conditional hazards, conditional means, conditional medians, conditional quantiles, conditional survival functions, among others [43]. Some applications of Super Learning include the estimation of propensity scores, dose–response functions [21], and optimal dynamic treatment rules [29], for example.

When used for standard prediction, the Super Learner algorithm is a supervised learning algorithm equivalent to *generalized stacking* [4,45], an ensemble learning technique that combines the output from a set of base learning algorithms via a second-level metalearning algorithm. The Super Learner is built on the theory of cross-validation and has been proven to represent an asymptotically optimal system for learning [42]. The framework allows for a general class of prediction algorithms to be considered for the ensemble.

In this chapter, we discuss some of the history of stacking, review the basic theoretical properties of Super Learning and provide a description of Online Super Learning. We discuss several practical implementations of the Super Learner algorithm and highlight the various ways in which the algorithm can scale to big data. In conclusion, we present examples of real-world applications that utilize Super Learning.

19.2 The Super Learner Algorithm

The Super Learner algorithm is a generalization of the stacking algorithm introduced in context of neural networks by Wolpert [45] in 1992 and adapted to regression problems by Breiman [4] in 1996. The *Super Learner* name was introduced due to the theoretical oracle property and its consequences as presented in [9,42].

The distinct characteristic of the Super Learner algorithm in the context of stacking is its theoretical foundation, discussed in Section 19.2.4, which shows that the Super Learner ensemble is asymptotically equivalent to the oracle. Under most conditions, the theory also guarantees that the Super Learner ensemble will perform as least as well as the best individual base learner. Therefore, if model performance is the primary objective in a machine learning problem, the Super Learner with a rich candidate learner library can be used to theoretically and practically guarantee better model performance than can be achieved by a single algorithm alone.

19.2.1 Stacking

Stacking or *stacked generalization* is a procedure for ensemble learning where a second-level learner, or a *metalearner*, is trained on the output (i.e., the cross-validated predictions, described below) of a collection of *base learners*. The output from the base learners, also called the *level-one* data, can be generated by using cross-validation. Accordingly, the original training dataset is often referred to as the *level-zero* data. Although not backed by theory, in the case of large training sets, it may be reasonable to construct the level-one data using predictions from a single, independent test set. In the original stacking literature, Wolpert proposed using *leave-one-out cross-validation* [45]; however, because of computational costs and empirical evidence of superior performance, Breiman suggested using 10-fold cross-validation to generate the level-one data [4]. The Super Learner theory requires cross-validation (usually *V-fold cross-validation*, in practice) to generate the level-one data.

The following describes in greater detail how to construct the level-one data. Assume that the training set comprises n independent and identically distributed observations $\{O_1, ..., O_n\}$, where $O_i = (X_i, Y_i)$, $X_i \in \mathbb{R}^p$ is a vector of covariate or feature values, and $Y_i \in \mathbb{R}$ is the outcome. Consider an ensemble comprising a set of L base learning algorithms, $\{\Psi^1, ..., \Psi^L\}$, each of which is indexed by an algorithm class and a specific set of model parameters. Then, the process of constructing the level-one data will involve generating an $n \times L$ matrix, $\boldsymbol{Z}$, of V-fold *cross-validated predicted values* as follows:

1. The original training set, $\boldsymbol{X}$, is divided at random into V roughly equal pieces (validation folds), $\boldsymbol{X}_{(1)}, ..., \boldsymbol{X}_{(V)}$.

2. For each base learner in the ensemble, Ψ^l, V-fold cross-validation is used to generate n cross-validated predicted values associated with the lth learner. These n-dimensional vectors of cross-validated predicted values become the L columns of $\boldsymbol{Z}$.

The level-one dataset, $\boldsymbol{Z}$, along with the original outcome, $\boldsymbol{y} \in \mathbb{R}^n$, is used to train the metalearning algorithm. As a final task, each of the L base learners will be fit on the full training set and these fits will be saved. The final *ensemble fit* comprises the L base learner fits along with the metalearner fit. To generate a prediction for new data using the ensemble, the algorithm first generates predicted values from each of the L base learner fits, and then passes those predicted values as input to the metalearner fit, which returns the final predicted value for the ensemble.

The historical definition of stacking does not specify restrictions on the type of algorithm used as a metalearner; however, the metalearner is often a method that minimizes the cross-validated risk of some loss function of interest. For example, ordinary least squares (OLS) can be used to minimize the sum of squared residuals, in the case of a linear model. The Super Learner algorithm can be thought of as the theoretically supported generalization of stacking to any estimation problem, where the goal is to minimize the cross-validated risk of some bounded loss function, including loss functions indexed by nuisance parameters.

19.2.2 Base Learners

It is recommended that the *base learner library* include a diverse set of learners (e.g., Linear Model, Support Vector Machine, Random Forest, Neural Net, etc.); however, the Super Learner theory does not require any specific level of diversity among the set of the base learners. The library can also include copies of the same algorithm, indexed by different sets of model parameters. For example, the user could specify multiple Random Forests [5], each with a different splitting criterion, tree depth or *mtry* value. Typically, in stacking-based ensemble methods, the prediction functions, $\hat{\Psi}^1, ..., \hat{\Psi}^L$, are fit by training each of base learning algorithms, $\Psi^1, ..., \Psi^L$, on the full training dataset and then combining these fits using a metalearning algorithm, Φ. However, there are variants of Super Learning, such as the Subsemble algorithm [36], which learn the prediction functions on subsets of the training data.

The base learners can be any parametric or nonparametric supervised machine learning algorithm. Stacking was originally presented by Wolpert, who used neural networks as base learners. Breiman extended the stacking framework to regression problems under the name *stacked regressions* and experimented with different base learners. For base learning algorithms, he evaluated ensembles of decision trees (with different numbers of terminal nodes), generalized linear models (GLMs) using subset variable regression (with a different number of predictor variables), or ridge regression [16] (with different ridge parameters). He also built ensembles by combining several subset variable regression models with ridge regression models and found that the added diversity among the base models increased performance. Both Wolpert and Breiman focused their work on using the same underlying algorithm (i.e., neural nets, decision trees, or GLMs) with unique tuning parameters as the set of base learners, although Breiman briefly suggested the idea of using heterogeneous base learning algorithms, such as neural nets and nearest-neighbor.

19.2.3 Metalearning Algorithm

The metalearner, Φ, is used to find the optimal combination of the L base learners. The $\boldsymbol{Z}$ matrix of cross-validated predicted values, as described in Section 19.2.1, is used as the input for the metalearning algorithm, along with the original outcome from the level-zero training data, $\boldsymbol{y} = (Y_1, ..., Y_n)$.

The metalearning algorithm is typically a method designed to minimize the cross-validated risk of some loss function. For example, if your goal is to minimize mean squared prediction error, you could use the least-squares algorithm to solve for $\boldsymbol{\alpha} = (\alpha_1, ..., \alpha_L)$, the weight vector that minimizes the following:

$$\sum_{i=1}^{n}\left(Y_i - \sum_{l=1}^{L}\alpha_l z_{li}\right)^2$$

Because the set of predictions from the various base learners may be highly correlated, it is advisable to choose a metalearning method that performs well in the presence of collinear predictors. Regularization via Ridge [17] or Lasso [39] regression is commonly used to overcome the issue of collinearity among the predictor variables that make up the level-one dataset. Empirically, Breiman found that using Ridge regression as the metalearner often yielded a lower prediction error than using unregularized least-squares regression. Of the regularization methods he considered, a linear combination achieved via nonnegative least squares (NNLS) [23] gave the best results in terms of prediction error. The NNLS algorithm minimizes the same objective function as the least-squares algorithm, but adds the constraint that $\alpha_l \geq 0$, for $l = 1, ..., L$. Le Blanc and Tibshirani [24] also came to the conclusion that nonnegativity constraints lead to the most accurate linear combinations of the base learners.

Breiman also discussed desirable theoretical properties that arise by enforcing the additional constraint that $\sum_l \alpha_l = 1$, where the ensemble is a *convex combination* of the base learners. However, in simulations, he shows that the prediction error is nearly the same whether or not $\sum_l \alpha_l = 1$. The convex combination is not only empirically motivated, but also supported by the theory. As mentioned in Section 19.2.4, the oracle results for the Super Learner require a uniformly bounded loss function and restricting to the convex combination implies that if each algorithm in the library is bounded, the convex combination will also be bounded. In practice, truncation of the predicted values to the range of the outcome variable in the training set is sufficient to allow for unbounded loss functions.

In the Super Learner algorithm, the metalearning method is specified as the minimizer of the cross-validated risk of a loss function of interest, such as *squared-error loss* or *rank loss* (1-AUC). If the loss function of interest is unique, unusual or complex, it may be difficult to find an existing machine learning algorithm (i.e., metalearner) that directly or indirectly minimizes this function. However, the optimal combination of the base learners can be estimated using a nonlinear optimization algorithm such as those that are available in the open source **NLopt** library [20]. This particular approach to metalearning provides a great deal of flexibility to the Super Learner, in the sense that the ensemble can be trained to optimize any complex objective. Historically, in stacking implementations, the metalearning algorithm is often some sort of regularized linear model; however, a variety of parametric and nonparametric methods can used as a metalearner to combine the output from the base fits.

19.2.4 Oracle Properties

The *oracle selector* is defined as the estimator, among all possible weighted combinations of the base prediction functions, which minimizes risk under the true data-generating distribution. The oracle result for the cross-validation selector among a set of candidate learners was established in [41] for general bounded loss functions, in [10] for unbounded loss functions under an exponential tail condition, and in [42] for its application to the

Super Learner. The oracle selector is considered to be optimal with respect to a particular loss function, given the set of base learners; however, it depends on both the observed data and the true distribution, P_0, and thus is unknown. If the true prediction function cannot be represented by a combination of the base learners in the library, then *optimal* will be the closest combination that could be determined to be optimal, if the true data-generating mechanism were known. If a training set is large enough, it would theoretically result in the oracle selector. In the original stacking literature, Breiman observed that the ensemble predictor almost always has lower prediction error than the single best base learner, although a proof was not presented in his work [4].

If one of the base learners is a parametric model that happens to contain the true prediction function, this base learner will achieve a parametric rate of convergence and thus the Super Learner achieves an almost parametric rate of convergence, $\log(n)/n$.

19.2.5 Comparison to Other Ensemble Learners

In the machine learning community, the term *ensemble learning* is often associated with *bagging* [3] or *boosting* [11] techniques or particular algorithms such as Random Forest [5]. Stacking is similar to bagging due to the independent training of the base learners; however, there are two notable distinctions. The first is that stacking uses a metalearning algorithm to optimally combine the output from the base learners instead of simple averaging, as in bagging. The second is that modern stacking is typically characterized by a diverse set of strong base learners, where bagging is often associated with a single, often weak, base learning algorithm. A popular example of bagging is the Random Forest algorithm that bags classification or regression trees trained on subsets of the feature space. A case could be made that bagging is a special case of stacking that uses the mean as the metalearning algorithm.

From a computational perspective, bagging, like stacking, is a particularly well-suited ensemble learning method for big data because models can be trained independently on different cores or machines within a cluster. However, because boosting utilizes an iterative, hence sequential, training approach, it does not scale as easily to big data problems.

A Bayesian ensemble learning algorithm that is often compared to stacking is Bayesian model averaging (BMA). A BMA model is a linear combination of the output from the base learners in which the weights are the posterior probabilities of models. Both BMA and Super Learner use cross-validation as part of the ensemble process. In the case where the true prediction function is contained within the base learner library, BMA is never worse than stacking and often is demonstrably better under reasonable conditions. However, if the true prediction function is not well approximated by the base learner library, then stacking will significantly outperform BMA [7].

19.3 Super Learner Software

This section serves as a broad overview of several implementations of the Super Learner ensemble algorithm and its variants. The original Super Learner implementation is the **SuperLearner** R package [34]; however, there are several ongoing projects that aim to create more scalable implementations of the algorithm that are suitable for big data. We will discuss a variety of approaches to scalingG the Super Learner algorithm:

1. Perform the cross-validation and base learning steps in parallel as these are computationally independent tasks.

2. Train the base learners on subsets of the original training dataset.
3. Utilize distributed or parallelized base learning algorithms.
4. Employ online learning techniques to avoid memory-wise scalability limitations.
5. Implement the ensemble (and/or base learners) in a scalable language, such as C++, Java, Scala, or Julia, for example.

Currently, there are three implementations of the Super Learner algorithm that have an R interface. The **SuperLearner** and **subsemble** [27] R packages are implemented entirely in R, although they can make use of base learning algorithms that are written in compiled languages as long as there is an R interface available. Often, the main computational tasks of machine learning algorithms accessible via R packages are written in Fortran (e.g., **randomForest**, **glmnet**) or C++ (e.g., **e1071**s interface to **LIBSVM** [6]), and the runtime of certain algorithms can be reduced by linking R to an optimized BLAS (Basic Linear Algebra Subprograms) library, such as **OpenBLAS** [46], **ATLAS** [44], or **Intel MKL** [19]. These techniques may provide additional speed in training, but do not necessarily curtail all memory-related scalability issues. Typically, because at least one copy of the full training dataset must reside in memory in R, this is an inherent limitation to the scalability of these implementations.

A more scalable implementation of the Super Learner algorithm is available in the **h2oEnsemble** R package [25]. The **H2O Ensemble** implementation uses R to interface with distributed base learning algorithms from the high-performance, open source Java machine learning library, **H2O** [14]. Each of these three Super Learner implementations is at a different stage of development and has benefits and drawbacks compared to the others, but all three projects are being actively developed and maintained.

The main challenge in writing a Super Learner implementation is not implementing the ensemble algorithm itself. In fact, the Super Learner algorithm simply organizes the cross-validated output from the base learners and applies the metalearning algorithm to this derived dataset. Some thought must be given to the parallelization aspects of the algorithm, but this is typically a straightforward exercise, given the computational independence of the cross-validation and base learning steps. One of the main software engineering tasks in any Super Learner implementation is creating a unified interface to a large collection of base learning and metalearning algorithms. A Super Learner implementation must include a novel or third-party machine learning algorithm interface that allows users to specify the base learners in a common format. Ideally, the users of the software should be able to define their own base learning functions that specify an algorithm and set of model parameters in addition to any default algorithms that are provided within the software. The performance of the Super Learner is determined by the combined performance of the base learners, so a having a rich library of machine learning algorithms accessible in the ensemble software is important.

The metalearning methods can use the same interface as the base learners simplifying the implementation. The metalearner is just another algorithm, although it is common for a nonnegative linear combination of the base algorithms to be created using a method like NNLS. However, if the loss function of interest to the user is unrelated to the objective functions associated with the base learning algorithms, then a linear combination of the base learners that minimizes the user-specified loss function can be learned using a nonlinear optimization library, such as NLopt. In classification problems, this is particularly relevant in the case where the outcome variable in the training set is highly imbalanced. NLopt provides a common interface to a number of different algorithms that can be used to solve this problem. There are also methods that allow for constraints, such as nonnegativity ($\alpha_l \geq 0$) and convexity ($\sum_{l=1}^{L} \alpha_l = 1$) of the weights. Using one of several nonlinear optimization algorithms, such as L-BFGS-B, Nelder-Mead, or COBYLA, it is possible to find a linear combination of the base learners that specifically minimizes the loss function of interest.

19.3.1 SuperLearner R Package

As is common for many statistical algorithms, the original implementation of the Super Learner algorithm was written in R. The **SuperLearner** R package, first released in 2010, is actively maintained with new features being added periodically. This package implements the Super Learner algorithm and provides a unified interface to a diverse set of machine learning algorithms that are available in the R language. The software is extensible in the sense that the user can define custom base-learner function wrappers and specify them as part of the ensemble; however, there are about 30 algorithm wrappers provided by the package by default. The main advantage of an R implementation is direct access to the rich collection of machine learning algorithms that already exist within the R ecosystem. The main disadvantage of an R implementation is memory-related scalability.

Because the base learners are trained independently from each other, the training of the constituent algorithms can be done in parallel. The embarrassingly parallel nature of the cross-validation and base learning steps of the Super Learner algorithm can be exploited in any language. If there are L base learners and V cross-validation folds, there are $L \times V$ independent computational tasks involved in creating the level-one data. The **SuperLearner** package provides functionality to parallelize the cross-validation step via multicore or SNOW (Simple Network of Workstations) [40] clusters.

The R language and its third-party libraries are not particularly well known for memory efficiency, so depending on the specifications of the machine or cluster that is being used, it is possible to run out of memory while attempting to train the ensemble on large training sets. Because the **SuperLearner** package relies on third-party implementations of the base learning algorithms, the scalability of **SuperLearner** is tied to the scalability of the base learner implementations used in the ensemble. When selecting a single model among a group of candidate algorithms based on cross-validated model performance, this is computationally equivalent to generating the level-one data in the Super Learner algorithm. If cross-validation is already being employed as a means of grid-search-based model selection among a group of candidate learning algorithms, the addition of the metalearning step is a computationally minimal burden. However, a Super Learner ensemble can result in a significant boost in overall model performance over a single base learner model.

19.3.2 Subsemble R Package

The **subsemble** R package implements the Subsemble algorithm [36], a variant of Super Learning, which ensembles base models trained on subsets of the original data. Specifically, the disjoint union of the subsets is the full training set. As a special case, where the number of subsets = 1, the package also implements the Super Learner algorithm.

The Subsemble algorithm can be used as a stand-alone ensemble algorithm or as the base learning algorithm in the Super Learner algorithm. Empirically, it has been shown that Subsemble can provide better prediction performance than fitting a single algorithm once on the full available dataset [36], although this is not always the case.

An oracle result shows that Subsemble performs as well as the best possible combination of the subset-specific fits. The Super Learner has more powerful asymptotic properties; it performs as well as the best possible combination of the base learners trained on the full dataset. However, when used as a stand-alone ensemble algorithm, Subsemble offers great computational flexibility, in that the training task can be scaled to any size by changing the number, or size, of the subsets. This allows the user to effectively *flatten* the training process into a task that is compatible with available computational resources. If parallelization is used effectively, all subset-specific fits can be trained at the same time, drastically increasing the speed of the training process. Because the subsets are typically much smaller than the original training set, this also reduces the memory requirements of each node in your cluster. The computational flexibility and speed of the Subsemble algorithm offer a unique solution to scaling ensemble learning to big data problems.

In the **subsemble** package, the J subsets can be created by the software at random, or the subsets can be explicitly specified by the user. Given L base learning algorithms and J subsets, a total of $L \times J$ subset-specific fits will be trained and included in the Subsemble (by default). This construction allows each base learning algorithm to see each subset of the training data, so in this sense, there is a similarity to ensembles trained on the full data. To distinguish the variations on this theme, this type of ensemble construction is referred to as a *cross-product* Subsemble. The **subsemble** package also implements what are called *divisor* Subsembles, a structure that can be created if the number of unique base learning algorithms is a divisor of the number of subsets. In this case, there are only J total subset-specific fits that make up the ensemble, and each learner only sees approximately n/J observations from the full training set (assuming that the subsets are of equal size). For example, if $L = 2$ and $J = 10$, then each of the two base learning algorithms would be used to train five subset-specific fits and would only see a total of 50% of the original training observations. This type of Subsemble allows for quicker training, but will typically result in less accurate models. Therefore, the *cross-product* method is the default Subsemble type in the software.

An algorithm called Supervised Regression Tree Subsemble or *SRT Subsemble* [35] is also on the development road map for the **subsemble** package. SRT Subsemble is an extension of the regular Subsemble algorithm, which provides a means of learning the optimal number and constituency of the subsets. This method incurs an additional computational cost, but can provide greater model performance for the Subsemble.

19.3.3 H2O Ensemble

The **H2O Ensemble** software contains an implementation of the Super Learner ensemble algorithm that is built on the distributed, open source, Java-based machine learning platform for big data, **H2O**. **H2O Ensemble** is currently implemented as a stand-alone R package called **h2oEnsemble** that makes use of the **h2o** package, the R interface to the **H2O** platform. There are a handful of powerful supervised machine learning algorithms supported by the **h2o** package, all of which can be used as base learners for the ensemble. This includes a high-performance method for deep learning, which allows the user to create ensembles of deep neural nets or combine the power of deep neural nets with other algorithms, such as Random Forest or Gradient Boosting Machines (GBMs) [12].

Because the **H2O** machine learning platform was designed with big data in mind, each of the **H2O** base learning algorithms is scalable to very large training sets and enables parallelism across multiple nodes and cores. The **H2O** platform comprises a distributed in-memory parallel computing architecture and has the ability to seamlessly use datasets stored in Hadoop Distributed File System (HDFS), Amazon's S3 cloud storage, NoSQL, and SQL databases in addition to CSV files stored locally or in distributed filesystems. The **H2O Ensemble** project aims to match the scalability of the **H2O** algorithms, so although the ensemble uses R as its main user interface, most of the computations are performed in Java via **H2O** in a distributed, scalable fashion.

There are several publicly available benchmarks of the **H2O** algorithms. Notably, the **H2O** GLM implementation has been benchmarked on a training set of one billion observations [13]. This benchmark training set is derived from the *Airline Dataset* [31], which has been called the *Iris dataset for big data*. The one billion row training set is a 42 Gb CSV file with 12 feature columns (9 numerical features, 3 categorical features with cardinalities 30, 376, and 380) and a binary outcome. Using a 48-node cluster (8 cores on each node, 15 Gb of RAM, and 1 Gb interconnect speed), the **H2O** GLM can be trained in 5.6 s. The **H2O** algorithm implementations aim to be scalable to any size dataset so that all of the available training set, rather than a subset, can be used for training models.

H2O Ensemble takes a different approach to scaling the Super Learner algorithm than the **subsemble** or **SuperLearner** R packages. Because the **subsemble** and **SuperLearner** ensembles rely on third-party R algorithm implementations that are typically single threaded, the parallelism of these two implementations occurs in the cross-validation and base learning steps. In the **SuperLearner** implementation, the ability to take advantage of multiple cores is strictly limited by the number of cross-validation folds and number of base learners. With **subsemble**, the scalability of the ensemble can be improved by increasing the number of subsets used; however, this may lead to a decrease in model performance. Unlike most third-party machine learning algorithms that are available in R, the **H2O** base learning algorithms are implemented in a distributed fashion and can scale to all available cores in a multicore or multinode cluster. In the current release of **H2O Ensemble**, the cross-validation and base learning steps of the ensemble algorithm are performed in serial; however, each serial training step is maximally parallelized across all available cores in a cluster. The **H2O Ensemble** implementation could possibly be re-architected to parallelize the cross-validation and base learning steps; however, it is unknown at this time how that may affect runtime performance.

19.3.3.1 R Code Example

The following R code example demonstrates how to create an ensemble of a Random Forest and two Deep Neural Nets using the **h2oEnsemble** R interface. In the code below, an example shows the current method for defining custom base-learner functions. The **h2oEnsemble** package comes with four base learner function wrappers; however, to create a base learner with nondefault model parameters, the user can pass along nondefault function arguments as shown. The user must also specify a metalearning algorithm, and in this example, a GLM wrapper function is used.

```
library("SuperLearner") # For "SL.nnls" metalearner function
library("h2oEnsemble")

# Create custom base learner functions using non-default model params:
h2o_rf_1 <- function(..., family = "binomial",
                              ntree = 500,
                              depth = 50,
                              mtries = 6,
                              sample.rate = 0.8,
                              nbins = 50,
                              nfolds = 0)
     h2o.randomForest.wrapper(..., family = family, ntree = ntree,
     depth = depth, mtries = mtries, sample.rate = sample.rate,
     nbins = nbins, nfolds = nfolds)
}
```

```
h2o_dl_1 <- function(..., family = "binomial",
                                      nfolds = 0,
                                      activation = "RectifierWithDropout",
                                      hidden = c(200,200),
                                      epochs = 100,
                                      l1 = 0,
                                      l2 = 0)
        h2o.deeplearning.wrapper(..., family = family, nfolds = nfolds,
        activation = activation, hidden = hidden, epochs = epochs,
        l1 = l1, l2 = l2)
}

h2o_dl_1 <- function(..., family = "binomial",
                                      nfolds = 0,
                                      activation = "Rectifier",
                                      hidden = c(200,200),
                                      epochs = 100,
                                      l1 = 0,
                                      l2 = 1e-05)
        h2o.deeplearning.wrapper(..., family = family, nfolds = nfolds,
        activation = activation, hidden = hidden, epochs = epochs,
        l1 = l1, l2 = l2)
}
```

The function interface for the `h2o.ensemble` function follows the same conventions as the other **h2o** R package algorithm functions. This includes the `x` and `y` arguments, which are the column names of the predictor variables and outcome variable, respectively. The `data` object is a reference to the training dataset, which exists in Java memory. The `family` argument is used to specify the type of prediction (i.e., classification or regression). The `predict.h2o.ensemble` function uses the `predict(object, newdata)` interface that is common to most machine learning software packages in R. After specifying the base learner library and the metalearner, the ensemble can be trained and tested:

```
# Set up the ensemble
learner <- c("h2o_rf_1", "h2o_dl_1", "h2o_dl_2")
metalearner <- "SL.nnls"

# Train the ensemble using 2-fold CV to generate level-one data
# More CV folds will increase runtime, but should increase performance
fit <- h2o.ensemble(x = x, y = y, data = data, family = "binomial",
                    learner = learner, metalearner = metalearner,
                    cvControl = list(V = 2))

# Generate predictions on the test set
pred <- predict(fit, newdata)
```

19.3.4 Performance Benchmarks

The **H2O Ensemble** was benchmarked on Amazon's Elastic Compute Cloud (EC2) to demonstrate the practical use of the Super Learner algorithm on big data. The instance type used across all benchmarks is EC2's *c3.8xlarge* type, which has 32 virtual CPUs (vCPUs) and 60 Gb RAM and 10 Gb interconnect speed. Because **H2O**'s algorithms are distributed and the benchmarks were performed on multinode clusters, the node interconnect speed is critical to performance. Further computational details are given in Section 19.3.5. A few different cluster architectures were evaluated, including a 320 vCPU and 96 vCPU cluster (10 and 3 nodes each, respectively), as well as a single workstation with 32 vCPUs.

The **h2oEnsemble** package currently provides four base learner function wrappers for the **H2O** algorithms. The following supervised learning algorithms are supported: GLMs with elastic net regularization, Gradient Boosting (GBM) with regression and classification trees, Random Forest and Deep Learning (multilayer feed-forward neural networks). These algorithms support both classification and regression problems, although this benchmark is a binary classification problem. Various subsets of the *HIGGS* dataset [1] (28 numeric features; binary outcome with balanced training classes) were used to assess the scalability of the ensemble. An independent test set of 500,000 observations (the same test set as in [1]) was used to measure the performance.

The base learner library consists of the three base learners that were defined in Section 19.3.3.1, which includes a Random Forest of 500 trees and two Deep Neural Nets (one with dropout [15] and the other with L_2-regularization). In the ensemble, twofold cross-validation was used to generate the level-one data and both a GLM and NNLS metalearner were evaluated. An increase in the number of validation folds will likely increase ensemble performance; however, this will increase training time (twofold is the recommended minimum required to retain the desirable asymptotic properties of the Super Learner algorithm). Although the performance is measured by AUC (area under the ROC curve) in the benchmarks, the metalearning algorithms used (GLM and NNLS) are not designed to maximize AUC. By using a higher number of cross-validation folds, an AUC-maximizing metalearning algorithm and a larger and more diverse base learning library, the performance of the ensemble will likely increase. Thus, the ensemble AUC estimates shown in Table 19.1 are conservative example of performance.

Memory profiling was not performed as part of the benchmarking process. The source code for the benchmarks is available on the author's GitHub page [26] (Figure 19.1).

19.3.5 Computational Details

All benchmarks were performed on 64-bit linux instances (type *c3.8xlarge* on Amazon EC2) running Ubuntu 14.04. Each instance has 32 vCPUs, 60 Gb RAM and uses Intel Xeon E5-2680 v2 (Ivy Bridge) processors. In the 10-node (320 vCPU) cluster and 3-node (96 vCPU) cluster that were used, the nodes have a 10 Gb interconnect speed. Because the **H2O** base learner algorithms are distributed across all the cores in a multinode cluster, it is recommended to use 10 Gb interconnect (or greater). These results are for **h2oEnsemble** R package version 0.0.3, R version 3.1.1, **H2O** version 2.9.0.1593, and Java version 1.7.0_65 using the **OpenJDK** Runtime Environment (IcedTea 2.5.3) (Table 19.2).

TABLE 19.1
Base learner model performance (test set AUC) compared to **h2oEnsemble** model performance using twofold CV (ensemble results for both GLM and NNLS metalearners).

Data Size	RF	DNN-Dropout	DNN-L_2	Ensemble: GLM, NNLS
$n = 1{,}000$	0.730	0.683	0.660	0.729, 0.730
$n = 10{,}000$	0.785	0.722	0.707	0.786, 0.788
$n = 100{,}000$	0.825	0.812	0.809	0.818, 0.819
$n = 1{,}000{,}000$	0.823	0.812	0.838	0.841, 0.841
$n = 5{,}000{,}000$	0.839	0.817	0.845	0.852, 0.851

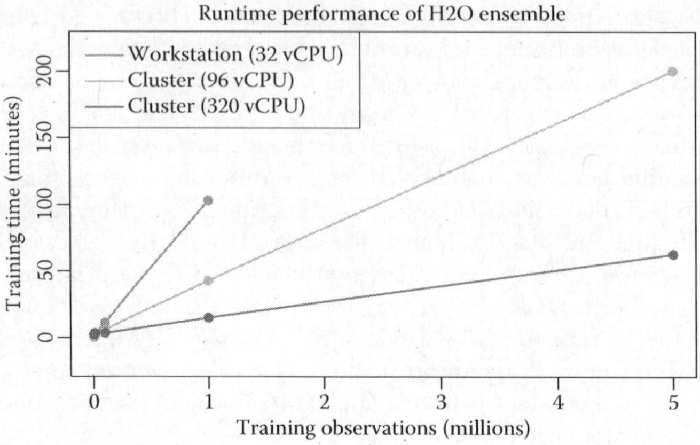

FIGURE 19.1
Training time for **H2O Ensemble** for training sets of increasing size (subsets of the HIGGS dataset). This ensemble included the three base learners, listed previously.

TABLE 19.2
Training times (minutes) for **H2O Ensemble** with a three-learner library using various cluster configurations, including a single workstation with 32 vCPUs.

Data Size	Cluster (320) (min)	Cluster (96) (min)	Workstation (32) (min)
$n = 1{,}000$	2.1	1.1	0.5
$n = 10{,}000$	3.3	2.5	2.0
$n = 100{,}000$	3.5	5.9	11.0
$n = 1{,}000{,}000$	14.9	42.6	102.9
$n = 5{,}000{,}000$	62.3	200.2	—

Note: The number of vCPUs for each cluster is noted in parentheses. Results for $n = 5$ million are not available for the single workstation setting.

19.4 Online Super Learning

Another approach to creating a scalable Super Learner implementation is by using sequential or *online learning* techniques. The Online Super Learner (OSL) uses both online base learners and an online metalearner to achieve out-of-core performance. Online learning methods offer a solution to the demanding memory requirements of *batch learning* (where the algorithm sees all the data at once), which typically requires the full training set to fit into RAM. A unique advantage of online learning, as opposed to batch learning, is that the algorithm fit can respond to changes or drift within the data-generating mechanism over time.

19.4.1 Optimization in Online Learning

Training an estimator typically reduces to some sort of optimization problem. There are many ways to solve different optimization problems, and one such way is gradient descent (GD). The algorithm is parameterized by γ, which controls the step size. If the number of training examples is very large, one iteration of the algorithm may take a long time because computing the gradient on the full dataset is slow.

An alternative to GD is stochastic GD (SGD). The algorithm is similar, except that a step is taken using an estimate of the gradient based on one or in the case of the minibatch version, $m \ll n$, observations. In [2], it is shown that SGD converges at the same rate as GD. Although SGD steps are noisy and more are required, each step uses only a small fraction of the data and therefore can be computed very quickly. Because of this, reasonably good results can be obtained in only a few passes through the data, which may take many passes in traditional GD. This results in a much faster algorithm. Another advantage of SGD is that it can be used in an online setting, where an essentially infinite stream of observations are being collected and consumed by the algorithm in a sequential process.

19.4.2 The OSL Algorithm

Assume a finite set, $X_1, ..., X_n$, or stream of observations, $X_1, ..., X_n, X_{n+1}, ...$, from some distribution, P_0, or some sequence of distributions. In the OSL algorithm, the base learning algorithms are online learners. We will consider the sequential learning case where we update each of the base learners after observing each new training point, X_i.

Because the online base learners are all observing the same training point at the same time, all of the base learners can be updated simultaneously at each iteration (either serially, or in parallel). In the batch version of Super Learning, after cross-validation is used to generate the level-one data from the base learners, a metalearning algorithm is fit using the level-one data. Because standard V-fold cross-validation is a batch operation, we must consider an alternative sequential approach to generating the level-one data and updating the metalearner fit in the OSL algorithm. There may be many possible ways to do this, but we will discuss one particular method, which was implemented in the **Vowpal Wabbit (VW) Ensemble** [28] described in Section 19.4.3.

Consider two types of sequential learning—single-pass and multipass mode, in which the training process is completed in one pass or multiple passes through the data, respectively. If the training samples are streaming in sequentially (in other words, the training set is not a previously collected set of examples), then the single-pass mode is necessary. However, if all of the training samples have already been collected, then it is possible to take multiple passes through the data.

In both the single-pass and multipass mode, there is an option to designate a *holdout set* of observations that are never used in training. This is not strictly necessary, but can be performed to collect information about estimated model performance (where model performance is evaluated incrementally on the holdout set). In practice, for single-pass mode, sequential validation of each observation is sufficient, and thus a designated holdout set is not required. This is because in single-pass mode, each observation can be used first as a test sample for the current fit, and then as a training sample in the next iteration of the algorithm. However, in multipass mode, a holdout set is required to generate an honest estimate of model performance.

To distinguish between two types of observations that are not used in training, we will reserve the term *holdout set* for observations used strictly for model evaluation. A second group of held-out observations, the *validation set*, will be set aside and used to generate predicted values using the existing model fit. The resulting predicted values will serve as the level-one data, which is used to train the metalearner.

We define two tuning parameters, ρ and ν, to control the construction of the level-one data for the metalearner. In multipass mode, the parameter ρ controls the *validation period*, or the number of training examples between each (non-holdout) validation sample, as observed in sequence. For example, if $\rho = 10$, then every 10th non-holdout sample would be set aside to be included in the rolling validation set. In this case, the algorithm sees 10 training samples for every validation sample. All nonvalidation, non-holdout sample points are used in training.

The second tuning parameter is ν, the *running validation size*, or the number of most recent (and non-holdout, if multipass) validation samples to be retained (at any iteration) for updating the metalearning fit. This parameter controls the amount of data that needs to reside in memory at any given time—bigger ν translates into a more informed metalearning fit, but demands higher memory requirements. In theory, the ν parameter could be adaptive; however, in this specification of the algorithm, we will consider it to be a fixed value.

Fixing or limiting the size of the level-one data for the ensemble at a given iteration via the ν parameter allows the user to make use of batch learning algorithms in the metalearning process. Regardless, this implementation of the OSL algorithm is still considered to be a sequential learner, because the ensemble fit is learned incrementally. When using a batch algorithm as part of the metalearning process, it is advisable to choose a large enough ν, or validation set size, to successfully train the metalearner. This is similar to minibatch learning in SGD, where $m > 1$ examples are retained at any given time for training (in that case, the m samples are used to estimate the gradient).

In an alternative formulation, where sequential learners are used for both the base learners and the metalearning algorithm, then $\nu = 1$ and the metalearner fit will be updated with one training sample at a time, in sync with the updates of the base learner fits. Or, in the case of minibatch SGD, then $\nu = m$ and m training observations are processed at each iteration.

19.4.3 A Practical Online Super Learner

VW [22] is fast out-of-core learning software developed by John Langford that was first released in 2007 and is still very actively maintained. **VW** implements SGD (and a few other optimization routines) for a variety of estimators with a primary goal of being computationally very fast and scaling well to large datasets. The software also allows for estimators to easily be fit on different subsets and cross-products of subsets of independent variables. **VW** is written in C++ and can be used as a library in other software.

The default learning algorithm in **VW** is a variant of online GD. Various extensions, such as conjugate gradient (CG), minibatch, and data-dependent learning rates, are included. **VW** is very useful for sparse data, so a **VW**-based OSL will also be useful for sparse data.

A proof-of-concept version of the OSL algorithm was implemented in C++, and uses the **VW** machine learning library to provide the base learners. The additional dependencies are the **Boost** C++ library [8] and a C implementation (**f2c** translation from Fortran) [37] of the NNLS algorithm for the metalearning process. The tuning parameters mentioned in Section 19.4.2 give the user fine-grained control over the sequential learning process.

To demonstrate computational performance, the OSL was trained on the *Malicious URL Dataset* [30] that has 2.4 million rows and 3.2 million sparse features. Using three algorithms to make up the ensemble, the OSL made a single pass over the data. The training process on a single 2.3 GHz Intel Core i7 processor took approximately 25 s.

19.5 Super Learner in Practice

There are many applications of the Super Learner algorithm; however, because of its superior performance over single algorithms and other ensemble learners, it is often used in situations where model performance is valued over other factors, such as training time and model simplicity. The algorithm has been used in a wide variety of applications in the field of biostatistics. In the context of prediction, Super Learner has been used to predict virologic failure among HIV-infected individuals [32], HIV-1 drug resistance [38], and mortality among patients in intensive care units [33], for example.

Super Learning can be used at iterative time points to evaluate the relative importance of each measured variable on an outcome. This can provide continuously changing prediction of the outcome and evaluation of which clinical variables likely drive a particular outcome. [18]

In the context of learning the optimal dynamic treatment rule, a nonsequential Super Learner seeks to directly maximize the mean outcome under the two-time-point rule [29]. This implementation relies on sequential candidate estimators based on various loss functions. Super Learner has also been used to estimate both the generalized propensity score and the dose–response function [21].

19.6 Concluding Remarks

In this chapter, we presented the Super Learner algorithm, a theoretically backed nonparametric ensemble prediction method. Super Learner fits a set of base learners and combines the fits through a second-level metalearning algorithm using cross-validation. We discussed several software implementations of the algorithm and provided code examples and benchmarks of a distributed, scalable implementation called **H2O Ensemble**. Further, an online implementation of the Super Learner algorithm was presented as an alternative to the batch version as another approach to achieving scalability for big data. Lastly, we described examples of practical applications of the Super Learner algorithm.

19.7 Glossary

Bagging: Bootstrap aggregating, or bagging, is an ensemble algorithm designed to improve the stability and accuracy of machine learning algorithms used in statistical classification and regression. Bagging is a special case of the model averaging approach.

Base learner: A supervised machine learning algorithm (with a specific set of tuning parameters) used as part of the ensemble.

Base learner library: A set of base learners that make up the ensemble.

Boosting: A boosting algorithm iteratively learns weak classifiers and adds them to a final strong classifier.

Batch learning: Any algorithm that learns by processing the entire dataset at once (which typically requires the entire dataset to fit in memory). This is the opposite of online or sequential learning.

Convex combination: A convex combination is a linear combination where the coefficients are nonnegative and sum to 1.

Cross-validated predicted values: Assuming n i.i.d. training examples and V-fold cross-validation, the cross-validated predicted values for a particular learner is the set of n predictions obtained by training on folds, $\{1, ..., V\} \setminus v$, and generating predictions on the held-out validation set, fold v. In the context of stacking, this is called the *level-one* data.

Ensemble learner: A machine learning algorithm that uses the input from multiple base learners to inform its predictions.

H2O: An open source machine learning library with a distributed, Java-based back-end.

Level-one data: The independent predictions generated from validation (typically V-fold cross-validation) of the base learners. This data is the input to the metalearner. This is also called the set of *cross-validated predicted values.*

Level-zero data: The original training dataset that is used to train the base learners.

Loss function, objective function: A loss function is a function that maps an event or values of one or more variables onto a real number intuitively representing some *cost* associated with the event. An optimization problem seeks to minimize a loss function.

Metalearner: A supervised machine learning algorithm that is used to learn the optimal combination of the base learners. This can also be an optimization method such as nonnegative least-squares (NNLS), COBYLA, or L-BFGS-B for finding the optimal linear combination of the base learners.

Online (or sequential) learning: Online learning, as opposed to batch learning, involves using a stream of data for training examples. In online methods, the model fit is updated, or learned, incrementally.

Online Super Learner (OSL): An online implementation of the Super Learner algorithm that uses stochastic gradient descent for incremental learning.

Oracle selector: The estimator, among all possible weighted combinations of the base prediction functions, which minimizes risk under the true data-generating distribution.

Rank loss: The rank loss is a name for the quantity, $1-$AUC, where AUC is the area under the ROC curve.

Squared-error loss: The squared-error loss of an estimator measures the average of the squares of the error or the difference between the estimator and what is estimated.

Stacking, stacked generalization, stacked regression: Stacking is a broad class of algorithms that involves training a second-level metalearner to ensemble a group of base learners. For prediction, the Super Learner algorithm is equivalent to generalized stacking.

Subsemble: Subsemble is a general subset ensemble prediction method which partitions the full dataset into subsets of observations, fits a specified underlying algorithm on each subset, and uses a unique form of V-fold cross-validation to output a prediction function that combines the subset-specific fits. An oracle result provides a theoretical performance guarantee for Subsemble.

Super Learner (SL): Super Learner is an ensemble algorithm takes as input a library of supervised learning algorithms and a metalearning algorithm. SL uses cross-validation to data-adaptively select the best way to combine the algorithms. It is general since it can be applied to any loss function $L(\psi)$ or $L_\eta(\psi)$ (and thus corresponding risk $R_0(\psi) = E_0L(\psi)$), or any risk function, $R_{P_0}(\psi)$. It is optimal in the sense of asymptotic equivalence with oracle selector as implied by oracle inequality.

V-fold cross-validation: Another name for k-fold cross-validation. In k-fold cross-validation, the data is partitioned into k folds, and then a model is trained using the observations from $k-1$ folds. Next, the model is evaluated on the held out set. This is repeated k times and estimates are averaged over the k-folds.

Vowpal Wabbit (VW): An open source, out-of-core, online machine learning library written in C++.

References

1. Pierre Baldi, Peter Sadowski, and Daniel Whiteson. Searching for exotic particles in high-energy physics with deep learning. *Nature Communications*, 5, 2014, doi:10.1038/ncomms5308.

2. Léon Bottou. Large-scale machine learning with stochastic gradient descent. In *Proceedings of COMPSTAT'2010*, pp. 177–186. Springer, Berlin, Germany, 2010.

3. Leo Breiman. Bagging predictors. *Machine Learning*, 24(2):123–140, 1996.

4. Leo Breiman. Stacked regressions. *Machine Learning*, 24(1):49–64, 1996.

5. Leo Breiman. Random forests. *Machine Learning*, 45(1):5–32, 2001.

6. Chih-Chung Chang and Chih-Jen Lin. *LIBSVM: A Library for Support Vector Machines*, 2001.

7. Bertrand Clarke and Bin Yu. Comparing bayes model averaging and stacking when model approximation error cannot be ignored. *Journal of Machine Learning Research*, 4:683-712, 2003.

8. Beman Dawes, David Abrahams, and Nicolai Josuttis. *Boost C++ Libraries*. http://www.boost.org/.

9. Sandrine Dudoit and Mark J. van der Laan. Asymptotics of cross-validated risk estimation in estimator selection and performance assessment. *Statistical Methodology*, 2(2):131–154, 2005.

10. Sandrine Dudoit, Mark J. van der Laan, and Aad W. van der Vaart. The cross-validated adaptive epsilon-net estimator. *Statistics and Decisions*, 24(2):373–395, 2006.

11. Yoav Freund and Robert E. Schapire. A decision-theoretic generalization of on-line learning and an application to boosting. *Journal of Computer and System Sciences*, 55(1):119–139, 1997.

12. Jerome H. Friedman. Greedy function approximation: A gradient boosting machine. *Annals of Statistics*, 29:1189–1232, 1999.

13. H2O. *H2O Performance Datasheet*, 2014. http://docs.h2o.ai/h2oclassic/resources/h2odatasheet.html.

14. H2O.ai. *H2O Machine Learning Platform*, 2014. version 2.9.0.1593. https://github.com/h2oai/h2o-2.

15. Geoffrey E. Hinton, Nitish Srivastava, Alex Krizhevsky, Ilya Sutskever, and Ruslan Salakhutdinov. Improving neural networks by preventing co-adaptation of feature detectors. *CoRR*, abs/1207.0580, 2012.

16. Arthur E. Hoerl. Application of ridge analysis to regression problems. *Chemical Engineering Progress*, 58:54–59, 1958.

17. Arthur E. Hoerl and Robert W. Kennard. Ridge regression: Bias estimation for nonorthogonal problems. *Technometrics*, 12:55–67, 1970.

18. Alan Hubbard, Ivn Daz, Anna Decker, John B. Holcomb, Eileen M. Bulger, Martin A. Schreiber, Karen J. Brasel et al. Time-dependent prediction and evaluation of variable importance using superlearning in high-dimensional clinical data. *Journal of Trauma and Acute Care Surgery*, 75:S53–S60, 2013.

19. Intel Corporation. *Intel Math Kernel Library* (*MKL*), 2003. https://software.intel.com/en-us/intel-mkl.

20. Steven G. Johnson. *The NLopt Nonlinear-Optimization Package*, 2014. http://ab-initio.mit.edu/nlopt.

21. Noemi Kreif, Ivn D. Muoz, and David Harrison. Health econometric evaluation of the effects of a continuous treatment: A machine learning approach. *The Selected Works of Ivn Daz*, 2013.

22. John Langford, Alex Strehl, and Lihong Li. *Vowpal Wabbit*, 2007. https://github.com/JohnLangford/vowpal_wabbit.

23. Charles L. Lawson and Richard J. Hanson. *Solving Least Squares Problems*. SIAM, Prentice-Hall, Englewood Cliffs, NJ, 1974.

24. Michael LeBlanc and Robert Tibshirani. Combining estimates in regression and classification. Technical report, Department of Statistics, University of Toronto, Canada, 1993; *Journal of the American Statistical Association*, 91:1641-1650, 1996.

25. Erin LeDell. *h2oEnsemble: H2O Ensemble Learning*. R package version 0.0.3, 2014. https://github.com/h2oai/h2o-3/tree/master/h2o-r/ensemble.

26. Erin LeDell. *h2oEnsemble Benchmarks*, 2015. https://github.com/ledell/h2oEnsemble-benchmarks/releases/tag/big-data-handbook.

27. Erin LeDell, Stephanie Sapp, and Mark van der Laan. *Subsemble: An Ensemble Method for Combining Subset-Specific Algorithm Fits*. R package version 0.0.9, 2014. https://github.com/ledell/subsemble.

28. Samuel Lendle and Erin LeDell. *Vowpal Wabbit Ensemble: Online Super Learner*, 2013.

29. Alexander R. Luedtke and Mark J. van der Laan. Super-learning of an optimal dynamic treatment rule. Technical Report 326, U.C. Division of Biostatistics Working Paper Series, University of California, Berkeley, CA, 2014.

30. Justin Ma, Lawrence K. Saul, Stefan Savage, and Geoffrey M. Voelker. *Malicious URL Dataset* (*UCSD*), 2009. https://archive.ics.uci.edu/ml/datasets/URL+Reputation.

31. ASA Sections on Statistical Computing. *Airline Dataset (1987–2008)*. http://stat-computing.org/dataexpo/2009/the-data.html.

32. Maya L. Petersen, Erin LeDell, Joshua Schwab, Varada Sarovar, Robert Gross, Nancy Reynolds, Jessica E. Haberer et al. Super learner analysis of electronic adherence data improves viral prediction and may provide strategies for selective HIV RNA monitoring. *Journal of Acquired Immune Deficiency Syndromes (JAIDS)*, 69(1):109–118, 2015.

33. Romain Pirracchio, Maya L. Petersen, Marco Carone, Mattieu R. Rigon, Sylvie Chevret, and Mark J. van der Laan. Mortality prediction in intensive care units with the super ICU learner algorithm (sicula): A population-based study. *Statistical Applications in Genetics and Molecular Biology*, 3(1):42–52, 2015.

34. Eric Polley and Mark van der Laan. *SuperLearner: Super Learner Prediction.* R package version 2.0-9, 2010. https://github.com/ecpolley/SuperLearner.

35. Stephanie Sapp and Mark J. van der Laan. A scalable supervised subsemble prediction algorithm. Technical Report 321, U.C. Berkeley Division of Biostatistics Working Paper Series, University of California, Berkeley, CA, April 2014.

36. Stephanie Sapp, Mark J. van der Laan, and John Canny. Subsemble: An ensemble method for combining subset-specific algorithm fits. *Journal of Applied Statistics*, 41(6):1247–1259, 2014.

37. Ed Schmahl. *NNLS C Implementation*, 2000. http://hesperia.gsfc.nasa.gov/~schmahl/nnls/nnls.c.

38. Sandra E. Sinisi, Eric C. Polley, Maya L. Petersen, Soo-Yon Rhee, and Mark J. van der Laan. Super learning: An application to the prediction of HIV-1 drug resistance. *Statistical Applications in Genetics and Molecular Biology*, 6(1), 2007, doi:10.2202/1544-6115.1240.

39. Robert Tibshirani. Regression shrinkage and selection via the lasso. *Journal of the Royal Statistical Society. Series B*, 58(1):267–288, 1996.

40. Luke Tierney. *Simple Network of Workstations for R (SNOW)*. http://homepage.stat.uiowa.edu/~luke/R/cluster/cluster.html.

41. Mark J. van der Laan, Sandrine Dudoit, and Aad W. van der Vaart. The cross-validated adaptive epsilon-net estimator. *Statistics and Decisions*, 24(3):373–395, 2006.

42. Mark J. van der Laan, Eric C. Polley, and Alan E. Hubbard. Super learner. *Statistical Applications in Genetics and Molecular Biology*, 6(1), 2007, doi:10.2202/1544-6115.1309.

43. Mark J. van der Laan and Sherri Rose. *Targeted Learning: Causal Inference for Observational and Experimental Data*, 1st edition. Springer Series in Statistics. Springer, New York, 2011.

44. R. Clint Whaley, Antoine Petitet, and Jack J. Dongarra. *Automatically Tuned Linear Algebra Software (ATLAS)*. http://math-atlas.sourceforge.net/.

45. David H. Wolpert. Stacked generalization. *Neural Networks*, 5(2):241–259, 1992.

46. Zhang Xianyi, Wang Qian, and Werner Saar. *OpenBLAS*, 2015. http://www.openblas.net/.

Part VII

Causal Inference

20

Tutorial for Causal Inference

Laura Balzer, Maya Petersen, and Mark van der Laan

CONTENTS

20.1 Why Bother with Causal Inference? 361
20.2 The Scientific Question 363
20.3 The Causal Model 363
20.4 The Target Causal Quantity 366
20.5 The Observed Data and Their Link to the Causal Model 368
20.6 Assessment of Identifiability 369
20.7 Estimation and Inference 373
20.8 Interpretation of the Results 376
20.9 Conclusion 377
Appendix: Extensions to Multiple Time Point Interventions 378
Acknowledgments 381
References 381

20.1 Why Bother with Causal Inference?

This book has mostly been dedicated to large-scale computing and machine learning algorithms. These tools help us describe the relationships between variables in vast, complex datasets. This chapter goes one step further by introducing methods, as well as their limitations, to learn causal relationships from these data. Consider, for example, the following questions:

1. What proportion of patients taking drug X suffered adverse side effects?
2. Which patients taking drug X are more likely to suffer adverse side effects?
3. Would the risk of adverse effects be lower if all patients took drug X instead of drug Y?

The first question is purely descriptive; the second can be characterized as a prediction problem, whereas the last is causal. Causal inference is distinct from statistical inference in that it seeks to make conclusions about the world under changed conditions [1]. In the third example, our goal is to make inferences about how the distribution of patient outcomes would differ if all patients had taken drug X versus if the same patients, over the same time frame and under the same conditions, had taken drug Y. Purely statistical analyses are sometimes endowed with causal interpretations. Furthermore, many of our noncausal questions have causal elements. For example, Geng et al. [2] sought to assess whether sex was an independent predictor of mortality among patients initiating drug therapy (i.e., describe a noncausal association) but in the absence of loss to follow up (i.e., a change to the existing conditions).

In this chapter, we review a formal framework for causal inference to (1) state the scientific question; (2) express our causal knowledge and limits of that knowledge; (3) specify the causal parameter; (4) specify the observed data and their link to the causal model; (5) assess identifiability of our causal parameter as some function of the observed data distribution; (6) estimate the corresponding statistical parameter, incorporating methods discussed in this book; and (7) interpret our results [3–5]. Access to millions of data points does not obviate the need for this framework. Analyses of big data are not immune to the problems of small data. Instead, one might argue that analyses of big data exacerbate many of the problems of small data. As illustrated in Figure 20.1, there are many sources of association between two variables, including direct effects, indirect effects, measured confounding, unmeasured confounding, and selection bias [6]. Methods to delineate causation from correlation are perhaps more pressing now than ever [7,8].

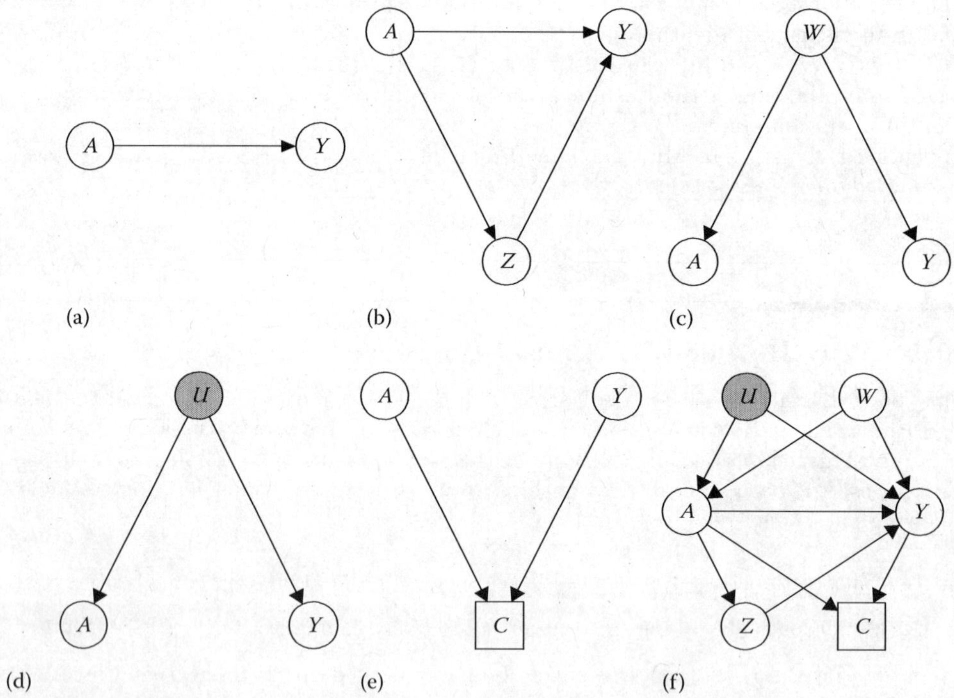

FIGURE 20.1
Some of the sources of dependence between an exposure A and an outcome Y: (a) the exposure A directly affects the outcome Y; (b) the exposure A directly affects the outcome Y as well as indirectly affects it through the mediator Z; (c) the exposure A has no effect on the outcome Y, but an association is induced by a measured common cause W; (d) the exposure A has no effect on the outcome Y, but an association is induced by an unmeasured common cause U; (e) the exposure A has no effect on the outcome Y, but an association is induced by only examining data among those not censored C; (f) all these sources of dependence are present. Please note this is *not* an exhaustive list.

20.2 The Scientific Question

The first step in the causal "roadmap" is to specify the scientific objective. As a running example, we will consider the timing of antiretroviral therapy (ART) initiation and its impact on outcomes among HIV+ individuals. Early ART initiation has been been shown to improve patient outcomes as well as reduce transmission between discordant couples [9,10]. Suppose we want to learn the effect of immediate ART initiation (i.e., irrespective of CD4+ T-cell count) on mortality. Large consortiums, such as the International Epidemiologic Databases to Evaluate AIDS and Sustainable East Africa Research in Community Health, are providing unprecedented quantities of data to answer this and other questions [12,13].

To sharply frame our scientific aim, we need to further specify the system, including the target population (e.g., patients and context), the exposure (e.g., criteria and timing), and the outcome. As a second try, consider our goal as learning the impact of initiating ART within 1 month of diagnosis on 5-year all-cause mortality among adults, recently diagnosed with HIV in Sub-Saharan Africa. This might seem like an insurmountable task, and it may seem safer to frame our question in terms of an association. Indeed, there seems to be a tendency to shy away from causal language when stating the scientific objective. However, we are not fundamentally interested in the correlation between early ART initiation and mortality among HIV+ adults. Instead, we want to isolate the effect of interest from the spurious sources of dependence (e.g., confounding, selection bias, informative censoring) as shown in Figure 20.1. The framework, discussed in this chapter, provides a pathway from our scientific aim to estimation of a statistical parameter that best approximates our causal effect, while keeping any assumptions transparent.

20.3 The Causal Model

The second step of the roadmap is to specify our causal model. Causal inference is distinct from statistics in that it requires something more than a sample from the observed data distribution. In particular, causal inference requires specification of background knowledge, and causal models provide a rigorous language for expressing this knowledge and its limits. In this chapter, we focus on *structural causal models* [14] to formally represent which variables potentially affect one another, the roles of unmeasured factors, and the functional form of those relationships. Structural causal models unify causal graphs [15], structural equations [16,17], and counterfactuals. We also briefly introduce the Neyman–Rubin potential outcomes framework [18–20] and discuss its relation to the structural causal model.

Consider again our running example. Let W denote the set of baseline covariates, including sociodemographics, clinical measurements, and social constructs. The exposure A is an indicator, equalling 1 if the patient initiated ART within 1 month of diagnosis and equalling 0 otherwise (i.e., initiation took longer than 1 month). Finally, the outcome Y is an indicator that the patient did not survive 5 years of follow-up. These factors have scientific meaning to the question and comprise the set of *endogenous variables*: $X = \{W, A, Y\}$. They can be measurable (e.g., age and sex) or unmeasurable and are affected by other variables in the model.

Each endogenous variable is associated with a set of background factors $U = (U_W, U_A, U_Y)$ with some joint distribution P_U. These represent all the unmeasured factors, affecting other variables in the model but not included in X. For example, U_A could include unknown clinic-level factors, influencing whether or not a patient initiates early ART.

Likewise, U_Y may include a patient's genetic risk profile. Furthermore, there might be shared unmeasured causes between the endogenous variables. For example, socioeconomic status may impact whether a patient initiates early ART as well as his/her 5-year mortality.

Each endogenous variable is also associated with a structural equation. These functions help encode our causal knowledge. Suppose, for example, we believe that the set of baseline covariates possibly impact whether a patient initiates early ART, and that both the covariates and the exposure may affect subsequent morality. Then we write each endogenous variable as a deterministic function of its "parents," variables that *may* impact its value:

$$
\begin{aligned}
W &= f_W(U_W) \\
A &= f_A(W, U_A) \\
Y &= f_Y(W, A, U_Y). \qquad (20.1)
\end{aligned}
$$

These functions $F = \{f_W, f_A, f_Y\}$ are left unspecified (nonparametric). For example, the third equation f_Y encodes that the covariates W and the exposure A may have influenced the value taken by the outcome Y. We have not, however, restricted their relationships: A and any member of W may interact on an additive (or any other) scale to affect Y and the impacts of A and W on Y may be nonlinear.

The structural causal model, denoted $\mathcal{M}^{\mathcal{F}}$, is defined by all possible distributions of P_U and all possible sets of functions F, which are compatible with our assumptions (if any). For the above example, there is some true joint distribution $P_{U,0}$ of health care access, personal preferences for ART use, socioeconomic factors, etc. Randomly sampling a patient from the population corresponds to drawing a particular realization u from $P_{U,0}$. Likewise, there are some true structural equations F_0 that would deterministically generate the endogenous variables $X = x$ if given input $U = u$. For a given distribution P_U and set of functions F, the structural causal model $\mathcal{M}^{\mathcal{F}}$ describes the following data generating process for (U, X):

1. Drawing the background factors U from some joint probability distribution P_U
2. Generating the baseline covariates W as some deterministic function f_W of U_W
3. Generating the exposure A as some deterministic function f_A of covariates W and U_A
4. Generating the outcome Y as some deterministic function f_Y of covariates W, the exposure A, and U_Y

Thus, the model $\mathcal{M}^{\mathcal{F}}$ is the collection of all possible probability distributions $P_{U,X}$ for the exogenous and endogenous variables (U, X). The true joint distribution is an element of the causal model: $P_{U,X,0} \in \mathcal{M}^{\mathcal{F}}$. The structural causal model is also sometimes also called a nonparametric structural equation model [14,21].

In other settings, we may have more in-depth knowledge about the data generating process. This knowledge is generally encoded in two ways. First, excluding a variable from the parent set of X_j encodes that this variable does not directly impact the value X_j takes. These assumptions are known as *exclusion restrictions.* Second, restricting the set of allowed distributions for P_U encodes that some variables do not have any unmeasured common causes. These assumptions are known as *independence assumptions.* Suppose, for example, that patients were randomized R to early ART initiation, but adherence A was imperfect. Then the treatment assignment R would only be determined by chance (e.g., a coin flip) and not influenced by the baseline covariates W. The unmeasured factors determining treatment assignment would be independent from all other unmeasured factors:

$$U_R \perp\!\!\!\perp (U_W, U_A, U_Y).$$

This is an independence assumption that restricts the allowed distribution of background factors P_U. Furthermore, suppose that randomization R only affects the mortality Y through its effect on adherence A. The resulting structural equations are then

$$\begin{aligned} W &= f_W(U_W) \\ R &= f_R(U_R) \\ A &= f_A(W, R, U_A) \\ Y &= f_Y(W, A, U_Y). \end{aligned} \tag{20.2}$$

We have made two exclusion restrictions: (1) the baseline covariates W do not influence randomization R and (2) randomization R has no direct effect on the outcome Y. The structural causal model is then defined by all probability distributions for U that are compatible with our independence assumptions and all sets of functions $F = (f_W, f_R, f_A, f_Y)$ that are compatible with our exclusion restrictions.

A causal graph can be drawn from the structural causal model [14]. Each endogenous variable (node) is connected to its parents and background error term with a directed arrow. The potential dependence between the background factors is encoded by the inclusion of a node representing any unmeasured common cause. Exclusion restrictions are encoded by absence of a directed arrow. Likewise, independence assumptions are encoded with the absence of a node representing an unmeasured common cause. The corresponding causal graphs for the two examples are given in Figure 20.2.

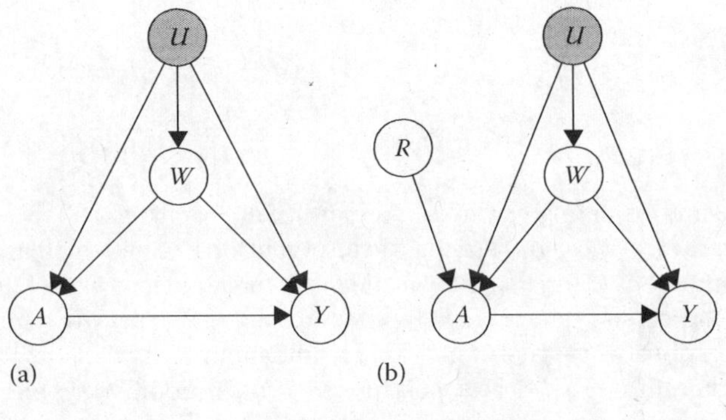

FIGURE 20.2
Directed acyclic graphs representing the structural causal model for our study (Equation 20.1) and for the hypothetical randomized trial (Equation 20.2). (a) This graph only encodes the time ordering between baseline covariates W, the exposure A, and the outcome Y. A single node U represents the unmeasured common causes of the endogenous variables. (b) This graph encodes the randomization R of some treatment with incomplete adherence A. There are two exclusion restrictions: The baseline covariates W do not impact the randomization R, and the randomization R has no direct effect on the outcome Y. There is also an independence assumption: the unmeasured factors contributing to randomization are independent of the unmeasured factors, contributing to the other variables.

Common Pitfall: Oversimplifying the Causal Model

Structural causal models and their corresponding graphs are powerful precisely because they do not impose unsubstantiated assumptions on the data generating process. There is a tendency, however, to present oversimplified models and graphs. It is crucial to remember that these are formal models, and every exclusion restriction or independence assumption (or equivalently, every arrow omitted) represents a real assumption about the true data generating system. Often, our knowledge is limited to the causal ordering of the variables in our system. Sometimes, we might not even have this information, forcing us to represent our knowledge using more than one possible model and graph.

20.4 The Target Causal Quantity

The structural causal model $\mathcal{M}^{\mathcal{F}}$ describes the system not only as it currently exists but also as it would exist under changed conditions. The structural equations are autonomous: an intervention on one equation does not affect the remaining ones. Therefore, we can modify a function and see how changes are transmitted through the system. For example, modifying the treatment decision does not change the effect of the treatment on the outcome. Therefore, we can make a targeted modification to represent our intervention of interest. In our running example (Equation 20.1 and Figure 20.2a), a self-selected group of patients initiated early ART. To answer our scientific question, we need to modify how this exposure variable was generated. Specifically, we can intervene to start all patients on ART within 1 month of testing HIV+ (i.e., deterministically set $A = 1$), and we can intervene to delay all patients from starting ART until 1 month after testing HIV+ (i.e., deterministically set $A = 0$):

$$\begin{aligned} W &= f_W(U_W) \qquad & W &= f_W(U_W) \\ A &= 1 & A &= 0 \\ Y_1 &= f_Y(W, 1, U_Y) & Y_0 &= f_Y(W, 0, U_Y) \end{aligned}$$

Alternative exposure mechanisms include dynamic interventions [22–25], which are responsive to patient characteristics, and stochastic interventions* [26], which are nondeterministic.

The *counterfactual outcome* Y_a is then the outcome a patient would have had, if possibly contrary to fact, he or she had received exposure level $A = a$. More formally, $Y_a = Y_a(u)$ is defined as the solution to the equation f_Y under an intervention to set $A = a$ (with input $U = u$). Therefore, $Y_a(U)$ is a postintervention random variable, whose probability distribution is induced by the set of structural equations F and the joint distribution of the background factors P_U. In other words, the structural causal model $\mathcal{M}^{\mathcal{F}}$ is also a model on the distribution of counterfactuals. In the Neyman–Rubin causal framework, these quantities are known as *potential outcomes* [18,19,27]. They are assumed to exist for all units under

*For simplicity, we have been considering the time-scale to be in months. Depending on our scientific question and the data resolution, we might be interested in shorter or longer intervals. If our time interval were days, then an intervention to start by day 30 (i.e., within 1 month) is a stochastic intervention. Alternatively, we could consider an intervention to initiate therapy on each day or not. For further discussion of longitudinal treatment regimes, see Appendix.

all treatment levels of interest. For this example, the *full data* would consist of baseline covariates and the outcomes under all possible exposures: $X^{\mathcal{F}} = \big(W, (Y_a : a \in \{0,1\})\big)$. The structural causal model $\mathcal{M}^{\mathcal{F}}$ also serves as a model for the set of possible full data distributions, each corresponding to a different intervention on the endogenous variables.

The distribution of these counterfactuals (potential outcomes) can then be used to define the target causal parameter. Consider, for example, the average treatment effect:

$$\Psi^{\mathcal{F}}(P_{U,X}) = \mathbb{E}_{U,X}(Y_1) - \mathbb{E}_{U,X}(Y_0),$$

where the subscript (U, X) denotes the expectation over the distribution $P_{U,X}$ (which implies the distribution of the counterfactual random variables (Y_1, Y_0)). In other words, $\Psi^{\mathcal{F}}(P_{U,X})$ is the difference in the expected counterfactual outcome if everyone in the population were exposed and the expected counterfactual outcome if everyone in the population were not exposed. Formally, $\Psi^{\mathcal{F}}$ is a mapping from a distribution $P_{U,X}$ in the causal model $\mathcal{M}^{\mathcal{F}}$ to the real number line. For our example, $\Psi^{\mathcal{F}}(P_{U,X})$ is the difference in the counterfactual risk of mortality if all patients immediately initiated ART and if all patients delayed ART initiation. For a binary outcome, this causal quantity corresponds the causal risk difference. We could also specify this contrast on the relative scale, within a certain stratum of the population (e.g., those with baseline CD4 counts above 350 cells/mm^3), for the actual study units (i.e., the sample average treatment effect [18]) or for some other population (i.e., transportability [28–30]).

Marginal structural models provide an alternative way to define our target parameter [31]. They are a summary measure of how the counterfactual outcome changes as a function of the exposure and possibly pretreatment covariates. Consider, for example, the impact of reducing the time (in months) between HIV diagnosis and treatment initiation. The intervention variable A would then be continuous. (An alternative approach would be to treat the exposure as a time-dependent binary variable as discussed in the Appendix.) To generate the relevant counterfactual outcomes,* we would repeatedly intervene on the structural causal model to set $A = a$ for all levels of a in the exposure set of interest $\mathcal{A} = \{1, 2, 3, \ldots\}$. If we knew the true shape of the relationship between the expected counterfactual outcome $\mathbb{E}_{U,X}(Y_a)$ and the treatment level a, we could summarize it with a parametric model [31], such as the following:

$$\begin{aligned} \text{logit}\big[\mathbb{E}_{U,X}(Y_a)\big] &= m(a|\beta) \\ \text{with } m(a|\beta) &= \beta_0 + \beta_1 a. \end{aligned}$$

where $\text{logit}(x) = \log(x/(1-x))$.

This model assumes that the counterfactual mortality risk is a function linear on the logistic scale of the time to treatment initiation a. This marginal structural model restricts the set of possible counterfactual distributions and therefore places an assumption on our causal model $\mathcal{M}^{\mathcal{F}}$.

In many cases, we do not have sufficient information to confidently specify a parametric model for this dose–response curve. Instead, we can use a *working marginal structural model* as a summary of the causal relationship of interest [32]. The target causal parameter is then the projection of the true causal curve onto a working model. Consider, for example,

$$\beta(P_{U,X}|m) = \text{argmin}_\beta \ \mathbb{E}_{U,X}\left[\sum_{a\in\mathcal{A}} -\log\left[m(a|\beta)^{Y_a}(1-m(a|\beta))^{(1-Y_a)}\right]\right],$$

*Under the Neyman–Rubin framework, we would assume the existence of the potential outcomes Y_a for all exposures $a \in \mathcal{A}$.

where our projection is the negative log-likehood loss. Intuitively, we can think of this projection as summarizing the full data (i.e., all counterfactuals) with a parametric regression curve. As usual, the quality of the summary depends on the underlying causal curve and the question of interest.

20.5 The Observed Data and Their Link to the Causal Model

Thus far, we have not specified the data that will be or have been collected in our study. Instead, we have discussed endogenous variables X (observable and possibly unobservable), background factors U (unobservable), and set of counterfactuals $(Y_a : a \in \mathcal{A})$. In this step, we specify the observed data, their link to the causal model and the resulting statistical model.

Suppose we have a simple random sample of n patients from our target population. On each patient, we measure some baseline covariates W, including sex, age, and CD4 count, the exposure A (whether or not the patient initiates ART within 1 month of diagnosis), and the outcome Y as the patient's 5-year mortality. Then the observed data for a given patient are $O = (W, A, Y)$, which has some true, but unknown distribution P_0. We assume that the observed data are generated by sampling n times from a distribution compatible with (contained in) the structural causal model. Recall the structural causal model provides a description of the data generating system under existing conditions as well as under specific interventions. The distribution of the background factors P_U and the structural equations F identify the distribution of the endogenous variables X as well as the distribution of the observed data O. The observed data O are a subset of (U, X). Suppose, for example, we observe all the endogenous nodes (i.e., if $O = X$). Then we have

$$P(O = o) = \sum_u P_{U,X}(X = x|U = u)P_U(U = u) = \sum_u \mathbb{I}(X(u) = x)P_U(U = u),$$

where the summation generalizes to an integral for continuous valued variables. This framework naturally accommodates more complicated links, such as case–control sampling and matched sampling [33,34].

Thereby, the structural causal model $\mathcal{M}^{\mathcal{F}}$, which is the set of possible distributions for (U, X), implies our statistical model $\mathcal{M}$, which is the set of possible distributions for the observed data O. The true distribution of the observed data P_0 is implied by the true distribution $P_{U,X,0}$ of (U, X) and is an element of the statistical model: $P_0 \in \mathcal{M}$. The causal model may, but often does not, place any restrictions on the statistical model. For example, the causal model, describing the data generating process for our observational study (Figure 20.2a), implies a *nonparametric* statistical model. There are no restrictions on the possible observed data distributions. In contrast, the causal model, corresponding to the randomized trial (Figure 20.2b), will only generate distributions, where the randomization R is independent of the baseline covariates W. This is a testable assumption and implies a *semiparametric* statistical model. We refer the reader to Pearl [14,15] for further discussion of a graphical criterion to evaluate independence between two variables as implied by a structural causal model or its corresponding directed acyclic graph.

Suppose that instead of specifying a structural causal model, we chose to follow the Neyman–Rubin framework. Specifically, we assumed the existence of the potential outcomes

$Y_a : a \in \mathcal{A}$ in Step 3. To relate these potential outcomes to the observed data, we need the stable unit treatment value assumption [35]. First, the potential outcomes for one unit must not be impacted by the treatment assignment of another unit (i.e., no interference)*. Second, there must not be multiple versions of the treatment $A = a$. With this assumption, we can map the potential outcomes to the observed outcomes:

$$Y_i = A_i Y_{1,i} + (1 - A_i) Y_{0,i}.$$

For unit i, we only get to see the outcome Y_i, corresponding to the unit's observed exposure A_i. As a result, causal inference can be treated as a missing data problem.

Common Pitfall: Specifying a Statistical Model Based on Convenience

Sometimes researchers specify a parametric multivariable model to relate the conditional mean of the observed outcome to the observed exposure and baseline covariates. We could, for example, assume that a main terms logistic regression describes the relationship between observed mortality risk, early ART initiation, and the measured covariates. Although these parametric models are often recognized as being misspecified, estimation and inference proceed as if they were true. Formally, the statistical model is the set of possible distributions for the observed data and should reflect real knowledge, however limited. Structural causal models make explicit the implications for background knowledge on the observed data distribution. In many cases, background knowledge is not sufficient to place any restrictions on the distribution of the observed data. Thereby, use of a formal causal model highlights that in many practical data applications, a nonparametric statistical model is appropriate.

20.6 Assessment of Identifiability

In Step 3 (Section 20.4), we specified our scientific question as a causal parameter $\Psi^{\mathcal{F}}(P_{U,X})$, a function of the distribution of counterfactuals (potential outcomes). In Step 4 (Section 20.5), we specified the observed data O and the statistical model $\mathcal{M}$. In this step, we establish whether our causal parameter can be written as some function of the observed data distribution. More formally, for each $P_{U,X}$ compatible with the structural causal model $\mathcal{M}^{\mathcal{F}}$, we want to establish the equivalence between the causal parameter $\Psi^{\mathcal{F}}(P_{U,X})$ and the statistical parameter $\Psi(P)$. If so, we state that the causal parameter is *identified.* If not, we explicitly state the additional assumptions needed to make inferences about the causal parameter using the observed data distribution. We keep these convenience-based assumptions separate from our knowledge-based assumptions, reflected in the structural causal model $\mathcal{M}^{\mathcal{F}}$.

Consider a simplified example, where we want to learn the 5-year mortality risk if, possibly contrary to the fact, all HIV+ adults initiated ART within 1 month of diagnosis:

*The structural causal model, given in Equation 20.1, implicitly assumes independence between study units. Recent work relaxing this assumption and considering a network of interacting units is given in the work by van der Laan [36].

$P_{U,X}(Y_1 = 1)$. Suppose we have not collected any baseline covariates; therefore, the observed data are simply $O = (A, Y)$. Then the causal parameter will only equal the observed mortality risk among exposed if the *only* source of association is due to the effect of interest:

$$P(Y = y|A = 1) = P_{U,X}(Y_1 = y|A = 1)$$
$$\stackrel{?}{=} P_{U,X}(Y_1 = y).$$

The first equality is by the definition of counterfactuals and then second holds if the counterfactual outcome Y_a is independent of the exposure A. In the absence of baseline covariates, the outcome is only a function of the exposure and the background error: $Y = f_Y(A, U_Y)$. Once we intervene to set $A = a$, the counterfactual outcome is only a function of its error: $Y_a(U) = f_Y(a, U_Y)$. If the unmeasured factors contributing to the outcome U_Y are independent of those contributing the exposure U_A, then the randomization assumption holds $Y_a \perp\!\!\!\perp A$, and the counterfactual risk $P_{U,X}(Y_1 = 1)$ is identified as the observed risk among those exposed $P(Y = 1|A = a)$. The randomization assumption is equivalent to stating that there are no unmeasured confounders of the exposure–outcome relation. Intuitively, this assumption holds by design a randomized trial.

In most observational settings, the assumption of no common (measured or unmeasured) causes of the exposure and outcome will not hold. We can weaken the randomization assumption by conditioning on a set of measured baseline covariates: $Y_a \perp\!\!\!\perp A|W$. The adjustment set W needs to block all spurious sources of association without creating any new sources of dependence or blocking any of the effect of A on Y. As illustrated in Figure 20.3, the *back-door criterion* can aid the evaluation of the randomization assumption [14]. A set of variables W satisfies the back-door criterion for the relationship of (A, Y) if (1) no node in W is a descendant of A and (2) W blocks all back-door paths from A to Y, where *back-door* refers to a path with an arrow into A. The rationale for condition 1 is to avoid blocking the path of interest or introducing spurious

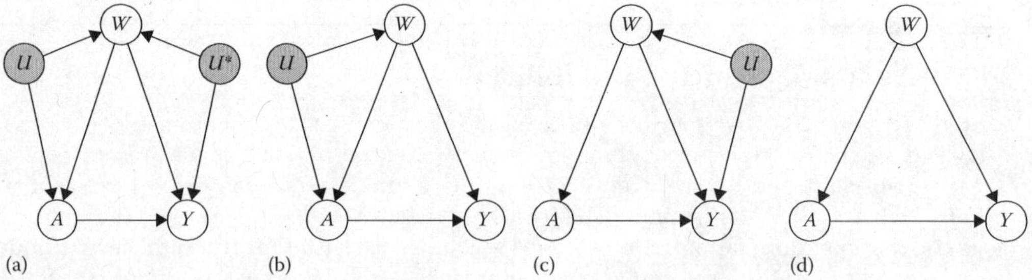

FIGURE 20.3
Considering the back-door criterion for the basic structure. For all the graphs, the exposure A and the outcome Y do not share an unmeasured common cause. (a) The covariates W are *not* sufficient to block all back-door paths. Conditioning covariates W blocks the path $Y \to W \to A$. However, conditioning on W (a collider of U and U^*) opens a new path: $Y \to U^* \to U \to A$. (b) The covariates W and the outcome Y also do not share an unmeasured common cause. The covariates W are sufficient to block all back-door paths. (c) The exposure A and the covariates W also do not share an unmeasured common cause. The covariates W are sufficient to block all back-door paths. (d) All the unmeasured background factors are independent. The covariates W are sufficient to block all back-door paths.

associations (i.e., conditioning on a collider). The rationale for condition 2 is to block any remaining spurious sources of association. For the basic structure (Figure 20.3), the randomization assumption will hold if the following independence assumptions are true:

$$U_A \perp\!\!\!\perp U_Y \text{ and } U_A \perp\!\!\!\perp U_W \text{ or } U_Y \perp\!\!\!\perp U_W.$$

There must not be any unmeasured common causes of the exposure and the outcome, and of the exposure and covariates or of the outcome and covariates. As illustrated in Figure 20.4, this graphical criteria can aid in the selection of an appropriate adjustment set.

When the randomization assumption holds, we can identify the distribution of counterfactuals within strata of covariates. Specifically, we have that for each $P_{U,X} \in \mathcal{M}^{\mathcal{F}}$

$$\begin{aligned} P_{U,X}(Y_a = y|W = w) &= P_{U,X}(Y_a = y|A = a, W = w) \\ &= P(Y = y|A = a, W = w), \end{aligned}$$

where the distribution P of the observed data is implied by $P_{U,X}$. This gives us the G-computation identifiability result [27] for the true distributions $P_{U,X,0}$ and P_0:

$$E_{U,X,0}(Y_a) = \sum_w E_0(Y|A = a, W = w)P_0(W = w),$$

where the summation generalizes to an integral for continuous covariates. Likewise, we can identify the difference in the expected counterfactual outcomes (i.e., the average treatment effect) in terms of the difference in the conditional mean outcomes, averaged with respect to the covariate distribution:

$$\underbrace{E_{U,X,0}(Y_1 - Y_0)}_{\Psi^{\mathcal{F}}(P_{U,X,0})} = \underbrace{\sum_w \left[E_0(Y|A = 1, W = w) - E_0(Y|A = 0, W = w)\right] P_0(W = w)}_{\Psi(P_0)}.$$

Identifiability also relies on having sufficient support in the data. The G-computation formula requires that the conditional mean $E_0(Y|A = a, W = w)$ is well defined for all possible values of w and levels of a of interest. In a nonparametric statistical model, each exposure of interest must occur with some positive probability for each possible covariate stratum:

$$\min_{a \in \mathcal{A}} P_0(A = a|W = w) > 0, \text{ for all } w \text{ for which } P_0(W = w) > 0.$$

This condition is known as the *positivity assumption* and as the experimental treatment assignment assumption.

Suppose, for example, that the randomization assumption holds conditionally on a single binary baseline covariate. Then our statistical estimand could be rewritten as

$$\begin{aligned} \Psi(P_0) = &\left[E_0(Y|A = 1, W = 1) - E_0(Y|A = 0, W = 1)\right] P_0(W = 1) \\ &+ \left[E_0(Y|A = 1, W = 0) - E_0(Y|A = 0, W = 0)\right] P_0(W = 0). \end{aligned}$$

As an extreme, suppose that in the population, there are zero exposed patients with this covariate: $P_0(A = 1|W = 1) = 0$. Then there would be no information about outcomes under the exposure for this subpopulation. To identify the treatment effect, we could consider a different target parameter (e.g., the effect among those with $W = 0$) or consider additional modeling assumptions (e.g., the effect is the same among those with $W = 1$ and $W = 0$).

Both options are a bit dissatisfying and other approaches may be taken [37]. The risk of violating the positivity assumption is exacerbated with higher dimensional data (i.e., as the number of covariates or their levels grow).

In many cases, our initial assumptions, encoded in the structural causal model $\mathcal{M}^{\mathcal{F}}$, are not sufficient to identify the causal effect $\Psi^{\mathcal{F}}(P_{U,X})$. Indeed, for our running example (Figure 20.2a), the set of baseline covariates is not sufficient to block the back-door paths from the outcome to the exposure. The question then becomes how to proceed? Possible options include giving up, gathering more data, or continuing to estimation while clearly acknowledging the lack of identifiability during the interpretation step. To facilitate the third option, we can use $\mathcal{M}^{\mathcal{F}*}$ to denote the structural causal model, augmented with additional *convenience-based* assumptions needed for identifiability. This gives us a way to proceed, while separating our real knowledge $\mathcal{M}^{\mathcal{F}}$ from our wished identifiability assumptions $\mathcal{M}^{\mathcal{F}*}$.

Overall, identifiability assumptions and resulting estimands are specific to the causal parameter $\Psi^{\mathcal{F}}(P_{U,X})$. We are focusing on a point treatment effect (i.e., distribution of counterfactuals under interventions on a single node or variable). Different identifiability results are needed for interventions on more than one node (e.g., longitudinal treatment effects and direct effects) and interventions responding to patient characteristics (e.g., dynamic regimes). Furthermore, a given causal parameter may have more than one identifiability result (e.g., instrumental variables and the front-door criterion). See, for example, Pearl [14].

Common Pitfall: Stating vs. Evaluating the Identifiability Assumptions

There is a temptation to simply state the identifiability assumptions and proceed to the analysis. The identifiability assumptions require careful consideration. Directed

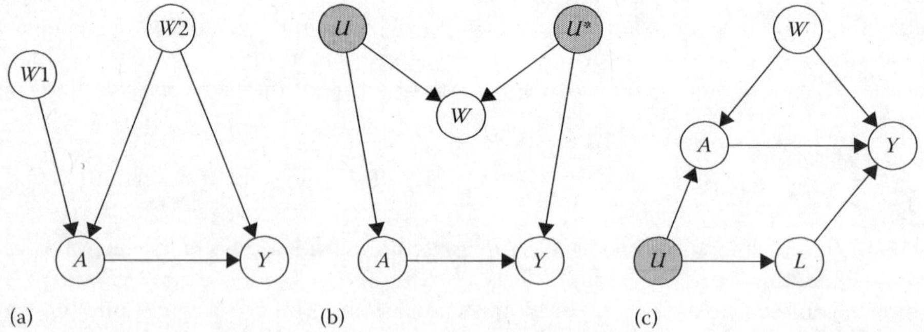

FIGURE 20.4
Considering the back-door criterion. (a) The set of covariates $W2$ is sufficient to block the back-door path from $Y \to W2 \to A$. Therefore, the randomization assumption will hold conditionally on $W2$. Further adjustment for $W1$ is unnecessary and potentially harmful. (b) The randomization assumption holds conditionally on $\emptyset$. Adjusting for W (i.e., conditioning on a collider of U and U^*) opens a back-door path and induces a spurious association between A and Y. (c) The randomization assumption holds conditionally on (W, L). The covariates L are needed to block the back-door path from $Y \to L \to U \to A$, even though L occurs temporally after the exposure A.

acyclic graphs facilitate the evaluation of assumptions by subject-matter experts without extensive statistical training. When interpreting the analysis, any convenience-based causal assumptions should be transparently stated and explained.

20.7 Estimation and Inference

In the previous step, we defined the parameter of interest as a mapping from the statistical model to the parameter space: $\Psi : \mathcal{M} \to \mathbb{R}$. In other words, the statistical parameter is a function, whose input is any distribution P compatible with the statistical model and whose output is a real number. The parameter mapping applied to the true observed data distribution P_0 is called the *estimand* and denoted $\Psi(P_0)$. Recall we have n independent, identically distributed (i.i.d.) copies of the random variable $O = (W, A, Y)$. The empirical distribution P_n corresponds to putting a weight $1/n$ on each copy of O_i. An *estimator* is a function, whose input is the observed data (a realization of P_n) and output a value in the parameter space.

In this chapter, we consider *substitution estimators* based on the G-computation identifiability result [27]:

$$\Psi(P_0) = E_0\big[E_0(Y|A=1,W) - E_0(Y|A=0,W)\big]. \tag{20.3}$$

A simple substitution estimator for $\Psi(P_0)$ can be implemented as follows:

1. Estimate the conditional expectation of the outcome, given the exposure and covariates, denoted $\hat{E}(Y|A,W)$.
2. Use this estimate to generate the predicted outcomes for each unit, setting $A = 1$ and $A = 0$.
3. Take the sample average of the difference in these predicted outcomes:

$$\hat{\Psi}(P_n) = \frac{1}{n}\sum_{i=1}^{n} \hat{E}(Y_i|A_i = 1, W_i) - \hat{E}(Y_i|A_i = 0, W_i).$$

The last step corresponds to estimating the marginal covariate distribution $P_0(W)$ with the sample proportion: $\frac{1}{n}\sum_i \mathbb{I}(W_i = w)$.

There are many options available for estimating the conditional expectation $E_0(Y|A,W)$. Often, parametric models are used to relate the conditional mean outcome to the possible predictor variables and the exposure. Suppose, for example, we knew that the conditional expectation of a continuous outcome could be described by the following parametric model:

$$E_0(Y|A,W) = \beta_0 + \beta_1 A + \beta_2 W_1 + \beta_3 W_2 + \beta_4 A^* W_1 + \beta_5 A^* W_2,$$

where $W = \{W_1, W_2\}$ denotes the set of covariates, needed for identifiability. Then this knowledge should have been encoded in our structural causal model $\mathcal{M}^{\mathcal{F}}$ with implied restrictions on our statistical model $\mathcal{M}$. (In other words, we avoid introducing new assumptions during the analysis.) The coefficients in this regression model could be estimated with maximum likelihood or with ordinary least squares regression. The estimate $\hat{\beta}_1$ does not, however, provide an estimate of the G-computation identifiability result. The exact interpretation of $\hat{\beta}_1$ depends on which variables and which interactions are included in the parametric model. To obtain an estimate of $\Psi(P_0)$, we need to average the predicted outcomes with respect to the distribution of covariates:

$$\hat{\Psi}(P_n) = \frac{1}{n}\sum_{i=1}^{n} \hat{E}(Y_i|A_i = 1, W_i) - \hat{E}(Y_i|A_i = 0, W_i)$$
$$= \frac{1}{n}\sum_{i=1}^{n} (\hat{\beta}_1 + \hat{\beta}_4 W_{1,i} + \hat{\beta}_5 W_{2,i}).$$

As a second example, suppose we knew that the conditional risk of a binary outcome could be described by the following parametric model:

$$\mathrm{logit}\left[\mathrm{E}_0(\mathrm{Y}|\mathrm{A}, \mathrm{W})\right] = \beta_0 + \beta_1 \mathrm{A} + \beta_2 \mathrm{W}_1 + \cdots + \beta_{11}\mathrm{W}_{10},$$

where $W = \{W_1 \ldots, W_{10}\}$ denotes the set of covariates, needed for identifiability. Then the estimate $\hat{\beta}_1$ would provide an estimate of the logarithm of the conditional odds ratio. An estimate of the G-computation identifiability result is given by averaging the expected outcomes under the exposure $A = 1$ and control $A = 0$:

$$\hat{\Psi}(P_n) = \frac{1}{n}\sum_{i=1}^{n}\left(\frac{1}{1+\exp^{-(\hat{\beta}_0+\hat{\beta}_1+\hat{\beta}_2\mathrm{W}_{1,i}+\cdots+\hat{\beta}_{11}\mathrm{W}_{10,i})}} - \frac{1}{1+\exp^{-(\hat{\beta}_0+\hat{\beta}_2\mathrm{W}_{1,i}+\cdots+\hat{\beta}_{11}\mathrm{W}_{10,i})}}\right).$$

In most cases, our background knowledge is inadequate to describe the conditional expectation $E_0(Y|A, W)$ with such parametric models. Indeed, with high dimensional data, the sheer number of potential covariates will likely make it impossible to correctly specify the functional form. If the assumed parametric model is incorrect, the point estimates will often be biased and inference misleading. In other words, the structural causal model $\mathcal{M}^{\mathcal{F}}$, representing our knowledge of the underlying data generating process, often implies a nonparametric statistical model $\mathcal{M}$. Our estimation approach should respect the statistical model.

To avoid unsubstantiated assumptions about functional form, it is sometimes possible to estimate $E_0(Y|A, W)$ with the empirical mean in each exposure–covariate stratum. Unfortunately, even when all covariates are discrete valued, nonparametric maximum likelihood estimators quickly become ill-defined due to the curse of dimensionality; the number of possible exposure–covariate combinations far exceeds the number of observations. Again, this problem becomes exacerbated with big data, where, for example, there are hundreds of potential covariates under consideration.

Various model selection routines can help alleviate these problems. For example, stepwise regression will add and subtract variables in hopes of minimizing the Akaike information criterion or the Bayesian information criterion. Other data-adaptive methods, based on cross-validation, involve splitting the data into training and validation sets. Each possible algorithm (e.g., various parametric models or semiparametric methods) is then fit on the training set and its performance assessed on the validation set. The measure of performance can be defined by a loss function, such as the L2-squared error or the negative log likelihood. Super learner, for example, uses cross-validation to select the candidate algorithm with the best performance or to build the optimal (convex) combination of estimates from candidate algorithms [38,39]. (For further details, see Chapter 19.) A point estimate could then be obtained by averaging the difference in predicted outcomes for each unit under the exposure and under the control.

Although these data-adaptive methods avoid betting on one *a priori* specified parametric regression model and are amenable to semiparametric algorithms, there is no reliable way to obtain statistical inference for parameters, such as the G-computation estimand $\Psi(P_0)$. Treating the final algorithm as if it were prespecified ignores the selection process. Furthermore, the selected algorithm was tailored to maximize/minimize some criterion with regard to the conditional expectation $E_0(Y|A, W)$ and will, in general, not provide the best bias–variance trade-off for estimating the statistical parameter $\Psi(P_0)$. Indeed, estimating the conditional mean outcome Y in every stratum of (A, W) is a much more ambitious task than estimating one number (the difference in conditional means, averaged with respect to the covariate distribution). Thus, without an additional step, the resulting estimator will be overly biased relative to its standard error, preventing accurate inference.

Targeted maximum likelihood estimation (TMLE) provides a way forward [3,40]. TMLE is a general algorithm for the construction of double robust, semiparametric, efficient substitution estimators. TMLE allows for data-adaptive estimation while obtaining valid statistical inference. The algorithm is detailed in Chapter 22. Although TMLE is a general algorithm for a wide range of parameters, we focus on its implementation for the G-computation estimand. Briefly, the TMLE algorithm uses information in the estimated exposure mechanism $\hat{P}(A|W)$ to update the initial estimator of the conditional mean $E_0(Y|A, W)$. The targeted estimates are then substituted into the parameter mapping. The updating step achieves a targeted bias reduction for the parameter of interest $\Psi(P_0)$ and serves to solve the efficient score equation. As a result, TMLE is a double robust estimator; it will be consistent for $\Psi(P_0)$ is either the conditional expectation $E_0(Y|A, W)$ or the exposure mechanism $P_0(A|W)$ is estimated consistently. When both functions are consistently estimated at a fast enough rate, the TMLE will be efficient in that it achieves the lowest asymptotic variance among a large class of estimators. These asymptotic properties typically translate into lower bias and variance in finite samples. The advantages of TMLE have been repeatedly demonstrated in both simulation studies and applied analyses [37,41–43]. The procedure is available with standard software such as the `tmle` and `ltmle` packages in `R` [44–46].

Thus far, we have discussed obtaining a point estimate from a simple or targeted substitution estimator. To create confidence intervals and test hypotheses, we also need to quantify uncertainty. A simple substitution estimator based on a correctly specified parametric model is asymptotically linear, and its variance can be approximated by the variance of its influence curve, divided by sample size n. It is worth emphasizing that our estimand $\Psi(P_0)$ often does not correspond to a single coefficient, and therefore we usually cannot read off the reported standard error from common software. Under reasonable conditions, the TMLE is also asymptotically linear and inference can be based on an estimate of its influence curve.

Overall, this chapter focused on substitution estimators (simple and targeted) of the G-computation identifiability result [27]. The simple substitution estimator only requires an estimate of the marginal distribution of baseline covariates $P_0(W)$ and the conditional expectation of the outcome, given the exposure and covariates $E_0(Y|A, W)$. TMLE also requires an estimate of the exposure mechanism $P_0(A|W)$. There are many other algorithms available for estimation of $\Psi(P_0)$. A popular class of estimators relies only on estimation of the exposure mechanism [47–49]. Inverse probability of treatment weighting (IPTW) estimators, for example, control for measured confounders by up-weighting exposure–covariate groups that are underrepresented and down-weighting exposure–covariate groups that are overrepresented (relative to what would be seen were the exposure randomized). Its double robust counterpart, augmented-IPTW, shares many of the same properties as TMLE [50,51]. A key distinction is that IPTW and augmented-IPTW are solutions to estimating equations and therefore respond differently in the face of challenges due to strong confounding and rare outcomes [37,52]. Throughout, we maintain that estimators should respect the knowledge encoded in the statistical model and not introduce new assumptions. An estimator should be selected for analysis based on its performance (e.g., bias, variance, robustness) as opposed to convenience or habit.

Common Pitfall: Confusing Estimation Methods with the Causal Parameters

Causal models and causal parameters help to specify a statistical estimation problem (i.e., the observed data, statistical model, and estimand) that is optimally informed by background knowledge and aims to answer the underlying scientific or policy question. However, there is nothing causal about the estimation step. A given estimand can be estimated in many different ways, and alternative algorithms can be compared simply based on their statistical properties, such as bias and variance. For example, (working) marginal structural models are often used to define a target counterfactual parameter equal, under needed causal assumptions, to a specific estimand. This estimand can be estimated with inverse probability weights [31,53], regression of the outcome on exposure and confounders, or double robust efficient methods [3,54]. There is nothing more or less causal about these estimators.

20.8 Interpretation of the Results

The last step of the roadmap is interpreting the results. In our running example, the identifiability assumptions did not hold. Nonetheless, the statistical estimand (Equation 20.3) always has a statistical interpretation as the difference in the expected outcome, given the exposure and covariates in the adjustment set, and the expected outcome, given the control and covariates in the adjustment set, standardized with respect to the covariate distribution in the population. For our example, $\Psi(P_0)$ can be interpreted as the marginal risk difference: the difference in the mortality risk among patients with early versus delayed ART initiation but the same values of the measured covariates (e.g., baseline CD4 count, age, and sex), averaged with respect to the distribution of these covariates. This estimand can be considered as the best approximation to the causal quantity of interest, given the limitations in the observed data. If the identifiability assumptions hold, our estimate would be endowed with a causal interpretation: a summary of how the distribution of the data would change under a specific intervention. For our example, the causal interpretation would be the difference in the 5-year counterfactual mortality risk if all patients initiated early ART versus if all patients delayed ART initiation. Further interpretation in terms of the impact of a real-world intervention or in terms of a randomized trial requires additional assumptions.

Common Pitfall: Lack of Identifiability Is Different from Statistical Bias

During the identifiability step, we advocate that a clear distinction be made between assumptions based on knowledge, encoded in the structural causal model $\mathcal{M}^{\mathcal{F}}$, and those based on convenience $\mathcal{M}^{\mathcal{F}*}$. This delineation emphasizes that the estimand may not equal the causal parameter. The discrepancy depends on unmeasured quantities and nontestable assumptions. In other words, the needed assumptions cannot be evaluated statistically using the observed data alone [1]. Nonetheless, sensitivity analyses can help in evaluating the potential magnitude of the deviations between the causal parameter and the statistical estimand [55–58]. By contrast, the statistical bias of an estimator is a statistical concept, characterizing how an estimator performs on average across multiple repetitions the experiment. Statistical bias can be evaluated through simulations and minimized with data-driven techniques.

20.9 Conclusion

In this chapter, we introduced a formal framework for causal inference [3,4]. Our running example was to estimate the effect of early ART initiation (within 1 month of diagnosis) on 5-year mortality risk among HIV+ adults in Sub-Saharan Africa. Our structural causal model $\mathcal{M}^{\mathcal{F}}$ only reflected the causal ordering of our variables; we did not make any exclusion restrictions, independence assumptions, or functional form assumptions. Counterfactual outcomes were generated by deterministically intervening on the data generating system, described by the structural causal model, to set $A = 1$ (i.e., early initiation) and also to set $A = 0$ (i.e., delayed initiation). We focused on the average treatment effect for this static exposure. The observed data $O = (W, A, Y)$ were assumed to be generated by sampling n independent times from a probability distribution compatible with the structural causal model $\mathcal{M}^{\mathcal{F}}$, which implied a non-parametric statistical model $\mathcal{M}$. Although our identifiability assumptions did not hold, we still defined a statistical estimand $\Psi(P_0)$ as a best approximation of our wished for causal quantity. We briefly discussed a simple (parametric) substitution estimator and a targeted substitution estimator (TMLE), which allows for data-adaptive estimation while obtaining valid inference. Because our needed identifiability assumptions were not met, we interpreted our estimate as the marginal difference in the mortality risk, given early ART initiation and the measured covariates, and the mortality risk, given delayed ART initiation and the measured covariates, standardized with respect to the covariate distribution.

This framework is easily extended to more complicated data structures. Consider, for example, the following scientific questions, corresponding to interventions on multiple exposure nodes and to alternate counterfactual treatment assignment mechanisms:

- *Longitudinal treatment effects* [31,51,53,54,59–69]: How does cumulative time until ART initiation affect mortality among recently diagnosed HIV+ adults? What is the effect of routine HIV viral load monitoring, compared to routine CD4+ T cell count monitoring, on mortality among patients initiating early ART? What would be impact of early ART initiation on the 5-year mortality if there were no losses to follow-up?

- *Dynamic regimes* (individualized treatment rules) [22–25,61,70–72]: How would mortality have differed if HIV+ adults initiated ART based on HIV RNA viral loads as opposed to CD4+ T cell counts?

- *Direct and indirect effects* [73–76]: What is the direct effect of early ART initiation on 5-year mortality that is not mediated through changes in HIV RNA viral load?

- *Stochastic interventions* (nondeteriministic interventions) [26]: What would be the 5-year mortality if the distribution of time until ART initiation shifted toward shorter wait times? What is the impact of early ART initiation on 5-year mortality if HIV RNA viral load, the intermediate, remained at the value it would have been in the absence of the exposure (i.e., the natural direct effect [77–79])?

Overall, access to unprecedented amounts of data does not undo the age-old adage: "correlation is not causation." Indeed, there are numerous sources of association (dependence) between two variables: direct effects, indirect effects, measured confounding, unmeasured confounding, and selection bias. The methods, introduced here, allow researchers to move from saying drug X is associated with an adverse side effect to saying (under the necessary and transparently stated assumptions) an adverse side effect is caused by drug X. Even if the needed identifiability assumptions are not expected to hold, this framework helps us to estimate a statistical parameter, coming as close to the wished causal parameter. In other words, this framework ensures that the scientific question is driving the analysis and not the other way around.

Appendix: Extensions to Multiple Time Point Interventions

As an introduction to causal inference, we focused on causal parameters corresponding to a static intervention on a single node. In this appendix, we step through the causal roadmap for an example of a longitudinal effect, corresponding to a multiple time point intervention.

Step 1—Specify the scientific question: What is the effect of delayed ART initiation on patient outcomes? As before, we want to be specific about the target population: recently diagnosed HIV+ adults in Sub-Saharan Africa. We also need to be clear about the definition and timing of the exposures. For simplicity, let us assume that the patients have monthly clinic visits and therefore could initiate ART or not each month. (This framework could easily be extended to shorter or longer time intervals.) Suppose the outcome is viral suppression after 12 months of follow-up.

Step 2—Specify the causal model: Let baseline ($t = 0$) be the time that the patient is diagnosed with HIV. Let L_0 represent the vector of baseline covariates, including sociodemographics, clinical measurements, and social constructs. Likewise, let L_t represent the vector of time-updated covariates (e.g., clinical measurements). Let A_t be an indicator that the patient initiated ART at time t. For example, $A_0 = 1$ represents starting ART on the same day as diagnosis (i.e., month 0), whereas $A_1 = 1$ represents initiation at the first month visit. Finally, let Y be an indicator that the patient had undetectable HIV RNA viral load at the end of follow-up. For simplicity, let us consider only three time points and assume complete follow-up. Our structural causal model $\mathcal{M}^{\mathcal{F}}$, only reflecting the causal ordering, is given by

Endogenous nodes: $X = (L_0, A_0, L_1, A_1, Y)$

Exogenous nodes: $U = (U_{L_0}, U_{A_0}, U_{L_1}, U_{A_1}, U_Y)$ with some true joint distribution $P_{U,0}$. We place no assumptions on the set of possible distributions for U. (During the identifiability step, we will need to make some independence assumptions. However, we want to keep our true knowledge, as specified by structural causal model $\mathcal{M}^{\mathcal{F}}$, separate from the additional assumptions needed for identifiability.)

Structural equations:

$$\begin{aligned} L_0 &= f_{L_0}(U_{L_0}) \\ A_0 &= f_{A_0}(L_0, U_{A_0}) \\ L_1 &= f_{L_1}(L_0, A_0, U_{L_1}) \\ A_1 &= f_{A_1}(L_0, A_0, L_1, U_{A_1}) \\ Y &= f_Y(L_0, A_0, L_1, A_1, U_Y). \end{aligned}$$

We have not made any exclusion restrictions or independence assumptions. The corresponding directed acyclic graph is given in Figure 20.5a.

Step 3—Specify the target causal quantity: Let $Y(a_0, a_1)$ denote the counterfactual outcome (viral suppression) if a patient, possibly contrary to fact, had treatment history (a_0, a_1). Counterfactuals are generated by intervening on the structural causal model:

$$\begin{aligned} L_0 &= f_{L_0}(U_{L_0}) \\ A_0 &= a_0 \\ L_1 &= f_{L_1}(L_0, a_0, U_{L_1}) \\ A_1 &= a_1 \\ Y &= f_Y(L_0, a_0, L_1, a_1, U_Y). \end{aligned}$$

For the two binary exposures (initiate or not at time t), the set of possible exposure combinations is $\mathcal{A} = \{10, 01, 00\}$. For example, $Y(0,1)$ corresponds to preventing ART initiation at month 0 and starting ART at the 1 month clinic visit. Suppose our goal is to contrast expected counterfactual outcome if, possibly contrary to fact, all patients immediately initiated ART with the the expected counterfactual outcome if, possibly contrary to fact, all patients delayed ART initiation until 1 month after diagnosis:

$$\Psi^{\mathcal{F}}(P_{U,X,0}) = E_{U,X,0}[Y(1,0) - Y(0,1)].$$

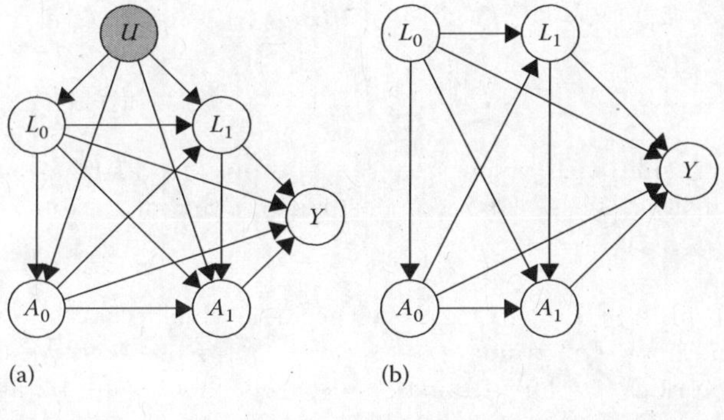

FIGURE 20.5
Directed acyclic graph corresponding to the longitudinal effect when (a) we make no independence assumptions on background factors and (b) when we assume that the background factors are all independent. L_0 denotes baseline covariates; A_0 denotes whether the patient initiated ART at $t = 0$; L_1 denotes time-updated covariates; A_1 denotes whether the patient initiated ART at $t = 1$; and Y denotes undetectable viral load.

Step 4—Specify the observed data and its link to the causal model: The observed data consist of n i.i.d. copies of

$$O = (L_0, A_0, L_1, A_1, Y) \sim P_0.$$

We assume that the observed data were generated by sampling n independent times from a data generating process compatible with $\mathcal{M}^{\mathcal{F}}$. The resulting statistical model $\mathcal{M}$, describing the possible observed data distributions, is nonparametric.

Step 5—Assess identifiability: For the purposes of discussion, suppose that the unmeasured factors $U = (U_{L_0}, U_{A_0}, U_{L_1}, U_{A_1}, U_Y)$ are all independent (Figure 20.5b). Even if this assumption held, there is not one set of covariates that simultaneously satisfy the back-door criterion for all intervention nodes. The baseline covariates L_0 alone fail, because there is an unblocked back-door path from Y through L_1 to A_1. In other words, the effect of initiation at 1 month A_1 on the outcome Y is confounded by time-updated covariates L_1. The baseline and time-updated covariates (L_0, L_1) jointly fail, because we are losing (blocking) the effect of early ART initiation A_0 on the outcome Y that goes through the covariates L_1. This challenge is generally known as *time-dependent confounding* [27,31,48]: time-varying covariates confound the effect of future exposures on the outcome, but are affected by past exposures.

To identify the effects of longitudinal interventions, we consider the problem sequentially. For each A_k in sequence, we ask if its effect on Y can be identified by conditioning on some subset of the observed past. This leads to the *sequential randomization assumption* [27]:

$$Y(a_0, a_1) \perp\!\!\!\perp A_0 \big| L_0 \text{ and } Y(a_0, a_1) \perp\!\!\!\perp A_1 \big| (L_0, A_0, L_1).$$

In words, we assume that the counterfactual outcome $Y(a_0, a_1)$ is independent from the intervention A_k at time k, given the observed past. With the sequential randomization assumption as well a longitudinal version of the positivity assumption, the expectation of counterfactual outcomes, indexed by multiple interventions, can be identified by the longitudinal G-computation formula [27]:

$$\begin{aligned} E_{U,X,0}[Y(a_0, a_1)] = \sum_{l_0, l_1} & E_0(Y | A_1 = a_1, L_1 = l_1, A_0 = a_0, L_0 = l_0) \\ & \times P_0(L_1 = l_1 | A_0 = a_0, L_0 = l_0) P_0(L_0 = l_0) = \Psi(P_0). \end{aligned}$$

Now we are averaging with respect to the appropriate distribution of covariates and thereby capturing the effect of both exposures (a_1, a_0) on the outcome Y through the covariates (L_0, L_1).

Step 6—Estimation and inference: As with single time point interventions, there are a variety of methods to estimate statistical parameters, corresponding under the necessary assumptions to longitudinal causal effects. Examples include longitudinal IPTW, "parametric G-computation" (maximum likelihood estimation of the longitudinal G-computation formula), and TMLE [31,51,53,54,59–69].

Step 7—Interpretation of the Results: As with the single time point setting, the strength of our interpretations depends on rigorous evaluation of the needed assumptions. Even when the identifiability assumptions do not hold, then we always have a statistical interpretation of $\Psi(P_0)$.

Acknowledgments

This work was supported, in part, by the National Institute of Allergy and Infectious Diseases of the National Institutes of Health under award number R01AI074345. The content is solely the responsibility of the authors and does not necessarily represent the officials views of the National Institutes of Health. Maya Petersen is a recipient of a Doris Duke Clinical Scientist Development Award.

References

1. J. Pearl. An introduction to causal inference. *International Journal of Biostatistics*, 6(2):Article 7, 2010.
2. E.H. Geng, D.V. Glidden, D.R. Bangsberg, M.B. Bwana, N. Musinguzi, D. Nash, J.Z. Metcalfe et al. A causal framework for understanding the effect of losses to follow-up on epidemiologic analyses in clinic-based cohorts: The case of HIV-infected patients on antiretroviral therapy in Africa. *American Journal of Epidemiology*, 175(10):1080–1087, 2012.
3. M. van der Laan and S. Rose. *Targeted Learning: Causal Inference for Observational and Experimental Data*. Springer, Berlin, Germany, 2011.
4. M.L. Petersen and M.J. van der Laan. Causal models and learning from data: Integrating causal modeling and statistical estimation. *Epidemiology*, 25(3):418–426, 2014.
5. J. Ahern and A. Hubbard. A roadmap for estimating and interpreting population intervention parameters. In J.M. Oakes and J.S. Kaufman, editors, *Methods in Social Epidemiology*. Jossey-Bass, San Francisco, CA, 2014.
6. M.A. Hernán, S. Hernández-Díaz, and J.M. Robins. A structural approach to selection bias. *Epidemiology*, 15(5):615–625, 2004.
7. S. Rose. Big data and the future. *Significance*, 9(4):47–48, 2012.
8. G. Marcus and E. Davis. Eight (no, nine!) problems with big data. *The New York Times*, A23, April 7, 2014.
9. S.D. Lawn and A.D. Harries. Reducing tuberculosis-associated early mortality in antiretroviral treatment programmes in sub-Saharan Africa. *AIDS*, 25(12):1554–1555, 2011.
10. M.S. Cohen, Y.Q. Chen, M. McCauley, T. Gamble, M.C. Hosseinipour, N. Kumarasamy et al. Prevention of HIV-1 infection with early antiretroviral therapy. *The New England Journal of Medicine*, 365(6):493–505, 2011.
11. World Health Organization. *Consolidated Guidelines on the Use of Antiretroviral Drugs for Treating and Preventing HIV Infection*. World Health Organization, Geneva, Switzerland, 2013.
12. M. Egger, D.K. Ekouevi, C. Williams, R.E. Lyamuya, H. Mukumbi, P. Braitstein et al. Cohort profile: The international epidemiological databases to evaluate AIDS (IeDEA) in Sub-Saharan Africa. *International Journal of Epidemiology*, 41(5):1256–1264, 2011.

13. University of California, San Francisco. Sustainable East Africa Research in Community Health (SEARCH). http://clinicaltrials.gov/show/NCT01864603, 2013.

14. J. Pearl. *Causality: Models, Reasoning and Inference.* Cambridge University Press, New York, 2000. (Second edition, 2009.)

15. J. Pearl. *Probabilistic Reasoning in Intelligent Systems.* Morgan Kaufmann, San Mateo, CA, 1988.

16. A. Goldberger. Structural equation models in the social sciences. *Econometrica: Journal of the Econometric Society*, 40:979–1001, 1972.

17. O. Duncan. *Introduction to Structural Equation Models.* Academic Press, New York, 1975.

18. J. Neyman. Sur les applications de la theorie des probabilites aux experiences agricoles: Essai des principes (in Polish). English translation by D.M. Dabrowska and T.P. Speed (1990). *Statistical Science*, 5:465–480, 1923.

19. D.B. Rubin. Estimating causal effects of treatments in randomized and nonrandomized studies. *Journal of Educational Psychology*, 66(5):688–701, 1974.

20. P.W. Holland. Statistics and causal inference. *Journal of the American Statistical Association*, 81(396):945–960, 1986.

21. J. Pearl. Causal diagrams for empirical research. *Biometrika*, 82:669–710, 1995.

22. M.A. Hernán, E. Lanoy, D. Costagliola, and J.M. Robins. Comparison of dynamic treatment regimes via inverse probability weighting. *Basic and Clinical Pharmacology and Toxicology*, 98(3):237–242, 2006.

23. M.J. van der Laan and M.L. Petersen. Causal effect models for realistic individualized treatment and intention to treat rules. *International Journal of Biostatistics*, 3(1): Article 3, 2007.

24. L.E. Cain, J.M. Robins, E. Lanoy, R. Logan, D. Costagliola, and M.A. Hernán. When to start treatment? A systematic approach to the comparison of dynamic regimes using observational data. *International Journal of Biostatistics*, 6(2):Article 18, 2010.

25. M.L. Petersen and M.J. van der Laan. Case study: Longitudinal HIV cohort data. In M.J. van der Laan and S. Rose, editors, *Targeted Learning: Causal Inference for Observational and Experimental Data.* Springer, New York, 397–417, 2011.

26. I. Díaz Muñoz and M. van der Laan. Population intervention causal effects based on stochastic interventions. *Biometrics*, 68(2):541–549, 2012.

27. J.M. Robins. A new approach to causal inference in mortality studies with sustained exposure periods—Application to control of the healthy worker survivor effect. *Mathematical Modeling*, 7:1393–1512, 1986.

28. M.A. Hernán and T.J. VanderWeele. Compound treatments and transportability of causal inference. *Epidemiology*, 22:368–377, 2011.

29. M.L. Petersen. Compound treatments, transportability, and the structural causal model: The power and simplicity of causal graphs. *Epidemiology*, 22:378–381, 2011.

30. J. Pearl and E. Bareinboim. Transportability across studies: A formal approach. Technical Report R-372, Computer Science Department, University of California, Los Angeles, CA, 2013.

31. J.M. Robins, M.A. Hernán, and B. Brumback. Marginal structural models and causal inference in epidemiology. *Epidemiology*, 11(5):550–560, 2000.

32. R. Neugebauer and M.J. van der Laan. Nonparametric causal effects based on marginal structural models. *Journal of Statistical Planning and Inference*, 137(2):419–434, 2007.

33. M.J. van der Laan. Estimation based on case-control designs with known prevalence probability. *International Journal of Biostatistics*, 4(1):Article 17, 2008.

34. S. Rose and M.J. van der Laan. Why match? Investigating matched case-control study designs with causal effect estimation. *International Journal of Biostatistics*, 5(1):Article 1, 2009.

35. D. Rubin. Randomization analysis of experimental data: The Fisher randomization test comment. *Journal of the American Statistical Association*, 75(371):591–593, 1980.

36. M.J. van der Laan. Causal inference for a population of causally connected units. *Journal of Causal Inference*, 2(1):13–74, 2014.

37. M.L. Petersen, K.E. Porter, S. Gruber, Y. Wang, and M.J. van der Laan. Diagnosing and responding to violations in the positivity assumption. *Statistical Methods in Medical Research*, 21(1):31–54, 2012.

38. E.C. Polley, S. Rose, and M.J. van der Laan. Super learner. In M.J. van der Laan and S. Rose, editors, *Targeted Learning: Causal Inference for Observational and Experimental Data*. Springer, New York, 43–66, 2011.

39. M.J. van der Laan, E.C. Polley, and A.E. Hubbard. Super learner. *Statistical Applications in Genetics and Molecular Biology*, 6(1):25, 2007.

40. M.J. van der Laan and D.B. Rubin. Targeted maximum likelihood learning. *International Journal of Biostatistics*, 2(1):Article 11, 2006.

41. S. Rose and M.J. van der Laan. Why TMLE? In M.J. van der Laan and S. Rose, editors, *Targeted Learning: Causal Inference for Observational and Experimental Data*. Springer, New York, 2011.

42. K.E. Porter, S. Gruber, M.J. van der Laan, and J.S. Sekhon. The relative performance of targeted maximum likelihood estimators. *International Journal of Biostatistics*, 7(1):Article 31, 2011.

43. O.M. Stitelman, V. De Gruttola, and M.J. van der Laan. A general implementation of tmle for longitudinal data applied to causal inference in survival analysis. *International Journal of Biostatistics*, 8(1), 2012. doi:10.1515/1557-4679.1334.

44. S. Gruber and M. van der Laan. Targeted maximum likelihood estimation. R package version 1.2.0-1. Available at http://CRAN.R-project.org/package=tmle, 2012.

45. J. Schwab, S. Lendle, M. Petersen, and M. van der Laan. LTMLE: Longitudinal Targeted Maximum Likelihood Estimation. R package version 0.9.3-1. Available at http://CRAN.R-project.org/package=ltmle, 2014.

46. R Core Team. *R: A Language and Environment for Statistical Computing.* R Foundation for Statistical Computing, Vienna, Austria, 2014.

47. M.A. Hernán and J.M. Robins. Estimating causal effects from epidemiological data. *Journal of Epidemiology and Community Health*, 60(7):578–586, 2006.

48. J.M. Robins and M.A. Hernán. Estimation of the causal effects of time-varying exposures. In G. Fitzmaurice, M. Davidian, G. Verbeke, and G. Molenberghs, editors, *Longitudinal Data Analysis*, chapter 23. Chapman & Hall/CRC Press, Boca Raton, FL, 2009.

49. M.L. Petersen, Y. Wang, M.J. van der Laan, and D.R. Bangsberg. Assessing the effectiveness of antiretroviral adherence interventions. Using marginal structural models to replicate the findings of randomized controlled trials. *Journal of Acquired Immune Deficiency Syndromes*, 43(Suppl 1):S96–S103, 2006.

50. J.M. Robins. Robust estimation in sequentially ignorable missing data and causal inference models. In *1999 Proceedings of the American Statistical Association.* American Statistical Association, Alexandria, VA, 2000, pp. 6–10.

51. M.J. van der Laan and J.M. Robins. *Unified Methods for Censored Longitudinal Data and Causality.* Springer-Verlag, New York, 2003.

52. L. Balzer, J. Ahern, S. Galea, and M.J. van der Laan. Estimating effects on rare outcomes: Knowledge is power. *Epidemiologic Methods*, In Press, 2015. Technical report available at http://biostats.bepress.com/ucbbiostat/paper310/, 2014.

53. L.M. Bodnar, M. Davidian, A.M. Siega-Riz, and A.A. Tsiatis. Marginal structural models for analyzing causal effects of time-dependent treatments: An application in perinatal epidemiology. *American Journal of Epidemiology*, 159(10):926–934, 2004.

54. M.L. Petersen, J. Schwab, S. Gruber, N. Blaser, M. Schomaker, and M.J. van der Laan. Targeted maximum likelihood estimation for dynamic and static longitudinal marginal structural working models. *Journal of Causal Inference*, 2(2):147–185, 2014.

55. J. Robins, A. Rotnitzky, and D. Scharfstein. Sensitivity analysis for selection bias and unmeasured confounding in missing data and causal inference models. In M. Halloran and D. Berry, editors, *Statistical Models in Epidemiology: The Environment and Clinical Trials.* Springer, New York, 1999.

56. K. Imai, L. Keele, and T. Yamamoto. Identification, inference, and sensitivity analysis for causal mediation effects. *Statistical Science*, 25:51–71, 2010.

57. T.J. VanderWeele and O.A. Arah. Bias formulas for sensitivity analysis of unmeasured confounding for general outcomes, treatments, and confounders. *Epidemiology*, 22: 42–52, 2011.

58. I. Díaz and M. van der Laan. Sensitivity analysis for causal inference under unmeasured confounding and measurement error problems. *International Journal of Biostatistics*, 9:149–160, 2013.

59. M.A. Hernán, B. Brumback, and J.M. Robins. Marginal structural models to estimate the causal effect of zidovudine on the survival of HIV-positive men. *Epidemiology*, 11(5):561–570, 2000.

60. S.R. Cole and M.A. Hernán. Constructing inverse probability weights for marginal structural models. *American Journal of Epidemiology*, 168(6):656–664, 2008.

61. J.M. Robins, L. Orellana, and A. Rotnitzky. Estimation and extrapolation of optimal treatment and testing strategies. *Statistics in Medicine*, 27(23):4678–4721, 2008.

62. S.L. Taubman, J.M. Robins, M.A. Mittleman, and M.A. Hernán. Intervening on risk factors for coronary heart disease: An application of the parametric g-formula. *International Journal of Epidemiology*, 38(6):1599–1611, 2009.

63. E.C. Polley and M.J. van der Laan. Super learning for right-censored data. In M.J. van der Laan and S. Rose, editors, *Targeted Learning: Causal Inference for Observational and Experimental Data*. Springer, New York, 249–258, 2011.

64. K.L. Moore and M.J. van der Laan. RCTs with time-to-event outcomes. In M.J. van der Laan and S. Rose, editors, *Targeted Learning: Causal Inference for Observational and Experimental Data*. Springer, New York, 259–269, 2011.

65. O.M. Stitelman and M.J. van der Laan. Collaborative targeted maximum likelihood for time-to-event data. *International Journal of Biostatistics*, 6(1):Article 21, 2010.

66. M.J. van der Laan and S. Gruber. Targeted minimum loss based estimation of causal effects of multiple time point interventions. *International Journal of Biostatistics*, 8(1), 2012. doi:10.1515/1557-4679.1370.

67. M.E. Schnitzer, E.E. Moodie, and R.W. Platt. Targeted maximum likelihood estimation for marginal time-dependent treatment effects under density misspecification. *Biostatistics*, 14(1):1–14, 2013.

68. M.E. Schnitzer, M.J. van der Laan, E.E. Moodie, and R.W. Platt. Effect of breastfeeding on gastrointestinal infection in infants: A targeted maximum likelihood approach for clustered longitudinal data. *Annals of Applied Statistics*, 8(2):703–725, 2014.

69. A.L. Decker, A. Hubbard, C.M. Crespi, E.Y.W. Seto, and M.C. Wang. Semiparametric estimation of the impacts of longitudinal interventions on adolescent obesity using targeted maximum-likelihood: Accessible estimation with the ltmle package. *Journal of Causal Inference*, 2(1):95–108, 2014.

70. O. Bembom and M.J. van der Laan. A practical illustration of the importance of realistic individualized treatment rules in causal inference. *Electronic Journal of Statistics*, 1:574–596, 2007.

71. M.M. Kitahata, S.J. Gange, A.G. Abraham, B. Merriman, M.S. Saag, A.C. Justice et al. Effect of early versus deferred antiretroviral therapy for HIV on survival. *The New England Journal of Medicine*, 360(18):1815–1826, 2009.

72. M.A. Hernán and J.M. Robins. Comment on: Early versus deferred antiretroviral therapy for HIV on survival. *The New England Journal of Medicine*, 361(8):823–824, 2009.

73. M.L. Petersen, S.E. Sinisi, and M.J. van der Laan. Estimation of direct causal effects. *Epidemiology*, 17(3):276–284, 2006.

74. M.J. van der Laan and M.L. Petersen. Direct effect models. *International Journal of Biostatistics*, 4(1):Article 23, 2008.

75. T.J. VanderWeele. Marginal structural models for the estimation of direct and indirect effects. *Epidemiology*, 20(1):18–26, 2009.

76. A.E. Hubbard, N.P. Jewell, and M.J. van der Laan. Direct effects and effect among the treated. In M.J. van der Laan and S. Rose, editors, *Targeted Learning: Causal Inference for Observational and Experimental Data*. Springer, New York, 133–143, 2011.

77. W. Zheng and M.J. van der Laan. Targeted maximum likelihood estimation for natural direct effects. *International Journal of Biostatistics*, 8(1):1–40, 2012.

78. W. Zheng and M.J. van der Laan. Causal mediation in a survival setting with time-dependent mediators. Technical Report 295, Division of Biostatistics, University of California, Berkeley, CA. Available at http://biostats.bepress.com/ucbbiostat/paper295/, 2012

79. S. Lendle, M.S. Subbaraman, and M.J. van der Laan. Identification and efficient estimation of the natural direct effect among the untreated. *Biometrics*, 69:310–317, 2013.

21

A Review of Some Recent Advances in Causal Inference

Marloes H. Maathuis and Preetam Nandy

CONTENTS

21.1 Introduction 388
21.1.1 Causal versus Noncausal Research Questions 388
21.1.2 Observational versus Experimental Data 389
21.1.2.1 Observational Data 389
21.1.2.2 Experimental Data 389
21.1.3 Problem Formulation 389
21.1.3.1 Outline of This Chapter 390
21.2 Estimating Causal Effects When the Causal Structure Is Known 390
21.2.1 Graph Terminology 391
21.2.2 Structural Equation Model 391
21.2.3 Postintervention Distributions and Causal Effects 393
21.2.3.1 Truncated Factorization Formula 393
21.2.3.2 Defining the Total Effect 393
21.2.3.3 Computing the Total Effect 394
21.3 Causal Structure Learning 394
21.3.1 Constraint-Based Methods 395
21.3.2 Score-Based Methods 396
21.3.3 Hybrid Methods 397
21.3.4 Learning SEMs with Additional Restrictions 397
21.4 Estimating the Size of Causal Effects When the Causal Structure Is Unknown 398
21.4.1 IDA 398
21.4.2 JointIDA 398
21.4.3 Application 399
21.5 Extensions 400
21.5.1 Local Causal Structure Learning 401
21.5.2 Causal Structure Learning in the Presence of Hidden Variables and Feedback Loops 401
21.5.3 Time Series Data 402
21.5.4 Causal Structure Learning from Heterogeneous Data 402
21.5.5 Covariate Adjustment 402
21.5.6 Measures of Uncertainty 402
21.6 Summary 403
References 403

21.1 Introduction

Causal questions are fundamental in all parts of science. Answering such questions from observational data is notoriously difficult, but there has been a lot of recent interest and progress in this field. This chapter gives a selective review of some of these results, intended for researchers who are not familiar with graphical models and causality, and with a focus on methods that are applicable to large datasets.

To clarify the problem formulation, we first discuss the difference between causal and noncausal questions, and between observational and experimental data. We then formulate the problem setting and give an overview of the rest of this chapter.

21.1.1 Causal versus Noncausal Research Questions

We use a small hypothetical example to illustrate the concepts.

Example 21.1 *Suppose that there is a new rehabilitation program for prisoners, aimed at lowering the recidivism rate. Among a random sample of* 1500 *prisoners,* 500 *participated in the program. All prisoners were followed for a period of* 2 *years after release from prison, and it was recorded whether or not they were rearrested within this period. Table* 21.1 *shows the (hypothetical) data. We note that the rearrest rate among the participants of the program* (20%) *is significantly lower than the rearrest rate among the nonparticipants* (50%).

We can ask various questions based on these data. For example:

1. Can we predict whether a prisoner will be rearrested, based on participation in the program (and possibly other variables)?
2. Does the program lower the rearrest rate?
3. What would the rearrest rate be if the program were compulsory for all prisoners?

Question 1 is *noncausal*, because it involves a *standard* prediction or classification problem. We note that this question can be very relevant in practice, for example in parole considerations. However, because we are interested in causality here, we will not consider questions of this type.

Questions 2 and 3 are *causal*. Question 2 asks if the program is the *cause* of the lower rearrest rate among the participants. In other words, it asks about the *mechanism* behind the data. Question 3 asks a prediction of the rearrest rate *after some novel outside intervention to the system*, namely after making the program compulsory for all prisoners. To make such a prediction, one needs to understand the causal structure of the system.

Example 21.2 *We consider gene expression levels of yeast cells. Suppose that we want to predict the average gene expression levels after knocking out one of the genes, or after knocking out multiple genes at a time. These are again causal questions, because we want to make predictions after interventions to the system.*

Thus, causal questions are about the *mechanism* behind the data or about predictions *after a novel intervention is applied to the system*. They arise in all parts of science. Application

TABLE 21.1
Hypothetical data about a rehabilitation program for prisoners.

	Rearrested	Not Rearrested	Rearrest Rate (%)
Participants	100	400	20
Nonparticipants	500	500	50

areas involving big data include, for example, systems biology (e.g., [12,19,30,32,40,62]), neuroscience (e.g., [8,20,49,58]), climate science (e.g., [16,17]), and marketing (e.g., [7]).

21.1.2 Observational versus Experimental Data

Going back to the prisoners example, which of the three posed questions can we answer? This depends on the origin of the data, and brings us to the distinction between observational and experimental data.

21.1.2.1 Observational Data

Suppose first that participation in the program was voluntary. Then we would have so-called *observational data*, because the subjects (prisoners) chose their own treatment (rehabilitation program or not), while the researchers just *observed* the results. From observational data, we can easily answer question 1. It is difficult, however, to answer questions 2 and 3.

Let us first consider question 2. Because the participants form a self-selected subgroup, there may be many differences between the participants and the nonparticipants. For example, the participants may be more motivated to change their lives, and this may contribute to the difference in rearrest rates. In this case, the effects of the program and the motivation of the prisoners are said to be mixed-up or *confounded.*

Next, let us consider question 3. At first sight, one may think that the answer is simply 20%, because this was the rearrest rate among the participants of the program. But again we have to keep in mind that the participants form a self-selected subgroup that is likely to have special characteristics. Hence, the rearrest rate of this subgroup cannot be extrapolated to the entire prisoners population.

21.1.2.2 Experimental Data

Now suppose that it was up to the researchers to decide which prisoners participated in the program. For example, suppose that the researchers rolled a die for each prisoner, and let him/her participate if the outcome was 1 or 2. Then we would have a so-called *randomized controlled experiment* and *experimental data.*

Let us look again at question 2. Because of the randomization, the motivation level of the prisoners is likely to be similar in the two groups. Moreover, any other factors of importance (such as social background, type of crime committed, and number of earlier crimes) are likely to be similar in the two groups. Hence, the groups are equal in all respects, except for participation in the program. The observed difference in rearrest rate must therefore be due to the program. This answers question 2.

Finally, the answer to question 3 is now 20%, because the randomized treatment assignment ensures that the participants form a representative sample of the population.

Thus, causal questions are best answered by experimental data, and we should work with such data whenever possible. Experimental data are not always available, however, because randomized controlled experiments can be unethical, infeasible, time consuming, or expensive. On the other hand, observational data are often relatively cheap and abundant. In this chapter, we therefore consider the problem of answering causal questions about large-scale systems from observational data.

21.1.3 Problem Formulation

It is relatively straightforward to make *standard* predictions based on observational data (see the *observational world* in Figure 21.1), or to estimate causal effects from randomized controlled experiments (see the *experimental world* in Figure 21.1). But we want to

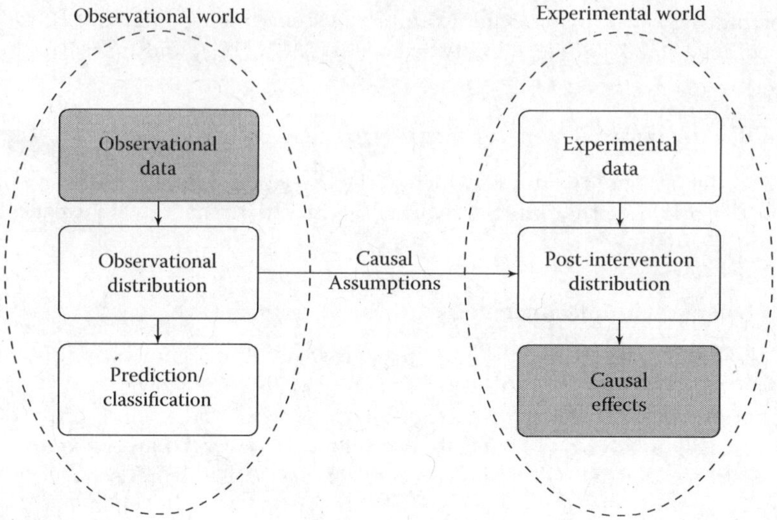

FIGURE 21.1
We want to estimate causal effects from observational data. This means that we need to move from the observational world to the experimental world. This can only be done by imposing causal assumptions.

estimate *causal effects* from *observational data*. This means that we need to move from the observational world to the experimental world. This step is fundamentally impossible without causal assumptions, even in the large sample limit with perfect knowledge about the observational distribution (cf. Section 2 of [43]). In other words, causal assumptions are needed to deduce the postintervention distribution from the observational distribution. In this chapter, we assume that the data were generated from a (known or unknown) causal structure that can be represented by a directed acyclic graph (DAG).

21.1.3.1 Outline of This Chapter

In the next section, we assume that the data were generated from a known DAG. In particular, we discuss the framework of a structural equation model (SEM) and its corresponding causal DAG. We also discuss the estimation of causal effects under such a model. In large-scale networks, however, the causal DAG is often unknown. Next, we therefore discuss causal structure learning, that is, learning information about the causal structure from observational data. We then combine these two parts and discuss methods to estimate (bounds on) causal effects from observational data when the causal structure is unknown. We also illustrate this method on a yeast gene expression dataset. We close by mentioning several extensions of the discussed work.

21.2 Estimating Causal Effects When the Causal Structure Is Known

Causal structures can be represented by graphs, where the random variables are represented by nodes (or vertices), and causal relationships between the variables are represented by edges between the corresponding nodes. Such causal graphs have two important practical advantages. First, a causal graph provides a transparent and compact description of the causal assumptions that are being made. This allows these assumptions to be discussed and debated among researchers. Next, after agreeing on a causal graph, one can easily determine causal effects. In particular, we can read off from the graph which sets of variables can or cannot be used for covariate adjustment to obtain a given causal effect. We refer to [43,44] for further details on the material in this section.

21.2.1 Graph Terminology

We consider graphs with *directed edges* ($\rightarrow$) and *undirected edges* ($-$). There can be at most one edge between any pair of distinct nodes. If all edges are directed (undirected), then the graph is called *directed* (*undirected*). A *partially directed graph* can contain both directed and undirected edges. The *skeleton* of a partially directed graph is the undirected graph that results from replacing all directed edges by undirected edges.

Two nodes are *adjacent* if they are connected by an edge. If $X \rightarrow Y$, then X is a parent of Y. The adjacency set and the parent set of a node X in a graph $\mathcal{G}$ are denoted by $adj(X, \mathcal{G})$ and $pa(X, \mathcal{G})$, respectively. A graph is *complete* if every pair of nodes is adjacent.

A *path* in a graph $\mathcal{G}$ is a distinct sequence of nodes, such that all successive pairs of nodes in the sequence are adjacent in $\mathcal{G}$. A *directed path* from X to Y is a path between X and Y in which all edges point toward Y, that is, $X \rightarrow \cdots \rightarrow Y$. A directed path from X to Y together with an edge $Y \rightarrow X$ forms a *directed cycle*. A directed graph is *acyclic* if it does not contain directed cycles. A *directed acyclic graph* is also called a *DAG*.

A node X is a *collider* on a path if the path has two colliding arrows at X, that is, the path contains $\rightarrow X \leftarrow$. Otherwise X is a *noncollider* on the path. We emphasize that the collider status of a node is relative to a path; a node can be a collider on one path, while it is a noncollider on another. The collider X is *unshielded* if the neighbors of X on the path are not adjacent to each other in the graph, that is, the path contains $W \rightarrow X \leftarrow Z$ and W and Z are not adjacent in the graph.

21.2.2 Structural Equation Model

We consider a collection of random variables $X_1, \ldots, X_p$ that are generated by structural equations (see, e.g., [6,69]):

$$X_i \leftarrow g_i(\mathbf{S}_i, \epsilon_i) \qquad i = 1, \ldots, p, \tag{21.1}$$

where $\mathbf{S}_i \subseteq \{X_1, \ldots, X_p\} \setminus \{X_i\}$ and ϵ_i is some random noise. We interpret these equations causally, as describing how each X_i is generated from the variables in $\mathbf{S}_i$ and the noise ϵ_i. Thus, changes to the variables in $\mathbf{S}_i$ can lead to changes in X_i, but not the other way around. We use the notation $\leftarrow$ in Equation 21.1 to emphasize this asymmetric relationship. Moreover, we assume that the structural equations are *autonomous*, in the sense that we can change one structural equation without affecting the others. This will allow the modeling of local interventions to the system.

The structural equations correspond to a directed graph $\mathcal{G}$ that is generated as follows: the nodes are given by $X_1, \ldots, X_p$, and the edges are drawn so that $\mathbf{S}_i$ is the parent set of X_i, $i = 1, \ldots, p$. The graph $\mathcal{G}$ then describes the causal structure and is called the *causal graph*: the presence of an edge $X_j \rightarrow X_i$ means that X_j is a potential direct cause of X_i (i.e., X_j may play a role in the generating mechanism of X_i), and the absence of an edge $X_k \rightarrow X_i$ means that X_k is definitely not a direct cause of X_i (i.e., X_k does not play a role in the generating mechanism of X_i).

Throughout, we make several assumptions about the model. The graph $\mathcal{G}$ is assumed to be acyclic (hence a DAG), and the error terms $\epsilon_1, \ldots, \epsilon_p$ are jointly independent. In terms of the causal interpretation, these assumptions mean that we do not allow feedback loops nor unmeasured confounding variables. The above model with these assumptions was called a *structural causal model* by [42]. We will simply refer to it as a *structural equation model* (*SEM*). If all structural equations are linear, we will call it a *linear SEM.*

We now discuss two important properties of SEMs, namely factorization and d-separation. If $X_1, \ldots, X_p$ are generated from an SEM with causal DAG $\mathcal{G}$, then the density $f(x_1, \ldots, x_p)$ of $X_1, \ldots, X_p$ (assuming it exists) factorizes as

$$f(x_1, \ldots, x_p) = \prod_{i=1}^{p} f_i(x_i | pa(x_i, \mathcal{G})) \tag{21.2}$$

where $f_i(x_i|pa(x_i, \mathcal{G}))$ is the conditional density of X_i given $pa(X_i, \mathcal{G})$.

If a density factorizes according to a DAG as in Equation 21.2, then one can use the DAG to read off conditional independencies that must hold in the distribution (regardless of the choice of the $f_i(\cdot)$'s), using a graphical criterion called *d-separation* (see, e.g., Definition 1 in [43]). In particular, the so-called global Markov property implies that when two disjoint sets $\mathbf{A}$ and $\mathbf{B}$ of vertices are d-separated by a third disjoint set $\mathbf{S}$, then $\mathbf{A}$ and $\mathbf{B}$ are conditionally independent given $\mathbf{S}$ ($\mathbf{A} \perp\!\!\!\perp \mathbf{B}|\mathbf{S}$) in any distribution that factorizes according to the DAG.

Example 21.3 *We consider the following structural equations and the corresponding causal DAG for the random variables P, S, R, and M:*

$$\begin{aligned} P &\leftarrow g_1(M, \epsilon_P) \\ S &\leftarrow g_2(P, \epsilon_S) \\ R &\leftarrow g_3(M, S, \epsilon_R) \\ M &\leftarrow g_4(\epsilon_M) \end{aligned}$$

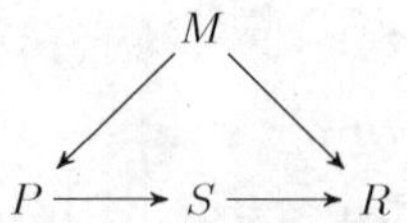

where ϵ_P, ϵ_S, ϵ_R, *and* ϵ_M *are mutually independent with arbitrary mean zero distributions. For each structural equation, the variables on the right-hand side appear in the causal DAG as the parents of the variable on the left-hand side.*

We denote the random variables by M, P, S, and R, because these structural equations can be used to describe a possible causal mechanism behind the prisoners data (Example 21.1), where $M =$ *measure of motivation,* $P =$ *participation in the program* ($P = 1$ *means participation,* $P = 0$ *otherwise),* $S =$ *measure of social skills taught by the program, and* $R =$ *rearrest* ($R = 1$ *means rearrest,* $R = 0$ *otherwise).*

We see that the causal DAG of this SEM indeed provides a clear and compact description its causal assumptions. In particular, it allows that motivation directly affects participation and rearrest. Moreover, it allows that participation directly affects social skills, and that social skills directly affect rearrest. The missing edge between M and S encodes the assumption that there is no direct effect from motivation on social skills. In other words, any effect of motivation on social skills goes entirely through participation (see the path $M \rightarrow P \rightarrow S$*). Similarly, the missing edge between P and R encodes the assumption that there is no direct effect of participation on rearrest; any effect of participation on rearrest must fully go through social skills (see the path* $P \rightarrow S \rightarrow R$*).*

21.2.3 Postintervention Distributions and Causal Effects

Now how does the framework of the SEM allow us to move between the observational and experimental worlds? This is straightforward, because an intervention at some variable X_i simply means that we change the generating mechanism of X_i, that is, we change the corresponding structural equation $g_i(\cdot)$ (and leave the other structural equations unchanged). For example, one can let $X_i \leftarrow \epsilon_i$, where ϵ_i has some given distribution, or $X_i \leftarrow x_i'$ for some fixed value x_i' in the support of X_i. The latter is often denoted as Pearl's do-intervention $do(X_i = x_i')$ and is interpreted as setting the variable X_i to the value x_i' by an outside intervention, uniformly over the entire population [43].

Example 21.4 *In the prisoners example (see Examples* 21.1 *and* 21.3*), the quantity* $P(R = 1|do(P = 1))$ *represents the rearrest probability when all prisoners are forced to participate in the program, while* $P(R = 1|do(P = 0))$ *is the rearrest probability if no prisoner is allowed to participate in the program. We emphasize that these quantities are generally not equal to the usual conditional probabilities* $P(R = 1|P = 1)$ *and* $P(R = 1|P = 0)$*, which represent the rearrest probabilities among prisoners who choose to participate or not to participate in the program.*

In the gene expression example (see Example 21.2*), let* X_i *and* X_j *represent the gene expression level of genes* i *and* j*. Then* $E(X_j|do(X_i = x_i'))$ *represents the average expression level of gene* j *after setting the gene expression level of gene* i *to the value* x_i' *by an outside intervention.*

21.2.3.1 Truncated Factorization Formula

A do-intervention on X_i means that X_i no longer depends on its former parents in the DAG, so that the incoming edges into X_i can be removed. This leads to a so-called truncated DAG. The postintervention distribution factorizes according to this truncated DAG, so that we get

$$f(x_1, \ldots, x_p|do(X_i = x_i')) = \begin{cases} \prod_{j \neq i} f_j(x_j|pa(x_j, \mathcal{G})) & \text{if } x_i = x_i', \\ 0 & \text{otherwise.} \end{cases} \tag{21.3}$$

This is called the truncated factorization formula [41], the manipulation formula [59] or the g-formula [52]. Note that this formula heavily uses the factorization formula (Equation 21.2) and the *autonomy assumption* (see page 391).

21.2.3.2 Defining the Total Effect

Summary measures of the postintervention distribution can be used to define total causal effects. In the prisoners example, it is natural to define the total effect of P on R as

$$P(R = 1|do(P = 1)) - P(R = 1|do(P = 0)).$$

Again, we emphasize that this is different from $P(R = 1|P = 1) - P(R = 1|P = 0)$.

In a setting with continuous variables, the total effect of X_i on Y can be defined as

$$\frac{\partial}{\partial x_i} E(Y|do(X_i = x_i))\Big|_{x_i = x_i'}.$$

21.2.3.3 Computing the Total Effect

A total effect can be computed using, for example, covariate adjustment [43,57], inverse probability weighting (IPW) [23,53], or instrumental variables (e.g., [4]). In all these methods, the causal DAG plays an important role, because it tells us which variables can be used for covariate adjustment, which variables can be used as instruments, or which weights should be used in IPW.

In this chapter, we focus mostly on linear SEMs. In this setting, the total effect of X_i on Y can be easily computed via linear regression with covariate adjustment. If $Y \in pa(X_i, \mathcal{G})$ then the effect of X_i on Y equals zero. Otherwise, it equals the regression coefficient of X_i in the linear regression of Y on X_i and $pa(X_i, \mathcal{G})$ (see Proposition 3.1 of [39]). In other words, we simply regress Y on X_i while adjusting for the parents of X_i in the causal DAG. This is also called *adjusting for direct causes of the intervention variable.*

Example 21.5 *We consider the following linear SEM:*

$$\begin{aligned} X_1 &\leftarrow 2X_4 + \epsilon_1 \\ X_2 &\leftarrow 3X_1 + \epsilon_2 \\ X_3 &\leftarrow 2X_2 + X_4 + \epsilon_3 \\ X_4 &\leftarrow \epsilon_4 \end{aligned}$$

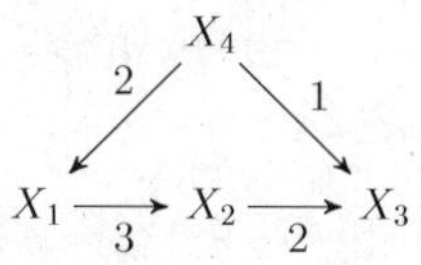

The errors are mutually independent with arbitrary mean zero distributions. We note that the coefficients in the structural equations are depicted as edge weights in the causal DAG.

Suppose we are interested in the total effect of X_1 on X_3. Then we consider an outside intervention that sets X_1 to the value x_1, that is, $do(X_1 = x_1)$. This means that we change the structural equation for X_1 to $X_1 \leftarrow x_1$. Because the other structural equations do not change, we then obtain $X_2 = 3x_1 + \epsilon_2$, $X_4 = \epsilon_4$, and $X_3 = 2X_2 + X_4 + \epsilon_3 = 6x_1 + 2\epsilon_2 + \epsilon_4 + \epsilon_3$. Hence, $E(X_3|do(X_1 = x_1)) = 6x_1$, and differentiating with respect to x_1 yields a total effect of 6.

We note that the total effect of X_1 on X_3 also equals the product of the edge weights along the directed path $X_1 \to X_2 \to X_3$. This is true in general for linear SEMs: the total effect of X_i on Y can be obtained by multiplying the edge weights along each directed path from X_i to Y, and then summing over the directed paths (if there is more than one).

The total effect can also be obtained via regression. Because $pa(X_1, \mathcal{G}) = \{X_4\}$, the total effect of X_1 on X_3 equals the coefficient of X_1 in the regression of X_3 on X_1 and X_4. It can be easily verified that this again yields 6. One can also verify that adjusting for any other subset of $\{X_2, X_4\}$ does not yield the correct total effect.

21.3 Causal Structure Learning

The material in the previous section can be used if the causal DAG is known. In settings with big data, however, it is rare that one can draw the causal DAG. In this section, we therefore consider methods for learning DAGs from observational data. Such methods are called *causal structure learning methods.*

Recall from Section 21.2.2 that DAGs encode conditional independencies via d-separation. Thus, by considering conditional independencies in the observational distribution, one may hope to reverse-engineer the causal DAG that generated the data. Unfortunately, this does not work in general, because the same set of d-separation relationships can be encoded by several DAGs. Such DAGs are called *Markov equivalent* and form a *Markov equivalence class.*

A Markov equivalence class can be described uniquely by a completed partially DAG (CPDAG) [3,9]. The skeleton of the CPDAG is defined as follows. Two nodes X_i and X_j are adjacent in the CPDAG if and only if, in any DAG in the Markov equivalence class, X_i and X_j cannot be d-separated by any set of the remaining nodes. The orientation of the edges in the CPDAG is as follows. A directed edge $X_i \to X_j$ in the CPDAG means that the edge $X_i \to X_j$ occurs in all DAGs in the Markov equivalence class. An undirected edge $X_i - X_j$ in the CPDAG means that there is a DAG in the Markov equivalence class with $X_i \to X_j$, as well as a DAG with $X_i \leftarrow X_j$.

It can happen that a distribution contains more conditional independence relationships than those that are encoded by the DAG via d-separation. If this is *not* the case, then the distribution is called *faithful* with respect to the DAG. If a distribution is both Markov and faithful with respect to a DAG, then the conditional independencies in the distribution correspond exactly to d-separation relationships in the DAG, and the DAG is called a *perfect map* of the distribution.

Problem setting. Throughout this section, we consider the following setting. We are given n i.i.d. observations of $\mathbf{X}$, where $\mathbf{X} = (X_1, \ldots, X_p)$ is generated from a SEM. We assume that the corresponding causal DAG $\mathcal{G}$ is a perfect map of the distribution of $\mathbf{X}$. We aim to learn the Markov equivalence class of $\mathcal{G}$.

In the following three subsections we discuss so-called constraint-based, score-based, and hybrid methods for this task. The discussed algorithms are available in the R-package `pcalg` [29]. In the last subsection we discuss a class of methods that can be used if one is willing to impose additional restrictions on the SEM that allow identification of the causal DAG (rather than its CPDAG).

21.3.1 Constraint-Based Methods

Constraint-based methods learn the CPDAG by exploiting conditional independence constraints in the observational distribution. The most prominent example of such a method is probably the PC algorithm [60]. This algorithm first estimates the skeleton of the underlying CPDAG, and then determines the orientation of as many edges as possible.

We discuss the estimation of the skeleton in more detail. Recall that, under the Markov and faithfulness assumptions, two nodes X_i and X_j are adjacent in the CPDAG if and only if they are conditionally dependent given all subsets of $\mathbf{X} \setminus \{X_i, X_j\}$. Therefore, adjacency of X_i and X_j can be determined by testing $X_i \perp\!\!\!\perp X_j | \mathbf{S}$ for all possible subsets $\mathbf{S} \subseteq \mathbf{X} \setminus \{X_i, X_j\}$. This naive approach is used in the SGS algorithm [60]. It quickly becomes computationally infeasible for a large number of variables.

The PC algorithm avoids this computational trap by using the following fact about DAGs: two nodes X_i and X_j in a DAG $\mathcal{G}$ are d-separated by some subset of the remaining nodes if and only if they are d-separated by $pa(X_i, \mathcal{G})$ or by $pa(X_j, \mathcal{G})$. This fact may seem of little help at first, because we do not know $pa(X_i, \mathcal{G})$ and $pa(X_j, \mathcal{G})$ (then we would know the DAG!). It is helpful, however, because it allows a clever ordering of the conditional independence tests in the PC algorithm, as follows. The algorithm starts with a complete undirected graph. It then assesses, for all pairs of variables, whether they are marginally independent. If a pair of variables is found to be independent, then the edge between them is removed. Next, for each pair of nodes (X_i, X_j) that are still adjacent, it tests conditional independence of the corresponding random variables given all possible subsets of size 1 of $adj(X_i, \mathcal{G}^*) \setminus \{X_j\}$ and of $adj(X_j, \mathcal{G}^*) \setminus \{X_i\}$, where $\mathcal{G}^*$ is the current graph. Again, it removes the edge if such a conditional independence is deemed to be true. The algorithm continues in this way, considering conditioning sets of increasing size, until the size of the conditioning sets is larger than the size of the adjacency sets of the nodes.

This procedure gives the correct skeleton when using perfect conditional independence information. To see this, note that at any point in the procedure, the current graph is a supergraph of the skeleton of the CPDAG. By construction of the algorithm, this ensures that $X_i \perp\!\!\!\perp X_j | pa(X_i, \mathcal{G})$ and $X_i \perp\!\!\!\perp X_j | pa(X_j, \mathcal{G})$ were assessed.

After applying certain edge orientation rules, the output of the PC algorithm is a partially directed graph, the estimated CPDAG. This output depends on the ordering of the variables (except in the limit of an infinite sample size), because the ordering determines which conditional independence tests are done. This issue was studied in [14], where it was shown that the order-dependence can be very severe in high-dimensional settings with many variables and a small sample size (see Section 21.4.3 for a data example). Moreover, an order-independent version of the PC algorithm, called PC-stable, was proposed in [14]. This version is now the default implementation in the R-package `pcalg` [29].

We note that the user has to specify a significance level α for the conditional independence tests. Because of multiple testing, this parameter does *not* play the role of an overall significance level. It should rather be viewed as a tuning parameter for the algorithm, where smaller values of α typically lead to sparser graphs.

The PC and PC-stable algorithms are computationally feasible for sparse graphs with thousands of variables. Both PC and PC-stable were shown to be consistent in sparse high-dimensional settings, when the joint distribution is multivariate Gaussian and conditional independence is assessed by testing for zero partial correlation [14,28]. By using Rank correlation, consistency can be achieved in sparse high-dimensional settings for a broader class of Gaussian copula or nonparanormal models [21].

21.3.2 Score-Based Methods

Score-based methods learn the CPDAG by (greedily) searching for an optimally scoring DAG, where the score measures how well the data fit to the DAG, while penalizing the complexity of the DAG.

A prominent example of such an algorithm is the greedy equivalence search (GES) algorithm [10]. GES is a grow–shrink algorithm that consists of two phases: a forward phase and a backward phase. The forward phase starts with an initial estimate (often the empty graph) of the CPDAG, and sequentially adds single edges, each time choosing the edge addition that yields the maximum improvement of the score, until the score can no longer be improved. The backward phase starts with the output of the forward phase, and sequentially deletes single edges, each time choosing the edge deletion that yields a maximum improvement of the score, until the score can no longer be improved. A computational advantage of GES over the traditional DAG-search methods is that it searches over the space of all possible CPDAGs, instead of over the space of all possible DAGs.

The GES algorithm requires the scoring criterion to be *score equivalent*, meaning that every DAG in a Markov equivalence class gets the same score. Moreover, the choice of scoring criterion is crucial for computational and statistical performances. The so-called *decomposability* property of a scoring criterion allows fast updates of scores during the forward and the backward phase. For example, (penalized) log-likelihood scores are decomposable, because Equation 21.2 implies that the (penalized) log-likelihood score of a DAG can be computed by summing up the (local) scores of each node given its parents in the DAG. Finally, the so-called *consistency* property of a scoring criterion ensures that the true CPDAG gets the highest score with probability approaching one (as the sample size tends to infinity).

GES was shown to be consistent when the scoring criterion is score equivalent, decomposable, and consistent. For multivariate Gaussian or multinomial distributions, penalized likelihood scores such as BIC satisfy these assumptions.

21.3.3 Hybrid Methods

Hybrid methods learn the CPDAG by combining the ideas of constraint-based and score-based methods. Typically, they first estimate (a supergraph of) the skeleton of the CPDAG using conditional independence tests, and then apply a search and score technique while restricting the set of allowed edges to the estimated skeleton. A prominent example is the Max-Min Hill-Climbing (MMHC) algorithm [66].

The restriction on the search space of hybrid methods provides a huge computational advantage when the estimated skeleton is sparse. This is why the hybrid methods scale well to thousands of variables, whereas the unrestricted score-based methods do not. However, this comes at the cost of inconsistency or at least at the cost of a lack of consistency proofs. Interestingly, empirical results have shown that a restriction on the search space can also help to improve the estimation quality [66].

This gap between theory and practice was addressed in [38], who proposed a consistent hybrid modification of GES, called ARGES. The search space of ARGES mainly depends on an estimated conditional independence graph. (This is an undirected graph containing an edge between X_i and X_j if and only if $X_i \not\perp\!\!\!\perp X_j | \mathbf{V} \setminus \{X_i, X_j\}$. It is a supergraph of the skeleton of the CPDAG.) But the search space also changes adaptively depending on the current state of the algorithm. This adaptive modification is necessary to achieve consistency in general. The fact that the modification is relatively minor may provide an explanation for the empirical success of (inconsistent) hybrid methods.

21.3.4 Learning SEMs with Additional Restrictions

Now that we have looked at various different methods to estimate the CPDAG, we close this section by discussing a slightly different approach that allows estimation of the causal DAG rather than its CPDAG. Identification of the DAG can be achieved by imposing additional restrictions on the generating SEM. Examples of this approach include the linear non-Gaussian acyclic model (LiNGAM) method for linear SEMs with non-Gaussian noise [54,55], methods for nonlinear SEMs [24] and methods for linear Gaussian SEMs with equal error variances [46].

We discuss the LiNGAM method in some more detail. A linear SEM can be written as $\mathbf{X} = B\mathbf{X} + \boldsymbol{\epsilon}$ or equivalently $\mathbf{X} = A\boldsymbol{\epsilon}$ with $A = (I - B)^{-1}$. The LiNGAM algorithm of [54] uses independent component analysis (ICA) to obtain estimates $\hat{A}$ and $\hat{B} = I - \hat{A}^{-1}$ of A and B. Ideally, rows and columns of $\hat{B}$ can be permuted to obtain a lower triangular matrix and hence an estimate of the causal DAG. This is not possible in general in the presence of sampling errors, but a lower triangular matrix can be obtained by setting some small nonzero entries to zero and permuting rows and columns of $\hat{B}$.

A more recent implementation of the LiNGAM algorithm, called DirectLiNGAM, was proposed in [55]. This implementation is not based on ICA. Rather, it estimates the variable ordering by iteratively finding an exogenous variable. DirectLiNGAM is suitable for settings with a larger number of variables.

21.4 Estimating the Size of Causal Effects When the Causal Structure Is Unknown

We now combine the previous two sections and discuss methods to estimate bounds on causal effects from observational data when the causal structure is unknown. We first define the problem setting.

Problem setting. We have n i.i.d. realizations of $\mathbf{X}$, where $\mathbf{X}$ is generated from a linear SEM with Gaussian errors. We do not know the corresponding causal DAG, but we assume that it is a perfect map of the distribution of $\mathbf{X}$. Our goal is to estimate the sizes of causal effects.

We first discuss the intervention-calculus when the DAG is absent (IDA) method [32,33] to estimate the effect of single interventions in this setting (e.g., a single gene knockout). Next, we consider a generalization of this approach for multiple simultaneous interventions, called jointIDA [39]. Finally, we present a data application from [14,32].

21.4.1 IDA

Suppose we want to estimate the total effect of X_1 on a response variable Y. The conceptual idea of IDA is as follows. We first estimate the CPDAG of the underlying causal DAG, using, for example, the PC algorithm. Next, we can list all the DAGs in the Markov equivalence class described by the estimated CPDAG. Under our assumptions and in the large sample limit, one of these DAGs is the true causal DAG. We can then apply covariate adjustment for each DAG, yielding an estimated total effect of X_1 on Y for each possible DAG. We collect all these effects in a multiset $\hat{\Theta}$. Bounds on $\hat{\Theta}$ are estimated bounds on the true causal effect.

For large graphs, it is computationally intensive to list all the DAGs in the Markov equivalence class. However, because we can always use the parent set of X_1 as adjustment set (see Section 21.2.3), it suffices to know the parent set of X_1 for each of the DAGs in the Markov equivalence class, rather than all DAGs. These possible parent sets of X_1 can be extracted easily from the CPDAG. It is then only left to count the number of DAGs in the Markov equivalence class with each of these parent sets. In [33] the authors used a shortcut, where they only looked whether a parent set is locally valid or not, instead of counting the number of DAGs in the Markov equivalence class. Here locally valid means that the parent set does not create a new unshielded collider with X_1 as a collider. This shortcut results in a set $\hat{\Theta}^L$ that contains the same distinct values as $\hat{\Theta}$, but might have different multiplicities. Hence, if one is only interested in bounds on causal effects, the information in $\hat{\Theta}^L$ is sufficient. In other cases, however, the information on multiplicities might be important, for example, if one is interested in the direction of the total effect ($\hat{\Theta} = \{1, 1, 1, 1, 1, -1\}$ would make us guess that the effect is positive, while $\hat{\Theta}^L = \{1, -1\}$ loses this information).

A schematic representation of IDA is given in Figure 21.2. IDA was shown to be consistent in certain sparse high-dimensional settings [33].

21.4.2 JointIDA

We can also estimate the effect of multiple simultaneous or joint interventions. For example, we may want to predict the effect of a double or triple gene knockout.

Generalizing IDA to this setting poses several nontrivial challenges. First, even if the parent sets of the intervention sets are known, it is nontrivial to estimate the size of a total joint effect, because a straightforward adjusted regression no longer works. The available methods for this purpose are IPW [53] and the recently developed methods recursive

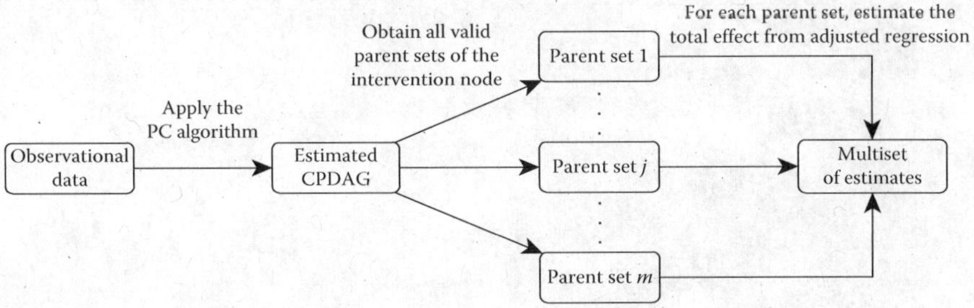

FIGURE 21.2
Schematic representation of the IDA algorithm. (From P. Nandy, M.H. Maathuis, and T.S. Richardson. Estimating the effect of joint interventions from observational data in sparse high-dimensional settings. arXiv:1407.2451v1, 2014. With permission.)

regressions for causal effects (RRC) [39] and modified cholesky decomposition (MCD) [39]. Under our assumptions, RRC recursively computes joint effects from single intervention effects, and MCD produces an estimate of the covariance matrix of the interventional distribution by iteratively modifying Cholesky decompositions of covariance matrices.

Second, we must extract possible parent sets for the intervention nodes from the estimated CPDAG. The local method of IDA can no longer be used for this purpose, because some combinations of locally valid parent sets of the intervention nodes may not yield a *jointly valid* combination of parent sets. In [39] the authors proposed a semilocal algorithm for obtaining jointly valid parent sets from a CPDAG. The runtime of this semilocal algorithm is comparable to the runtime of the local algorithm in sparse settings. Moreover, the semilocal algorithm has the advantage that it (asymptotically) produces a multiset of joint intervention effects with correct multiplicities (up to a constant factor). It can therefore also be used in IDA if the multiplicity information is important.

JointIDA based on RRC or MCD was shown to be consistent in sparse high-dimensional settings [39].

21.4.3 Application

The IDA method is based on various assumptions, including multivariate Gaussianity, faithfulness, no hidden variables, and no feedback loops. In practice, some of these assumptions are typically violated. It is therefore very important to see how the method performs on real data.

Validations were conducted in [32] on the yeast gene expression compendium of [26], and in [62] on gene expression data of *Arabidopsis Thaliana*. JointIDA was validated in [39] on the DREAM4 in silico network challenge [34]. We refer to these papers for details.

In the remainder, we want to highlight the severity of the order dependence of the PC algorithm in high-dimensional settings (see Section 21.3.1), and also advocate the use of subsampling methods. We will discuss these issues in the context of the yeast gene expression data of [26]. These data contain both observational and experimental data, obtained under similar conditions. We focus here on the observational data, which contain gene expression levels of 5361 genes for 63 wild-type yeast organisms.

Let us first consider the order dependence. The ordering of the columns in our 63×5361 observational data matrix should be irrelevant for our problem. But permuting the order of the columns (genes) dramatically changed the estimated skeleton. This is visualized in Figure 21.3 for 25 random orderings. Each estimated skeleton contained roughly 5000 edges. Only about 2000 of those were stable, in the sense that they occurred in almost all

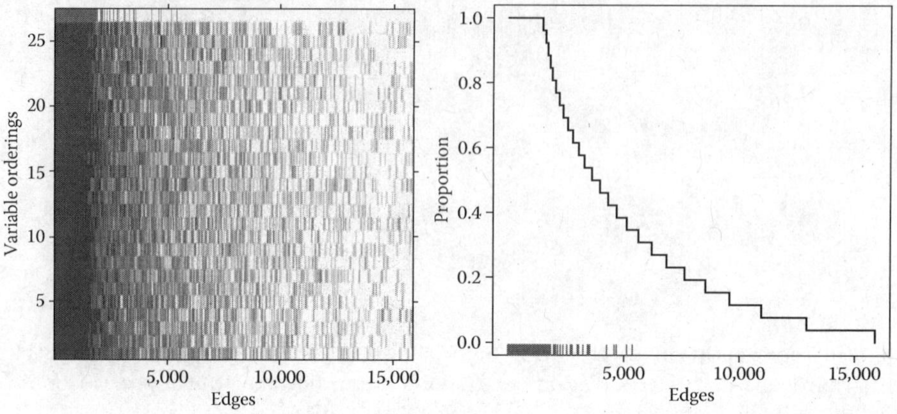

FIGURE 21.3
Analysis of estimated skeletons of the CPDAGs for the yeast gene expression data [26], using the PC and PC-stable algorithms with the tuning parameter $\alpha = 0.01$. The PC-stable algorithm yields an order-independent skeleton that roughly captures the edges that were stable among the different variable orderings for the original PC algorithm. (a) Black entries indicate edges occurring in the estimated skeletons using the PC algorithm, where each row in the figure corresponds to a different random variable ordering. The original ordering is shown as variable ordering 26. The edges along the x-axis are ordered from edges that occur in the estimated skeletons for all orderings, to edges that only occur in the skeleton for one of the orderings. Red entries denote edges in the uniquely estimated skeleton using the PC-stable algorithm over the same 26 variable orderings (shown as variable ordering 27). (b) The step function shows the proportion of the 26 variable orderings in which the edges were present for the original PC algorithm, where the edges are ordered as in (a). The red bars show the edges present in the estimated skeleton using the PC-stable algorithm. (From D. Colombo and M.H. Maathuis. Order-independent constraint-based causal structure learning. *J. Mach. Learn. Res.* 15:3741–82, 2014. With permission.)

estimated skeletons. We see that PC-stable (in red) selected the more stable edges. Perhaps surprisingly, it did this via a small modification of the algorithm (and not by actually estimating skeletons for many different variable orderings).

Next, we consider adding subsampling. Figure 21.4 shows receiver operating characteristic curves for various versions of IDA. In particular, there are three versions of PC: PC, PC-stable, and MPC-stable. Here PC-stable yields an order-independent skeleton, and MPC-stable also stabilizes the edge orientations. For each version of IDA, one can add stability selection (SS) or stability selection where the variable ordering is permuted in each subsample (SSP). We note that adding SSP yields an approximately order-independent algorithm. The best choice in this setting seems PC-stable + SSP.

21.5 Extensions

There are various extensions of the methods described in the previous sections. We only mention some directions here.

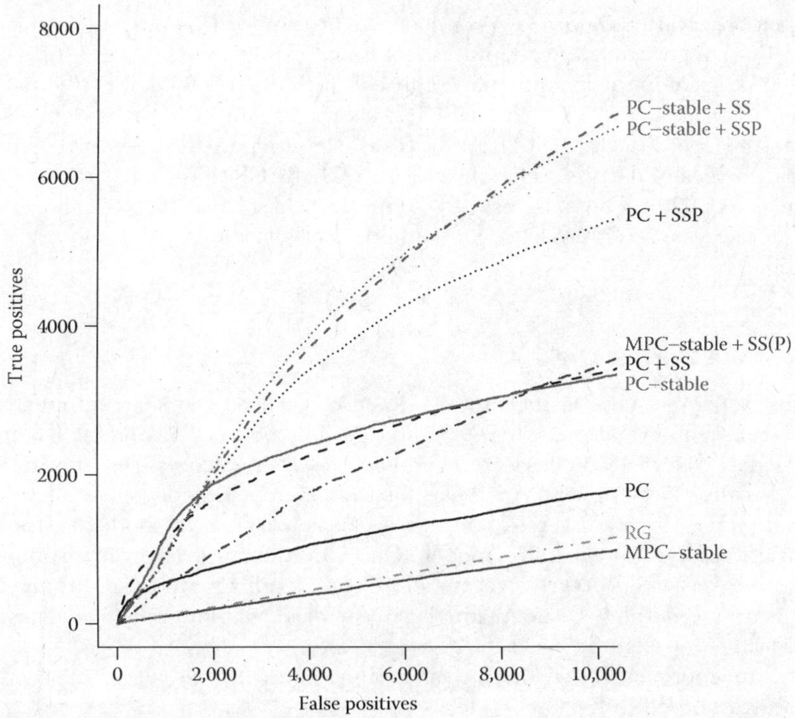

FIGURE 21.4
Analysis of the yeast gene expression data (From T.R. Hughes, M.J. Marton, A.R. Jones, C.J. Roberts, R. Stoughton, C.D. Armour, H.A. Bennett et al. Functional discovery via a compendium of expression profiles. *Cell* 102:109–126, 2000. With permission.) with PC (black lines), PC-stable (red lines), and MPC-stable (blue lines), using the original ordering over the variables (solid lines), using 100 runs stability selection without permuting the variable orderings (dashed lines, labeled as "+ SS"), and using 100 runs stability selection with permuting the variable orderings (dotted lines, labeled as "+ SSP"). The gray line labeled as "RG" represents random guessing. (From D. Colombo and M.H. Maathuis. Order-independent constraint-based causal structure learning. *J. Mach. Learn. Res.* 15:3741–82, 2014. With permission.)

21.5.1 Local Causal Structure Learning

Recall from Section 21.2.3 that we can determine the total effect of X_i on Y by adjusting for the direct causes, that is, by adjusting for the parents of X_i in the causal graph. Hence, if one is interested in a specific intervention variable X_i, it is not necessary to learn the entire CPDAG. Instead, one can try to learn the local structure around X_i. Algorithms for this purpose include, for example, [1,2,48,65].

21.5.2 Causal Structure Learning in the Presence of Hidden Variables and Feedback Loops

Maximal ancestral graphs (MAGs) can represent conditional independence information and causal relationships in DAGs that include unmeasured (hidden) variables [51]. Partial ancestral graphs (PAGs) describe a Markov equivalence class of MAGs. PAGs can be learned from observational data. A prominent algorithm for this purpose is the fast causal inference (FCI) algorithm, an adaptation of the PC algorithm [59–61,70]. Adaptations of FCI that are computationally more efficient include RFCI and FCI+ [13,15]. High-dimensional consistency of FCI and RFCI is shown in [15]. The order-dependence issues studied in [14] (see Section 21.3.1) apply to all these algorithms, and order-independent versions can be easily derived. The algorithms FCI, RFCI, and FCI+ are available in the R-package `pcalg` [29]. There is also an adaptation of LiNGAM that allows for hidden variables [25]. Causal structure learning methods that allow for feedback loops can be found in [36,37,50].

21.5.3 Time Series Data

Time series data are suitable for causal inference, because the time component contains important causal information. There are adaptations of the PC and FCI algorithms for time series data [11,16,18]. These are computationally intensive when considering several time lags, because they replicate variables for the different time lags.

Another approach for discrete time series data consists of modeling the system as a structural vector autoregressive model. One can then use a two-step approach, first estimating the vector autoregressive model and its residuals, and then applying a causal structure learning method to the residuals to learn the contemporaneous causal structure. This approach is for example used in [27].

Finally, an approach based on Bayesian time series models, applicable to large-scale systems, was proposed in [7].

21.5.4 Causal Structure Learning from Heterogeneous Data

There is interesting work on causal structure learning from heterogeneous data. For example, one can consider a mix of observational and various experimental datasets [22,47], or different datasets with overlapping sets of variables [63,64], or a combination of both [67]. A related line of work is concerned with transportability of causal effects [5].

21.5.5 Covariate Adjustment

Given a DAG and a set of intervention variables $\mathbf{X}$ and a set of target variables $\mathbf{Y}$, Pearl's backdoor criterion is a sufficient graphical criterion to determine whether a certain set of variables can be used for adjustment to compute the effect of $\mathbf{X}$ on $\mathbf{Y}$. This result was strengthened to a necessary and sufficient condition for DAGs in [56] and for MAGs in [68]. Pearl's backdoor criterion was generalized to CPDAGs, MAGs and PAGs in [31], and the necessary and sufficient condition of [56] was generalized to all these graph types in [45].

21.5.6 Measures of Uncertainty

The estimates of IDA come without a measure of uncertainty. (The regression estimates in IDA do produce standard errors, but these assume that the estimated CPDAG was correct. Hence, they underestimate the true uncertainty.) Asymptotically valid confidence intervals could be obtained using sample splitting methods (cf. [35]), but their performance is not satisfactory for small samples. Another approach that provides a measure of uncertainty for the presence of direct effects is given in [47]. More work toward quantifying uncertainty would be highly desirable.

21.6 Summary

In this chapter, we discussed the estimation of causal effects from observational data. This problem is relevant in many fields of science, because understanding cause–effect relationships is fundamental and randomized controlled experiments are not always possible. There is a lot of recent progress in this field. We have tried to give an overview of some of the theory behind selected methods, as well as some pointers to further literature.

Finally, we want to emphasize that the estimation of causal effects based on observational data cannot replace randomized controlled experiments. Ideally, such predictions from observational data are followed up by validation experiments. In this sense, such predictions could help in the design of experiments, by prioritizing experiments that are likely to show a large effect.

References

1. C.F. Aliferis, A. Statnikov, I. Tsamardinos, S. Mani, and X.D. Koutsoukos. Local causal and Markov blanket induction for causal discovery and feature selection for classification: part i. Algorithms and empirical evaluation. *J. Mach. Learn. Res.* 11: 171–234, 2010.

2. C.F. Aliferis, A. Statnikov, I. Tsamardinos, S. Mani, and X.D. Koutsoukos. Local causal and Markov blanket induction for causal discovery and feature selection for classification: part ii. Analysis and extensions. *J. Mach. Learn. Res.* 11:235–284, 2010.

3. S.A. Andersson, D. Madigan, and M.D. Perlman. A characterization of Markov equivalence classes for acyclic digraphs. *Ann. Stat.* 25:505–541, 1997.

4. J.D. Angrist, G.W. Imbens, and D.B. Rubin. Identification of causal effects using instrumental variables. *J. Am. Stat. Assoc.* 91:444–455, 1996.

5. E. Bareinboim and J. Pearl. Transportability from multiple environments with limited experiments: Completeness results. In *Advances in Neural Information Processing Systems 27 (NIPS 2014)*, pp. 280–288. Curran Associates, Inc., 2014.

6. K. Bollen. *Structural Equations with Latent Variables.* Wiley, New York, 1989.

7. K.H. Brodersen, F. Gallusser, J. Koehler, N. Remy, and S.L. Scott. Inferring causal impact using Bayesian structural time-series models. *Ann. Appl. Stat.* 9:247–274, 2015.

8. D. Chicharro and S. Panzeri. Algorithms of causal inference for the analysis of effective connectivity among brain regions. *Front. Neuroinform.* 8:64 2014.

9. D.M. Chickering. Learning equivalence classes of Bayesian-network structures. *J. Mach. Learn. Res.* 2:445–498, 2002.

10. D.M. Chickering. Optimal structure identification with greedy search. *J. Mach. Learn. Res.* 3:507–554, 2003.

11. T. Chu and C. Glymour. Search for additive nonlinear time series causal models. *J. Mach. Learn. Res.* 9:967–991, 2008.

12. T. Chu, C. Glymour, R. Scheines, and P. Spirtes. A statistical problem for inference to regulatory structure from associations of gene expression measurements with microarrays. *Bioinformatics* 19:1147–1152, 2003.

13. T. Claassen, J. Mooij, and T. Heskes. Learning sparse causal models is not NP-hard. In *Proceedings of the 29th Conference on Uncertainty in Artificial Intelligence (UAI-13)*, pp. 172–181. AUAI Press, Corvallis, OR, 2013.

14. D. Colombo and M.H. Maathuis. Order-independent constraint-based causal structure learning. *J. Mach. Learn. Res.* 15:3741–82, 2014.

15. D. Colombo, M.H. Maathuis, M. Kalisch, and T.S. Richardson. Learning high-dimensional directed acyclic graphs with latent and selection variables. *Ann. Stat.* 40:294–321, 2012.

16. I. Ebert-Uphoff and Y. Deng. Causal discovery for climate research using graphical models. *J. Climate* 25:5648–5665, 2012.

17. I. Ebert-Uphoff and Y. Deng. Using causal discovery algorithms to learn about our planet's climate. In *Machine Learning and Data Mining to Climate Science. Proceedings of the 4th International Workshop on Climate Informatics*, pp. 113–126. Springer, New York, 2015.

18. D. Entner and P.O. Hoyer. On causal discovery from time series data using FCI. In *Proceedings of the 5th European Workshop on Probabilistic Graphical Models (PGM 2010)*, pp. 121–129. HIIT Publications, 2010.

19. N. Friedman, M. Linial, I. Nachman, and D. Pe'er. Using Bayesian networks to analyze expression data. *J. Comput. Biol.* 7:601–620, 2000.

20. C. Hanson, S.J. Hanson, J. Ramsey, and C. Glymour. Atypical effective connectivity of social brain networks in individuals with autism. *Brain Connect.* 3:578–589, 2013.

21. N. Harris and M. Drton. PC algorithm for nonparanormal graphical models. *J. Mach. Learn. Res.* 14:3365–3383, 2013.

22. A. Hauser and P. Bühlmann. Characterization and greedy learning of interventional Markov equivalence classes of directed acyclic graphs. *J. Mach. Learn. Res.* 13: 2409–2464, 2012.

23. M.Á. Hernán, B. Brumback, and J.M. Robins. Marginal structural models to estimate the causal effect of zidovudine on the survival of HIV-positive men. *Epidemiology* 11:561–570, 2000.

24. P.O. Hoyer, D. Janzing, J. Mooij, J. Peters, and B. Schölkopf. Nonlinear causal discovery with additive noise models. In *Advances in Neural Information Processing Systems 21 (NIPS 2008)*, pp. 689–696. Curran Associates, Inc., 2008.

25. P.O. Hoyer, S. Shimizu, A.J. Kerminen, and M. Palviainen. Estimation of causal effects using linear non-Gaussian causal models with hidden variables. *Int. J. Approx. Reason.* 49:362–378, 2008.

26. T.R. Hughes, M.J. Marton, A.R. Jones, C.J. Roberts, R. Stoughton, C.D. Armour, H.A. Bennett et al. Functional discovery via a compendium of expression profiles. *Cell* 102:109–126, 2000.

27. A. Hyvärinen, K. Zhang, S. Shimizu, and P.O. Hoyer. Estimation of a structural vector autoregression model using non-Gaussianity. *J. Mach. Learn. Res.* 11:1709–1731, 2010.

28. M. Kalisch and P. Bühlmann. Estimating high-dimensional directed acyclic graphs with the PC-algorithm. *J. Mach. Learn. Res.* 8:613–636, 2007.

29. M. Kalisch, M. Mächler, D. Colombo, M.H. Maathuis, and P. Bühlmann. Causal inference using graphical models with the R package `pcalg`. *J. Stat. Softw.* 47(11):1–26, 2012.

30. S. Ma, P. Kemmeren, D. Gresham, and A. Statnikov. De-novo learning of genome-scale regulatory networks in S. cerevisiae. *PLoS ONE* 9:e106479, 2014.

31. M.H. Maathuis and D. Colombo. A generalized back-door criterion. *Ann. Stat.* 43: 1060–1088, 2015.

32. M.H. Maathuis, D. Colombo, M. Kalisch, and P. Bühlmann. Predicting causal effects in large-scale systems from observational data. *Nat. Methods* 7:247–248, 2010.

33. M.H. Maathuis, M. Kalisch, and P. Bühlmann. Estimating high-dimensional intervention effects from observational data. *Ann. Stat.* 37:3133–3164, 2009.

34. D. Marbach, T. Schaffter, C. Mattiussi, and D. Floreano. Generating realistic in silico gene networks for performance assessment of reverse engineering methods. *J. Comput. Biol.* 16:229–239, 2009.

35. N. Meinshausen, L. Meier, and P. Bühlmann. P-values for high-dimensional regression. *J. Am. Stat. Assoc.* 104:1671–1681, 2009.

36. J.M. Mooij and T. Heskes. Cyclic causal discovery from continuous equilibrium data. In *Proceedings of the 29th Conference on Uncertainty in Artificial Intelligence (UAI-13)*, pp. 431–439. AUAI Press, Corvallis, OR, 2013.

37. J.M. Mooij, D. Janzing, T. Heskes, and B. Schölkopf. On causal discovery with cyclic additive noise models. In *Advances in Neural Information Processing Systems 24 (NIPS 2011)*, pp. 639–647. Curran Associates, Inc., 2011.

38. P. Nandy, A. Hauser, and M.H. Maathuis. Understanding consistency in hybrid causal structure learning. arXiv:1507.02608, 2015.

39. P. Nandy, M.H. Maathuis, and T.S. Richardson. Estimating the effect of joint interventions from observational data in sparse high-dimensional settings. arXiv:1407.2451, 2014.

40. R. Opgen-Rhein and K. Strimmer. From correlation to causation networks: A simple approximate learning algorithm and its application to high-dimensional plant gene expression data. *BMC Syst. Biol.* 1:37, 2007.

41. J. Pearl. Comment: Graphical models, causality and intervention. *Stat. Sci.* 8:266–269, 1993.

42. J. Pearl. Causal diagrams for empirical research. *Biometrika* 82:669–710, 1995. (With discussion and a rejoinder by the author.)

43. J. Pearl. Causal inference in statistics: An overview. *Stat. Surv.* 3:96–146, 2009.

44. J. Pearl. *Causality: Models, Reasoning and Inference*, 2nd edition. Cambridge University Press, Cambridge, 2009.

45. E. Perkovic, J. Textor, M. Kalisch, and M.H. Maathuis. A complete generalized adjustment criterion. In *Proceedings of the 31st Conference on Uncertainty in Artificial Intelligence (UAI-15)*, pp. 682–691. AUAI Press, Corvallis, OR, 2015.

46. J. Peters and P. Bühlmann. Identifiability of Gaussian structural equation models with equal error variances. *Biometrika* 101:219–228, 2014.

47. J. Peters, P. Bühlmann, and N. Meinshausen. Causal inference using invariant prediction: Identification and confidence intervals. *J. Roy. Stat. Soc. B*, to appear, 2015.

48. J. Ramsey. A PC-style Markov blanket search for high dimensional datasets. Technical Report CMU-PHIL-177, Carnegie Mellon University, Pittsburgh, PA, 2006.

49. J.D. Ramsey, S.J. Hanson, C. Hanson, Y.O. Halchenko, R.A. Poldrack, and C. Glymour. Six problems for causal inference from fMRI. *Neuroimage* 49:1545–1558, 2010.

50. T.S. Richardson. A discovery algorithm for directed cyclic graphs. In *Proceedings of the 12th Conference on Uncertainty in Artificial Intelligence (UAI-96)*, pp. 454–461. Morgan Kaufmann, San Francisco, CA, 1996.

51. T.S. Richardson and P. Spirtes. Ancestral graph Markov models. *Ann. Stat.* 30: 962–1030, 2002.

52. J.M. Robins. A new approach to causal inference in mortality studies with a sustained exposure period-application to control of the healthy worker survivor effect. *Math. Model.* 7:1393–1512, 1986.

53. J.M. Robins, M.Á. Hernán, and B. Brumback. Marginal structural models and causal inference in epidemiology. *Epidemiology* 11:550–560, 2000.

54. S. Shimizu, P.O. Hoyer, A. Hyvärinen, and A. Kerminen. A linear non-Gaussian acyclic model for causal discovery. *J. Mach. Learn. Res.* 7:2003–2030, 2006.

55. S. Shimizu, A. Hyvärinen, Y. Kawahara, and T. Washio. A direct method for estimating a causal ordering in a linear non-Gaussian acyclic model. In *Proceedings of the 25th Conference on Uncertainty in Artificial Intelligence (UAI-09)*, pp. 506–513. AUAI Press, Corvallis, OR, 2009.

56. I. Shpitser and J. Pearl. Identification of conditional interventional distributions. In *Proceedings of the 22nd Conference on Uncertainty in Artificial Intelligence (UAI-06)*, pp. 437–444. AUAI Press, Arlington, VA, 2006.

57. I. Shpitser, T. Van der Weele, and J.M. Robins. On the validity of covariate adjustment for estimating causal effects. In *Proceedings of the 26th Conference on Uncertainty in Artificial Intelligence (UAI-10)*, pp. 527–536. AUAI Press, Corvallis, OR, 2010.

58. S.M. Smith, K.L. Miller, G. Salimi-Khorshidi, M. Webster, C.F. Beckmann, T.E. Nichols, J.D. Ramsey, and M.W. Woolrich. Network modelling methods for fMRI. *Neuroimage* 54:875–891, 2011.

59. P. Spirtes, C. Glymour, and R. Scheines. *Causation, Prediction, and Search.* Springer-Verlag, New York, 1993.

60. P. Spirtes, C. Glymour, and R. Scheines. *Causation, Prediction, and Search*, 2nd edition. MIT Press, Cambridge, MA, 2000.

61. P. Spirtes, C. Meek, and T.S. Richardson. Causal inference in the presence of latent variables and selection bias. In *Proceedings of the 11th Conference on Uncertainty in Artificial Intelligence (UAI-95)*, pp. 499–506. Morgan Kaufmann, San Francisco, CA, 1995.

62. D.J. Stekhoven, L. Hennig, G. Sveinbjörnsson, I. Moraes, M.H. Maathuis, and P. Bühlmann. Causal stability ranking. *Bioinformatics* 28:2819–2823, 2012.

63. R.E. Tillman, D. Danks, and C. Glymour. Integrating locally learned causal structures with overlapping variables. *Adv. Neural Inf. Process. Syst.* 21:1665–1672, 2008.

64. S. Triantafilou, I. Tsamardinos, and I.G. Tollis. Learning causal structure from overlapping variable sets. In *Proceedings of the 13th International Conference on Artificial Intelligence and Statistics (AISTATS 2010). J. Mach. Learn. Res. W&CP*, 9:860–867, 2010.

65. I. Tsamardinos, C.F. Aliferis, and A. Statnikov. Algorithms for large scale Markov blanket discovery. In *Proceedings of the 16th International Florida Artificial Intelligence Research Society Conference (FLAIRS 2003)*, pp. 376–380. AAAI Press, Menlo Park, CA, 2003.

66. I. Tsamardinos, L.E. Brown, and C.F. Aliferis. The max-min hill-climbing Bayesian network structure learning algorithm. *Mach. Learn.* 65:31–78, 2006.

67. I. Tsamardinos, S. Triantafillou, and V. Lagani. Towards integrative causal analysis of heterogeneous data sets and studies. *J. Mach. Learn. Res.* 13:1097–1157, 2012.

68. B. Van der Zander, M. Liśkiewicz, and J. Textor. Constructing separators and adjustment sets in ancestral graphs. In *Proceedings of the 13th Conference on Uncertainty in Artificial Intelligence (UAI-14)*, pp. 907–916. AUAI Press, Corvallis, OR, 2014.

69. S. Wright. Correlation and causation. *J. Agric. Res.* 20:557–585, 1921.

70. J. Zhang. On the completeness of orientation rules for causal discovery in the presence of latent confounders and selection bias. *Artif. Intell.* 172:1873–1896, 2008.

Part VIII

Targeted Learning

22

Targeted Learning for Variable Importance

Sherri Rose

CONTENTS

22.1 Introduction 411
22.2 Literature 412
22.2.1 Biomarkers and Genomics 413
22.2.1.1 Treatment Resistance in HIV 413
22.2.1.2 Quantitative Trait Loci Mapping 414
22.2.2 Complex Data Structures 415
22.3 Road Map for Estimation and Inference 416
22.3.1 Defining the Research Question 416
22.3.1.1 Data 416
22.3.1.2 Model and Parameter 417
22.3.1.3 Causal Assumptions 417
22.3.2 Estimation 418
22.3.2.1 TMLE Algorithm for Quantitative Trait Loci Mapping 419
22.3.3 Inference 420
22.4 Programming 421
22.5 Discussion: Variable Importance and Big Data 422
Acknowledgments 423
References 423

22.1 Introduction

Targeted learning methods build machine learning-based estimators of parameters defined as features of the probability distribution of the data, while also providing influence-curve or bootstrap-based confidence internals. The theory offers a general template for creating targeted maximum likelihood estimators for a data structure, nonparametric or semiparametric statistical model, and parameter mapping. The targeted learning framework for efficient estimation was introduced nearly a decade ago [62], following key advances where efficient influence curves were used as estimating functions for effect estimation [27–30,59], and unified loss-based machine learning methods were developed for fitting infinite-dimensional parameters of the probability distribution of the data [54,58]. Targeted maximum likelihood estimation (TMLE) built on the loss-based *super learning* system such that lower dimensional parameters could be targeted; the remaining bias for the (low-dimensional) target feature of the probability distribution was removed. It also represents the first class of estimators that provide inference in concert with the use of machine learning.

Targeted learning for effect estimation allows for the complete integration of machine learning advances in prediction while providing statistical inference for the target parameter(s) of interest. Targeted maximum likelihood estimators are well-defined (i.e., have one solution) loss-based double robust substitution estimators that respect the global constraints of the statistical model. As noted, the advances in ensembled loss-based learning, namely, (1) defining an infinite-dimensional parameter as a minimizer of the expected loss function and (2) cross-validated estimator selection, were not tailored to lower-dimensional parameters that are often of interest in causal inference and variable importance.

While estimating function approaches may estimate the effect parameters of interest, estimating functions are not loss-based or substitution estimators. Thus, they may have multiple solutions, or produce a solution that falls outside the global constraints of the model. (A detailed comparison of the statistical properties of various maximum-likelihood-based estimators, including targeted learning, and estimating-equation-based estimators can be found elsewhere [61].) Therefore, the introduction of targeted learning was a considerable advance, with super learning and TMLE methods labeled "new statistical paradigms" [5].

Targeted Learning

The targeted learning methodology template involves the following:

1. Starting with a (possibly super-learner-based) initial estimator.
2. Positing a parametric working submodel through this initial estimator, which provides a family of candidate fluctuations of the initial estimator.
3. Holding the initial estimator fixed and choosing the fluctuation that minimizes the selected loss function.
4. Iterating until the updated initial estimator solves the estimating equation defined by the efficient influence curve.

The continued development of targeted learning has led to new solutions for existing problems in many data structures in addition to discoveries in varied applied areas. This has included work in randomized controlled trials [18–20,40,42], parameters defined by a marginal structural model [41], case-control studies [34,35,37,38,50], collaborative TMLE [9,47,55], missing and censored data [36,47], effect modification [25,48], longitudinal data [52,56], networks [53], community-based interventions [51], comparative effectiveness research [13,22], aging [2,32], cancer [25], occupational exposures [3], mental health [12], and HIV [39], as well as many others. A text on targeted learning was also published [61], and contains both introductory and advanced topics.

In this chapter, we focus on the development of targeted learning methods for variable importance problems. Specifically, we are interested in understanding the effect of a list of variables *individually* on an outcome, such as in a genomic profile, while providing statistical inference that accounts for multiple testing. We discuss a few motivating examples from the published literature on targeted learning for variable importance, and then walk through a road map for estimation and inference in variable importance settings.

22.2 Literature

Some of the earliest works on targeted learning developed methodology for variable importance, and this activity has continued into the present. The articles in this review all consider an experiment where a unit is randomly sampled from a target population and a list of variables is measured on the unit aside from additional baseline characteristics. An outcome is also measured, and we wish to estimate the effect of each variable in the list on this outcome. Variables in the list may be binary or continuous. In contrast to standard approaches, targeted learning isolates the effect of each variable in the list *separately.*

22.2.1 Biomarkers and Genomics

There has been considerable work in targeted learning methods for variable importance in biomarker detection and genomics applications. We examine several of these works here, in an effort to highlight the flexibility of the targeted learning framework to address various variable importance research questions while incorporating investigator knowledge. Additional variable importance articles in this area that focus on methodology development, simulations, and data applications include: procedures for semiparametric variable importance and a demonstration in Golub et al. [8], leukemia dataset [49], and sophisticated dimension reduction procedures incorporated into targeted learning for variable importance measures [65].

22.2.1.1 Treatment Resistance in HIV

Bembom et al. [1] studied a list of candidate mutations in an HIV protease enzyme in an effort to identify mutations that reduce the clinical response to antiretroviral treatments. Specifically, they were interested in subjects taking combinations of drugs that contained the protease inhibitor lopinavir who also had a treatment change episode. The ultimate goal was to produce a ranked list of mutations based on their relative contributions to clinical virologic response. In their analysis, it was of particular importance to control for confounding variables that could have been predictive of both the mutation and clinical virologic response through another mechanism aside from the mutation. Without this step, the marginal effect of a mutation in the list may not have reflected an effect due to resistance.

Their study data was derived from two clinical observational data sources: the Stanford Drug Resistance Database and the Kaiser Permanente Medical Care Program, Northern California. They considered a total of 30 candidate protease inhibitor mutations, all of which had been isolated as possibly related to resistance to protease inhibitor drug treatments based on the Stanford HIVdb algorithm. As previously noted, they controlled for a large set of additional baseline variables, including past treatment and prior clinical measurements. The selection of the appropriate variables to control for in the analysis required substantial clinical background, and a complete discussion of these choices, as well as exclusion criteria, can be found in the paper. The list of candidate mutations was treated as a vector of binary variables, where the variable was equal to 1 when the mutation was present in that subject.

The authors implemented targeted learning for variable importance using the deletion/substitution/addition (D/S/A) algorithm [21] to estimate the conditional expectation of the outcome given the list of mutations and other covariates, as well as the conditional distribution of the biomarker given covariates, for each mutation in the list. The estimate of the conditional distribution of the biomarker given covariates was used in the update to the initial estimate of the conditional expectation for the outcome. This is the step where a parametric working submodel is determined to fluctuate the initial estimator. The initial estimator is held fixed while the fluctuation that minimizes the loss function is chosen. This involves using a function of the conditional distribution of the biomarker given covariates as a covariate in the parametric working model. Prior to estimating these components, the authors performed dimension reduction on their set of non-mutation covariates using the unadjusted association of each covariate with the outcome. They retained the top 50 covariates with the smallest p-values to include in the D/S/A algorithm.

This targeted maximum likelihood estimator was compared to multiple implementations of g-computation, each using a different initial estimator, in simulations. Their g-computation estimators did not converge to the true known value in their simulations, whereas the targeted learning estimator did. In the HIV data, they implemented an unadjusted marginal estimator, along with g-computation and TMLE. The false discovery rate was used to adjust for multiple testing and control the expected proportion of false positives at 5%.

The targeted learning estimator identified five out of seven known major mutations and three minor mutations. G-computation did not include one of these major mutations, and, along with the unadjusted estimator, also identified two mutations that were not thought to be associated with resistance. The unadjusted estimator identified two major mutations previously thought to be associated with resistance that neither g-computation nor TMLE identified as significant. One of these major mutations, however, lacked variation within the strata of the adjustment covariates (i.e., a positivity violation), and there is *in vitro* evidence that the other mutation may not play a substantial role in resistance.

22.2.1.2 Quantitative Trait Loci Mapping

Several works have developed targeted learning methods for variable importance in the area of quantitative train loci mapping. The three Wang et al. articles [63,64,66] present novel semiparametric algorithms for targeted learning, including comparisons to existing approaches, simulations, and three data analyses. The goal of quantitative trait loci mapping is to identify genes that underlie a particular observed trait using genetic markers across the genome. Current standard techniques for quantitative trait loci mapping include interval mapping, composite interval mapping, and multiple interval mapping. Interval mapping methods are fully parametric and require the (unrealistic) assumption that only a single quantitative trait loci accounts for the observed trait. Composite and multiple interval mapping techniques allow for multiple quantitative trait loci, but are also restrictive, relying on parametric assumptions. These parametric models tend to oversimplify the (unknown) underlying genetic mechanisms.

In each work, the authors consider a backcross design to demonstrate the methodology development, although the procedures are general. Backcross is generated by backcrossing the first generation to one of its parental strains, with two possible genotypes at a locus. They propose a semiparametric model that assumes the phenotypic trait changes linearly with the quantitative trait loci. Both TMLEs [63,66] and collaborative TMLEs [63,64] are developed, where collaborative TMLE is an extension of TMLE that tailors the estimation of the nuisance parameter(s) for the target parameter.

The TMLEs in Wang et al. [66] were implemented with adjustment for flanking markers both 10 centimorgans (cM) away and 20 cM away, and compared to univariate regression and composite interval mapping in simulations of 100 markers on 600 backcross subjects, as well as iterative adaptive least absolute shrinkage and selection operator (lasso) and a penalized likelihood approach in additional simulations. In these settings, the TMLE adjusting for flanking markers 10 cM away had the best overall performance. Notably, univariate regression failed to identify the correct quantitative trait loci, composite interval mapping had mixed results, and the TMLE adjusting for flanking markers 20 cM away had a performance between composite interval mapping and the other TMLE. The lasso isolated all the main effects but none of the markers carrying epistatic effects, and effect estimates were biased downward, while the penalized likelihood approach improved on a linear main effects model but did not outperform TMLE. Further simulations results can be found in the paper and supplementary materials. The authors also studied a barely dataset containing 150 doubled haploid lines aiming to identify quantitative trait loci underlying measured agronomic traits. TMLE was compared to composite interval mapping, with TMLE finding fewer quantitative trait loci.

The collaborative TMLE developed in [64] allowed the authors to use the information in the data to decide which additional markers to include in the updating stage of the estimator. This is the step where, with fewer covariates under consideration, it would not be challenging to simply estimate the conditional distribution of the marker under consideration given the set of other markers. This could then be used to define a parametric working model that codes fluctuations of the initial estimator. However, the number of markers is too numerous, and collaborative TMLE provides an algorithmic procedure to select the most appropriate adjustment set. Readers interested in additional details on theory, implementation, and application of collaborative TMLE are referred to the corresponding works [63,64] as well as other literature [9,47,55,61].

Collaborative TMLE was compared to composite interval mapping in a dataset of 116 female mice that followed their survival time after infection with *Listeria monocytogenes*. They wished to map genetic factors underlying susceptibility to *L. monocytogenes* with the phenotypic trait as time to death in hours. The collaborative TMLE was found to be less noisy than composite interval mapping, with the composite interval mapping identifying many suspicious positives. Another advance in this paper was the proposal of a two-part super learner, which was developed for specific nuances related to the nonnormality of the outcome in this dataset, although we leave the specifics out of our summary [64].

Finally, a genome-wide scan of 119 markers in 633 mice was used to understand the quantitative trait loci involved in wound healing [63]. Estimators included TMLE, collaborative TMLE, and composite interval mapping. The two targeted learning methods were initialized using the D/S/A algorithm. Approximately 400 quantitative trait loci positions were examined in 2 cM increments with *p*-values adjusted using the false discovery rate. The results for TMLE and collaborative TMLE were similar, and they identified the same quantitative trait loci as composite interval mapping, although the targeted learning approaches had improved resolution.

22.2.2 Complex Data Structures

Further methodological work for variable importance has been developed in a series of recent works, each with many areas of potential application beyond those considered within the articles. Chambaz et al. [4] also examine the setting where the list of candidate variables has a continuous measure. Their motivating example is that of cancer cells and the continuous *exposure* is DNA copy number. They rank the genes based on the effect of DNA copy number on expression level, controlling for a measure of DNA methylation. Their methods are fully semiparametric and respect a set reference level for the exposure.

Another new contribution to the literature is the manuscript by Sapp et al. [45], which studies interval-censored outcomes. This work provides variable importance estimators for the practical setting where data is not collected continuously, but at specific monitoring times. Along with simulation studies, the authors assessed the importance of a list of covariates among injection drug users in the InC3 cohort for spontaneous viral clearance of HCV. Covariates in the list included gender, age, genotype status, and others.

Finally, Díaz et al. [6] developed techniques for variable importance in longitudinal data with continuous and binary exposures. As the use of longitudinal big data repositories, such as electronic health records, becomes increasingly common, estimating target parameters that respect the longitudinal nature of the data will become more common as well. Here, the authors apply their methods to the ACIT study of severe trauma patients to estimate variable importance measures for the effect of a list of physiological and clinical measurements on death.

22.3 Road Map for Estimation and Inference

The targeted learning framework provides a template for translating variable importance research questions into statistical questions, developing and applying estimators, and assessing uncertainty in the effect measures. We use the motivating examples from the earlier discussed work in quantitative trait loci mapping [63,64,66] to illustrate this road map for estimation and inference, as estimated in [66].

Variable Importance Measures

In this chapter, we focus on a TMLE of the variable importance measure described in Section 22.3 under a semiparametric regression model. This is a flexible definition that can handle both continuous and binary list variables. While we use quantitative trait loci mapping to illustrate the methodology concretely, the applications of these methods are vast. As discussed earlier, the list of variables could involve clinical or epidemiological data [6,45], and these tools also have important implications for testing for possible effect modification (e.g., an intervention modified by the variables in the list) and in controlled randomized trial data [61].

22.3.1 Defining the Research Question

The first step is to define the research question, which includes accurately specifying your data, model, and target parameters. Recall that we are interested in understanding which quantitative trait loci underlie a particular phenotypic trait value. Quantitative trait loci mapping for experimental organisms typically involves crossing two inbred lines that have substantial differences in a trait. The trait is then scored in the segregating progeny. Markers along the genome are genotyped in the segregating progeny, and associations between the trait and the quantitative trait loci are evaluated. The positions and effect sizes of quantitative trait loci are of primary interest. Typical segregating designs include the backcross design, the intercross (F2) design, and the double haploid (DH) design. Backcross is produced by back-crossing the first generation (F1) to one of its parental strains, and there are two possible genotypes, Aa and aa at any locus. For the ease of presentation, as the authors do in the original work [66], we focus most heavily on backcross to demonstrate our method. All the derivations can be readily extended to F2 and other types of experimental crosses.

22.3.1.1 Data

The observed data are given as n i.i.d. realizations of

$$O_i = (Y_i, M_i) \sim P_0 \quad i = 1, \ldots, n$$

Here, Y is the phenotypic trait value and M is a vector of the marker genotypic values, with i indexing the ith subject and the 0 subscript, indicating that P_0 is the true distribution of the data. The true probability distribution P_0 is contained within the set of possible probability distributions that make up the statistical model $\mathcal{M}$.

We introduce the notation A to represent the genotypic value of the quantitative trait loci currently under consideration. A is observed when it lies on a marker, although it can also lie between markers, where it will be unobserved. When A is unobserved, it is imputed using the expected value returned from a multinomial distribution computed from

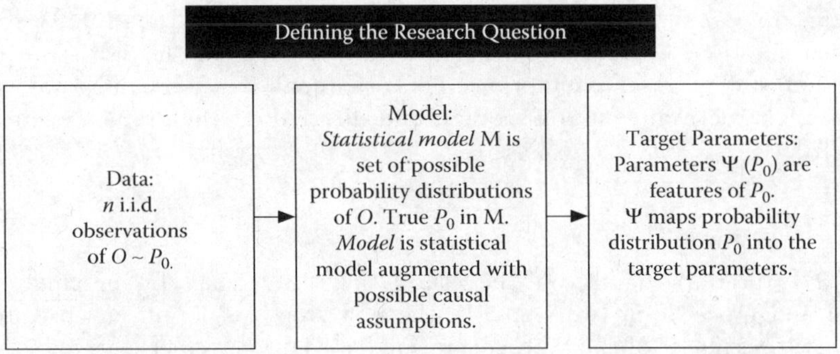

the locations and genotypes locations of the flanking markers. This is also the approach used in Haley–Knott regression [11]. In this case, the effect is therefore only an estimate of the effect of imputed A for these locations.

22.3.1.2 Model and Parameter

We use a semiparametric model that assumes that the phenotypic trait changes linearly with the quantitative trait loci. This regression model for the effect of A at a value $A = a$ relative to $A = 0$, adjusted for the set of other markers, denoted M^-, is

$$E_0(Y \mid A = a, M^-) - E_0(Y \mid A = 0, M^-) = \beta_0 a \tag{22.1}$$

Our target parameter is therefore β_0, which is also equivalent to the average marginal effect given by averaging this conditional effect over the distribution of M^-. The target parameter is defined formally as a mapping $\Psi : \mathcal{M} \to \mathbb{R}$ that maps the probability distribution of the data into the (finite dimensional) feature of interest $\Psi(P_0) = \beta_0$. Additional discussion of this parameter can be found in earlier literature [49,63].

For our application, the parameter measures the difference in the phenotypic trait outcome Y when A shifts from heterozygote to homozygote. This can be understood due to the coding: aa (homozygote) is given the value 0 and Aa (heterozygote) is set to 1 in a backcross population and, for an F2 population, the coding is $(AA, Aa, aa) = (1, 0, -1)$.

The linearity assumption discussed above can be seen explicitly in Equation 22.1. It is important to stress that only the effect of our genotypic value A on the mean outcome of quantitative trait loci Y is modeled using a parametric form in the semiparametric model. We do not impose any distributional assumptions on the data. We also do not make assumptions about the functional form of all functions $f(M^-)$ of M^-. We do additionally make the assumption that A is not a perfect surrogate of M^- in order for the parameter to be well defined and estimable. Finally, we make the positivity assumption $0 < P_0(A = a \mid M^-) < 1$. The model given in Equation 22.1 is general and may be specified in alternative ways, depending on the target parameter of interest. To include effect modification by markers V_j, we would write: $a \sum_{j=1}^{J} \beta_j V_j$.

22.3.1.3 Causal Assumptions

We do not discuss causal assumptions in detail here for brevity and also given that, in many variable importance settings, these causal assumptions will be violated. In particular, the no unmeasured confounding assumption (also referred to as the *randomization assumption*) will frequently not hold. Researchers may also not be interested in drawing causal inferences in variable importance settings. However, a case could be made that the exercise of walking through the causal assumptions and articulating the role of endogenous and exogenous variables in nonparametric structural equations is still useful for a full description of the research question. One could then decide not to augment the statistical model with additional untestable causal assumptions. For a thorough treatment of causal assumptions, nonparametric structural equation models, and directed acyclic graphs, we refer to other literature [23,61].

22.3.2 Estimation

The TMLE procedure builds on the foundation established by maximum likelihood estimation and proceeds in two steps. In the first step, we obtain an ensemble machine learning-based estimator of the data-generating distribution. Super learning is appropriate for this task [32,58,61]. It allows the user to consider multiple algorithms, without the need to select the *best* algorithm a priori. The super learner returns the best weighted combination of the algorithms considered, selected based on a chosen loss function. Cross-validation is employed to protect against overfitting. The second stage of TMLE fluctuates the initial super learner-based estimator in a submodel focusing on the optimal bias–variance trade-off for the target parameter. This second step can also be thought of as a bias reduction step. We must reduce the bias remaining in the initial estimator for the target parameter, since it was fitted based on a bias–variance trade-off for the data-generating distribution, not the target parameter.

The procedure can also be understood intuitively in the context of our motivating quantitative trait loci example as well. In stage one, the conditional expectation for the phenotypic trait value Y given the vector M is not targeted toward our parameter of interest. Here, its bias–variance trade-off is for the overall density. Stage two incorporates the conditional expectation for genotypic value A of the quantitative trait loci currently being considered to shrink the bias of the conditional expectation of Y, our initial estimate. We now also introduce a subset of M^- denoted W for each A. The vector W contains the subset of markers that are potential confounders for the effect of genotypic value A on phenotypic trait Y.

To define our TMLE concretely for this problem, we must begin by calculating the pathwise derivative of our parameter $\Psi(P) = \beta$ at P and its corresponding canonical gradient (efficient influence curve) $D(P, O)$:

$$D(P, O) = \frac{1}{\sigma^2(A, W)} h(A, W)(Y - Q(A, W)) \tag{22.2}$$

where

$$h(A, W) = \frac{d}{d\beta} m(A \mid \beta) - \frac{E(\frac{d}{d\beta} m(A \mid \beta)/\sigma^2(A, W) \mid W)}{E(1/\sigma^2(A, W) \mid W)} \tag{22.3}$$

and $\sigma^2(A, W)$ is the conditional variance of Y given A and W.

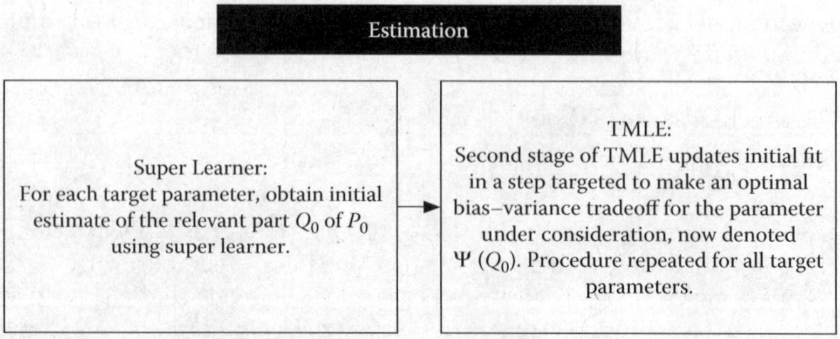

The TMLE requires choosing a loss function $L(O, Q)$ for candidate function Q applied to an observation O and then specifying a submodel $\{Q(\epsilon) : \epsilon\} \subset \mathcal{M}$ to fluctuate the initial estimator. Here, we use the squared-error loss function:

$$L(O, Q) = \frac{(Y - Q(A, W))^2}{\sigma^2(A, W)}.$$

The submodel $\{Q(\epsilon) : \epsilon\} \subset \mathcal{M}$ through Q at $\epsilon = 0$ is selected such that the linear span of $d/d\epsilon\, L(Q(\epsilon))$ at $\epsilon = 0$ includes the efficient influence curve in Equation 22.2. The specific steps of the TMLE algorithm for the target parameter β_0 are enumerated below.

22.3.2.1 TMLE Algorithm for Quantitative Trait Loci Mapping

Estimating $E_0(Y \mid A, M^-) = Q_0(A, M^-)$. Generate a super learner-based initial estimator that respects the semiparametric model in Equation 22.1 and also takes the form

$$Q_n^0 = \beta_n^0 A + f_n(M^-)$$

We introduce the subscript n to denote estimators and estimates.

Estimating $E_0(A \mid W) = g_0(W)$. Recall that we introduced a subset W of M^- for each A. Thus, M^- is replaced with W and we can refer to the function $g_0(W) = E_0(A \mid W)$ as a *marker confounding mechanism.* For the applications considered here, as in Wang et al. [66], the set of markers W are those that lie on the same chromosome as A.

However, the choice for $E_0(A \mid W)$, in general, is still a complicated one. The selection of flanking markers to include in the marker confounding mechanism can be further simplified to including only two flanking markers, possibly capturing a good portion of the confounding. But, there is still then the issue of distance for A for the selection of these two flanking markers. Those that are too close to A may be too predictive of A, thus failing to isolate the contribution of A when estimating β_0. On the other hand, if the selected markers are too great a distance from A, they may not contribute to reducing bias for the target parameter of interest. Collaborative TMLE, as discussed briefly in our literature review, may also be employed to data-adaptively select the most appropriate adjustment set. We leave further discussion of this issue to other literature [49,63].

Determine parametric working model to fluctuate initial estimator. The targeted step uses an estimate $g_n(W)$ of $g_0(W)$ to correct the bias remaining in the initial estimator. This involves defining a so-called clever covariate in a parametric working model coding fluctuations of our initial estimator Q_n^0. For our parameter β_0, the clever covariate is given by

$$h(A, W) = A - g_n(W)$$

the residual of $g_n(W)$, under a condition we describe below.

The clever covariate $h(A, W)$ was defined earlier in Equation 22.3 and derived based on the efficient influence curve in Equation 22.2. When $\sigma^2(A, W)$ is a function of W only, it drops out of the efficient influence curve. We choose to estimate $\sigma^2(A, W)$ with the constant 1, which gives us the simplified clever covariate $h(A, W) = A - g_n(W)$ as above. The estimation of the nuisance parameter $\sigma^2(A, W)$ does not impact the consistency properties of the TMLE, but TMLE will only be efficient if, in addition to estimating Q_0 and g_0 consistently, $\sigma^2(A, W)$ is in fact only a function of W [49].

Update Q_n^0. The regression of Y on $h(A, W)$ can be reformulated as

$$Y' \sim \epsilon h(A, W)$$

where

$$Y' = Y - Q_n^0(A, M^-)$$

The estimate of the regression coefficient is denoted ϵ_n. Our initial estimate β_n^0 is updated with ϵ_n:

$$\beta_n^1 = \beta_n^0 + \epsilon_n$$

Convergence of the algorithm for this target parameter occurs in one step. Since our TMLE is double robust, we have the following properties for this estimator of β_0: this TMLE is (1) consistent when either Q_n^0 or $g_n(W)$ is consistent and (2) is efficient when both Q_n^0 and $g_n(W)$ are consistent (and $\sigma^2(A, W)$ is a function of W only).

Implementation Summary

The TMLE of the target parameter β_0, defined in Equation 22.1, requires an initial fit of $E_0(Y \mid M)$. Our best *fit* of $E_0(Y \mid M)$ will be based on minimizing the chosen error loss function. This initial estimator yields a fit of $E_0(Y \mid A = 0, M^-)$, which we can map to a first-stage estimator of β_0 in our semiparametric model.

We now complete the second-stage targeted updating step. This single update (convergence is achieved in one step) is completed by fitting a coefficient ϵ in front of an estimate of $A - E_0(A \mid W)$ with univariate regression, using the initial estimator of $E_0(Y \mid A, M^-)$ as an offset. We can show that the TMLE of β_0 is $\beta_n^0 + \epsilon_n$.

22.3.3 Inference

The variance σ_n^2 for each variable importance measure β_n^1 can be calculated using influence-curve-based methods [66], with the variance σ_n^2 given by

$$\sigma_n^2 = \frac{\sum_i (Y_i - Q_n^1(A_i, M_i^-))^2 h(A_i, W_i)^2}{(\sum_i A_i h(A_i, W_i))^2}$$

A detailed discussion of multiple hypothesis testing and inference for variable importance measures is presented in [7]. The authors in the corresponding quantitative trait loci work [66] adjusted for multiple testing using the false discovery rate and interpreted each variable importance measure as a W-adjusted effect estimate.

In general, variance estimates for TMLE rely on δ-method conditions [61,62], and, as such, the asymptotic normal limit distribution of the estimator is characterized by its influence curve. The estimator β_n^1 of our target parameter is asymptotically linear; therefore, it behaves as an empirical mean, with bias converging to 0 in sample size faster than a rate of $1/\sqrt{n}$ and is approximately normally distributed (for sample size n reasonably large). The variance of the estimator is thus well approximated by the variance of the influence curve divided by n. One can also use the covariance in variable importance questions with a multivariate vector of parameters, where the covariance matrix of the estimator vector is well approximated by the covariance matrix of the corresponding multivariate influence curve divided by n [61].

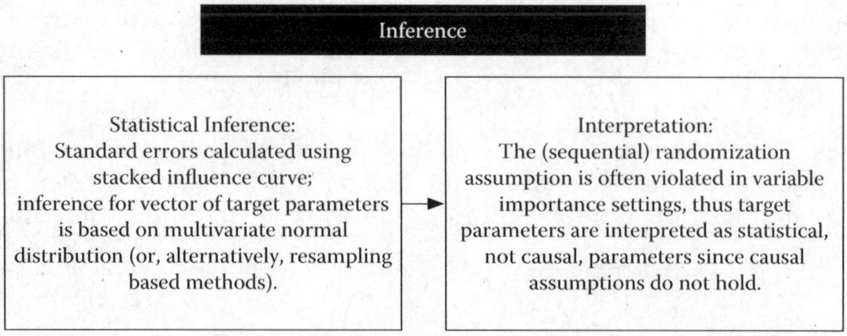

22.4 Programming

Practical tools for the implementation of targeted learning methods for variable importance have developed alongside the theoretical and methodological advances. While some work has been done to develop computational tools for targeted learning in proprietary programming languages, such as `SAS`, the majority of the code has been built in `R`. TMLE and collaborative TMLE `R` code specifically tailored to answer quantitative trait loci mapping questions, such as those discussed throughout this chapter, is available in the supplementary material of Wang et al. [64]. Each `R` package discussed in this section is available on The Comprehensive R Archive Network (`www.cran.r-project.org`).

Of key importance are the two `R` packages `SuperLearner` and `tmle` [10,24]. The `SuperLearner` package, authored by Eric Polley (NCI), is flexible, allowing for the integration of dozens of prespecified potential algorithms as well as a system of wrappers that provide the user with the ability to design their own algorithms, or include newer algorithms not yet added to the package. The package returns multiple useful objects, including the cross-validated predicted values, final predicted values, vector of weights, and fitted objects for each of the included algorithms, among others. The `tmle` package, authored by Susan Gruber (Reagan-Udall Foundation, Washington, DC), allows for the estimation of both average treatment effects and parameters defined by a marginal structural model in cross-sectional data with a binary intervention. This package also includes the ability to incorporate missingness in the outcome and the intervention, use `SuperLearner` to estimate the relevant components of the likelihood, and use data with a mediating variable.

The `multiPIM` package [26], authored by Stephan Ritter (Omicia, Inc., Oakland, CA), is designed specifically for variable importance analysis, and estimates an attributable-risk-type parameter using TMLE. This package also allows the use of `SuperLearner` to estimate nuisance parameters and produces additional estimates using estimating-equation-based estimators and g-computation. The package includes its own internal bootstrapping function to calculate standard errors if this is preferred over the use of influence curves, or influence curves are not valid for the chosen estimator.

Four additional prediction-focused packages are `casecontrolSL` [17], `cvAUC` [15], `subsemble` [16], and `h2oEnsemble` [14], all primarily authored by Erin LeDell (Berkeley). The `casecontrolSL` package relies on `SuperLearner` and performs subsampling in a case-control design with inverse-probability-of-censoring-weighting, which may be particularly useful in settings with rare outcomes. The `cvAUC` package is a tool kit to evaluate area under the ROC curve estimators when using cross-validation. The `subsemble` package was developed based on a new approach [44] to ensembling that fits each algorithm on a subset of the data and combines these fits using cross-validation. This technique can be used in datasets of all size, but has been demonstrated to be particularly useful in smaller datasets.

A new implementation of super learner can be found in the Java-based `h2oEnsemble` package, which was designed for big data. The package uses the H2O R interface to run super learning in R with a selection of prespecified algorithms.

Another TMLE package is `ltmle` [46], primarily authored by Joshua Schwab (Berkeley). This package mainly focuses on parameters in longitudinal data structures, including the treatment-specific mean outcome and parameters defined by a marginal structural model. The package returns estimates for TMLE, g-computation, and estimating-equation-based estimators.

22.5 Discussion: Variable Importance and Big Data

While the development of targeted learning for variable importance has demonstrated promise, its potential has yet to be fully realized. The data we are collecting in biology, social sciences, health care, medicine, business analytics, and ecology, among others, continue to grow in both dimensions (n and p), and are frequently observational in nature [31,43]. Statisticians are armed with a unique set of rigorous and practical tools to tackle these challenges. To face this growth in data going forward, targeted learning provides a framework for incorporating advances in machine learning and TMLE for problems of variable importance [33,60].

It is always important to remember that sophisticated statistical methods will never be able to overcome weak or problematic big data. Misclassification, missingness, and unmeasured confounding are frequently found in these new streams of data. A thorough understanding of the data and associated research questions, often only ascertained by working in interdisciplinary teams, is required before leaping toward analysis. This will not change as technologies continue to advance.

> To call in the statistician after the experiment is done may be no more than asking him to perform a postmortem examination: he may be able to say what the experiment died of.
>
> R.A. Fisher
> 1938

We will also need to address the increasing computational challenges presented by these data. For example, online targeted learning [57] is a new proposed method for data that arrives sequentially, another common feature of big data applications. Advances will not only be found in statistical theory and methodology development, however. Existing approaches to merge data systems and statistics currently mainly use database systems to serve, for example, `R` requests in the background. Movement toward integrated native big data systems may be a key component in the adoption of rigorous targeted learning tools for variable importance in massive datasets.

Targeted learning is one of many new statistical innovations that are poised for further theoretical and methodological development in this new era of big data, inspired by these real-world challenges. Advances in dimension-reduction for imaging analyses, for example, will improve our ability to use features of these images as covariates in variable importance analyses, and also move us toward the ability to estimate variable importance measures of a list of images. The future of statistical and scientific discovery with big data is bright, as we look forward to the creation of automated big data machines that incorporate investigator knowledge, are statistically sound, and can handle the computational burden of our data.

Acknowledgments

The author acknowledges funding from the University of Utah fund P0 163947.

References

1. O. Bembom, M.L. Petersen, S.-Y. Rhee, W.J. Fessel, S.E. Sinisi, R.W. Shafer, and M.J. van der Laan. Biomarker discovery using targeted maximum likelihood estimation: Application to the treatment of antiretroviral resistant HIV infection. *Stat Med*, 28: 152–72, 2009.

2. O. Bembom and M.J. van der Laan. A practical illustration of the importance of realistic individualized treatment rules in causal inference. *Electron J Stat*, 1:574–596, 2007.

3. A. Chambaz, D. Choudat, C. Huber, J.C. Pairon, and M.J. van der Laan. Analysis of the effect of occupational exposure to asbestos based on threshold regression modeling of case–control data. *Biostatistics*, 15(2):327–340, 2014.

4. A. Chambaz, P. Neuvial, and M.J. van der Laan. Estimation of a non-parametric variable importance measure of a continuous exposure. *Electron J Stat*, 6:1059–1099, 2012.

5. S. Datta and H.C. van Houwelingen. Statistics in biological and medical sciences. *Stat Prob Lett*, 81(7):715–716, 2011.

6. I. Diaz, A.E. Hubbard, A. Decker, and M. Cohen. Variable importance and prediction methods for longitudinal problems with missing variables. Technical Report 318, Division of Biostatistics, University of California, Berkeley, CA, 2013.

7. S. Dudoit and M.J. van der Laan. *Resampling Based Multiple Testing with Applications to Genomics*. Springer, Berlin, Germany, 2008.

8. T.R. Golub, D.K. Slonim, P. Tamayo et al. Molecular classification of cancer: Class discovery and class prediction by gene expression monitoring. *Science*, 286:531–537, 1999.

9. S. Gruber and M.J. van der Laan. An application of collaborative targeted maximum likelihood estimation in causal inference and genomics. *Int J Biostat*, 6(1):Article 18, 2010.

10. S. Gruber and M.J. van der Laan. tmle: An R package for targeted maximum likelihood estimation. *J Stat Softw*, 51(13):1–35, 2012.

11. C.S. Haley and S.A. Knott. A simple regression method for mapping quantitative trait loci in line crosses using flanking markers. *Heredity*, 69(4):315–324, 1992.

12. R. Kessler, S. Rose, and K. Koenen et al. How well can post-traumatic stress disorder be predicted from pre-trauma risk factors? An exploratory study in the WHO world mental health surveys. *World Psychiatry*, 13(3):265–274, 2014.

13. L. Kunz, S. Rose, and S.-L. Normand. An overview of statistical approaches for comparative effectiveness research. In C. Gatsonis and S.C. Morton, editors, *Methods in Comparative Effectiveness Research.* Chapman & Hall, Boca Raton, FL, 2015.

14. E. LeDell. *h2oEnsemble: H2O Ensemble.* R package version 0.0.1, 2014.

15. E. LeDell, M. Petersen, and M.J. van der Laan. *cvAUC: Cross-Validated Area Under the ROC Curve Confidence Intervals.* R package version 1.0-0, 2014.

16. E. LeDell, S. Sapp, and M.J. van der Laan. *Subsemble: An Ensemble Method for Combining Subset-Specific Algorithm Fits.* R package version 0.0.9, 2014.

17. E. LeDell, M.J. van der Laan, and M. Petersen. *casecontrolSL: Case-Control Subsampling for SuperLearner.* R package version 0.1-5, 2014.

18. K.L. Moore and M.J. van der Laan. Application of time-to-event methods in the assessment of safety in clinical trials. In Karl E. Peace, editor, *Design, Summarization, Analysis & Interpretation of Clinical Trials with Time-to-Event Endpoints.* Chapman & Hall, Boca Raton, FL, 2009.

19. K.L. Moore and M.J. van der Laan. Covariate adjustment in randomized trials with binary outcomes: targeted maximum likelihood estimation. *Stat Med*, 28(1):39–64, 2009.

20. K.L. Moore and M.J. van der Laan. Increasing power in randomized trials with right censored outcomes through covariate adjustment. *J Biopharm Stat*, 19(6):1099–1131, 2009.

21. R. Neugebauer and J. Bullard. *DSA: Data-Adaptive Estimation with Cross-Validation and the D/S/A Algorithm.* R package version 3.1.3, 2009.

22. R. Neugebauer, J.A. Schmittdiel, and M.J. Laan. Targeted learning in real-world comparative effectiveness research with time-varying interventions. *Stat Med*, 33(14): 2480–2520, 2014.

23. J. Pearl. On a class of bias-amplifying variables that endanger effect estimates. In *Proceedings of the Uncertainty in Artificial Intelligence*, Catalina Island, CA, 2010.

24. E. Polley and M.J. van der Laan. *SuperLearner: Super Learner Prediction.* R package version 2.0-10, 2013.

25. E.C. Polley and M.J. van der Laan. Predicting optimal treatment assignment based on prognostic factors in cancer patients. In K.E. Peace, editor, *Design, Summarization, Analysis & Interpretation of Clinical Trials with Time-to-Event Endpoints*, Chapman & Hall, Boca Raton, FL, 2009.

26. S.J. Ritter, N.P. Jewell, and A.E. Hubbard. R package multiPIM: A causal inference approach to variable importance analysis. *J Stat Softw*, 57(8), 2014.

27. J.M. Robins. Robust estimation in sequentially ignorable missing data and causal inference models. In *Proceedings of the American Statistical Association*, Indianapolis, IN, 2000.

28. J.M. Robins and A. Rotnitzky. Recovery of information and adjustment for dependent censoring using surrogate markers. In N.P. Jewell, K. Dietz and V.T. Farewell, editors, *AIDS Epidemiology*, pp. 297–331. Birkhäuser, Basel, Switzerland, 1992.

29. J.M. Robins and A. Rotnitzky. Comment on the Bickel and Kwon article, "Inference for semiparametric models: Some questions and an answer." *Stat Sinica*, 11(4):920–936, 2001.

30. J.M. Robins, A. Rotnitzky, and M.J. van der Laan. Comment on "On profile likelihood." *J Am Stat Assoc*, 450:431–435, 2000.

31. S. Rose. Big data and the future. *Significance*, 9(4):47–48, 2012.

32. S. Rose. Mortality risk score prediction in an elderly population using machine learning. *Am J Epidemiol*, 177(5):443–452, 2013.

33. S. Rose. Statisticians' place in big data. *Amstat News*, 428:28, 2013.

34. S. Rose and M.J. van der Laan. Simple optimal weighting of cases and controls in case-control studies. *Int J Biostat*, 4(1):Article 19, 2008.

35. S. Rose and M.J. van der Laan. Why match? Investigating matched case-control study designs with causal effect estimation. *Int J Biostat*, 5(1):Article 1, 2009.

36. S. Rose and M.J. van der Laan. A targeted maximum likelihood estimator for two-stage designs. *Int J Biostat*, 7(1):Article 17, 2011.

37. S. Rose and M.J. van der Laan. A double robust approach to causal effects in case-control studies. *Am J Epidemiol*, 179(6):663–669, 2014.

38. S. Rose and M.J. van der Laan. Rose and van der laan respond to "Some advantages of RERI." *Am J Epidemiol*, 179(6):672–673, 2014.

39. M. Rosenblum, S.G. Deeks, M.J. van der Laan, and D.R. Bangsberg. The risk of virologic failure decreases with duration of HIV suppression, at greater than 50% adherence to antiretroviral therapy. *PLoS ONE*, 4(9): e7196. doi:10.1371/journal.pone.0007196, 2009.

40. M. Rosenblum and M.J. van der Laan. Using regression models to analyze randomized trials: Asymptotically valid hypothesis tests despite incorrectly specified models. *Biometrics*, 65(3):937–945, 2009.

41. M. Rosenblum and M.J. van der Laan. Targeted maximum likelihood estimation of the parameter of a marginal structural model. *Int J Biostat*, 6(2):Article 19, 2010.

42. D.B. Rubin and M.J. van der Laan. Empirical efficiency maximization: Improved locally efficient covariate adjustment in randomized experiments and survival analysis. *Int J Biostat*, 4(1):Article 5, 2008.

43. C. Rudin and D. Dunson, R. Irizarry et al. Discovery with data: Leveraging statistics and computer science to transform science and society. Technical report, American Statistical Association, Alexandria, VA, 2014.

44. S. Sapp, M.J. van der Laan, and J. Canny. Subsemble: An ensemble method for combining subset-specific algorithm fits. *Journal of Applied Statistics*, 41(6):1247–1259, 2014.

45. S. Sapp, M.J. van der Laan, and K. Page. Targeted estimation of binary variable importance measures with interval-censored outcomes. *Int J Biostat*, 10(1):77–97, 2014.

46. J. Schwab, S. Lendle, M. Petersen, and M. van der Laan. *ltmle: Longitudinal Targeted Maximum Likelihood Estimation*. R package version 0.9.3, 2013.

47. O.M. Stitelman and M.J. van der Laan. Collaborative targeted maximum likelihood for time-to-event data. *Int J Biostat*, 6(1):Article 21, 2010.

48. O.M. Stitelman and M.J. van der Laan. Targeted maximum likelihood estimation of effect modification parameters in survival analysis. *Int J Biostat*, 7(1), 2011.

49. C. Tuglus and M.J. van der Laan. Targeted methods for biomarker discovery. In M.J. van der Laan and S. Rose, editors, *Targeted Learning: Causal Inference for Observational and Experimental Data*, pp. 367–382. Springer, Berlin, Germany, 2011.

50. M.J. van der Laan. Estimation based on case-control designs with known prevalence probability. *Int J Biostat*, 4(1):Article 17, 2008.

51. M.J. van der Laan. Estimation of causal effects of community-based interventions. Technical Report 268, Division of Biostatistics, University of California, Berkeley, CA, 2010.

52. M.J. van der Laan. Targeted maximum likelihood based causal inference: Part I. *Int J Biostat*, 6(2):Article 2, 2010.

53. M.J. van der Laan. Causal inference for networks. *J Causal Inference*, 2(1):13–74, 2014.

54. M.J. van der Laan and S. Dudoit. Unified cross-validation methodology for selection among estimators and a general cross-validated adaptive epsilon-net estimator: Finite sample oracle inequalities and examples. Technical Report 130, Division of Biostatistics, University of California, Berkeley, CA, 2003.

55. M.J. van der Laan and S. Gruber. Collaborative double robust penalized targeted maximum likelihood estimation. *Int J Biostat*, 6(1):Article 17, 2010.

56. M.J. van der Laan and S. Gruber. Targeted minimum loss based estimation of causal effects of multiple time point interventions. *Int J Biostat*, 8(1), 2012.

57. M.J. van der Laan and S. Lendle. Online targeted learning. Technical Report 330, Division of Biostatistics, University of California, Berkeley, CA, 2014.

58. M.J. van der Laan, E.C. Polley, and A.E. Hubbard. Super learner. *Stat Appl Genet Mol*, 6(1):Article 25, 2007.

59. M.J. van der Laan and J.M. Robins. *Unified Methods for Censored Longitudinal Data and Causality*. Springer, Berlin, Germany, 2003.

60. M.J. van der Laan and S. Rose. Statistics ready for a revolution: Next generation of statisticians must build tools for massive data sets. *Amstat News*, 399:38–39, 2010.

61. M.J. van der Laan and S. Rose. *Targeted Learning: Causal Inference for Observational and Experimental Data*. Springer, Berlin, Germany, 2011.

62. M.J. van der Laan and D.B. Rubin. Targeted maximum likelihood learning. *Int J Biostat*, 2(1):Article 11, 2006.

63. H. Wang, S. Rose, and M.J. van der Laan. Finding quantitative trait loci genes. In M.J. van der Laan and S. Rose, editors, *Targeted Learning: Causal Inference for Observational and Experimental Data*, pp. 383–394. Springer, Berlin, Germany, 2011.

64. H. Wang, S. Rose, and M.J. van der Laan. Finding quantitative trait loci genes with collaborative targeted maximum likelihood learning. *Stat Prob Lett*, 81(7):792–796, 2011.

65. H. Wang and M.J. van der Laan. Dimension reduction with gene expression data using targeted variable importance measurement. *BMC Bioinformatics*, 12(1):312, 2011.

66. H. Wang, Z. Zhang, S. Rose, and M.J. van der Laan. A novel targeted learning methods for quantitative trait loci mapping. *Genetics*, 198(4):1369–1376, 2014.

23

Online Estimation of the Average Treatment Effect

Sam Lendle

CONTENTS

23.1 Introduction ... 429
23.2 Preliminaries ... 430
23.2.1 Causal Parameter and Assumptions ... 430
23.2.2 Statistical Model ... 430
23.3 Batch Estimation of the ATE ... 431
23.4 Online One-Step Estimation of the ATE ... 432
23.5 Example and Simulation ... 433
23.5.1 Data-Generating Distribution ... 433
23.5.2 SGD for Logistic Regression ... 434
23.5.3 Results ... 434
23.6 Discussion ... 436
References ... 437

23.1 Introduction

Drawing causal inferences from observational data requires making strong assumptions about the causal process from which the data are generated, followed by a statistical analysis of the observational dataset. Though we must make *causal* assumptions, we often know little about the data-generating distribution. This means we generally cannot make strong *statistical* assumptions so we estimate a statistical parameter in a nonparametric or semiparametric statistical model. Semiparametric efficient estimators, that is, estimators that achieve the minimum asymptotic variance bound, such as augmented inverse probability of treatment weighted (A-IPTW) estimators [11] and targeted minimum loss-based estimators (TMLE) [15,18], have been developed for a variety of statistical parameters with applications in causal inference.

Typically, the computational efficiency and scalability of these estimators are not taken into account. Borrowing language from the large-scale machine learning literature, we call these batch estimators, because they process the entire dataset at one time. They rely on estimation of one or more parts of the data-generating distribution. With traditional statistical methods, estimating each of these parts may require many passes through the data that can quickly become impractical as the size of datasets grow.

In this chapter, we demonstrate an online method for estimating the average treatment effect (ATE) that is doubly robust and statistically efficient with only a single pass through the dataset. In Section 23.2, we introduce the observed data structure, the causal parameter, causal assumptions required for identification of the parameter, and the statistical parameter. In Section 23.3, we review a batch method for estimating the ATE. In Section 23.4, we describe an online approach to estimating the ATE. In Section 23.5, we demonstrate the performance of the online estimator in simulations. We conclude with a discussion of extensions and future work in Section 23.6.

23.2 Preliminaries

23.2.1 Causal Parameter and Assumptions

We define the ATE using the counterfactual framework [14]. For a single observation, let Y_a be the counterfactual value of some outcome had exposure A been set to level a for $a \in \{0, 1\}$. These values are called *counterfactual* because we can only observe a sample's outcome under the observed treatment that it received. Because at least one of Y_1 or Y_0 is not observed, we can never calculate for a given observation the value $Y_1 - Y_0$, which can be interpreted as the treatment effect for that observation. Under some conditions, however, we can estimate the average of this quantity, $E_0(Y_1 - Y_0)$. This is known as the ATE, where E_0 denotes expectation with respect to the true distribution of the counterfactual random variables.

Before attempting to estimate the ATE, we first consider the structure of our observed dataset. Let $O = (W, A, Y)$ be an observed sample where W is a vector of covariates measured before A, a binary exposure or treatment, and Y is the observed outcome. We make the counterfactual consistency assumption that the observed outcome Y is equal to the counterfactual under the observed treatment A. That is, we assume $Y = Y_A$.

The ATE is a function of the distribution of counterfactuals Y_1 and Y_0. To estimate the ATE, we must be able to write it as a function of the distribution of the observed data. When we can do this, the ATE is said to be identifiable. To do this, we need to make some assumptions. The first is the randomization assumption where we assume $A \perp (Y_1, Y_0) \mid W$. That is, we assume that if there are any common causes of the exposure A and outcome Y, they are measured and included in W. This is sometimes called the *no unmeasured confounders* assumption. This is called an untestable assumption, because it is not possible to test if this assumption is true using the observed data. Making the randomization assumption requires expert domain knowledge and careful study design. We also make the experimental treatment assignment assumption or positivity assumption: that for any value of W, there is some possibility of either treatment being assigned. Formally, we assume $0 < P_0(A = 1 \mid W) < 1$ almost everywhere. Under these assumptions, we can write the ATE as [12]

$$E_0(Y_1 - Y_0) = E_0[E_0(Y \mid A = 1, W) - E_0(Y \mid A = 0, W)]$$

23.2.2 Statistical Model

Now that we have posed some causal assumptions that allow us to write the ATE as a parameter of the distribution of the observed data, we need to specify a statistical model and target parameter. A statistical model $\mathcal{M}$ is a set of possible probability distributions of the observed data.

Suppose that we observe a dataset of n independent and identically distributed observations, $O_1, \ldots, O_n$, with distribution P_0. For a distribution $P \in \mathcal{M}$, let $p = dP/d\mu$

be the density of O with respect to some dominating measure μ. We can factorize the density as

$$p(o) = Q_W(w)G(a \mid w)Q_Y(y \mid a, w)$$

where:

Q_W is the marginal density of W
G is the conditional probability that $A = a$, given W
Q_Y is the conditional density of Y, given A and W

Let $Q = (Q_Y, Q_W)$ and $\bar{Q}(a, w) = E_{Q_Y}(Y \mid A = a, W = w)$. We can parameterize the model as $\mathcal{M} = \{P : Q \in \mathcal{Q}, G \in \mathcal{G}\}$.

The randomization assumption puts no restriction on the distribution of the observed data, and the positivity assumption only requires that $G(1 \mid W)$ be bounded away from 0 and 1. To ensure the true distribution P_0 is in $\mathcal{M}$, we make no additional assumptions on Q so $\mathcal{Q}$ is nonparametric. In some cases, we may know something about the treatment mechanism G. For instance, we may know that the probability of treatment only depends on a subset of covariates. In that case, we put some restriction on the set $\mathcal{G}$ in addition to assuming $0 < G(1 \mid W) < 0$. In general, our model $\mathcal{M}$ is semiparametric.

We define the parameter mapping $\Psi : \mathcal{M} \to \mathbb{R}$ as

$$\Psi(P) = E_P[E_P(Y \mid A = 1, W) - E_P(Y \mid A = 0, W)]$$

where E_P denotes expectation with respect to the distribution P. Let $\psi = \Psi(P)$ be the parameter mapping applied to distribution P. The target parameter we wish to estimate is $\psi_0 = \Psi(P_0)$, the parameter mapping applied to the true distribution. We note that $\Psi(P)$ only depends on P through Q, so recognizing the abuse of notation, we sometimes write $\Psi(Q)$. Throughout, we will use subscript n to denote that a quantity is an estimate based on n observations, and subscript 0 to denote the truth. For example $\bar{Q}_n$ is an estimate of $\bar{Q}_0$, defined as $E_0(Y \mid A = a,\ W = w)$, where E_0 is expectation with respect to the true distribution P_0.

23.3 Batch Estimation of the ATE

An asymptotically linear estimator is one that can be written as a sum of some mean zero function called an influence curve plus a small remainder. An efficient estimator is an estimator that achieves the minimum asymptotic variance among the class of regular estimators. In particular, an efficient estimator is asymptotically linear with the influence curve equal to the efficient influence curve, which depends on the particular parameter and model. The asymptotic variance of an efficient estimator is the variance of the efficient influence curve [2]. For our model $\mathcal{M}$ and parameter mapping Ψ, the efficient influence curve is given by

$$D^*(P)(O) = \frac{2A - 1}{G(A \mid W)}(Y - \bar{Q}(A, W)) + \bar{Q}(1, W) - \bar{Q}(0, W) - \Psi(Q).$$

To denote the dependence of D^* on P through Q and G, we sometimes also write $D^*(Q, G)$.

There are many ways to construct an efficient estimator, for example TMLE or A-IPTW. We now review the A-IPTW estimator in the batch setting. An A-IPTW estimate is calculated as

$$\psi_n = \frac{1}{n}\sum_{i=1}^{n} \frac{2A_i - 1}{G_n(A_i \mid W_i)}(Y_i - \bar{Q}_n(A_i, W_i)) + \bar{Q}_n(1, W_i) - \bar{Q}_n(0, W_i)$$

where $\bar{Q}_n$ and G_n are estimates of Q_0 and G_0, respectively. The A-IPTW estimator treats $D^*(P)$ as an estimating function in ψ and nuisance parameters Q and G and solves for ψ. The A-IPTW is also a one-step estimator, which starts with a plug in estimator for ψ_0 and takes a step in the direction of the efficient influence curve. That is,

$$\psi_n = \Psi(Q_n) + \frac{1}{n}\sum_{i=1}^{n} D^*(Q_n, G_n)$$

where

$$\Psi(Q_n) = \frac{1}{n}\sum_{i=1}^{n} \bar{Q}_n(1, W_i) - \bar{Q}_n(0, W_i).$$

Under regularity conditions, the A-IPTW estimator is efficient if both $\bar{Q}_n$ and G_n are consistent for $\bar{Q}_0$ and G_0, respectively. Additionally, the A-IPTW estimator is doubly robust, meaning that if either of $\bar{Q}_n$ or G_n is consistent, then ψ_n is consistent.

23.4 Online One-Step Estimation of the ATE

The batch A-IPTW in Section 23.3 has some nice statistical properties. In particular, it is efficient and doubly robust. Our goal now is to construct an estimator of ψ_0 that has these same properties, but we only want to make a single pass through the dataset. Additionally, we only want to process a relatively small number of observations, a *minibatch*, at one time.

Let $0 = n_0 < n_1 < \cdots < n_K = n$. Here $n = n_K$ represents the total sample size, and n_j is the sample size accumulated up to minibatch j. Suppose $n_j - n_{j-1}$ is bounded for all j, and for simplicity let $n_j - n_{j-1} = m$ be constant. Let $O_{n_i:n_j}$ denote the observations $O_{n_i+1}, O_{n_i+2}, \ldots, O_{n_j}$ for $i < j$.

In Section 23.3, we computed an estimate of ψ_0 with estimates $\bar{Q}_n$ and G_n, which were fit on the full dataset. Now suppose we have estimates $\bar{Q}_{n_{j-1}}$ and $G_{n_{j-1}}$ for $\bar{Q}_0$ and G_0, respectively, that are based on observations $O_{n_0:n_{j-1}}$. We will return to the problem of computing $\bar{Q}_{n_{j-1}}$ and $G_{n_{j-1}}$ later. Using those estimates of $\bar{Q}_0$ and G_0, we compute a new estimate of ψ_0 on the next minibatch as

$$\psi_{n_{j-1}:n_j} = \frac{1}{m}\sum_{i=n_{j-1}+1}^{n_j}\left[\frac{2A_i - 1}{G_{n_{j-1}}(A_i \mid W_i)}(Y_i - \bar{Q}_{n_{j-1}}(A_i, W_i)) + \bar{Q}_{n_{j-1}}(1, W_i) - \bar{Q}_{n_{j-1}}(0, W_i)\right].$$

That is, $\psi_{n_{j-1}:n_j}$ is a one-step estimator computed on minibatch j using initial estimates of $\bar{Q}_0$ and G_0 from the previous minibatches. We compute the final estimate of ψ_0 by taking the mean of estimates $\psi_{n_{j-1}:n_j}$ from each minibatch. Let

$$\psi_{n_K} = \frac{1}{K}\sum_{j=1}^{K} \psi_{n_{j-1}:n_j},$$

and call this procedure the online one-step (OLOS) estimator.

Under regularity conditions and if $\bar{Q}_{n_K}$ and G_{n_K} converge faster than rate $n_K^{-(1/4)}$ and are both consistent for $\bar{Q}_0$ and G_0, then the OLOS estimator is asymptotically efficient as $K \to \infty$. Additionally, the OLOS estimator has the double robustness property, so if either of $\bar{Q}_{n_K}$ or G_{n_K} is consistent, then ψ_{n_K} is consistent [16, Theorem 1].

We now turn to estimating $\bar{Q}_0$ and G_0, both of which are conditional means. To be truly scalable, ideally we want an estimation procedure that has a constant computational time and storage per minibatch up to K, but we need that the estimates converge fast enough as $K \to \infty$. This rules out estimates of $\bar{Q}_0$ and G_0 that are fit on data from one or a fixed number of minibatches. Stochastic gradient descent-based methods, however, can achieve an appropriate rate of convergence in some circumstances [8,20].

Stochastic gradient descent (SGD) is an optimization procedure similar to traditional batch gradient descent, where the gradient of the objective function for the whole dataset is replaced by the gradient of the objective function at a single observation (or a minibatch). The convergence rate to the empirical optimum of the objective function in terms of number of iterations is very poor relative to batch gradient descent. However, a single iteration of SGD or minibatch gradient descent takes constant time regardless of the size of the dataset, while a single iteration of batch gradient descent takes $O(n)$ time [4].

SGD can be used to fit the parameters of generalized linear models (GLMs). Despite the slow convergence rate, with an appropriately chosen step size, the parameters of a GLM fit with SGD can achieve $\sqrt{n_K}$ consistency in a single pass [8]. If curvature information is taken into account, parameters fit by so-called second-order SGD can achieve the same variance as directly optimizing the empirical objective function [8], but this is often computationally infeasible and rarely done in practice [4]. We note that the class of models for which SGD will obtain $\sqrt{n_K}$ consistency is larger than just generalized linear models that we use as an example here [6].

Averaged stochastic gradient descent (ASGD) is a variant of SGD where parameter estimates are computed with SGD and then averaged. With an appropriate step size, parameters fit by ASDG have been shown to achieve the same variance in a single pass as those fit by directly optimizing the objective function [10,20]. ASGD is much simpler to implement than second-order SGD but has not been popular in practice. This may be because it takes a very large sample size to reach the asymptotic regime [20].

Some variants of SGD allow for a step size for each parameter, such as SGD-QN [3], Adagrad [7], and Adadelta [21], which tend to work well in practice. For information about other variants and implementation details, see [5]. We provide a simple concrete implementation of SGD in Section 23.5.2.

Despite the drawbacks, if $\bar{Q}_0$ and G_0 can be well approximated by GLMs, SGD-based optimization routines are a good way to compute the estimates in one pass.

23.5 Example and Simulation

23.5.1 Data-Generating Distribution

We evaluate the statistical performance of the OLOS estimator and discuss practical implementation details in the context of a simulation study. For each observation, W is generated by making $p = 2000$ independent draws from a uniform distribution on $[-1, 1]$. Given W, A is drawn from a Bernoulli distribution with success probability

$$\frac{1}{1 + \exp(-0.75Z)}$$

where Z is the sum of the first four components of W. Finally, Y is drawn from a Bernoulli distribution with success probability

$$\frac{1}{1+\exp(1+0.5Z-0.3A)}.$$

The first four components of W are related to both A and Y so they are confounders. In general, failing to adjust for confounding variables will result in a biased estimate of the ATE. The other components of W are not counfounders and just add noise to the data. The true parameter ψ_0 is approximately 0.0602. A naive estimate of ψ_0 that fails to adjust for W is approximately -0.026. In this simulation, confounding is strong enough that a naive estimate of ψ_0 that does not adjust for W will be quite biased.

23.5.2 SGD for Logistic Regression

We estimate both G_0 and $\bar{Q}_0$ with main term logistic regression with parameters computed with minibatch gradient descent.

We estimate G_0 with a logistic regression model with main terms for each component of W, and $\bar{Q}_0$ with a logistic regression model with main terms for A and each component of W. To investigate the double robustness of the estimator, we misspecify models for G_0 and $\bar{Q}_0$ by leaving out W. The parameters for both $\bar{Q}_0$ and G_0 are computed with minibatch gradient descent.

For concreteness, we describe the SGD algorithm for logistic regression to estimate $\bar{Q}_0$. Estimating G_0 is analogous. Let X_i be a d-dimensional vector of predictor variables including a constant, A_i, and when the correctly specified, W_i. Let θ be a vector of the same dimension of X_i. For a particular θ, $\bar{Q}(A_i, W_i)$ is computed as

$$\frac{1}{1+\exp(-\theta' X_i)}.$$

Initializing θ_0 to a vector of 0s, θ_j at minibatch j is computed as

$$\theta_j = \theta_{j-1} - \eta_j \frac{1}{m} \sum_{i=n_{j-1}+1}^{n_j} - \left(Y_i - \frac{1}{1+\exp(-\theta'_{j-1} X_i)}\right) X_i$$

where η_j is the step size.

We use minibatches of size 100 and step size

$$\eta_j = \frac{0.05}{1+j0.05\alpha}$$

for minibatch j where α is 0.01 for $\bar{Q}_0$ and 0.1 for G_0.

23.5.3 Results

We constructed datasets of size $n = 10^6$. Using double precision floating point numbers for storage, a single dataset is more than 15 GB uncompressed, so computing a batch estimate of ψ_0 on a typical personal computer is non-trivial. For each simulated dataset, the OLOS estimator is run using either correctly or incorrectly specified initial estimators of $\bar{Q}_0$ and G_0. The current estimate ψ_{n_j} is recorded at each minibatch j.

To investigate the performance of the estimator as a function of sample size, we compute the observed bias and variance at each minibatch across 1000 simulated datasets. Figure 23.1 shows the bias as a function of sample size scaled by the square root of the accumulated sample size.

For an estimator to be asymptotically linear, the bias should be $o_P(1/\sqrt{n})$. This means that we want to see that the scaled bias converge to zero as n increases. We see that in all cases, bias is quite high when sample size is small. This is because estimates of $\bar{Q}_0$ and G_0 are far from the truth for the first few hundred minibatches. When only one of $\bar{Q}_0$ or G_0 is correctly specified, bias moves toward zero slowly, because we are relying on the double robustness of the OLOS. When both $\bar{Q}_0$ and G_0 are estimated by a correctly specified model, the scaled bias approaches 0 reasonably quickly.

Bias is high in early minibatches and it takes many steps to recover. To avoid some of the initial bias, it is sometimes helpful to discard estimates of ψ_0 in early minibatches and compute the final estimate of ψ_0 as

$$\frac{1}{K - K_0} \sum_{j=K_0+1}^{K} \psi_{n_{j-1}:n_j}$$

where K_0 is the number of discarded minibatches. This allows estimates of $\bar{Q}_0$ and G_0 to get *warmed up* with the first K_0 minibatches, and in experiments we see this can reduce bias substantially. (Results not shown.)

Figure 23.2 plots the variance of the OLOS estimates scaled by accumulated sample size. The red line denotes the variance of the efficient influence curve at P_0, which is approximately 0.95 in this simulation. If an estimator is efficient, its variance scaled by the sample size will approach the variance of the efficient influence curve as $n \to \infty$. As expected, we see that when both $\bar{Q}_0$ and G_0 are consistently estimated, the OLOS estimator is efficient. When only one of $\bar{Q}_0$ or G_0 is consistently estimated, the OLOS estimator is not efficient in general, but in this simulation we see that the variance is close to the efficiency bound.

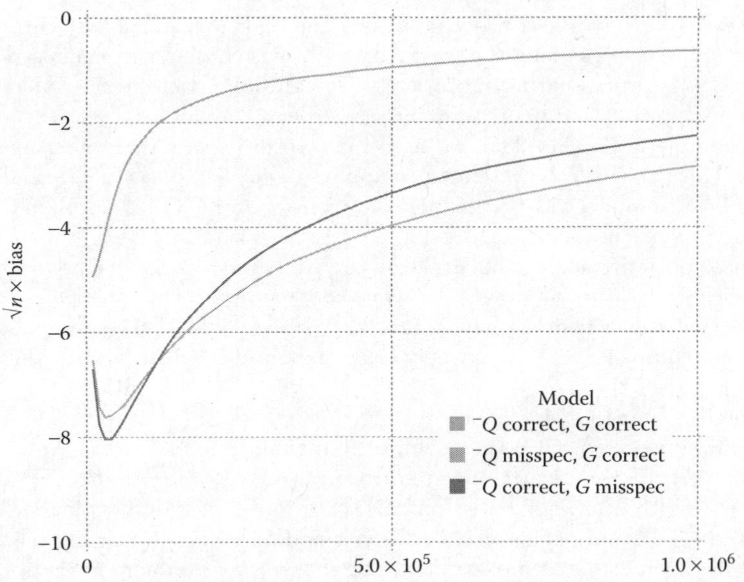

FIGURE 23.1
Bias scaled by $\sqrt{n}$ by sample size.

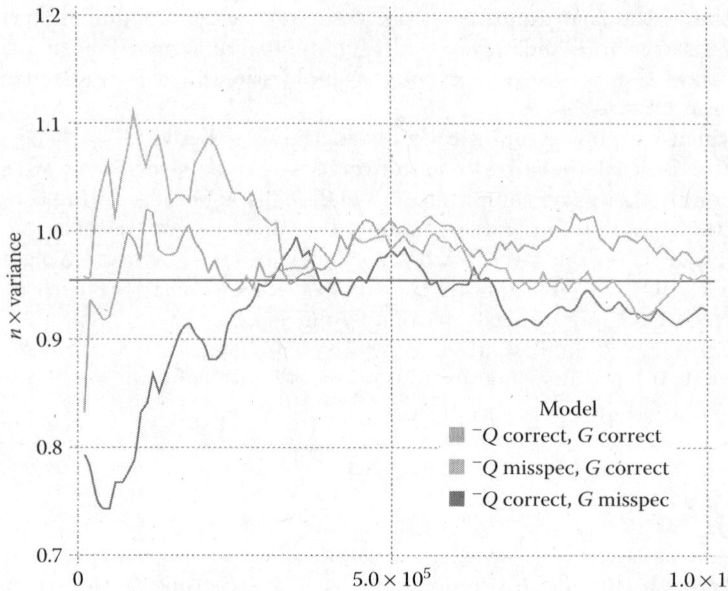

FIGURE 23.2
Variance scaled by n by sample size with a horizontal line at the optimal asymptotic variance.

23.6 Discussion

The OLOS estimator gives us a way to estimate the ATE in a single pass through a dataset, getting running estimates along the way. Although bias can be high when a relatively small amount of data is processed, asymptotically we can do as well as we would with a batch estimator that typically requires many passes through the dataset.

In the example in Section 23.5, we used main term logistic regression to estimate both $\bar{Q}_0$ and G_0. This can easily be extended to any user-specified basis function of W. However, generalized linear models will not include the true $\bar{Q}_0$ and G_0 in general, and more flexible online estimators are needed.

SGD-based optimization is a natural way to turn batch algorithms into online algorithms and is applicable to a wide range of estimation methods. One such class of estimators is multilayer neural networks, which are incredibly flexible. Typically, because of the computational complexity of neural networks, they are fit with SGD in the batch setting with multiple passes through the dataset. In principle, one could fit a neural network as an online estimator, though a single pass through even very large datasets may not be enough for the neural network to reach the asymptotic regime.

There are other examples in the literature of estimators that have been extended to the online setting that are not based on SGD. Examples include bagging and boosting [9], random forests [1,13], and generalized additive models [19].

It is not clear when one estimator should be chosen over another. There are also typically some choices of tuning parameters, for example level of regularization. For online methods, fitting procedures may have their own set of choices. For example, there are a number of variants of SGD for optimization, each of which has some tuning parameters. In the batch setting, cross-validation can be used to select between many estimators, or a model stacking approach such as the super learner algorithm [17] can be used to choose a combination of estimators. A similar approach can be taken in an online setting by using each new minibatch as an independent validation set to estimate out-of-sample performance before updating an estimator with that minibatch. In this way, many estimators with different choices of tuning parameters can be fit concurrently, and the best or a combination can be selected based on the estimated out-of-sample performance.

References

1. Hanady Abdulsalam, David B. Skillicorn, and Patrick Martin. Streaming random forests. In *Database Engineering and Applications Symposium, IDEAS 2007. 11th International*, pp. 225–232. IEEE, Alberta, Canada, 2007.

2. Peter J. Bickel, Chris A.J. Klaassen, Ya'acov Ritov, and Jon A. Wellner. *Efficient and Adaptive Estimation for Semiparametric Models.* Johns Hopkins University Press, Baltimore, MD, 1993.

3. Antoine Bordes, Léon Bottou, and Patrick Gallinari. SGD-QN: Careful quasi-Newton stochastic gradient descent. *The Journal of Machine Learning Research*, 10:1737–1754, 2009.

4. Léon Bottou. Large-scale machine learning with stochastic gradient descent. In *Proceedings of COMPSTAT*, pp. 177–186. Springer, Berlin, Germany, 2010.

5. Léon Bottou. Stochastic gradient descent tricks. In Grégoire Montavon; Geneviève B. Orr; Klaus-Robert Müller, editors, *Neural Networks: Tricks of the Trade*, pp. 421–436. Springer, Berlin, Germany, 2012.

6. Léon Bottou and Yann L. Cun. On-line learning for very large data sets. *Applied Stochastic Models in Business and Industry*, 21(2):137–151, 2005.

7. John Duchi, Elad Hazan, and Yoram Singer. Adaptive subgradient methods for online learning and stochastic optimization. *The Journal of Machine Learning Research*, 12:2121–2159, 2011.

8. Noboru Murata. *A Statistical Study of On-Line Learning: Online Learning and Neural Networks.* Cambridge University Press, Cambridge, 1998.

9. Nikunj C. Oza. Online bagging and boosting. In *IEEE International Conference on Systems, Man and Cybernetics*, volume 3, pp. 2340–2345. IEEE, 2005.

10. Boris T. Polyak and Anatoli B. Juditsky. Acceleration of stochastic approximation by averaging. *SIAM Journal on Control and Optimization*, 30(4):838–855, 1992.

11. James M. Robins, Andrea Rotnitzky, and Lue P. Zhao. Estimation of regression coefficients when some regressors are not always observed. *Journal of the American Statistical Association*, 89(427):846–866, 1994.

12. Paul R. Rosenbaum and Donald B. Rubin. The central role of the propensity score in observational studies for causal effects. *Biometrika*, 70(1):41–55, 1983.

13. Amir Saffari, Christian Leistner, Jakob Santner, Martin Godec, and Horst Bischof. On-line random forests. In *IEEE 12th International Conference on Computer Vision Workshops*, pp. 1393–1400. IEEE, Kyoto, Japan, 2009.

14. Janet M. Box-Steffensmeier, Henry E. Brady, and David Collier. *The Oxford Handbook of Political Methodology*, Oxford University Press, Oxford, New York, 2008.

15. Mark J. van der Laan. Targeted maximum likelihood based causal inference: Part I. *The International Journal of Biostatistics*, 6(2), 2010.

16. Mark J. van der Laan and Samuel D. Lendle. Online Targeted Learning. Working Paper 330, U.C. Berkeley Division of Biostatistics, University of California, Berkeley, CA, September 2014.

17. Mark J. van der Laan, Eric C. Polley, and Alan E. Hubbard. Super learner. *Statistical Applications in Genetics and Molecular Biology*, 6(1):1–23, 2007.

18. Mark J. van der Laan and Sherri Rose. *Targeted Learning: Causal Inference for Observational and Experimental Data*. Springer-Verlag, New York, 2011.

19. Simon N. Wood, Yannig Goude, and Simon Shaw. Generalized additive models for large data sets. *Journal of the Royal Statistical Society: Series C (Applied Statistics)*, 139–155, 2014.

20. Wei Xu. Towards optimal one pass large scale learning with averaged stochastic gradient descent. *CoRR*, abs/1107.2490, 2011.

21. Matthew D. Zeiler. Adadelta: An adaptive learning rate method. arXiv preprint arXiv:1212.5701, 2012.

24

Mining with Inference: Data-Adaptive Target Parameters

Alan Hubbard and Mark van der Laan

CONTENTS

24.1 Introduction 439
24.1.1 Motivating Example 439
24.2 General Methodology 441
24.3 Examples 443
24.3.1 Inference for Sample-Split Cluster-Specific Target Parameters, Where the Data are Used to Define Clusters 443
24.4 Data Analysis: ACIT Variable Importance Trauma Study 444
24.4.1 Results 447
24.5 Concluding Remarks 450
Acknowledgments 451
References 451

24.1 Introduction

There has been an explosion of empirical approaches to scientific questions driven by the growing systematic collection of data. Though there has been great progress in developing quantitative statistical methods well suited to exploratory, data-driven analysis, there still remains much to be done for deriving estimators and robust inference of relevant parameters in such a context. The growth of so-called big data has inspired pattern-finding procedures, for instance, its use in evidenced-based methods for optimizing health care [1].

However, less emphasis has been given to formally defining the parameters such procedures *discover*. Thus, an obvious first step necessary for driving theoretical results is to explicitly define such data-adaptive parameters. The goal of this chapter is to address this gap, by providing formal definitions of data-adaptive parameters, as well as general methodology for estimation and statistical inference (see also [2]).

24.1.1 Motivating Example

Though the methodology described in this chapter is quite general, we illustrate the method by a particularly challenging causal inference/variable importance estimation problem. Consider data from the Activation of Coagulation and Inflammation in Trauma (ACIT) study [3,4]. The ACIT study is designed to identify clinically important mechanisms by which the inflammatory and coagulation pathways are altered following major trauma.

Detailed and somewhat messy data were collected from as near the original injury as possible. These data are used to characterize coagulation and inflammation after injury, and *to identify variables important for impacting outcomes, like death.* Beginning in the emergency department (generally, soon after injury), blood was prospectively sampled from severely injured trauma patients. In addition, comprehensive demographic and injury variables were also collected. The result is a wide dataset, with detailed, though irregularly collected longitudinal measurements of many patient-level factors that could contribute to clinical outcomes, such as multiple organ failure and death. In our case, we examine early factors and their impact on death within the first 24 hours after injury.

This chapter is about using the data to both define a target parameter, and yet estimate and draw inferences about a well-defined parameter. As a concrete example, consider that we have a large number of predictors, R (e.g., injury severity, measures of platelets, presence of alcohol in blood, etc.) all measured from time of injury, an outcome death between 6 and 24 hours: $Y = 1$ for death, $Y = 0$ for alive at 24 hours. We want to know which of these variables is *most important* for explaining (predicting) Y among those alive at 6 hours. Thus, this is a *variable importance measure* (VIM) estimation problem. As opposed to deriving VIMs as a byproduct of some parametric model or machine learning procedure [5].

We [6] have advocated for targeted estimation of parameters motivated by causal inference, for example, see [7]. We have previously applied such techniques to look at variable importance for related trauma data [8]. Define the data, for a particular variable of interest ($A \in R$), as $O = (W, \Delta, \Delta * (A, Y))$, where W is the original covariate vector with the current variable of interest, A, removed (this definition is repeated for each variable that comprises W), and Δ is missingness indicator for either A or Y (=1 if both not missing, 0 otherwise). Assume for now that A is discrete and there is an a priori *highest risk* level (a_H) and a lowest risk level (a_L). Then, a candidate for variable importance that would allow comparisons across different candidate predictors (each with their own (a_L, a_H)) is:

$$E_W\{E(Y \mid A = a_H, W) - E(Y \mid A = a_L, W)\} \tag{24.1}$$

or a weighted average of the stratified mean differences comparing, within strata W, subjects with a_H versus those with a_L. Though we do not emphasize such identifiability conditions for this application, under assumptions Equation 24.1 identifies $E\{Y(a_H) - Y(a_L)\}$, where $Y(a)$ is the counterfactual outcome for patients if, possibly contrary to the fact, their A was set to a. In any case, it is a VIM that can be compared across different covariates and is a pathwise differentiable parameter, and thus one can derive semiparametrically efficient, asymptotically normal estimators.

However, the reality is that candidates for A are not always discrete and even when they are, there is no objectively defined high- and low-risk levels for many if not most of the potential predictors. Thus, we need to use the data (data adaptively) to define levels a_H and a_L. Let P_n define the empirical distribution of our sample; one could apply an algorithm of some kind to P_n to define by these high- and low-risk sets in A or in shorthand $(a_L(P_n), a_H(P_n))$. For instance, if A were discrete with arbitrary levels $\mathcal{A} = (a_1, a_2, ..., a_i, ..., a_K)$, we could define $a_L(P_n)$ as

$$a_L(P_n) = \underset{a \in \mathcal{A}}{\text{argmin}} \frac{1}{n} \sum_{i=1}^{n} Q_n(a, W_i)$$

$$a_H(P_n) = \underset{a \in \mathcal{A}}{\text{argmin}} \frac{1}{n} \sum_{i=1}^{n} Q_n(a, W_i)$$

where $Q_n(A, W)$ is an estimate (based on P_n) of $Q(A, W) \equiv E(Y \mid A, W)$. Simply, one finds the levels $(a_L(P_n), a_H(P_n))$ that maximize the substitution estimate of Equation 24.1 according to some regression estimate $Q_n(A, W)$ (we discuss below how to *optimize* Q_n).

Thus, we have a data-adaptive target parameter: $E_W\{E(Y \mid A = a_H(P_n), W) - E(Y \mid A = a_L(P_n), W)\}$, for which the substitution estimator

$$\frac{1}{n}\sum_{i=1} Q_n(a_H(P_n), W_i) - Q_n(a_L(P_n), W_i) \tag{24.2}$$

can suffer from serious bias due to overfitting. For instance, under the statistical null that $E_W\{E(Y \mid A = a_H(P_n), W) - E(Y \mid A = a_L(P_n), W)\} = 0$, the estimate (Equation 24.2) will always be positively biased (it is always ≥ 0). Others have noted dangers of false positives from the combination of high-dimensional data and flexible methodologies [9,10]. However, if one had done sample splitting such that (1) a training sample was used to define $(a_L(P_{n,\text{tr}}), a_H(P_{n,\text{tr}}))$, and (2) an estimation sample was used to estimate $E_W\{E(Y \mid A = a_L(P_{n,\text{tr}}), W) - E(Y \mid A = a_L(P_{n,\text{tr}}), W)\}$, then consistent estimation is possible. However, estimation has lower power as the sample size is split into two. What one would like is a data-adaptive procedure that can use the data to define the target parameter, but still estimate it consistently and derive robust inference. Thus, we discuss methods that use sample splitting to avoid bias from overfitting, but still can use the entire dataset to estimate a data-adaptive parameter. These methods apply in circumstances where there is little constraint on how the data are explored to generate potential parameters of interest. Such methods can capitalize on the very large sample sizes and/or very high dimension associated with *big data.*

We present the material in the following order: in Section 24.2, we will define our general methodology, using sample splitting or not, present theorems establishing the asymptotic statistical performance, and discuss its implications, as well as present influence curve-based inference. In Section 24.3, we discuss an example of an interesting target parameter generated via the data-adaptive methodology presented in Section 24.2. In Section 24.4, we revisit the example of VIMs in the acute trauma study, and end with concluding a remark.

24.2 General Methodology

Let $O_1, \ldots, O_n$ be i.i.d. with probability distribution P_0, an element of the statistical model $\mathcal{M}$; let P_n represent the empirical distribution of a sample. We discuss our estimator in the context of V-fold cross-validation. Let us assume that we have divided up the sample into equal numbers of observations randomly of size n/V by randomly assigning integers $(1, 2, \ldots, V)$ of length n – we can call a particular permutation of these sets of integers, Z. In this way, we can define random splits of the O_i into an estimation sample $(Z = v)$ and into the parameter-generating (training) sample $(Z \neq v)$. Thus, this corresponds with a V-fold cross-validation scheme: (1) $\{1, \ldots, n\}$ are divided into V equal size subgroups, (2) an estimation sample is defined by one of the subgroups, and (3) the parameter-generating sample is its complement resulting in V such splits of the sample.

For a given random split v, let P_{n,v^c} be the empirical distribution of the parameter-generating sample, and $P_{n,v}$ be the empirical distribution of the estimation sample. Thus, for a particular sample split, $\Psi_{P_{n,v^c}} : \mathcal{M} \to \mathbb{R}$ is the target parameter mapping indexed by the parameter-generating sample P_{n,v^c} , and $\hat{\Psi}_{P_{n,v^c}} : \mathcal{M}_{NP} \to \mathbb{R}$ the corresponding estimator of this target parameter. Here $\mathcal{M}_{\text{NP}}$ is the nonparametric model and an estimator is defined as a mapping/algorithm from a nonparametric model, including the empirical distributions, to the parameter space. Assume that the parameter is real valued.

The choice of target parameter mapping and corresponding estimator can be informed by the data P_{n,v^c}, but not by the corresponding estimation sample $P_{n,v}$. Define the sample-split data-adaptive statistical target parameter as $\Psi_n : \mathcal{M} \to \mathbb{R}$ with

$$\Psi_n(P) = \text{Ave}\{\Psi_{P_{n,v^c}}(P)\} \equiv \frac{1}{V}\sum_{v=1}^{V} \Psi_{P_{n,v^c}}(P)$$

and the statistical estimand of interest is thus

$$\psi_{n,0} = \Psi_n(P_0) = \text{Ave}\{\Psi_{P_{n,v^c}}(P_0)\}. \tag{24.3}$$

This target parameter mapping depends on the data, and thus we call it a *data-adaptive target parameter.* A corresponding estimator of the data-adaptive estimand $\psi_{n,0}$ is given by

$$\psi_n = \hat{\Psi}(P_n) = \text{Ave}\{\hat{\Psi}_{P_{n,v^c}}(P_{n,v})\}. \tag{24.4}$$

We show below that $\sqrt{n}(\psi_n - \psi_{n,0})$ converges to a mean zero normal distribution with variance σ^2 that can be consistently estimated, allowing the construction of confidence intervals for $\psi_{n,0}$ and also allowing testing a null hypothesis such as $H_0 : \psi_{n,0} \leq 0$. In particular, this would hold if $\psi_n = \hat{\Psi}(P_n)$ is an asymptotically linear estimator of $\psi_{n,0}$ with the influence curve $IC(P_0)$:

$$\psi_n - \psi_{n,0} = (P_n - P_0)IC(P_0) + o_P(1/\sqrt{n})$$

where we use the notation $Pf \equiv \int f(o)dP(o)$ for the expectation of $f(O)$ w.r.t. P. Because $(P_n - P_0)IC(P_0) = 1/n\sum_i IC(P_0)(O_i)$ is a sum of mean zero-independent random variables, this asymptotic linearity implies that $\sqrt{n}(\psi_n - \psi_{n,0})$ converges to a mean zero normal distribution with variance $\sigma^2 = P_0 IC(P_0)^2$.

Theorem 24.1 *Suppose that, given* (P_{n,v^c}), $\hat{\Psi}_{P_{n,v^c}}$ *is an asymptotically linear estimator of* $\Psi_{P_{n,v^c}}(P_0)$ *at* P_0 *with the influence curve* $IC_{v,P_{n,v^c}}(P_0)$ *indexed by* (v, P_{n,v^c}):

$$\hat{\Psi}_{P_{n,v^c}}(P_{n,v}) - \Psi_{P_{n,v^c}}(P_0) = (P_{n,v} - P_0)IC_{P_{n,v^c}}(P_0) + R_{n,v}$$

where (unconditional) $R_{n,v} = o_P(1/\sqrt{n})$. *Assume* V*-fold cross-validation, and for a given split* v, *assume that* $P_0 IC^2_{v,P^0_{n,v}}(P_0) - P_0 IC^2_v(P_0) \to 0$ *in probability, where* $IC_v(P_0)$ *is a limit influence curve that can still be indexed by the split* v.

Then, $\sqrt{n}(\psi_n - \psi_{n,0}) = \frac{1}{V}\sum_v \sqrt{V}\sqrt{n/V}(P_{n,v} - P_0)IC_{v,P^0_{n,v}}(P_0) + o_P(1/\sqrt{n})$ *converges to a mean zero normal distribution with variance*

$$\sigma^2 = \frac{1}{V}\sum_{v=1}^{V} \sigma_v^2$$

where $\sigma_v^2 = P_0 IC_v^2(P_0)$. *A consistent estimator of* σ^2 *is given by*

$$\sigma_n^2 = \frac{1}{V}\sum_{v=1}^{V} P_n IC_{v,n}^2$$

where $IC_{v,n}$ *is an* $L^2(P_0)$*-consistent estimator of* $IC_v(P_0)$. *Alternatively, one can use*

$$\sigma_n^2 = \frac{1}{V}\sum_{v=1}^{V} P_{n,v} IC_{v,P_{n,v^c}}(P_{n,v})^2 \tag{24.5}$$

where $IC_{v,P_{n,v^c}}(P_{n,v})$ is an $L^2(P_0)$-consistent estimator of $IC_{v,P_{n,v^c}}(P_0)$ based on the sample $P_{n,v}$.

See [2] for proof.

Note that these results generalize to cases where the mapping also relies on the split itself. For instance, the general theory covers the case that each training sample is sent to separate research groups that are told to derive a mapping to estimate some parameter, and then each of these mappings is applied to the corresponding training sample, where to estimate the resulting data-adaptive parameter one does not need to know how the mapping was done, and whether it was a common algorithm applied in all training sample. However, we emphasize for the rest of the chapter, as we have implied by the notation above (by not indexing Equation 24.3 by Z in addition to P_{n,v^c}), those cases where the mapping is based on a fixed algorithm and so only a function of the empirical distribution of the training sample.

We note that in some circumstances, one can improve the efficiency of the data-adaptive parameter estimates by using a cross-validated, targeted maximum likelihood approach (CV-TMLE; see Chapter 27 in [11]).

For advice on the number of splits, V, see [2]. In addition, we also derived results for the classic data-mining procedure, where the entire sample is used both to define the parameter and then subsequently to estimate it (Theorem 3 in [2]). The conditions of this theorem imply greater restrictions (detailed in [2]) on the use of algorithms for defining data-adaptive target parameters.

24.3 Examples

24.3.1 Inference for Sample-Split Cluster-Specific Target Parameters, Where the Data are Used to Define Clusters

Suppose one has a very high dimensional set of variables, potentially correlated in relatively distinct groups, but for which the definition of such groups is not known a priori, and thus must be determined empirically. Furthermore, the summaries of the values of the variables in these blocks represent meaningful summaries of their joint relationship with an explanatory variable. One such situation might be genomic experiments, where the expression of highly correlated genes represents distinct pathways that might be simultaneously triggered by the same intervention (e.g., drug). Thus, one might derive significant variable reduction by creating summaries of the highly correlated gene expression in these blocks, as well as exploratory summaries of potential pathways to more efficiently measure the impact of the intervention of interest. Because this involves an exploratory part (forming the blocks/clusters), but still with the need for formal statistical inference to determine the significance of the relationship of these clusters with the intervention, it is an ideal application for the methodologies in this chapter.

Suppose that one observes on each subject a p-dimensional gene-expression profile $Y \in \mathbb{R}^p$, a binary treatment/exposure A, and a vector of baseline characteristics W. Thus, $O = (W, A, Y)$ and we observe n i.i.d. copies $O_1, \ldots, O_n$. Consider an algorithm that maps a dataset $O_1, \ldots, O_n$ into a cluster $C \subset \{1, \ldots, p\}$ of genes. Denote this cluster estimator with $\hat{C} : \mathcal{M}_{NP} \rightarrow \mathcal{C}$, where $\mathcal{C}$ is the space of possible cluster values. Given a realized cluster C, let $\Psi_C : \mathcal{M} \rightarrow \mathbb{R}$ be a desired parameter of interest such as the effect of treatment A on $Y(M(C))$, controlling for the baseline covariates W, where $M(C)$ is the medoid/center of the cluster C, defined as

$$\Psi_C(P_0) = E_0\{E_0(Y(M(C)) \mid A = 1, W) - E_0(Y(M(C)) \mid A = 0, W)\}$$

Alternatively, one might define $\Psi_C(P_0)$ as the average over all genes j in cluster C of the effect of treatment A on $Y(j)$, controlling for W, defined as

$$\Psi_C(P_0) = \frac{1}{|C|}\sum_{j=1}^{|C|} E_0\{E_0(Y(j) \mid A=1, W) - E_0(Y(j) \mid A=0, W)\}$$

Let $\hat{\Psi}_C : \mathcal{M}_{\text{NP}} \to \mathbb{R}$ be an estimator of $\Psi_C(P_0)$, for instance, inverse probability of treatment weighted (IPTW [12]), or targeted maximum likelihood estimator (TMLE [11,13]). If one assumes that the regularity conditions hold so that, for instance, the TMLE estimator, $\hat{\Psi}_C(P_n)$, is asymptotically linear with the influence curve $IC_C(P_0)$, then

$$\hat{\Psi}_C(P_n) - \Psi_C(P_0) = (P_n - P_0)IC_C(P_0) + R_{C,n}$$

where $R_{C,n} = o_P(1/\sqrt{n})$. We define $\Psi_{P_{n,v^c}} : \mathcal{M} \to \mathbb{R}$ as $\Psi_{P_{n,v^c}} = \Psi_{\hat{C}(P_{n,v^c})}$, that is, the causal effect of treatment on the data-adaptively determined cluster $\hat{C}(P_{n,v^c})$. Similarly, we define $\hat{\Psi}_{P_{n,v^c}} : \mathcal{M}_{\text{NP}} \to \mathbb{R}$ as $\hat{\Psi}_{P_{n,v^c}} = \hat{\Psi}_{\hat{C}(P_{n,v^c})}$, that is, the TMLE of the W-controlled effect of treatment of this data-adaptively determined cluster, treating the latter as given. The estimand of interest is thus defined as $\psi_{n,0} = \text{Ave}\{\Psi_{P_{n,v^c}}(P_0)\}$ and its estimator is $\psi_n = \text{Ave}\{\hat{\Psi}_{P_{n,v^c}}(P_{n,v})\}$. Thus, for a given split, we use the parameter-generating sample P_{n,v^c} to generate a cluster $\hat{C}(P_{n,v^c})$ and the corresponding TMLE of $\hat{\Psi}_{\hat{C}(P_{n,v^c})}(P_0)$ applied to the estimation sample $P_{n,v}$, and these sample-split specific estimators are averaged across the V sample splits. By assumption we have for each split v:

$$\hat{\Psi}_{\hat{C}(P_{n,v^c})}(P_{n,v}) - \Psi_{\hat{C}(P_{n,v^c})}(P_0) = (P_{n,v} - P_0)IC_{\hat{C}(P_{n,v^c})}(P_0) + R_{\hat{C}(P_{n,v^c}),n}$$

where we now assume that (unconditionally) $R_{\hat{C}(P_{n,v^c}),n} = o_P(1/\sqrt{n})$. In addition, we assume that $P_0\{IC_{\hat{C}(P_{n,v^c})}(P_0)\}^2$ converges to $P_0\{IC_{\hat{C}(P_0)}(P_0)\}^2$ for a limit cluster $\hat{C}(P_0)$. Application of Theorem 24.1 now proves that $\psi_n - \psi_{n,0}$ is asymptotically linear with the influence curve $IC_{\hat{C}(P_0)}(P_0)$ so that it is asymptotically normally distributed with mean zero and variance $\sigma^2 = P_0 IC_{\hat{C}(P_0)}(P_0)^2$.

There are many examples of potential applications of this approach too numerous to list (see [2] for more examples and extensive simulations). However, one particularly important one is the estimation of the causal effect of particular treatment rules that are learned from data. This one has obvious practical implications in all sorts of fields, including medicine, political science, and any discipline where of interest is the impact of an approach that tailors an intervention to the characteristics of the statistical units, and the data must be used to learn the best approach.

24.4 Data Analysis: ACIT Variable Importance Trauma Study

We revisit estimating VIMs of the form 24.2 for the ACIT trauma data. The target population are those patients that survive up to 6 hours after their injury, and the outcome Y is the indicator of death from 6 to 24 hours, where, among the $n = 1277$ observations (subjects) alive at 6 hours, the proportion of deaths in this next interval is 3.5%. We estimate the variable importance from a combination of ordered continuous variables, ordered discrete, and factors for a total of 108 potential predictors. Each of these 108 variables is treated as the variable of interest, A, and the remainder as covariates. This is an extremely messy data (missing values, sparsity, etc.), and thus, for each variable importance we undergo a number of automated data-processing steps to make estimation viable. These include:

1. Drop variables missing for more than 50% of observations.
2. Automatically determine which variables are ordered and unordered factors.
3. Drop observations variables for which there distribution is too *uneven* so that there is not enough experimentation across different levels to estimate a VIM.

Then, for each variable (when current variable of interest), we performed the following steps.

1. For a continuous variable, we constructed new ordered discrete variables (integers) that map the original value into intervals defined by the empirical deciles of the variable. This results in new ordered variables with values $1, ..., \max(A)$, where $\max(A) = 10$ unless the original variable has fewer unique values. We then further lump these values into groups by histogram density estimation using the penalized likelihood approach [14,15] to bin values, avoiding very small cell sizes in the distribution A.
2. For each variable, we generated basis functions that indicate which observations have missing values, so that for each original variable, say W_j, there is a new basis $(\Delta_j, \Delta_j * W_j)$, where $\Delta_j = 1$ if W_j is not missing for an observation, 0 otherwise (see below for how this is used in the algorithm).
3. Use hierarchical clustering routine HOPACH [16] to cluster adjustment variables (the matrices of all other predictors besides the current A as well as the matrix of associated missingness indicators) to reduce the dimension of the adjustment set.

Each of these processing steps is tunable depending on sample size to the point where the data are very close to the original form. These steps allow a very general messy dataset of mixed variable types that can be automatically processed for VIM analysis. Thus, after processing, for each VIM analysis we can represent the data as i.i.d., $O = (W, A, Y) \sim P_0 \in \mathcal{M}$, W being all other covariates besides the current A as well as the basis functions related to missingness observations for covariates.

We estimate our data-adaptive, VIM based on algorithms motivated by both theorems above. Specifically, we use the approach of Theorem 24.1 by performing sample splitting using two-fold cross-validation (splitting randomly in equal samples). The parameter is first defined by using the training sample to define $a_L(P_{n,v^c})$. To do so, we estimate, for each of values, a, of the discretized $A \in \mathcal{A}$, an estimand motivated by the *causal* parameter $E(Y_a)$. Under identifiability assumptions (e.g., randomization, positivity; see Chapter 4 in [11]), we can identify $E(Y_a)$ as

$$E_0\{E_0(Y \mid A = a, W)\} = E_0\{Q_0(a, W)\} \tag{24.6}$$

where 0 indicated under P_0, and $Q_0(a, W)$ is the true regression (conditional mean) function of Y on (A, W). If we knew Q_0, we would know the *true* levels of A to compare, that is,

$$\begin{aligned} a_L &\equiv \mathrm{argmin}_{\mathrm{a} \in \mathcal{A}} \mathrm{E}_0\{\mathrm{Q}_0(\mathrm{a}, \mathrm{W})\} \\ a_H &\equiv \mathrm{argmax}_{\mathrm{a} \in \mathcal{A}} \mathrm{E}_0\{\mathrm{Q}_0(\mathrm{a}, \mathrm{W})\} \end{aligned}$$

so we could then estimate Equation 24.1 without having to *discover* values of (a_L, a_H) using the data. However, we do not know Q_0 and must estimate it to estimate Equation 24.6 to empirically define (a_L, a_H). In the context of Theorem 24.1, we then use the training sample to define these levels. We do so using the following algorithm:

1. Estimate $\theta_0(a) \equiv E_{0,W}\{Q_0(a,W)\}$ for all levels $a \in \mathcal{A}$ using a semi-parametric, locally efficient data-adaptive method TMLE [11].
   a. To do so requires an initial estimate of the regression $Q_0(A,W)$ and we use the *SuperLearner* algorithm [17], an ensemble learner that itself uses cross-validation to derive an optimal weighted combination of selected learners. For this we used (1) LASSO via the glmnet package in R [18], (2) ADD OTHERS.
   b. This also requires an estimate of the so-called treatment mechanism ($g_0(a;W) \equiv P_0(A = a \mid W)$) and the glmnet package was also used for this.

   We can define these estimates for a specific training sample v^c as $\hat{\theta}_{P_{n,v^c}}(a)$.
2. Select the levels of A to compare in the corresponding training sample as

$$\begin{aligned} a_L(P_{n,v^c}) &= \text{argmin}_{a \in \mathcal{A}} \hat{\theta}_{P_{n,v^c}}(a) \\ a_H(P_{n,v^c}) &= \text{argmax}_{a \in \mathcal{A}} \hat{\theta}_{P_{n,v^c}}(a) \end{aligned}$$

3. On the corresponding estimation sample, estimate the parameter

$$\Psi_{P_{n,v^c}}(P_0) \equiv \theta_0(a_H(P_{n,v^c})) - \theta_0(a_L(P_{n,v^c})) \tag{24.7}$$

   We estimated $\Psi_{P_{n,v^c}}(P_0)$ on the corresponding estimation sample (say $\hat{\Psi}_{P_{n,v^c}}(P_{n,v})$) using the same combination of SuperLearner and TMLE described above as used for defining $(a_L(P_{n,v^c}), a_H(P_{n,v^c}))$.
4. Derive the influence curve of these estimators on the validation sample. In this case, the estimated influence curve is

$$\begin{aligned} IC_{P_{n,v^c}}(P_{n,v}) &= Y - \left[\frac{I\{A=a_H(P_{n,v^c})\}}{g_{P_{n,v}}(a_H(P_{n,v^c});W)} - \frac{I\{A=a_L(P_{n,v^c})\}}{g_{P_{n,v}}(a_L(P_{n,v^c});W)}\right]\{Y - Q_{P_{n,v}}(A,W)\} \\ &+ \left[Q_{P_{n,v}}(a_H(P_{n,v^c}),W) - Q_{P_{n,v}}(a_L(P_{n,v^c}),W)\right] - \Psi_{P_{n,v^c}}(P_{n,v}) \end{aligned}$$

   where $Q_{P_{n,v}}$ and $g_{P_{n,v}}$ indicate that these functions were estimated on the estimation sample $P_{n,v}$.
5. Derive the estimated sample variance of the influence curve: $\sigma^2_{n,v} \equiv P_{n,v} IC_{P_{n,v^c}}(P_{n,v})^2$.
6. Repeat steps 1–5 above for every combination of estimation and validation sample to get the entire set of parameter and variance estimates, $(\hat{\Psi}_{P_{n,v^c}}(P_{n,v}), \sigma^2_{P_{n,v}}), v = 1, \ldots, V$.
7. Average the estimates to get the estimate (Equation 24.4) of the average parameter: $\psi_n = \text{Ave}\{\hat{\Psi}_{P_{n,v^c}}(P_{n,v})\}$, as well as the average estimated variances, $\sigma^2_n = \text{Ave}\{\sigma^2_{n,v}\}$.
8. Derive confidence intervals, and p-values based using quantities calculated in 7.
9. Repeat steps 1–8 for every variable to consider as an A by switching places with the current A and one of the W.
10. Based on the p-value of the test of null: $H_0 : \psi_{n,0} \leq 0$, adjust for multiple comparisons by controlling the false discovery rate (FDR; [19])

The results are an ordered list (by statistical significance) of the VIM (the ψ_n), statistical inference adjusted for multiple comparisons, along with information about the estimates and the levels of $(a_L(P_{n,v^c}), a_H(P_{n,v^c}))$ chosen for each combination of training and estimation samples.

24.4.1 Results

The names of the potential predictors along with the type of variable (ordered or unordered factor) are listed in Table 24.1. This table is ordered by the p-value of the test: $H_0 : \psi_n \leq 0$, so most significant estimates at top. There were 108 original variables examined, but only 72 with sufficient data to estimate a VIM. Table 24.2 has the estimation sample-specific results for the same ordered list. The definition of the $(a_L(P_{n,v^c}), a_H(P_{n,v^c}))$ for the two training samples is related to the original discretization, so, for instance, if it states that $a_L(P_{n,v^c})$ is $(x, 1]$, then $a_L(P_{n,v^c})$ is the indicator of being in the lowest decile. One can see some shortcomings of the data from these results. The outcome is rare enough, that

TABLE 24.1
ACIT variables and description—note variables are ordered by statistical significance.

Name	Var. type	Description
tbi	Factor	Traumatic brain injury
hr6_basedefexc	Ordered	Hour 6 base deficit/excess
ortho	Factor	Orthopedic injury
alcabuse	Factor	Alcohol use
race	Factor	Race
hr0_factorviii	Ordered	Hour 0 factor VIII
hr0_ptt	Ordered	Hour 0 partial thromboplastin time
heightcm	Ordered	Height
edworsttemp	Ordered	ED worst temp
aisface2	Ordered	Abbreviated injury scale: face
hr0_factorv	Ordered	Hour 0 factor V
hr0_atiii	Ordered	Hour 0 antithrombin III
aisextremity5	Ordered	Abbreviated injury scale: extremity
male	Factor	Gender male?
edlowestsbp	Ordered	ED lowest SBP
latino	Factor	Latino
pbw	Ordered	Predicted body weight
edlowesthr	Ordered	ED lowest HR
hr0_temp	Ordered	Hour 0 temperature
blunt	Factor	Mechanism of injury—blunt?
hr0_map	Ordered	Hour 0 mean arterial pressure
aisabdomen4	Ordered	Abbreviated injury scale: abdomen
iss	Ordered	Injury severity score
hr0_resprate	Ordered	Hour 0 respiratory rate
numribfxs	Ordered	Number of rib fractures
hr0_factorx	Ordered	Hour 0 factor X
patientbloodtype	Factor	Patient blood type
edadmittemp	Ordered	ED admit temp
edhighestsbp	Ordered	ED highest SBP
age	Ordered	AGE at time of injury
insurancesource	Factor	Insurance source
mechtype	Factor	Mechanism type
hr0_basedefexc	Ordered	Hour 0 base deficit/excess
hr0_ph	Ordered	Hour 0 pH
ali	Factor	Acute lung injury
hr0_pc	Ordered	Hour 0 protein C
hr0_factorix	Ordered	Hour 0 factor IX
edworstrr	Ordered	ED worst RR
aischest3	Ordered	Abbreviated injury scale: chest

TABLE 24.2
ACIT variable importance results by the estimation sample.

Predictor	$\hat{\Psi}_{P_{n,(v=1)^c}}$	$\hat{\Psi}_{P_{n,(v=2)^c}}$	$a_L(P_{n,(v=1)^c})$	$a_H(P_{n,(v=1)^c})$	$a_L(P_{n,(v=2)^c})$	$a_H(P_{n,(v=2)^c})$
tbi	0.0636	0.1130	No	Yes	No	Yes
hr6_basedefexc	0.1283	0.2141	(1,10.1]	(0.95,1]	(1,10]	(0.9,1]
ortho	0.0300	0.0554	Yes	No	Yes	No
alcabuse	0.0565	0.0588	No	Unknown	No	Unknown
race	0.0961	0.0407	White	Asian	White	Asian
hr0_factorviii	0.1753	0.0947	(1,10]	(0.9,1]	(1,10.1]	(0.9,1]
hr0_ptt	0.0895	0.0431	(1,9]	(9,10]	(0.9,6]	(6,10]
heightcm	0.0800	0.0156	(1,10]	(0.9,1]	(1,10.1]	(0.9,1]
edworsttemp	0.0506	0.0582	(1,10.1]	(0.95,1]	(3,10.1]	(0.9,1]
aisface2	0.0085	0.0266	(1,4]	(0.97,1]	(1,4]	(0.97,1]
hr0_factorv	0.0166	0.059	(1,10]	(0.9,1]	(1,10.1]	(0.9,1]
hr0_atiii	0.0159	0.0322	(1,10]	(0.9,1]	(1,10]	(0.9,1]
aisextremity5	0.0164	0.0189	(1,5]	(0.96,1]	(1,5]	(0.96,1]
male	0.0648	−0.0159	Male	Female	Male	Female
edlowestsbp	0.0334	0.0311	(1,10]	(0.9,1]	(1,10]	(0.9,1]
latino	0.019	0.0154	Yes	No	Yes	No
pbw	0.0577	0.0107	(1,10]	(0.9,1]	(1,10.1]	(0.9,1]
edlowesthr	0.0317	0.0557	(1,10.1]	(0.9,1]	(1,10]	(0.9,1]
hr0_temp	0.029	0.0401	(1,10.1]	(0.9,1]	(1,10.1]	(0.9,1]
blunt	0.0293	−0.0018	Penetrating	Blunt	Penetrating	Blunt
hr0_map	0.0506	0.0053	(0.9,1]	(9,10]	(0.9,1]	(1,10]
aisabdomen4	0.0159	0.0059	(1,4]	(0.97,1]	(1,4]	(0.97,1]
iss	0.0329	0.0634	(0.9,5]	(5,9]	(1,7]	(7,9]
hr0_resprate	−0.0059	0.0268	(1,10]	(0.9,1]	(2,10]	(1,2]
numribfxs	0.0179	0.0103	(1,4]	(0.97,1]	(1,4]	(0.97,1]
hr0_factorx	0.0461	−0.0087	(1,10]	(0.9,1]	(6,10]	(0.9,1]
patientbloodtype	0.0219	0.0298	A+	A−	A+	A−
edadmittemp	−0.0008	0.0220	(1,10.1]	(0.9,1]	(3,10.1]	(1,3]
edhighestsbp	0.0120	0.0150	(1,9]	(9,10]	(1,10]	(0.9,1]
age	−0.0095	0.0280	(1,10]	(0.9,1]	(1,9]	(9,10]
insurancesource	0.0235	−0.0124	No insurance	Medical	No insurance	Medicare
mechtype	0.0801	−0.0328	PVA	Found down	Found down	PVA
hr0_basedefexc	0.0083	0.0095	(1,10.1]	(0.9,1]	(1,10]	(0.9,1]
hr0_ph	0.0509	−0.0316	(1,10]	(0.9,1]	(0.9,1]	(1,10]
ali	−0.0275	0.0116	No	Yes	Yes	No
hr0_pc	0.0058	−0.0477	(1,10]	(0.9,1]	(0.9,1]	(1,10]
hr0_factorix	−0.0293	−0.0192	(1,10]	(0.9,1]	(0.9,1]	(1,10]
edworstrr	−0.0106	−0.0644	(1,9.1]	(0.9,1]	(0.9,1]	(1,9]
aischest3	−0.s0270	−0.0326	(1,5.1]	(0.97,1]	(0.96,1]	(1,5]

given the modest sample size, for some variables there is inconsistency in how (a_L, a_H) are defined from one training sample to the next. This will partially explain how the estimates of the VIM will also vary, as they are comparing very different groups. We can use this to subset the results further below.

The final estimates, ψ_n, with confidence intervals and both raw and adjusted (for multiple testing by controlling FDR) p-values are shown in Table 24.3. We subset this table by statistical significance using the FDR cutoff of 0.1, as well as exclude those variables for which (a_L, a_H) were inconsistent across training samples (either not the same for the factors or in opposite directions for ordered variables), resulting in Table 24.4. This list indicates

TABLE 24.3
ACIT variable importance results for combined estimates.

Name	ψ_n	95% CI	*p*-value	FDF (Q-value)
tbi	0.0883	(0.0577 – 0.119)	0.0000	0.0000
hr6_basedefexc	0.1712	(0.102 – 0.241)	0.0000	0.0000
ortho	0.0427	(0.0254 – 0.06)	0.0000	0.0000
alcabuse	0.0576	(0.0331 – 0.0822)	0.0000	0.0000
race	0.0684	(0.0257 – 0.111)	0.0008	0.0065
hr0_factorviii	0.1350	(0.0379 – 0.232)	0.0032	0.0210
hr0_ptt	0.0663	(0.0154 – 0.117)	0.0053	0.0297
heightcm	0.0478	(0.00509 – 0.0905)	0.0141	0.0689
edworsttemp	0.0544	(0.000437 – 0.108)	0.0241	0.1044
aisface2	0.0176	(−0.000284 – 0.0354)	0.0269	0.1048
hr0_factorv	0.0382	(−0.00414 – 0.0806)	0.0385	0.1146
hr0_atiii	0.0240	(−0.00264 – 0.0507)	0.0387	0.1146
aisextremity5	0.0177	(−0.0022 – 0.0376)	0.0406	0.1146
male	0.0244	(−0.00355 – 0.0524)	0.0435	0.1146
edlowestsbp	0.0323	(−0.00502 – 0.0695)	0.0450	0.1146
latino	0.0176	(−0.00351 – 0.0388)	0.0510	0.1146
pbw	0.0342	(−0.00729 – 0.0757)	0.0531	0.1146
edlowesthr	0.0437	(−0.0101 – 0.0976)	0.0557	0.1146
hr0_temp	0.0350	(−0.00812 – 0.0781)	0.0558	0.1146
blunt	0.0137	(−0.00728 – 0.0347)	0.1001	0.1952
hr0_map	0.0279	(−0.0177 – 0.0736)	0.1154	0.2143
aisabdomen4	0.0109	(−0.0112 – 0.033)	0.1664	0.2950
iss	0.0481	(−0.0578 – 0.154)	0.1866	0.3165
hr0_resprate	0.0105	(−0.0163 – 0.0373)	0.2218	0.3604
numribfxs	0.0141	(−0.0266 – 0.0548)	0.2485	0.3745
hr0_factorx	0.0187	(−0.0368 – 0.0741)	0.2546	0.3745
patientbloodtype	0.0259	(−0.0527 – 0.104)	0.2593	0.3745
edadmittemp	0.0106	(−0.0249 – 0.0461)	0.2793	0.3890
edhighestsbp	0.0135	(−0.0351 – 0.0621)	0.2931	0.3941
age	0.0093	(−0.0281 – 0.0466)	0.3134	0.4074
insurancesource	0.0056	(−0.0246 – 0.0358)	0.3583	0.4455
mechtype	0.0236	(−0.111 – 0.158)	0.3655	0.4455
hr0_basedefexc	0.0089	(−0.0521 – 0.0699)	0.3875	0.4579
hr0_ph	0.0096	(−0.0772 – 0.0965)	0.4138	0.4747
ali	−0.0080	(−0.0353 – 0.0193)	0.7161	0.7980
hr0_pc	−0.0209	(−0.0571 – 0.0153)	0.8713	0.9405
hr0_factorix	−0.0243	(−0.0627 – 0.0141)	0.8922	0.9405
edworstrr	−0.0375	(−0.0767 – 0.00172)	0.9695	0.9951
aischest3	−0.0298	(−0.0469 – −0.0127)	0.9997	0.9997

TABLE 24.4
Subset of significant and *consistent* results.

Name	ψ_n	**95% CI**
tbi	0.0883	(0.0577 – 0.119)
hr6_basedefexc	0.1712	(0.102 – 0.241)
ortho	0.0427	(0.0254 – 0.06)
alcabuse	0.0576	(0.0331 – 0.0822)
race	0.0684	(0.0257 – 0.111)
hr0_factorviii	0.1350	(0.0379 – 0.232)
hr0_ptt	0.0663	(0.0154 – 0.117)

both variables that are thought to be important for their association with coagulopathy (e.g., Base Deficit, Factor VIII, and partial thromboplastin time), and injury characteristics that either are *relatively* more (traumatic brain injury) or less (orthopedic injury) likely to lead to death. One variable (alcohol use) appears to be chosen because a label of *Unknown* is potentially a proxy for the seriousness of the condition of the patient (i.e., the inability to collect the data at baseline could indicate a more serious patient at greater risk of death). It is also noted that the potential known indicators of coagulopathy are generally the procedure estimated to have high importance by our algorithm, also choose the relative levels (i.e., the *high* versus *low* risk levels) consistent with the existing understanding of their associations with potential for uncontrolled bleeding. Specifically, current understanding suggests that smaller values of base deficit (hr6_basedefexc) and factor VIII (hr0_factorviii) results in higher risk of poor outcomes, where as the association is expected to be in opposite direction (higher value is higher risk) for thromboplastin time (hr0_ptt). Finally, the magnitude of the estimates ψ_n indicates that these variables are potentially very important for predicting death, for instance, hr6_basedefexc for the high risk (lower value) versus low risk (higher value) suggests a near 20% increase in death. This is particularly large given the proportion of subjects who died in the data was only 3.5%. In any case, the results are consistent with the current understanding of survival and the dangers of coagulopahthy [20].

24.5 Concluding Remarks

Much scientific progress has been achieved by generating target parameters based on past studies, and evaluating them for future studies. However, such costly splitting of a stream of data is by no means necessary, and the proposed data-adaptive target parameter and the corresponding statistical procedure studied in this chapter allow for general sample splits, and averaging the results across such splits. Our formal results show that statistical inference is preserved under minimal conditions, even though the estimators are now based on all the data. To obtain valid finite sample inference, it is important to utilize our corresponding variance estimator (Equation 24.5), and that the sample size for the estimation sample is chosen large enough so that the second-order terms of a possible nonlinear estimator are controlled. We also note that one can often gain greater efficiency by using the related CV-TMLE procedure [21].

We have demonstrate that the data-adaptive target parameter framework provides a formalized approach for estimating target parameters that are either very hard or impossible to pre-specify. There are many examples of interest that have not been highlighted in this chapter, where the motivation can come from dimension reduction, or complex causal parameters. In our example, we derived comparable and interpretable VIMs, where comparison groups defined by the variable of interest are data-adaptively determined by a search algorithm using a combination of machine learning and causal inference. This situation is particularly prone to over fitting, and thus the estimator that uses the same data to both define the parameter and estimate it probably does not satisfy the conditions of Theorem 3 in [2]. It is easy to propose other situations in a big data context where one would like to similar types of aggressive data-mining procedures to implicitly define the parameter while still deriving a consistent estimator and accurate inference. The general methodology presented here puts few constraints on how one uses the data to define interesting parameters, and we expect that there are many applications in big data situations for which this approach is particularly well suited.

Acknowledgments

This work was partially supported through a Patient-Centered Outcomes Research Institute (PCORI) Pilot Project Program Award (ME-1306-02735).

DISCLAIMER: All statements in this report, including its findings and conclusions, are solely those of the authors and do not necessarily represent the views of the Patient-Centered Outcomes Research Institute (PCORI), its Board of Governors or Methodology Committee.

References

1. Sebastian Schneeweiss. Learning from big health care data. *New England Journal of Medicine*, 370(23):2161–2163, 2014.

2. Mark J. van der Laan, Alan E. Hubbard, and Sara K. Pajouh. Statistical inference for data adaptive target parameters. Technical Report 314, Division of Biostatistics Working Paper Series, University of California, Berkeley, CA, 2013.

3. Mitchell J. Cohen, Karim Brohi, Carolyn S. Calfee, Pamela Rahn, Brian B. Chesebro, Sarah C. Christiaans, Michel Carles et al. Early release of high mobility group box nuclear protein 1 after severe trauma in humans: Role of injury severity and tissue hypoperfusion. *Critical Care*, 13(6):R174, 2009.

4. Mitchell J. Cohen, Natasha Bir, Pamela Rahn, Rachel Dotson, Karim Brohi, Brian B. Chesebro, Robert Mackersie et al. Protein c depletion early after trauma increases the risk of ventilator-associated pneumonia. *Journal of Trauma*, 67(6):1176–1181, 2009.

5. Ulrike Grömping. Variable importance assessment in regression: Linear regression versus random forest. *The American Statistician*, 63(4):308–319, 2009.

6. Mark J. van der Laan. Statistical inference for variable importance. *The International Journal of Biostatistics*, 2(1), 2006, doi:10.2202/1557-4679.1008.

7. Stephan J. Ritter, Nicholas P. Jewell, and Alan E. Hubbard. R Package multiPIM: A causal inference approach to variable importance analysis. *Journal of Statistical Software*, 57(8):1–29, 2014.

8. Alan Hubbard, Ivan D. Munoz, Anna Decker, John B. Holcomb, Martin A. Schreiber, Eileen M. Bulger, Karen J. Brasel et al. Time-dependent prediction and evaluation of variable importance using superlearning in high-dimensional clinical data. *Journal of Trauma-Injury, Infection, and Critical Care*, 75(1):S53–S60, 2013.

9. John P.A. Ioannidis. Why most discovered true associations are inflated. *Epidemiology*, 19(5):640–648, 2008.

10. David I. Broadhurst and Douglas B. Kell. Statistical strategies for avoiding false discoveries in metabolomics and related experiments. *Metabolomics*, 2(4):171–196, 2006.

11. Mark J. van der Laan and Sherri Rose. *Targeted Learning: Causal Inference for Observational and Experimental Data*. Springer, New York, 2011.

12. James M. Robins, Miguel A. Hernan, and Babette Brumback. Marginal structural models and causal inference in epidemiology. *Epidemiology*, 11:550–560, 2000.

13. Mark J. van der Laan and Daniel Rubin. Targeted maximum likelihood learning. *International Journal of Biostatistics*, 2(1):11, 2006.

14. Yves Rozenholca, Thoralf Mildenbergerb and Ursula Gatherb. Combining regular and irregular histograms by penalized likelihood. *Computational Statistics & Data Analysis*, 54(12):3313–3323, 2010.

15. Thoralf Mildenberger, Yves Rozenholc, and David Zasada. Histogram: Construction of regular and irregular histograms with different options for automatic choice of bins. R package version 0.0-23, 2009.

16. Mark J. van der Laan and Katherine S. Pollard. Hybrid clustering of gene expression data with visualization and the bootstrap. *Journal of Statistical Planning and Inference*, 117:275–303, 2003.

17. Mark J. van der Laan, Eric C. Polley, and Alan E. Hubbard. Super learner. *Statistical Applications in Genetics and Molecular Biology*, 6:25, 2007.

18. Jerome Friedman, Trevor Hastie, and Rob Tibshirani. Regularization paths for generalized linear models via coordinate descent. *Journal of Statistical Software*, 33(1):1–22, 2010.

19. Yoav Benjamini and Yosef Hochberg. Controlling the false discovery rate: A practical and powerful approach to multiple testing. *Journal of the Royal Statistical Society*, 57:289–300, 1995.

20. Jana B.A. MacLeod, Mauricio Lynn, Mark G. McKenney, Stephen M. Cohn, and Mary Murtha. Early coagulopathy predicts mortality in trauma. *Journal of Trauma-Injury, Infection, and Critical Care*, 55(1):39–44, 2003.

21. Wenjing Zheng and Mark J. van der Laan. Asymptotic theory for cross-validated targeted maximum likelihood estimation. Technical report 273, Division of Biostatistics, University of California, Berkeley, CA, http://biostats.bepress.com/ucbbiostat/paper273, 2010.

Index

Note: Locators followed by '*f*' and '*t*' denote figures and tables in the text.

A

Activation of Coagulation and Inflammation in Trauma (ACIT) study, 439
  variable importance results
    for combined estimates, 449*t*
    by estimation sample, 448*t*
  variable importance trauma study, 444–450
  variables and description, 447*t*
Active query model, 163–164
AdaGrad method, 252
Adaptive SGD method, 251
Adjacency list, 194
Adjustees, 95–96, 97*f*
Adjustors, 95–96, 97*f*
Aggregation of structured distributions, 271
Algorithm
  loss function, 291–295
    ADMM, 294–295, 294*t*
    BCD, 292–293, 292*t*
    PGM, 293–294, 293*t*
  online EM algorithm, 254–256
  with semi-ring matrix-vector products, 205–206
  with standard matrix-vector products, 205
  Subsemble algorithm, 325–327
  two-stage algorithm for CSSP, 144
Alternating direction method of multipliers (ADMM), 294–295
  algorithm, 294*t*, 295
  for graphical lasso, 298*t*
Amplification process, 109
Analysis of variance (ANOVA), 99
Andersen–Chung–Lang (ACL) push procedure, 202–203
Anscombe's quartet, 61, 62*f*
Antiretroviral therapy (ART) initiation, 363, 367
Application program interface (API), 66, 69
Arcs, 193
Area under curve (AUC), 230–231, 230*f*
Association Navigator (AN), 73
  creating and programming instances of, 100–102
  graphical displays, 75–86
    blockplots, 75–78
    large correlation tables, 78–80
    marginal and bivariate plots, 82–85, 83*f*
    uses of, 80–82
    variations on, 85–86
  operation of, 86–98
    color brushing in scatterplots, 94
    complete pairs, 89
    correlations, 89
    crosshair placement, panning, and zooming, 87–88
    future of, 98
    graphical parameters, 88–89
    highlighting rectangle, 90–91
    highlighting strips, 90
    lenses, 92–94
    linear adjustment, 94–98
    missing pairs, 89
    to prevent confusion, 87
    p-values, 89
    reference variables, 91, 92*f*
    searching variables, 91–92, 93*f*
    starting up, 87
  overview, 74–75
  versatility of correlation analysis, 98–100
Atlantis motif, 10
Augmented inverse probability of treatment weighted (A-IPTW) estimators, 429, 431–432

Augmented Lanczos bidiagonalization method, 128–131
Autism instruments, 91
Averaged SGD (ASGD), 252–253
Averaged stochastic gradient descent (ASGD), 433
Average mixture (AVGM) procedure, 324
Average treatment effect (ATE), 429
  batch estimation of, 431–432
  OLOS estimation of, 432–433, 435
  preliminaries
    causal parameter and assumptions, 430
    statistical model, 430–431

B
Back-door criterion, 370, 370*f*, 372*f*
Bacon, Francis (1561–1626), 12
Bagging algorithm, 323–324, 343
Ball carving, LSH, 110
Base learner library, 324–325, 341, 349
Base learners, 328–329, 340–341
  algorithm, 324, 326
  Subsemble procedure using single, 326*f*
Batch estimation of ATE, 431–432
Batch learning, 350
Bayesian model, 244
Bayesian model averaging (BMA) model, 343
Bias-variance tradeoffs, 182
Big data
  ancient professions and organizations, 7
  aspect, 9
  Big-n. *See* Big-n method, case of
  Big-p. *See* Big-p method, case of
  concept, 6
  and data science, 5–7
  discoveries in history of, 7–8
  integrating, 48–58
  interactive visualization. *See* Interactive visualization of big data
  power systems
    and acquisition, 48
    characteristics, 47
    integration quality challenges in, 48
  problems, 7
  rough taxonomy of, 22–23
  statistical challenges, 285–286
  statistics with, 21–22
  Subsemble for, 325–331
    algorithm, 325–327
    oracle result, 327–328
    performance benchmarks, 330–331, 331*f*
    practical Subsemble implementation, 328–330
  variable importance and, 422–423
  visualization systems, 62, 63*f*
Big Data: A Revolution That Will Transform How We Live, Work and Think (2013), 5
Big-n method, case of, 23–25
  basic method, 23–24
  complexity analysis, 24–25
  examples, 25
  validity of SA method, 24
Big-p method, case of, 26–30
  COD, 26–28
    data sparsity, 26–27
    variable sparsity, 27–28
  example, 30
  linear regression and PCA, 26
  PEV, 28–29
  theoretical literature, 29–30
Binning, data, 64–67
Biomarkers and genomics, targeted learning, 413–415
  quantitative trait loci mapping, 414–415
  treatment resistance in HIV, 413–414
Bit sampling, LSH, 110
BlinkDB, 67
Blockplot, 73, 75–78
  of 757 variables, 78*f*
  aspect of, 86
  block size in, 88
  example of, 76*f*
  uses
    fraction of missing/complete pairs of values, 81–82, 82*f*
    p-values, 80–81, 81*f*
  variations on, 85–86
  vs. heatmap, 86*f*
Blockwise coordinate descent (BCD), 292–293, 292*t*
  for multivariate regression with group lasso, 296*t*
Body mass index (BMI), 183–184
Boosting method, 324
Bootstrap aggregating, 323–324
Bootstrap resampling, 226

Borges motif, 10
Bow tie network, 184*f*

C

`casecontrolSL` package, 421
Categorical variables, 83
Causal effects
known causal structure, 390–394
graph terminology, 391
postintervention distributions and, 393–394
SEM, 391–392
uknown causal structure, 398–400
application, 399–400
IDA, 398, 399*f*
jointIDA, 398–399
Causal graph, 391
Causal inference
assessment of identifiability, 369–373
estimation and inference, 373–376
extensions, 400–402
formal framework for, 362
interpretation of results, 376–377
multiple time point interventions, 378–380
observational *vs.* experimental data, 389, 390*f*
problem formulation, 389–390
scientific objective, 363
vs. noncausal research questions, 388–389
Causal model, 363–366
assumptions, 417–418
observed data and their link to, 368–369
oversimplifying, 366
Causal structure learning methods, 394–397
constraint-based methods, 395–396
hybrid methods, 397
score-based methods, 396–397
SEMs with additional restrictions, 397
`cex` (character expansion), 86
Chemicals, classification of, 227
cross-validated risk for algorithm to, 230*t*, 233*t*
estimated risks and standard deviations in, 236*t*
weights of prediction algorithm in, 232*t*
Classical inference procedures, extending, 308–312
covariance test, 311–312
extension to GLMs, 311
lasso projection, 309–311
ridge projection, 308–309
Classical statistical theory, 288
Classification and Regression Tree (CART) algorithm, 333–334
Cluster dendrogram of dataset, 315*f*
Cognostics, 42
Coherency aggregation method vs. DEAR method, 57*f*
Coherent groups clustering, 54*f*
Collaborative TMLE, 415
Color brushing in scatterplots, 94
Column subset selection problem (CSSP), 139
data analysis and machine learning, 145–146
open question on, 145
theory, 143–145
two-stage algorithm for, 144*t*
The Communications of Pure and Applied Mathematics, 3
Community detection, 211–212
Completed partially DAG (CPDAG), 395–397
analysis of estimated skeletons of, 400*f*
Computer science, project of, 7–8
Conditional risk, estimator, 233
Confidence intervals, group-bound, 316, 317*f*
Connected components, graph mining, 194
Constraint-based methods, 395–396
Contagion, 172
Contrastive divergence method, 258
Controversy, big data, 13–16
antithesis, 14–15
EDA, 13–14
synthesis, 15–16
thesis, 14
Convex combination, 342
Core descriptive variables, 76
Counterfactual values, 430
Covariance test, 311–312
Covariate adjustment, 402
Covariate space, 332–334
Cross-product Subsemble, 346
Cross-validated estimator selector, asymptotic for, 233–235
Cross-validated risk estimator, asymptotic for, 227*f*, 235–237

Cross-validation process, 29, 326
with correlated units, 228
Cross-wise highlight strips, 90
Curse of dimensionality (COD), 26–28, 105
data sparsity, 26–27
variable sparsity, 27–28
`cvAUC` package, 421

D

Data-adaptive target parameter, 441–442
data analysis, 444–450
examples, 443–444
general methodology, 441–443
overview, 439–441
Data analysis algorithms for model reduction, 49–58
case study, 52–58
DEAR algorithm, 49–52
k-means clustering-based model reduction, 49
Data binning, 64–67
Data cubes, 65
Data-dependent space partitions, 111–112
Data dredging fallacy, 74
Data-generating distribution, 433–436
Data–Information–Knowledge concept, 4
Data science
Bacon and emergence of, 11–12
big data and, 5–7
Data sparsity, COD, 26–27
Data-splitting techniques, 226
Davenport, Thomas, 5
Decision tree, 161–162
Deep analysis, data, 36–37
Deep architectures, 258
Deletion/substitution/addition (D/S/A) algorithm, 413
Diffusion neighborhood-based graph mining, 199, 201–204
ACL push methods, 203
random walks with restart, 203–204
small/large, 202*f*
Dimensionality, notation and notions of, 22
Dimension reduction, 106–107
Directed acyclic graph (DAG), 390–391, 398
absent (IDA), 365*f*, 398, 399*f*
to longitudinal effect, 379*f*
of structural causal model, 365*f*
Directed graph, 391
DirectLiNGAM, 397
Discrete model selection, 228–231
Discrete super learner, 229
Distance threshold estimation problem (DTEP), 115
Distortion (approximation), 112
Distributed data frame, 40
Distributed data objects (DDOs), 36, 40
Divide and recombine (D&R), 35–36, 38–41
computational environment for, 43–45
back ends, 43–45
front end, 43
data structures and computation, 40
division approaches, 39
recombination approaches, 39–40
research in, 41
statistical/computational framework, 38*f*
Divisor Subsembles, 346
Dose–response curve, estimation of, 224–225
Doubling dimension, 117
Dummy variable, 99
Dyad, 171
Dynamic-feature extraction, attribution, and reconstruction (DEAR) algorithm, 49–52
coherency aggregation method *vs.*, 57*f*
dynamic-feature extraction, 50
feature attribution, 51
feature reconstruction, 51–52
generalization to high-order models, 52
online application of, 52

E

Earthmover distance (EMD), 114
Eco-motif, 10
Edge list, 194
Edges, 193
Edit distance (Levenstein distance), 114
Efficient estimator, 431
Egonet, 199
Embarrassingly parallel (EP), 24
Endogenous variable, 363
Erdos–Renyi–Gilbert model, 173–174, 174*f*
Estimator, 441
Exclusion restrictions, 364–365
Expectation-Maximization (EM) algorithm, 241
online, 254–256
Experiments in networks, 179–182
estimation of causal effects, 181–182
Fisherian hypothesis testing, 180–181
Exploratory data analysis (EDA), 7, 13–14

Exposure model, 182
Extensions of SGD method, 251–254
  ASGD, 252–253
  Monte Carlo SGD, 253–254
  second-order methods, 251–252
Extremal eigenvalues, graph mining, 195

F
Fast causal inference (FCI) algorithm, 402
Fast JL transform technique, 107
Fisherian hypothesis testing, 180–181
Fisherian randomization-based inference, 180–181
Fisher, Ronald, 8, 13
Fisher scoring, 242
Fixed rank nominations scheme, 177
Fluctuation diagram, 75, 85
Functions, data
  testing properties of, 160–164
    alternative query and sampling models, 163–164
    data quality, 162–163
    feature selection, 161
    model selection, 161–162
  types of, 204
The Future of Data Analysis, 14–15

G
G-computation estimator, 414
Gelfand, Israel, 4
Generalized additive model (GAM), 229
Generalized estimating equations (GEEs), 182–183
Generalized gradient descent, 293
Generalized linear models (GLMs), 182–183, 229, 305, 311, 341, 347, 433
Generalized matrix-vector products graph mining, 199, 204–208
  algorithms with semi-ring, 205–206
  algorithms with standard, 205
  complexities with power-law graphs, 208
  edge-oriented updates, 207
  general updates, 207
  implementations in SQL, 208
Generalized stacking, 339–340
General latent space model, 176–177
Generator group, 53–54
  Dg of characteristic, 58, 58*t*
  rotor angle dynamics of, 57*f*, 58*f*
Geodesic neighborhood-based graph mining, 198–201
  all neighborhoods, 200
  complexities with power-law graphs, 200–201
  in Newman's netscience graph, 202*f*
  single neighborhood, 199–200
Golub–Kahan–Lanczos bidiagonalization (GKLB) procedure, 125–128
Google, 192
Gradient Boosting Machines (GBMs), 346, 349
Gradient descent (GD), 350–351
Graph cluster randomization, 181
Graphical displays of AN, 75–86
  blockplots, 75–78
  large correlation tables, 78–80
  marginal and bivariate plots, 82–85
  uses of blockplots, 80–82
  variations on blockplots, 85–86
Graphical model, 288
  with lasso, 297–298
Graphics processing units (GPUs), 65
Graphs, testing properties of, 159–160
  diameter, 159–160
  vertex cover, 160
Graph terminology, 391
Greedy equivalence search (GES) algorithm, 396–397
Grid partitioning, LSH, 110
Group-bound confidence intervals, 316, 317*f*
Group lasso, 290
  ADMM for, 298*t*
  multivariate regression with, 295–296
Guilt by association mining, 201–202

H
`h2oEnsemble` package, 422
H2O R interface, 422
H2O Ensemble software, 344, 346–348
  training time for, 350*f*, 350*t*
Hadamard transform, 107
Hadoop Distributed File System (HDFS), 40, 346
Hamiltonian dynamics, 256
Hamiltonian Monte Carlo (HMC) method, 256
Hausdoff distance, 114
Heatmaps, 85
  vs. blockplot, 86*f*
Hegel, G.F.W., 15

Hessian matrix, 242
Heuristic approach, 175
Hierarchical approaches, 314–316
High-dimensional computational geometry, 106
  dimension reduction, 106–107
  embeddings, 112–115
    distortion for metrics, 114, 114*t*
    of norms, 113
    of specialized metrics, 113–115
  sketching, 115–117
    amplified sketch, 115
    constructions, 116–117
  small dimension, 117
  space partitions, 107–112
    ℓ_∞ norm, 112
    data-dependent, 111–112
    LSH families, 109–111
    from LSH to NNS, 108–109
    optimality of LSH, 111
High-dimensional Euclidean space, 106
High-dimensional geometry 101 technique, 106
Histogram regression, 332–333
Horwitz–Thompson estimators, 182
Hybrid methods, 397

I
IDA. *See* Directed acyclic graph (DAG), absent (IDA)
IEEE 50 machine system, 52, 53*f*
  10 coherency groups in, 55*f*
  blue solid lines, 56*f*
  red dashed lines, 56*f*
imMens, 65–66
Implicitly restarted Arnoldi method (IRAM), 125–126
Implicitly restarted Lanczos bidiagonalization algorithm (IRLBA), 125–126
  augmented with Ritz vectors, 131
  numerical performance, 132
  overview, 125–126
  software implementations of, 132
Implicit SGD methods, computation of, 250–251
Independence assumptions, 364
Induction, 172
Influence curve, estimated, 446
Influence-curve theory, 17
Instrumental variable (IV) methods, 183–184
Insulated neighbors randomization, 181
Interactive visualization of big data
  binning, 64–67
  graphical considerations, 68
  outlook and open issues, 68–69
  overview, 61–64
  sampling, 67–68
Interpolative decomposition, 147
Interval mapping methods, 414
Intrinsic dimension, 117
Inverse probability of treatment weighting (IPTW) estimators, 375
Inverse probability weighting (IPW), 394
Iris dataset for big data, 347
Iteratively re-weighted least-squares (IRLS) algorithm, 311

J
Jaccard coefficient, 111
Johnson-Lindenstrauss (JL) lemma, 106–107, 113
JointIDA, 398–399
Junta testing problem, 161

K
k-exposure, 181
Key-value store, 40
k-means clustering-based model reduction, 49
Knot, 230
Knowledge, apory of complete, 9–11
Komolgorov–Smirnov test statistic, 181

L
Langevin dynamics, 256
Large complex data, 37
  analysis of, 37–38
Large graph mining
  canonical types, 198–199
  with diffusion neighborhoods, 199, 201–204
    ACL push methods, 203
    random walks with restart, 203–204
  in future
    with generalized matrix–matrix products, 214–215
    with streaming procedures, 214
  with generalized matrix-vector products, 199, 204–208

algorithms with semi-ring, 205–206
algorithms with standard, 205
complexities with power-law graphs, 208
edge-oriented updates, 207
general updates, 207
implementations in SQL, 208
with geodesic neighborhoods, 198–201
all neighborhoods, 200
complexities with power-law graphs, 200–201
single neighborhood, 199–200
limitations and tradeoffs in, 208–214
communities and modularity, 211–214
graph drawing, 209–210, 210*f*
viral propagation, 210–211
preliminaries, 193–198
classification of large graphs, 195–197
graph representations, 193–194
sources for data, 197–198
systems, 197–198
tasks, 194–195, 196*t*
scope and overview, 192–193
Large graphs (100M–10B vertices), 197
LARGE graphs (over 10B vertices), 197
Large-n problem, 74
Large-p problem, 74
Large small graph (10k–1M vertices), 196
Lasso, 288–290
graphical models with, 297–298, 298*t*
penalty, 289
projection, 309–311
ridge regression and, 307
LASSO regression, 27, 29–30
Latent distance model, 176
Learning rate parameter, 242
Learning rate sequence, 242
Leave-one-out cross-validation, 226, 340
Level-one data, 325
Level-zero data, 325, 340
Levenstein distance, 114
Linear adjustment, AN, 94–98
menu, 95*f*
results of, 96*f*
Linear model, 231, 305
Linear nongaussian acyclic model (LiNGAM) method, 397, 402
Linear regression model, 287, 306
Links, 193
Lipschitz property, 162–163
Local causal structure learning, 401
covariate adjustment, 402
from heterogeneous data, 402
hidden variables and feedback loops, 401–402
measures of uncertainty, 402
time series data, 402
Local distributed algorithms, 160
Locality-sensitive hash (LSH) functions, 108
families, 109–111
to NNS, 108–109
optimality of, 111
Loss functions, 287–288
algorithms, 291–295
ADMM, 294–295, 294*t*
BCD, 292–293, 292*t*
PGM, 293–294, 293*t*
applications, 295–298
graphical models with lasso, 297–298
matrix completion with nuclear norm, 296–297
multivariate regression with group lasso, 295–296
linear regression, 287
matrix completion, 287–288
natural, 295
precision matrix estimation, 288
squared-error, 287
Loss + penalty framework, 286–287, 291, 293, 298
Low-rank matrix approximation problems, 139
random projections for, 146–148
`ltmle` package, 422

M
Mann–Whitney statistic, 180
MapReduce, 40, 201
Marginal structural models, 367
Marker confounding mechanism, 419
Markov chain Monte Carlo (MCMC) sampling, 245, 256–257
Markov equivalent, 395
MATLAB® clustering toolbox, 53
MATLAB code, 132
Matrix completion problem, 287–288
with nuclear norm, 296–297
PGM for, 297*t*
Maximal ancestral graphs (MAGs), 401
Maximum likelihood estimation (MLE), 14, 16–17, 270, 273

Metalearner, 329
Metalearning algorithm, 341–342, 344
Metric entropy numbers, 271
Min-hash, LSH, 111
Minibatch, 432, 435
Model-driven approach, 175
Model reduction, data analysis algorithms for, 49–58
case study, 52–58
DEAR algorithm, 49–52
k-means clustering-based, 49
reduction ratio, 54–55
Model selection approach, 225
and parameter estimation, 306–307
problem, 161
Model stacking and super learning, 231–233
Modified cholesky decomposition (MCD), 399
Modified GKLB (MGKLB) decomposition, 130–131
Modularity, 211–214
as cut measure, 212–214
defined, 212
Monotone distributions, 274–275
Monot hazard rate (MHR) distributions, 276–277
Monotonicity, 163, 274
Monte Carlo resampling, 226
Monte Carlo SGD method, 253–254
Multifold cross-validation, 226
`multiPIM` package, 421
Multiple time point interventions, 378–380
Multisample splitting algorithm, 314
Multivariate adaptive regression splines (MARS), 230–231
Multivariate regression with group lasso, 295–296, 296*t*
Multivariate structured distributions, 277–278

N
Nanocubes, 65–66
Natural loss function, 295
Nearest neighbor preserving embedding, 113
Nearest neighbor search (NNS), 105–106
Neeman's theorem, 158
Negative log-likelihood loss, 325
Neighborhood, graph mining
diffusion, 199, 201–204
ACL push methods, 203
random walks with restart, 203–204
small/large, 202*f*
geodesic, 198–201
all neighborhoods, 200
complexities with power-law graphs, 200–201
in Newman's netscience graph, 202*f*
single neighborhood, 199–200
Network models, 173–178
bow tie network, 184*f*
Erdos–Renyi–Gilbert model, 173–174, 174*f*
future directions, 185–186
general latent space model, 176–177
observations sampled from nodes of, 178–185
experiments. *See* Experiments in networks
observational studies, 182–185
terminology and notation, 179
overview, 171–173
stochastic blockmodel, 174–176
structure testing, 177–178
Bickel and Sarkar (2013), 177
Volfovsky and Hoff (2014), 177–178
Newton–Raphson methods, 242
Nodes, 193
Nonnegative least squares (NNLS), 325, 342
Nonparametric structural equation model, 364
Nonproper learning, 268
Normalized least mean squares (NLMS) filter, 244
No unmeasured confounders assumption, 430
Nuclear norm, 291
Nuisance parameter, 224–225
Numerical linear algebra (NLA), 137–138
Nyström-based machine learning, 148–149

O
Observational studies, network, 182–185
dependence, 185
IV methods, 183–184
peer effects, 182–183
TMLE for causal effects, 185
Oddball anomaly detection method, 200
Online EM algorithm, 254–256
Online one-step (OLOS) estimation of ATE, 432–433, 435
data-generating distribution, 433–436

results, 434–436, 435*f*, 436*f*
SGD for logistic regression, 434
Online Super Learner (OSL), 350–352
algorithm, 351–352
optimization in, 350–351
practical, 352
Operation of AN, 86–98
color brushing in scatterplots, 94
complete pairs, 89
correlations, 89
crosshair placement, panning, and zooming, 87–88
future of, 98
graphical parameters, 88–89
highlighting rectangle, 90–91
highlighting strips, 90
lenses, 92–94
linear adjustment, 94–98
missing pairs, 89
to prevent confusion, 87
p-values, 89
reference variables, 91, 92*f*
searching variables, 91–92, 93*f*
starting up, 87
Optimal risk, estimator, 233
Oracle result for Subsemble, 327–328
Oracle selector, estimator, 233, 342–343
Ordinary least squares (OLS), 341
Out-of-sample extension, 106, 113

P
PageRank, graph mining, 194, 205
Panel, 41
Parallel matrix-vector product, 205
Parameter learning, 268–269
Parameter mapping, 431
Partial ancestral graphs (PAGs), 401–402
Patil, D.J., 5
Pearson, Karl, 8, 16–17
Peer effects, 172, 182–183
Phasor measurement units (PMU), 47
Piecewise polynomials, 273
agnostically learning, 276–277
Point sets, testing properties of, 157–159
clustering, 157–158
surface area, 158–159
Poisson binomial distributions (PBDs), 272–273
Polyak–Ruppert averaging scheme, 253
Power-law graphs, complexities with, 200–201, 208
Precision matrix estimation, 288
Prediction error
estimation of, 227–228
of stacked predictor, 232–233
Principal components analysis (PCA), 24, 98–99, 137
linear regression and, 26
Principle of extreme values (PEV), 28–29
Programming, targeted learning methods, 421–422
Proper learning, 268
Property testing, 155
Proximal gradient method (PGM), 293–294, 293*t*
for matrix completion, 297*t*
Proximal operator, 293

Q
Quantitative structure-activity relationship (QSAR) dataset, 227
Quantitative trait loci mapping, 414–415
current standard techniques for, 414
goal of, 414
TMLE algorithm for, 419–420
Quasi-Newton methods, 242

R
Random forests (RFs), 225, 229–230
Random graph, 172
Randomization assumption, 417, 431
Randomized NLA (RandNLA), 138
applications of main technical result, 143–149
data analysis and machine learning, 145–146
Nyström-based machine learning, 148–149
random projections, 146–148
theory, 143–145
main technical result, 140–142
popular special case, 141–142
proof of, 142
statement of, 140–141
overview, 138–140
sketching matrix, 139
Random projection, LSH, 110
Random walk, graph mining, 194
with restart, 203–204
R Code, 237
Receiver effect, 176

Receiver operating characteristic (ROC) curves, 230, 230*f*
Recombination approaches, 39–40
Recursive estimation methods, 243
Recursive regressions for causal effects (RRC), 398–399
Reference variables, AN, 91, 92*f*
Regression trees, 332–333
Research question, defining, 416–418
  causal assumptions, 417–418
  data, 416–417
  model and parameter, 417
Restricted Boltzmann Machine (RBM), 258
Ridge projection, 308–309
Ridge regression and lasso, 307
Ritz values and vectors, 129
  IRLBA augmented with, 131
Robbins–Monro procedure, 245

S
Sakrison's recursive estimation method, 246
Sample splitting and p-value aggregation, 313–314
Sampling engines, 67–68
Sampling model, 163–164
Scagnostics, 42
Scatterplot matrices, 82–85, 84*f*
Score-based methods, 396–397
Score vector $Z^{(j)}$, 309–310
Second-order SGD method, 251–252
Selection frequencies to stability selection, 312–313
Selector, 228–229
Semiparametric efficient estimators, 429
Semi-ring matrix-vector products, algorithms with, 205–206
Sender effect, 176
Sequential learning, types of, 351
Sequential randomization assumption, 380
Shape-constrained distributions, 270
Sharp null hypothesis, 180
Sim-hash, LSH, 111
Simons Simplex Collection (SSC), 75, 100, 101*t*
Single neighborhood, graph mining, 199–200
Singular value decomposition (SVD), 49, 52, 125, 137
Six degrees of separation theory, 159
Sketching matrix, 139–140
Small graphs (under 10k vertices), 196
  geodesic propagation in, 211*f*
Small large graphs (1M–100M vertices), 196
Small world theory, 159
Social Responsiveness Scale (SRS), 95–96
Software alchemy (SA) method, 23
  validity of, 24
Spectral gap error bound method, 149
Spillover effects, 179
Splitting criterion, 333
Sploms, 84
Squared-error loss function, 287, 333, 342, 419
Stacked generalization, 340
Stacking method, 324–325, 340–341
Standard errors, 22
Standard matrix-vector products, algorithms with, 205
Statistical Methods for Research Workers (1925) (book), 13
Stochastic approximation, 245–246
Stochastic blockmodel, 174–176
Stochastic gradient descent (SGD), 242–243, 245, 351–352, 433
  estimation with, 247–254
    bias and variance, 247–248
    computation of implicit methods, 250–251
    extensions, 251–254
    learning rate sequence, 249–250
    stability, 248–249
  for logistic regression, 434
  other applications, 254–259
    deep learning, 258–259
    MCMC sampling, 256–257
    online EM algorithm, 254–256
    reinforcement learning, 257–258
Structural causal model, 363–366, 365*f*, 392
Structural equation model (SEM), 390–392
  with additional restrictions, 397
Structured distributions
  cover method and sample bounds, 271–273
  definitions, 269–270
  future directions, 279
  historical background, 268–269
  multivariate, 277–278
  preliminaries, 269–270
  statistical distance, 269
  types of, 270–271
    aggregation, 271
    shape-constrained distributions, 270
  univariate, 273–277

agnostically learning histograms, 275–276
agnostically learning piecewise polynomials, 276–277
monotone distributions, 274–275
Structure-inducing convex penalties, 288–291, 289*t*
group lasso, 290
lasso, 288–290
nuclear norm, 291
Subsampled average mixture (SAVGM) procedure, 324
Subsemble method
for big data, 325–331
algorithm, 325–327, 327*f*
oracle result, 327–328
performance benchmarks, 330–331
practical Subsemble implementation, 328–330
using single base learner, 326*f*
with subset supervision, 331–335
SRT Subsemble algorithm, 333–334
SRT Subsemble in practice, 334–335
supervised Subsembles, 332–333
training time for, 332*f*
`subsemble` package, 421
subsemble R package, 329, 345–346
Super Learner algorithm, 324, 340–343
base learners, 341
implementation, 344, 347
metalearning algorithm, 341–342
oracle properties, 342–343
other ensemble learners vs., 343
in practice, 352–353
software, 343–350
computational details, 349–350
H2O Ensemble, 346–348
performance benchmarks, 348–349, 349*t*
subsemble R package, 345–346
SuperLearner R package, 329, 345, 421
stacking, 340–341
Supervised Regression Tree (SRT) Subsemble, 328, 332, 346
algorithm, 333–334
in practice, 334–335
Supervised Subsembles, 332–333
Support vector machines (SVM), 225, 229, 229*f*
Surface area of point sets, 158–159
Sweep cut, 203
Symmetric positive semi-definite (SPSD) matrices, 148

T
Target causal quantity, 366–368
Targeted learning methods, 411–412
estimation, 418–420
inference, 420–421
literature, 412–415
biomarkers and genomics, 413–415
complex data structures, 415
programming, 421–422
research question, 416–418
causal assumptions, 417–418
data, 416–417
model and parameter, 417
template, 412
variable importance and big data, 422–423
Targeted maximum likelihood estimation (TMLE), 16, 375, 411–412, 414, 444
algorithm for quantitative trait loci mapping, 419–420
collaborative, 415
of target parameter, 420
variance estimates for, 420
Targeted minimum loss-based estimation, 185
Target, graph mining, 199
Temporal differences (TD) learning algorithm, 258
Tessera, 36
back ends, 43–45
large scale, 44
large scale in memory, 44–45
medium scale, 44
small scale, 44
front end, 43
Testing by implicit learning technique, 162
Testing properties
of functions, 160–164
alternative query and sampling models, 163–164
data quality, 162–163
feature selection, 161
model selection, 161–162
of graphs, 159–160
diameter, 159–160
vertex cover, 160

of point sets, 157–159
clustering, 157–158
surface area, 158–159
Theoretical computer science (TCS), 138
Thick-restarted Lanczos tridiagonalization, 125–126
Time-dependent confounding, 380
Time synchronization, 47–48
`tmle` R package, 421
Trelliscope system, 36, 41–43
scaling trellis display, 41–42
trellis display/small multiples, 41
Triangle counting, graph mining, 195
Truncated factorization formula, 393
Tufte, Edward, 41
Tukey, John W. (1915–2000), 13, 37
unorthodox approach in EDA, 14
Turing machine, 7

U
Ulam distance, 114
Unit-level causal effects, 179
Unit-level potential outcome, 179
Univariate structured distributions, 273–277
agnostically learning histograms, 275–276
piecewise polynomials, 276–277
monotone distributions, 274–275
Untestable assumption, 430

V
Vapnik–Chervonenkis (VC)-dimension, 275
Variable importance measure (VIM) estimation, 440, 444–445
Variables, description of, 238–239
Velupillai, Vela, 4
Venter process, 246
Verne, Jules, 10
Vertex cover of graph, 160
Vertices, 193
V-fold cross-validation, 325–326, 351, 441
Viral propagation, 210–211
Visualization database, 43
Vowpal Wabbit (VW) Ensemble, 351–352

W
Warm start, 292–294
Wells, H. G., 10
Wigner, Eugene Paul (1902–1995), 3
Wigner *vs.* Google, 3–5

Y
Yeast gene expression data, analysis of, 401*f*